STALEY@CLARA.CO.UK

ELPIS ISRAEL

John Thomas, aged 64, during his third visit to Britain in 1869

ELPIS ISRAEL

an Exposition of the
KINGDOM OF GOD
with reference to
THE TIME OF THE END
and THE AGE TO COME

JOHN THOMAS, M.D.

"For the hope of Israel I am bound with this chain."—*Paul*

Fifteenth Edition

THE CHRISTADELPHIAN
404 SHAFTMOOR LANE
BIRMINGHAM B28 8SZ

2000

1st	Edition	1849	10th Edition	1917
2nd	Edition	1851	11th Edition	1924
3rd	Edition	1859	12th Edition	1939
4th	Edition	1866	13th Edition	1942
5th	Edition	1884	14th Edition	1949
6th	Edition	1888	15th Edition	2000
7th	Edition	1897		
8th	Edition	1903		
9th	Edition	1910		

ISBN 0 85189 027 X

Colour picture depicting the author—digitally reproduced by D. J. Miles from an original oil painting by W. Bromley (1886).

Cover photograph of Earth amidst a starry background, courtesy of the Telegraph Colour Library.

Thanks also to Mary Knechtl for photographing the Shield of Clovis in Innsbruck (see page 409).

Prefaces and Notes to this Edition

THE 1st edition of *Elpis Israel* commenced with the Author's own Preface to his work. In subsequent editions, both Author and Publisher added further explanatory notes; moreover, in editions subsequent to the death of John Thomas, Biographical Notes of his life were included.

So much prefatory material has now been accumulated that a brief listing may be helpful to readers of this 15th (reset) edition:

PRINTED BY CROMWELL PRESS LTD., TROWBRIDGE

AUTHOR'S PREFACE

(Condensed from the four Prefaces appearing in the Fourth Edition, and covering a period of eighteen years, 1848-1866)

THE year 1848 has been well and truly styled the "Annus Mirabilis", or Wonderful Year. So, indeed, it proved itself in Europe; for though this division of the globe was overspread with numerous large, well-appointed, and highly-disciplined armies, maintained to uphold what remained of the work of the Congress of Vienna in 1815, and to prevent the rising of the people against their destroyers, yet did the wild and ill-armed Democracy of Europe break their bonds asunder as a rotten thread, and shake its kingdoms to their foundations.

Great excitement was produced in the United States by the news of what was going on in Europe. Many who had for years before been predicting "the end of all things" were now persuaded that it had come at last. Others came to a different conclusion, and rejoiced in the supposition that the kingdoms of the world were about to become republics, after the model of the United States. Both these imaginations, however, serve to show how little the "sure word of prophecy" was understood or heeded by the people. The author endeavoured, as far as he could obtain the ears of the public, to disabuse it of these vain conceits. He opposed to them "the testimony of God", which testifies the continuance of "the times of the Gentiles" until Nebuchadnezzar's Image be broken to pieces upon the mountains of Israel; and the perpetuity of the kingdoms until after this event, when Christ shall encounter their kings in battle, and annex their realms to his kingdom by conquest; for, by his kingdom, and not by popular violence, will he break in pieces and consume them all. But the author was as one that spoke parables in the ears of the deaf. Time, however, has verified his interpretation in part. Though terribly shaken, the kingdoms still exist, and republics are at a discount and the "Order", in which God's enemies rejoice, has been provisionally re-established.

The events in 1848 caused many in the United States to revisit their native lands. Among these was the author of this volume. Believing he could irradiate the light of the prophetic word upon the political tragedies of the time, and, by so doing, be of use to those who desire to know the truth, he determined to intermit his labours in America, where he had been operating for about sixteen years in the same vocation, and to see if "a door of utterance" might not be opened in England for the same purpose. He was the more induced to take this step by a desire to be nearer the scene of action, that he might avail himself of the more frequent and copious details furnished by the British than the American Press, to the end that he might as speedily as possible obtain a comprehensive view of the crisis; which is the most important that has yet happened to the world, because it is pregnant of consequences for good and evil, which will leave their mark upon society for a thousand years.

AUTHOR'S PREFACE

Having made his arrangements accordingly, he arrived in London, June 28th, 1848; and in July following he received an invitation to visit Nottingham, and to deliver a course of lectures upon the times, in connection with the prophetic word. The interest created during his short stay was great and encouraging, and became the occasion of invitation to visit other towns and cities also. During this tour he visited Derby, Belper, Lincoln, Edinburgh, Glasgow, and Paisley, and addressed thousands of the people. who heard him gladly. Those who opened the way for him were neither the rich nor the noble, but intelligent men of industrious and steady habits, who desired to know and disseminate the truth according to their means. As the author's labours were gratuitous, they were the better able to afford him facilities; and he would add here the testimony of his experience, that not only is the gospel, when preached, "preached to the poor", and received by them, but it is the poor also who devote themselves to its proclamation, and who do most for its support. If it had not been for the poor and humble during the last 1,849 years, the gospel would have perished from the earth; for the rich have not been the persons to leave the comforts of their homes, and to go forth, without fee or reward, to enlighten their fellow men, for the truth's sake.

It is a gratification to the author to be able to say that he has left his home, 4,000 miles in the south-west; that he has travelled twice through Britain; delivered 170 addresses to the people ; sat up early and late conversing with them on the things of the kingdom, and written this work, that he may leave a testimony behind him, and as yet has received no more than four shillings over his travelling expenses. He mentions this that the reader may be able to acquit him of being a trader in religion; and that what he says in this book concerning "spiritual merchants" may not lose its point, under the supposition that he is also one of the wealthy and thriving firm. Rich men have not yet learned to "make themselves friends of the mammon of unrighteousness; that when they fail, they may receive them into everlasting habitations". All the opposition the author has had to contend against since his arrival in Britain has proceeded from them: but he is gratified in being able to state, that they have failed to obstruct him, and their waywardness has recoiled on their own pates.

The interest created in the thousands who listened to the author's discourses has originated the work now offered to the world. A request was publicly made to him in Edinburgh and Glasgow, that what had been spoken should be printed; and that, as it was not to be expected that he should publish at a mere venture, committees would be formed to promote a subscription. Although the author had concluded to return to America in October or November, he could not find it in his heart to leave his work unfinished, seeing that such a volume was now desired. Trusting, therefore, to the good faith of those who had become interested in the truth, he acceded to their request, and on his return to London entered upon the labour, which has proved sufficiently laborious by the close application required to do much in a limited time.

Having at length finished the manuscript, the author made a second tour in June, 1849. In addition to the former places, he visited Birmingham, Newark, Dundee, Aberdeen and Liverpool. The result of his labours was a list of upwards of a thousand subscribers, which encouraged him to go to press on his return to London in September. But on revising the manuscript, he found some things omitted, others touched too lightly, and other parts too diffuse; so that, upon the whole, he condemned it as unsuitable, and imposed upon himself the task of writing it over again—which, after four months he has accomplished, and now offers it to the public for its "edification, exhortation, and comfort."

The nature of the work is indicated on the title-page. It is a work showing what the Bible teaches as a whole, and not the elaboration of a new or fantastical theological theory, or the new vamping of an old one. It demonstrates the great subject of the Scriptures, namely: "the Kingdom of God and of His Anointed", without which they would be as a nut whose kernel had perished. It is a book for all classes, lay and clerical, without respect of persons, for all are concluded under sin, being all ignorant of "the gospel of the kingdom". Judging from the lucubrations of public writers of the ministerial class, the nature of the times demands something out of the ordinary periodical and public routine to awake "the churches" to spiritual life, lest they sleep the sleep of death. They are truly in a Laodicean state, and already spued out of the mouth of the Lord. They say they are "rich and increased in goods, and have need of nothing"; but some of their doctors have discernment enough to see that they are "wretched, and miserable, and poor, and blind, and naked". But, alas for them, they know not how to remedy the evil! They do not perceive that the fault is in their systems; which have made them what they are, and which they are pledged to support on pain of "suffering the loss of all things."

The great desideratum of the crisis is *the Gospel of the Kingdom*. The State-clergy and the Dissenting-ministry are ignorant of the Gospel; and "like priest like people". "The churches" are full of darkness, for the Gospel doth not shine into them being neither believed nor preached among them. Here, then, is a book peculiarly adapted to the times. It will show the people what the gospel is—what is the obedience it requires—and enable them to discern the times; that the Lord may not come upon them at unawares, and take them unprepared. It is a book, not for these times only, but for all the years preceding "the time of the end", and thence to the epoch of the restoration of the kingdom and throne of David, It is named ELPIS ISRAEL, or *Israel's Hope*: for the kingdom of which it treats is that which is longed for by all intelligent Israelites, and for which, said Paul, "I am bound with this chain."

Elpis Israel's subject-matter is national, not sectarian. It treats of a nation, and of its civil and ecclesiastical institutions in a past and *future age*. It is designed to enlighten both Jews and Gentiles in Israel's Hope, that by conforming to the proclamation of their King, they may be prepared for the administration of its affairs in concert with him, when all nations shall be as politically subject to his dominion, as Hindostan and Britain are to Queen Victoria's. It is designed to show men how they may attain to eternal life in this theocracy, and obtain a crown which shall never fade away. To accomplish this, the reader must, in justice to himself and the truth, study it with the Bible at his right hand, for he will find but few pages in which frequent reference is not made to its authority, and without which nothing can or ought to be determined.

AUTHOR'S PREFACE

A copy of this work has been ordered for presentation to the Autocrat of all the Russias. He will find in it much concerning his dominions. The high priest of the Jews showed Alexander the Great the prophecy in Daniel concerning himself; and although it spoke of his power being broken, the knowledge of it did not deter him from endeavouring to found a universal dominion. So it will be with the Autocrat. He will, doubtless, receive all that speaks of the extension of his empire over Europe and Turkey, because his ambition will be flattered by it; but being impressed with the idea of his being God's Vicegerent upon earth, he will probably disregard what relates to the breaking of his power on the Mountains of Israel by the Lord from heaven; arguing, as a natural man, that it is not likely that God will destroy His Grand Vizier among the nations. But whatever the Autocrat may think of the destiny marked out for him, the reader's attention is particularly invited to what is said respecting it in this volume. The future movements of Russia are notable signs of the times, because they are predicted in the Scriptures of truth. The Russian Autocracy in its plenitude, and on the verge of dissolution, is the Image of Nebuchadnezzar standing upon the Mountains of Israel, ready to be smitten by the Stone. When Russia makes its grand move for the building-up of its Image-empire then let the reader know that the end of all things, as at present constituted, is at hand, The long-expected, but stealthy, advent of the King of Israel will be on the eve of becoming a fact; and salvation will be to those who not only looked for it, but have trimmed their lamps by believing the gospel of the kingdom unto the obedience of faith, and the perfection thereof in "fruits meet for repentance".

As to the reviewers, the author presents his compliments to them, and respectfully invites them to examine this work impartially. While he has no wish to propitiate them, it would afford him great pleasure to turn them to what he believes to be "the truth as it is in Jesus", as opposed to the dogmas of their creeds. It is not to be expected that they can approve the work, seeing that, if the things exhibited be received, Sectarianism is dethroned, at least in the hearts of those who receive the principles inculcated. By Sectarianism the author means *everything professedly Christian, not according to "the law and the testimony"*. He therefore uses the word as representative of all state religions, as well as of the forms opposed to them. Being the echo of no living sect, but the advocate only of *what is written in the oracles of God*, of the faith and practice of that "sect" which in Paul's time "was everywhere spoken against", he has shown no favour to the Heresies (αἱρέσεις) which destroy it, and therefore he expects none. The perils to which he is exposed are only to be despised by those whose houses are founded upon the rock. The author is free to admit his weakness and inferiority in every respect that can be imagined. In one thing, however, he feels strong, and armed at all points for a conflict with the giants—*he knows what is written* in *"the law and the testimony", and he understands the meaning of it*. If they undertake to review this work, they must put it through the evolutions of the Spirit; and if they enter into combat with it, he would advise them to throw away their wooden swords, and encounter it with "the two-edged sword of the Spirit, which is the Word of God"; for no other weapon can do more than raise the Author's mirth.

But perhaps prudence, which is sometimes the better part of valour, may dictate the expediency of saying nothing about it. This might be very good policy if *Elpis Israel* were born from the press only to gasp and die. But editors must remember that, before a single copy reaches them, it will be in the hands of upwards of a thousand people. This is a fact not to be despised. Such a number of intelligent persons is calculated to make a troublesome impression upon the public mind; and if the press do not check it, there is no telling whereunto the evil may grow! Let "the Ministry" be up and doing. It is not the "infidel" their influence hath to fear; but the Word of the Living God understood by the people. The author has some of them among his subscribers. He trusts that for their own sakes they will read this work with candour, impartiality, and tranquillity of mind.As individuals. he has no controversy with them. His opposition is to their systems, which he trusts they will abandon for the gospel of the kingdom. If *Elpis Israel* convinces them of error, then, like the apostle, may they esteem their worldly honours and profits as mere dross for the excellency of the truth. Let them leave the fat things of the apostasy to those who mind "earthly things"; and let them put on the whole armour of God, and go forth among the people with the two-edged sword of the Spirit, and do battle for the truth.

In conclusion, then, the author respectfully hands over to the subscribers this work, as an ample fulfilment of his part of the covenant between them. They can now form their own judgment of its merits or defects, according to the evidence a candid perusal may afford. And, may God Almighty bless their honest endeavours to know and understand His truth, which is intrinsically invincible, and needs only to come in contact with "good and honest hearts", to become triumphantly defiant of all the wiles and "power of the enemy". May the spirit of the truth enter into them, and lead them into its liberty and fraternity; that at the coming of the Son of Man in celestial majesty and power, they may share with him in his joy, and inherit the kingdom of God with eternal glory.

London, January 1, 1850.

FROM THE PREFACE TO SECOND EDITION

IN the Preface to the first edition I stated that "a copy of this work had been ordered for presentation to the Autocrat of all the Russias This was the fact. It was ordered by a friend in Dundee, in Scotland, whence a great trade is carried on with the Emperor's dominions. Now, what I have to add, is rendered necessary, that the reader may not be misled. He will probably have concluded that the Autocrat is in possession of *Elpis Israel*, and acquainted with its contents. This however is not the case, as far as I am at present informed. My friend in Dundee did his best to get the work transmitted. He applied to several captains of vessels trading to St Petersburg, but they all declined to take it, lest it might bring them into trouble there.

AUTHOR'S PREFACE

[Then Dr. Thomas tried Baron Brunnow, the Russian Ambassador. He retained the book sixteen days, and then returned it, with a polite letter in French explaining that "the rules of the service" forbade its transmission. The rest of this preface contains Dr. Thomas's letters to Baron Brunnow and Czar Nicholas. It is dated Richmond, Va., June, 1851.]

FROM THE PREFACE TO THIRD EDITION

NEARLY ten years have elapsed since this work was originally published in London, England. A year after, an edition was published in New York, the two editions collectively consisting of two thousand three hundred copies. These have all been disposed of, so that for the past three years the author has been unable to supply a considerable additional demand for the work. He has been urged by many who have read the book to publish a new edition ... A friend writes: "Apart from all other considerations than the real merit of the book, you have nothing to fear as to its success. I would recommend you to give *at once* a public announcement of your intention to issue a new edition, and invite orders; you may find a larger edition wanted than you anticipate." Encouraged, therefore, by many similar assurances from others, I have published this *third edition of Elpis Israel.*

When the work was written, the times were of a highly exciting and stirring character. Nor have they materially changed to the present hour. During the past ten years a succession of events has demonstrated that a fixed and predetermined purpose is in process of development, unknown, indeed, to "the Powers that be", but known of God, revealed in His word, and guided by His hand. That purpose is *the gathering together of the hosts of the nations against Jerusalem to war; that the Eternal Spirit, by Jesus, the King of kings, may smite them upon the mountains of Israel; and in concert with resurrected and living saints, at the head of the armies of Israel, re-establish the throne and kingdom of David and subjugate all other kingdoms to this New Power in the earth.* If the reader desire to assure himself of the verity of this purpose, he may consult the following testimonies: Isaiah 14:24-27; 27:1-6; Joel 3:1,2,9-17; Micah 5:1-6; Zechariah 12:1-9; 14:1-11; Daniel 11:40-45; 12:1,2; Revelation 19:11-16; 17:14; 11:15-17; 5:9, 10; 2:26,27; Acts 15:16; Amos 9:11-15; Isaiah 9:6,7; Luke 1:31-33—and so forth. The past history of Israel, of Jesus and the Saints, and of the world at large, all prove that this purpose has never yet been fulfilled; so that the reader has no alternative but to believe the purpose, or reject the truth of the Bible, and write himself an infidel. There is no neutral ground. Every man in "Christendom", falsely so-called, is on the side of the purpose or against it Jesus and his apostles preached that *"Salvation is of the Jews"*—a salvation dependent upon the development of the purpose defined. Hence, "when ye see certain things coming to pass, then look up, and lift up your heads; for your redemption draweth nigh"—a saying which intimates that the approach of redemption, whatever it may consist in, may be known by a current fulfilment of predicted things, shortly preceding its manifestation.

We may remark here, that on page 149, second paragraph, we are supposed to say, that "the work of the law was written upon the hearts" of Gentiles who had heard nothing of it. This was not our meaning. We there endeavour to account for the moral difference between the mere savage and the peoples of the four empires; that the little light they had came from the law through their intercourse with Israel; it came "from without": but where there was no intercourse with this peculiar people, the darkness was total; and there was no accusing or excusing, no conscience; but a blind, impulsive instinct, unsentimental as that of the beasts that perish. We agree entirely with our intelligent friend whose letter has been already quoted from at the beginning, that "Paul, in Romans 2:15, is labouring to check the presumption of the Jews who were claiming pre-eminence in the congregation at Rome, because of their superior knowledge of the law of Moses, by showing their pretensions vain because they had not kept the law; whereas *the Gentiles in the Church*, who never were under the law of Moses, showed that the work of the law was written in their hearts by the word of the truth of the gospel by faith, and therefore they kept the righteousness of the law; and by so doing they proved that they were the true circumcision, all of which is clearly and beautifully argued out to the close of the chapter."

Mott Haven, Westchester, N.Y., May 6, 1859

FROM THE PREFACE TO FOURTH EDITION

SEVEN years have elapsed since the issue of the third edition of this work. For a considerable time there have been no copies of it for sale, being, as the phrase is, "out of print". A fourth edition has been called for both in Britain and America. To this call the author has reluctantly responded; not that he did not think it desirable; but because of the additional labour it would append to that already on hand in the preparation of the manuscript of the third volume of the *Exposition of the Apocalypse*, styled EUREKA. The earnest request, however, of many acquainted with ELPIS ISRAEL; and the commencement of a subscription in Britain and the States to induce compliance, at length overcame this reluctance. For the first time since correcting the proof of the first edition in 1849, he has read the work again. He knew what ought to be there; but memory after seventeen years did not serve him with the assurance that he would so find it. It was reasonable to suppose that a longer and maturer study of "The Word" might render him dissatisfied with much originally written; and that he would have to strike out many pages that could not now be endorsed.

But on reviewing the original, the author was agreeably surprised on finding he had so few corrections to make. He has made about half-adozen in the first part; and less than that number in the second. In the third part he found it necessary to make the most. If he were to re-write the book, he might go more into detail upon some points; while other parts, perhaps, he might retrench; but upon the whole, considering that it is designed for an elementary work, he does not know that it would thereby be much improved. The emendations made will place this revise in accord with the author's latest work; so that he considers this revised edition is the best.

The most important correction has been that emendatory of allusions to the resurrection. The understanding of this *"element of the beginning of the oracles of the Deity"*—στοιχεῖα τῆς ἀρχῆς τῶν λογίον τού Θεού—Hebrews 5:12; 6:2—has been enlarged in the author's mind since 1849. The question was not then the resurrection in its detail; but the necessity of resurrection and judgment at all in view of the immortality of the soul and its instantaneous translation to heaven or hell at the death of the body. Such a dogma as this is a logical denial of both resurrection and judgment. It makes them both superfluous, and absolutely unnecessary. It was, therefore, met at that time by a testimony, pure and simple, for resurrection of the body, as indispensable to the incorruptibility and immortality of the dead. But the times are now changed. The Laodiceanism of the Clerical Apostasy has been fully exposed and refuted; and the resurrection and judgment are just at hand. The time had therefore overtaken us in which the author found it necessary, in *Eureka*, to expound more in detail so important a consequence of the speedy and thief-like advent of Christ. Some, who have no objection to resurrection *in general*, are very much dissatisfied with it *in its particulars*. The resurrection ordained of the Deity does not suit them; and, therefore, they loudly disapprove it! They contend,

1.   That the judgment of the righteous, in which they are giving account of themselves to God, is in the present life, after which they will have no account to give.

2.   That resurrection of an imperfect body is not taught directly or indirectly in the word.

3.   That the righteous are not brought to judgment.

4.   That the Scriptures teach positively and without reservation, that the righteous are raised incorruptible.

With such theorists it is judgment first, and resurrection afterwards! This is an inversion of the divine order, by which the whole subject is confused. The author believes that the divine order is the best; and he believes, too, that the righteous are raised incorruptible; but also, that *the raising* is not one instantaneous event like the lightning's flash, but *an order of development*, initiated in the dust, and ultimating after *judgment* in incorruptibility and deathlessness of body.

[The rest of this Preface has to do with the progress of the world to date, namely, to December, 1866.]

PUBLISHER'S NOTES
(to the 11th Edition)

THE Publisher has not hesitated to make such emendations as he believes the Author will approve on his reappearance in the land of the living.

These emendations and changes are, however, very slight, and are here mentioned only for the information of the community that so justly values *Elpis Israel* and its Author; and also "to cut off occasion" from some who would not be slow to accuse the publisher of "tampering" with the work of the deceased.

The changes made, in the main range themselves round two or three heads as follows:—Improved translations; improved expositions due to increased knowledge; expunged errors; notes on the Author's wonderful political prevision.

With regard to TRANSLATIONS, it must be admitted that Dr. Thomas sometimes altered "the Authorized Version", as it is called, without improving matters, illustrating somewhat the remark of Mr. Fowler, the phrenologist; who said that he would sometimes "use rather extravagant language" in his expositions. The present edition of *Elpis Israel* restores the A.V. rendering of 2 Timothy 3:16 (page 5 and elsewhere). "All Scripture *is* given by inspiration." The R.V. rendering will not be defended by those who know the truth of the matter. On page 9, "word" has been substituted for "will and testament", as defining the Lord's purpose, the reason for which appears in another note. On page 68, the A.V. translation of Romans 13:1-5 has been restored. On page 72, the Hebrew idiom should not be lifted into the English. The footnote illustrates the matter. Some mistaken expositions have arisen out of this; hence it is here mentioned. On pages 142-3 "justification" has been restored, and "pardon" deleted; also "in" has been restored, and "by" deleted in the expressions "in the name of Jesus", etc. On page 195, the usage of *Elohim* in the singular is referred to in the footnote, and the suggestion that it should be rendered "gods" throughout Genesis is deleted. Other changes in translation are very few and are too unimportant to mention. The publisher is indebted to an esteemed fellow-labourer for valued help in the revisions here noted.

With regard to IMPROVED EXPOSITIONS due to increased knowledge the following notes may suffice. In the section on "The Sabbath", the author speaks of "the first day of the week" as "the Lord's day". But it is never so styled in the scriptures, and the author in *Eureka*, Vol. I, p.159 (a later writing), himself more forcibly draws the true distinction between "Sunday" and "the Lord's day". The latter phrase has therefore been deleted from this edition of *Elpis Israel*.

On page 53, the reference to the nature of the resurrection-body on its emergence from the grave is corrected, in harmony with the author's preface to the fourth edition, and *Anastasis*, a later work on Resurrection and Judgment.

PUBLISHER'S NOTES

On page 178, the publisher has ventured to suggest in a footnote that the scriptures do here and there suggest *reasons* for the expression of God's will in His appointed "principles of religion". He believes that his impressions on this matter are derived from Dr. Thomas' other expositions.

On page 251, the author speaks of the Lord's "*covenant* with Abraham" and a footnote gives the publisher's reasons for retaining this scriptural term and rejecting "will" and "testament" in the argument following. For the expression "substitutional testator" (page 256), the publisher has substituted the term "Mediator", which is the true equivalent of the inspired original. Those who choose to compare closely the old and new editions of *Elpis Israel* in these pages, will see that the author's argument gains in lucidity and force by the change.

On pages 381, 382, paragraphs indicated which were either lacking in clearness, or rendered erroneous by lapse of time, have been re-written on the basis of later expositions by the author.

There are very few EXPUNGED ERRORS. Among these is the erroneous paraphrase of Christ's reply to the thief on the cross (omitted in this edition from the exposition on page 63), and mentioned here only because it has, unfortunately, gained considerable currency.

On page 316, the erroneous supposition that Exodus 17 and Numbers 20 refer to one and the same incident (the smiting of the rock by Moses), is corrected by a slight change in the wording. The first incident was before the giving of the law, in Horeb, and the smiting was in *obedience* to a command of God. The second incident was nearly forty years later, at Kadesh, about 150 miles north of Horeb, and smiting was *not* commanded—only *speaking* to the rock.

From pages 388, 446 and 448, some erroneous anticipations that the efflux of time has manifested concerning the end of the age, have been omitted as a matter of course.

A more agreeable class of notes is that referring to the author's wonderful POLITICAL PREVISION on the basis of the prophecies. A mere reference to some of the footnotes in this edition will suffice for illustration. See pages 123, 358, 403, 405, 411 412, etc. Also the paragraph at the end of the preceding "Biographical Notes".

C. C. Walker, Birmingham, July, 1924

FOREWORD
to the 15th Edition

ELPIS ISRAEL was written over 150 years ago: it was a pioneer work. As appears from the Biographical Notes which follow, it was written at the request of those who had heard Dr. Thomas's lectures on the Bible, and particularly on Bible prophecies, while he was on a visit from the United States to get a closer view of the stirring events of 1848 and to lecture on the Gospel of the Kingdom of God. It is a testimony to Dr. Thomas's extensive knowledge of the Bible that he was able in four months, away from his books and lexicons, to write a work so massive in its understanding of the revealed purpose of God. At the time when it was written, frank speech expressed in robust language was indulged in without offence, and in this matter the book reflects its age. The forthrightness of the writer is seen in the vigour of his words and modern readers must make some allowance for this. The main substance of the book has stood the test of study by five generations of believers in God's Word. In the edition of 1903 some minor blemishes were removed, as explained under the heading of Publisher's Notes.

As the title implies, great emphasis is given to the doctrine of the Kingdom of God, while the doctrine of the Atonement receives what might appear to be only incidental reference. Those who may criticize the balance of the work should bear in mind the conditions of the time when it was written. The doctrine of the Kingdom was neglected or misinterpreted; on the necessity of the Cross there was general agreement even though atonement was distorted into the appeasing of an angry Deity. The disproportionate emphasis in Dr. Thomas's work is the converse of that prevailing at the time, and met a contemporary need. Were Dr. Thomas writing in the present conditions of widespread unbelief he would doubtless respond to the current needs with no less vigour of mind. In judging this work his immediate object must be kept in view.

The third part of the book deals with prophecy in relation to world affairs. Here understanding was influenced by an expectation of the Lord's early advent, which proved premature, and much that has now to be treated with reserve derived from this outlook. Whilst some things looked for came to pass, others did not; but it must be recognized that the world is conforming in general to the pattern expected. even though on a larger scale than was looked for 150 years ago. The whole world is knit together by modern means of communication; yet it is clear that as a result of the stresses of two world wars, the world is divided into two groups which might in general terms be called the land-mass group and the maritime group of nations. This is what was expected, and the impending clash of the rival forces, equipped as they are with unimagined powers of destruction, will inevitably take place in the near East. Shining brightly amidst the general distress and perplexity is the rise of the State of Israel. This is a landmark, clear and unmistakable, which shows that we are nearing the end of Gentile times. The seeker for truth will find much to help, and in view of the times and circumstances of the book's origin, will bear with the imperfections time has revealed.

FOREWORD

The Biographical Notes, the extracts from the Author's Prefaces, and the Publisher's Notes are as printed in the 1924 edition.

The reader should remember, especially when reading the Third Part of the work, that the references to recent events or existing institutions are to what were recent or existing in 1849, when the book was first written. In order not to interfere with the author's argument, these passages are left unaltered, but this note is made here to prevent misunderstanding. Examples are to be found on pages 401, 413, 437, 445, 461, 468, 475.

This edition represents the first major re-setting of the work since 1910. Opportunity has been taken to improve readability, and in this regard all scripture references have been stated in full and moved into the main body of the text. As a result, it should be noted that the number of pages has increased, and specific page references made in other publications will no longer apply.

Birmingham 2000

BIOGRAPHICAL NOTES

JOHN THOMAS was born in Hoxton Square, London, on April 12th, 1805. Information concerning his ancestry is meagre, and interest centres more in his work than in his extraction. He studied medicine at an early age in Chorley and London, and contributed to *The Lancet* occasionally as far back as 1830. His English degree, of that year's date, is M.R.C.S., his M.D. being an American degree of date 1848. Some insinuations of unfriendly critics have been met by the brief statement of facts that appears in *The Christadelphian* for April, 1886, page 152.

In 1832 Dr. Thomas emigrated to America, making the passage as surgeon to the ship *Marquis of Wellesley*. The vessel ran ashore on Sable Island, and it was supposed she would be lost with all hands. Dr. Thomas was naturally exercised as to the future state, and finding himself in a state of hopeless ignorance on the matter, resolved, if his life should be spared, that he would end the uncertainty and search out the truth upon the matter.

On getting safely ashore he did not forget this resolution; and in the course of his travels, having been introduced to Mr. Walter Scott, of "Campbellite" associations, and by him convinced of the necessity of baptism, he submitted to immersion as an ordinance appointed of God. From this time onward he became involved with Campbellism and theological expositions and discussions which were altogether distasteful to him, and from which he would fain have escaped. But it was not to be. At Wellsburg, Va., in 1833, he made the acquaintance of Alexander Campbell, and was by him constrained to speak in his meeting-place; which he did, on Daniel's prophecies, and on the subject of The Apostasy spoken of by Paul.

From this time forth wherever he went he was in demand in this connection. At Baltimore, Md., and at Philadelphia, Pa., he was likewise constrained to set forth what he then believed to be the truth. At Philadelphia he set up as a medical practitioner; but his practice was somewhat hampered by the Biblical studies and speaking in which he had become involved.

In 1834 Dr. Thomas started a monthly magazine called *The Apostolic Advocate*, in the pages of which he manifested an understanding of the Scriptures, and especially of the Apocalypse, that was rare in those times (and, indeed, in any), and gave promise of the fruit of after years, of which *Elpis Israel* is a good sample.

About this time, by the growing influence of "the Word", Dr. Thomas was rapidly becoming "wiser than his teachers", and trouble ensued. He perceived that the knowledge and belief of the gospel must in God's appointments precede baptism, and was thereupon re-immersed upon the belief of what he then supposed to be the gospel, and which was certainly much nearer to it than the very rudimentary belief with which he had been immersed a few years previously. Upon this there naturally arose a cry against what Alexander Campbell and his followers called

BIOGRAPHICAL NOTES

"Anabaptism". Mr. Campbell controverted Dr. Thomas in *The Millennial Harbinger*, and he replied vigorously in *The Apostolic Advocate*, in which, in December, 1835, he published an article in all good faith under the heading, "Information Wanted", putting forward a series of 34 questions intended to elucidate the Scriptural doctrines of eternal life, the Kingdom of God, and related topics.

This was treated by Campbellism as heretical speculation, and a rupture followed which was never healed.

In 1839, becoming tired of theological strife, Dr. Thomas migrated westward into the State of Illinois, and settled at Longrove upon some 300 acres of land and took to farming, with experiences of an arduous and sometimes amusing character. 1841 found him editing a weekly newspaper at St. Charles, and in 1842 a monthly magazine called *The Investigator*.

About this time a taste of Job's experience befell him, for, having removed to Louisville, Va., and determined to sell the farm in Illinois, he entrusted the sale to an agent who absconded with the proceeds, leaving Dr. Thomas not only minus the price but saddled with debt as well.

In 1844 he started a monthly magazine called *The Herald of the Future Age*, and settled at Richmond, Va., and soon after finally broke with Campbellism, the oppositions of which had done so much to force his attention to the accurate and thorough study of the Scriptures.

In 1847 he had elaborated from the Scriptures the doctrines that find such lucid and ample exhibition in *Elpis Israel*; and, perceiving that he had after all only just arrived at "the truth of the gospel", he published in March, 1847, "A Confession and Abjuration" of past erroneous belief and contentions, and was re-immersed for "the hope of Israel", which Paul preached to the Jews at Rome. About this time also he paid a visit to New York, where afterwards he was to settle. Also about this time he proposed to Alexander Campbell a full and exhaustive written discussion upon the immortality of the soul and related topics. The proposal, however, met with so contemptuous a refusal that several of Mr. Campbell's friends were alienated by his manner.

An interesting episode occurred also about this time, namely, the phrenological examination of both Alexander Campbell and John Thomas by Mr. L. N. Fowler, of New York. It was a quite independent examination and interestingly illustrated the natural tendencies of the disputants, and is strikingly borne out by the portraits of each.

In 1848 Dr. Thomas visited Britain. He was deeply stirred by the revolutionary upheavals of the time, and before his departure wrote on the subject to the *New York Star*, which, in publishing his letter, spoke of him as "A Missionary for Europe", which indeed he was, but of an unusual type. Arriving at Liverpool in June, 1848, he made his way South; and by a series of providences a door of utterance was opened for him by the interactions of Campbellite rivalries. He travelled through Nottingham, Derby, Birmingham, Plymouth, Lincoln, Newark, and other places, speaking upon the gospel of the Kingdom of God as occasion offered. Afterwards he made his way to Glasgow, and lectured there, and at Paisley, attracting much attention by his expositions of the prophetic word in its bearings upon the signs of the times.

Elpis Israel itself came out of this visit, as is explained by Dr. Thomas himself in the foregoing PREFACE.

Returning to London, he occupied some months in writing *Elpis Israel*, and during the time attended a Peace meeting in the British Institution, Cowper Street, at which he moved an amendment to the effect that war was a divine institution in this age of sin and death, and that the coming years were by the prophetic word defined to be "a time of war", and not "a time of peace". The amendment was derisively rejected; but the past hundred years have only too sadly well attested the soundness of Dr. Thomas' views.

Having completed *Elpis Israel*, Dr. Thomas made a second journey through England and Scotland, among other things contributing a pamphlet to "the Gorham controversy", under the title *Clerical Theology Unscriptural*, now out of print; and, in a breezy dialogue between "Boanerges" and "Heresian", exhibits the Bible truth concerning "original sin", "remission of sins", etc., as graphically set forth in other style in *Elpis Israel*.

After over two years' absence from America, Dr. Thomas returned, and resumed the publication of *The Herald of the Kingdom,* which he continued for eleven years, until the outbreak of the American Civil War in 1860-61 brought about its suspension.

In 1862 Dr. Thomas revisited Britain and found that, notwithstanding the fact that *Elpis Israel* had in many cases been burnt in disgust upon its receipt by subscribers, some small communities of believers of the gospel had arisen. For the edification of these, he travelled and lectured through the country once more, returning to America shortly afterwards.

His next, and greatest and last work, was *Eureka*, an exposition of the Apocalypse, in three volumes (over 2,000 pages), published by subscription, of which the first volume was published in 1862, and the third in 1868. It is a work which none of "the servants of God" should fail to possess.

In 1864, as *The Herald of the Kingdom* had been suspended, and Dr. Thomas was engaged upon *Eureka*, at his suggestion *The Ambassador of the Coming Age* was started under the editorship of Robert Roberts, of Birmingham, England, who continued it (as *The Christadelphian*) to the day of his death in September, 1898.

The progress of the American Civil War bore hardly upon the brethren of Christ, who were found in both the opposing camps, and who abhorred the taking of the sword as a thing forbidden by their Lord and Master, whose dictum is, "All they that take the sword, shall perish with the sword". In their extremity they desired Dr. Thomas to formulate some appeal to the authorities for exemption from military service on account of their conscientious objections, and subject to such conditions as might be thought fit to be imposed. To save his friends from being called Thomasites, it was necessary to adopt some distinctive name. The name Christian, as Dr. Thomas pointed out, had been appropriated by every Anti-Christian thing under the sun, and was no longer distinctive as it was in the first century. So Dr. Thomas hit upon the name CHRISTADELPHIAN, which, after many years' "earnest contention for the faith", conquered for itself a recognition in the allotment of about three inches of space in the *Encyclopaedia Britannica*, after this manner:—

"CHRISTADELPHIANS (Χριστού ἀδελφοί), a community founded by John Thomas (1848), who studied medicine in London and then migrated to America. There he first joined the 'Campbellites', but afterwards struck out independently, preaching largely on the application of Hebrew prophecy and of the language of the Apocalypse to current and future political events. In America and in Great Britain he gathered a number of adherents, and formed a community which is said to have extended to most English speaking countries. It consists of exclusive 'Ecclesias', with neither ministry nor organization. The members meet on Sundays to 'break bread' and discuss the Bible. Their theology is strongly Millenarian, centring in the hope of a world-wide theocracy, with its seat at Jerusalem. They believe that they alone have the true exegesis of Scripture, and that the 'faith of Christendom' is 'compounded of the fables predicted by Paul'. No statistics are published."

In 1869, after the completion of *Eureka*, Dr. Thomas visited Britain for the last time. He found that the truth had taken root through his labours, and decided to transfer his residence to England for the rest of his days. But it was not to be. Upon his advice the name of *The Ambassador* was changed to *The Christadelphian*, which it still bears. After travelling and lecturing among the people created by "the truth" illustrated by his writings, Dr. Thomas returned to New York, but was soon afterwards attacked by illness, and died March 5th, 1871. He is buried in Greenwood Cemetery, Brooklyn, where, by a remarkable coincidence, Robert Roberts, who for many years continued his work, was laid beside him in September, 1898.

Of the correctness of Dr. Thomas' political anticipations from the prophets, the following is offered as proof, in addition to what may be found in the text and footnotes of this edition of *Elpis Israel*. The subjoined extract is from *Dr. Thomas: His Life and Work*, a biography by Robert Roberts, with copious extracts from Dr. Thomas' letters and articles.

"Dr. Thomas's political prognostications, based on prophecy, have been too signally realized to admit of the supposition that he was radically mistaken in his chronological scheme. He predicted the failure of the Hungarian revolt (*Herald of the Kingdom*, vol. i., p. 98); the uprise of Napoleon III, without mentioning his name (*Herald of the Future Age*, vol. iv., p. 48); the political and war-developing ascendancy of France under him for a series of years (*Herald of the Kingdom*, vol. ii., p. 37; vol. iii., p. 16); his interference in the affairs of Italy (*Herald of the Future Age*, vol. iii., p. 262); his expulsion of the Austrians from that country (vol.v., p. 205); the war between Austria and Italy, resulting in Austria losing her hold on Italy (vol. iii., p.262); the dismemberment of the Austrian Empire by France (ibid., p.263); the downfall of the French Empire (*Herald of the Kingdom*, vol. iii., p. 17); the co-existence of the Pope and King of Italy in Rome (*Herald of the Future Age*, vol. iii., p. 288) and a number of other things, such as the efforts of Egypt for independence, the attempt of Russia on Turkey in 1854, etc., etc."—*Dr. Thomas: His Life and Work*, page 316.

CONTENTS

PART FIRST

THE RUDIMENTS OF THE WORLD

CHAPTER I

THE NECESSITY OF A REVELATION

CHAPTER II

THE CREATION OF THE EARTH AND MAN

CHAPTER III

GOD'S LAW, AND HOW SIN ENTERED INTO THE WORLD

CONTENTS

CHAPTER IV

THE SENTENCE OF DEATH—THE RUIN OF THE OLD WORLD AND THE PRESERVATION OF A REMNANT

CHAPTER V

IMMORTALITY—RELIGION—"CLERGY" AND "LAITY"

CHAPTER VI

THE PRESENT WORLD IN RELATION TO THE WORLD TO COME

PART SECOND

THE THINGS OF THE KINGDOM OF GOD, AND THE NAME OF JESUS CHRIST

CHAPTER I

THE GOSPEL OF THE KINGDOM IN RELATION TO ISRAEL AND THE GENTILES

CHAPTER II

THE GOSPEL PREACHED TO ABRAHAM HIS FAITH AND WORKS

CHAPTER III

THE GOSPEL PREACHED TO ISAAC AND JACOB:
THE SCRIPTURE DOCTRINE OF ELECTION

.

CHAPTER IV

THE GOSPEL IN RELATION TO THE MOSAIC ECONOMY

CHAPTER V

THINGS CONCERNING THE NAME OF JESUS CHRIST

CONTENTS

PART THIRD

THE KINGDOMS OF THE WORLD IN THEIR RELATION TO THE KINGDOM OF GOD

CHAPTER I

NEBUCHADNEZZAR'S IMAGE—THE HAND OF GOD IN HUMAN HISTORY

The pandemonianism of the world—The Press its organ to a great extent—Its conductors greatly deficient in political prevision—A divine agency the real source of the world's revolutions—God hath revealed what shall come to pass—Nebuchadnezzar's Image explained—It represents an Autocracy to be manifested in these Latter Days—The Toe-kingdoms enumerated—The Vision of the Four Beasts—Of the Saints and the two Witnesses

CHAPTER II

ROMAN BABYLON AND THE RESURRECTION OF THE WITNESSES

The Sin-Power in its war against the seed of the woman in the West, symbolized by the Beasts and their Image—God will surely avenge His saints—The crimes for which the nations are to be judged stated—The geography of the "Lake of Fire" where the judgment sits—The saints the executioners of the Little Horn—They are raised from political death for this purpose—Events connected with their resurrection—The three days and a half of their unburied state explained—Their ascension—End of 1,260 years—Of the time of the Beast

CHAPTER III

THE "VIALS OF THE WRATH OF GOD"—ARMAGEDDON

Doings of the witnesses when invested with power—They execute justice on their enemies—A great earthquake—The seventh trum-

CHAPTER IV

THE EASTERN QUESTION BEFORE CHRIST

CHAPTER V

THE EASTERN QUESTION IN "THE TIME OF THE END"

CHAPTER VI

THE RESURRECTION OF ISRAEL—THE SECOND
EXODUS—THE MILLENNIUM—"THE END"

CONTENTS

SUBJECT INDEX

SCRIPTURE INDEX

ELPIS ISRAEL

PART FIRST

THE RUDIMENTS OF THE WORLD

CHAPTER I

THE NECESSITY OF A REVELATION

The necessity of a Revelation to make known the origin, reason, and tendency of things in relation to man and the world around him—An intelligible Mystery, and the only source of true wisdom; but practically repudiated by the Moderns—The study of the Bible urged, to facilitate and promote which is the object of this volume

REVOLVING upon its own axis, and describing an ample circuit through the boundless fields of space, is a planet of the solar system bearing upon its surface a population of over a thousand millions subject to sin, disease, and death. This orb of the starry heavens shines with a glory similar to that of its kindred spheres. Viewed from them, it is seen sparkling "like a diamond in the sky"; and with the rest of the heavens, declares the glory of God, and shows forth the handiwork of Him that did create it.

This celestial orb, which is a world or system of itself, is styled THE EARTH. It is the habitation of races of animals which graze its fields, lurk in its forests, soar through its atmosphere, and pass through the paths of its seas. At the head of all these is a creature like themselves, animal, sensual and mortal. He is called MAN. He has replenished the earth and subdued it, and filled it with his renown. His crimes, however, rather than his virtues, have illustrated and distinguished him with an unhappy pre-eminence above all other created things. His heart is evil; and, left to its uncontrolled impulses, he becomes licentious, merciless, and more cruel than the fiercest beast of prey.

Such is the being that claims the independent sovereignty of the globe. He has founded dominions, principalities, and powers; he has built great cities, and vaunted himself in the works of his hands, saying, "Are not these by the might of my power, and for the honour of my majesty?" He repudiates all lordship over him, and claims the inalienable and inherent right of self-government,

1

and of establishing whatever civil and ecclesiastical institutions are best suited to his sensuality and caprice. Hence, at successive periods, the earth has become the arena of fierce and pandemoniac conflicts; its tragedies have baptized its soil in blood, and the mingled cries of the oppressor and the victim have ascended to the throne of the Most High.

Skilled in the wisdom which comes from beneath, he is by nature ignorant of that which is "first pure, and then peaceable, gentle, and easy to be entreated, full of mercy and good fruits, without partiality and without hypocrisy". This is a disposition to which the animal man under the guidance of his fleshly mind has no affinity. His propensity is to obey the lust of his nature; and to do its evil works, "which are adultery, fornication, uncleanness, lasciviousness, idolatry, witchcraft, hatred, variance, emulations, wrath, strife, seditions, sects, envying, murders, drunkenness, revellings, and such like" (Galatians 5:19-21). All these make up the character of the world, "the lust of the flesh, the lust of the eye, and the pride of life", upon which is enstamped the seal of God's eternal reprobation. "They who do such things shall not inherit the kingdom of God," but "they shall die".

Such is the world of human kind! The great and impious enemy of God upon the earth. Its mind is not subject to His law, neither indeed can it be. What shall we say to these things? Is the world as we behold it a finality? Are generations of men, rebellious against God, and destroyers of the earth, to occupy it successively through an endless series of ages? Are men to repeat the history of the past for ever? Is the earth always to be cursed, and sin and death to reign victorious? Who can answer these inquiries? If we survey the starry canopy, thence no sign or voice is given expressive of the truth. They declare the eternal power and divinity of their Creator, but they speak not of the destiny of the earth or of man upon it. If we question the mountains and hills, the plains and valleys, the rivers, seas, and oceans of the earth, and demand their origin, why they were produced, to what end they were created; their rocks, their strata, their fossils, or deposits, afford us no response. Turn we to man and ask him, "Whence comest thou, and what is thy destiny? Whence all the evil of thy nature, why art thou mortal, who made thee, who involved thee in the wide-spread ruin and calamity on every side?"

Ask an infant of days the history of the past, and he can as well detail it, as man can answer these inquiries without a revelation from Him who is before all, and to whom is known from the beginning all He intends shall come to pass. So true is it, that, unaided by light from heaven, "since the beginning of the world men have not heard, nor perceived by the ear, neither hath the eye seen, O God, beside thee, what is prepared for him that waiteth for him"; but, adds the apostle in his comment upon these words of the prophet, "God hath revealed these things unto us by his spirit ... which things we (apostles) speak, not in the words which man's wisdom teacheth, but which the holy spirit teacheth; interpreting spiritual things in spiritual words" (1 Corinthians 2:9,10,13).

To the Bible, then, all must come at last if they would be truly wise in spiritual things. This is a great truth which few of the sons of men have learned to appreciate according to its importance. A man may be a theologian profoundly skilled in all questions of "divinity"; he may be well versed in the mythology of the heathen world; be able to speak all languages of the nations; compute the distances of orb from orb, and weigh them in the scales of rigid calculation; he may know all science and be able to solve all mysteries,—but if, with all this, he be ignorant of "the things of the spirit"; if he know not the true meaning of the Bible; he seemeth only to be wise, while he is, in fact, a fool. Therefore, the apostle saith, "let no man deceive himself. If any man among you seemeth to be wise in this world, let him become a fool, that he may be wise. For the wisdom of this world is foolishness with God. For it is written, He taketh the wise in their own craftiness. And again, the Lord knoweth the thoughts of the wise, that they are vain. Therefore *let no man glory in men*" (1 Corinthians 3:18-21). If our contemporaries could only attain to the adoption of this great precept, "let no man glory in men", they would have overleaped a barrier which as a fatal obstacle prevents myriads from understanding and obeying the truth.

But while God lightly esteems the wisdom of the reputed wise, there is a wisdom which He invites all men to embrace. This is styled *"the wisdom of God in a mystery"*; it is also termed "the *hidden wisdom* which God ordained before the world, which none of the princes of this world knew". It is said to be hidden in a mystery, because until the apostolic age, it was not clearly made known. This will appear from the following texts: "Now to him that is of power to establish you according to the revelation of THE MYSTERY, *which was kept secret* (χρόνοις αἰωνίοις) in the times of the ages, but *now* (in the time, or age, of the apostles) is made manifest, and by the scriptures of the prophets made known to all nations *for the obedience of faith*" (Romans 16:25,26). "By revelation God made known unto me, Paul, THE MYSTERY, which in other ages (former ages under the law of Moses) was not made known unto the sons of men *as it is now revealed* unto the holy apostles and prophets by the spirit, *that the Gentiles should be fellow heirs, and of the same body, and*

3

partakers of his promise in Christ by the gospel" (Ephesians 3:3,5,6).

Here is "the knowledge of God", in which are contained "exceeding great and precious promises", the understanding of which is able to make a man wise, and "a partaker of the divine nature". Now, although these hidden things have been clearly made known, they still continued to be styled the mystery; not because of their unintelligibility, but because they were once secret. Hence, the things preached unto the Gentiles, and by them believed, are styled by Paul, "the mystery of the faith", and "the mystery of godliness", some of the items of which he enumerates; such as, "God manifest in the flesh, justified by the spirit, seen of angels, preached unto the Gentiles, believed on in the world, received up in glory" (1 Timothy 3:9,16). Thus an *intelligible mystery* characterizes the once hidden wisdom of God, and becomes the subject matter of an enlightened faith. This, however, is not the case with regard to religious systems which are not of the truth. Unintelligible mystery is the *ultima ratio* for all difficulties which are insoluble by the symbols of ecclesiastical communities, whose text of universal application is, that "secret things belong to God, but the things which are revealed, to us and to our children". This is true; but, then, these things which were secret in the days of Moses, have been revealed by God to the apostles and prophets for our information.

No one has any right to set up his own ignorance as the limit of what God hath revealed. A thing may be unknown to such a man, but it doth not therefore follow that it is either absolutely unintelligible or a secret. He may not know of it, or, if explained to him, he may not have intellect enough to comprehend it, or his prejudices, or sectarian bias may darken his understanding—this by no means makes the thing unintelligible or mysterious to other people. All that such persons have a right to say is, "We do not know anything about it". They may confess their own ignorance, and resolve to look into the matter, or not; but they are presumptuously overstepping the bounds of propriety to venture to do more. Those who have no secondary interests to subserve apart from the truth only desire to know that they may believe and do. But where to know more would jeopardize the "vested interests" of a sect, and extort the confessions of its leaders and members that they were in error and knew not the truth, investigation is discouraged, and the things proscribed as too speculative and mysterious for comprehension, or, if understood, of no practical utility. In this way mankind infold themselves as in the mantle of their self-esteem. They repress all progress, and glorify their own ignorance by detracting from things which they fear to look into, or apprehend are far above their reach.

Beside glorying in men, this unfortunate peculiarity of the human mind has developed the organization of a system of things impiously hostile to the institutions and wisdom of Jehovah. It is a system of many subordinate parts. It is animated by one spirit which, under various modifications, pervades and actuates the whole. It is an evil spirit, and may be detected wherever the dogma of unintelligible mystery is at work. The name of this system is "MYSTERY". Its baneful effects began to be visible in the apostolic age. It was then styled, *the Mystery of iniquity*, which, as was predicted, has, like a cancer, eaten out the truth, and submitted in place thereof a civil and ecclesiastical constitution, styled "Harlots and the Abominations of the Earth", such as we behold on every side.

"Wisdom", say the scriptures, "is the principal thing; therefore get wisdom; and with all thy getting get understanding. Exalt her, and she shall promote thee: she shall bring thee to honour, when thou dost embrace her. She shall give to thy head an ornament of grace; *a crown of glory* shall she deliver to thee." If thou wouldst, O reader, get this wisdom, happy art thou if thou findest it. "For the merchandise of it is better than the merchandise of silver, and the gain thereof than fine gold. She is more precious than rubies, and all things thou canst desire are not to be compared to her. Length of days is in her right hand; and in her left hand riches and honour. Her ways are ways of pleasantness, and all her paths are peace. She is A TREE OF LIFE to them that lay hold upon her; and happy is every one that retaineth her" (Proverbs 3:14-18).

Before the Son of God sent forth his apostles to proclaim the gospel of the kingdom in his name, "He opened their understanding that they might understand the scriptures". If thou wouldst gain the knowledge of the wisdom of God which is so inestimable, and which is contained in the word they preached, thou must also be the subject of the same illumination. This is indispensable; for there is no obtaining of this commodity except through the scriptures of truth. These "are able to make thee wise unto salvation through faith which is in Christ Jesus. For all scripture is given by inspiration of God, and is profitable for teaching, for conviction, for correction, for instruction in righteousness: that the man of God may be perfect, throughly furnished unto all good works" (2 Timothy 3:15-17). What more dost thou want than perfection, and a crown of life and glory in the age to come? Search the scriptures with the teachableness of a little child, and thy labour will not be in vain. Cast away to the owls and to the bats the traditions of men, and the prejudices indoctrinated into thy mind by their means; make a whole burnt offering of their creeds, confessions, catechisms, and articles of religion; and, after the example of the Ephesian disciples, hand over your books of curious theological arts, and burn them before all (Acts 19:19). These mountains of rubbish have served the purpose of a dark and barbarous age; the word, the word of the living God alone, can meet the necessities of the times.

Let the example of the noble-minded Bereans be ours. They searched the scriptures daily to see if the things taught by the apostles were worthy of belief; "therefore they believed" (Acts 17:11,12). If, then, not even the preaching of an apostle was credited unaccompanied by scriptural investigation, is it not infinitely more incumbent on us that we should bring to a like test the opinions and precepts of the uninspired and fallible professional theologists of our day? Let us believe nothing that comes from "the pulpit", "the altar", or the press, not demonstrated by the grammatical sense of the scriptures. Let us be contented with nothing less than a "thus it is written", and a "thus saith the Lord"; for He has laid it down in His law, that no one is worthy of belief who does not speak after His rule. "To *the law and to the testimony*: if they speak not according to THIS WORD, it is because there is no light in them" (Isaiah 8:20). If then their light be darkness, how great is that darkness.

The scriptures can do everything for us in relation to the light. This is known, felt, and keenly appreciated by all interested in the support of error. Hence, in the days of Diocletian, one of the pagan predecessors of Constantine, a decree was issued commanding the surrender of all copies of the Holy Scriptures: for it was found that so long as they obtained circulation the Christian doctrine could never be suppressed. The Popes, as deadly, and more insidious, enemies of the truth than the pagan Roman emperors, followed the example of Diocletian. The Bible and popery are as mutually hostile as the light of the sun and the thick darkness of Egypt that might be felt. But it is not paganism and popery alone that are practically hostile to a free and untrammelled investigation of the word of God. The Protestant world, while it deludes itself with the conceit that "the Bible, the Bible *alone*, is the religion of Protestants"—while it spends its thousands for its circulation among the nations in their native tongues—is itself hostile to the belief and practice of what it proclaims. The "Bible *alone*" is not its religion; for if it were, why encumber its professors with the "Common Prayer", "Thirty-nine Articles", and all the other "notions" of a similar kind? To believe and practise the Bible alone would be a sufficient ground of exclusion from all "orthodox churches". When Chillingworth uttered the sentiment, there was more truth in it than at this day; but now it is as far from the fact as that Protestantism is the religion of Christ.

To protest against an error, such as Romanism, and to affirm that every man has a right to worship God according to the dictates of his own conscience, is a very different thing to believing and obeying the gospel of the Kingdom of God, and walking in all the institutions of the Lord blameless. To do this would unchristianize a man in the estimation of State churches and sectarian denominations; for the Bible religion requires a man to *"contend earnestly for the faith once delivered to the saints"* (Jude 3), which in these times cannot be done without upheaving the very foundations of the self-complacent, self-glorifying, and self-laudatory communions of the antipapal constitution of things. It is true that no man or power has a right to interfere between God and the conscience; but it is also true that no man has a right to worship God as he pleases. This is a Protestant fallacy. *Man has a right to worship God only in the way God has Himself appointed.* "In vain do ye worship me, teaching for doctrines the commandments of men." This is the judgment pronounced by the wisdom of God upon all worship which He has not instituted. He declares it to be *vain worship*; concerning which the apostle to the Gentiles says: "Let no man judge you *in meat*, or *in drink*, or in respect of *a holy-day*, or of the new moon, or of *the Sabbath*; let no man beguile you of your reward in a *voluntary humility* and worshipping of angels. Be not subject to dogmatisms (δογματίζεσθε) after the commandments and traditions of men; which things have indeed a *show of wisdom in* WILL-WORSHIP and humility" (Colossians 2:16-23).

These exhortations apply to all faith and worship, Papal and Protestant. If Popery judges men in meats, Protestantism doth the same in drinks, and in the Sabbath; they both judge men in holy-days and "movable feasts"; and though Protestantism repudiates the worshipping of angels, it proclaims in its "fasts", "preparations", "concerts", etc., a voluntary humility, and celebration of "saints and martyrs", renowned in legendary tales for "the pride that apes humility". Let the reader search the scriptures from beginning to end, and he will nowhere find such systems of faith and worship as those comprehended in the Papal and Protestant systems. The gospel of the Kingdom of God in the name of Jesus is not preached among them; they are communions which are uncircumcised of heart; theological dissertations on texts, called "sermons", are substituted for "reasoning out of the scriptures"—for "expounding and testifying the Kingdom of God, and persuading men concerning Jesus, both out of the law of Moses, and out of the prophets" (Acts 28:23,31). Puseyism, Swedenborgianism, and all sorts of *isms*, to which in apostolic times the world was a total stranger, run riot among them; the lusts of the flesh, of the eye, and of the pride of life have extinguished even the energy and zeal of the antipapal rebellion out of which they have arisen; they are dead, twice dead, plucked up by the roots, and therefore the time is come to cut them off as a rotten branch from the good olive tree (Romans 11:17,20,22). Let therefore every man that would eschew the wrath which is begun, and who would become an heir of the kingdom of God, save himself from the unholy, lifeless, and effete denominations of these "Latter Days". By remaining in them, a man partakes of their evil deeds, and subjects himself to their evil influences. The word of man has silenced the word of God in their midst; and religion has degenerated into a professional commodity sold for cash according to the taste which most prevails in the soul-makers of the world.

Let us then "cease from men, whose breath is in their nostrils; for wherein are they to be accounted of?" "They be blind leaders of the blind", in whom is no light, because they speak not according to the law and the testimony of God. Let us repudiate their dogmatisms; let us renounce their mysteries; and let us declare our independence of all human authority in matters of faith and practice outside the word of God. The scriptures are able to make us wise, which the traditions of "divines" are not. Let us then come to these scriptures, for we have the assurance that he who seeks shall find. But we must seek by the light of scripture, and not permit that light to be obscured by high thoughts and vain imaginations which exalt themselves against the knowledge of God. Great is the consolation that "the wise shall understand", and "shall shine as the brightness of the firmament". Be this then our happiness, to understand, believe, and do, that we may be blessed in our deed, and attain to the glorious liberty and manifestation of the sons of God.

To the Bible then let us turn, as to "a light shining in a dark place", and, with humility, teachableness, and independence of mind, let us diligently inquire into the things which it reveals for the obedience and confirmation of faith. The object before us then will be, to present such a connected view of this truthful and wonderful book as will open the reader's eyes, and enable him to understand it, and expound it to others, that he may become "a workman that needeth not to be ashamed, rightly dividing the word of truth"; and be able intelligently to "contend for the faith"; and by "turning many to righteousness, to shine as the stars for ever and ever".

In effecting this purpose, we must proceed as we would with any other book, or in teaching any of the arts and sciences; namely, begin at the beginning, or with the elements of things. This was the method adopted by the spirit of God in the instruction of the Israelites by Moses. He began His revelations by giving them, and us through them, an account of the creation of the heavens and the earth; of animals; and of man. This then would seem to be the proper place for us to start from; and as we have the system completely revealed, which they had not, we may extend our enquiries into the reason, or philosophy of things farther than they. Be this, then, our commencement; and may the Lord himself prosper our endeavours to decipher and understand His word, and to disentangle it from the crude traditions and dogmatisms of contemporary theologies, useful in their beginnings as *"oppositions"* to the Mystery of Iniquity, but now "waxed old and ready to vanish away" with the thing they have antagonized; but which, though consumptive of the civil and ecclesiastical tyranny of the Image of the Beast, have by their glosses in effect taken from the people "the Key of Knowledge", and thus shut up the Kingdom of Heaven against men. Our endeavour will be to restore this "Key", that they may understand "the mysteries of the kingdom", and "have right to the tree of life, and enter in through the gates into the city" (Revelation 22:14). And this we will do if God permit.

RUDIMENTS OF THE WORLD

CHAPTER II

THE CREATION OF THE EARTH AND MAN

The earth before the creation of Adam the habitation of the angels who kept not their first estate—A geological error corrected—The Sabbath day and the Lord's day—The formation of man and woman—The "great mystery" of her formation out of man explained—Eden—The Garden of Eden—The original and future paradises considered—Man's primitive dominion confined to the inferior creatures and his own immediate family—Of the two trees of the garden—And man in his original estate

THE *general* account of the work of the six days is contained in the first chapter of Genesis; while in the second is presented among other things, a more particular narrative of the work of the sixth day in the formation of the first human pair.

Let the reader peruse the history of the creation as a revelation to himself as an inhabitant of the earth. It informs him of the order in which the things narrated would have developed themselves to his view, had he been placed on some projecting rock, the spectator of the events detailed. He must remember this. The Mosaic account is not a revelation to the inhabitants of other orbs remote from the earth of the formation of the boundless universe; but to man, as a constituent of the terrestrial system. This will explain why light is said to have been created four days before the sun, moon, and stars. To an observer on the earth this was *the order of their appearance*; and in relation to him a *primary* creation, though absolutely preexistent for millions of ages before the Adamic era.

The *duration* of the earth's revolutions round the sun previous to the work of the first day is not revealed: but the evidences produced by the strata of our globe show that the period was long continued. There are indeed hints, casually dropped in the scriptures, which would seem to indicate that our planet was inhabited by a race of beings anterior to the formation of man. The apostle Peter, speaking of the "false teachers" that would arise among Christians "by reason of whom the way of truth would be evil spoken of" illustrates the certainty of their "damnation" by citing three cases in point; namely, that of certain angels; that of the antediluvian world; and that of Sodom and Gomorrah. Now the earth, we know, was the place of judgment to the contemporaries of Noah and Lot, and seeing that these three are warnings to inhabitants of earth, it is probable that they are all related to things pertaining to our globe in the order of their enumeration—first, judgment upon its pre-Adamic inhabitants; secondly, upon the antediluvian world, which succeeded them; and thirdly, upon Sodom after the flood.

Peter says that "the Angels", or pre-Adamic inhabitants of the Earth, "sinned"; and Jude, in speaking of the same subject, reveals to us the nature of their transgression. He says (verse 6), "the angels maintained not their original state, but forsook their own habitation". From which it would appear that they had the ability to leave their dwelling if they pleased; secondly, that they were sometimes employed as messengers to other parts of the universe; this their name (ἄγγελος, angelos, *one sent*) implies; thirdly, that they were forbidden to leave their habitation without special command to do so; and fourthly, that they violated this injunction and left it. Having transgressed the divine law, God would not forgive them; "but casting them down", or driving them back, "he committed them to everlasting chains of intense darkness to be reserved for judgment" (2 Peter 2:4). Hence, it is clear, when they were driven back to their habitation, some further catastrophe befell them by which their committal to darkness was effected. This probably consisted in the total wreck of their abode, and their entire submergence, with all the mammoths of their estate, under the waters of an overwhelming flood. Reduced to this extremity, the earth became "without form and empty; and darkness overspread the deep waters" (Genesis 1:2). Its mountains, hills, valleys, plains, seas, rivers, and fountains of waters, which gave diversity of "*form*" to the surface of our globe, all disappeared; and it became "*void*", or empty, no living creatures, angels, quadrupeds, birds, or fishes, being found any more upon it.

Fragments, however, of the wreck of this pre-Adamic world have been brought to light by geological research, to the records of which we refer the reader, for a detailed account of its discoveries, with this remark, that its organic remains, coal fields, and strata, belong to the ages before the formation of man, rather than to the era of the creation, or the Noachic flood. This view of the matter will remove a host of difficulties, which have hitherto disturbed the harmony between the conclusions of geologists and the Mosaic account of the physical constitution of our globe.

Geologists have endeavoured to extend the six days into six thousand years. But this, with the scriptural data we have adduced, is quite unnecessary. Instead of six thousand, they can avail themselves of sixty thousand; for the scriptures reveal no length of time during which the terrene angels dwelt upon our globe. The six days of Genesis were unquestionably six diurnal revolutions of the earth upon its axis. This is clear from the tenor of the sabbath law. "Six days shalt thou labour (O Israel) and do all thy work; but the seventh day is the sabbath of the LORD thy God: in it thou shalt not do any work: for in six days the LORD made heaven and earth, the sea, and all that in them is, and rested the seventh day: wherefore the LORD blessed the sabbath day, and hallowed it." Would it be any fit reason that, because the Lord worked six periods of a thousand or more years each, and had ceased about two thousand until the giving of the law, therefore the Israelites were to work six periods of twelve hours, and do no work on a seventh period or day of like duration? Would any Israelite or Gentile, unspoiled by vain philosophy, come to the conclusion of the geologists by reading the sabbath law? We believe not. Six days of ordinary length were ample time for Omnipotence, with all the power of the universe at command, to re-form the earth, and to place the few animals upon it necessary for the beginning of a new order of things upon the globe.

But what is to become of the Evil Angels in everlasting chains of darkness, and who shall be their judge? Jude says, they were committed "for *the judgment of* THE GREAT DAY". He alludes to this great day in his quotation of the prophecy of Enoch, saying: "Behold, the Lord cometh with ten thousand of his Holy Ones (angels of his might—2 Thessalonians 1:7) *to execute judgment* upon all", etc. This coming of the Lord to judgment is termed by Paul, "the Day of Christ"—"A DAY in which he will judge the world in righteousness by Jesus Christ"—during which, the saints, with angels ministering to them, having lived again, will reign with Christ a thousand years on the earth (2 Thessalonians 2:2; Revelation 5:10; 20:4,11-15). This is the Great Day of Judgment, a period of one thousand years, in which Christ and his saints will govern the nations righteously; judge the raised dead in his kingdom according to their works; and award to the rebel angels the recompense awaiting their transgression. "Know ye not", saith Paul, "that *we* (the saints) *shall judge angels*? How much more, things that pertain to this life?" (1 Corinthians 6:3). From these data, then, we conclude that these angels will be judged in the Day of Christ by Jesus and the saints.

In the period between the wreck of the globe as the habitation of the rebel angels and the epoch of the first day, the earth was as described in Genesis 1:2, "without form and void, and darkness upon the face of the deep"—a globe of mineral structure, submerged in water, and mantled in impenetrable night. Out of these crude materials, a new habitation was constructed, and adapted to the abode of new races of living creatures. On the first day, light was caused to shine through the darkness, and disclose the face of the waters; on the second, the atmosphere called Heaven was formed, by which the fog was enabled to float in masses above the deep; on the third, the waters were gathered together into seas, and the dry land, called the *Earth*, appeared. It was then clothed with verdure, and with fruit and forest trees, preparatory to the introduction of herbivorous creatures to inhabit it. On the fourth day, the expanded atmosphere became transparent, and the shining orbs of the universe could be seen from the surface of the earth. Our globe was then placed in such astronomical relation to them as to be subjected by their influences to the vicissitudes of day and night, summer and winter; and that they might serve for signs, and for years. Thus, the sun, moon, and stars which God had made, by giving the earth's axis a certain inclination to the plane of the ecliptic, became diffusive of the most genial influences over the land and sea. It was now a fit and beautiful abode for animals of every kind. The dwelling-place was perfected, well aired, and gloriously illuminated by the lights of heaven; food was abundantly provided; and the man-sional estate waited only a joyous tenantry to be complete.

This was the work of the fifth and sixth days. On the fifth, fish and water-fowl were produced from the teeming waters; and on the sixth, cattle, reptiles, land-fowl, and the beasts of the earth, came out of "the dust of the ground", male and female, after their several kinds (Genesis 1:20-25; 2:19).

But among all these there was not one fit to exercise *dominion over the animal world*, or to reflect the divine attributes. Therefore the Elohim said, "Let *us* make man in *our* image, after *our* likeness: and let them have dominion over the living creatures". So Elohim created man in His image; male and female created He them. Further details concerning the formation of the human pair are given in the second chapter of Genesis, verses 7,18,21-25. These passages belong to the work of the sixth day; while that from verse 8 to 14 pertains to the record of the third; and from 15 to 17 is parallel with chapter 1:28-31, which completes the history of the sixth.

"Thus the heavens and the earth were finished, and all the host of them"; and the Jehovah Elohim, on reviewing the stupendous and glorious creation elaborated by the Spirit, pronounced it "VERY GOOD". Then the Elohim or "Morning Stars sang together, and all the sons of God shouted for joy" (Job 38:4-7).

OF THE SABBATH DAY

ON the seventh day, which was neither longer nor shorter than the days which preceded it, "God ended his work which he had made"; and because of this notable event, "he blessed and sanctified it". A day is blessed, because of what is or will be imparted to those who are commanded to observe it. The sanctification of the day implies the setting of it apart that it might be kept in some way different from other days. The manner of its original observance may be inferred from the law concerning it when it was enjoined upon the Israelites. To them it was said, "Remember the sabbath day to keep it holy". If it be asked, how was it to be kept holy? the answer is, "in it thou shalt not do any work, thou, nor any one or thing belonging to thee"; and the reason for this total abstinence from work is referred to the Lord's own example in that "he rested the seventh day". The nature of its observance in the ages and generations, and the recompense thereof, is well expressed in the words of Isaiah:—"If thou turn away thy foot from the sabbath, from doing thy pleasure on my holy day; and call the sabbath a delight, the holy of the LORD, honourable: and shalt honour him, not doing thine own ways, nor finding thine own pleasure, nor speaking thine own words: then shalt thou delight thyself in the LORD, and I will cause thee to ride upon the high places of the earth, and feed thee with the heritage of Jacob thy father: for the mouth of the LORD hath spoken it" (Isaiah 58:13,14).

In this passage, the conditions are stated upon which faithful Israelites might inherit the blessing typified by the rest of the seventh day. They were joyfully to devote themselves to the way of the Lord. They were not simply to abstain from work, yawning and grumbling over the tediousness of the day, and wishing it were gone, that they might return to their ordinary course of life; but they were to esteem it as a delightful, holy, and honourable day. Their pleasure was to consist in doing what the Lord required, and in talking of "the exceeding great and precious promises" He had made. To do this was "not speaking their own words", but the Lord's words. Such an observance as this, however, of the sabbath day, implies a faithful mind and a gracious disposition as the result of knowing the truth. Neither antediluvian nor postdiluvian could "call the sabbath a delight" who was either ignorant or faithless of the import of the promise, "thou shalt delight thyself in the LORD, and ride upon the high places of the earth, and feed with the heritage of Jacob". A man who simply looked at the seventh day as a sabbath in which he was interdicted from pleasures, and conversation agreeable to him, and from the money-making pursuits in which he delighted, would regard the day more as a weekly punishment, than as joyous and honourable. Though he might mechanically abstain from work, he did not keep it so as to be entitled to the blessing which belonged to the observance of the day of the Lord. It was irksome to him, because, being faithless, he perceived no reward in keeping it; and "without faith it is impossible to please God".

The reward to antediluvian and postdiluvian patriarchs and Israelites, for a faithful observance, or commemoration of

Jehovah's rest from His creation-work, was "delight in the LORD, riding upon the high places of the earth, and feeding with the heritage of Jacob". This was neither more nor less than a promise of inheriting the Kingdom of God, which is a summary of "the things hoped for and the things unseen", or the subject matter of the faith that pleases God. When that kingdom is established, all who are accounted worthy of it will "delight or joy in the LORD"; and occupy "the high places of the earth", ruling over the nations as His associate kings and priests; and share in the "new heavens and earth," in which dwells righteousness, when Jerusalem shall be made a rejoicing, and her people Israel a joy (Matthew 25:23,24; Revelation 2:26,27; 3:21; 5:9,10; 20:4; Daniel 7:18,22,27; Isaiah 65:17,18). The knowledge and belief of these things was the powerful and transforming motive which caused Abel, Abraham, Moses, Jesus, etc., to "call the sabbath a delight, holy of the LORD, and honourable"; and to observe it as the sons of Belial cannot possibly do. But while this was the motive, even faith, which actuated the sons of God in their keeping holy the seventh day, Jehovah did not permit the faithless to transgress or desecrate it with impunity. We know not what penalty, if any, was attached to its violation before the flood; but its desecration under the Mosaic constitution was attended with signal and summary vengeance, as will appear from the following testimonies: —

1.   "And the LORD spake unto Moses, saying, Speak thou unto the children of Israel, saying, Verily my sabbaths ye shall keep; for it is *a sign between me and you throughout your generations*; that ye may know that I am the LORD that doth sanctify you. Ye shall keep the sabbath therefore: for it is holy *unto you*. Every one that defileth it shall surely be put to death; for whosoever doeth *any work* therein, that soul shall be cut off from among his people. Six days may work be done, but in the *seventh* is the sabbath of rest, holy to the LORD; *whosoever doeth any work on the sabbath day shall surely be put to death*. Wherefore *the children of Israel* shall keep the sabbath, to observe the sabbath throughout their generations, for a perpetual covenant. It is *a sign between me and the children of Israel for ever*; for in six days the LORD made heaven and earth, and on the seventh day he rested and was *refreshed*" (Exodus 31:12-17).

2.   "Remember (O Israel), that thou wast a servant in the land of Egypt, and the LORD thy God brought thee out thence through a mighty hand and by a stretched out arm; therefore the LORD thy God commanded thee to keep the sabbath day" (Deuteronomy 5:15).

3.   "Six days shall work be done, but on the *seventh* day there shall be to you a holy day, a sabbath of rest to the LORD:

whosoever doeth work therein shall be put to death. *Ye shall kindle no fire throughout your habitations on the sabbath day*" (Exodus 35:2,3).

4. "And while the children of Israel were in the wilderness, they found a man that gathered sticks upon the sabbath day. And they that found him gathering sticks brought him unto Moses and Aaron, and unto all the congregation. And they put him in ward, because it was not declared what should be done to him. And the LORD said unto Moses, The man shall surely be put to death; all the congregation shall stone him with stones without the camp. And all the congregation brought him without the camp, and stoned him with stones, and he died; as the LORD commanded Moses" (Numbers 15:32-36).

5. "Thus saith the LORD; Take heed to yourselves, and *bear no burden* on the sabbath day, nor bring it in by the gates of Jerusalem: neither carry forth a burden out of your houses on the sabbath day, neither do ye any work, but hallow ye the sabbath day, as I commanded your fathers ... And it shall come to pass, if ye diligently hearken unto me, saith the LORD, to bring in no burden through the gates of this city on the sabbath day, to do no work therein: *then shall there enter into the gates of this city kings and princes sitting upon the throne of David*, riding in chariots and upon horses, they, and their princes, the men of Judah, and the inhabitants of Jerusalem: and this city shall remain for ever. And they shall come from the cities of Judah, and from the places about Jerusalem, and from the land of Benjamin and from the plain, and from the mountains, and from the south, bringing burnt offerings, and sacrifices, and meat-offerings, and incense, and bringing sacrifices of praise, unto the temple of the LORD. But if ye will not hearken unto me to hallow the sabbath day, and not to bear a burden, even entering in at the gates of Jerusalem on the sabbath day; then I will kindle a fire in the gates thereof, and it shall devour the palaces of Jerusalem, and it shall not be quenched" (Jeremiah 17:21-27).

6. "Abide ye every man in his place; let no man go out of his place on the seventh day. So the people rested on the seventh day" (Exodus 16:29,30).

From these testimonies it is clear that it was unlawful for servants in the families of Israel to light fires, cook dinners, harness horses, drive out families to the synagogues, or priests to the temple to officiate in the service of the Lord. The visiting of families on the sabbath day, the taking of excursions for health or for preaching, and conversing about worldly, or family, or any kind of secular affairs, was also illegal, and punishable with death. The law, it will be observed also, had regard to the *seventh*, and to no other day of the week. It was lawful to do all these things on the *first* or *eighth* day (some particular ones, however, excepted), but not on the seventh. On this day, however, it was "lawful to do good"; but then, this good was not arbitrary. Neither the priests nor the people were the judges of the good or evil, but the law only which defined it. "On the sabbath days the priests in the temple profaned the sabbath, and were blameless" (Matthew 12:5); for the law enjoined them to offer "two lambs of the first year, without spot, as the burnt-offering of every sabbath" (Numbers 28:9-10). This was a profanation of the seventh-day law, which prohibited "any work" from being done; and had not God commanded it, they would have been "guilty of death". It was upon this ground that Jesus was "guiltless"; for he did the work of God on that day in healing the sick as the Father had commanded him.

"The sabbath was made for man, and not man for the sabbath: therefore", said Jesus, "the Son of Man is Lord also of the sabbath Day" (Mark 2:27,28). It was a wise and beneficent institution. It prevented the Israelites from wearing out themselves and their dependants by incessant toil; and revived in them a weekly remembrance of the law and promises of God. It was, however, only "*a* SHADOW *of things to come*", the substance of which is found in the things which pertain to the Anointed One of God (Colossians 2:14,16-17). It was a part of "the rudiments of the world" inscribed on "the handwriting of ordinances that was against us, which was contrary to us", and which the Lord Jesus "took out of the way, nailing it to his cross". When he lay entombed he rested from his labours, abiding in his place all the seventh day. Having ended his work, he arose on the eighth day, "and was refreshed". The shadowy sabbath disappeared before the brightness of the rising of the sun of righteousness; who, having become the accursed of the law, delivered his brethren from its sentence upon all.

The ordinances of the law of Moses are styled by Paul "the rudiments", or "elements of the world", which, in Galatians, he also terms "weak and beggarly elements, whereunto they desired again to be in bondage". They evinced this desire by "observing *days*, and months, and times, and years" (Galatians 4:3,5,9,10); not being satisfied with the things of Christ, but seeking to combine the Mosaic institutions with the gospel. This was Judaizing, and the first step to that awful apostasy by which the world has been cursed for so many ages. When the Mosaic constitution, as "the *representation* of the knowledge and the truth", had "waxed old" by the manifestation of the substance to a sufficient extent to nullify it, it "vanished away" by being "cast down to the ground" by the Roman power, and with it the law of the seventh day. Even before its abolition, Paul expressed his fear of the Galatians, "lest he should have bestowed labour upon them in vain", seeing that they were becoming zealous of the ordinances of the law. They seemed not to understand that the Mosaic economy was only a temporary constitution of things, "added because of transgressions, *till the seed should come*"; that when he came, "he redeemed them from the curse of the law, being made a curse for them"; and that therefore they had nothing to fear, nor to hope for from keeping, or transgressing its methods. They had got it into their heads that "except they were circumcised and kept the law of Moses", as well as believed and obeyed the gospel of the kingdom, they could not be saved (Acts 15:1,5). Therefore they "desired to be under the law", and began to busy themselves about "keeping the sabbath", and doing other works which Moses had enjoined upon Israel. Paul was very much distressed at this, and describes himself as "travailing in birth again until Christ be formed in them". They had been delivered from "the yoke of bondage", by putting on Christ, but by seeking to renew their connexion with Moses' law, they were selling their birth-right for a mess of pottage. "I say unto you", saith Paul, "that if ye be circumcised, Christ shall profit you nothing. For I testify again to every man that is circumcised, that *he is a debtor to do the whole law.* Christ is become of no effect unto you, whosoever of you are justified by the law; ye are fallen from grace". A partial observance of the law can do no one any good. If he kept the sabbath in the most approved manner, but neglected the sacrifices, or ate swine's flesh, he was as accursed as a thief or a robber; for to one under the law it saith, "Cursed is every one that continueth not in *all things* which are written in the book of the law to do them"; hence even the sinless Jesus was cursed by it, because he was crucified; for it is written, "Cursed is every one that hangeth on a tree" (Galatians 3:10; 5:4). What hope then is there for Jew or Gentile of escaping the curse of the law, seeing that from the very nature of things connected with the present state of Jerusalem it is impossible to observe it, save in the few particulars of "meat and drink, or in respect of the sabbath" partially, etc. The observance of the seventh day was regulated by the Mosaic law, and the penalties due to its "desecration", or "profanation", are pronounced by it alone; but it is clear that the law being taken out of the way, or abolished, by Jesus, who nailed it to his cross, there remain no more retributions for the non-observance of its appointments; and therefore there is no transgression in working or pleasure-taking, or in speaking one's own words on the seventh day.

On the first day of the creation-week God said, "Let there be light, and there was light"; so on the first day of the week "THE

TRUE LIGHT" came forth from the darkness of the tomb "like dew from the womb of the morning". It is a day to be much remembered by his people, because it assures them of their justification "in him", of their own resurrection to life, and of the certainty of his ruling or "judging the world in righteousness" as Jehovah's king, when they shall also reign with him as kings and priests to God (Romans 4:25; 8:11; 1 Corinthians 15:14,20; Acts 17:31; Revelation 5:9,10). This day is also notable on account of the special interviews which occurred between Jesus and his disciples after his resurrection (John 20:19,26). He ascended to heaven on this day, even the forty-third from his crucifixion; and seven days after, that is the fiftieth, being "the day of Pentecost", the gift of the Holy Spirit was poured out upon the apostles, and the gospel of the kingdom preached for the first time *in his name*.

Power being in the hands of their enemies, the Christians of the Hebrew nation still continued to observe the seventh day according to the custom. Hence we find the apostles frequenting the synagogues on the sabbath days and reasoning with the people out of the scriptures (Acts 17:2,17; 18:4; 19:8). To have done otherwise would have been to create an unnecessary prejudice, and to let slip one of the best opportunities of introducing the gospel to the attention of the Jewish public. They did not forsake the synagogues until they were expelled. While they frequented these, however, on the seventh day, they assembled themselves together with the disciples whose assemblies constituted the churches of the saints and of God. They ordained elders over these societies, and "taught them to observe all things whatsoever Jesus had commanded them" (Matthew 28:20; Acts 2:42; 14:22,23). In his letter to the Hebrew Christians, Paul exhorts them "not to forsake the assembling of themselves together" (Hebrews 10:25). Such an exhortation as this implies *a stated time* and place of assembly. On what day, then, did the churches of the saints meet to exhort one another so as to provoke to love and to good works? Certainly not on the seventh day, for then the apostles were in the synagogues. What day then more appropriate than the first day of the week? Now it cannot be affirmed that the saints were commanded to meet on this day, because there is no testimony to that effect in the New Testament. But it is beyond dispute that they did assemble themselves together on the first day of the week, and the most reasonable inference is that they did so in obedience to the instruction of the apostles, from whose teaching they derived all their faith and practice, which constituted them the disciples of Jesus.

To keep the first day of the week to the Lord is possible only for the saints. There is no law, except the emperor Constantine's, that commands *sinners* to keep *holy* the first, or eighth, day, or

Sunday, as the Gentiles term it. For a sinner to keep this day unto the Lord he must become one of the Lord's people. He must believe the gospel of the kingdom and name of Christ, and become obedient to it, before any religious service he can offer will be accepted. He must come under law to Christ by putting on Christ before he can keep the Lord's day. Having become a Christian, if he would keep the day to the Lord, he must assemble with a congregation of New Testament saints, and assist in edifying and provoking them to love and good works, in showing forth the death of Jesus, in giving thanks to the Father, in celebrating the resurrection of Christ, and in praising and blessing God. Under the gospel, or "law of liberty", he is subjected to no "yoke of bondage" concerning a sabbath day. It is his delight when an opportunity presents, to celebrate in this way the day of the resurrection. He requires no penal statutes to compel him to a formal and disagreeable self-denial, or "duty"; for it is his meat and drink to do the will of his Father who is in heaven.

The law of Moses was delivered to the Israelites and not to the Gentiles, who were therefore "without the law". "What things soever the law saith, it says it to them who are under the law"; consequently the nations were not amenable to it; and though they obtained not the blessings of Mount Gerizim (unless they became faithful Jews by adoption), neither were they obnoxious to the curses of Mount Ebal (Deuteronomy 27:9-26). The faithless Jews and Gentiles are equally aliens from the precepts of Christ and his apostles. What these prescribe is enjoined upon the disciples of Jesus. They only are "under law to Christ". "What have I", says Paul, "to do to judge them that are without? God judgeth them" (1 Corinthians 5:12,13). He has caused the gospel of the kingdom to be preached to sinners "for the obedience of faith". When they are judged, it will be for "not obeying the gospel of the Lord Jesus Christ" (2 Thessalonians 1:7-10), and not because they do not "go to church", or do not keep a sabbath instituted by a semi-pagan emperor of the fourth century. The sabbath God requires sinful men to observe is to *cease from the works of the flesh*, as completely as He rested from the work of creation on the seventh day, that they may enter into the millennial rest that remaineth for the people of God (Hebrews 4:9-11).

Men frequently err in their speculations from inattention to the marked distinction which subsists in the scriptures between those classes of mankind termed "saints" and "sinners". They confound what is said to, or concerning, the one, with what is said in relation to the other. Relatively to the institutions of God they are as near or afar off as are "citizens" and "foreigners" to the laws and constitution of the United States. "What the law saith, it saith to them who are under the law." This is a principle laid down by Paul concerning the law of Moses, which is equally true of the codes of all nations. "Citizens" are the saints, or separated ones, of the particular code by which they are insulated from all other people; while "foreigners" or "aliens" from their commonwealth are sinners in relation to it; for they live in other countries in total disregard of its institutions, and doing contrary to its laws, and yet are blameless: so that if they were to visit the country of that commonwealth, they would not be punished for their former course, because they were not under law to it. Let them, however, while sojourning there continue their native customs, and they would become guilty and worthy of the punishment made and provided for such offenders.

It is a fact, that "God blessed and sanctified" or set apart, "the seventh day"; and doubtless, Adam and his wife rested, or intermitted, their horticultural tendance upon that day. Yea, we may go further and say, that it is extremely probable that "the sons of God" before the flood, worshipped God according to "His way" upon that day; but in all the history of that long period, which intervened from the sanctification of the seventh day to the raining down bread from heaven for the Israelites in the wilderness (Exodus 16), there is not the least hint of any punishment for breaking the sabbath day. Guiltiness before God cannot therefore be argued against the Gentiles so as to entitle them to death or reprobation, predicated on the threatenings of the patriarchal code. Whatever the appointment might be, it was no doubt significative of the blessings to be obtained through observing it; not alone, but in connexion with the other matters which made up "the way of God".

As I have shown, the observance of the seventh day was obligatory only upon the Israelites so long as the Mosaic code was in force, being "a sign" between God and them. The sabbaths belong to the land and people of Israel, and can be only kept according to the law while they reside in the country. This will appear from the fact that the law requires that "two lambs of the first year without spot" should be offered with other things "as the burnt-offering of every sabbath"; an offering which, like all the offerings, etc., must be offered in a temple in Jerusalem where the Lord has placed His name, and not in the dwelling places of Jacob. Israel must therefore be restored to their own country before even they can keep the sabbath. Then, when "the throne is established in mercy, and he (the Lord Jesus) shall sit upon it in truth in the tabernacle of David, judging, and seeking judgment, and hasting righteousness" (Isaiah 16:5), then, I say "shall the priests, the Levites, the sons of Zadok, that kept the charge of my sanctuary when the children of Israel went astray from me, come near to me to minister unto me, and they shall stand before me to offer unto me the fat and the blood, saith the Lord GOD ... and *they shall hallow my sabbaths*" (Ezekiel 44:15,24).

But these sabbaths will be no longer celebrated on the seventh day. They will be changed from the seventh to the eighth, or first day of the week, which are the same. The *"dispensation of the fulness of times"* (Ephesians 1:10), popularly styled the Millennium, will be the antitype, or substance, of the Mosaic feast of tabernacles which was "a shadow of things to come". In this type, or pattern, Israel were to rejoice before the Lord for seven days, beginning "on the fifteenth day of the seventh month, when they had gathered the fruit of the land". In relation to the *first day* of the seven, the law says, "it shall be a holy convocation: *ye shall do no servile work therein*". This was what we call Sunday. The statute then continues, "on the *eighth* day", also Sunday, "shall be a holy convocation unto you, and ye shall offer an offering made by fire unto the LORD: it is a solemn assembly; and *ye shall do no servile work therein*". Again, "on the first day shall be a sabbath and on the eighth day shall be a sabbath" (Leviticus 23:34-43). Thus, in this "pattern of things in the heavens", the first and eighth days are constituted holy days in which no work was to be done. It also represents the palm-bearing or victorious ingathering of the twelve tribes of Israel from their present dispersion to the land of their fathers, "when the Lord shall set his hand *a second time* to recover the remnant of his people" (Isaiah 11:11).

Three times in four verses does Zechariah style the yearly going up of the Gentiles to Jerusalem to worship the King, the Lord of Hosts, there, the keeping of the feast of tabernacles (Zechariah 14:16-19); an event which is consequent upon the destruction of the dominion represented by Nebuchadnezzar's image, and the re-establishment of the kingdom and throne of David. This national confluence of the Gentiles to Jerusalem is characteristic of Messiah's times; and of the true or real festival of tabernacles, when he will "confess to God among the Gentiles, and sing unto his name", and "they shall rejoice with his people", Israel (Romans 15:9,10). Referring to this time, the Lord says, "the place of my throne, and the place of the soles of my feet, where I will dwell in the midst of the children of Israel *for ever*, and my holy name shall the House of Israel *no more* defile, neither they, nor their kings, by their whoredom, nor by the carcases of their kings in their high places ... They have even defiled my holy name by their abominations that they have committed: wherefore I have consumed them in mine anger. Now let them put away their whoredom, and the carcases of their kings, far from me, and *I will dwell in the midst of them for ever*" (Ezekiel 43:7-9). This is clearly a prophecy of what shall be hereafter, because the House of Israel still continues to defile God's holy name by their abominations; but when this comes to pass they shall defile it *"no more"*.

After the declaration of these things, Ezekiel is commanded to show them the description of the temple which is destined to be "the house of prayer for all nations", with the ordinances, forms, and laws thereof. The Lord God then declares, "the ordinances of the altar *in the day when they shall make it"*, and when the Levites of the seed of Zadok shall approach unto Him. The "cleansing of the altar", and the consecration of the priests, is then effected by the offerings of *seven days*. "And when these days are expired, it shall be that *upon the eighth day, and* SO FORWARD, the priests shall make your burnt offerings upon the altar, and your peace offerings; and I will accept you (O Israel), saith the LORD" (verse 27). Thus, the day of the Lord's resurrection from his seventh-day incarceration in the tomb, becomes *the sabbath day of the future age* which shall be hallowed by the priests of Israel, and be observed by all nations as a day of holy convocation in which they shall rejoice, and do no manner of servile work at all.

Constantine, though not a Christian himself, paid homage to the truth so far as to compel the world to respect the day on which Christ Jesus rose from the dead. Hence, in 328, he ordained that the day should be kept religiously, which a Judaizing clergy construed into sabbatical observance according to the Mosaic law concerning the seventh day. This is the origin of that sabbatarianism which so ludicrously, yet mischievously, illustrates the Blue Laws of Connecticut (by these a woman was forbidden to kiss her child on the sabbath!), the zeal of the Agnews and Plumptres of the House of Commons, and the rhapsodies of the pietists of the passing day. These well-meaning persons, whose zeal outruns their knowledge, seem not to be aware that Christ and his apostles did not promulge a civil and ecclesiastical code for the nations, when they preached the gospel of the kingdom. Their object was not to give them laws and constitutions; but to separate a peculiar people from the nations who should afterwards rule them justly and in fear of the Lord, when the dispensation of the fulness of times should be introduced (Acts 15:14; 1 Corinthians 6:2; 2 Samuel 23:3,4; Titus 2:11). To be able to do this, these peculiars were required to be "holy, unblameable, and unreprovable before God" (Colossians 1:22,23; 1 Thessalonians 2:19; 3:13). To this end instructions were delivered to them, that under the divine tuition "they might be renewed in the spirit of their mind; and put on the new man which after God's image is created in righteousness and true holiness".

As for "those without" "who receive not the love of the truth, that they might be saved, God sent them a strong delusion, that they should believe a lie" (2 Thessalonians 2:10-12) as a punishment. They are left to govern themselves by their own laws until the time arrives for Christ to take away their dominion and assume the sovereignty over them conjointly with "the people of the saints". If they please to impose upon themselves yokes of bondage, binding themselves to keep the *first* day of the week according to the Mosaic law of the *seventh* day, they are left at liberty to do so. But for this act of "voluntary humility" they are entitled to no recompense from God, seeing that He has not required it of them. The reward due for observing a Judaized Lord's day voluntarily inflicted upon themselves; or, the pains and penalties to which they may be entitled for its "profanation", are such, and such only, as result from the will and pleasure of the unenlightened lawgivers of the nations. It is a wise regulation to decree a cessation from labour and toil for man and beast during one day in seven; but it betrays egregious misunderstanding of the scriptures and singular superstition to proclaim perdition to men's souls in flaming brimstone, if they do not keep it according to the Mosaic law of the seventh day.

All I need say in conclusion is, that if it be necessary to keep Sunday as the Jews were required to keep Saturday by the law of Moses, then those who make so much ado about sabbath-breaking are themselves as guilty as those they denounce for the unholy and profane. "He that offendeth in one point is guilty of the whole." If they do not keep open shop, or perambulate the parks and fields, or take excursions, or go to places of public resort and amusement on the Lord's day—yet, they light fires in the dwellings and meeting houses, they entertain their friends at comfortable warm dinners, drive to church in splendid equipages, annoy the sick and distract the sober-minded with noisy bells, bury the dead, speak their own words, etc.—all of which is a violation of the divine law which saith, "Thou shalt not do *any work*, thy man-servant, nor thy maid-servant, nor thy cattle"; and "Thou shalt not speak *thine own words*". This would certainly put to silence nearly all the preachers of the day; whose "sermons", when made by themselves, are emphatically *their own* in thoughts and *words* without dispute. It is not only ridiculous, but downright Pharisaism, the fuss that is made about breaking the sabbath. Let the zealots "first cast the beam out of their own eyes; and then will they see clearly to cast out the mote from the eyes of others". If they would "keep the day to the Lord," let them believe and obey the gospel of the kingdom in the name of Jesus; and then "continue steadfastly in the apostles' doctrine and fellowship, and in breaking of bread, and in prayers" (Acts 2:42), on the "first day"; and cease from the works of sinful flesh (Galatians 5:19) every day of the week; and they will doubtless "delight in the LORD, and ride upon the high places of the earth, and feed with the heritage of Jacob" in the Kingdom of God, as the mouth of the Lord hath spoken.

Of the things then which have been written under this head this is the sum.

1.   The six creation-days were each as long as the seventh, whose duration is defined by the Mosaic law; and consequently the geological notion of their being six several periods of many centuries each, falls to the ground as a mere conceit of infidel philosophy.

2.   The Lord God ended His work on the seventh day, "and was refreshed" by the songs of the Morning Stars, and the joyous shouts of the Sons of God.

3.   To celebrate His rest, He constituted it holy and a day of blessing. Hence it was commemorative of the past, and "*a shadow of things to come*".

4.   The seventh day was observed by Adam and Eve as a day of delight before they became sinners. The immediate cause of their joyousness on the day of rest is not testified. It is certain it was not a burdensome day; for sin had not yet marred their enjoyments. It was probably because of the gracious interviews granted them by the Lord God on that day; and of the revelations made to them of the things contained in the blessing pronounced upon it when He "blessed and sanctified it".

5.   There is no record, or hint, of the existence of a penal statute for not observing the seventh day, from the sanctification of it till the raining down bread from heaven for the Israelites in the wilderness of Egypt.

6.   The observance of the seventh day by absolute rest from every kind of work and pleasure-taking, accompanied by a peculiar sacrifice on the brazen altar of the temple, and spiritual delight in its blessedness, was its Mosaic celebration enjoined upon the Israelites, and their dependants in Palestine, and upon them alone.

7.   Its profanation by citizens of the commonwealth of Israel was punishable with death by stoning.

8.   Israel was especially commanded to remember the seventh day and keep it as appointed by the law; because God in creating their world brought them out of Egypt, and rested from the work of its creation when He gave them a temporary and typical rest under Joshua in the land of Canaan.

9. For an Israelite to remember the seventh day to keep it holy, spiritually as well as ceremonially, so as to obtain the blessing which it shadowed forth, he must have had an Abrahamic faith (Romans 4:12,18-22—read the whole chapter diligently) in the promised blessing, and have ceased or rested from the works of "sinful flesh".

10. The blessing promised to Israelites, who were Abraham's sons by faith as well as by flesh descent, for a spiritual observance of the seventh day (and which, until "the handwriting", or Mosaic law, was blotted out and nailed to the cross, could not be spiritually observed and ceremonially profaned) was, that they should "delight in the LORD, ride upon the high places of the earth, and feed with the heritage of Jacob their father", when the time to fulfil the promises made to Abraham, Isaac, and Jacob should arrive.

11. The blessing pronounced on a national observance of the seventh day was the uninterrupted continuance of the throne of David, and great national prosperity. Its desecration to be punished by the breaking up of the commonwealth of Israel and desolation of their country.

12. The Mosaic observance of the seventh day was appointed as *"a sign"* between God and the twelve tribes of Israel. It was a holy day *to them*, and to be observed perpetually throughout their generations (Matthew 1:17—the forty-two generations from Abraham to Christ).

13. It was lawful for Israelites to do good on the seventh day; but they were not permitted to be the judges of the good or evil. This was defined by the law. The priests profaned the sabbath by hard work in slaying and burning the seventh day sacrifices on the altar, yet they were blameless; because this was a good work which the Lord of the sabbath commanded them to do.

14. Having *finished the work* the Father had given him to do (John 17:4), on the *sixth* day of the week, Jesus, while suspended on the accursed tree, cried with a loud voice, *"It is finished!"* (John 19:28-30). "All things were now accomplished", so that the Mosaic handwriting was blotted out, being nailed with him to the cross, and taken out of the way as a rule of life. The Lord Jesus, "rested from his labours" on the seventh day in the silent tomb, and "his disciples rested according to the commandment" (Luke 23:56). He abode in his place, and did not go out of it until the sabbath was at an end (Mark 16:1). But on the eighth day, styled also the first day, God gave him liberty (Matthew 28:2), he left the tomb, and "was refreshed". Having "spoiled the principalities and the powers" constituted by the handwriting, he made the spoliation manifest, "triumphing over them in himself" (ἐν αὐτῷ),

27

that is, in his resurrection; thus, for ever delivering men from the bondage of the law, which, Peter says, was a yoke which neither our fathers nor we were able to bear" (Acts 15:10). With the abolition of the Mosaic handwriting the obligation to keep the seventh day as a rule of spiritual life was cancelled as a matter of course.

15. The apostles and Christians (Acts 21:20) of the Hebrew nation in Palestine continued a ceremonial observance of the Mosaic festivals (verses 24-26) (the annual atonement for sin excepted) and of the seventh day, until the destruction of the commonwealth by the Romans, on the same principle that New Testament Christians among the nations now observe Sunday and the laws; not as a means of justification before God, but as mere national customs for the regulation of society.

16. Hebrew Christians who proposed to blend the law of Moses with that of Jesus as a spiritual rule, or means of justification, and consequently to keep holy the seventh day, were severely reproved by the apostles, who stigmatised it as "Judaizing" (Galatians 2:14) ('Ιουδαΐζειν).

17. The Judaizing Christians endeavoured to impose the observance of the law upon the Gentile converts, which would have compelled them to keep holy the seventh day. But the apostles and elders of the Christian community at Jerusalem positively forbade it, and wrote to them, saying, "We have heard that certain who went out from us have troubled you with words subverting your souls, saying, Be circumcised, and *keep the law*: to whom we gave no such commandment". On the contrary, "it seemed good to the Holy Spirit, and to us, to lay upon you no greater burden than these necessary things: that ye abstain from meats offered to idols, and from blood, and from things strangled, and from fornication; from which if ye keep yourselves, ye shall do well" (Acts 15:24-29).

18. Upon the first day of the week (or day after the seventh, and therefore sometimes styled the eighth day), the disciples of Christ assembled to show forth his death, and to celebrate his resurrection; which, with an enduring rest from the works of "sinful flesh", was all the sabbatizing they practised.

19. There is no law in the scriptures requiring the nations to keep this day in any manner whatever during his absence at the right hand of the Majesty in the heavens. So long as they continue faithless and disobedient to the gospel of the kingdom, neither nations nor individuals can present an acceptable observance of the day before the Lord; on the principle that "Jehovah is far from the wicked, whose way and sacrifice are an abomination to the LORD" (Proverbs 15:8,9,26-29)—and,

20.   The "first day" was Judaized by Constantine, the man-child of sin (Revelation 12:2,5), and his clergy. His present representative is the Italian high priest of Papal Christendom. When his power, and that of his kings, is finally destroyed in "the burning flame"; when Israel is engrafted into their own olive again, and the nations are subdued to the glorious sceptre of the king of saints—then will this day become the holy sabbath, "blessed and sanctified of God" instead of the shadowy seventh day, which was merely "a sign" of the things which will then have come to pass.

THE FORMATION OF MAN

"Out of the ground wast thou taken; for dust thou art."

THAT "the sabbath was made for man, and not man for the sabbath", is a truth of general application to all the institutions of God. Upon this principle, man was not made for religion, but religion was made for him. If this be true, then it follows that it was adapted to man as God had formed him. Hence, the institutions of religion, if it be of God, will always be found in harmony with his constitution and not at variance with it. They are devised as a remedy for certain irregularities which have invaded his intellectual and moral nature; by which, phenomena have been superinduced which are destructive of his being. Now the exact adaptation of the Bible religion to the curative indications suggested by the intellectual, moral, and physical infirmities of human nature, which everyone who understands it cannot fail to perceive, proves that the mind which framed it is divine; and that the religion of the scriptures, and the constitution of man, are the work of one and the same Creator. God is truly the only wise physician, whose practice is based upon perfect knowledge; for He alone (and they to whom He hath revealed it) knows *"what is in man"* (John 2:25). Hence, no incongruities are discoverable in "His way" when His method of cure is understood.

In medicine, a scientific practice is directed, and founded, upon a knowledge of the structure or mechanism of the body, the motive power thereof, and of the functions which are manifested by the working of this power on its several parts. The absence of this knowledge in a professional, constitutes empiricism; and is one cause of such vast multitudes *"dying"*, as it is said, *"of the doctor"*. Being ignorant of the motive power of the living creature, they are as unsuccessful in correcting its irregularities as a watchmaker, who was ignorant of the principles and laws by which a timepiece was moved, would be in rectifying its errors. Now this may be taken in illustration of the predicament of others

29

who undertake the *"cure of souls"*. To treat these as "a workman that needeth not to be ashamed", a man should be acquainted with "souls" as God hath formed and constituted them. He should know what "a living soul" is; what its condition in a healthy state; what the peculiar morbid affection under which it languishes; what the nature of the cure indicated; and what the divinely appointed means by which the indications may be infallibly fulfilled. An attempt to "cure souls" without understanding the constitution of man as revealed by Him who created him, is mere theological experimentalism; and as bootless, and more fatally destructive than the empiricism of the most ignorant pretenders to the healing art. What! men undertake to "cure souls", and not to know what a soul is; or to imagine it a something, which it is admitted cannot be demonstrated by "the testimony of God". This is like pretending to repair a timepiece without knowing what constitutes a watch or clock, or while imagining it to be a musical box, or any other conceivable thing.

Speculation has assumed that the soul is something in the human body capable of living out of the body, and of eating, drinking, feeling, tasting, smelling, thinking, singing, and so forth; and of the same essence as God Himself. In times past some have busied themselves in calculating how many such souls could stand on the point of a needle; a problem, however, which still remains unsolved. A vast deal is said in "sermons" and systems about this idea; about its supposed nature, its wonderful capacity, its infinite value, its immortality, and its destiny. I shall not, however, trouble the reader with it. We have to do with "the law and the testimony"; and as they are altogether silent about such a supposed existence, we shall not occupy our pages in superadding to the obsolete print concerning its attributes, which has already merged into the oblivion of the past. I allude to so much as this, because it is made the foundation cornerstone, as it were, of those experimental systems of spiritual cure, which are so popular with the world, and so utterly exclusive and proscriptive of the divine method.

Upon the supposition of the existence of this kind of a soul in the human body are based the current notions of heaven, hell, immortality, infant salvation, purgatory, saint-worship, Mariolatry, spiritual millenniumism, metempsychosis, etc., etc. Its existence both in the body and out of the body being assumed, it is assumed also to be immortal. An immortal disembodied existence requires a dwelling place, because something must be somewhere; and, as it is said to be virtuous or vicious according to its supposed life in the body, and *post mortem* rewards and punishments are affirmed—this dwelling-place is exhibited as an elysium, or, as an orthodox poet sings, "a place of goblins damn'd".

To deter men from crime, and to move them to "get religion" that their souls may be cured of sin, frightful pictures are painted, sometimes on canvas, sometimes on the imagination, and sometimes sculptured on stones, of the crackling and sulphurous flames, hideous devils, and horrid shapes, which fill the Tartarian habitation of the immortal ghosts of wicked men. This destiny of condemned ghosts was a part of the "vain philosophy" of the Greeks and Romans before the advent of Christ. It was introduced into the churches of the saints soon after "God granted repentance to the Gentiles" (Acts 11:18). But, as the apostles taught the resurrection of the mortal body (Romans 8:11; 1 Corinthians 15:42-54), the dogmatism of the Greeks was variously modified. Some admitted the resurrection of the dead; but, as it interfered with their hypothesis about souls, they said it was already past (2 Timothy 2:18); and consequently, that "there is no resurrection of the dead" (1 Corinthians 15:12). This gentilizing the hope of the gospel filled Paul with zeal, and caused him to pen the fifteenth chapter of his first letter to the Corinthians to counteract its pernicious influence. He wrote to Timothy to put him on his guard against it; and styles the gentilisms, "profane vain babblings; and oppositions of science falsely so called" (1 Timothy 6:20). He exhorts him to shun them, and "not to strive about words to no profit"; for they *would eat as doth a canker*" (2 Timothy 2:14,16,17).

If there were no other evidence in Paul's writings of inspiration, this prediction would be sufficient to establish it. It has come to pass exactly as he foretold it. The dogma of an immortal soul in mortal sinful flesh has eaten out the marrow and fatness, the flesh and sinew, of the doctrine of Christ; and has left behind only an ill-conditioned and ulcerated skeleton of Christianity, whose dry bones rattle in the "winds of doctrine" that are blowing around us, chopping and changing to every point of the compass. The apostles taught two resurrections of the dead; one at "the manifestation of his presence" (τῇ ἐπιφανείᾳ τῆς παρουσίας αὐτοῦ—TÉ EPIPHANEIA *tēs parousias autou*) (1 Thessalonians 4:14-17; 2 Thessalonians 1:7-8; 2:8), the other, at the delivering up of the kingdom to God at the end (Revelation 20:5; 1 Corinthians 15:24) of the dispensation of the fulness of times. But this did not suit the theory of dogmatists. They resolved the first into what they term "a glorious resurrection of spiritual life in the soul"; and the second, into a re-union of disembodied ghosts with their old mortalities to be sent back whence they came. In this way they reduce the second resurrection to a very useless and superfluous affair. Their systems send "souls" to their account as soon as death strikes the bodies down. Some torment them in purgatory, or in an intermediate state; others send them direct into unmitigated punishment; while both, after they have suffered for thousands of years before trial and conviction, re-unite them to their bodies; and if it be asked for what purpose? system replies, "to be judged!" Punish souls first and judge them after! This is truly human, but it is certainly not divine justice. The truth is, that this article of the creed is brought in to defend "orthodoxy" against the imputation of denying the resurrection of the body, which would be a very inconvenient charge in the face of the testimony of God. But this will not avail; for, to believe dogmas that make the resurrection of the mortal body unnecessary and absurd is equivalent to a denial of it. In saying that there was no future resurrection, Paul charged the Corinthians with the mortal sin of repudiating the resurrection of Jesus; "for", said he, "if the dead rise not", as ye say, "then Christ is not raised". Their heresy ate out this truth, which stands or falls with the reality of the "*first* resurrection" at his coming (1 Corinthians 15:23).

The question of "infant salvation" and "non-elect infant damnation", also rests upon the dogma before us. "Orthodoxy" sends some infants to hell and some to heaven; though many "orthodox" persons are getting heartily ashamed of this part of the creed. The apprehension of the damnation of their "immortal souls" on account of "original sin", has given rise to the Romish conceit of the rhantismal regeneration of infants by the Holy Spirit in the scattering of a few drops of water upon the face, and the use of a certain form of words. This has been recently declared to be regenerative of infant souls by an English court of law! This question was actually gravely discussed by bishops, priests, lawyers and ministers, in the year of grace 1849! So true is it that "great men are not always wise; neither do the aged understand judgment" (Job 32:9).

As far as the infant is itself concerned, this Romish ceremony is of no importance, for it does it neither good nor harm. In one sense, however, the subject of "the ordinance" is deeply injured. He is indoctrinated by system into the notion that he was truly baptized when rhantismally "regenerated": and, therefore, when he is grown he troubles himself no more about the matter. Alas, what havoc the apostasy has made with the doctrine of Christ! Believers' baptism transmuted into rhantizing an unconscious babe for the regeneration of its "immortal soul"! Would such a thing ever have been thought of but for the Nicolaitan "oppositions of science", "which", says the Lord Jesus, "I hate"? (Revelation 2:6,15) I trow not.

How important, then, it is that we should have a scriptural understanding of the constitution of man. If it should appear by an exposition of the truth, that there is no such kind of soul in the universe as that conceited by the pagan Greeks and Romans, and gentilized into the doctrine of the apostles by contemporary perverters (Galatians 1:7-9) of the gospel, the faith and hope of which it hath ulcerously consumed—and handed down to us by "orthodox divines"—and fondled in these times as an essential ingredient of a true faith:—what becomes of the "cure of souls" by the dogmatical specifics of the day? They are resolved into theological empiricism, which is destined to recede like darkness before the orient brightness of the rising truth.

Let us then endeavour to understand ourselves as God has revealed our nature in His word. On the sixth day, the Elohim gave the word, saying, "Let us make man in our image, after our likeness". In this word was life, spirit, or energy. "It was God. All things were made by it, and without it was not anything made that was made" (John 1:1-5). Hence, says Elihu, "the *Spirit* of God hath made me, and the *breath* of the Almighty hath given me *life*" (Job 33:4); or, as Moses testifies, "the LORD God formed man of the dust of the ground, and breathed into his nostrils the breath of lives and *man* became *a* LIVING SOUL" (Genesis 2:7).

Now, if it be asked, what do the scriptures define "a living soul" to be?—the answer is, a living natural, or animal, body, whether of birds, beasts, fish or men. The phrase living creature is the exact synonym of living soul. The Hebrew words *nephesh chayiah* are the signs of the ideas expressed by Moses. *Nephesh* signifies *creature*, also *life*, *soul*, or *breathing frame*, from the verb *to breathe*: *chayiah* is *of life*—a noun from the verb *to live*. *Nephesh chayiah* is the *genus* which includes all *species* of living creatures; namely, *Adam*, man; *beme*, beast of the field; *chitu*, wild beast; *remesh*, reptile; and *ouph*, fowl, etc. In the common version of the scriptures, it is rendered *living soul*; so that under this form of expression the scriptures speak of "all flesh" which breathes in air, earth, and sea.

Writing about *body*, the apostle says, "There is *a natural body* and there is *a spiritual body*". But, he does not content himself with simply declaring this truth; he goes further, and proves it by quoting the words of Moses, saying, "For so it is written, the first man Adam was made into *a living soul*"—εἰς ψυχὴν ζῶσαν; and then adds, "the last Adam *into a spirit* giving life"—εἰς πνεῦμα ζωοποιοῦν (1 Corinthians 15:44,45). Hence, in another place, speaking of the latter, he says of him "Now the Lord is the spirit"—ὁ δὲ κύριος τὸ πνεῦμά ἐστιν. "And we all, with unveiled face, beholding as in a mirror the glory of the Lord, are changed into his image from glory into glory, as by *the Lord the Spirit"* — ἀπό κυρίου πνεύματος (2 Corinthians 3:17,18).

The proof of the apostle's proposition that there is *a natural body* as distinct from a spiritual body, lies in the testimony, that "Adam was made into *a living soul*"; showing that he considered a natural, or animal body, and a living soul, as one and the same thing. If he did not, then there was no proof in the quotation, of what he affirmed.

A man then is a body of life in the sense of his being an animal, or living creature — *nephesh chayiah adam*. As a natural man, he has no other pre-eminence over the creatures God made than what his peculiar organization confers upon him. Moses makes no distinction between him and them; for he styles them all living souls, breathing the breath of lives. Thus, literally rendered, he says, "The Elohim said, The waters shall produce abundantly *sheretz chayiah nephesh*, the *reptile living soul*"; and again, "*kal nephesh, chayiah erameshat*, every living soul creeping". In another verse, "Let the earth bring forth *nephesh chayiah*, the living soul after its kind, cattle, and creeping thing, and beast of the earth", etc.; and "*lekol rumesh ol eretz asher bu nephesh chayiah*, to every thing creeping upon the earth which (has) in it living breath" (Genesis 1:20,21,24,30), that is, breath of lives. And lastly, "Whatsoever Adam called *nephesh chayiah*, the living soul, that was the name thereof" (Genesis 2:19).

Quadrupeds and men, however, are not only "living souls" but they are vivified by the same breath and spirit. In proof of this, I remark first, that the phrase "*breath of life*" in the text of the common version is *neshemet chayim* in the Hebrew; and that, as *chayim* is in the plural, it should be rendered *breath of lives*. Secondly, this *neshemet chayim* is said to be in the inferior creatures as well as in man. Thus, God said, "I bring a flood of waters upon the earth to destroy *all flesh* wherein is *ruach chayim*, spirit of lives" (Genesis 6:17). And in another place, "They went in to Noah into the ark, two and two of *all flesh*, in which is *ruach chayim*, spirit of lives". "And *all flesh* died that moved upon the earth, both of fowl, and of cattle, and of beast, and of every creeping thing, and every man; all in whose nostrils was *neshemet ruach chayim*, BREATH OF SPIRIT OF LIVES" (Genesis 7:15,21,22). Now, as I have said, it was the *neshemet chayim* with which Moses testifies God inflated the nostrils of Adam; if, therefore, this were *divina particula auræ*, particle of the divine essence, as it is affirmed, which became the "immortal soul" in man, then all other animals have "immortal souls" likewise; for they all received "breath of spirit of lives" in common with man.

From these testimonies, I think, it must be obvious to the most unlearned, that the argument for the existence of an "immortal soul" in "sinful flesh", hereditarily derived from the first sinner, predicated on the inspiration of his nostrils with *"the breath of lives"* by the Lord God, and the consequent application to him of the phrase *"living* soul", if admitted as good logic, proves too much, and therefore nothing to the purpose. For if man be proved to be immortal in this sense, and upon such premises as these, then all quadrupeds are similarly immortal; which none, I suppose, but believers in the transmigration of souls, would be disposed to admit.

The original condition of the animal world was *"very good"*. Unperverted by the production of evil, all its constituents fulfilled the purposes of its existence. Begotten of the same power, and formed from the substance of a common mother, they were all animated by the same spirit, and lived in peace and harmony together. Formed to be *living breathing frames,* though of different species, in God they lived, and moved, and had their continued being; and displayed His wisdom, power, and handiwork.

But, to return to the philology of our subject, I remark that by a metonymy, or figure of speech in which the container is put for the thing contained, and *vice-versa,* nephesh, *"breathing frame",* is put for *neshemet ruach chayim,* which, when in motion, the frame respires. Hence, *nephesh* signifies "life", also "breath" and "soul"—*Life,* or those mutually effective, positive and negative principles in all living creatures, whose closed circuits cause motion of and in their frames. These principles or qualities, perhaps, of the same thing, are styled by Moses *Ruach Elohim* (Genesis 1:2), or Spirit of Him "who only hath immortality, dwelling in the light which no man can approach unto, which no man hath seen, nor can see" (1 Timothy 6:16), and which, when the word was spoken by "the Holy Gods" (Daniel 4:8), first caused a motion upon the waters, and afterwards disengaged the light, evolved the expanse, aggregated the waters, produced vegetation, manifested the celestial universe, vitalized the breathing frames of the dry land, expanse, and seas; and formed man in *their* image and likeness. This *ruach,* or spirit, is neither the Uncreated One who dwells in light, the Lord God, nor the Elohim, His co-workers, who co-operated in the elaboration of the natural world. It was the *instrumental principle* by which they executed the commission of the glorious INCREATE to erect this earthly house, and furnish it with living souls of every species.

It is this *ruach,* or instrumentally formative power, together with the *neshemeh* or breath, which keeps them all from perishing, or returning to the dust. Thus, "If God set His heart against man, He will withdraw to himself *ruachu veneshmetu, i.e., his*

35

spirit and his breath; all flesh shall perish together, and man shall turn again to dust" (Job 34:14,15). In another place, "By the *neshemet el*, or *breath of God*, frost is given" (Job 37:10). Speaking of reptiles and beasts, David saith, "Thou withdrawest *ruachem, i.e., their spirit*—they die; and to their dust they return. Thou sendest forth *ruhech, i.e., thy spirit*—they are created" (Psalm 104:30). And again, "Whither shall I fly, *meruhech*, from thy spirit" (Psalm 139:7).

From these testimonies it is manifest that the *ruach* or spirit is all pervading. It is in heaven, in sheol, or the dust of the deepest hollow, in the uttermost depths of the sea, in the darkness, in the light, and in all things animate, and without life. It is a *universal* principle in the broadest, or rather, in an illimitable sense. It is the substratum of all motion, whether manifested in the diurnal and ellipsoidal revolutions of the planets, in the flux and reflux of the sea, in the storms and tempests of the expanse, or in the organism of reptiles, cattle, beasts, fish, fowl, vegetables, or men. The atmospheric expanse is charged with it; but it is not the air: plants and animals of all species breathe it; but it is not their breath: yet without it, though filled with air, they would die.

The atmosphere, which extends some forty-five miles in altitude, and encircles the globe, is styled the expanse, by Moses; and the breath of God, in Job. It is a compound body, consisting, when pure, of nitrogen and oxygen, in the proportion of 79 of the former and 21 of the latter, in 100 parts.* These are considered as simple bodies, because they have not yet been decomposed; though it is probable they have a base, which may be the *ruach*. This may exist free or combined with the elementary constituents of the *neshemeh*. Uncombined, it is that wonderful fluid, whose explosions are heard in the thunder, whose fiery bolts overthrow the loftiest towers, and rive the sturdy monarchs of the woods; and in less intensity gives polarity to light, the needle, and the brain. These three together, the oxygen, nitrogen, and electricity, constitute *"the breath"* and *"spirit"* of the lives of all God's living souls.

Thus, from the centre of the earth, and extending throughout all space in every direction, is the *Ruach Elohim*, the existence of which is demonstrable from the phenomena of the natural system of things. It penetrates where the *neshemet el*, or atmospheric air, cannot. When speaking, however, of the motivity and sustentation of organized dust, or souls, they are co-existent within

---

* Since this was written argon and other rare gases have been discovered but the statement is otherwise true.—*Publisher*.

them. In this case, the *ruach Elohim* becomes the *ruach chayim*, or "spirit of lives"; and the *neshemet el*, the *neshemet chayim*, or "breath of lives"; and both combined in the elaboration and support of life, the *neshemet ruach chayim*, or "breath of the spirit of lives". Living creatures, or souls, are not animated, as physiologists and speculative "divines" erroneously imagine, by "*a vital principle*", capable of disembodied existence as the ghost of a man, or the transmigrating spectres of other animal species: — ghostly things, the laws and functions of which in the animal economy physiologists are unable to discover; and theologists are nonplussed to prove the existence of from the word of God. On the contrary, "*souls*" are "*made living*" by the coetaneous operation of the *ruach chayim* and *neshemet chayim* upon their organized tissues according to certain fixed laws. When the as yet occult laws of the all-pervading *ruach*, or spirit, shall be known, this subject will be understood; and men will then be as astonished at the ignorance of the "divines" and physiologists of this "cloudy and dark day", respecting "living souls", as we are at the notion of the ancients, that their "immortal gods" resided in the stocks and stones they so stupidly adored. This, however, is quite as reasonable a theory as that of "immortal souls" dwelling in sinners of Adam's race.

The *ruach chayim* and *neshemet chayim* are lent to the creatures of the natural world for the appointed period of their living existence. But, though lent to them, they are still God's breath, and God's spirit; nevertheless, to distinguish them from the expanse of air and spirit in their totality, they are sometimes styled, "the spirit of man", and "the spirit of the beast"; or collectively, "the spirits of all flesh", and "*their* breath". Thus, it is written, "They have all *one ruach*, or spirit; so that man hath no pre-eminence over a beast; for all is vanity or vapour." "All go to one place; all are of the dust, and all turn to dust again" (Ecclesiastes 3:19,20). And in the sense of supplying to every living creature, or soul, "spirit" and "breath", Jehovah is styled by Moses, "God of the *spirits* of *all flesh*" (Numbers 27:16).

Besides the *ruach* and *neshemeh* without, there are certain elementary principles, in a state of combination, within all living souls, which are related to them by fixed and appropriate laws, for the manifestation of living actions. The light to the eye, and the eye to the light; so also, the breath and the spirit of God to the constituents of blood, and the blood to them. These, acting and re-acting upon each other in the lungs of all breathing frames, cause that motion throughout their structure which is termed *life*. The following testimonies will throw some light upon this part of our subject.

"Flesh, *be-nephesh-u*, with the life thereof, which is the blood thereof, shall ye not eat." This teaches that blood is the *nephesh*, or life of the flesh; hence it continues, "and surely your blood, *lah-nephesh-tikam*, for your lives will I require" (Genesis 9:5). We often find life put for blood, and blood for life, as elsewhere in the context. "Be sure that thou eat not the blood, for the blood is the *nephesh* or life; and thou mayest not eat the life, *nephesh*, with the flesh" (Deuteronomy 12:23) But, to this it might be objected, that if the blood be the life, then so long as it is in the body it ought to live; on the contrary it dies with the blood in it. True. Moses, however, does not teach the dogma of an *abstract vital principle*; but life, the result and consequence of the decomposition and re-combination of the elements of certain compounds. The blood abstractly considered is not life; yet relatively, it is "the life of the flesh". The following testimony will show the sense in which the phrase "the blood is the life" is used. "I will set my face against that soul that eateth blood. For the life of the flesh is IN *the blood itself*. I have given it to you upon the altar to make an atonement for *nephesh-tikem*, your lives: for it is the blood that atones, *be-nephesh*, for the soul" or life. Whosoever catcheth any fowl that may be eaten, he shall even pour out the blood thereof, and *cover it with dust*. For it is the life of *all* flesh; the blood of it is *for the life* thereof. Ye shall eat the blood of no manner of flesh; for the life of all flesh is the blood thereof" (Leviticus 17:11-14). Nothing can be plainer than this.

There are three kinds of living manifestations, which are characterized by the *nature* of the organization, or being, through which they occur. Hence, we have *vegetable* life, *animal* life, and *incorruptible* life. The last is *immortality*; because the body through which the life is manifested, being incorruptible, never wears out; so that being once put into motion by the spirit of God, *it lives for ever*. Vegetable and animal life, on the contrary, is terminable or mortal; because the materials through which it is revealed are perishably organized. Mortality, then, is *life manifested through a corruptible body*; and immortality, *life manifested through an incorruptible body*. Hence, the necessity laid down in the saying of the apostle, "This corruptible body must put on incorruption, and this mortal put on immortality", before death can be "swallowed up in victory" (1 Corinthians 15:53,54). This doctrine of "life and incorruptibility" (ζωὴ καὶ ἀφθαρσία) was new to the Greeks and Romans; and brought to light only through the gospel of the kingdom and name of Jesus Christ. It was to them foolishness: and is to the moderns incredible, because they understand not the glad tidings of the age to come.

Incorruptible life might with equal propriety be styled *spiritual life*, as indicative of that with which spiritual bodies are endowed. But here I use not the word spiritual, lest it should be confounded with that intellectual and moral life a man possesses when the "incorruptible seed" of the kingdom takes root in his heart; and when, in "obedience of faith", he passes from under the sentence of death to the sentence of justification unto life eternal. But, at present, we have to do with animal or natural life, which is all the life the fleshy sons of the first Adam can boast of. Enough, however, I think has been advanced to show the scriptural import of the text already quoted, that "the LORD God formed man, the dust of the ground, and breathed into his nostrils the breath of lives, and man became a living soul".

The simple, obvious and undogmatic meaning of this, is that the dust was first formed into *"clay"*, which was then modelled by Jehovah Elohim into the form of the soul called "man", as a potter shapes the substance of his vessels. Thus, Elihu said to Job, *"I* also am formed out of the clay" (Job 33:6) and again, "We are the clay, and thou our potter; and we are the work of thy hand" (Isaiah 64:8). The fashioning of the clay being accomplished in all its component parts, which in the aggregate constitute man; that is, the dust being animalized, and then organized, the next thing was to set all the parts of this exquisite mechanism into motion. This was effected by the inrush of the air through his nostrils into his lungs according to the natural laws. This phenomenon was the *neshemet el*, or "breath of God", breathing into him; and as it was the pabulum of life to all creatures formed from the dust, it is very expressively styled "the breath of *lives*" in the plural number. Some imagine that Jehovah Elohim placed His mouth to the nostrils to the yet clay-cold man-soul prostrate before Him, and so breathed into them. Be this as it may; of this, however, we are without doubt, that God breathes into every man at his birth the breath of lives to this day; and I see no scriptural reason why we should deny that He breathed into Adam and He hath done into the nostrils of his posterity, namely, by the operation of the natural, or pneumatic, laws. Hitherto, man, though a soul formed from the ground, had been *inanimate*; but as soon as he began to respire, like the embryo passing from foetal to infant life, he "became a *living* soul", not an *everliving*, but simply *nephesh chayiah*, a living breathing frame, or *body of life*.

MAN IN THE IMAGE AND LIKENESS OF THE
ELOHIM

"Thou hast made him a little lower than the angels."

MEN and beasts, say the scriptures, "have all one *ruach* or spirit; so that a man hath no pre-eminence over a beast". The reason assigned for this equality is the *oneness of their spirit*, which is proved by the fact of their common destiny; as it is written, "for all are vanity": that is, "all go unto one place; all are of the dust, and all turn to dust again". Yet this one spirit manifests its tendencies differently in men and other creatures. In the former it is aspiring and God-defying, rejoicing in its own works, and devoted to the vanity of the passing hour; while in the latter, its disposition is grovelling to the earth in all things. Thus, the heart of man being "deceitful above all things and desperately wicked, who can know or fathom it?"—Solomon was led to exclaim, "Who knoweth the spirit of the sons of Adam, *ruach beni headam*, which exalts itself to the highest, and the spirit of a beast which inclines to the earth?" (Ecclesiastes 3:19-21). We may answer, "None, but God only"; He knoweth what is in man, and needs not that any should testify of him (John 2:25).

But, from this testimony someone might infer that, as man was made only "a *little lower* than the angels", and yet has "no pre-eminence over a beast", the beast also is but a little lower than the angels. This, however, would be a very erroneous conclusion. The equality of men and other animals consists in the *kind of life* they possess in common with each other. Vanity, or mortality is all that pertains to any kind of living flesh. The whole animal world has been made subject to it; and as it affects all living souls alike, bringing them back to the dust again, no one species can claim pre-eminence over the other; for "one thing befalleth them; as the one dieth, so dieth the other".

Man, however, differs from other creatures in having been modelled after a divine type, or pattern. In *form* and *capacity* he was made like to the angels, though in *nature* inferior to them. This appears from the testimony that he was made "in their image, after their likeness", and "a *little lower* than the *angels*", or Elohim (Psalm 8:5). I say, he was made in the image of the angels, as the interpretation of the co-operative imperative, "Let *us* make man in *our* image, after *our* likeness". The work of the six days, though elaborated by the power of Him "who dwelleth in the light", was executed by "his angels, that excel in strength, and do his commandments, hearkening unto the voice of his word" (Psalm 103:20). These are styled Elohim, or "gods," in numerous passages. David says, "Worship him, all *ye gods*" (Psalm 97:7); which Paul applies to Jesus, saying,* "Let all *the angels* of God worship him" (Hebrews 1:6). Man, then, was made after the image and likeness of Elohim, but for a while inferior in nature. But the race will not always be inferior in this respect. It is destined to advance to a higher nature; not all the individuals of it; but those of the race "who shall be accounted worthy to obtain that age (*αἰὼν μέλλων*, the future age) and the resurrection from among the dead (*ἐκ νεκρῶν*) ... who can die no more; for they are equal to the angels (*ἰσάγγελοι*) and are the sons of God, being the sons of the resurrection" (Luke 20:35,36).

The import of the phrase "in the image, after the likeness" is suggested by the testimony, that "Adam begat a son in his own likeness, after his image, and called his name Seth" (Genesis 5:3). In this respect, Seth stands related to Adam, as Adam did to the Elohim; but differing in this, that the nature of Adam and Seth was identical; whereas those of Adam and the Elohim were dissimilar. Would any one be at a loss to know the meaning of Seth's being in the image of his father? The very same thing is meant by Adam being in the image of the Elohim. An image is the representation of some *form* or shape; metaphorically, it may signify the exact resemblance of one character to another. But in the case before us, the parties had no characters at the time of their birth. They were simply innocent of actual transgression; no scope having been afforded them to develop character. The Elohim, however, were personages of dignity and holiness, as well as of incorruptible, or spiritual, nature. The resemblance, therefore, of Adam to the Elohim as their image was of *bodily form*, not of intellectual and moral attainment; and this I apprehend to be the reason why the Elohim are styled *"men"* when their visits to the sons of Adam are recorded in the scriptures of truth. In shape, Seth was like Adam, Adam like the Elohim, and the Elohim, the image of the invisible Increate; the great and glorious archetype of the intelligent universe.

Seth was also "in Adam's own likeness". While *image*, then, hath reference to form or shape, *"likeness"* hath regard to mental constitution, or *capacity*. From the shape of his head, as compared with other creatures, it is evident that man has a mental capacity which distinguishes him above them all. Their *likeness* to him is faint. They can think; but their thoughts are only sensual. They have no moral sentiments, or high intellectual aspirations; but are grovelling in all their instincts, which incline only to the earth. In proportion as their heads assume the human

---

* Paul's *quotation* is verbatim from Deuteronomy 32:43 (LXX)—not Psalm 97.

form in the same ratio do they excel each other in sagacity; and, as in the monkey tribe, display a greater likeness to man. But, let the case be reversed; let the human head degenerate from the godlike perfection of the Elohim, the standard of beauty in shape and feature; let it diverge to the image of an ape's, and the human animal no longer presents the image and likeness of the Elohim; but rather, the chattering imbecility of the creature most resembling it in form. Adam's mental capacity enabled him to comprehend and receive spiritual ideas, which moved him to veneration, hope, conscientiousness, the expression of his views, affections, and so forth. Seth was capable of the like display of intellectual and moral phenomena; and of an assimilation of character to that of his father. He was therefore in the likeness as well as in the image of Adam; and, in the same sense, they were both "after the likeness of the Elohim".

But, though Adam was "made in the image and after the likeness" of the "Holy Ones", the similitude has been so greatly marred, that his posterity present but a faint representation of either. The almost uncontrolled and continuous operation of "the law of sin and death" (Romans 7:23), styled by philosophers "the law of nature", which is an indwelling and inseparable constituent of our present economy, has exceedingly deformed the image, and effaced the likeness of God, which man originally presented. It required, therefore, the appearance of a New Man, in whom the image and likeness should re-appear, as in the beginning. This was "the man Christ Jesus", whom Paul styles "the last Adam". He is "the *Image* of the invisible God" (Colossians 1:15) (εἰκών τοῦ Θεοῦ); "the effulgent mirror of the glory, and the exact likeness of his person" (Hebrews 1:3) (ἀπαύγασμα τῆς δόξης καὶ χαρακτὴρ τῆς ὑποστάσεως αὐτοῦ). Hence, in another place, Paul says, he was "in the *form* of God" (Philippians 2:6-8) (ἐν μορφῇ Θεοῦ) and also "made in the likeness of men, and in the form of a man". Being thus the image and likeness of the invisible God, as well as of man, who was created in the image and likeness of the Elohim, he made himself equal with God in claiming God for his Father (John 5:18), though born of "sinful flesh". Though thus highly related in paternity, image and character, he was yet "made a little lower than the angels"; for he appeared not in the higher nature of Elohim, but in the inferior nature of the seed of Abraham (Hebrews 2:16). This was the first stage of his manifestation, as the present is of the saints who are his brethren. But he is the appointed "heir of all things, on account of whom" (δι᾿ οὗ), "the ages were rearranged (κατηρτίσθαι τοὺς αἰῶνας) by the word of God, so that the things seen exist not from things apparent" (Hebrews 1:2; 11:3). But, says the apostle, "we do not yet see all things put under him: but we see Jesus, who was made a little lower than the angels *for the suffering of death*, crowned with glory and honour; that by the grace of God he should taste death for every man" (Hebrews 2:8,9). Having been thus laid low, and for this gracious purpose, he is no longer "lower than the angels". He is equal to them in body: and made so much superior to them in rank, dignity, honour, and glory, "as he hath by inheritance obtained a more excellent name than they" (Hebrews 1:4).

In Jesus, then, raised from the dead incorruptible, and clothed with brightness as when he was transfigured upon the Holy Mount (Matthew 17:2), we behold the image and likeness of the invisible God. When we contemplate him by faith, as we shall hereafter by sight, we see A MIRROR from which the glory of Jehovah is reflected in intellectual, moral, and physical grandeur. He that would know God, must behold Him in Christ. If he be acquainted with Him as He is portrayed in the prophets and apostles, he will understand the character of God, whom no man hath seen, nor can see; Who chargeth His angels with folly, and before Whom the heavens are not clean. Jesus was the true light shining in the darkness of Judea, whose inhabitants "comprehended it not". Through him, God, who commanded the light to shine out of darkness, shone into the hearts of as many as received him; to give them the light of the knowledge of the glory of God in the face of Jesus Christ; that so they might receive power to become the sons of God, believing on his name (2 Corinthians 3:18; 4:6; John 1:5,12).

How consoling and cheering is it, then, amid all the evils of the present state, that God hath found a ransom, who is willing and able to deliver us from the power of the grave; and not only so, but that "at the manifestation of the sons of God" (Romans 8:17-25), when he shall appear in power and great glory, *"we shall be like him*; because we shall see him as he is" (1 John 3:2). Then will the saints be "changed into the same image from glory", now only a matter of hope, "into glory", as seen and actually possessed, "even as the Lord" himself was changed, when he became "the spirit giving life", or "a quickening spirit".

THE SPIRITUAL BODY

"There is a spiritual body"

THE subject of this section is the second member of the apostle's proposition, that "there is a natural body, and there is a spiritual body". It is contained in his reply to some of the Corinthian disciples, who, to their shame, had not the knowledge of God, and therefore foolishly inquired, "How are the dead raised up? and with *what body* do they come?" He showed them that the *animal body* had a similar relation to the *spiritual body* that *naked grain* has to the *plant* produced from it according to the law of its reproduction. He explained, that before a plant could be reproduced from a seed, the seed must be put into the soil, and die, or decay away. By the time the plant is established, all vestige of the seed is gone from the root; yet, the identity of the seed with the plant is not lost, inasmuch as the same kind of seed reappears in the fruit of the plant. The plant is the secondary body of the seed-body, which is the first. There are different kinds of vegetable seed-bodies; and also of animal seed-bodies. These classes of seeds are terrestrial bodies, and have their glory in the bodies produced from them. But there are also celestial bodies, whose glory is of a different character. It is a light blazing and sparkling in the vault of heaven, as may be seen by every eye. Such is the apostle's illustration of the resurrection from the dead; or, of how they are raised, and for what kind of body they spring forth. "So also", says he, "is the resurrection of the dead." We are in this state of the naked grain. We die and are buried, and go to corruption; leaving only our characters behind us written in the book of God. When decayed, a little dust alone remains, as the nucleus of our future selves. When the time comes for the righteous dead to rise, then "He that raised up Christ from the dead will also make alive their mortal bodies by his spirit", operating through Jesus upon their dust, and fashioning it into the image of the Lord from heaven (Romans 8:11; 2 Corinthians 4:14). Thus, as the Elohim made man out of the dust in their own image and likeness; so, the Lord Jesus, by the same spirit, will also re-fashion from the dust, the righteous of the posterity of the first Adam, into his own image and likeness. This is wonderful, that by a man should come the resurrection of the dead (1 Corinthians 15:21). Truly may he be called the "Wonderful" (Isaiah 9:6). Once a babe fondled at the breast, and hereafter the creator of myriads, now only dust and ashes, but then equal to the angels of God; and "sons of the resurrection", of which he is himself "the First Fruits".

Having shown "how", or upon what principles, the righteous dead are raised, the apostle gives us to understand, that their "glory" will consist in brightness; for he cites the splendour of the celestial bodies as illustrative of theirs. This reminds us of the testimony in Daniel, that "They that be wise shall shine as the brightness of the firmament, and they that turn many to righteousness as the stars for ever and ever" (Daniel 12:3). This is repeated by the Lord Jesus, who says, "Then shall the righteous shine forth as the sun *in the kingdom* of their Father" (Matthew

13:43), which assurance Paul also revives in his letter to the saints at Philippi, saying, "Our commonwealth (ἡμῶν τὸ πολίτευμα) has a beginning (Daniel 2:44; Luke 19:12,15) (ὑπάρχει) in the heavens (ἐν οὐρανοῖς), out of which also we wait for the Saviour, the Lord Jesus Christ: who will transfigure the body of our humiliation, that it may become of like form with the body of his glory, by the power of that which enables him even to subdue all things to himself" (Philippians 3:20,21).

When we die we are buried, or "sown" like so many seeds in the earth. We are sown, says the apostle, "in corruption", "in dishonour", "in weakness", and with an animal nature; but, when we are raised to inherit the kingdom, we become incorruptible, glorious, powerful, and possessed of a spiritual nature, such as Jesus and the Elohim rejoice in. Now, a spiritual body is as material, or substantial and tangible, a body as that which we now possess. It is a body purified from "the law of sin and death". Hence it is termed "holy" and "spiritual", because it is born of the spirit from the dust, is incorruptible, and sustained by the *ruach*, or spirit, independently of the *neshemeh*, or atmospheric air. "That which is born of the flesh", in the ordinary way, "is flesh", or an animal body: and "that which is born of the spirit", by a resurrection to life, *"is spirit"*, or a spiritual body (John 3:6). Hence, in speaking of Jesus, Paul says, "born of David's seed according to the flesh; and constituted the son of God in power, according to the spirit of holiness, through the resurrection from the dead" (Romans 1:3,4). Thus, he was born of the spirit, and therefore became "a spirit"; and, because highly exalted, and possessing a name which is above every name (Philippians 2:9-11), he is styled *"the Lord the Spirit"*.

That the spiritual body is independent of atmospheric air for its support, is clear from the ascension of the Lord Jesus. An animal body can only exist in water, or in atmospheric air, and at a comparatively low altitude above the surface of the earth. Now, the air does not extend beyond forty-five miles; consequently beyond that limit, if they could even attain to it, creatures supported by breath in the nostrils, could no more live than fish in the air. Beyond our atmosphere is the *ether*; through which they only can pass, who, like the Lord Jesus and the angels, possess a nature adapted to it. This is the case with the spiritual nature. Jesus was changed εἰς πνεῦμα, *into a spirit*, and was therefore enabled to pass through it to the right hand of the Majesty in the heavens. Enoch, Elijah, and Moses, are also cases to the point.

The spiritual body is constituted of flesh and bones vitalized by the spirit. This appears from the testimony concerning Jesus. On a certain occasion, he unexpectedly stood in the midst of his disciples, at which they were exceedingly alarmed, supposing

45

they beheld a spirit, or phantasm, as at a former time. But, that they might be assured that it was really he himself, he invited them to handle him, and examine his hands and feet: "For", said he, "a spirit hath not flesh and bones as ye see me have". Incredulous for joy, he gave them further proof by eating a piece of broiled fish and of a honeycomb (Luke 24:36-43). Thomas thrust his hand into his side, and was convinced that he was the same who had been crucified (John 20:27). What stronger proof can we need of the substantial and tangible nature of the spiritual body? It is the animal body purified, not evaporated into gas, or vapour. It is a bloodless body; for in the case of Jesus he had poured out his blood on the cross. The life of the animal body is in the blood; but not so that of the spiritual body: the life of this resides in that mighty power which suspends "the earth upon nothing", and is diffused through the immensity of space.

When the Lord Jesus said, "A *spirit* hath not flesh and bones as ye see me have", he did not mean to say that *a spiritual body* had not; but a spirit such as they thought they saw. "They supposed they had seen a spirit." In the received reading the same word, πνεῦμα, is used here as in the text which speaks of Jesus as "the Lord the Spirit"; but evidently, not in the same sense. Indeed, the reading in Griesbach's edition of the original text is clearly the correct one. The word rendered spirit is properly φάντασμα, a phantom or mere optical illusion; and not πνεῦμα, spirit.* When Jesus walked upon the sea both Matthew (14:26) and Mark (Mark 6:49) make use of the same phrase as Luke, and say that the disciples when they saw him, "supposed they had seen a spirit, and they cried out for fear". In both these places the word is *phantasma*, and not *pneuma*.

Having affirmed that man stands related to two kinds of body, the apostle gives us to understand, that in the arrangements of God the spiritual system of things is elaborated out of the animal, and not the animal out of the spiritual. The natural world is the raw material, as it were, of the spiritual; the bricks and mortar, so to speak, of the mansion which is to endure for ever. In relation to human nature, two men are presented as its types in the two phases it is to assume. These Paul styles "the First Adam", and "the Last Adam", or "the first man", and "the second man". The former, he terms "earthy"; because he came from the ground, and goes thither again: and, the latter, "the Lord from heaven"; because, being "known no more after the flesh", he is expected from heaven as the place of his final manifestation in

---

*The R.V. retains *pneuma*, spirit; but in Matthew and Mark renders *phantasma*, apparition.

"the body of his glory". Then, says John, *"we shall be like him"*. If, therefore, we have been successful in depicting the Lord as he is now, while seated at the right hand of God; namely, an incorruptible, honourable, powerful, living person, substantial and tangible, shining as the sun, and able to eat and drink, and to display all mental and other phenomena in perfection: if the reader be able to comprehend such an "Image of the invisible God", he can understand what they are to be, who are accounted worthy to inherit His kingdom. Therefore, says Paul, "As we have borne the image of the earthy, we shall also bear the image of the heavenly" (1 Corinthians 15:49), or, Lord from heaven.

This corporeal change of those, who have first been morally "renewed unto knowledge after the image of him that hath created them" (Colossians 3:10) from "sinful flesh" into spirit, is an absolute necessity, before they can inherit the Kingdom of God. When we come to understand the nature of this Kingdom, which has to be exhibited in these pages, we shall see that it is a necessity which cannot be dispensed with. "That which is corruptible cannot inherit incorruptibility", says the apostle. This is the reason why animal men must die, or be transformed. Our animal nature is corruptible; but the Kingdom of God is indestructible, as the prophet testifies, saying, "It shall never be destroyed, nor left to other people; but shall stand for ever" (Daniel 2:44). Because, therefore, of the nature of this Kingdom, "flesh and blood cannot inherit it"; and hence the necessity of a man being "born of the spirit', or "he cannot enter into the Kingdom of God" (John 3:5,6; 1 Corinthians 15:50). He must be "changed into spirit", put on incorruptibility and immortality of body, or he will be physically incapable of retaining the honour, glory, and power of the Kingdom for ever, or even for a thousand years.

But, before the apostle concludes his interesting exposition of "the kind of body for which the dead come", he makes known a secret which was previously concealed from the disciples at Corinth. It would probably have occurred to them, that if flesh and blood could not inherit the Kingdom of God, then those who were living at the epoch of its establishment, being men in the flesh, could have no part in it. But to remove this difficulty, the apostle wrote, saying, "Behold, I tell you a mystery. We shall not all sleep (κοιμηθησόμεθα, *met.* to die, be dead), but we shall all be changed, in a moment, in the twinkling of an eye, at the last trumpet; for it (the seventh trumpet—Revelation 11:15,18; 15:8; 20:4) shall sound, and the dead shall be raised incorruptible (ἰσάγγελοι, equal to the angels—Luke 20:36), and we shall be changed (εἰς πνεῦμα, into spirit—1 Corinthians 15:45). For this corruptible (body) must put on incorruptibility (ἀφθαρσίαν), and this mortal (body) must put on immortality (ἀθανασίαν). Then

47

shall be brought to pass the saying that is written, "Death is swallowed up in victory" (Isaiah 25:8).

But, that the saints might not misapprehend the matter, especially those of them who may be contemporary with the seventh trumpet-period, he gave further particulars of the secret in another letter. The disciples at Thessalonica were deeply sorrowing for the loss of some of their body who had fallen asleep in death; probably victims to persecution. The apostle wrote to comfort them, and exhorted them "not to sorrow as the others (ο ι λοιποί, i.e., the unbelievers), who have no hope. For if we (the disciples) believe that Jesus died and rose again"; and be not like those, who, by saying, "There is no resurrection of the dead", in effect deny it; "even so", as he rose, "them also who sleep in Jesus will God bring forth (ἄξει, lead out, or produce), with him" (2 Corinthians 4:14). He then proceeds to show the "order" (1 Corinthians 15:23) in which the saints are changed into spirit, or immortalized, by the Son of Man (John 5:21,25,26,28,29). "For", says he, "this we say unto you by the word of the Lord, that we, the living, who remain at the Lord's coming, shall not anticipate them who are asleep. For the Lord himself shall come down from heaven with a shout, with the voice of the archangel, and with the trumpet of God: and *the dead in Christ shall rise* FIRST: *after that* we, the living, who remain, shall be snatched away together with them in clouds to a meeting of the Lord in the air: and thus we shall be with the Lord at all times. Wherefore comfort one another with these words" (1 Thessalonians 4:13-18).

It will be seen from this, that survivors of the dead were not consoled in the first age of Christianity for the loss of their friends as they are now by those who "improve the death" of the influential among them. In "funeral sermons", the "immortal souls" of the deceased are transported "on angels' wings to heaven", and the living are consoled with the assurance that they are singing the praises of God around the throne; feasting with Abraham, and the prophets, with the saints and martyrs, and with Jesus and his apostles in the Kingdom of God; and they are themselves persuaded, that the souls of their relations, now become angels, are watching over them, and praying for them; and that when they die their own souls will be re-united with them in the realms of bliss. Need I say to the man enlightened in the word, that there is no such comfort, or consolation, as this in the law and the testimony of God? Such traditions are purely mythological; and come of the Nicolaitan dogma of "saved ghosts, and goblins damn'd", which has cancerously extirpated "the truth as it is in Jesus". No, the apostles did not point men to the day of their death, and its immediate consequents, for comfort; nor did they administer the consolations of the gospel to any who had not obeyed it. They offered comfort only to the disciples; for they only are the heirs with Jesus of the Kingdom of God. They taught these to look to the coming of Christ, and to the resurrection, as the time of a re-union with their brethren in the faith. At death, they should "rest from their labours, and their works should follow them" and "to them that look for him shall he appear the second time without sin unto salvation" (Hebrews 9:28) Such were the practical and intelligible "words" with which the apostles comforted their brethren; but words which have become sealed and cabalistic, both to the unlearned and "the wise".

In conclusion, then, as far as power is concerned, God could have created all things upon a spiritual or incorruptible basis at once. The globe could have been filled with men and women, equal to the angels in nature, power, and intellect, on the sixth day; but the world would have been without a history, and its population characterless. This, however, would not have been according to the plan. The animal must precede the spiritual as the acorn goes before the oak. This will explain many difficulties which are created by systems; and which will for ever remain inexplicable upon the hypotheses they invent. The Bible has to do with things, not imaginations; with bodies, not phantasmata; with "living souls" of every species; with *corporeal* beings of other worlds; and with incorruptible and undying men; but it is as mute as death, and silent as the grave, having nothing at all to say about such "souls" as men pretend to "*cure*"; except to repudiate them as a part of that "philosophy and vain deceit" (Colossians 2:8), "which some professing have erred concerning the faith" (1 Timothy 6:21).

THE FORMATION OF WOMAN

"The woman was of the man."

ADAM, having been formed in the image, after the likeness of the Elohim on the sixth day, remained for a short time alone in the midst of the earthborns of the field. He had no companion who could reciprocate his intelligence; none who could minister to his wants, or rejoice with him in the delights of creation; and reflect the glory of his nature. The Elohim are a society, rejoicing in the love and attachment of one another; and Adam, being like them though of inferior nature, required an object which should be calculated to evoke the latent resemblances of his similitude to theirs. It was no better for man to be alone than for them. Formed in their image, he had social feelings as well as intellectual and moral faculties, which required scope for their practical and harmonious exercise. A purely intellectual and abstractly moral society, untempered by domesticism, is an imperfect state. It may be very enlightened, very dignified and immaculate; but it would also be very formal, and frigid as the poles. A being might know all things, and he might scrupulously observe the divine law from a sense of duty; but something more is requisite to make him amiable, and beloved by either God or his fellows. This amiability the social feelings enable him to develop; which, however, if unfurnished with a proper object, or wholesome excitation, react upon him unfavourably, and make him disagreeable. Well aware of this, Yahweh Elohim said, "It is not good that the man should be alone. I will make him a help fit for him" (Genesis 2:18).

But previous to the formation of this help, God caused "every living soul" (*kol nephesh chayiah*) to pass in review before Adam, that he might name them. He saw that each one had its mate; "but for him there was not found a suitable companion". It was necessary, therefore, to form one, the last and fairest of His handiworks. The Lord had created man in His own "image and glory"; but He had yet to subdivide him into two; a negative and a positive division; an active and a passive half; male and female, yet one flesh. The negatives, or females, of all other species of animals, were formed out of the ground (verse 19); and not out of the sides of their positive mates: so that the lion could not say of the lioness, "This is bone of my bone, and flesh of my flesh; therefore shall a lion leave his sire and dam, and cleave unto the same lioness for ever". The inferior creatures are under no such law as this; as primaries, indeed, the earth is their common mother, and the Lord, the "God of all their spirits". They have no second selves; the sexes in the beginning were from the ground direct; the female was not of the male, though the male is by her: therefore, there is no natural basis for a social, or domestic, law to them.

But in the formation of a companion for the first man, the Lord Elohim created her upon a different principle. She was to be a dependent creature; and a sympathy was to be established between them, by which they should be attached inseparably. It would not have been fit, therefore, to have given her an independent origin from the dust of the ground. Had this been the case, there would have been about the same kind of attachment between men and women as subsists among the creatures below them. The woman's companionship was designed to be intellectually and morally sympathetic with "the image and glory of God", whom she was to revere as her superior. The sympathy of the mutually independent earthborns of the field, is purely sensual;

and in proportion as generations of mankind lose their intellectual and moral likeness to the Elohim, and fall under the dominion of sensuality; so the sympathy between men and women evaporates into mere animalism. But, I say, such a degenerate result as this was not the end of her formation. She was not simply to be "the mother of all living"; but to reflect the glory of man as he reflected the glory of God.

To give being to such a creature, it was necessary she should be formed out of man. This necessity is found in the law which pervades the flesh. If the feeblest member of the body suffer, all the other members suffer with it; that is, pain even in the little finger will produce distress throughout the system. Bone sympathizes with bone, and flesh with flesh, in all pleasurable, healthful, and painful feelings. Hence, to separate a portion of Adam's living substance, and from it to build a woman, would be to transfer to her the sympathies of Adam's nature; and though by her organization able to maintain an independent existence, she would never lose from her nature a sympathy with his, in all its intellectual, moral, and physical manifestations. According to this natural law, then, the Lord Elohim made woman in the likeness of the man, out of his substance. He might have formed her from his body before he became a *living* soul; but this would have defeated the law of sympathy; for in inanimate matter there is no mental sympathy. She must, therefore, be formed from the living bone and flesh of the man. To do this was to inflict pain; for to cut out a portion of flesh would have created the same sensations in Adam as in any of his posterity. To avoid such an infliction, "the Lord God caused *a deep sleep* to fall upon Adam, and he slept". While thus unconscious of what was doing, and perfectly insensible to all corporeal impressions, the Lord "took out one of his ribs, and then closed up the flesh in its place". This was a delicate operation; and consisted in separating the rib from the breast bone and spine. But nothing is too difficult for God. The most wonderful part of the work had yet to be performed. The quivering rib, with its nerves and vessels, had to be increased in magnitude, and formed into a human figure, capable of reflecting the glory of the man. This was soon accomplished; for, on the sixth day, "male and female created he them": and "the rib which the LORD God had taken from man, he made a woman, and brought her unto the man". And "God blessed them, and said unto them, Be fruitful, and multiply, and replenish (fill again) the earth, and subdue it: and have dominion over the fish of the sea, and over the fowl of the air, and over every living thing that creepeth upon the earth".

Believing this portion of the testimony of God, need our faith be staggered at the resurrection of the body from the little dust that remains after its entire reduction? Surely, the Lord Jesus Christ by the same power that formed woman from a rib, and that increased a few loaves and fishes to twelve baskets of fragments after five thousand were fed and satisfied, can create multitudes of immortal men from a few proportions of the former selves: and as capable of resuming their individual identity, as was Adam's rib of reflecting his mental and physical similitude. It is blind unbelief alone that requires the continuance of some sort of existence to preserve the identity of the resurrected man with his former self. Faith confides in the ability of God to do what He has promised, although the believer has not the knowledge of how He is to accomplish it. Believing the wonders of the past, "he staggers not at the promise of God through unbelief; but is strong in faith, giving glory to God" (Romans 4:20).

The testimony of Moses in regard to the formation of woman brings to light a very interesting phenomenon, which has since been amply proved to be the result of a natural law. It is that *man may be made insensible to pain by being placed in a deep sleep*. The Lord Elohim availed Himself of this law, and subjected the man He had made to its operation; and man, because be is in His likeness, is also able to influence his fellow-man in the same way. The art of applying the law is called various names, and may be practised variously. The name does not alter the thing. A man's rib might be extracted now with as little inconvenience as Adam experienced, by throwing him into a deep sleep, which in numerous cases may be easily effected; but there our imitative ability ceases. We could not build up a woman from the rib. Greater wonders, however, than this will man do hereafter; for by "the *Man* Christ Jesus" will his Bride be created from the dust, in his own image after his own likeness, "to the glory of God, throughout all ages, world without end. Amen".

When the Lord God presented the newly formed creature to her parent flesh, Adam said, "This is now bone of my bone, and flesh of my flesh; she shall be called *Ishah* (or Outman), because she was taken out of *Ish*, or man. Therefore shall a man leave his father and his mother, and shall cleave unto his wife; and they shall be one flesh" (Genesis 2:21-24). Thus, Adam pronounced upon himself the sentence that was to bind them together for weal or woe, until death should dissolve the union, and set them free for ever. This was marriage. It was based upon the great fact of her formation out of man; and consisted in Adam taking her to himself with her unconstrained consent. There was no religious ceremonial to sanctify the institution; for the Lord Himself even abstained from pronouncing the union. No human ceremony can make marriage more holy than it is in the nature of things. Superstition has made it "a sacrament", and inconsistently enough, denied it, though "a *holy* sacrament", to the very priests she has appointed to administer it. But priests and superstition have no right to meddle with the matter; they only disturb the harmony, and destroy the beauty, of God's arrangements. A declaration in the presence of the Lord Elohim, and the consent of the woman, before religion was instituted, is the only ceremonial recorded in the case. This, I believe, is the order of things among "the Friends", or nearly so; and, if all their peculiarities were as scriptural as this, there would be but little cause of complaint against them.

"Man", says the apostle, "is the image and glory of God; but the woman is the glory of the man"; and the reason he assigns is, because "The man is not of the woman; but the woman of the man. Neither was the man created for the woman; but the woman for the man" (1 Corinthians 11:7-9). She was not formed in the image of man, though she may have been in the image of some of the Elohim. "Man" is generic of both sexes. When, therefore, Elohim said, "Let us make *man* in *our* image"; and it is added, "male and female created he *them*", it would seem that both the man and the woman were created in the image and likeness of Elohim. In this case some of the Elohim are represented by Adam's form, and some by Eve's. I see no reason why it should not be so. When mankind rises from the dead, they will doubtless become immortal men and women; and then, says Jesus, "they are equal to the angels"; on an equality with them in every respect. Adam only was in the image of Him that created him; but then, the Elohim that do the commandments of the invisible God, are the virile portion of their community: Eve was not in their image. Theirs was restricted to Adam; nevertheless, she was after the image and likeness of some of those comprehended in the pronoun "*our*". Be this as it may, though not in the image, she was in the likeness of Adam; and both "very good" according to the subangelic nature they possessed.

A GREAT MYSTERY

"We are members of his body, of his flesh, and of his bones."

IN writing to the disciples at Ephesus, the apostle illustrated the submission due from wives to their husbands by the obedience rendered to Christ by the community of the faithful in his day. "As the church is subject unto Christ, so let the wives be to their own husbands in every thing." This was an injunction of absolute submission to their Christian husbands as unto the Lord himself; because "the husband is the head of the wife, even as Christ is the head of the Church". But, while he enjoins this unqualified obedience, he exhorts their husbands to return them due benevolence, not to treat them with bitterness, but to love them "even as Christ loved the church, and gave himself up *for it*" (Ephesians 5:25). If unbelieving wives, however, were disobedient and perverse, and chose to depart, "let them; a brother is not under bondage, in such cases" (1 Corinthians 7:15). The love which should subsist between Christian brethren and sisters in the married state, is such as Christ manifested for the church by anticipation. "While *we* were yet sinners Christ died for *us*", says the apostle (Romans 5:6,8). This is the greatest love a man can possibly show, that he should die for his enemies; and this is the kind of love which Paul commends to the attention of the Ephesians; though always on the supposition, that the wives "adorn the hidden man of the heart with that which is incorruptible, even a meek and quiet spirit, which is in the sight of God of great price. For after this manner in the old time the holy women also, who trusted in God, adorned themselves, being in subjection to their own husbands: even as Sara obeyed Abraham, calling him lord: whose daughters such women are, *as long as they do well*, and are not dismayed at any threat" (1 Peter 3:3-6).

As he had introduced the subject of matrimonial love and obedience, and had adduced the love of Christ for them all as his church, by way of illustration; he proceeds to show the object for which he loved them even unto death; the relationship which was subsequently established between them; and the sacrifice which they ought cheerfully to make for him, who had loved them so devotedly. His object in giving himself for the church before it was formed, was that those who should afterwards compose it "might be sanctified and cleansed *in the laver of the water* (τῷ λουτρῷ τοῦ ὕδατος) *by the word* (ἐν ῥήματι), that", at the resurrection, "he might present it to himself a glorious church, not having spot, or wrinkle, or any such thing; but holy and without blemish". "Ye are clean", said Jesus to his disciples "through *the word* which I have spoken to you" (John 15:3). This word, which is defined to be "the law and the testimony" (Isaiah 8:20), is the great instrument of holiness and purification. It changes men's minds; loosens their attachment to earthly things; causes them to place their affection on things above; creates a new and right spirit within them; diffuses the love of God abroad in their hearts; separates them from sinners; leads them into Christ; and develops in their lives, fruit characteristic of that repentance which needs not to be repented of. The Lord Jesus styles it, "the word of the kingdom" (Matthew 13:19); and Peter, the incorruptible seed (1 Peter 1:23); and Paul, "the word of the truth of the gospel" (Colossians 1:5); and John, "God's seed" (1 John 3:9); and by James it is termed, "the word of truth" (James 1:18), with which the invariable and unvacillating Father of lights begets His children, that they should be "a kind of firstfruits of his creatures". It is by this word that an individual is renewed or renovated; so as, in an intellectual and moral sense, to become a "new man", as appears from what the apostle says to the brethren at Colossae: "Ye have put on the new man, which is *renewed unto knowledge* (Colossians 3:10) after the image of him that created him". This renewing affects the spirit of the mind (Ephesians 4:23,24), which may be known to be renovated by a man having turned from his natural subserviency to "the lust of the flesh, the lust of the eye, and the pride of life", to "righteousness and *true* holiness". When the mental disposition, called "the heart", is renewed, it becomes a mirror, as it were, in which one skilled in the word of the kingdom, can discern the spirit, or behold a reflection of the Divine Nature. This image of God in a man's character can only be created by the word of the truth of the gospel of the kingdom. A man may be very "pious" according to the standard of piety set up fellow men; but, if he be ignorant of the renewing elements, if he neither know nor understand, and consequently be faithless of the law and testimony of God, "there is no light in him". He is walking in a vain show; "in the vanity of his mind, having his understanding darkened, being alienated from the life of God *through the ignorance that is in him*, because of the blindness of his heart" (verse 18). The law and the testimony are styled by Peter, "God's knowledge"; "whereby are given unto us *exceeding great and precious promises*, that BY THESE", *i.e.*, by the understanding and belief of these, "ye might be partakers of the Divine Nature, having escaped the corruption that is in the world through lust" (2 Peter 1:2-4). Now, the "testimony of God" came by the Holy Spirit, by which God testified in His prophets (Nehemiah 9:30); and, in the last days, spoke through His Son (Hebrews 1:1,2; John 3:34; 5:47; 6:63; 7:16; 12:48,49) and the apostles (Matthew 10:19,20). Hence, the effects of the word believed are attributed to the spirit; and because the word sets men to breathing in God's moral atmosphere, it is termed "spirit and life". These remarks will explain the saying of the apostle to Titus, "According to his mercy God saved us through the laver of regeneration, and *renewal of the Holy Spirit*" (Titus 3:5). This is parallel to the saying, "Sanctified and cleansed in the laver of the water *by the word*"; for the reader must not suppose, that any man, woman, or child, who is ignorant of the word, can be regenerated, or born again, by being plunged into a bath. The Holy Spirit does not renew the heart of man as he renews the mortal body, when through Jesus he raises it from the dead. In this case, the power is purely physical. But, when the heart is the subject of renewal it is by the knowledge of the written testimony of God, or the word. "God", says Peter, speaking of the Gentile believers, "purified their hearts by faith" (Acts 15:9); and Paul prays, "That Christ may dwell in their hearts by faith" (Ephesians 3:17). Now, faith comes by hearing the word of God (Romans 10:17); in other words, it is the belief of God's testimony concerning things to come, which are not seen (Hebrews 11:1); and without which, it is impossible to please Him (verse 6). When a man is renewed by the truth, he is renewed by the spirit, and not before. There is no such thing in the scriptures as a renewed ignorant man. Ignorance of the testimony of God, and regeneration, are utterly incompatible. The truth is the purifier to those only who understand and obey it (1 Peter 1:22); and there is no moral purity, or sanctification of spirit before God, without it. It is only believers of the truth, then, who can be the subjects of a regeneration by being submerged "in the laver of the water". When they come out of this, they have been "washed, sanctified, and justified in the name of the Lord Jesus, by the spirit of God" (1 Corinthians 6:11).

The truth to be believed is the gospel of the kingdom and name of Jesus Christ (Acts 8:12). When this is understood, and heartily received, it produces a *disposition of mind*, such as was in Abraham and Jesus, and which is called repentance. Believers, so disposed, are the begotten of God, and have become as little children. They believe "the exceeding great and precious promises", together with the things testified concerning the sufferings and resurrection of Jesus. He fell into *a deep sleep*; and, while thus unconscious and insensible, his side was opened by a spear, and forthwith rushed blood and water (John 19:33,34). Being awakened out of his sleep, he was built up a spiritual body, flesh and bones; and, by his ascension, presented to the Father as the federal representative of his church. This is the aggregate of those, who, believing these things, have been introduced into Christ through the laver of the water; according to the saying of the scriptures, "Ye are all the children of God in Christ Jesus through the faith. For as many as have been baptized into Christ have put on Christ" (ἐνεδύσασθε) ..."Ye are all one *in* Christ Jesus. And *if* ye be Christ's, *then* are ye Abraham's seed, and HEIRS according to the promise" (Galatians 3:26-29). A community of such individuals as these constitutes the mystical body of Christ. By faith, its elements are "members of his body, of his flesh, and of his bones". Hence, they are "bone of his bone, and flesh of his flesh"; and therefore, the beloved Eve of the last Adam, the Lord who is to come from heaven, and make her of the same holy spiritual nature as his own. Thus, the church is figuratively taken out of the side of her Lord; for every member of it believes in the remission of sins through his shed blood; and they all believe in the real resurrection of his flesh and bones, for their justification unto life by a similar revival from the dead. "Your bodies are the members", or flesh and bones, "of Christ; ... and he that is joined unto the Lord is one spirit" (1 Corinthians 6:15,17). "I have espoused you to one husband," says Paul, "that I may present you as a chaste virgin to Christ" (2 Corinthians 11:2). It will be perceived, then, that the church as defined, is in the present state *the espoused of Christ*, but not actually married. She is in the formative state, being moulded under the hand of God. When she shall be completed, God will then present her to the Man from heaven, "arrayed in fine linen, clean and white" (Revelation 19:7,8). This is she of whom the psalmist sings, "Hearken, O daughter, and consider, and incline thine ear; forget also thine own people and thy father's house; so shall the king greatly desire thy beauty: for he is thy Lord; and worship thou him. The king's daughter is all glorious within; her clothing is of wrought gold. She shall be brought unto the king in raiment of needlework; the virgins, her companions that follow her, shall be brought unto thee. With gladness and rejoicing shall they be brought: *they shall enter into the king's palace*" (Psalm 45:10-15). The presentation of Eve to the first Adam was the signal of rejoicing to the Morning Stars; and we perceive that the manifestation of Messiah's Queen will he attended with the *"Alleluia"* of a great multitude, sounding like the roaring of many waters, and the echoes of mighty thunderings, saying, "Let us be glad and rejoice, and give honour to the Lord God omnipotent: for the marriage of the Lamb is come, and his betrothed hath made herself ready".

Such is the relationship and destiny of the true church, styled by Paul, "the One Body". It is forming by the word; or, taking it as formed in the apostolic age, but not presented, the apprehension of the apostle has been sadly realised. "I fear", says he, "lest by any means, as the serpent beguiled Eve through his subtlety, so your minds should be corrupted from the simplicity that is in Christ" (2 Corinthians 11:3). The tempter has seduced the betrothed. The simplicity in Christ is no longer characteristic of a community. It is corrupted on every side; and the ruin of the transgression alone prevails. Nevertheless, although there be no hope for the professing world, seeing that it is too "wise in its own conceit"; too self-satisfied with its supposed illumination; glorifying itself, and saying, "I am rich, and increased with goods, and have need of nothing", and knows not, and will not be persuaded, "that it is wretched, and miserable, and poor, and blind, and naked" (Revelation 3:17)—seeing, I say, that this is the irremediable condition of the religious public, yet there remains scope for the deliverance of those who are disposed to obey God rather than men. If they would become bone of Christ's bone, and flesh of his flesh, they must "leave father and mother, and be joined unto the wife". They find themselves now, perhaps, members of denominations as they happen to be led. These are their parentage according to the fleshly mind. They must be forsaken, and men must become "one flesh" and "one spirit" in the Lord, if they would inherit the kingdom of God (Matthew 10:37). "This is *a great mystery*", says Paul; "but I speak concerning Christ and the church" (Ephesians 5:22-32). This mystery, I have endeavoured to elucidate in these remarks, though necessarily in a very brief, and therefore imperfect manner. When I shall have finished the work before me, it will have been more minutely unfolded, and, I trust, convincingly explained.

EDEN

"In Eden"

WHEN Moses penned the words "*in Eden*" (Genesis 2:8), he was westward in "the wilderness of the land of Egypt". From the expression, then, we are to understand that there was a country styled Eden in his day, which lay to the eastward of his position. Adam and Eve were its aborigines. It was "*the East*" of the Egyptians, as Ohio, Indiana, and Illinois are "the West" to the Atlantic American States. It was quite an extensive range of country, and in after times became the seat of powerful dominions. It appears to have been well watered by the branches, or tributaries, of "a river that went", or flowed, "out of it" (verse 10). These were four principal streams, whose names, as given by Moses, are the Pison, "which compasseth the whole land of Havilah"; the Gihon, "the same is it which compasseth the whole land of Khush", or Khushistan; the third, the Hiddekel, or Tigris, "that is it which goeth eastward to Assyria. And the fourth river is the Euphrates" (verses 11-14), frequently styled in the scriptures, "the Great River" (Genesis 15:18). On the map before me, there are four rivers which flow together, and at length form a river which falls into the Persian Gulf. This indicates the country called Eden, namely, that which is watered by these rivers; so that we may reasonably conclude that in early times it comprehended the land east of the Jordan, Syria, Assyria, part of Persia, Khushistan, and the original settlements of Ishmael (Genesis 25:18).

This country, in after ages, came to be denominated "the Garden of the LORD"; and the kings who reigned in it, "the Trees of Eden". It was no doubt termed the Lord's garden as a whole, from the fact of His having, in the beginning, planted a garden in it, where He put the man; so that the name of a small part of Eden came to be applied by his family in the time of Seth, Noah, Shem, Abraham, and Moses, to the whole region; more especially as the future paradise is to occupy a considerable portion of its ancient limits.

The plain of Jordan appears to have been part of Eden from the following texts. "Lot beheld all the plain of Jordan, that it was well watered everywhere as *the garden of the Lord*. Then Lot chose him all the plain of Jordan; and Lot journeyed *east*; and dwelled in the cities of the plain" (Genesis 13:10-12); that is, in the East, or Eden.

There is a prophecy in Ezekiel, predicting the overthrow of the Egyptian Pharaoh by the King of Babylon, "the mighty one of the heathen". In setting forth the certainty of his overthrow, God recapitulates the power and dominion of the Ninevite dynasty of Assyria; which, however, was not able to withstand the King of Babylon, and therefore there was no hope for Egypt of a successful resistance. In the recapitulation, the Ninevite Assyrian is styled, *"a cedar in Lebanon"*; that is, his dominion extended over the land of the ten tribes of Israel, in which are the cedar-crowned mountains of Lebanon. After describing the greatness of his power by the magnitude of the cedar, the Lord says, "the cedars in the garden of God could not hide him; nor was any tree in the garden of God like unto him in his beauty. I made him fair by the multitude of his branches; so that all the trees of Eden, in the garden of God, envied him" (Ezekiel 31:3,8,9). These trees (Daniel 4:20,22) are representative of the royalties of Mesopotamia, Syria, Israel, etc., which the king of Assyria had abolished (Isaiah 37:12-13); and which "could not hide him", or prevent him getting the ascendancy over them. It is clear, then, from the terms of this beautiful allegory, that the countries I have indicated are comprehended in Eden; that as a whole it is styled the garden of the Lord; and that the trees are the royalties of the land.

That Eden extended to the Mediterranean, or "Great Sea", appears from Ezekiel's prophecy against Tyre. Addressing the Tyrian royalty, he says, "Thou hast been in Eden, the garden of God ... Thou wast upon the holy mountain of God. Thou wast perfect in thy ways from the day that thou wast created, till iniquity was found in thee. Therefore I will cast thee as profane out of the mountain of God. Thou shalt be a terror, and never shalt thou be any more (Ezekiel 28:13,16,19). The meaning of this is obvious to one acquainted with the history of the kingdom of Tyre. It was a royalty of Palestine in Upper Galilee, whose king,

Hiram, was in intimate alliance with Solomon. He appears to have been a proselyte worshipper of the God of Israel; whom his successors some time afterwards forsook; and therefore God suppressed the kingdom of Tyre by Nebuchadnezzar for seventy years; and finally by the Greeks.

Eden has been a field of blood from the beginning of the contest between the "Seed of the Woman" and the "Seed of the Serpent", until now; and will yet continue to be until the serpent power be broken upon the mountains of Israel. It was in Eden that Abel died by the hand of Cain. There also Abel's antitype was wounded in the heel, when put to death upon the accursed tree; and lastly, to fill up the measure of iniquity of the blood-defiled land, the serpents of Israel slew the son of Barachias between the temple and altar. But the blood of God's saints shed in Eden, did not cry to Him for vengeance without effect: for as the Lord Jesus declared, so it came to pass. "Behold", said he to the vipers of his day, "I send you prophets, and wise men, and scribes; and some of them ye will kill and crucify; and some of them ye will scourge in your synagogues, and persecute from city to city; that upon you may come all the righteous blood shed upon the land, from the blood of righteous Abel unto the blood of Zecharias, son of Barachias, whom ye slew between the temple and the altar" (Matthew 23:35).

Eden is emphatically the Lord's land, or garden; and from the creation till the breaking off of Israel's olive branch, the principal, and almost only, theatre upon which He exhibited His wonders to the nations in the days of old. Egypt and its wilderness may be excepted for forty years. Beyond its limits was outer darkness. Eden only was favoured with light, until the gospel found its way among the nations of the west; and although darkness covers the land, and gross darkness the people; yet the Lord, its light, will arise upon it and His glory shall be seen there (Isaiah 60:1,2).

THE GARDEN OF EDEN

"And the LORD God planted a garden eastward in Eden."

WHILE Eden was "the East" eastward of the wilderness, the garden of Eden was eastward in Eden. "Eden the garden of the LORD", and "the garden of Eden", are quite different ideas. The former designates the whole of Eden as the Lord's garden; the latter, as merely a plantation in some part of it. To plant a garden is to fence in a certain piece of land, and to adorn it with fruit and ornamental trees and shrubs. If unenclosed, and consequently unguarded, it is not a garden. The name of the plantation implies that its surface was protected from the invasion of the animals, whose habits made them unfit tenants of a garden. The place, then, was an enclosure, planted with "every tree that is pleasant to the sight and good for food". Its situation, Moses says, was "eastward", having a river flowing through it to water it. I suspect from this, that it lay somewhere between the Gulf of Persia, and the junction of the Euphrates and the Tigris. The text reads, "And a river went out of Eden to water the garden; and *from thence* it was parted, and became into four heads"; which I should interpret thus:—a river flowing out of Eden was caused to water the garden on its way to the sea; and from the garden northward, the river diverged into its branches, which terminated at four several heads. The heads were not in the garden, but at remote distances from it. The garden of Eden was watered by only one, and not by four rivers; as it is written, "*a river went out to water it*"; which certainly excludes the four from its enclosure.

In the Septuagint of this text, the word *garden* is expressed παράδειοος, which is transferred into our language without translation. *Paradise* is a Persian word adopted into the Greek, and expressed in Hebrew by *parades* or *pardes*. It signifies a park, a forest, or preserve; a garden of trees of various kinds, a delightful grove, etc. It is found in these texts: "I made me gardens (*paradises*) and orchards, and I planted trees in them of all kinds of fruits" (Ecclesiastes 2:5); and, "A garden enclosed (*a paradise*) is my sister spouse ... ; thy plants are an orchard of pomegranates", etc. (Song of Solomon 4:12,13). The latter text is part of a description of Solomon's vineyard, representative of that part of Eden over which he reigned; and metaphorical of its beauty, fertility, and glory, when the Heir of the vineyard, the "greater than Solomon", shall come to Zion, and "marry the land" of Eden, as defined in the everlasting covenant made with Abraham (Genesis 15:18). For so it is written, "Thy land, O Zion, shall no more be termed desolate: but thou shalt be called Hephzibah (*i.e., my beloved is in her*), and thy land Beulah (*i.e., married*): for Jehovah delighteth in thee, and thy land shall be married. For as a young man marrieth a virgin, so shall thy sons marry, thee: and as the bridegroom rejoiceth over the bride, so shall thy God rejoice over thee" (Isaiah 62:4,5).

When the marriage, or union, takes place between the sons of Zion, and their king, with the Land of Promise in Eden, it will again become the garden of the Lord, or Paradise, which His own right hand hath planted. For "the LORD shall comfort Zion: he will comfort all her waste places; and he will make her wilderness like Eden, and her desert like the garden of the LORD; joy and gladness shall be found therein, thanksgiving, and the voice of melody" (Isaiah 51:3). "Instead of the thorn shall come up the fir tree, and instead of the brier shall come up the myrtle tree: and it shall be to the LORD for a name, for an everlasting sign that shall not be cut off" (Isaiah 55:13). At that time, "I will open rivers in high places, and fountains in the midst of the valleys: I will make the wilderness a pool of water, and the dry land springs of water. I will plant in the wilderness the cedar, the shittah tree, and the myrtle tree, and the oil tree; I will set in the desert the fir tree, and the pine, and the box together: that they (Israel) may see, and know, and consider, and understand together, that the hand of the Lord hath done this, and the Holy One of Israel hath created it" (Isaiah 41:18-20).

These testimonies reveal a future state in regard to Eden, of which its primitive garden is a beautiful and appropriate representation. Once the seat of *a paradise* on a small scale, it is destined to be transformed from its present desolation into *"the Paradise of God"*. The country of the four rivers, even to the west from sea to sea, is predetermined to shine forth as "the glory of all lands". Paradise hath no other locality. Other orbs may have their paradises: but as far as man is concerned, the Paradise of God will be by Him planted in Eden according to *"the promise"*. "In that day, shall Israel be the third with Egypt and Assyria, even a blessing *in the midst* of the land"; that is, of Eden: "whom the LORD of Hosts shall bless, saying, Blessed be Egypt, my people, and Assyria, the work of my hands, and Israel, mine inheritance" (Isaiah 19:24,25).

In the letter to the congregation at Ephesus, the Spirit says, "To him that overcometh will I give to eat of the Tree of Life, which is in the midst of the paradise of God" (Revelation 2:7). The simple import of this is as follows. The saints of God are termed in scripture, "Trees of Righteousness", which bring forth good fruit; and the King of Saints, the Tree of Life. This, then, is the symbol of Christ as the giver of life. "As the living Father hath sent me, and I live by the Father; so *he that eateth me*", says Christ, "even he *shall live by me*" (John 6:57). Hence, to give a man to eat of the Tree of Life, is for the Lord Jesus to raise a true believer from among the dead to incorruptible life. He will then eat, or partake, of that life, which he is ordained to bestow, who said of himself, "I am the way, and the truth, and *the life*". But none of the believers, or heirs of life, can partake of the life-giving tree, until it is manifested in the Paradise of God; that is, until the Lord appears in his Kingdom (2 Timothy 4:1,8; 1 Peter 1:7,13). We shall see in the second part of this work the particulars concerning this Kingdom. I shall, therefore, content myself with remarking here, that when it is manifested, it will be established in the Lord's land; that is, in Eden: hence, the promise, interpreted into plain English, is — "To the believer that overcomes the world (1 John 5:4), will I, the Lord, who am the life, give glory, honour, and immortality, when I come to stand on the Mount of Olives (Zechariah 14:4), and to re-establish the kingdom and throne of David, as in the days of old" (Amos 9:11). There is no immortality, nor Paradise until then; neither can any attain to them unless they "overcome the world"; for the promise is only "to him that overcometh".

But to this doctrine sceptics object, that Paradise must have a present existence somewhere ; seeing that, on the day of his crucifixion, Jesus told the thief that he should be with them in Paradise on that day; as it is written, "I say to thee, *to-day* shalt thou be with me in Paradise" (Luke 23:43). I admit, that it is so written in English; but I find there are various readings and punctuations in the Greek. In the first place, the thief's petition is differently worded in some manuscripts. In the common version it reads "Remember me, Lord, when thou comest *in thy kingdom*", ἐν τῇ βασιλεία σου, but in others, it is various, though in sense the same — as, "Remember me when thou comest *in the day of thy coming*", ἐν τῇ ἡμέρα τῆς ἐλεύσεως σου. Now the Lord "comes in his kingdom" "in the day of his coming"; therefore, I say, the two phrases are in sense the same, only the latter more plainly suggests to "the unskilful in the word of righteousness" (Hebrews 5:13), the import of the term "to-day", in the answer to the petition.

In the next place, Jesus did not evade the thief's prayer, but gave him a direct and intelligible reply. He told him, in effect, that what he requested should be granted: in other words, that when he was himself in his kingdom he should be there too. But does the reader imagine, that Jesus told him *the time when*, seeing that he was not even himself acquainted with the time when the Jewish State, as constituted by the Mosaic code, should be abolished? And, till this was set aside, he could not come in his kingdom; for then he is to sit and rule, and be a priest upon his throne (Zechariah 6:12,13,15); which he could not be co-existent with the law: because the law of Moses would permit no one to officiate as a priest, who was not of the tribe of Levi; and Jesus was descended from Judah (Hebrews 7:12-14). "Heaven and earth", or the Mosaic constitution of things in Eden, "shall pass away", said Jesus: "but of that day and hour knoweth no man — no, not the angels which are in heaven, *neither the Son*, but the Father" (Mark 13:31-32).

Furthermore, does the reader suppose, that the Lord informed the thief of the time when he would come in his kingdom; or that it could possibly be, that he came in his kingdom on the day of his suffering; seeing that on the forty-third day afterwards, he refused to tell even the apostles, the times and the seasons when he would "*restore* AGAIN the kingdom to Israel"? "It is not *for you* to know the times and the seasons, which the Father hath put in his own power" (Acts 1:3,6,7). This was his language to the apostles. The kingdom could not be restored again to Israel under the Mosaic code. This had "decayed, and waxed old, and was ready to vanish away" (Hebrews 8:13). It was to be "cast down to the ground", the daily sacrifice was to be taken away, and the temple and city to be demolished, by the Little Horn of the Goat, or Roman power (Daniel 8:9-12,24; 9:26). To tell *them* of the times and the seasons of the kingdom, would have been to have informed them of this national catastrophe; of which they were kept in ignorance, that they might not fall asleep, but be continually on the watch.

But, though Jesus did not then know the times and the seasons of the kingdom, he knows them now; for, about thirty years after the destruction of Jerusalem, "God gave him a revelation of the things which shortly must come to pass" (Revelation 1:1); and in this apocalypse, the times and seasons are set forth in order. But, to return to the case of the thief. In saying "to-day", Jesus did not, and could not, tell him the precise time when he should be with him in Paradise. In some translations, there is a various, and no doubt the correct, punctuation. The comma, instead of being after "thee", is placed after "to-day"; as, "I say unto thee to-day,*—thou shalt be with me in *the* Paradise, ἐν τῷ παραδείσῳ": that is, "At this time, or, I now say to thee, thou shalt be with me in my kingdom in the day of my coming".

But, if the objector insist upon an interpretation of the passage as it stands in the common version, then let it be so; his position will be by no means less easy to carry. His instantaneous translation of souls to Paradise at death, as far as it is fortified by this passage, hangs upon a thread, like the sword of the Syracusan tyrant; and that is, the word "to-day". This is a scripture term, and must be explained by the scripture use of it. In the sacred writings, then, the term is used to express a period of *over two thousand years*. The use of it occurs in David, as it is written, "To-day if ye will hear his voice, harden not your hearts, lest ye enter not into my rest" (Psalm 95:7-11). The apostle, commenting upon this passage about one thousand years after it was written, says, "Exhort one another daily, *while it is called* to-day"; and, "Labour to enter into the rest that remaineth for the

---

* *Sēmeron* (to-day), thus qualifies the preceding verb in Luke 2:11, and many other passages in the N.T. Also in the LXX. of Deuteronomy 8:19; 9:1; 30:18,19; and other places.

people of God" (Hebrews 3:13; 4:11,9). Thus, it was called "to-day", when David wrote; and "to-day", when Paul commented upon it. This was a long day; but one, however, which is not yet finished; and will continue unclosed until the manifestation of the rest in the Paradise of God. If it be admitted, that we are still in "the day of salvation", then it must be received as true, that we are living "while it is called to-day"—that "to-day" is *now*; and this "now" will be present until the Lord Jesus enters into his rest (Psalm 132:13-18) which he cannot do until he has finished the work God has given him to do (Isaiah 49:5,6,8; 40:10). "Behold, *now* is the time of acceptance; behold, *now* is *the day*", or the "to-day" "*of salvation*" (2 Corinthians 6:2), a period of time from Joshua to the future glorious manifestation of Christ in the kingdom, to say nothing of "the accepted time" to the patriarchs, before the typical rest of Israel in the promised land.

Lastly, is it not the very climax of absurdity to talk of Jesus being "in his kingdom", or "in the Paradise", which were synonymous, while he was lying dead in the tomb? Is his kingdom among the dead? He told the Pharisees it was among the living. "Oh, but", says one, "he descended into hell."

"True", says another, "and while he was there he preached the gospel to the dead, and proclaimed repentance to the spirits in prison. He and the thief, that is to say, their souls, were there together as soon as death released them. This was Paradise". "Not exactly so", adds a third. "That savours too much of purgatory. They were in an intermediate state of blessedness before the throne of God, in the kingdoms beyond the skies." "How can that be", says a fourth; "is the blessedness in God's presence only intermediate? They went straight to the fulness of joy for evermore." Why, then, was Jesus raised that he might go to the Father (John 16:17), if he were with the Father before; and, where did he *leave* the thief, for he was not raised; and if not raised, but left behind, how can he be with the Lord in Paradise? When this question is answered, it will be time enough to glance at the traditions extant upon this subject—dogmatisms, however, which none who understand the gospel of the kingdom can possibly entertain.

MAN'S DOMINION

"Let them have dominion."

THE garden being prepared in Eden, the Lord placed the man there whom He had formed. It was there the "deep sleep" came over him, and he first beheld his bride. They were now settled in

Paradise; and, protected by its enclosure from the intrusion of the inferior creatures, they passed their days in blissful tranquillity; innocent of transgression, and in peaceful harmony with God and the creatures He had made. Adam dressed the garden and kept it. This was his occupation. Though as yet sinless, it was no part of his enjoyments to be idle. To eat bread in the sweat of the face is sorrowful; but to work without toil is an element of health and cheerfulness; and is doubtless the rule of life to all the intelligences of the universe of God.

But he was not simply an inhabitant of the Paradise, placed there "to dress and keep it". The work before him was to begin the replenishing and subjugation of the earth. For in the blessing pronounced upon them, God said, "Be fruitful, and multiply, and *replenish* the earth, and subdue it". The material was all before him. The earth was to be peopled; and the culture of the garden, as the model of improvement, to be extended as his posterity spread themselves over its surface.

This command to "replenish the earth" strengthens my previous conclusion, that the earth had been inhabited at some period anterior to the creation of the six days; and that its population had all been swept away by a catastrophe similar to the Noachic flood. That "replenish" means to *fill* the earth *again*, is manifest from the use of the word in the blessing pronounced upon Noah. As it is written, "And God blessed Noah and his sons, and said unto them, Be fruitful, and multiply, and *replenish* the earth". There is no room for dispute here. Every one must admit that it signifies to *fill again*; for, having been filled by Adam, all his posterity, except eight persons, were swept away by the deluge; and Noah and his sons were to supply their place, or refill it, as at this day. I see, therefore, no good reason why the same word should not be similarly interpreted in both cases; which I have concluded to do.*

Man's conquests in a sinless state were to be over rocks, mountains, seas and rivers, by which he might subdue them to his own convenience and enjoyment; and, perhaps, had he continued innocent of transgression until his mission was accomplished; that is, until by his faithfulness he had filled the earth again with people, and had subdued it from its natural wildness to a paradise state—his nature would have been exalted to an equality with the Elohim; and the earth, without any violent changes, have become his dwelling-place for ever. But, the Creator foreseeing that man would transgress, laid the founda-

---

* But the Heb. *maleh* (to fill) must not be strained. It does not of itself convey the idea, *re*plenish.

tion of the earth upon such principles as would afterwards accommodate it to his altered circumstances. Had He foreseen a result different from what has actually come to pass, He would, doubtless, have framed or constituted it with reference to that result. But, while He did not necessitate man's transgression, His plan was to constitute a natural world with reference to it as its basis; and then, on the other hand, without necessitating man's obedience, to constitute a spiritual, or incorruptible, order of things upon the earth, having an intelligent and voluntary conformity to His precepts, as the foundation upon which it should be built. This, then, is the present order of things. Man is replenishing the earth and subduing it. He is reducing it from its natural wildness. Subduing land and sea to the convenience of nations; and subjugating, likewise, the wild creatures of his own species to law and order, and exterminating the untameable; — he is preparing the world for an advance to *a more exalted*, yet not perfect, *state*, which the Man from heaven shall introduce, and establish; not, however, upon the destruction of nature and society, but upon the improvement of the first, and the regeneration of the last; which shall continue for a thousand years, *as the intermediate state* between the present purely animal and natural, and the final purely spiritual, or incorruptible, and unchangeable constitution of the globe.

In carrying his mission into effect, it was necessary that the animal man should have dominion. He was too feeble to execute it without assistance; and there was no source from which he could receive *voluntary* aid. It was needful, therefore, that he should receive power by which he could compel the co-operation he required. For this reason, as well as for his own defence against the inconvenient familiarity of the inferior creatures with their lord, God gave him dominion over them all. "Have dominion", said He, "over the fish of the sea, and over the fowl of the air, and over the cattle, and over all the earth, and over every creeping thing that creepeth upon the earth." This was the charter of man's sovereignty over flesh and blood. Himself the king, and all living creatures the subjects of his dominion. As to his own species, however, he was permitted to be *neither a law to himself, nor to his fellows*.

The right of man to exercise lordship over his fellow-man beyond the circle of his own family, was not granted to him "*by the grace of God*". God's grace only conferred upon him what I have already stated. Even his domestic sovereignty was to cease, when the time came for one to leave father and mother. After this separation, all paternal rule ended, and the only bondage which continued was the yoke of affection. Man rules in his family by the grace of God, which says, "Children, obey your parents *in the Lord*; for this is right. Honour thy father and mother; which is the first commandment *with promise*; that it may be well with thee, and thou mayest live long in the land" (Ephesians 6:1-3). This obedience is founded on the fitness of things; but even this is not enjoined absolutely. It is only "parents *in the Lord*", who have a divine right to expect unqualified obedience from the Christian children of their household. If parents *not* in the Lord, require their children to do contrary to, or to abstain from doing, His will, obedience should be firmly, but affectionately, refused. This would probably produce trouble and division in the family, if the parent were an uncultivated man of the flesh, or a bigot. In that case, he would behave like a tyrant, and endeavour to coerce them to obey him, rather than their conviction of the truth; whose nature it is to divide between flesh and spirit, sinners and saints, and to create a man's foes out of the members of his own household (Matthew 10:35-36). But such children should remember that "it is better to obey God than man" (Acts 4:19; 5:29) and that he that loves parents more than Jesus, is not worthy of him. Better leave the paternal roof as an outcast, than dishonour him by preferring their laws to his.

If man's domestic sovereignty be thus qualified and limited by the grace of God, shall we say that he conferred on man "a divine right" to govern his species in its spiritual and civil concerns? To found kingdoms and empires, and to invent religions as a means of imparting durability to their thrones? What God permits and regulates is one thing; and what He appoints is another. He permits thrones and dominions, principalities and powers, to exist; He regulates them, setting over them the basest of men (Daniel 4:17), if such answer His intentions best; prevents them circumventing His purposes; and commands His saints to "be subject unto the higher powers. For there is no power but of God; the powers that be are ordained of God. Whosoever therefore resisteth the power, resisteth the ordinance of God: and they that resist shall receive to themselves punishment. For the magistrates are not a terror to good deeds, but to the evil ... Do that which is good, and thou shalt have praise of the same: for he is a servant of God unto that which is good for thee" (Romans 13:1-5).

God did not commission man to set up these powers. All He required of him was to obey whatsoever He chose to appoint. But, when man became a rebel, his rebellious spirit was transmitted to his posterity; and, refusing to be governed by the grace of God, they founded dominions of their own, upon principles which were utterly subversive of the government of God upon the earth. He could as easily have quashed their treasonable proceedings as He stopped the building of Babel; but in His wisdom He chose rather to give them scope, and to subject their usurpations to such regulations as would in the end promote His own glory and their confusion. Therefore it is that Paul says every power is of God; and the powers that be are ordained of Him. This is matter of great consolation and rejoicing to His saints; for, though the tyrants may propose, it is God only that disposes events. The saints who understand the word will keep aloof from politics. None are more interested in them than they; but they will mix themselves up neither with one party nor another; for God regulates them all: therefore to be found in any such strife would be to contend in some way or other against Him. The servant of the Lord must not strive, except "for the faith once delivered to the saints". For this he is commanded to "contend earnestly" (Jude 3), because such a contention is to "fight the good fight of faith", and to "lay hold on eternal life".

In the beginning, then, God reserved to Himself the right of dominion over the human race. He gave it not to Adam, nor to his posterity; but claimed the undivided sovereignty over all man's concerns for Himself by right of creation; and for him whom He might ordain as His representative upon earth. All the kingdoms that exist, or have existed, with the exception of the Commonwealth of Israel, are based upon the usurpation of the rights of God, and of His Son, Jesus Christ; nor is there a king or queen, pope or emperor, among the Gentiles, who reigns "by the grace of God". They reign by the same grace, or favour, by which sin reigns over the nations. They have no favour in the eyes of God. He bears with them for a time: and makes use of them as His sword to maintain order among the lawless; until His gracious purposes in favour of His saints shall be manifested, according to the arrangement of the times He has disposed. Then "will his Saints be joyful in glory; and the high praises of God be in their mouth, and a two-edged sword in their hand; to execute vengeance upon the heathen, and punishments upon the people; to bind their kings with chains, and their nobles with fetters of iron; to execute upon them the judgment written: this honour have all his saints. Praise ye the LORD" (Psalm 149:5-9).

THE TREE OF KNOWLEDGE OF GOOD AND EVIL

"Out of the ground made the LORD God to grow the Tree of Life in the midst of the garden, and the Tree of Knowledge of good and evil."

THESE are the most remarkable trees that have ever appeared in the vegetable kingdom. They were "pleasant to the sight, and *good for food*". This, however, is all that is said about their nature and appearance. They would seem to have been the only trees of their kind; for, if they had been common, Eve's desire to taste the fruit of the Tree of Knowledge, and their inclination to eat of that of the Tree of Life, could have been gratified by eating of other similar trees. What the fruits were we cannot tell; not is it important to know. Supposition says, that the Tree of Knowledge was an apple tree; but testimony makes no deposition on the subject; therefore we can believe nothing in the case.

These trees, however, are interesting to us, not on account of their natural characteristics, but because of *the interdict* which rested upon them. Adam and Eve were permitted to take freely of all the other trees in the garden, "but of the Tree of Knowledge of good and evil", said the Lord God, "thou shalt not eat of it, neither shall ye touch it: for *in the day that thou eatest thereof thou shalt surely die*" (Genesis 2:17; 3:3). Naturally, it was as good for food as any other tree; but, as soon as the Lord God laid His interdict upon it, its fruit became death to the eater; not instant death, however, for their eyes were to be opened (Genesis 3:5,7), and they were to become as the gods, or Elohim, being acquainted with good and evil even as they (Genesis 3:5,22). The final consequence of eating of this tree being death, it may be styled the *Tree of Death* in contradistinction to the *Tree of Life*. Decay of body, and consequent termination of life, ending in corruption, or *mortality*, was the attribute which this fatal tree was prepared to *bestow* upon the individual who should presume to touch it.

In the sentence, *"Thou shalt surely die"*, death is mentioned in the Bible for the first time. But Adam lived several centuries after he had eaten of the tree, which has proved a difficulty in the definition of the death there indicated, hitherto insuperable upon the principles of the creeds. Creed theology paraphrases the sentence thus—"In the day thou eatest thereof thou shalt die figuratively, thine immortal soul becoming liable to the pains of hell for ever; and thy body shall die literally afterwards". But, it is very evident to one unspoiled by the philosophy of the creeds, that this interpretation is not contained in the text. The obscurity which creates the difficulty does not lie in the words spoken, but in the English version of them. The phrase *"in the day"* is supposed to mean that *on the very day itself* upon which Adam transgressed, he was to die in some sense. But this is not the use of the phrase even in the English of the same chapter. For in the fourth verse of the second chapter, it is written, *"in the day* that the LORD God made the earth and the heavens, and every plant of the field before it was in the earth, and every herb of the field before it grew". This, we know, was the work of six days; so that "in the day" is expressive of that period. But in the text before us, the same phrase represents a much longer period, for Adam did not die until he was 930 years old; therefore, the day in which he died did not terminate till then.

But it may be objected that the day in the text must be limited to the day of the eating; because it says, "in the day *that thou eatest thereof* thou shalt surely die": and as he was not eating of it 930 years, but only partook of it once on a certain natural day, it cannot mean that long period. But I am not prepared to admit that the physical action of eating is the only eating indicated in the text. Adam fed upon the fruit of the Tree of Knowledge all the time from his eating of the natural fruit until he died. The natural fruit in its effect was figurative of the fruit of transgressing the interdict, which said, "Thou shalt not eat of it". The figurative fruit was of a mixed character. It was *"good"*, or *pleasant* to the flesh; but *"evil"* in its consequences. "By the *law*", says the apostle, "is the *knowledge of sin*"; for "sin is the transgression of law" (Romans 3:20; 1 John 3:4). Sin is pleasant to the flesh; because the deeds forbidden are natural to it. It is that *"good"* fruit which the animal man delights to eat. The flesh, the eyes, and life, have all their desires, or lusts, which, when gratified, constitute the *chiefest good* that men under their dominion seek after.

But God has forbidden indulgence in these lusts. He says, "Love not the world, neither the things that are in the world. If any man love the world, the love of the Father is not in him. For all that is in the world, the lust of the flesh, the lust of the eyes, and the pride of life, is not of the Father, but is of the world" (1 John 2:15,16). And again, "The friendship of the world is enmity with God. Whosoever therefore will be a friend of the world is the enemy of God" (James 4:4): and, "If ye live after the flesh ye shall die" (Romans 8:13). This language is unmistakable. To indulge, then, in the lawless pleasures, which "sinful flesh" terms "good", is to *"bring forth sin"* (James 1:15), or to bear fruit unto death; because the "wages of sin is death" (Romans 6:21-23). "Whatsoever a man *soweth*, that shall he also reap. For he that soweth to the flesh, shall of the flesh reap corruption" (Galatians 6:7,8). All "the ills that flesh is heir to" make up the "evil" which has come upon man as the result of transgressing the law of God, which said to Adam, "Thou shalt not eat thereof". The fruit of his eating was the gratification of his flesh in the lusts thereof, and the subjection of himself and posterity to the *"evil"* of eating of the cursed ground in sorrow all the days of their lives (Genesis 3:17-19).

All the posterity of Adam, when they attain the age of puberty, and their eyes are in the opening crisis, begin to eat of the Tree of the Knowledge of good and evil. Previous to that natural change, they are in their innocency. But, thenceforth, the world,

71

as a serpent-entwined fruit tree, stands before the mind, enticing it to take and eat, and enjoy the *good* things it affords. To speculate upon the lawfulness of compliance is partly to give consent. There must be no reasoning upon the harmlessness of conforming to the world. Its enticements without, and the sympathizing instincts of the flesh within, must be instantly suppressed; for, to hold a parley with its lusts, is dangerous. When one is seduced by "the deceitfulness of sin", "he is drawn away of his own lusts, and enticed. Then when lust hath conceived, it bringeth forth sin; and sin when it is finished, bringeth forth death" (James 1:14,15): in other words, he plucks the forbidden fruit, and dies, if not forgiven.

Furthermore, the sentence *"Thou shalt surely die"*, is proof that the phrase *"in the day"* relates to a longer period than the day of the natural eating. This was not a sentence to be consummated in a moment, as when a man is shot or guillotined. It required time; for the death threatened was the result, or finishing, of a certain process which is very clearly indicated in the original Hebrew. In this language the phrase is *muth temuth*, which literally rendered is, DYING THOU SHALT DIE.* The sentence, then, as a whole reads thus—*"In the day of thy eating from it dying thou shalt die"*. From this reading, it is evident, that Adam was to be subjected to a process, but not to an endless process; but to one which should commence with the transgression, and end with his extinction. The process is expressed by *muth, dying*; and the last stage of the process by *temuth*, thou SHALT DIE.

This view is fully sustained by the paraphrase found in the following words:—"Cursed is the ground for thy sake: in sorrow shalt thou eat of it all the days of thy life. In the sweat of thy face shalt thou eat bread TILL *thou return unto the ground*; for out of it wast thou taken; for dust thou art, and unto dust thou shalt return" (Genesis 3:19). The context of this informs us, that Adam, having transgressed, had been summoned to trial and judgment for the offence. The Lord God interrogated him, saying, "Hast thou eaten of the tree of which I commanded thee that thou shouldest not eat?" Adam confessed his guilt, which was sufficiently manifest before by his timidity, and shame at his nakedness. The offence being proved, the Judge then proceeded to pass sentence upon the transgressors. This He did in the order of transgression; first upon the Serpent; then upon Eve; and lastly upon Adam, in the words of the text. In these, the ground is cursed, and the man sentenced to a life of sorrowful labour, and

---

* The Hebrew idiom is correctly represented by the text of the A.V. Compare Genesis 2:16 (marg.), "Eating thou shalt eat"; and Deuteronomy 13:15, lit., "Smiting thou shalt smite".

to *a resolution into his original and parent dust*. The terms in which the last particular of his sentence is expressed, are explanatory of the penalty annexed to the law. "Thou shalt return unto the ground", and "Unto dust shalt thou return", are phrases equivalent to "Dying thou shalt die". Hence, the divine interpretation of the sentence, "In the day thou eatest thereof thou shalt surely die", is, "In the day of thy eating all the days of thy life of sorrow, returning thou shalt return unto the dust of the ground whence thou wast taken". Thus, *"dying"*, in the meaning of the text, is to be the subject of *a sorrowful*, painful, and *laborious* existence, which wears a man *out*, and brings him down to the brink of the grave; and, by *"die"*, is signified the end, or last stage of corporeal existence, which is marked by *a ceasing to breathe, and decomposition into dust*. Thus, man's life from the womb to the grave is a dying existence; and, so long as he retains his *form*, as in the case of Jesus in the sepulchre, he is existent in death; for what is termed *being* is corporeal existence in life and death. The end of our being is the end of that process by which we are resolved into dust—*we cease to be*. This was Adam's state, if we may so speak, before he was created. He had no being. And at this non-existence he arrived after a lapse of 930 years from his formation; and thus were practically illustrated the penalty of the law and the sentence of the Judge. For from the day of his transgression, he began his pilgrimage to the grave, at which he surely arrived. He made his couch in the dust, and saw corruption; and with its mother earth commingled all that was known as Adam, the federal head, and chief father of mankind.

TREE OF LIFE

"Eat and live for ever."

THIS was planted "in the midst of the garden". It was also a fruit-bearing tree. It would seem to have been as accessible as the Tree of Knowledge; for after the man had eaten of this, he was driven out of the garden that he might not touch that likewise. Its fruit, however, was of a quality entirely opposite to that of which they had eaten. Both trees bore good fruit; but that of the Tree of Life had the quality of perpetuating the living existence of the eater for ever. This appears from the testimony of Moses, who reports that after the transgressors had received judgment, "the LORD God said, Behold the man has become as one of us, to know good and evil: and now, *lest* he put forth his hand, and take also of the Tree of Life, *and eat and live for ever*:

73

therefore the LORD God sent him forth from the garden of Eden, to till the ground whence he was taken" (Genesis 3:22,23). From this, we learn that the Lord God had instituted this tree to give life, and that Adam was aware of what would result from eating of its fruit. It is probable that, had he been obedient to the law of the Tree of Knowledge, he would have been permitted to eat of the Tree of Life, after he had fulfilled his destiny as an animal man; and, instead of dying away into dust, have been "changed in the twinkling of an eye", as Enoch was; and as they are to be who shall be ready for the Lord at his coming. But of this we can say nothing certain, because nothing is testified on the subject; and beyond the testimony our faith cannot go, though opinion and credulity may.

If, then, Adam had eaten of the Tree of Life, he would have been changed from a living soul into a soul capable of living for ever: and not only capable, but it would seem, that being immortal, the Lord God would have permitted him to remain so. For, we are not to suppose, that, if a thing become capable of undecaying existence, therefore its creator cannot destroy it; consequently, if Adam as a sinner had eaten of the Tree of Life, his immortality would have been only permitted, and not necessitated contrary to the power of the Lord God.

To have permitted Adam and Eve to become deathless, and to remain so, in a state of good and evil such as the world experiences, would have been a disproportionate and unmerciful punishment. It would have been to populate the earth with deathless sinners; and to convert it into the abode of deathless giants in crime; in other words, the earth would have become, what creed theologians describe "hell" to be in their imagination. The good work of the sixth day would then have proved a terrible mishap, instead of the nucleus of a glorious manifestation of divine wisdom and power. But a world of undying sinners in a state of good and evil, was not according to the divine plan. This required first the sanctification of sinners; then their probation; and afterwards, their exaltation, or humiliation, according to their works. Therefore, lest Adam should invert this order, and "put on immortality" before he should be morally renewed, or purified from sin, and the moral likeness of God be formed in him again; the Lord God expelled him from the dangerous vicinity of the Tree of Life. He drove him forth that he should not then become incorruptible and deathless.

The first intimation of immortality for man is contained in the text before us. But, in this instance it eluded his grasp. He was expelled "lest he should eat, and live for ever". It was because immortality belonged to this tree; or rather, was communicable by or through it to the eater, that it was styled *etz ha-chayim*, that is, the Tree of the Lives; for that is its name when literally rendered. The phrase "of the lives" is particularly appropriate; for it was the tree of endless life both to Adam and Eve, if permitted to eat of it. If the world enticing to sin, be fitly represented by the serpent-entwined tree, imparting death to its victim, Christ, who "has overcome the world" (John 16:33), as a giver of life to his people, is well set forth by the other tree in the garden; which was a beautiful emblem of the incarnated power and wisdom (Proverbs 3:13,18; 1 Corinthians 1:24) of the Deity, planted as the Tree of Life in the future Paradise of God (Revelation 22:2).

MAN IN HIS NOVITIATE

"God made man upright."

WHEN the work of the six days was completed, the Lord God reviewed all that He had made, and pronounced it "very good". This quality pertained to everything terrestrial. The beasts of the field, the fowls of the air, reptiles, and man, were all "very good"; and all made up a natural system of things, or world, as perfect as the nature of things required. Its excellence, however, had relation solely to its physical quality. Man, though "very good", was so only as a piece of divine workmanship. He was made different from what he afterwards became. Being made in the image, after the likeness of the Elohim, he was "made upright". He had no conscience of evil; for he did not know what it was. He was neither virtuous, nor vicious; holy, nor unholy; but in his beginning simply innocent of good or evil deeds. Being without a history, he was without character. This had to be developed; and could only be formed for good or evil, by his own independent action under the divine law. In short, when Adam and Eve came forth from the hand of their potter, they were morally in a similar condition to a new-born babe; excepting that a babe is born under the constitution of sin, and *involuntarily* subjected to "vanity" (Romans 8:20); while they first beheld the light in a state of things where evil had as yet no place. They were created in the stature of a perfect man and woman; but with their sexual feelings undeveloped; in ignorance, and without experience.

The interval between their formation and their transgression was the period of their novitiate. The Spirit of God had made them; and during this time, "the inspiration of the Almighty was giving them understanding" (Job 33:4; 32:8). In this way, knowledge was imparted to them. It became power, and enabled them to meet all the demands of their situation. Thus, they were "taught of God", and became the depositories of those arts and sciences, in which they afterwards instructed their sons and daughters, to enable them to till the ground, tend the flocks and herds, provide the conveniences of life, and subdue the earth.

Guided by the precepts of the Lord God, his conscience continued good, and his heart courageous. "They were naked, both the man and his wife, and were not ashamed" (Genesis 2:25). They were no more abashed than children in their nudity; for, though adults in stature, yet, being in the infancy of nature, they stood before the Elohim, and in the face of one another, without embarrassment. This fact was not accidentally recorded. As we shall see hereafter, it is a clue, as it were, given to enable us to understand the nature of the transgression.

While in the state of good unmixed with evil, were Adam and Eve mortal or immortal? This is a question which presents itself to many who study the Mosaic account of the origin of things. It is an interesting question, and worthy of all attention. Some hastily reply, they were mortal; that is, if they had not sinned they would nevertheless have died. It is probable they would after a long time, if no further change had been operated upon their nature. But the Tree of Life seems to have been provided for the purpose of this change being effected, through the eating of its fruit, if they had proved themselves worthy of the favour. The animal nature will sooner or later dissolve. It was not constituted so as to continue in life for ever, independent of any further modification. We may admit, therefore, the corruptibility, and consequent mortality, of their nature, without saying that they were mortal. The inherent tendency of their nature to death would have been arrested; and they would have been changed as Enoch and Elijah were; and as they of whom Paul says, "*We shall not all die*" The "*we*" here indicated possess an animal, and therefore corruptible nature; and, if not "changed", would surely die: but inasmuch as they are to "be changed in the twinkling of an eye at the last trumpet", though corruptible, they are not mortal. In this sense, therefore, I say, that in their novitiate, Adam and his betrothed had a nature *capable* of corruption, but were not subject to death, or mortal. The penalty was "dying thou shalt die"; that is, "You shall not be permitted to eat of the Tree of Life in arrest of dissolution; but the inherent tendency of your animal nature shall take its course, and return you to the dust whence you originally came". Mortality was in disobedience as the wages of sin, and not a necessity.

But, if they were not mortal in their novitiate, it is also true that they were not immortal. To say that immortals were expelled from the garden of Eden, that they might live for ever by eating of the tree, is absurd. The truth is in few words, man was created with a nature endued with certain susceptibilities. He was capable of death; and capable of endless life; but, whether he should merge into mortality; or, by a physical change be clothed with immortality, was predicated on his choosing to do good or evil. Capacity must not be confounded with impletion. A vessel may be capable of holding a pint of fluid; but it does not therefore follow that there is a pint in it, or any at all. In the Paradise of Eden, mortality and immortality were set before the man and his companion. They were external to them. They were to avoid the former, and seek after the latter, by obedience to the law of God. They were capable of being filled with either; but with which depended upon their actions; for immortality is the end of holiness (Romans 6:22), without which no man can see the Lord.

We meet with no traces in the Mosaic history of ceremonial observances, or religious worship, pertaining to the novitiate. To rest one day in seven; believe that the Lord God would perform His word if they transgressed; and to abstain from touching the Tree of knowledge, was all their gracious benefactor required. There was no "religion" in the garden of Eden—no sacrifices, or offerings; for sin was as yet a stranger there. The tenure of the Paradise was predicated upon their abstinence from sin; so that it could be forfeited only by transgression of the law of the Lord.

RUDIMENTS OF THE WORLD

CHAPTER III

GOD'S LAW, AND HOW SIN ENTERED INTO THE WORLD

Probation before exaltation, the law of the moral universe of God—The temptation of the Lord Jesus by Satan the trial of his faith by the Father—The Temptation explained—God's foreknowledge does not necessitate; nor does He justify, or condemn, by anticipation—The Serpent an intellectual animal, but not a moral agent, nor inspired—He deceives the woman—The nature of the transgression—Eve becomes the tempter to Adam—The transgression consummated in the conception of Cain—A good conscience, and an evil conscience, defined—Man cannot cover his own sin—The carnal mind illustrated by the reasoning of the Serpent—It is metaphorically the serpent in the flesh—God's truth the only rule of right and wrong—The Serpent in the flesh is manifested in the wickedness of individuals; and in the spiritual and temporal institutions of the world—Serpent-sin in the flesh identified with "the Wicked One"—The Prince of the World—The Kingdom of Satan and the World identical—The Wiles of the Devil—The "*Prince*" shown to be *sin*, working and reigning in all sinners—How he was "cast out" by Jesus—"The works of the Devil"—"Bound of Satan"; delivering to Satan—The Great Dragon—The Devil and Satan—The Man of Sin.

M AN in the first estate is "a little lower than the angels" but, in the second, or higher, estate, he is to be "crowned with glory and honour"; and to take his stand in the universe upon an equality with them in nature and renown. Man's first estate is the natural and animal; his second, the spiritual, or incorruptible. To be exalted from the present to the future state and inheritance, he must be subjected to trial. From the examples recorded in the scriptures, it is evident, that God has established it as the rule of His grace; that is, the principle upon which He bestows His honours and rewards to prove men before He exalts them. Probation, then, is the indispensable ordeal, to which every man is subjected in the providence of God, before he is accepted as "fit for the Master's use" (2 Timothy 2:20,21). By these examples, also, it appears, that man's probation is made to bear upon *the trial of his faith* by testing *his obedience*. An untried faith is worth nothing; but a faith that stands the test of trial, "is much more precious than gold which perisheth, though it be tried with fire"; because the sustained trial will be "found unto praise, and honour, and glory, *at the appearance* of Jesus Christ" (1 Peter 1:5-7).

An untried faith is a dead faith, being alone. Faith without trial finds no scope for demonstration, or evidence of its existence. Thus, it is written, "Faith, if it hath not works, is dead, being alone. Yea, a man may say, Thou hast faith, and I have works: *show* me thy faith without thy works, and I will show thee my faith *by my works.* Thou believest that there is one God: thou doest well; the devils also believe, and tremble. But wilt thou know, O vain man, that faith without works is dead? Was not Abraham our father justified by works, when he had offered Isaac his son upon the altar? Seest thou how faith wrought with his works, and *by works was faith made perfect?* ... Ye see then how that by works a man is justified, and NOT *by faith* ALONE" (James 2:17-24). "Without faith", says Paul, "it is impossible to please God" and it is also apparent from James' testimony just recited, that the faith with which He is pleased, is a faith that is made manifest by works; of which Noah, Abraham, Job, and Jesus, are pre-eminent examples.

Now, this "precious faith" can only be educed by trial; for the trial elaborates the works. This is the use of persecution, or tribulation, to believers; which in the divine economy is appointed for their refinement. Peter styles the "manifold persecutions" to which his brethren were subjected, "the trial of their faith"; and Paul testified to others of them, that "it is through much tribulation they must enter the Kingdom". Probation is a refining process. It purges out a man's dross, and brings out the image of Christ in his character; and prepares him for exaltation to his throne (Revelation 3:21). We can only enter the Kingdom through the fire (1 Corinthians 3:13); but, if a man be courageous, and "hold fast the confidence and rejoicing of the hope firm unto the end", he will emerge from it unscorched; and be presented holy, unblameable, and unrebukeable (Colossians 1:22-23) before the King.

A man cannot "honour God" more than in believing *what He promises*, and doing what He commands; although to repudiate that belief, and to neglect, or disobey, those commands, should highly gratify all his senses, and place at his disposal the kingdoms of the world, and all their glory. Not to believe the promises of God is in effect to call God a liar; and no offence, even to men of integrity in the world, is so insulting and intolerable as this. "Let God be true", saith the scripture. His veracity must not be impeached in word or deed; if it be, then "judgment without mercy" is the "sorer punishment" which awaits the calumniator. The unswerving obedience of faith, is the "faith made perfect by works", tried by fire. God is pleased with this faith, because it honours Him. It is a working faith. There is life in it; and its exercise proves that the believer loves Him. Such a man it is God's delight to honour; and, though like Jesus he be for the present, "despised and rejected of men, a man of sorrows and acquainted with grief", the time will certainly come, when God will acknowledge him in the presence of the Elohim, and overwhelm his enemies with confusion of face.

Probation before exaltation, then, is upon the principle of *a faith in the promises of God, made precious by trial well sustained*. There is no exemption from this ordeal. Even Christ himself was subjected to it. "By the grace of God he tasted death for every man. For it was fitting for God, that in bringing many sons to glory, He should make the Captain of their salvation *perfect through sufferings* ... For in that he himself hath suffered *being put to the proof* (πειρασθείς), he is able to succour them who are tried" (Hebrews 2:9-18). And "though he were a Son, yet learned he obedience *by the things which he suffered*: and being made perfect, he became the author of eternal salvation *unto all them that* OBEY *him*" (Hebrews 5:8-9). He was first morally perfected through suffering, and then corporeally, by being "made into a spirit" by the spirit of holiness in his resurrection from the dead. I say, "morally perfected"; for, although he was without transgression, his perfection of character is predicated upon his "obedience unto death".

The probation of the Lord Jesus is an interesting and important study, especially that part of it styled the Temptation of Satan. Paul, speaking of him as the High Priest under the New Constitution, says, "He was put to the proof in all things according to our likeness, without transgression" (Hebrews 4:15); that is, "having taken hold of the seed of Abraham", "being found in fashion as a man", the infirmities of human nature were thus laid upon him. He could sympathize with them experimentally; being, by the feelings excited within him when enticed, well acquainted with all its weak points. By examining the narrative of his trial in the wilderness, we shall find that he was proved in all the assailable points of human nature. As soon as he was filled with the Spirit (Luke 4:1) at his baptism in the Jordan, it immediately drove him (Mark 1:12) into the wilderness to be tempted of the devil (Matthew 4:1). This was very remarkable. The Spirit led him there that he might be put to the proof; but not to tempt him; for, says the apostle, "Let no man say when he is tempted, I am tempted of God: for God cannot be tempted with evil, *neither tempteth he any man*" (James 1:13). God, then, did not tempt Jesus; though His Spirit conducted him thither to be tempted, and that, too, "by the devil", or the enemy.

This enemy within the human nature is the mind of the flesh, which is enmity against God; it is not subject to His law, neither indeed can be (Romans 8:7). The commandment of God, which is "holy, just and good", being so restrictive of the propensities, which in purely animal men display themselves with uncontrolled violence, makes them appear in their true colours. These turbulent propensities the apostle styles "sin in the flesh", of which it is full; hence, he also terms it "sinful flesh". This is human nature; and the evil in it, made so apparent by the law of God, he personifies as *"pre-eminently* A SINNER", καθ ὑπερβολὴν ἁμαρτωλός (Romans 7:12,13,17,18).

This is the accuser, adversary, and calumniator of God, whose stronghold is the flesh. It is the devil and Satan within the human nature; so that "when a man is tempted, he is drawn away of his own lust and enticed". If a man examine himself, he will perceive within him something at work, craving after things which the law of God forbids. The best of men are conscious of this enemy within them. It troubled the apostle so much, that he exclaimed, "O, wretched man that I am! who shall deliver me from the body of this death" (Romans 7:24), or, this mortal body? He thanked God that the Lord Jesus Christ would do it; that is, as he had himself been delivered from it, by God raising him from the dead by His Spirit (Romans 8:11).

Human nature, or "sinful flesh", has three principal channels through which it displays its waywardness against the law of God. These are expressed by "the lust of the flesh, the lust of the eyes, and the pride of life". All that is in the world stands related to these points of our nature; and there is no temptation that can be devised, but what assails it in one, or more, of these three particulars. The world without is the seducer, which finds in all animal men, unsubdued by the law and testimony of God, a sympathizing and friendly principle, ready at all times to eat of its forbidden fruit. This sinful nature we inherit. It is our misfortune, not our crime, that we possess it. We are only blameworthy when, being supplied with the power of subduing it, we permit it to reign over us. This power resides in "the testimony of God" believed; so that we "are kept by the power of God *through faith* unto salvation" (1 Peter 1:5). This testimony ought to dwell in us as it dwelt in the Lord Jesus; so that, as with the shield of faith, the fiery assaults of the world may be quenched (Ephesians 6:16) by a "thus it is written", and a "thus saith the LORD".

Jesus was prepared by the exhaustion of a long fast, for an appeal to the desire of his flesh for food. Hunger, it is said, will break through stone walls. "He was hungry." At this crisis, "the Tempter came to him". Who he was does not appear. Perhaps, Paul refers to him, saying "Satan himself is transformed into an angel of light" (2 Corinthians 11:14). Some one "came to him" who was his adversary, and who desired his ruin or, at least, acted the part of one on the same principle that the adversary was permitted to put the fidelity of Job to the proof. The trial of this eminent son of God, was perhaps recorded as an illustration of the temptation of the Son of God, even Jesus, to whom "there was none like in the earth, a perfect and upright man, one that feared God, and eschewed evil" (Job 1:8). From his birth to his baptism in the Jordan, he was faultless. But in the words of Satan concerning Job, "Did Jesus fear God for nought? Had not God made a hedge about him?" Yes; God was his defence: and "in keeping his testimony there is great reward". But, the adversary calumniated Jesus, in suggesting that his obedience to God had been prompted by mercenary motives. He "feared" (Hebrews 5:7), not simply for what he should get, but because of his love for his Father's character as revealed in the divine testimonies. The adversary affected to disbelieve this, and to suppose that, if God would just leave him in the position of any other man, he would distrust Him; and eat of the world's forbidden fruit, by embracing all it would afford him. Thus, the adversary may be supposed to have moved the Lord to permit him to put the fidelity of Jesus to the test. God, therefore, allowed the experiment to be tried; and by His spirit sent him into the wilderness for the purpose. So the adversary went forth from the presence of the Lord, and came to him there.

Having arrived at the crisis when Jesus was suffering from the keenest hunger, the adversary assumed the character of an angel, or messenger of light to him. Being acquainted with "the law and the testimony", for which he knew Jesus had a profound regard, he adduced it in support of his suggestions. He invited him to gratify the *cravings of the flesh* by helping himself. He was God's son; but then his Father seemed to have abandoned him; why not therefore use the power he possessed, whose presence in him was of itself a proof of God's approval of its exercise, and "command that the stones be made bread"? But Jesus disregarded the reasoning; and set it aside by "*It is written*, Man shall not live by bread alone, but by every word that proceedeth out of the mouth of God" (Deuteronomy 8:3).

Failing in this, the scene of the temptation was then removed to "the pinnacle of the temple"; and, as Jesus fortified himself by the word, the adversary determined to be even with him; and in appealing to *the pride of life*, so strong in the nature laid upon him, to strengthen himself with the testimony likewise. "*If* thou be the son of God, as thou proudly assumest to be, cast thyself down: for *it is written*, He shall give his angels charge concerning thee: and they shall bear thee up in their hands, lest at any time thou dash thy foot against a stone" (Psalm 91:11,12). But Jesus met him with "Again *it is written*, Thou shalt not tempt the Lord thy God" (Deuteronomy 6:16).

Lastly, the scene was shifted to a lofty mountain. From this position, by the power granted him, he showed Jesus "all the kingdoms of the world", visible from that elevation; "and the glory of them". He knew that Jesus was destined to possess them all; but that he was also to obtain them through suffering. Jesus knew this, too. Now, as the flesh dislikes suffering, the tempter proposed to gratify *the desire of his eyes* by giving him all he saw, on the easy condition of doing homage to him as the god of the world. "All this power", said he, "will I give thee, and the glory of them for that is delivered to me, and to whomsoever I will, I give it. If thou therefore wilt worship me, all shall be thine" (Luke 4:6,7). But Jesus resisted the enticement; and said, "Get thee hence, adversary: for *it is written*, Thou shalt worship the Lord thy God, and him only shalt thou serve". "Having ended all the temptation he departed from him *for a season*." And Jesus returned in *the power* of the Spirit into Galilee.

In this manner, then, was he put to the proof in all things according to the likeness of his nature to ours, but without transgression. He believed not this angel of light (Galatians 1:8) and power, and would have none of his favours. He preferred the grace of God with suffering, to the gratification of his flesh with all the pomp and pageantry of this vain and transitory world. Its *"glory"* is indeed delivered to the adversary of God, His people, and His truth: and to whomsoever he wills he gives it. The knowledge of this truth ought to deter every righteous man from seeking after it; or even accepting it, when offered upon conditions derogatory to the truth of God. And, if those who possess it, such as kings, priests, nobles, etc., were what they pretended to be, they would follow Jesus' and Paul's examples, and renounce them all. Christianity in high places, is Christ falling down before the adversary; and doing homage to him for the honour, riches, and power of the world. What fellowship hath Christ with Belial? Certainly none.

If the principles upon which the temptation of the Lord Jesus was permitted, be understood, the necessity of putting the first Adam to the proof will be readily perceived. Would he retain his integrity, if placed in a situation of trial? Or, would he disbelieve God and die? The Lord God well knew what the result would be; and had made all necessary provision for the altered circumstances which He foresaw would arise. His knowledge, however, of what would be, did not necessitate it. He had placed all things in a *provisional state*. If the man maintained his integrity, there was the Tree of

Lives as the germ of a superior order of things; but, if he transgressed, then the natural and animal system would continue unchanged; and the spiritualization of the earth and its population be deferred to a future period.

God's knowledge of what a man's character will be, does not cause Him to exempt him from trial. He rewards and punishes none upon foregone conclusions. He does not say to this man, "I know you are certain to turn out a reprobate, therefore I will punish you for what you would do"; nor does He say to another, "I know thee that thou wouldst do well all the days of thy life: therefore, I will promote thee to glory and honour, without subjecting thee to the tribulation of the world". His principle is to recompense men according to what they *have done*, not for what they would do. Thus he dealt with the Two Adams; and with Israel: to whom Moses says, "The LORD thy God led thee these forty years in the wilderness to humble thee, and to prove thee, to know what was in thy heart, whether thou wouldest keep His commandments, or no" (Deuteronomy 8:2). And thus also the Lord Jesus treated Judas. He knew he was a thief, and would betray him; yet he trusted him with the bag, and made no difference between him and the rest, until his character was revealed. The Lord knew what was in the heart of Israel, and whether they would obey Him; but He subjected them to such a trial as would cause them to reveal themselves in their true character, and thereby justify Him in his conduct towards them. With these remarks, then, by way of preface, I shall now proceed to the further exposition of things connected with this subject in the Mosaic account.

THE SERPENT

"It was more subtle than any beast of the field."

THE Serpent was one of "the living things that moved upon the earth", and which the Lord God pronounced "very good". Moses says, it was more subtle, or shrewd, than any of the creatures the Lord God had made. It was, probably, because of this quality of shrewdness, or *quickness of perception*, that Adam named it *nachash*; which is rendered by δράκων in the New Testament, from δέρκομαι *to see*; as, δράκοντα τὸν ὄφιν τὸν ἀρχαῖων, *the Dragon, the old serpent* (Revelation 20:2). It was doubtless, the chief of the serpent tribe, as it is styled *"the"* serpent; and, seeing that it was afterwards condemned to go upon its belly as a part of its sentence, it is probable it was a winged-serpent in the beginning: fiery, but afterwards deprived of the power of flight and made to move as at present.

Its subtlety, or quickness of perception by eye and ear, and skilfulness in the use of them (πανουργία) (2 Corinthians 11:3), was a part of the goodness of its nature. It was not an evil quality by any means; for Jesus exhorts his disciples to "be *wise* as the serpents; and unsophisticated (ἀκέραιοι) as the doves". This quality of shrewdness, or instinctive wisdom, is that which principally strikes us in all that is said about it. It was an observant spectator of what was passing around it in the garden, since the Lord God had planted it eastward in Eden. It had seen the Lord God and His companion Elohim. He had heard their discourse. He was acquainted with the existence of the Tree of Knowledge, and the Tree of Lives; and knew that the Lord God had forbidden Adam and his wife to eat of the good and evil fruit; or so much as to touch the tree. He was aware from what he had heard, that the Elohim knew what good and evil were experimentally; and that in this particular, Adam and Eve were not so wise as they. But, all this knowledge was shut up in his own cranium, from which it could never have made its exit, had not the Lord God bestowed upon it the power of expressing its thoughts in speech.

And what use should we naturally expect such a creature would make of this faculty? Such a one, certainly, as its cerebral constitution would enable it to manifest. It was an intellectual, but not a moral, creature. It had no "moral sentiments". No part of its brain was appropriated to the exercise of benevolence, veneration, conscientiousness, and so forth. To speak phrenologically, it was destitute of these organs; having only "intellectual faculties" and "propensities". Hence, its cerebral mechanism, under the excitation of external phenomena, would only develop what I would term *an animal intellectuality*. Moral, or spiritual, ideas would make no impression upon its mental constitution; for it was incapable, from its formation, of responding to them. It would be physically impossible for it to reason in harmony with the mind of God; or with the mind of man, whose reasoning was regulated by divinely enlightened moral sentiments. Its wisdom would be that of the untutored savage race, whose "sentiments", by the desuetude of ages, had become as nothing. In short, we should expect that, if the faculty of speech were bestowed upon it, it would make just such a use of it, as Moses narrates of the serpent in the garden of Eden. Its mind was purely and emphatically a "Carnal Mind", of a more shrewd description than that of any of the inferior creatures. It was "very good"; but, when he undertook to converse upon things too high for him; to speak of what he had seen and heard; and to comment upon the law of the Lord, he lost himself in his dialogisms, and became *the inventor of a lie*.

Thus prepared, he commenced a conversation with the woman. "Yea", said he, as though he were familiar with the saying, "hath God said, Ye shall not eat of *every* tree of the garden?" In this manner he spoke, as if he had been pondering over the matter to find out the meaning of things; but, not being able to make anything of it, he invited her attention inquiringly. She replied, "We may eat of the fruit of the trees of the garden: but of the fruit of the tree in the midst of the garden, God hath said, Ye shall not eat of it, neither shall ye touch it, lest ye die". This was enunciating "the law of the spirit of life", or *the truth*; for "the law of God is the truth" (Psalm 119:142). Had she adhered to the letter of this, she would have been safe. But the serpent began to intellectualize; and, in so doing "abode not in the truth; because there was no truth in him". When he may be speaking the falsehood (ὅταν λαλῇ τὸ ψεῦδος) he speaks out of his own (John 8:44) reasonings (ἐκ τῶν ἰδίων λαλεῖ). He could not comprehend the moral obligation necessitating obedience to the divine law; for there was nothing in him that responded to it. Hence, says Jesus, "there was no truth in him".

This, however, was not the case with Eve. There was truth in her; but she also began to intellectualize at the suggestion of the Serpent; and from his reasonings to doubt, and finally to conclude, that the Lord God *did not mean exactly what He said*. This was an error of which all the world is guilty to this day. It admits that God has spoken; that He has promulgated laws; that He has made promises; and that He has said, "He that believeth the gospel, and is baptized, shall be saved; but he that believeth not shall be condemned". All this professors admit in theory; while, as in the case of Eve, in practice they deny it. They say He is too kind, too loving, too merciful, to act according to a rigid construction of the word: for if He did, multitudes of the good and pious, and excellent of the earth, would be condemned. This is doubtless true. Sceptics, however, of this class should remember that they only are "the salt of the earth" who delight in the law of the Lord, *and do it*. Every sect has its "good and pious" ones, who are thought little or nothing of by adverse denominations. The law of God is the only true standard of goodness and piety; and men may depend upon it, attested by the examples in Scripture, that they who treat Him as not meaning exactly what He says in His word, "make God a liar" (1 John 5:10), and are anything but good and pious in His esteem.

Eve having repeated the law in the hearing of the Serpent, he remarked that *they should not surely die*: "for", said he, "God doth know that in the day ye eat thereof, then your eyes shall be opened, and ye shall be as gods, knowing good and evil". The falsehood of this assertion consisted in the declaration, "Ye shall not surely die", when God had said, "Dying ye shall die". It was truth that God did know that in the day of their eating *their eyes would be opened*; and it was also true that they should then become *as the Elohim*, in the sense of *knowing good and evil*. This appears from the testimony of Moses, that when they had eaten "the eyes of them both were opened" (Genesis 3:7); and from the admission of God Himself, who said, "Behold, the man is become like one of us, to know good and evil" (Genesis 3:22). The Serpent's declaration was therefore an admixture of truth and falsehood, which so blended itself with what Eve knew to exist, that "she was beguiled by his shrewdness" from the simplicity of the law of God.

But how did the Serpent know that the Lord knew that these things would happen to them in the day of their eating? How came he to know anything about the gods, and their acquaintance with good and evil? And upon what grounds did he affirm that they should not surely die? The answer is, one of two ways—by *inspiration*; or, by *observation*. If we say by inspiration, then we make God the author of the lie; but if we say that he obtained his knowledge by observation—by the use of his eyes and ears upon things transpiring around him—then we confirm the words of Moses, that he was the shrewdest of the creatures the Lord God had made. "Hath God said, Ye shall not eat of *every* tree?" This question shows that he was aware of some exceptions. He had heard of the Tree of Knowledge and of the Tree of Lives, which were both in the midst of the garden. He had heard the Lord Elohim, and the other Elohim, conversing on their own experience of good and evil; and of the enlightenment of the man and woman in the same qualities through the eating of the Tree of Knowledge: and of their living for ever, if obedient, by eating of the Tree of Life. In reasoning upon these things, he concluded that, if they did eat of the forbidden fruit, they would not surely die; for they would have nothing more to do than to go and eat of the Tree of Life, and it would prevent all fatal consequences. Therefore, he said, "Ye shall not surely die". The Lord God, it is evident, was apprehensive of the effect of this reasoning upon the mind of Adam and his wife; for He forthwith expelled them from the garden, to prevent all possibility of access to the tree, lest they should eat, and put on immortality in sin.

The reasoning of the Serpent operated upon the woman by exciting the lust of her flesh, the lust of her eyes, and the pride of life. This appears from the testimony. An appetite, or longing for it, that she might eat it, was created within her.

The fruit also was very beautiful. It hung upon the tree in a very attractive and inviting manner. "She saw that it was *good for food*, and that it was *pleasant to the eyes*". But there was a greater inducement still than even this. The flesh and the eyes would soon be satisfied. Her pride of life had been aroused by the suggestion that by eating it their eyes would be opened: and that she would be "made wise" as the glorious Elohim she had so often seen in the garden. To become "as the gods"; to know good and evil as they knew it—was a consideration too cogent to be resisted. She not only saw that it was good for food and pleasant to the eyes, but that it was "a tree to be desired as making one wise" as the gods; therefore "she took of the fruit thereof, and did eat". Thus, as far as she was concerned, the transgression was complete.

THE NATURE OF THE TRANSGRESSION

"The eyes of them both were opened, and they knew that they were naked."

THE effect produced upon the woman by the eating of the forbidden fruit, was the excitation of the propensities. By the transgression of the law of God, she had placed herself in *a state of sin*; in which she had acquired that maturity of feeling which is known to exist when females attain to womanhood. The Serpent's part had been performed in her deception; and sorely was she deceived. Expecting to be equal to the gods, the hitherto latent passions of her animal nature only were set free; and though she now knew what evil sensations and impulses were, as they had done before her, she had failed in attaining to the pride of her life—an equality with them as she had seen them in their power and glory.

In this state of animal excitation, she presented herself before the man, with the fruit so "pleasant to the eyes". Standing now in his presence, she became the tempter, soliciting him to sin. She became to him an "evil woman flattering with her tongue"; "whose lips dropped as a honeycomb, and her mouth was smoother than oil". She found him "a young man void of understanding" like herself. We can imagine how "she caught him, and kissed him; and with an impudent face, and her much fair speech, she caused him to yield". He accepted the fatal fruit, "and ate with her", consenting to her enticement, "not knowing that it was for his life": though God had said, transgression should surely be punished with death. As yet inexperienced in the certainty of the literal execution of the divine law, and depending upon the remedial efficacy of the Tree of Lives, he did not believe that he should *surely die*. He saw everything delightful around him, and his beautiful companion with the tempting fruit; and yet he was told that his eyes were shut! What wonderful things might he not see if his eyes were opened. And to be "as the gods", too, "knowing good and evil", was not this a wisdom much to be desired? The fair deceiver had, at length, succeeded in kindling in the man the same lusts that had taken possession of herself. His flesh, his eyes, and his pride of life, were all inflamed; and he followed her in her evil way "as a fool to the correction of the stocks". They had both fallen into unbelief. They did not believe God would do what He had promised. This was a fatal mistake. They afterwards found by experience, that in their sin they had charged God falsely; and that what He promises, He will certainly perform to the letter of His word. Thus, unbelief prepared them for disobedience; and disobedience separated them from God.

As the Mosaic narrative gives an account of *things natural*, upon which *things spiritual* were afterwards to be established in word and substance; the key to his testimony is found in *what actually exists*. When, therefore, he tells us that the eyes of Adam and Eve were closed at first, in that he says they were opened by sin, we have to examine ourselves as natural beings for the meaning of his words. Moses, indeed, informs us in what sense, or to what phenomena, their eyes were closed, in saying, "They were both naked, the man and his wife, and they were not ashamed". If their eyes had been surreptitiously opened, they would have been ashamed of standing before the Lord Elohim in a state of nudity; and they would have had emotions towards one another, which would have been inconvenient. But, in their unsinning ignorance of the latent possibilities of their nature, shame, which makes the subject of it feel as though he would hide himself in a nutshell, and be buried in the depths of the sea, found no place within them. They were unabashed; and had they been created with their eyes open, they would have been equally so at all times. But, seeing that their eyes were opened in connexion with, and as the consequence of doing what was forbidden, having "yielded their members servants to uncleanness, and to iniquity unto iniquity"; and their superior faculties being constituted susceptible of the feeling, they were ashamed; and "the uncomely parts of the body" became "their shame"; and from that time have been esteemed dishonourable, and invariably "hid". The inferior creatures have no such feeling as this, because they have never sinned: but *the parents of Cain* in their transgression, having served themselves of the members they afterwards concealed, were deeply affected both with shame and fear; and their posterity have ever since more or less partaken of it after the same form.

Having transgressed the divine law, and "solaced themselves with loves", "the eyes of them both were opened" as the consequence; and when opened, "they *knew* that they were naked", which they did not comprehend before. "By the law is the knowledge of sin", and "sin is the transgression of the law"; so, having transgressed the law, "they knew they were naked" without waiting for the Lord to reveal it to them, and to permit them the lawful use of one another in His own time. They were quite chagrined at the discovery they had made and sought to mitigate it by a contrivance of their own: so "they sewed fig-leaves together, and made themselves aprons".

Although thus corporeally defended from mutual observation, the nakedness of their minds was still exposed. They heard the voice of the Elohim, which had now become terrible; and they hid themselves from His presence amongst the trees. They had not yet learned, however, that the Lord was not only a God at hand, but a God also afar off; and that none can hide in secret places and He not see them; for He fills both the heaven and the earth (Jeremiah 23:23,24). Their concealment was ineffectual against the voice of the Lord, who called out to him, "Where art thou Adam?" And he answered, "I heard thy voice in the garden, and *I was afraid, because I was naked*; and I hid myself." Adam's heart had condemned him, therefore he lost confidence before God (1 John 3:19-22).

A GOOD, AND AN EVIL CONSCIENCE

THE reader, by contemplating Adam and Eve in innocency, and afterwards in guilt, will perceive in the facts of their case the nature of *a good conscience*, and of an evil one. When they rejoiced in "the answer of a good conscience", they were destitute of shame and fear. They could stand naked in God's presence unabashed; and instead of trembling at His voice, they rejoiced to hear it as the harbinger of good things. They were then pure and undefiled, being devoid of all conscience of sin. They were then of the truth, living in obedience to it as expressed in the law; and therefore their hearts were assured before Him. No doubts and fears oppressed them then. But mark the change that afterwards came over them. When they lost their good conscience, terror seized upon them at the voice of God, and shame possessed their souls; and they sought to get out of His sight, and to remove as far from Him as possible. Now, what was the cause of this? There is but one answer that can be given, and that is—SIN.

Sin, then, takes away "the answer of a good conscience towards God", and converts it into an evil conscience; which may be certainly known to exist, when the subject of it is *ashamed* of the truth, and harassed by "doubts and fears". They are ashamed of the truth, who, being enlightened, feel themselves condemned; or, being ignorant, apprehend it. Such, on account of unbelief, or of "a dead faith", may well be ashamed and afraid; for to be ashamed of God's truth is to be ashamed of His wisdom and power. People of this description proscribe all conversation about the truth as unfashionable, and vulgar; or as calculated to disturb the peace of the family circle; others, again, make a great outcry against controversy as dangerous to religion; as though God's truth could be planted in the hearts of men, already prepossessed by God's enemy, without controversy: others subjected to the timidity of sin, reduce everything to opinion, and inculcate "charity"; not that they are more liberal and kind than other people; but that they fear lest their own nakedness may be discovered, and "men see their shame"; while another class of bashful professors cry out, "Disturb not that which is quiet", which is a capital maxim for a rotten cause, especially where its subversion would break up all "vested interests", and pecuniary emoluments. So it is; while "the righteous are bold as a lion, the wicked flee when no man pursueth". Sinners, however "pious" they may be reputed to be, are invariably cowards; they are ashamed of a bold stand for their own *profession*; and afraid of an independent and impartial examination of the law and testimony of God.

Understanding then, that *sin*, or the transgression of God's law, evinced by doubts, fears, and shamefacedness, is *the morbid principle* of an evil conscience, what is the obvious indication to be fulfilled in its removal? The answer is, *blot out the sin*, and the conscience of the patient will be cured. The morbid phenomena will disappear and "the answer of a good conscience towards God" (1 Peter 3:21) remain. From the nature of things, it is obvious that the sinner cannot cure himself; though superstition has taught him to attempt it by fastings, and penances, and all "the voluntary humility and vain deceit," inculcated by "the blind". Adam and Eve vainly imagined they could *cover their own sin*, and efface it from divine scrutiny; but the very clumsy device they contrived, betrayed the defilement of their consciences. Their posterity have not learned wisdom by the failure of their endeavour; but, to this day, they are as industriously engaged in inventing cloaks for their evil consciences, as were their first parents, when stitching fig-leaves together to cover their shame. So true is it that, though God made man upright, he hath sought out many inventions (Ecclesiastes 7:29). But after all the patching and altering, and scouring, they are but like "the filthy garments" taken from the high priest, Joshua (Zechariah 3:3,4); to which all the iniquity laid upon him adhered with the inveteracy of a leprous plague.

Men have not yet learned the lesson, that all they are called upon by God to do is to *believe His word and obey His laws.* He requires nothing more at their hands than this. If they neither believe nor do, or believe but do not obey, they are evil doers, and at enmity with Him. He asks men for actions, not words; for He will judge them "according to their works" in the light of His law, and not according to their suppositious feelings and traditions. The reason why He will not permit men to prescribe for their own moral evils is because He is the physician, they the lepers; He their sovereign, they the rebels against His law. It is His prerogative, and His alone, to dictate the terms of reconciliation. Man has offended God. It becomes him, therefore, to surrender unconditionally; and, with the humility and teachableness of a child, to receive with open heart and grateful feelings, whatever in the wisdom, and justice, and benevolence of God, He may condescend to prescribe.

Until they do this, they may preach in His name (Matthew 7:21-23); make broad the phylacteries (Matthew 23:5-7); sound trumpets in the synagogues and in the streets (Matthew 6:1-4), make long prayers in public (verses 5-7; 23:14); disfigure their countenances with grimace that they may appear to fast (Matthew 6:16-18); build churches; compass sea and land to make proselytes (Matthew 23:15); found hospitals and fill the world with their benevolences:—all is reducible to mere fig-leaf invention as a substitute for "the righteousness of God". "Blessed are they whose iniquities are forgiven, and whose *sins are covered*" (Romans 4:7); but this blessedness came not upon Adam, nor upon any of his posterity, by garments of their own device. The Lord's covering for sin is "a change of raiment", even "white raiment", which He counsels men to buy, "that they may be clothed, and that the shame of their nakedness do not appear" (Revelation 3:18). He alone can furnish it. His price is that men should believe, and put it on.

THE CARNAL MIND

"The thinking of the flesh is enmity against God."

WHEN the Lord bestowed the faculty of speech upon the Serpent, He enabled it to give utterance to its thoughts. The possession of this power did not, however, confer upon it moral accountability. This depends on a different constitution of "the flesh". Where no "moral sentiments" exist as part of "the flesh", or brain, there is no *ability* in the creature to *render an account* for its aberrations from the requirements of moral, or spiritual, institutions. Speech only enables it to utter the thinkings of its unsentimentalized intellect. It spoke, like Balaam's ass, under the impulse of the sensations excited by what it had seen and heard. The thinkings of its flesh could not ascend to faith, being destitute of the organic ability to believe; therefore its speech could express only fleshly thoughts. Faith was too high an attainment for it. The light of God's law could not shine into it. Like all the inferior animals, it was a creature of mere sensation; and could utter only sentences formed of combinations resulting from the impressions of sensible objects transmitted to its sensorium by the five senses; it transcended them, however, in being more observant and reasoning than they.

What it *had done*, and not what it *intended* to do, was made the ground of the Serpent's condemnation. "*Because thou hast done this*", said the Lord God, "thou art cursed above all cattle", etc. It was incapable of moral intention. It did not intend to deceive; but it did deceive; therefore, it was a deceiver. It did not intend to lie; but it did lie; therefore, it was a liar, and the father of a lie. It did not intend to cause the woman's death; but still it brought her under sentence of death; therefore, it was a murderer: and became the spiritual father of all intentional liars, deceivers, unbelievers, and man-killers, who are styled "the Serpent's seed".

The Serpent had propensities and intellect, and so had the woman; but her mental constitution differed from his, in having "moral sentiments" superadded to her propensities and intellect. By the sentiments she was made a morally accountable being capable of believing, and able to control and direct her other faculties in their application. The propensities enable a creature to propagate its species, take care of its young, defend itself against enemies, collect food, and so forth: *intellect* enables it to do these things, for the gratification of its sensations; but when, in addition to these, a being is endowed with the sentiments of conscientiousness, hope, veneration, benevolence, wonder, etc., it possesses a spiritual, or sentimental, organization, which makes it capable of reflecting as from a mirror, the likeness and glory of God. The appropriate sphere of the propensities is on things sensual and fleshly; while that of spiritual, or sentimentallized, intellect, is on "the things of the spirit of God". In the mental constitution of man, God designed that the sentiments, *enlightened by His truth*, should have the ascendancy, and preside over, and govern his actions. Under such an arrangement, the thoughts of the man would have resulted from spiritual thinking as opposed to the thoughts of the inferior creatures, which are purely the thinking of the flesh. Where the truth has possession of the sentiments, setting them to work and so forming the thoughts, it becomes the law of God to them; which the apostle styles "*the law of his mind*"; and because it is written there through the hearing of "the law and the testimony", which came to the prophets and apostles through the spirit, he terms it, "*the law of the spirit*" (Romans 7:23; 8:2) inscribed "on fleshy tables of the heart" (2 Corinthians 3:3) and "the law of the spirit of *life*" because, while obeyed, it confers a right to eternal life.

But in the absence of this law and testimony, the "moral sentiments" are as incapable of directing a man aright, as though he were all intellect, or all propensities. By a right direction, I mean, according to the mind of God. The sentiments are as blind as the propensities when intellect is unenlightened by divine revelation. The truth of this is illustrated by the excesses into which mankind has plunged in the name of religion. Mohammedanism, Romanism, Paganism, and the infinite varieties of Protestantism, are all the result of the coworkings of the intellect, and sentiments, under the impulse of the propensities. They are all the thinkings of the flesh, predicated on ignorance, or misconception, of the truth. Hence, they are either altogether false; or, like the dialogisms of the shrewd Serpent, a clumsy mixture of truth and error.

The *Carnal Mind* is an expression used by Paul; or rather, it is the translation of words used by him, in his epistle to the Romans. It is not so explicit as the original. The words he wrote are φρόνημα τῆς σαρκὸς, *the thinking of the flesh* (Romans 8:7). In this phrase, he intimates to us, that *the flesh is the thinking substance*, that is, the brain; which, in another place, he terms "*the fleshy tablet of the heart*". The kind of thinking, therefore, depends upon the conformation of this organ. Hence, the more elaborate and perfect its mechanism, the more precise and comprehensive the thought; and *vice versa*. It is upon this principle such a diversity of mental manifestation is observable among men and other animals; but after all, how diverse soever they may be, they are all referable to one and the same thing—*the thinking of the flesh, whose elaborations are excited by the propensities, and the sensible phenomena of the world*.

Now, the law of God is given, that the thinking of the flesh, instead of being excited by the propensities within and the world without, may be conducted according to its direction. So long as Adam and Eve yielded to its guidance, they were happy and contented. Their thoughts were the result of right thinking, and obedience was the consequence. But when they adopted the Serpent's reasonings as their own, these being at variance with the truth, caused an "enmity" against it in their thinkings, which is equivalent to "enmity against God". When their sin was perfected, the propensities, or lusts, having been inflamed, became *"a law in their members"*; and because it was implanted in their flesh by transgression, it is styled, "the law of sin"; and death being the wages of sin, it is also termed, "the law of sin and death"; but by philosophy, "the law of nature".

The thinking of the flesh, uninfluenced by the ameliorating agency of divine truth, is so degenerating in its effects, that it reduces man to savagery. There is nothing elevating or ennobling in fleshly thoughts; on the contrary, they tend to physical deterioration and death; for "to be carnally minded is death; but to be spiritually minded is life and peace" (Romans 8:6). If ferocious creatures become tame, or civilized, it is the result of what may be termed spiritual influences; which, operating from without the animal, call into exercise its highest powers, by which the more turbulent are subdued, or kept in check. The law in the members when uncontrolled in its mental operations is so vicious in its influence as to endanger the continuance of the race. Notwithstanding the antagonism established between God's law and the flesh, by which a wholesome conflict has been maintained in the world, a vast proportion of its people are "blind of heart" and "past feeling", in consequence of their intellect and sentiments having fallen into moral desuetude; or of being exercised upon the reasonings of the flesh, as were Eve's upon the speculations of the Serpent.

The unilluminated thinking of the flesh gives birth to the works of the flesh; which are, adultery, fornication, uncleanness, lasciviousness, idolatry, witchcraft, hatred. variance, emulations, wrath, strife, dissensions, sects, envyings, murders, drunkenness, revellings and such like" (Galatians 5:19). Unchecked by the truth and judgments of God, the world would have been composed solely of such characters. Indeed, notwithstanding all His interference to save it from the ruinous consequences of its vicious enmity against His law, it seems to have attained a state of immorality in the apostolic age well nigh to reprobation. "They were", says the apostle, "without excuse: because that when they knew God, they glorified him not as God, neither were thankful; but became *vain in their imaginations, and their foolish heart was darkened.* Professing themselves to be wise (or philosophers) they became fools, and changed the glory of the Incorruptible God into an image made like to corruptible men, and to birds, and four-footed beasts, and creeping things. Wherefore God also *gave them up* to uncleanness *through the lusts of their own hearts*, to dishonour their own bodies between themselves: who changed the truth of God into a lie, and worshipped and served the creature more than the Creator, who is blessed for ever. For this cause, God gave them up unto vile affections: working that which is unseemly, and receiving in themselves that recompense of their error which was meet. And even as they did not like to retain God in their knowledge, *God gave them over to a reprobate mind* to do those things which are not convenient; being filled with all unrighteousness, fornication, wickedness, covetousness, maliciousness; full of envy, murder, debate, deceit, malignity, whisperers, backbiters, haters of God, despiteful, proud, boasters, inventors of evil things, disobedient to parents, without understanding, covenant breakers, without natural affection, implacable, unmerciful" (Romans 1:20-31).

Such is the carnal mind, or thinking of the flesh, as illustrated by the works of the flesh: a hideous deformity, whose conception is referable to the infidelity and disobedience of our first parents: by whom "sin entered into the world, and death by sin" (Romans 5:12). It is *the serpent mind*; because it was through his untruthful reasonings believed, that a like mode of thinking to his was generated in the heart of Eve and her husband. The seed sown there by the Serpent was corruptible seed. Hence the carnal mind, or thinking of the flesh, unenlightened by the truth, is *the serpent in the flesh*. It was for this reason that Jesus styled his enemies "serpents, and a generation of vipers" (Matthew 23:33). Their actions all emanated from the serpent-thinking of the flesh, which displayed "a wisdom not from above", which was at once "earthly, sensual, and devilish"; as opposed to that which "is from above", and which is *"first* pure, *then* peaceful, gentle, and easy to be entreated, full of mercy and good fruits, without partiality, and without hypocrisy" (James 3:15,17).

The carnal mind, or serpent in the flesh, is the subject of a two-fold manifestation—namely, *individually and collectively*. An individual manifestation is more or less observable in persons who "mind the things of the flesh" or "earthly things" (Romans 8:5; Philippians 3:18,19; Colossians 3:2; 1 John 2:15). To do this is to be *"after the flesh"*, and *"in the flesh"*; of whom it is testified, "they cannot please God". By a figure, *sin is put for the serpent*, the effect for the cause; seeing that he was *the suggester* of unbelief and disobedience to man, by whom it entered into the world. Hence, the idea of the serpent in the flesh is expressed by "sin in the flesh"; which was "condemned in the flesh" when Jesus was crucified for, or on account of, sin, "in the likeness of sinful flesh". In the animal man there dwelleth no good thing. The apostle affirms this of himself, considered as an unenlightened son of the flesh. "In me, that is, in my flesh", says he, "dwelleth no good thing." Hence, whatever good was in him, did not originate from the thinking of the flesh excited by the propensities, and traditions of Gamaliel; but from "the law of the spirit of life in Christ Jesus"; that is, from the influence of "the testimony of God" concerning "the things of the kingdom and name of Jesus Christ", upon "the fleshy tablet of his heart", most assuredly believed. Submission to this "made me free", says he, "from the law of sin and death". This attests the truth of the Lord's saying, that "if the truth made a man free, he should be free indeed". Sin, though still in the flesh, should no more reign in his mortal body, nor have dominion over him.

If it were not for the law, or truth, of God, we should not know what sin is; for, says the apostle, "I had not known sin, but by the law"; "for without the law, *sin is dead*". If a man committed theft, or adultery, or any other thing, he would not know whether he did right or wrong in God's esteem, if God had not said they shall not be done. The lower animals steal, kill, and obey their propensities uncontrolled; but, in so doing, they do not sin, because God has made them with the ability and disposition so to do, and has not forbidden them. *Wrong* consists not in any particular act of which we are capable; but in that act being contrary to the letter and spirit of the divine testimony: in other words, *right* is the doing of the will of God. Hence, if we saw a man bowing down, before an image of the Virgin Mary, which is death by His law, and He commanded us to kill him, we should do wrong to refuse, although He has said, "Thou shalt not kill". Men have lost sight of this truth. They know not, or seem not to know, that the only true standard of right and wrong, truth and error, is the divine law. Hence, they inflict upon themselves and one another all sorts of pains and penalties, making their lives miserable, because of nonconformity to standards of faith and morals, which know no other paternity than the serpent-thinking of sinful flesh.

Sin was in the world from the fall to the giving of the law through Moses. But it did not appear to be sin to those who obeyed its impulses; because, there being no such law as the Mosaic, "the sons of God" did not know when they might have erred. They were not held accountable to any future retribution for doing things, which, under Moses' law, were punishable with death. They were amenable only to "the way of the LORD", even as the disciples of Jesus are at this day. This required them to walk by faith in the nurture and admonition of the Lord, whose love was shed abroad in their hearts by the testimony they believed (Romans 5:13).

The Serpent in the flesh shows itself in individuals in all the colours of its skin. It manifests itself in all the deceptions men practise upon themselves and one another. Its most insidious and dangerous manifestations emanate from the pulpit, and ecclesiastical thrones. In these, the Serpent presents himself to mankind, presumptuously entertaining them with things he does not understand. From thence he delights them with the assurance of wisdom upon principles in harmony with their nature. "God doth not mean", saith he, "exactly what He says. Trouble not your consciences about the letter of His word. He knows that the circumstances in which you are placed prevent a rigid construction of it. Besides, the times are changed, and the world is better than it used to be. He takes the will for the deed. The spirit is everything; the letter is nothing; for the letter killeth, but the spirit giveth life. Eat, then, and drink, and be merry. Be diligent in business, fervent in the cause of your church, serving your clergy; and when you die, ye shall be as gods in the elysian fields!"

But the serpent in the flesh manifests itself in *all* the high places of the earth. It obtrudes itself upon all occasions, and through all the channels of human life. Popes, cardinals, and priests; bishops, ministers, and deacons; emperors, kings. and presidents; with all who sustain them, and execute their behests, are but the fleshly media through which the thinking of the flesh finds expression. They are "the high things that exalt themselves against *the knowledge* of God", which are to be cast down (2 Corinthians 10:5). They are faithless of this knowledge, which they make of no effect by their traditions; and "whatsoever is not of faith is sin". My business will be to show what this knowledge is; and, if it be found that I speak not according to "the law and the testimony" it will be because there is no light in me; and that, like them, I speak my own thoughts as of the flesh, and not according to the gospel of the kingdom of God.

As I have remarked before, *sin* is personified by Paul as "pre-eminently *a sinner*"; and by another apostle, as "the Wicked One" (1 John 3:12). In this text, he says, "Cain was of that Wicked One, and slew his brother". There is precision in this language which is not to be disregarded in the interpretation. Cain was of the Wicked One; that is, he was *a son of sin* — of the serpent-sin, or original transgression. The Mosaic narrative of facts is interrupted at the end of the sixth verse of the third chapter. The fact passed over there, though implied in the seventh verse, is plainly stated in the first verse of the fourth chapter. These texts conjoined read thus: "And Eve gave unto her husband, and he did eat with her. And Adam knew Eve his wife; and she conceived. And the eyes of them were both opened, and they knew that they were naked". Now, here was a conception in sin, the originator of which was the Serpent. When, therefore, in the "set time" afterwards, "Eve bare Cain", though procreated by Adam, he was of the Serpent, seeing that he suggested the transgression which ended in the conception of Cain. In this way, sin in the flesh being put for the Serpent, Cain was of that Wicked One, the pre-eminent sinner, and the first-born of the Serpent's seed.

Now, they who do the works of flesh are the children of the Wicked one, or of sin in the flesh; on the principle that those Jews only were the children of Abraham who did the works of Abraham. But they did not the deeds of Abraham, but evil deeds. They were liars, hypocrites and murderers: therefore, said Jesus, "Ye are of your father the devil, and the lusts of your father you are willing to do. He was a murderer from the beginning, and stood not in the truth, because there is no truth in him" (John 8:39,44). We have seen in what sense it is affirmed of the Serpent, the unaccountable and irresponsible author of sin. Every son of Adam is "conceived in sin and shapen in iniquity", and therefore "sinful flesh"; on the principle that "what is born of flesh is flesh." If he obey the impulses of his flesh, he is like Cain, "of the Wicked One"; but if he believe the "exceeding great and precious promises of God", obey the law of faith, and put to death unlawful obedience to his propensities, he becomes a son of the living God, and a brother and a joint-heir of the Lord Jesus Christ of the glory to be revealed in the last time.

But serpent-sin, being a constituent of human nature, is treated of in the scripture in the aggregate, as well as in its individual manifestations. The "lust of the flesh, the lust of the eyes, and the pride of life", generated in our nature by sin, and displayed in all the children of sin, taken in the aggregate constitute "*the world*", which stands opposed to God. Serpent-sin in the flesh is the god of the world, who possesses the glory of it. Hence, to overcome the world is to overcome the Wicked One; because sin finds in its expression in the things of the world. These things are the civil and ecclesiastical polities, and social institutions of the nations, which are based upon "the wisdom that descendeth not from above"—the serpent wisdom of the flesh. If this be admitted, it is easy to appreciate the full force of the saying, "The friendship of the world is enmity against God. Whosoever therefore will be a friend of the world is the enemy of God" (James 4:4). Let no more, then, who would have God's favour, seek the honour and glory of the world in *Church* or State; for promotion in either of them can only be attained by sacrificing the principles of God's truth upon the altar of popular favour, or of princely patronage. Let no man envy men in place and power. It is their misfortune, and will be their ruin; and though many of them profess to be very pious, and to have great zeal for religion; yea, zeal as flaming as the scribes and Pharisees of old; they are in friendship with the world, which in return heaps upon them its riches, and honour, and therefore they are the enemies of God. It is unnecessary to indicate them in detail. If the reader understand the scripture, he can easily discern them. Wherever the gospel of the kingdom is supplanted by sectarian theology, there is a stronghold of "the carnal mind, which is enmity against God; for it is not subject to the law of God, neither indeed can be" (Romans 8:7). This is a rule to which there is no exception; and the grand secret of that formality, coldness, and spiritual death, which are said to paralyse "the churches". They are rich in all things, but *the truth*; and of that there is a worse than Egyptian scarcity.

THE PRINCE OF THIS WORLD

"The prince of this world shall be cast out."

SIN made flesh, whose character is revealed in the works of the flesh, is the Wicked One of the world. He is styled by Jesus ὁ ἄρχων τοῦ κόρμου τούτου, the Prince of this world (John 12:31). *Kosmos*, rendered world in this phrase, signifies, that *order of things* constituted upon the basis of sin in the flesh, and styled *the kingdom of Satan* (Matthew 12:26), as opposed to the kingdom of God: which is to be established upon the foundation of "the word made flesh" obedient unto death. Incarnated sin, and incarnated obedience, are the bases of the two hostile kingdoms, of God and of the adversary. The world is Satan's kingdom; therefore it is, that "the saints", or people of God, both Israelites outwardly (Romans 2:28,29; 9:6,7), and "Israelites indeed" (John 1:47), are a dispersed and persecuted community. Satan's kingdom is the kingdom of sin. It is a kingdom in which "sin reigns in the mortal body", and thus has dominion over men.

It is quite fabulous to locate it in a region of ghosts and hobgoblins, remote from, or under the earth, where Pluto reigns as "God of Hell". This notion is a part of the wisdom of those fleshly thinkers, who, as the apostle says, "professing themselves to be wise, became fools", a wisdom, too, which "God hath made foolishness" (1 Corinthians 1:19,20) by "the light of the glorious gospel of Christ" (2 Corinthians 4:3,4,6). The kingdom of sin is among the living upon the earth; and it is called the kingdom of Satan, because "all the power of the enemy", or adversary, of God and His people, is concentrated and incarnated in it. It is a kingdom teeming with religion, or rather forms of superstition, all of which have sprung from the thinking of sinful flesh. This is the reason why men hate, or neglect, or disparage, the Bible. If the leaders of the people were to speak honestly they would confess that they did not understand it. Their systems of divinity are the untoward thinkings of sinful flesh; and they know that they cannot interpret the Bible intelligibly according to their principles. At all events they have not yet accomplished it. Hence, one class have forbidden their people the use of the scriptures at all, and have placed it among prohibited books. Another class advocates them, not because it walks by the light of them, but because they hate the tyranny of Rome. These, in their public exhibitions, substitute their sermonizings for "reasoning out of the scriptures", and "expounding out of the law of Moses and the Prophets" (Acts 28:23,31). Thus they neglect the Bible, or use it only as a book of maxims and mottoes for their sermons; which, for the most part, have as much to do with the subject treated of in the text as with the science of gymnastics, or perpetual motion.

But the carnal policy does not end here. The neglect of the preachers might be supplied by the searching of the scriptures by the people themselves. But this is discouraged by disparagements from the pulpit. The word is proclaimed to be "a dead letter"; the prophecies are said to be unintelligible; the Apocalypse incomprehensible, and utterly bewildering; that it is necessary to go to college to study divinity before it can be *judiciously* explained; and so forth. The people for whom I write, know this to be the truth. But what is the English of all this? It is that the pulpit orators and newspaper scribes are consciously ignorant of "the sure word of prophecy": so that, in order to maintain their ascendancy, they must repress the enterprise of the people, lest they should become "wiser than their teachers"; and find that they could do infinitely better without their services than with them, and thus their occupation would be gone.

As for a college education in divinity qualifying boys for *"preaching the word"*, the absurdity of the conceit is manifest in the fact that the "college-bred divines" are all at variance among themselves upon its meaning. Call a convention of priests and preachers of all religious sects and parties, and assign to them the work of publishing a scriptural and *unani-*

mous reply to the simple question, *What do the scriptures teach as the measure of faith, and rule of conduct, to him who would inherit the Kingdom?* Let it be such a reply as would stand the scrutiny of deep and earnest investigation—and what does the reader expect would be the result? Would their knowldege of all the languages living and dead; of Euclid's Elements; of Liguori, Bellarmine, Luther, Calvin, and Arminius; of the mythologies of the Greeks and Romans; of all the creeds, confessions, catechisms and articles of "Christendom"; of logic, ancient and modern; of the art of sermonizing; and of all religious controversies extant:—would their acquaintance with such lore as this bring them to unanimity; and cause them to manifest themselves as "workmen that need not to be ashamed, rightly dividing the word of truth?" What can we reason upon this point, but from what we know? Experience, then, teaches us that their performance of such a thing so simple and easy in itself, would be utterly impracticable; for "the thinking of the flesh is enmity against God"; and until they throw away their traditions. and study the Word, which is very different from "studying divinity", they will continue as they are, perhaps unconsciously, the perverters and enemies of the truth.

The kingdom of Satan is manifested under various phases. When the Word was embodied in sinful flesh, and dwelt among the Jews, the Kosmos was constituted of the Roman world, which was then based upon the institutions of paganism. After these were suppressed, the kingdom of the adversary assumed the Constantinian form, which was subsequently changed in the west to the Papal and Protestant order of things; and in the east to the Mohammedan. These phases, however, no more affect the nature of the kingdom than the changes of the moon alter her substance. The lord that dominates over them all from the days of Jesus to the present time is SIN, the incarnate accuser and adversary of the law of God, and therefore styled "the Devil and Satan".

The words ὁ ἄρχων signify *the prince*, or one invested with power. All persons in authority are styled ἄρχοντες in the New Testament, such as magistrates, and chiefs among the people. Hence, the *archōn* of the *archōns* would be the chief magistrate of the kingdom. Now, sin in its sovereign manifestations among the nations executes its will and pleasure through the civil and ecclesiastical authorities of a state. What, then, is decreed by emperors, kings, popes, and subordinate rulers, are the mandates of "the Prince of the World", who works in them all to gratify their own lusts, oppress the people, and "make war against the saints", with all the energy they possess. Taken collectively from the chief magistrate to the lowest, they are styled ἀρχαί and ἐξουσίαι, *principali-*

103

ties and powers; the κοσμοκράτορες τοῦ σκότους τοῦ αἰῶνος τούτου, *the world-rulers of the darkness of this age*; who are τὰ πνευματικὰ τῆς πονηρίας ἐν τοῖς ἐπουρανίοις, *the spirituals of wickedness in the high places of the kingdoms* (Ephesians 6:12). So the apostle writes of the rulers of the world in his day; and from the conduct they now exhibit before the nations in all their kingdoms, it is clear that the style is as characteristic of the rulers, and of these times, as it was in the first century of the Christian era. Iniquity has only changed its form and mode of attack against the truth. The world's rulers, temporal and spiritual, are as essentially hostile to the gospel of the kingdom as ever. They could not embrace it and retain the friendship of the world. This is as impossible now as at the beginning. But things are now quiet with respect to the gospel; not because the world is reconciled to it, but because there are scarcely any to be found who have intelligence of it, faith and courage enough earnestly to contend for it as it was originally delivered to the saints (Jude 3).

In apostolic times, it was the privilege of the church to make known to the world-rulers "the manifold wisdom of God" (Ephesians 3:10). This mission brought the disciples of Christ into contact with them, as is related in the Acts. When they stood before these men of sin, in whom the thinking of sinful flesh worked strongly, the truth of God proclaimed to them brought out the evil of the flesh in all its malignity. They imprisoned the disciples of Christ; threatened them with death; tempted them with rewards; and when they could not shake their fidelity to the truth, tormented them with the cruellest tortures they could invent. The apostle styles these the μεθοδεῖαι τοῦ διαβόλου, the artifices, or *wiles of the accuser* (Ephesians 6:11): against which he exhorts believers to stand firm, being panoplied with the whole armour of God. The war being thus commenced by an attack upon the strongholds of power, the magistrates, urged on by the priests, were not content to take vengeance against them when they came in their way; but they obtained imperial decrees to hunt them out, and destroy them. This they did with destructive energy and effect. They *calumniated* the disciples, charging them with the most licentious and impious practices; and employed spies and informers, who personated brethren, to walk among them, and watch an opportunity of *accusing* them before the judge. These *adversaries* of the Christian, being actuated by the same spirit of sinful flesh, the apostle terms ὁ ἀντίδικος ὑμῶν διάβολος, *your adversary the accuser*; and to express the ferocious spirit that impelled the enemy, he compared him to a roaring lion, walking about, on the look out for prey. "Resist him", says he; not by wrestling with flesh and blood in personal combat; but by continuing "steadfast in the faith, knowing that *the same sufferings* are inflicted in the world upon your brethren" (1 Peter 5:8,9).

To walk being dead in trespasses and sins, is to live according to *the course (αἰών)* of this world. So says the apostle (Ephesians 2:1,2). The *course of the world* is according to the thinking of sinful flesh, in whatever way it may be manifested or expressed. If a man embrace one of the religions of Satan's kingdom, he is still "dead in trespasses and sins", and walks according to the course of the world. In brief, anything short of faith in the gospel of the kingdom, and obedience to the law of faith, is walking according to the course of the world. To walk in sin is to walk in this course. Hence, the apostle terms walking according to the course of the world, walking according to *the Prince of the Power of the Air—ὁ ἄρχων τῆς ἐξουσίας τοῦ ἀέρος*: which he explains as *"the Spirit now working* in the children of disobedience". The *"power of the air"*, or aerial power, is *the political power of the world*, which is animated and pervaded by *the spirit of disobedience*, which is sin in the flesh; and styled above, the Prince of the Power of the Air. This is that prince of whom Jesus spoke, saying, "Now is the judgment *(κρίσις)* of this world; now shall the Prince of this World be cast out" (John 12:31), that is "judged" (John 16:11). The key to this is suggested in what follows: "And I, if I be lifted up from the earth, will draw all unto me. This he said, signifying *what death he should die."*

The judgment of the Prince of the World by God, was exhibited in the contest between Jesus and the civil and spiritual power of Judea. "Its poison was like the poison of a serpent" (Psalm 58:4), when "the iniquity of his heels compassed him about". "The battle was against him" for a time. They bruised him in the heel (Genesis 3:15). "The enemy smote his life down to the ground; and made him to dwell in darkness, as those that had been long dead" (Psalm 143:3). But here the Serpent-power of sin ended. It had stung him to death by the strength of the law, which cursed every one that was hanged upon a tree. Jesus being cursed upon this ground, God "condemned sin in the flesh" through him (Galatians 3:13; Romans 8:3). Thus was sin, the Prince of the World, condemned, and the world with him according to the existing course of it. But Jesus rose again, leading captivity captive; and so giving to the world an earnest, that the time would come when death should be abolished and sin, the power of death, destroyed. Sinful flesh was laid upon him, "that through death, he might destroy *him* that had the power of death, that is, the devil", or sin in the flesh (Hebrews 2:14): for, *"for this purpose* the Son of God was manifested, that he might destroy the works of the devil".

THE WORKS OF THE DEVIL (1 John 3:8)

IT is clear to my mind that *sin* is the thing referred to by the apostle in the word *devil*. The sting of the Serpent is its power of destruction. The "sting of death" is the power of death; and that, the apostle says, in one place, *"is sin"*; and in another, *"is the devil"*. There are not two powers of death; but one only. Hence, the *devil* and *sin*, though different words, represent the same thing. "Sin *had* the power of death", and would have retained it, if the man, who was *obedient* unto death, had not gained the victory over it. But, thanks be to God, the earth is not to be a charnel house for ever; for he that overcame the world in his own person (John 16:33), is destined hereafter to "take away the sin of the world", and to "make all things new" (Revelation 21:5). Every curse will then cease (Revelation 22:3), and death be swallowed up in victory; for death shall be no more (Revelation 21:4).

The works of the devil, or evil one, are *the works of sin*. Individually, they are "the works of the flesh" exhibited in the lives of sinners; collectively, they are on a larger scale, as displayed in the polities of the world. All the institutions of the kingdom of the adversary are the works which have resulted from the thinking of sinful flesh; though happily for the saints of God, *"the powers that be"* are controlled by Him. They cannot do what they please. Though defiant of His truth, and His hypocritical and malignant enemies, He serves Himself of them; and dashes them against one another when the enormity of their crimes, reaching to heaven, demands His terrible rebuke.

Among the works of sin are the numerous diseases which transgression has brought upon the world. The Hebrews, the idiom of whose language is derived from the Mosaic narrative of the origin of things, referred disease to sin under the names of the devil and Satan. Hence, they inquired, "Who sinned, this man or his parents, that he was born blind?" A woman "bowed together with a spirit of infirmity for eighteen years", is said to have been "bound of Satan", or the adversary, for that time; and her restoration to health is termed "loosing her from the bond" (Luke 13:10-17). Paul also writes in the same idiom to the disciples at Corinth, commanding them to deliver the incestuous brother "unto Satan for the destruction of the flesh"; that is, inflict disease upon him, that he may be brought to repentance, "that the spirit may be saved in the day of the Lord Jesus" (1 Corinthians 5:5). Thus he was "judged and chastened of the Lord that he might not be condemned with the world" (1 Corinthians 11:32). This had the desired effect; for he was overwhelmed with sorrow. Wherefore, he exhorts the spiritually gifted men of the body

(James 5:14) to forgive and comfort, or restore him to health, "lest Satan should get an advantage over them" by the offender being reduced to despair: "for", says the apostle "we are not ignorant of his devices", or those of sin in the flesh (2 Corinthians 2:6-11), which is very deceitful. Other of the Corinthians were offenders in another way. They were very disorderly in the celebration of the Lord's Supper, eating and drinking condemnation to themselves. "For this cause", says he—that is, because they sinned thus—"many are weak and *sickly* among you, and *many sleep*", or are dead. Many other cases might be adduced from scripture to show the connection between sin and disease; but these are sufficient. If there were no moral evil in the world, there would be no physical evils. Sin and punishment are as cause and effect in the divine economy. God does not willingly afflict, but is long-suffering and kind. If men, however, will work sin, they must lay their account with "the wages of sin", which is disease, famine, pestilence, the sword, misery and death. But let the righteous rejoice that the enemy will not always triumph in the earth. The Son of God was manifested to destroy him and all his works; which, by the power and blessing of the Father, he will assuredly do.

THE GREAT DRAGON

Ὁ ὄφις ὁ ἀρχαῖος ὁ καλούμενος Διάβολος, καὶ ὁ Σατανᾶς, ὁ πλανῶν τὴν οἰκουμένην ὅλην.

"The old Serpent, surnamed the Accuser and the Adversary, who deceives the whole habitable."

THE οἰκουμένη ὅλη, or *whole habitable*, in the days of the apostles, was that part of the earth's surface which acknowledged the dominion of Rome. Upon this platform had been erected the largest empire then known to the world. By its imperial constitution was aggregated in one dominion all "the lust of the flesh, the lust of the eyes, and the pride of life". These lusts found free course through the constituted authorities of the pagan church and state. Of the horrors perpetrated upon the world lying under them by their wanton riot, the reader will find an ample account in the history of pagan Rome. In the progress and maturity of this dominion, sin reigned triumphant over the human race. Its lusts were let loose, and the propensities alone directed the policy of the world.

The only antagonism experienced by sin was established in Judea. There, as we have seen, the first battle was fought, and the first victory won over sin, by the Son of Mary. These were the two combatants—*sin*, working in the children of disobedience; and *"the truth"*, in the person of Jesus. Sin bruised him in the heel; but God healed him of his wound, and so prepared him for the future contest, when he should bruise sin in the head. Now, sin could only have crucified him by the hands of power; for as this world is a concrete, and not an indigested concourse of abstractions, sin, which in the abstract "is a transgression of law", must be incorporate to be competent to act. Sin corporealized attacked Jesus through the Roman power instigated by the chief priests of Israel. At this crisis, sin was brought to a head, and ready to sting its victim to death. The event was now about to happen, which the Lord God predicted, saying to the Serpent, *"Thou* shalt bruise his heel"* (Genesis 3:15). No one would be simple enough to suppose that the literal Serpent was to do this *in propria persona*. He was, however, to do it, in the sense of his being the instrumental cause of sin; which, through those that should afterwards obey it, should inflict a violent death upon the son of the woman. Hence, the Roman power, which put Jesus to death (for the Jews had not power to do it) represented the Serpent in the transaction. And, as sin had been working in the children of disobedience for 4,000 years; and manifesting itself in the Ninevite, Assyrian, Chaldean, Persian, and Macedonian empires, whose power was at length absorbed into the Roman, the last came to be symbolized as *"the Old Serpent"*.

When the woman's seed rose from among the dead, and "led captivity captive", the war upon the Old Serpent began in good earnest. The manner in which it was conducted on both sides, may be learned from the Acts of the Apostles. The parties were the Jewish and the Roman power on the one hand, and the apostles and their brethren on the other. These enemies were the two seeds; the former, the *"Seed of the Serpent"*; and the latter, by constitution in Christ Jesus, the *"Seed of the Woman"*. Hence, in the Apocalypse, "the Old Serpent" (Revelation 12:3,9; 21:2), and "the Woman" (12:1,4,6,13,14-17), became the symbols by which they are represented. During 280 years; that is, from the Day of Pentecost, A.D. 33, to A.D. 313, when Constantine established himself in Rome, the contest raged between the pagan power and the woman with intense fury. She was calumniated, *accused*, and tortured, by the Old Serpent without pity. Hence the Spirit of God surnamed him Διάβολος, or the *Accuser*; and Σατανᾶς, or the *Adversary*; so that, when he was "cast out" from the government of the empire, "a loud voice" is represented as "saying in the heaven, Now is come deliverance, and power, and the kingdom of our God, and the dominion of his Christ: for *the Accuser* of our brethren, *who accuseth* them before God day and night, is cast down" (12:10). The history of this period is a striking illustration of the *"enmity"* (Genesis 3:15) God has put between the seed of the Serpent and the seed of the woman. In the war between them the heel of her seed was bruised by the Serpent power, as it had bruised that of their great Captain; but thanks be to God who gives them the victory, the time is at the door, when they will leave the dead, and with him bruise the Old Serpent's head upon the mountains of Israel (Ezekiel 39:4). There can be no friendship between these parties. Death or victory is the only alternative. There can be no peace in the world till one or other he suppressed. The "enmity" is the essential hostility betwixt sin and God's law, which is the truth. Either truth must conquer sin, or sin must abolish the truth; but compromise there can be none. I have great faith in the power of truth, because I have faith in God. He is pledged to give it the victory; and though deceivers in church and state may triumph for the time, and tyrants "destroy the earth", their end is certain and their destruction sure.

The Dragon is the organic symbol of the Old Serpent power, as the Leopard with *four heads* and *four wings* (Daniel 7:6) was of the quadrupartite constitution of the Macedonian. The Dragon appears in four principal scenes in the Apocalypse; *first*, in taking him who hindered out of the way (2 Thessalonians 2:7) A.D. 313; *second*, in the surrendering of the power, throne, and extensive dominion of the west, to papalized imperio-regal Europe, A.D. 800 (Revelation 13:2,4); *third*, in the present crisis of the gathering of "the powers that be" to their last conflict for the world's dominion (Revelation 16:13); and *fourth*, in the suppression of the Serpent-power by the Lord Jesus, when he bruises his head, and restrains him for 1,000 years (Revelation 20:2). As the symbol of the Old Serpent in its pagan constitution, with Rome as his satanic seat, he is styled "the great Red Dragon, having seven heads and ten horns, and seven crowns upon his heads"; but after the revolution by which paganism was suppressed, the serpent-power of Rome is simply styled "the Dragon". About A.D. 334, a new capital was built, and dedicated, by Constantine, and called NEW ROME by an imperial edict; which, however, was afterwards superseded by the name of *Constantinople*. Old and New Rome were now the top capitals of the Dragon-dominion; and so continued to be until Old Rome was surrendered to the imperio-papal power of the West. New Rome, or Constantinople, then became the sole capital of the Dragon empire; and Old Rome the capital of the Seven-headed and Ten-horned Beast; an arrangement which continued for more than a thousand years: so that "they do homage to the Dragon, and they do homage to the Beast" (13:4), that is, they of the east are subject to Constantinople; and they of the west, to Rome.

But the time is at hand when the dominion, divided between the Dragon and the Beast, may be re-united; and the old Roman territory, the ὀικουμένη ὄλη, with an immense addition of domain, again subject to one sovereign. This may be by the fall of the Two-horned Beast (13:11; Daniel 7:11), and the expulsion of the Turks from Constantinople, which will then become the throne of the dominion, represented by Nebuchadnezzar's Image, which is to be broken to pieces in "the latter-days" (Daniel 2:28,34,35). The establishment of this sovereignty being accomplished, it stands upon the earth as the Accuser and Adversary of God's people Israel; and will make war upon them (Daniel 11:41,45; Ezekiel 38:8-12); and will combat with the faithful and True One, and his saints (Revelation 19:11,14), as did the Old Serpent-power against *Michael* (Revelation 12:7) Constantine and his confederates in the early part of the fourth century. The result will be the same. The victory will be with Jesus, the Great Prince of Israel (Daniel 12:1), who will break his power to pieces upon the mountains of Israel in the Battle of Armageddon (Revelation 16:16; Ezekiel 39:4). This great Adversary of the latter days, is the Northern Autocrat for the time being. He is styled Gog by Ezekiel (38:2). In him will be acuminated "all the power of the enemy"; that is, of SIN, imperially manifested in a dominion, such as the world has never seen before. Because of this, it is styled the Old Serpent; and because it will exist upon the old Roman territory, it is called the Dragon: and from its hostility to God and His truth, it is "surnamed the Devil and Satan".

THE MAN OF SIN

"The Man of Sin, the Son of Perdition."

THE Dragon, the Old Serpent, surnamed the Devil and Satan, being representative of SIN *in its imperial constitution*, as manifested in the past, present, and future, upon *"the Habitable"*, or Roman territory; the Man of Sin is that dynasty, "whose coming was after the energy of the Adversary with all power, and tokens, and prodigies of falsehood, and with all the deceit of iniquity in them that perish" (2 Thessalonians 2:9,10). This is what he was in his coming, or presence. The power is styled, "the Man of Sin", not because it is to be found in only one man, but because it is sin pre-eminently incarnate in an order of men. This order occupying one throne, was to "be revealed" out of *an apostasy* from the original apostolic faith; but before its presence could be manifested, a certain obstacle was to "be taken out of the way". No order of men such as the apostle describes, could make its appearance upon the territory of the Roman Dragon, so long as the constitution of the empire continued pagan. This, then, was the obstacle to be removed. While it continued, the elements of the new power were at work in the Christian body; but incapable of the exercise of political authority. These elements are collectively styled "the Mystery of Iniquity", the open manifestation of which was withheld for a time.

When the *"Red"* or pagan aspect of the Dragon was changed for the *"Catholic"*, by the victories of Constantine, the *opposing power* was removed; in fact, the Adversary, or Satan, now a *professor* of Christianity, took "the Mystery of Iniquity" under his patronage; and as he found paganism no longer fit for the contest against the apostolic faith, he determined to change his weapon, and to fight it with the apostasy in the name of Christ. Hence, the first thing he did was to impose this apostasy on the world as its religion. He married it to the state, and established it by law. The National Establishment, as it now became, assumed the character of "Mother Church"; and the community in Old Rome, with its bishop now converted into the chief magistrate of the city at its head, claimed to be the mistress of all churches. The apostasy being united to Satan, became the open enemy of God, and the worse than pagan persecutor of His truth. Its name is Catholic; and since the division of the Dragon territory into east and west, and the great schism about *image-worship*, it is surnamed Greek Catholic, and Roman Catholic. The undivided catholic apostasy in its first establishment is represented in the Apocalypse by "a woman clothed with the sun, and the moon under her feet, and upon her head a crown of twelve stars" (Revelation 12:1). This woman, after *nine months of years*, or "a set time", and not long before she was clothed with the imperial robes, was "pained to be delivered" of her child, which had been conceived in her by sin. As the betrothed of the Second Adam, the Serpent had beguiled her, and had corrupted her mind from the simplicity that is in Christ. Part of her body had embraced another Jesus, another Spirit, and another gospel (2 Corinthians 11:2-4); by which they were so corrupted that they were prepared to take the sword; declare for the first military chieftain, whose anti-pagan ambition of supreme power should induce him to embrace their cause; and to turn Christianity into a State Religion. This party found a semi-pagan suited to their purpose in Constantine, surnamed "the Great". When he avowed himself their champion, all the power of the Old Serpent was brought to bear against him and his confederates. They fought; and victory perched upon the standard of the Cross, now become "the mark" of the Apostasy.

Constantine was the man-child of sin, who began that iron-rule, which, in the name of Christianity, has soaked the dust of the earth with the best and noblest blood of its inhabitants. He set himself up as the arbiter of faith, and the corrector of heretics; and though pretending to believe, yet refusing to be immersed till within three days of his death, that he might commit all the sins he would be likely to do before he was baptized for remission of sins—yet he is belauded by ecclesiastics as a great and pious Christian! What Constantine began, his successors on the Dragon throne, Julian excepted, perfected. For the Bishop of Old Rome, they conceived an especial veneration and regard; seeing that he was more of a hypocrite, and as much of a serpent as themselves. They energized him with all power, and set him up as the supreme pontiff of the world. This God upon earth, whom the pagan predecessors knew not, they "honoured with gold, with silver, and with precious stones, and pleasant things". A humble bishop of an obscure society in Rome, they acknowledged as a god, and increased with glory (Daniel 11:38,39); so that "by the energy of Satan with all power", the dominion founded by the man-child of the apostasy was matured; and at length possessed by the Roman bishop as the full-grown Man of Sin.

The presence of the Man of Sin in Rome for upwards of twelve centuries past may be determined by Paul's description of him. If we find an order of men there answering to the character recorded against them, we may know that the Man of Sin has been revealed. He describes him as one *"who opposes and exalts himself above every one called a god, or an object of veneration; so that he sits in the temple of the god as a god, exhibiting himself that he is a god"* (2 Thessalonians 2:4). This in few words is highly descriptive of the Popes. "God" in the passage signifies *a ruler* of whatever kind; for "god" in the Scriptures is applied to angels, magistrates, and the whole nation of Israel; as "I said, ye are gods; but ye shall die as one of the princes"; and "worship him, ye gods"; the former being addressed to Israel; the latter, to the angels concerning Jesus. The *"temple of the god"* is St. Peter's at Rome. Now, the history of the papacy shows the applicability of the description to the Popes, and to them exclusively. They have systematically opposed and exalted themselves above every ruler, whether emperors or kings, and above all bishops and priests; so that they have sat in St. Peter's as gods, exhibiting themselves thus, because they claim to be gods upon earth. The incarnate devilism of these blasphemers of God's name, and of His people (Revelation 13:6,7; 18:24), and murderers of His saints, cannot be surpassed by any power that could possibly arise. They are essentially sin corporealized in human shape and therefore most emphatically the order of the Man of Sin; as "the Holy, Apostolic, and Roman Catholic Church" is the "Mother of Harlots, and of all the abominations of the earth".

Paul styles this dynastic order ὁ ἄνομος, *the Lawless One*; and because of its destiny, *"the Son of Perdition"*. In the Apocalypse, it is represented by an Eighth Head (Revelation 17:11) of the Beast, which divides *"the habitable"* with the Dragon. Of this head, the Spirit saith, *"It goeth to perdition"*. It is a head, which exercised both civil and pontifical dominion over the west; and when resolved into other symbols its conjoint dominion is represented by a Two-horned Beast (Revelation 13:11); and an image of the sixth head of the Seven-headed Beast (verse 14,15); the former symbolizing the Austrian power; and the latter, his ally, the Lawless One. These are both doomed to perdition together. Their present intrigues are contributing to kindle a flame in Europe, that will convert it into "a lake of fire burning with brimstone" (Revelation 19:20; Daniel 7:26; 2 Thessalonians 2:8). Into this will the Beast, and the Lawless One, his pseudo-prophet, be "cast alive". The dominions they represent will be utterly destroyed by the lightning and thunderbolts of war; and their power transferred to the Dragon, the Old Serpent, surnamed the Devil and Satan, of whom I have already spoken in the last section. The binding of the Dragon will terminate the struggle which began in 1848. Sin will then be chained; and all flesh implicated in maintaining its ascendancy, be put to shame before the universe of God.

RUDIMENTS OF THE WORLD

CHAPTER IV

THE SENTENCE OF DEATH—THE RUIN OF THE OLD
WORLD, AND THE PRESERVATION OF A
REMNANT

The trial of the Transgressors—Of the Literal and the Allegorical—The
sentence upon the Serpent particularized—The "Peace and Safety" cry—
Jesus came not to send peace, but a sword—The Peace Society the
enemy of God—Cain, Abel, and Seth—Atheism defined—Cain rejected
as the progenitor of the Woman's Seed, and Seth appointed—The
Antediluvian apostasy—The Cainites and Sethites distinct Societies—
Their union the ruin of the old world, of which eight sons of Seth only
survive—The Foundation of the World—The sentence upon Woman—
Her social position defined—The sentence upon Adam—The Constitution
of Sin—Of sin as a physical quality of the flesh—Of the hereditary
nature of Jesus—Of "original sin"—Men, sinners in a two-fold sense—
The Constitution of Righteousness—Men become saints by adoption—
The Three Witnesses—The "new birth" explained—The Two Principles—
Of "the light within"—The scripture revelation the divine principle of
illumination—The awful condition of "the church"—Of the Hidden Man
of the Heart.

IN the previous chapter, I have treated of the introduction
of sin into the world; its immediate effects upon the transgressors; and of some of its remoter consequences upon
their posterity. We left Adam and his companion hid among
the trees of the garden, greatly alarmed at the voice of God;
and overwhelmed with shame at the condition to which they
had reduced themselves. But, though hid, as they supposed,
they soon found the truth of the saying that is written, that
"there is not any creature that is not manifest in his sight;
but all things are naked and open unto the eyes of him with
whom we have to do" (Hebrews 4:13). When the Lord God
called to Adam, he said, in answer to the question, "Where art
thou? I was *afraid*, because I was *naked*; and I *hid* myself".

This was the truth as far as it went; but it was not the
whole truth. Fear, shame, and concealment are plainly
avowed; but why he was ashamed he was not ingenuous
enough to confess. The Lord God, however, knowing from the
mental constitution He had bestowed upon him, that man
could not be ashamed unless his conscience was defiled by
transgression of His law in fact or supposition, directed His
next inquiry so as at once to elicit a confession of the whole

115

truth. "Who told thee", said He, "that thou wast naked?" Did I tell thee, or did any of the Elohim? Or, "Hast thou eaten of the tree whereof I commanded thee that thou shouldest not eat?" Thou hast no cause to be afraid of Me, or ashamed of thine appearance as I have formed thee; unless thou hast sinned against Me by transgressing My law. Thou hast heard My voice, and stood upright and naked in My presence before, and wert not ashamed; what hast thou done? Why coverest thou thy transgression by hiding thine iniquity in thy bosom? (Job 31:33).

But Adam, still unwilling to be blamed according to his demerits, in confessing reflected upon the Lord God, and turned evidence against Eve. "The woman", said he, "whom *thou* gavest to be with me, *she* gave me of the tree, and I did eat." As much as to say, If thou hadst not put her in my way, and I had been left to myself, I should not have done it. It is she who is chiefly to blame; for she not only ate herself, but tempted me.

The offence being traced to Eve, the Lord Elohim said to her, "what is this that *thou* hast done?" But her ingenuousness was no more conspicuous than Adam's. She confessed that she had eaten, but excused herself on the ground of a deception having been practised upon her by the serpent: "The serpent beguiled me", said she, "and I did eat."

There is no evidence that the Serpent either touched the tree, or ate of its fruit. Indeed, if he had he would have committed no offence; for the law was not given to him, but to Adam and Eve only; and "where there is no law there is no transgression". Besides, Paul says Eve was the first in the transgression. The Lord God, therefore, did not interrogate the Serpent as He had the others. He had, by his clumsy interpretation of what he had seen and heard, corrupted Eve's mind from the simplicity of faith, and obedience to the divine law; but he was incapable of showing upon what moral grounds he had called in question its *literality*. He *thought* they would not surely die; because he *thought* they could as well eat of the tree of life as of the tree of knowledge of good and evil. He thought nothing of the immorality of the Lord God's solemnly declaring a thing, and not performing it. Cognizance of the morality of thoughts and actions was beyond the sphere of his mentality. With all his superior shrewdness, he was neither responsible, nor able to give an account.

All the evidence in the case being elicited, the Lord God proceeded to pass sentence upon the accused in the order of their conviction. Being incriminated by Eve, and having, in effect, accused God of lying, the Lord began with him, and said, "Because thou hast *done* this, thou art cursed above all cattle, and above every beast of the field; upon thy belly shalt thou go, and dust shalt thou eat all the days of thy life; and I will put *enmity* between *thee* and the *woman*, and between *thy seed* and *her seed*: He shall bruise *thy head*, and thou shalt bruise *his heel*."

This sentence was both *literal* and *allegorical*, like the rest of the things exhibited in the Mosaic account; being "representations of the knowledge and the truth" (Romans 2:20; Hebrews 8:5; 9:9,23,24; 10:1; Romans 5:14; Galatians 4:24). For the information of the unlearned reader I remark, that to allegorize is to speak in such a way that something else is intended than is contained in the words literally construed. The historical allegory has *a double sense*, namely, the *literal* and the *figurative*; and the latter is as *real*, as the former is essential to its existence. Thus, the *literal* serpent was *allegorical* of "sin in the flesh"; which is therefore figuratively styled the serpent, etc., as before explained. The literal formation of Eve out of Adam's side was allegorical of the formation of the church out of him, of whom Adam was the figure; therefore, the church is the figurative Eve, and its temptation illustrated by that of the literal one. The examples of this are almost infinite. That of Abraham, Sarah and Hagar as allegorized by Paul in the text below, is a beautiful illustration of the relation between the literal and the figurative, as they are employed in the scriptures of truth. The discernment of the due limit between them is acquired, not by rules, but by much and diligent study of the word.

The literal is the exact construction of the sentence as it reads, and is found in strict accordance with their natural habit, and mutual antipathy between serpents and mankind. They go upon the belly, and lick the dust; and by the deadly quality of their venom, or "sting", they are esteemed more hateful than any other creatures. In walking *with a naked foot* one would be bitten in the *heel*, whose retaliation would be instinctively to bruise the reptile's *head*. This is all perfectly natural; but what does it suggest?

Much that might be said upon the allegorical meaning of this passage is already before the reader. I shall add, therefore, by way of summary, the following particulars: —

1. The Serpent as the author of sin is allegorical of "sin in the flesh"; which is therefore called ὁ πονηρός, "the Wicked One"; and symbolized in its personal and political agency by "the Serpent".

2. The putting of "enmity" between the Serpent and the woman is allegorical of the establishment of enmity between sin, incorporate in the institutions of the world, or the serpent: and the obedience of faith, embodied in the congregation of the Lord, which is the woman.

3.   The *"seed of the Serpent"* is allegorical of those over whom sin reigns, as evinced in their obeying it in the lusts thereof. They are styled *"the servants of sin"* (Romans 6:12,17,19); or, "the tares" (Matthew 13:25,38).

4.   The *"seed of the woman"* is allegorical of *"the children of the kingdom"* (Matthew 13:25,38), or "the servants of right-eousness" (Romans 6:12,17,19). They are also termed "the good seed" (Matthew 13:23,38), who hear and understand the word of the kingdom, sown in their hearts as "incorruptible seed" (1 Peter 1:23).

5.   The seed of the Serpent, and the seed of the woman, are phrases to be taken in the singular and plural numbers. Plurally, in the sense of the fourth particular; and singularly, *of two separate hostile personages.*

6.   The serpent-bruiser of the heel is the sixth, or Imperial, head of the Dragon, to be crushed at the period of its binding, in the person of the last of the Autocrats.

7.   The head-bruiser of the dragon, the old serpent, sur-named the Devil and Satan, is emphatically the Seed of the woman, but not of the man.

The allegorical reading of the text founded upon these par-ticulars is as follows: "I will put the enmity (Romans 8:7) of that mode of thinking thou hast elicited in Eve and her hus-band against My law, between the powers that shall be here-after, in consequence of what thou hast done, and the faithful and unblemished corporation I shall constitute: and I will put this enmity of the spirit against the flesh, and of the flesh against the spirit (Galatians 5:16-17; 4:29), between all who obey the lusts of the flesh which thou hast excited, and those of My institution who shall serve me: their Chief shall bear away the world's sin (John 1:29) which thou hast originated, and shall destroy all the works (1 John 3:8) that have grown out of it: and the sin-power (John 19:10) shall wound him to death; but he shall recover it, and accomplish the work I now pre-ordain him to do."

THE PEACE AND SAFETY CRY

"There is no peace to the wicked, saith God."

THE allegorical signification of the sentence became the plan of "the foundation of the world", under the altered circum-stances which sin had introduced. It constitutes the earth the arena of a terrible strife between two hostile powers, which was not to terminate until His law gained the ascendancy over the sin of the world, and but one sovereign will be obeyed by the sons of men. The enmity He put between these parties was not a mere unfriendly verbal disputation, but one which reeked of blood. It began with the dispute which caused Abel to lose his life, and has continued unto this day. For nearly 6,000 years has this enmity made the earth a field of blood, and yet the war is not ended. The sin-power still lords it over the world, and is marshalling its forces for a last decisive blow. The "powers that be" have laid low the saints of God in all the countries of their dominion; they have bruised them in the heel; and are now taking up their positions, and preparing themselves to arbitrate their relative and future destiny by the sword. They have forgotten, or are indifferent to, the enormities of the past. They know not that the righteous blood they have shed upon the earth cries loudly for vengeance in the ears of God. Truth, justice, and equity their souls hate; and all that they propose is to destroy the liberty and happiness of mankind; and to make eternal their own vicious and hateful rule.

But God is as just as He is full of goodness, mercy, and truth. "The death of his saints is precious in the sight of the LORD": and He will not permit them to go unavenged. The "powers that be" can, therefore, no more perpetually exist than convicted robbers and murderers can escape the punishment due to their crimes. The law of retribution to which God has assigned the adjudication of their punishment says, "Give them blood to drink, for they are deserving; *because they have shed the blood of saints and prophets*" (Revelation 16:6); "Reward them even as they have rewarded you, and double unto them double according to their works; in the cup which they have filled, fill to them double" (Revelation 18:6).

But, though the scriptures of truth are so explicit with respect to the blasphemous and felonious character of the governments of the world; though they denounce the judgments of war, pestilence, and famine upon the nations subject to them; though they declare that the wicked are the Lord's sword to execute his judgments upon one another; though they most emphatically and solemnly aver that God says "there shall be no peace to the wicked" (Isaiah 57:21); and though men see, and *profess* to deplore, the whoredoms and witchcrafts of the Roman Jezebel, and the enormities of the cruel tyrants who pour out their victims' blood like water to uphold her: notwithstanding all this, there are multitudes of people who pretend to take the Bible as the rule of their faith; who claim to be "pious", and class themselves among the saints of the Lord: I say, men of these pretensions, headed by political and spiritual guides, are clamouring for the abolition of war, and the settlement of all international differences by arbitration!

Such persons may be very benevolent, or very covetous; but they are certainly not very wise. Their outcry about "peace" evinces their ignorance of the nature of "sinful flesh", and of the testimony of God; or, if cognizant of them, their infidelity, and shallowness of mind. Before peace can be established in the world, "the enmity" which God has put between good and evil, in word and deed, must be abolished. Peace is to be deprecated as a calamity by the faithful, so long as the Roman Jezebel and her paramours are found among the living. "What peace, so long as her whoredoms and witchcrafts are so many?" (2 Kings 9:22). Will they destroy the divisions among powers and people, which God's truth is ever calculated to make where it is received in whole or part? Arbitration indeed! And who are to be the arbitrators? The popes, cardinals, priests, emperors, and kings of the nations? Can justice, integrity, and good faith, proceed from such reprobates? Do the Quakers, and financial, or acquisitive, reformers imagine that a righteous arbitration could emanate from them upon any question in which the interests of nations as opposed to theirs were concerned? Really, the conceit of pious infidelity is egregiously presumptuous. If this peace mania be a specimen of *"the light within"*, alas! how great is the darkness of that place which professes to be enlightened by it.

But the most absurd thing imaginable is that the arbitrationists profess to advocate peace upon scriptural grounds! Because one of the titles of the Lord is "the Prince of Peace", they argue that war is displeasing to God: and that Jesus came to establish peace as the result of preaching. But war is not displeasing to God any more than a rod is displeasing to him that uses it for correction. *God instituted war when He put enmity between the serpent and the woman.* It is a divine institution for the punishment of the transgressors of His law; and a most beneficent one too: for all the little liberty the world enjoys is attributable to the controversy of the tongue, the pen, and the sword. What would have been the fate of the thirteen trans-Atlantic Colonies, if they had been left to the arbitrative justice of George the Third's contemporaries? The heel of spiritual tyranny backed by the civil power, would have trampled upon them to this moment. The weak who contend for liberty and truth, have everything to dread from arbitration. With sword in hand, they may extort justice from the strong; but, if under the necessity of expecting it at the conscience and tender mercies of "the powers that be", the award will be a mockery of justice, and an insult to the sufferings of the oppressed.

Yes, verily, the Lord Jesus is "the *Prince* of Peace"; and therefore, no peace society can give peace to the world. It is he alone who can establish "peace on earth and good will among men"; for he only is morally fit and potentially competent to do it. The peace of the arbitrationists is based upon the transgression of the divine law; and the hostility of the covenanters to the gospel of the kingdom. It is an impure peace; peace with the serpent power reigning over the blood-stained earth. Such a peace as this avaunt! Eternal war is better for the world than such a compromise with sin. The peace Messiah brings is *"first pure"*. It is a peace the result of conquest; the tranquillity which succeeds the bruising of the Serpent's head. It is consequent upon the establishment of God's sovereignty over the nations, by the hand of him whom he hath prepared to "break in pieces the oppressor", and let the oppressed go free. *"In his days* shall the righteous flourish; and *abundance of peace* so long as the moon endures. His enemies shall lick the dust; all nations shall serve him, and call him blessed" (Psalm 72:4,7,11,17; Revelation 11:18). Then shall he judge among them, and rebuke them, and speak peace to them (Zechariah 9:10); and "they shall beat their swords into ploughshares, and their spears into pruning hooks: nation shall not lift up sword against nation, neither shall they learn war any more" (Isaiah 2:4).

But the Father did not send Jesus with the idea of bringing about this mighty revolution among the nations by preaching the gospel; neither did He propose to effect it in the absence of His Son. *When he appeared in humiliation he came to take away peace from the earth*, as both his words and history prove. "Suppose ye that I am come to give peace on earth? I tell you, Nay; but rather division. I am come to send fire upon the earth; and what will I if it be already kindled?" (Luke 12:49,51) "I come not to send peace, but a sword. For I am come to set man at variance against his nearest and dearest relations. So that man's foes shall be they of his own household" (Matthew 10:34-36). This is the way the Prince of Peace spoke when on earth. The doctrine he taught is distasteful to the natural mind; and, by the purity of its principles, and astonishing nature of its promises, excites the enmity and incredulity of the flesh. Loving sin and hating righteousness, the carnal mind becomes the enemy and persecutor of those who advocate it. The enmity on the part of the faithless is inveterate: and where they have the power, they stir up war even at the domestic health. If the believer will agree to be silent, or to renounce his faith, there will then be "peace and love" such as the world, that "loves its own", is able to afford. But the true believers are not permitted to make any compromise of the kind. They are commanded to "contend earnestly for the faith once delivered to the saints" (Jude 3), and so long as they do this, they may lay their account with tribulation of various kinds. There is a vast deal of this false peace and spurious charity in the Protestant world. Men have become traitors to Christ, and betray him with their lips. They say, "O how we love the Lord!" and were he here they would doubtless kiss him; but, like Judas, they have colleagued with his enemies, and are as popular with the world as its god can possibly desire.

The truth is, judging from their arguments, the peace-mongers are not so man-loving as they pretend. The cry for peace is a piece of ventriloquism emanating from the pocket. Their strongest argument against war is based upon its cost. The taxes are burdensome because of the extravagance and warlike habits of past governments. This pinches them in the iron chest; and diminishes the profits of trade; and curtails the means of indulging the lusts of their flesh, of their eyes, and the pride of life. It is well these mammon-worshippers should feel the pinch. They are the enemies of God, and oblivious of His slaughtered saints, and, therefore, richly deserving of all the punishment the recklessness of "the powers" has entailed upon the world. Those who escape the sword and the famine groan under the expense of *punishing the wicked at their own cost*. Thus, the punishment re-acts upon all classes. I say, these peace-criers are the enemies of God; for with all their profession of piety, they are at peace with the world, and in high esteem and friendship with it; and *"whosoever"*, says the scripture, *"is a friend of the world is the enemy of God"*.

Look at the peace congress at Paris,* composed of popish priests, dissenting ministers, French politicians, self-illuminati of the Quaker School, English radicals, American priests of all colours, rationalists, infidels, etc., etc.; all in such high favour with the *liberticide dynasty* of France, as to be let into *"Egypt and Sodom"* (Revelation 11:8) without passports, or custom-house scrutiny; and to be *fêted* by one of the state officials. In what way can the world show its friendship to the Peace Society more palpably; or the Society its reciprocity of feeling with the most godless and Christless portion of it? The Peace Society is the world's beloved friend. The world wants peace, that it may find a respite from the judgments of God for its iniquity; and that it may enrich itself by commerce, and enjoy itself in all the good things of life. The Society is the world's *employee*; its zealous, utopian, missionary; and, therefore, individually and collectively *"the enemy of God"*.

Still, even out of so impious a speculation as this Peace Society, "the wise who understand" (Daniel 12:10) may extract encouragement. They will discern a providence in the

---

* Opened in August, 1849.

foundation of the Quaker sect. The unscriptural cry of "peace and safety" emanated from them. They have gained wealth in the temple of their god; and this, with their friend "the world", is a sufficient guarantee of their worth and respectability. Whatever they were in the beginning matters not; they are now the most popular of all religionists with the masses; to please whom a man must pander to their propensities. All sorts of anti-government factions colleague with the Quakers in their cry of peace; not because they love peace for its own sake; but by curtailing the resources of the state, and so necessitating the reduction of armies, they think they can the more easily supersede the existing tyrannies by a still worse one of their own, as it would doubtless prove. This unhallowed coalition proclaims its outcry to be *"the world's cry"*.

We accept it as such. It is the cry of the world, which echoes in tones of thunder in the ears of the true believers. It is a cry, in the providence of God, which is a great "sign of the times"; announcing that "the Lord standeth at the door and knocks" (Revelation 3:20), and is about quickly and unexpectedly to appear (16:15; 22:7,20) It is the world's cry, as the cry of a woman in travail, which has been extorted by sudden and tormenting pains. It blows a trumpet in the wise and understanding ear, sounding the approach of "the day of the Lord as a thief in the night" for "so it cometh; and *when they shall say*, PEACE *and* SAFETY; *then sudden destruction cometh upon them*, as travail upon a woman with child; and they shall not escape" (1 Thessalonians 5:1-3). Such is the divine mission of the Quakers, and their allies the Cobdenite Reformers. Not satisfied with crying peace, they cry "SAFETY" likewise. This is a peculiar feature of Cobdenism, which urges the disbandment of regiments, and the dismantling of ships, on the perverse presumption that danger there is none! Blind leaders of the blind! The groans of nations ascending to heaven on every side; the kindling embers of war smoking in Rome, Vienna,

---

*CONSTANTINOPLE.—In October, 1853, "the embers" blazed up in Constantinople, and the Sultan declared war against Russia. In February, 1854, Mr. J. Sturge and other Quakers of the Bright and Cobden School were received at St. Petersburg by Czar Nicholas, who spoke peace and fought on. In March, England and France declared war against Russia. VIENNA—In 1859 the fire blazed up in Vienna. Napoleon III picked a quarrel with Austria. "A mission of peace", in the hands of Lord Cowley, was only the prelude to the Austro-Sardinian war. ROME.—The Peace Congress of Geneva (September, 1867), at which Garibaldi was present, was immediately followed by the revolution; and the Fall of the Temporal Power followed in 1870. So afterwards, when we saw the Peace Congress at the Hague (1899) followed in the same year by the war in South Africa; and still more recently, the "Peace of Munich" followed by the outbreak of the Second "World War".

and Constantinople*—and yet ye cry "Peace and safety"; surely ye are incorrigibly demented, and ripe for capture and destruction.

CAIN, ABEL, AND SETH

"If thou doest well, shalt thou not be accepted?"

THE allegorical signification of the sentence upon the Serpent kindled the first scintillation of hope in the human heart of the appearance of One, who should deliver the world from all its ills, and advance it to a higher state. The promise of such a personage, and of such a consummation, was the nucleus of that "faith, which is the assured expectation of things hoped for, and the conviction of things unseen" (Hebrews 11:1). The belief, and spiritualizing influence, of this hope, became the ground of acceptance with God in the earliest times. Faith in this promise was established as the principle of classification among the sons of Adam. Belief in what He promises is belief in God; and its influence upon "the fleshy tablet of the heart" is most edifying in its effect, making the subject of it "a partaker of the divine nature". Atheism in its scriptural import is not the denial of God's existence. None but a fool would say, "There is no God" (Psalm 14:1). It is worse than this. It is to believe that He exists, and yet to treat Him as a liar. To do this, is not to believe His promises; and he that is faithless of these, is "without God", ἄθεος—i.e., an atheist in the world (Ephesians 2:12).

In the beginning, this kind of atheism soon manifested itself in the family of Adam. Cain, who was conceived in sin, true to his paternity, was as faithless of God's word as the Serpent; while Abel believed on God. Hence, the apostle says, "By faith Abel offered unto God a fuller sacrifice (πλείονα θυσίαν) than Cain, by which he obtained witness that he was righteous, God testifying of his gifts; and by it he being dead yet speaketh" (Hebrews 11:4). This is an important intimation, importing that no religious services are acceptable to God, which are not predicated on the belief of His promises; for without faith it is impossible to please God" (Hebrews 11:6).

This was, therefore, the ground of Cain's reprobation. "The Lord had respect unto Abel and to his offering: but unto Cain and his offering he had not respect". This made Cain fierce and sullen. He refused to "bring the firstlings of the flock, and of the fat thereof". He did not believe in its necessity, having no faith in the remission of sins by the shedding of sacrificial blood (Hebrews 9:22; 10:4-14); nor in the fulfilment of God's promise concerning him, who, being "bruised in the heel", or slain as Abel's accepted lamb, should arise, and "bruise the Serpent's head", *in destroying the works of sin* (1 John 3:8). This is what Cain did not believe; and his faithlessness expressed itself in neglecting to walk in "the way of the LORD." Nevertheless, he continued "a professor of religion"; for "he brought of the fruit of the ground an offering to the LORD". But the Lord paid no respect to him or his offering; because, in neglecting the sacrifice, he had set up his judgment against God; and in being faithless had in effect treated God as a liar; for, saith the scripture, "he that believeth not God hath made him a liar" (1 John 5:10).

But Cain's sullen anger against God could only wound himself. His refusal to obey Him could not injure the Most High. He insulted God with his "will-worship and voluntary humility" (Colossians 2:18,23), and convicted himself as an *evil-doer*. Self-condemned and impotent, he vented his rage against his brother, whom God respected and had accepted. He was wroth against him: "because his own works were evil, and his brother's righteous" (1 John 3:12,15). He was now a murderer in principle; and with this fratricidal feeling rankling in his heart, brought his gift to the altar (Matthew 5:22-24). But God, who "discerns the thoughts and intents of the heart" (Hebrews 4:12), called him to account for his lowering aspect, and anger against his brother, and said, "If thou *doest well*, shalt thou not be accepted? And if thou doest not well, a sin-offering lieth at the door. And his hope shall be towards thee, and thou shalt rule over him", or have the excellency as the first-born and progenitor of the Seed. But Cain was a genuine "seed of the Serpent". The thinking of *the flesh* called by Adam the Serpent, was strong within him. He talked with Abel, who doubtless, pleaded for the things repudiated by Cain. But Cain's reasonings were perverse; well-doing was not at all to his taste; so that, having no faith in the *promise*, he preferred to follow his own waywardness; and being determined to rid himself of his brother's expostulations, he mingled his blood with the dust of the ground.

Thus was slain by a brother's hand the protomartyr of the faith. A righteous man, respected and beloved of God. His only offence was, that, in believing the promises of God and doing well, his brother was reproved. The fleshly mind hates righteousness, and those who practise it; so that between the two parties *the truth and righteousness of God* (Matthew 6:33; Romans 1:16,17; 3:21,22,25,26) lie as an apple of discord. Abel was the first of Eve's sons of whom honourable mention is made on account of "the obedience of faith" (Romans 16:25,26; 1:5). As Cain was of the evil one by transgression; so Abel was

125

of God by the obedience of faith, which evinced that "God's seed remained in him". Hence though both of them were born of Eve according to the flesh, their spiritual paternity was as opposite as light and darkness. Cain was a man of sin; and Abel an accepted son of God. In these characters, they stood at the head of two divisions of their father's family; and proximately represented the seed of the Serpent, and the seed of the Woman. Cain bruised his brother's heel; but God appointed a substitute for Abel in the person of Seth, by whom Cain's headship was bruised, and his posterity superseded in the earth. Eve, says Moses, "bare a son, and called his name Seth: for, said she, God hath *appointed me* another seed *instead* of Abel, whom Cain slew".

She had many other sons, but none of them are mentioned except Cain, Abel, and Seth. When, therefore, we are informed that Seth was "appointed *instead* of Abel", and trace the posterity of Seth terminating through a certain line in Jesus of Nazareth, the Son of God; we are taught that Cain lost his excellency by sin, and was therefore set aside; and Abel provisionally appointed to be the progenitor of the seed, who is to bruise the Serpent's headship over the world. But, Abel having been bruised in the heel, it became necessary, in order to carry out the divine purpose, and to answer allegorically the indications of the sentence upon the Serpent, to appoint another son of Eve in the place of Abel. According to this arrangement, Abel became the type of Jesus, wounded in the heel; but whose sprinkled blood speaks better things than Abel's (Hebrews 12:24), which cried only for vengeance: while Seth typifies him in his re-appearance among the sons of men to bruise sin under foot, and to exterminate in the course of his reign the Serpent's seed from the face of the earth.

Notwithstanding his crime Cain was permitted to live. But the seed of evil-doers never gets renown. Sooner or later their deeds of villainy consign their names to reprobation. God hid His face from Cain, and exiled him from the settlements in Eden. He wandered still further to the east, "and dwelt in the land of Nod". There he founded a city, and called it Enoch. His offspring multiplied, and found out many inventions. They became wandering tribes, dwelling in tents and tending cattle; others of them musicians; and artificers in brass and iron. Their women were beautiful, and as the descendants of Cain, untrained in the nurture and admonition of the Lord, were vain in their imaginations, and demoralizing in their associations.

Seth's descendants in the direct line ended in Noah and Japheth at the time of the flood. His posterity, in this and the collateral branches, multiplied considerably; but for a time constituted a separate community from the progeny of Cain.

During the lifetime of Enos, son of Seth, "they began to call themselves by the name of the LORD", or *"sons of God"* (Genesis 4:26; 6:2): while the faithless and corrupt worshippers of the land of Nod were simply styled *"men"*.

THE ANTEDILUVIAN APOSTASY

THE Sethites and the Cainites stood related to one another as the church of God and the world; or, as the Woman and the Serpent. So long as the sons of God maintained their integrity, and walked in *"the way of the Tree of Life"*, the two communities had no religious associations, or family intercourse. The time, however, arrived when the middle wall of partition was about to be laid low by a general apostasy. A spirit of liberalism had arisen among the sons and daughters of Seth, the result of an expiring faith, which predisposed them to a fraternity, or mixed community, with the Cainites; who, like their father, were religionists of a wilful stamp. The Serpent's seed enjoyed themselves in those days as they do now. They were men of the flesh, grovelling in their tastes, habits, and pursuits; and devoted to the lust of the flesh, the lust of the eyes, and the pride of life. Their religion sanctified what pleased them best; and doubtless afforded a fair specimen of the same sort of thing in all subsequent ages.

It is probable that the precepts and example of the sons of God had considerably modified the original impiety of the Cainites so as to bring things to a similar state to that observable in our day. Sects, between whom there were no more dealings in their beginning than between the Jews and the Samaritans, are now so liberal that they agree to be silent upon all controversial topics for which they once contended to the death, and to recognize one another as brethren in the Lord! Thus, if they ever had the truth they have suppressed it by a tacit compromise; and have become highly respectable, and singularly amiable and polite; so that they "have need of nothing", but to enjoy the good things of the world within their reach.

The serpents had become so harmless, and even pious, under the influence abroad, and were withal so fair to look upon, and so enchanting in their ways, that the Sethites took them into their bosoms, and cherished them with the affection of their own flesh.

"They saw", says Moses, "that the daughters of men were fair; and they took wives of all they chose." This was a fatal step. Can a man take fire into his bosom and not be burned? The sons of God corrupted themselves in marrying the daughters of Cain. Instead of bringing them over to *"the Way of the*

Tree of Life", they were beguiled into "*the Way of Cain*" (Jude 11). For sons of God to marry daughters of Belial is to jeopardize their fidelity to God. This practice has ever been fruitful of apostasy.

Balaam was well aware of this; and knowing that the only way to bring a curse upon Israel was to involve them in transgression, he therefore taught Balak, the King of Moab, to tempt them with the fair daughters of his people, as the readiest way of beguiling them into the worship of their idols; which would cause God to hate them, and so facilitate their conquest by the Moabites. The policy succeeded but too well for the honour and happiness of Israel. Moses says, "They began to commit whoredom with the daughters of Moab". The consequence of this licentiousness was that the women invited Israel unto the sacrifices of their gods: and they did eat, and bowed down to them. And Israel joined himself unto Baal-Peor (Numbers 25:1,2). And the anger of the Lord was kindled against them; so that He slew four and twenty-thousand of them.

After the same example, the union of the Sethites and Cainites was productive of the worst results. The offspring of this union were "mighty men of renown", whose wickedness "was great in the earth"; for "every imagination of the thoughts of their hearts was only evil continually" (Genesis 6:1-5). Their apostasy, however, was not perfected without remonstrance on the part of God. There was one eminent man of whom it was testified, that "he pleased God". He "walked with God" in the way of the Tree of Life for three hundred years after the birth of Methuselah. His name is Enoch. The spirit of prophecy was in him; and the gigantic wickedness of the Antediluvians aroused him to reprove their iniquity. Animated by the hope of the promise concerning the woman's seed, he prophesied of the serpents of his own and future time, saying, "Behold, the Lord cometh with myriads of his saints, to dispense justice towards all, and to convict all that are ungodly among them of their ungodly deeds which they have impiously committed; and of all their hard speeches, which ungodly sinners have spoken against him" (Jude 14,15). But his expostulation was unheeded; and God graciously "translated him that he should not see death" (Hebrews 11:5,26); thus rewarding him for his constancy, and *giving the faithful a notable illustration and earnest* of "the recompense of the reward", and the certainty of the punishment of the world.

Things went on from bad to worse "for *all* flesh had corrupted *His Way* upon the earth"; "and the earth was filled with violence". Before, however, things had come to the worst the Lord made another effort to reclaim the Antediluvians.

He had resolved to put an end to the wickedness of man upon the earth; for, said He, "*My Spirit* shall *not always* strive with him because he is but flesh" (Genesis 6:3). This intimates a limit to His forbearance; that it should have an end, but not immediately; for it is added, "Yet his days shall be a hundred and twenty years".

Four hundred and eighty years before the announcement of this determination, a son was born to Lamech, the grandson of Enoch, whom he named Noah; that is, Comfort, saying, "This same shall comfort us concerning our work and toil of our hands, because of the ground which the LORD hath cursed". This was the hope of those who remained faithful of the sons of Seth. They laboured in hope of a translation into a rest from their labours, when the curse should be removed from the earth (Revelation 22:3). In process of time, Noah was "warned of God of things not seen as yet". Noah believed them; and "God *by his spirit*" in him, "went and preached to the spirits (now) in prison" (1 Peter 3:19), that is, to the Antediluvians "who were disobedient in the days of Noah". He warned them of the coming flood, which would "destroy them from the earth"; and proved to them his own conviction of its certainty by "preparing an ark for the safety of his own house; by the which he condemned the world, and became heir of the righteousness which is by faith" (Hebrews 11:7). But, his faith thus made perfect by his works, made no salutary impression upon his contemporaries. "They were eating and drinking, marrying and giving in marriage, until the day that Noah entered into the ark, and knew not till the flood came, and took them all away" (Matthew 24:38-39); leaving only eight persons *of the sons of Seth* alive.

Thus was the mingled seed of Seth and Cain exterminated from the earth. Cain's race became utterly extinct, and those only of Seth remained, who were upright in their generations, and who walked with God. The distinction of seeds was temporarily suspended. The generation of vipers was extinct; but sin in the flesh survived—a principle, destined in after times to produce the most hideous and terrible results.

THE FOUNDATION OF THE WORLD

"Inherit the Kingdom prepared from the Foundation of the World."

AS the woman had so wilfully sought the gratification of her flesh, when the Lord God passed sentence upon her He made it the ground of her punishment. "I will", said He, "greatly multiply thy sorrow and thy conception; in sorrow thou shalt bring forth children: and thy desire shall be subject to thy husband, and he shall rule over thee." This being her portion as the consequence of sin, the reverse would have been her condition, so long as her animal nature should have continued unchanged, if she had remained obedient. She would have brought forth children without pain, and would have had fewer of them; nor would she have been deprived of that equality she enjoyed in the garden, and consequently she would have escaped that degradation she has experienced in all the countries of the world.

The punishment, however, was not inflicted simply as an individual sorrow. The pain was personal, and the subjection likewise; but the multiplication of woman's conception became necessary from the altered circumstances of things; which were then being constituted for the ensuing seven thousand years. In the war divinely instituted between the seeds of the Serpent and the Woman, there would be a great loss of life. The population of the world would be greatly thinned; besides which great havoc would be made by pestilence, famine, and the ordinary diseases of the flesh. To compensate this waste, and still to maintain an increase, so that the earth might be filled, necessitated that part of woman's punishment involved in the multiplication of the conception, which is a great domestic calamity under the Serpent-dominion of sin.

We hear much in some parts of the world of the political rights and equality of women with men; and of their preaching and teaching in public assemblies. We need wonder at nothing which emanates from the unenlightened thinking of sinful flesh. There is no absurdity too monstrous to be sanctified by unspiritualized animal intellect. Men do not think according to God's thinking, and therefore it is they run into the most unscriptural conceits; among which may be enumerated the political and social equality of women. Trained to usefulness, of cultivated intellect and with moral sentiments purified and ennobled by the nurture and admonition of the Lord's truth, women are "helps meet" for the Elohim; and much too good for men of ordinary stamp. The sex is susceptible of this exaltation; though I despair of witnessing it in many instances till "the Age to come". But, even women of this excellency of mind and disposition, were it able for such to do so, would be guilty of indiscretion, presumption, and rebellion against God's law, in assuming equality of rank, equality of rights, and authority over man, which is implied in teaching and preaching. It is the old ambition of the sex to be equal to the gods; but in taking steps to attain it, they involved themselves in subjection to men. Preaching, and lecturing, women are but species of actresses, who exhibit upon the boards for the amusement of sinful and foolish men. They

aim at an equality for which they are not physically constituted; they degrade themselves by the exhibition, and in proportion as they rise in assurance, they sink in all that really
adorns a woman.

The law, which forms a part of the foundation of the world,
says to the woman, "*He* shall reign over thee". The nature of
this subjection is well exhibited in the Mosaic law (Numbers
30:3-15). A daughter being yet in her youth in her father's
house, could only make a vow subject to his will. If he held
his peace, and said nothing for or against, she was bound by
her word; but if when he heard it, he disallowed it, she was
not bound to perform; and the Lord forgave the failure of the
vow. The same law applied to a wife. A widow, or divorced
woman, were both bound to fulfil; unless their husbands had
made them void before separation. If not, being subject to
God, they had no release.

This throws light upon the apostle's instructions concerning women. "They are commanded to be under obedience, as
also saith the law." And "Let the woman learn in silence with
all subjection. But I suffer not a woman to teach, nor to *usurp*
authority over man, but to be in silence". The reason he gives
for imposing silence and subjection, is remarkable. He
adduces the priority of Adam's formation; and the unhappy
consequences of Eve's talkativeness and leadership in transgression; as it is written, "Adam was first formed, then Eve.
And Adam was not deceived, but the woman being deceived
was in the transgression" (1 Timothy 2:11-14) first. And then,
as to their public ministrations, he says, "Let women keep
silence in the congregations; for it is not permitted unto them
to speak; but to be under obedience, as saith the law. And if
they will learn any thing, let them ask their husbands at
home: for it is a shame for women to speak in the congregation" (1 Corinthians 14:34,35). It is true, that in another place
the apostle says, "Let the aged women be teachers of good
things"; but then this teaching is not to be in the congregation, or in the brazen attitude of a public oratrix. They are to
exercise their gift of teaching privately among their own sex,
"that they may teach the young women to be sober, to love
their husbands, to love their children, to be discreet, chaste,
keepers at home, good, obedient to their own husbands, that
the word of God (which they profess), be not blasphemed"
(Titus 2:4,5).

Christian women should not copy after the god-aspiring
Eve, but after Sarah, the faithful mother of Israel, who sub-
mitted herself in all things to Abraham, "calling him lord"
(Genesis 18:12). Nor should their obedience be restricted to
Christian husbands only. They should also obey them "*with-
out the word*"; that is, those who have not submitted to it, in

order that they may be won over to the faith when they behold the chaste and respectful behaviour of their wives, produced by a belief of the truth (1 Peter 3:1-6).

Such are the statutory provisions enacted in the world's constitution at the beginning, with respect to the position of women in the body social and political. Any attempt to alter the arrangement is rebellion against God, and usurpation of the rights of men to whom God has subjected them. Their wisdom is to be quiet, and to make their influence felt by their excellent qualities. They will then rule in the hearts of their rulers, and so ameliorate their own subjection as to convert it into a desirable and sovereign obedience.

A man should never permit the words of a woman to intervene between him and the laws of God. This is a rock upon which myriads have made shipwreck of the faith. Adam sinned in consequence of listening to Eve's silvery discourse. No temptation has proved more irresistible to the flesh than the enticing words of woman's lips. "They drop as a honeycomb, and her mouth is smoother than oil: but her end is bitter as wormwood, and sharp as a two-edged sword. Her feet go down to death; and her steps take hold on hell" (Proverbs 5:3-5). Adam was a striking illustration of this truth, as appears from the sentence pronounced upon him. "Because", said the Lord God, "thou hast hearkened to the voice of thy wife, and hast eaten of the tree of which I commanded thee, saying, Thou shalt not eat of it: cursed is the ground for thy sake: in sorrow shalt thou eat of it all the days of thy life; thorns also and thistles shall it bring forth to thee; and thou shalt eat the herb of the field: in the sweat of thy face shalt thou eat bread, till thou return unto the ground; for out of it was thou taken: for dust thou art, and unto dust shalt thou return." Thus, having passed sentence upon the serpent, the woman, and the man, the Lord appointed them *a new law*, and expelled them from the garden He had made.

These three sentences, and the New Law, constitute *the foundation of the world*. This is a phrase which occurs in various passages of the Bible. It occupies a prominent place in the following text: "Then shall the King say unto them on his right hand, Come, ye blessed of my Father, inherit the kingdom prepared for you from the foundation of the world" (Matthew 25:34). The words in the Greek are ἀπὸ καταβολῆς κόσμου, which, more literally rendered, signify, *from laying the world's foundation*. The globe is the platform; the world that which is constituted, or built, upon it and the Builder is God; for "he that built all things is God" (Hebrews 3:4). Now, the world was not built out of nothing. The materials had been prepared by the work of the six days; and by the moral phenomena of the fall. At this crisis, there appeared a natural system of things, with two transgressors, in whom sin had enthroned itself; and who were endued with the power of multiplying such as themselves to an unlimited extent. This population, then, was either to act for itself under the uncontrolled dominion of sin; or, things must be so constituted as to bring it into order and subjection to the sovereignty of God. The result of the former alternative would have been to barbarize mankind, and to fill the earth with violence. This is demonstrated by what actually occurred before the flood when the divine constitution of things was corrupted and abolished by the world. *Man when left to himself never improves.* God made man upright; but look at the wretched specimens of humanity which are presented in those regions where God has left them to their natural tendency, under the impulse of their uncontrolled propensities. Man thus abandoned of God, degenerates into an ignorant savage, ferocious as the beasts of prey.

If the Lord God had renounced all interest in the earth, this would have been the consummation of His work. Man by his vices would have destroyed his own race. But, though transgression upon transgression marked his career, "God so loved the world" (John 3:16), that He determined that it should not perish, but should be rescued from evil in spite of itself. This He purposed to do in such a way as to make man reflect the divine nature in his character: and to display his own wisdom, glory, and power in the earth. But chance could not bring this to pass. Human life, therefore, was not to be a mere chapter of accidents; but the result of a well-digested and unvarying plan. Things, then, were to be arranged according to this purpose; so that in their original constitution should be contained *the rudiments* of a "glorious manifestation"; which, as a grain of mustard seed, should so unfold themselves under the fostering hand of God as to become "a tree, which is the greatest among herbs" (Matthew 13:31,32), in whose branches the family of man might be refreshed.

In the acorn, it is said, can be traced by aid of the microscope the branches of the future oak. So in "the Rudiments of the World" are traceable the things of the future Kingdom of God. These rudiments, or elements, are exhibited in the sentences upon the serpent, the woman, and the man; and in that institution styled "The Way of the Tree of Life". Out of these things was afterwards to arise the Kingdom of God; so that in constituting them, *a foundation was laid* upon which "the world to come" should be built; even that world of which Abraham was constituted the heir (Romans 4:13); and which, when finished at the end of six days of a thousand years each, will manifest the woman's Seed triumphant over the Serpent-power; resting from his work in the Sabbatism which remains for the people of God (Hebrews 4:3,8,9,11).

The things laid, or fixed, in the rudimental constitution of the world, may be summarily stated in the following particulars: —

1.   Sin in the flesh, the enemy of God, contending for the dominion of the world.

2.   Mankind in a state of nature, subject to the propensities; and to pain, trouble and death.

3.   Labour and toil the condition of existence in the present state.

4.   The subjection of woman to the lordship of man.

To these things was established a divine antagonism, by which they might be controlled; and a system of things elaborated in conformity with the purpose of God. This part of the foundation may be stated as:

1.   The law and truth of God as expressed in "His Way", demanding unreserved submission to its authority.

2.   Mankind under the influence of this truth assuredly believed, contending for it.

3.   Divine power exhibited in the punishment of men, and in the performance of His promises.

The action and re-action of these agencies upon one another was to produce:

1.   An enmity and war in the earth between the Sin-power and the Institution opposed to it.

2.   A bloody persecution of the adherents of the truth.

3.   The destruction of the Sin-power by a personage to be manifested for the purpose; and

4.   The consequent victory of divine truth, and establishment of the Kingdom of God.

That *the crisis of the fall was the period of laying the foundation of the world*, in its civil, social, and spiritual relations, appears from the use of the phrase in the apostolic writings. The Lord Jesus, speaking of what was about to come upon the generation then living in Judea, said, "The blood of all the prophets shed from the foundation of the world shall be required of this generation"; and to show to what period of the world he referred, he added by way of explanation, "from the blood of Abel" (Luke 11:50-51), the prophet of his day. The phrase is also applied by the apostle to the work of the six days (Hebrews 4:3-4); that is, as the basis, or substratum, in or upon which the social and political system was constituted. There is further proof of the judgment of the transgressors being the institutional foundation of the world, in the words, "all that dwell upon the earth shall do homage to him", the ten-horned papal Beast, "whose names are not written in the Book of Life of the Lamb *slain from the laying of the world's foundations*" (Revelation 13:8). By this is signified that, when the Lord God appointed coats of skins to cover the man's and woman's shame, lambs were slain, which they were taught to understand were representative of the Seed, who should be slain for the sins of all the faithful; and with whose righteousness they should be clothed, after the type of their covering by the skins of their sacrifices. Thus, from the institution of sacrifice in Paradise till the death of Jesus on the cross, he was typically slain; and the *accepted* worshippers, being full of faith in the divine promise, like Abel and Enoch, understood to what the slaughtered lambs referred. Their names were consequently written in the remembrance of God (Malachi 3:16; Revelation 17:8; 20:12; 21:27), as inheritors of the kingdom; whose foundation was commenced in Paradise, and has been preparing ever since, that when finished it may be manifested "in Eden the garden of the LORD".

THE CONSTITUTION OF SIN

"The creature was made subject to evil, not willingly, but by reason of him who subjected it in hope."

THE introduction of *sin* into the world necessitated the constitution of things as they were laid in the beginning. If there had been no sin there would have been no *"enmity"* between God and man; and consequently no antagonism by which to educe good out of evil. Sin and evil are as cause and effect. God is the author of evil, but not of sin; for the evil is the punishment of sin. "I form the light, and create darkness: I make peace, *and create evil*: I, the LORD, do all these things" (Isaiah 45:7). "Shall there be evil in a city, and the LORD hath not done it?" (Amos 3:6). The evil then to which man is subjected is the Lord's doing. War, famine, pestilence, flood, earthquake, disease, and death, are the terrible evils which God inflicts upon mankind for their transgressions. Nations cannot go to war when they please, any more than they can shake the earth at their will and pleasure; neither can they preserve peace, when He proclaims war. Evil is the artillery with which He combats the enemies of His law, and of His saints; consequently, there will be neither peace nor blessedness for the nations, until sin is put down, His people avenged, and truth and righteousness be established in the earth.

135

This is the constituted order of things. It is the constitution of the world; and as the world is sin's dominion, or the kingdom of the adversary, it is the constitution of the kingdom of sin.

The word *sin* is used in two principal acceptations in the scripture. It signifies in the first place, *"the transgression of the law"*; and in the next, it represents that physical principle of the animal nature, which is the cause of all its diseases, death, and resolution into dust. It is that in the flesh *"which has the power of death"*; and it is called *sin*, because the development, or fixation, of this evil in the flesh, was the result of transgression. Inasmuch as this evil principle pervades every part of the flesh, the animal nature is styled "sinful flesh," that is, *"flesh full of sin"*; so that *sin*, in the sacred style, came to stand for the substance called *man*. In human flesh "dwells no good thing"; and all the evil a man does is the result of this principle dwelling in him (Romans 7:18,17). Operating upon the brain, it excites the "propensities", and these set the "intellect" and "sentiments" to work. The propensities are blind, and so are the intellect and sentiments in a purely natural state; when therefore, the latter operate under the sole impulse of the propensities, "the understanding is darkened through ignorance, because of the blindness of the heart" (Ephesians 4:18). The nature of the lower animals is as full of this physical evil principle as the nature of man; though it cannot be styled *sin* with the same expressiveness; because it does not possess them as the result of their own transgression; the name, however, does not alter the nature of the thing.

A defective piece of mechanism cannot do good work. The principle must be perfect, and the adaptation true, for the working to be faultless. Man in his physical constitution is imperfect; and this imperfection is traceable to the physical organization of his flesh, being based on the principle of decay and reproduction from the blood; which, acted upon by the air, becomes the life of his flesh. All the phenomena which pertain to this arrangement of things are summed up in the simple word *sin*; which is, therefore, not an individual abstraction, but a concretion of relations in all animal bodies; and the source of all their physical infirmities. Now, the apostle says, that the flesh thinks—τὸ φρόνημα τῆς σαρκός—that is, the brain, as all who think are well assured from their own consciousness. If, then, this thinking organ be commanded not to do what is natural for it to do under blind impulse, will it not naturally disobey? Now this disobedience is wrong, because what God commands to be done is right, and only right; so that "by his law is the knowledge of sin"; and this law requiring an obedience which is not natural, flesh is sure to think in opposition to it. The philosophy of superstition is—*religion in harmony with the thinking of the flesh*; while true religion is religion in accordance with the thoughts of God as expressed in His law. Hence, it need excite no astonishment that religion and superstition are so hostile; and that all the world should uphold the latter; while so few are to be found who are identified with the religion of God. They are as opposite as flesh and spirit.

Sin, I say, is a synonym for human nature. Hence, the flesh is invariably regarded as *unclean*. It is therefore written, "How can he be clean who is born of a woman?" (Job 25:4) "Who can bring a clean thing out of an unclean? Not one" (Job 14:4). "What is man that he should be clean? And he which is born of a woman that he should be righteous? Behold, God putteth no trust in his saints; yea, the heavens are not clean in his sight. How much more abominable and filthy is man, who drinketh iniquity like water?" (Job 15:14-16). This view of sin in the flesh is enlightening in the things concerning Jesus. The apostle says, "God *made him to be sin* for us, who knew no sin" (2 Corinthians 5:21); and this he explains in another place by saying, that "He sent his own son *in the likeness of sinful flesh*, and for sin, condemned sin *in the flesh*" (Romans 8:3) in the offering of his body once (Hebrews 10:10,12,14). Sin could not have been condemned in the body of Jesus, if it had not existed there. His body was as unclean as the bodies of those for whom he died; for he was born of a woman, and "not one" can bring a clean body out of a defiled body; for "that", says Jesus himself, "which is born of the flesh is flesh" (John 3:6).

According to this physical law, the Seed of the woman was born into the world. The nature of Mary was as unclean as that of other women; and therefore could give birth only to "*a body*" like her own, though especially "*prepared* of God" (Hebrews 10:5). Had Mary's nature been immaculate, as her idolatrous worshippers contend, an immaculate body would have been born of her; which, therefore, would not have answered the purpose of God; which was to condemn sin in the flesh; a thing that could not have been accomplished, if there were no sin there.

Speaking of the conception and preparation of the Seed, the prophet as a typical person, says, "Behold, I was shapen in iniquity; and in sin did my mother conceive me" (Psalm 51:5). This is nothing more than affirming that he was born of sinful flesh; and not of the pure and incorruptible angelic nature.

Sinful flesh being the hereditary nature of the Lord Jesus, he was a fit and proper sacrifice for sin; especially as he was himself "innocent of the great transgression", having been

137

obedient in all things. Appearing in the nature of the seed of Abraham (Hebrews 2:16-18), he was subject to all the emotions by which we are troubled; so that he was enabled to sympathize with our infirmities (Hebrews 4:15), being "made *in all things* like unto his brethren". But, when he was "born of the Spirit", in the quickening of his mortal body by the spirit (Romans 8:11), he became a spirit; for "that which is born of the spirit *is spirit*". Hence, he is "the Lord the Spirit", incorruptible flesh and bones.

Sin in the flesh is hereditary; and entailed upon mankind as the consequence of Adam's violation of the Eden law. The *"original sin"* was such as I have shown in previous pages. Adam and Eve committed it; and their posterity are suffering the consequence of it. The tribe of Levi paid tithes to Melchisedec many years before Levi was born. The apostle says, "Levi, who receiveth tithes, paid tithes in Abraham". Upon the same federal principle, all mankind ate of the forbidden fruit, being in the loins of Adam when he transgressed. This is the only way men can by any possibility be guilty of the original sin. Because they sinned in Adam, therefore they return to the dust from which Adam came—ἐφ ᾧ, says the apostle, *"in whom* all sinned" (Romans 5:12).* There is much foolishness spoken and written about "original sin". Infants are made the subjects of a religious ceremony to regenerate them because of original sin; on account of which, according to Geneva philosophy they are liable to the flames of hell for ever! If original sin, which is in fact sin in the flesh, were neutralized, then all "baptismally regenerated" babes ought to live for ever, as Adam would have done had he eaten of the Tree of Life after he had sinned. But they die; which is a proof that the "regeneration" does not "cure their souls"; and is, therefore, mere theological quackery.

Mankind being born of the flesh, and of the will of man, are born into the world under the constitution of sin. That is, they are the natural born citizens of Satan's kingdom. By their fleshly birth, they are entitled to all that *sin* can impart to them. What creates the distinction of bodies politic among the sons of Adam? It is constitution, or covenant. By constitution, then, one man is English, and another American. The former is British because he is born of the flesh under the British constitution. In this case, he is worthy of neither praise nor blame. He was made subject to the constitution, not willingly, but by reason of them who chose that he should be born under it. But when he comes of age, the same man may become an American. He may put off the old man of the

---

*This marginal reading of the AV cannot be sustained. The Revised Version has struck it out.

political flesh, and put on the new man, which is created by the constitution of the United States; so that by constitution, he becomes an American in every particular but the accident of birth. This will be exact enough to illustrate what I am about to say.

There are two states or kingdoms, in God's arrangements, which are distinguished by constitution. These are the Kingdom of Satan and the Kingdom of God. The citizens of the former are all *sinners*; the heirs of the latter are *saints*. Men cannot be born heirs by the will of the flesh; for natural birth confers no right to God's Kingdom. Men must be born sinners before they can become saints; even as one must be born a foreigner before he can be an *adopted* citizen of the States. It is absurd to say that children are born holy, except in the sense of their being legitimate. None are born holy, but such as are born of the Spirit into the Kingdom of God. Children are born sinners or unclean, because they are born of sinful flesh; and "that which is born of the flesh is flesh", or sin. This is a misfortune, not a crime. They did not will to be born sinners. They have no choice in the case; for it is written, "The creature was *made subject, τῇ ματαιότητι, to the evil,* not willingly, but by reason of him who subjected it *in hope*" (Romans 8:20). Hence, the apostle says, "By Adam's disobedience the many were *made sinners*" (Romans 5:19); that is, they were endowed with a nature like his, which had become unclean, as the result of disobedience; and by the constitution of the economy into which they were introduced by the will of the flesh, they were constituted transgressors before they were able to discern between right and wrong.

Upon this principle, he that is born of sinful flesh is a sinner as he that is born of English parents is an English child. Such a sinner is an heir of all that is derivable from sin. Hence, new-born babes suffer all the evil of the peculiar department of Satan, or sin's kingdom, to which they belong. Thus, in the case of the Amalekites, when the divine vengeance fell upon them, the decree was—"Utterly destroy all that they have, and spare them not; but slay both man and woman, *infant and suckling,* ox and sheep, camel and ass" (1 Samuel 15:3). The destruction of "infants and sucklings" is especially commanded in divers parts of scripture. Not because they were responsible transgressors; but, on the same principle that men not only destroy all adult serpents that come in their way, but the thread-like progeny also; for in these is the germ of venomous and malignant reptiles. Had God spared the infants and sucklings of the Canaanitish nations, when they had attained to manhood, even though they had been trained by Israel, they would have reverted to the iniquities of their fathers. Even Israel itself proved a stiff-necked and perverse race, notwithstanding all the pains bestowed upon their education by the Lord God; how much more perverse would such a seed of evil serpents as the Canaanitish offspring have turned out to be?

It is a law of the flesh that "like produces like". Wild and truthless men reproduce themselves in their sons and daughters. The experiment has been tried on Indian infants. They have been taken from their parents, and carefully educated in the learning and civilization of the white man; but when they have returned to their tribe as men, they have thrown off the habits of their patrons, and adopted the practices of savage life. The same tendency is seen in other animals. Hatch the eggs of the wild turkey under a tame one; and as soon as they are able to shift for themselves they will leave the poultry yard, and associate with the wild species of the woods. So strong is habit, that it becomes a law to the flesh, when continued through generations for a series of years.

But men are not only made, or constituted sinners by the disobedience of Adam, but they become sinners even as he, *by actual transgression*. Having attained the maturity of their nature, they become accountable and responsible creatures. At this crisis, they may be placed by the divine arranging in a relation to His word. It becomes to them a Tree of Life (Proverbs 3:18), inviting them to "take, and eat, and live for ever". If, however, they prefer to eat of the world's forbidden fruit, they come under the sentence of death in their own behalf. They are thus doubly condemned. They are "condemned already" to the dust as natural born sinners; and, secondarily, condemned to a resurrection to judgment for rejecting the gospel of the kingdom of God: by which they become obnoxious to "*the* SECOND *Death*" (Revelation 20:14).

Thus men are sinners in a twofold sense; first, by natural birth; and next, by transgression. In the former sense, it is manifest they could not help themselves. They will not be condemned to the Second Death because they were born sinners; nor to any other pains and penalties than those which are the common lot of humanity in the present life. They are simply under that provision of the constitution of sin which says, "Dust thou art, and unto dust thou shalt return". Now, if the Lord God had made no other arrangement than that expressed in the sentence upon the woman and the man, they and all their posterity in all their generations would have incessantly gone to dust and there have remained for ever. "The wages of sin is death." Sinful flesh confers no good thing upon its offspring; for holiness, righteousness, incorruptibility, and life for ever are not hereditary. None of these are inherent in animal flesh. Sinners *can only acquire* them by a conformity to the law of God; who offers them freely to all who thirst after the water of life eternal (Revelation 22:17; Isaiah 55:1-3).

THE CONSTITUTION OF RIGHTEOUSNESS

"Constituted the righteousness of God in Christ."

THE former things being admitted, if men would be righteous in God's esteem, they must become such *by constitution* also. The "good actions" of a pious sinner are mere "dead works"; for the actions of a sinner to be of any worth in relation to the future state, he must be "constituted righteous"; and this can only be by his coming under a constitution made and provided for the purpose. A stranger and foreigner from the commonwealth of the States, can only become a fellow-citizen with Americans, by taking the oath of abjuration, fulfilling the time of his probation, and taking the oath of allegiance according to the provisions of the constitution.

Now, the Kingdom of God has a constitution as well as the Kingdom of Satan, or that province of it styled the United States. Before sinners come under it, they are characterized as "without Christ, being aliens from the *Commonwealth of Israel*, and strangers from the covenants of promise, having no hope, and without God (ἄθεοι, *atheists*) in the world" (Ephesians 2:12,13,19). They are termed "far off", "strangers and foreigners" "walking in the vanity of their mind, having the understanding darkened, being alienated from the life of God through the ignorance that is in them, because of the blindness of their heart" (Ephesians 4:17,18). But, mark the sacred style descriptive of sinners after they have been placed under the constitution of Israel's Commonwealth, which is the Kingdom of God. "You that were far off are made nigh by the blood of Christ"; "through him you have access by one spirit to the Father; and are no more strangers and foreigners, but fellow-citizens with the saints, and of the household of God"—"fellow-heirs, and of the same body, and partakers of God's promise *in* Christ *by the gospel*" (Ephesians 3:6). In this remarkable contrast is discoverable a great change in *state* and *character* predicated of the same persons. How was this transformation effected? This question is answered by the phrase, "*In* Christ *by* the gospel". The "*in*" expresses the state; the "*by*" the instrumentality by which the state and character are changed.

As the constitution of sin hath its root in the disobedience of the First Adam, so also hath the constitution of righteousness root in the obedience of the Second Adam. Hence, the apostle says, "As through one offence (sentence was pronounced) upon all men unto condemnation; so also through one righteousness (sentence was pronounced) upon all men (that is, Jews and Gentiles) unto *a justification of life*. For as through the disobedience of the one man *the many* were *constituted (κατεστάθησαν) sinners*; so also through the obedience of the one the many shall be *constituted righteous*" (Romans 5:18,19). The two Adams are *two federal chiefs*; the first being figurative of the second (verse 14), in these relations. All sinners are *in* the first Adam; and all the righteous *in* the second, only on a different principle. Sinners were in the loins of the former when he transgressed; but not in the loins of the latter, when he was obedient unto death; therefore, "the flesh profiteth nothing". For this cause, then, for sons of Adam to become sons of God, they must be the subjects of an *adoption*, which is attainable only by some divinely appointed means.

The apostle then brings to light *two sentences*, which are co-extensive, but not co-etaneous in their bearing upon mankind. The one is the sentence of condemnation, which consigns "*the many*", both believing Jews and Gentiles, to the dust of the ground; the other is a sentence which affects the same "many", and brings them out of the ground again to return thither no more. Hence, of the saints it is said, "The body is dead because of sin; but the spirit (gives) life because of righteousness" (Romans 8:10,11); for "since by man came death, by a man also came a resurrection of dead persons (*ἀνάστασις νεκρῶν*). For as in Adam they all die, so also in Christ shall they all be made alive. But every one in his own order: Christ the first fruits; afterward *they that are Christ's* at his coming" (1 Corinthians 15:21-23). It is obvious that the apostle is not writing of all the individuals of the human race; but only of that portion of them that become the subject of "*a justification of life*", *δικαίωσις ζωῆς*. It is true, that all men do die; but it is not true that they are all the subjects of justification. Those who are justified are "the many", *οἱ πολλοί*, who are sentenced to live for ever. Of the rest we shall speak hereafter.

The sentence to justification of life is through Jesus Christ. In being made a sacrifice for sin by the pouring out of his blood upon the cross, he was set forth as *a blood-sprinkled mercy seat* to all believers of the gospel of the kingdom, who have faith in this remission of sins through the shedding of his blood. "He was delivered for our offences, and raised again for our justification" (Romans 4:25); that is, for the pardon of those *who believe in the gospel*; as it is written, "He that believeth the gospel and is baptized shall be saved" (Mark 16:15,16). Hence, "*the obedience of faith*" (Romans 1:5) is made the condition of righteousness; and this obedience implies the existence of a "*law of faith*", as attested by that of

Moses, which is *the law of works*" (Romans 3:27,21). The law of faith says to him who believes the gospel of the kingdom, "Be renewed, and be ye every one of you baptized in the name (ἐπὶ τῷ ὀνόματι) of Jesus Christ for remission of sins" (Acts 2:38).

Here is a command which meets a man as a dividing line between *the State of Sin* and *the State of Righteousness*. The obedience of faith finds expression *in the name of Jesus* as "the mercy seat through faith in his blood". Hence the apostle says to the disciples in Corinth, "Know ye not that *the unrighteous shall not inherit the Kingdom of God*? Be not deceived; neither fornicators, idolaters, adulterers, effeminate, abusers of themselves with mankind, nor covetous, nor drunkards, nor revilers, nor extortioners; shall inherit the kingdom of God. And *such were some of you*: but ye were *washed, sanctified*, and *made righteous* (ἐδικαιώθητε) in the name (ἐν τῷ ὀνόματι) of the Lord Jesus, and *in the spirit* (ἐν τῷ πνεύματι) of our God" (1 Corinthians 6:9-11). Thus, the spirit, which is put for the gospel of the kingdom and name, renewed these profligates; the divine law and testimony attested by the spirit with signs, and wonders, and divers miracles, and gifts (Hebrews 2:3,4), and believed with a full assurance of conviction that worked in them by love to will and to do— caused them to be *"washed in the name"*, to be *"sanctified in the name"*, and to be *"made righteous in the name* of Jesus Christ".

It must be clear to any man, unspoiled by a vain and deceitful philosophy, that to be washed in a name is impossible, unless the individual have *faith in the name*, and be subjected to the use of a fluid in some way. Now when a man is "washed in the name of Jesus Christ", there are three witnesses to the fact, by whose testimony everything is established. These are the spirit, the water, and the blood, and they all agree in one statement. Jesus Christ was made manifest *by water* at his baptism (John 1:31); and *by blood* in his death; and *by the spirit* in his resurrection: therefore, the spirit *who is the truth* (τὸ πνεῦμά ἐστιν ἡ ἀλήθεια), and the water, and the blood, or the truth concerning the Messiahship, sacrificial character, and resurrection of Jesus, are constituted the witnesses who bear testimony to a man's being the subject of "the righteousness of God" (Romans 1:17; 3:21,22,25,26) set forth in the gospel of His Kingdom. The testimony of these witnesses is termed "the witness of God", which every believer of the Kingdom and Name hath as *"the witness in himself"* (1 John 5:6-10).

Water, then, is the medium in which the washing occurs. But, although water is so accessible in all parts of the world where the gospel has been preached, it is one of the most dif-

143

ficult things under heaven to use it so as to *wash* a man *in the name of Jesus Christ*. What! says one, is it difficult to get a man to be dipped in water as a religious action? No; it is very easy. Thousands in society go into the water on very slender grounds. But going into the water, and having certain words pronounced over the subject, is not washing in the name. The difficulty lies, not in getting men to be dipped, but in *first* getting them to believe "the things concerning the Kingdom of God and the Name of Jesus Christ" (Acts 8:12); or "the exceeding great and precious promises", by the faith of which they can alone become the "partakers of the divine nature" (2 Peter 1:4). Without faith in these things, there is no true washing, no sanctification, or purification, from moral defilement, and no constitution of righteousness by the name of Jesus for the sons of men; for, says the scripture, "without faith it is impossible to please God".

It was the renewing efficacy of the exceeding great and precious promises of God assuredly believed, that changed the gay and profligate Corinthians into "the sanctified in Christ Jesus, called to be saints"; of whom it is testified that "hearing, they believed and were baptized" (Acts 18:8). Now, to these baptized believers he writes, and tells them that "God *made* (ἐποίησεν) Jesus, who knew not sin, to be sin (that is, sinful flesh) for them, that they might be *constituted* (γινῶνται) God's righteousness *in* Him" (2 Corinthians 5:21); so that, being introduced into Him (for an individual cannot be *in* a federal person unless *introduced into* him) the crucified and resurrected Jesus became "the LORD their righteousness" (Jeremiah 23:6); as it is written, "Of Him, Corinthians, are ye IN Christ Jesus, who of God was *constituted* (ἐγενήθη) for us wisdom, righteousness, sanctification, and redemption" (1 Corinthians 1:30). So that, whosoever is in him, is said to be "*complete in him*"; in whom he is circumcised "*in putting off* THE BODY OF THE SINS *of the flesh*"; that is, *all past sins*; being buried with Christ in the baptism, in which also he rises with him through the belief of the power of God evinced in raising him from among the dead (Colossians 2:10-12).

Now, because the unconstituted, or unrighteous, cannot inherit the kingdom of God, the law is revealed which says, "*Ye must be born again*"; for says the King, "Except a man be born again he cannot behold the kingdom of God". This saying is unintelligible to men whose thinking is guided by the flesh. They cannot comprehend "how these things can be": and, though they *profess* to be "teachers of Israel", "Masters of Arts", and "Bachelors", and "Doctors of Divinity", and of "Canon and Civil Law", they are as mystified upon the subject of "the new birth" as Nicodemus himself. But to those who understand "the word of the kingdom" these "heavenly things" are distinguished by the obviousness and simplicity of truth. To be born again, as the Lord Jesus expounds it, is to be "born of the water and the spirit"; as it is written, "Except a man be born, *out of water* (ἐξ ὕδατος) and of the spirit, he cannot enter into the kingdom of God" (John 3:3-10). This is surely very explicit and very intelligible; who can misunderstand it, unless it be against his will to receive it?

The New Birth, like the old one of the flesh, is not an abstract principle, but a process. It begins with the begettal and ends with the having been born. A son of God is a character, which is developed out of the "incorruptible seed" (1 Peter 1:23) of God, sown into the fleshy table of the heart (Matthew 13:19). When this seed, or word of the Kingdom, is received, it begins to work in a man until he becomes a believer of the truth. When things have come to this pass, he is a changed man. He has acquired a new mode of thinking; for he thinks in harmony with the thoughts of God as revealed in His law and testimony. He sees himself, and the world around him, in a new light. He is convinced of sin; and experiences an aversion to the things in which he formerly delighted. His views, disposition, temper, and affections are transformed. He is humble, child-like, teachable, and obediently disposed; and his simple anxiety is to know what God would have him to do. Having ascertained this, he does it; and in doing it is *"born out of the water"*. Having been begotten by the Father by the word of truth (James 1:18), and born of water, the first stage of the process is completed. He is *constitutionally* "in Christ".

When a child is born, the next thing is to train him up in the way he should go, that when he is old he may not depart from it. This is also the arrangement of God in relation to those who are born out of water into His family on earth. He disciplines and tries them, that He may "exalt them in due time". Having believed the gospel and been baptized, such a person is required to "walk worthy of the vocation", or calling, "wherewith he has been called" (Ephesians 4:1), that by so doing he may be "accounted worthy" of being "born of spirit", that he may become "spirit", or a spiritual body; and so enter the kingdom of God, crowned with "glory, honour, incorruptibility, and life" (Romans 2:7). When, therefore, such a believer comes *out* of the ground by a resurrection from among the dead, the spirit of God, worked by the Lord Jesus, first opens the grave, and forms him in the image, and after the likeness of Christ; and then gives him life. He is then an incorruptible and living man, "equal to the angels"; and like them capable of reflecting the glory of Him that made him. This is the end of the process. He is like Jesus himself, the great exemplar of God's family, born out of water by the moral power of the truth; and out of the grave by the physical power of spirit; but all things of God through Jesus Christ the Lord.

In the way described, sinners are transformed into saints; and it is the only way; their conversion being the result of the transforming influence of "the testimony of God". Those who are ignorant of "the law and the testimony", and who yet claim to be saints, and "teachers of divine mysteries", may demur *in toto* to this conclusion, because "in saying this thou condemnest us also". But truth knows no respect of persons; and while the oracles of God declare, that men are "renewed by knowledge", and "alienated from the life of God through ignorance", I feel entrenched impregnably in the position here assumed. According to the constitution of the human intellect, the knowledge of truth must precede the belief of it. There is no exception to this. If cases be cited as exceptions, the faith is spurious, and not that with which God is pleased. It is credulity; the faith of opinion, such as characterizes the spiritual philosophy of the age.

Lastly, the *act* demanded of a *renewed* sinner by the constitution of righteousness, that he may be inducted into Christ, and so "constituted the righteousness of God in him", is *a burial in water into death*. The energy of the word of truth is twofold. It makes a man "*dead* to sin" and "*alive* to God". Now, as Christ died to sin once and was buried, so the believer, having become dead to sin, must be buried also; for after death, burial. The death and burial of the believer is connected with the death and burial of Christ by the individual's faith in the testimony concerning them. Hence, he is said to be "dead with Christ", and to be "buried with Christ"; but, how buried? "*By baptism into death*", saith the scripture.

But is this all? By no means; for the object of the burial in water is not to extinguish animal life; but, by preserving it to afford the believer scope to "walk in newness of life", moral and intellectual. He is, therefore, *raised up* out of the water. This action is representative of his *faith* in the resurrection of Jesus; and of his *hope*, that as he had been planted with him in the similitude of his death, he shall hereafter be also in the likeness of his resurrection (Romans 6:3-11), and so enter the kingdom of God. To such persons the scripture saith, "Ye are all sons of God *in* Christ Jesus *through the faith*"; and the ground of this honourable and divine relationship is assigned in these words: "*For* as many of you as have been *baptized* INTO *Christ* have put on Christ; and *if* ye be Christ's, *then* are ye the seed of Abraham, and *heirs* according to the promise" (Galatians 3:26-29). They have thus received the spirit of adoption by which they can address God as their Father who is in heaven.

THE TWO PRINCIPLES

"With the mind I myself serve the Law of God; but with the flesh the Law of Sin."

ALTHOUGH a sinner may have been "delivered from the power of darkness", or ignorance, and have been "translated into" (Colossians 1:13) the hope of "the Kingdom of God and of his Christ" (Revelation 11:15), by faith in the divine testimony and baptism into Christ—yet, if he turn his thoughts back into his own heart, and note the impulses which work there, he will perceive a something that, if he were to yield to it, would impel him to the violation of the divine law. These impulses are styled *"the motions of sins"* (Romans 7:5). Before he was enlightened, they "worked in his members", until they were manifested in evil action, or sin; which is termed, "bringing forth fruit unto death". The remote cause of these "motions" is that physical principle, or quality, of the flesh, styled indwelling sin, which returns the mortal body to the dust; and that which excites the latent disposition is the law of God forbidding to do thus and so; for, I had not known sin, but by the law".

Now, while a righteous man feels this law involuntarily at work in his members, the law of sin, or of nature within him; he also perceives there a something which condemns "the motions of sins", and suppresses them; so that they shall not impel him to do what he ought not to do. The best of men— and I quote Paul as an illustration of the class—are conscious of the co-existence of these hostile principles within them. "I find", says he, a law that, when I would do good, *evil* is present with me." Yes; *the principle of evil* and *the principle of good* are the two laws which abide in the saints of God so long as they continue subject to mortality.

The reader is invited to re-peruse pages ninety-five and ninety-six on the subject of these laws, as it will prevent repetition in this place.

The law of sin and death is *hereditary*, and derived from the federal sinner of the race; but the law of the mind is an intellectual and moral *acquisition*. The law of sin pervades every particle of the flesh; but in the thinking flesh it reigns especially in the propensities. In the savage, it is the only law to which he is subject; so that with his flesh, he serves only the law of sin and death. This is to him *"the light within"*; which is best illustrated by the darkness of Egypt, which might be felt. It was this internal light which illuminated "the princes of the world, who crucified the Lord of glory". It shined forth in the philosophy of Plato, and in the logic of

Aristotle, who walked in it while "dwelling in the land of the shadow of death" (Isaiah 9:2) and it is "the light within" all babes who are born of blood, of the will of the flesh, and of man under the constitution of sin, in all countries of the world.

Now, the scripture saith, "The commandment of God is a lamp; and his law is light" (Proverbs 6:23); so that the prophet says, "Thy word is a lamp unto my feet, and a light unto my path" (Psalm 119:105). And to this agrees the saying of the apostle, that the sure word of prophecy is "a light that shineth in a dark place" (2 Peter 1:19). Now, Isaiah testifies, that the Word is made up of God's law and testimony, and that those who do not speak according to it, have no light in them (Isaiah 8:20). This is the reason that the savage has no light in him; because he is intensely ignorant of the law of God. Light does not emanate from within; for sin, blood, and flesh can give out none. It can only reflect it after the fashion of a mirror. The light is not in the mirror; but its surface is so constituted that when light falls upon it, it can throw it back, or reflect it, according to the law of light, that the images of objects are seen on the surface, whence the light proceeding from the objects is last reflected to the eye. Neither is light innate in the heart. This is simply *a tablet*; a polished tablet, or mirror, in some; but a tarnished, rusty tablet in others. It is called "the fleshy tablet of the heart". It was polished in the beginning, when God formed man after His likeness; but sin, "the god of this world", hath so tarnished it that there are but few who reflect His similitude.

No; it is a mere conceit of the fleshly mind that man is born into the world with the light within; which requires only to be cherished to be sufficient to guide him in the right way. God only is the source of light; He is the glorious illuminator of the moral universe; and He transmits His enlightening radiance through the medium, sometimes of angels, sometimes of prophets, and at others through that of His Son and the apostles, by His all-pervading Spirit. Hence it is that the scripture saith, "God is light", whose truth "enlightens the eyes". But what is the truth? It is "the light of the glorious gospel of Christ", who is the polished incorruptible fleshly mirror, which reflects the Image of God—an image, at present, but obscurely impressed upon the fleshy tablets of our hearts; because we know only in part, perceiving things by the eye of faith, until hope shall disappear in the possession of the prize.

God, then, is the *source* of light; the gospel of the kingdom in the name of Jesus is *the light*; and Christ is the *medium* through which it shines; hence he is styled THE SUN OF RIGHTEOUSNESS; also, "the true light, which enlighteneth every man, that cometh into the world"; "a light to enlighten the Gentiles, and the glory of his people Israel". Now, the enlightening of every man is thus explained by the apostle: "God", saith he, "who commanded the light to shine out of darkness, is he who hath shined into our (the saints') hearts, with the illumination of *the knowledge* (πρὸς φωτισμὸν τῆς γνώσεως) of the glory of God in the face of Jesus Christ" (2 Corinthians 4:6). But "every man" is not enlightened by this glorious knowledge; for to some it is hid. The tablets of their hearts are so corroded and encrusted with opaque and sordid matter that they are destitute of all reflecting power. Light will not shine in a black surface. Hence, saith the apostle, "If our gospel be hid, it is hid to them that are lost: in whom the god of the world hath blinded the minds of them who believe not, lest the light of the glorious gospel of Christ should shine into them" (2 Corinthians 4:3,4). He darkens the tablets of their hearts by "the care of the world, and the deceitfulness of riches" (Matthew 13:22); and thus prevents them from opening their ears to hear the words of eternal life.

If a man have light, then, it is very evident that it is *acquired from without*, and not an hereditary spark within. When the Lord Jesus appeared in Israel "he shined in the darkness". This nation was so darkened by the propensities and human tradition, that they did not perceive the light when it shined among them; "the darkness comprehended it not" (John 1:5). If this were the condition of Israel, how intensely dark must have been the world at large. Still, the Gentile mind was not so totally eclipsed as that of the savage. The nations of the Four Empires had been greatly mixed up with the Israelites in their history; so that the light of their law must have been considerably diffused among them; though not given to them for their obedience. Hence, "the work of the law was written upon their hearts" to some extent; and created in them "a conscience, by the thoughts of which they accused or excused one another" (Romans 2:14,15).

This shining of the truth in the darkness of the nations was considerably increased by the apostolic labours; for "their sound went into all the land, and their words unto the end of the habitable" (τῆς οἰκουμένης, or *Roman Empire*) (Romans 10:18). Now, although this light was almost extinguished by the apostasy, lamps were still kept burning in its presence (Revelation 11:4); so that the eclipse was not so total that the darkness of the Gentile mind was reduced to a savage state. When the scriptures were again disseminated in the tongues of the nations in the sixteenth century, the light of the truth began again to stream in upon them. The scriptures were then like a book just fallen from heaven. The world was astonished at their contents; but "comprehended them not". Men discussed it, tortured it, perverted it, fought about it; until the stronger party established the foundation of the world as at present constituted.

This world, called "Christendom", is much after the order of things in the days of Jesus. Were he to appear now, he would "shine in the darkness" as when among the Jews. These professed to know God, while in works they denied Him. Their clergy said, *"We see"*; but Jesus characterized them as "blind leaders of the blind"; therefore, "their sin remained". They boasted in the law; yet through breaking it, dishonoured God. They professed to be more conscientious and pious than Jesus; but he charged them with being hypocrites and serpents. They strained out gnats, and swallowed camels; and gave tithe of mint and cummin, and despoiled the fatherless and the widow. And, "like priest, like people". They crowded to the synagogues and the temple in splendid apparel. The bejewelled worshippers exhibited themselves in conspicuous seats; while the poor stood, or if seated, sat on footstools near the door. They made a great show of piety, sang the psalms of David with holy rapture, devoutly listened to the reading of the law and the prophets; and expelled Jesus and his apostles with great fury from their midst, when they showed the meaning of them. With the worship of God they combined the worship of Mammon. They heaped up gold and silver, and apparel till it was moth eaten; oppressed the hirelings in his wages; and ground the faces of the poor.

Such was the state of "the church" when Jesus and his apostles were members of it; and such is its condition now that "he standeth at the door, and knocks". *"The Church"* of the 20th century (by which I understand, not the *"One Body"* (Ephesians 4:4); but that thousand-headed monster presented by the ecclesiastical aggregate of "Christendom") is that Laodicean antitype which is neither cold nor hot, but lukewarm, and which saith, "I am rich, and increased in goods, and have need of nothing: but knows not that it is wretched, and miserable, and poor, and blind, and naked" (Revelation 3:17); the sputa once "spewed out of the Lord's mouth". Its eyes are blinded by the god of the world. Its zeal for faction: its devotion to Mammon; its ignorance of the scriptures; and its subjection to the dogmas and commandments of men—have made its heart fat, its ears heavy, and closed its eyes. "The people of the Lord, the people of the Lord are we!" ascends as its cry to heaven from myriads of throats; but in the tablets of their hearts the light of the glorious gospel of Christ's kingdom and name finds no surface of reflection. Many who mean well lament "the decline of spirituality in the Churches"; but they fail to perceive the cause.

150

The scriptures have fallen into comparative disuse among them. They are superseded by shallow speculations—mere unintelligible pulpit disquisitions, the contradictory thinking of the flesh, trained to excogitate the creedism of the community that glorifies itself in the orator of its choice. *The gospel is neither believed nor preached in the churches.* In fact, it is hid from their eyes; and the time is come to break off the wild olive branch for its saplessness; to cut off these churches for their unbelief (Romans 11:20,22,25).

The principle, or spirit, that works in these children of disobedience, is neither the law of sin as exhibited in the savage; nor the law of God as it appears in the genuine disciples of Christ. It is a blending of the two; so as to make of none effect (Matthew 15:6,9) the little truth believed, as far as inheriting the Kingdom of God is concerned. This proportion of truth in the public mind is the measure of its morality, and exegetical of its conscience; and constitutes that scintillation, or "light within", which is struck out by the collision of ideas in the world around. Educational bias makes men what they are— sinners, whose habitude of thought and action is "pious", or impious, civilised or savage, according to the school in which their young ideas have been taught to shoot. The divine law and testimony alone can turn these into reflectors of the moral image and similitude of God.

The *"intellect"* and *"sentiments"* of the apostle's brain, constituting "the fleshly tablet of his heart", had been inscribed by the Spirit of the living God, in a way that all believers are not the subject of. He was inspired; and consequently received much of "the light of the knowledge of the glory of God" by divine suggestion, or revelation (Galatians 1:11,12); others receive the same knowledge, in words spoken, or written, by "earthen vessels" like himself, in whom "this treasure" was deposited (2 Corinthians 4:7). The means by which the knowledge is communicated matters not, so that it is written on the heart. When it gets possession of this, it forms that *"mind"* or *mode of thinking or feeling* (νοῦς) with which the apostle said he "served the Law of God". Being renewed by the divine testimony, his intellect and sentiments were sure to think and feel in harmony with the thoughts of God. Nevertheless, his "propensities" were only checked in their emotions. He kept his body under. This was all that he could do; for no spiritual perfection of thought and feeling could eradicate from the particles of his flesh the all-pervading principle of its corruption. While, therefore, with his mind he served the Law of God, his flesh obeyed the law of sin, which finally mingled it with its parent dust.

This *new mode of thinking and feeling* created in a true believer by the divine law and testimony, is variously designated in scripture. It is styled "a clean heart and a right spirit" (Psalm 51:10); "a new spirit" and "a heart of flesh" (Ezekiel 11:19); the "inward man" (2 Corinthians 4:16; Romans 7:22); "new creature" (2 Corinthians 5:17); "the new man created in righteousness and true holiness"; and "renewed unto knowledge after the image of him that created him" (Ephesians 4:24; Colossians 3:10); the "hidden man of the heart" (1 Peter 3:4); and so forth. This new and hidden man is manifested in the life, which is virtuous as becomes the gospel. He delights in the law of the Lord, and speaks often of His testimonies. He denies himself of all ungodliness and worldly lusts, and walks soberly, righteously and godly in the world. His hope is the glorious manifestation of Jesus Christ, with the crown of righteousness, even glory, honour, and immortality, promised to all who look for him, and "*love* his appearing", and desire his kingdom (Titus 2:11-14; 2 Timothy 4:1,8; Hebrews 9:28). Nevertheless, the law of sin, through the weakness of the flesh, fails not to remind him of imperfection. Being delivered from the fear of death, he looks forward to it as to the period of his change, knowing that, when he falls asleep in the dust, he will afterwards be delivered from the principle of evil by a resurrection to incorruptibility and unalloyed existence in the Paradise of God.

CHAPTER V

IMMORTALITY, RELIGION, "CLERGY" AND "LAITY"

Immortality in the present state a positive evil—Immortality in misery unscriptural—The professing world religious from fear—The world's religions useful as a system of Ecclesiastical Police—The Religion of Christ destitute of all worldly goods till his return, when it will possess all things—The doctrine of immortality a divine revelation—The Heathens baffled in their endeavour to discover it—The Mosaic Cherubim God's throne in Israel—The Cherubim of Ezekiel and John—The Cherubic Veil—The Faces of the Lord—The Flaming Sword—Illustrated by Ezekiel's description of the glory of the GOD of Israel—The brightness of the Spiritual Body—The Way of the Tree of Life—The etymology of the word RELIGION—False religion based upon the idea of appeasing the wrath of God—God already reconciled to the world—The "Word of Reconciliation" committed to the apostles in the beginning—The apostles the only ambassadors of Christ—"The word" preached by the apostles entrusted to the disciples of Christ—"Clergy" and "Laity" distinctions of the apostasy—Religion defined—Its grand desideratum—No true religion without belief of the truth—The word "faith" scripturally defined—How faith comes—The "religious world" infidel of "the faith"—"Love" scripturally defined by "obedience"—The religious world destitute of the Spirit of God—Religion contemporary only with sin—Summary of principles.

THE LORD God, having arranged the foundation of the world, in the sentences pronounced upon the transgressors; and commenced the preparation of the kingdom in the stipulations of the New Law: decreed their expulsion from the garden eastward in Eden. As the Serpent had said, the man had become "as the gods", or Elohim, "to know good and evil", in consequence of eating the forbidden fruit. He had known good only in his novitiate; but, being lifted up with pride, he had fallen into the condemnation of the devil (1 Timothy 3:6), and had come to know also by experience both sorrow and pain. This was a great calamity; but not so great as that a greater might not befall him, even in Paradise. He had eaten of one tree, and his presumption might cause him to take and eat of the other. The consequences of this eating, superadded to the first, would have rendered his situation still more deplorable than it was. He now knew evil, as the Elohim had done before him; but there was hope of deliverance from it when he should return to the dust whence he was taken; but if he should eat of the Tree of the Lives, this hope would be cut off, and he would live for ever the subject of weeping, sorrow, and pain. The misery of being the subject of evil for ever is forcibly expressed by Job. When reduced to the deepest distress, he laments, saying, "When I say, My bed shall comfort me, my couch shall ease my complaint; then thou scarest me with dreams, and terrifiest me through visions: so that my soul chooseth strangling, and death rather than my life. I loathe it; *I would not live alway*: let me alone; for my days are vanity" (Job 7:13-16). But, if Adam had eaten of the Tree of Life, when reduced to such misery as this he would have sought death, but it would have fled from him. He would have found no deliverance. This, however, would not have been the worst of it. He would have involved all his posterity in the same interminable calamity. The earth would at length have become crowded with undying generations of sensual and devilish men; who, if any virtue should survive, would afflict it a hundredfold. For this awful consummation there would have been no remedy but to break up the fountains of the abyss, and cast them down under chains of intense darkness, after the example of the terrene angels who sinned under a previous constitution of the globe.

But the repetition of the scenes of the pre-Adamic drama was not designed, although men were afterwards permitted to imitate it with a similar result; with this difference, however, that the race of the angels was one generation, while that of men was composed of many. To prevent, then, the replenishment of the earth with undying sinners, the Lord God said to Elohim, "Behold, the man *has become as one of us*, to know good and evil: and now *lest he* put forth his hand and take also of the Tree of the Lives, and eat, and *live for ever*: therefore the Lord God sent him forth from the garden of Eden, to till the ground from whence he was taken. So he drove out the man".

This is a very remarkable passage of scripture. It contains much in a few words. The points which stand out, shining like two stars, are the acknowledgement that *man had become as the gods* by his offence; and, secondly, that he was expelled from Paradise *that he might not live for ever*. I shall defer to another place the exposition of the things suggested by his godlikeness in evil; and after what has already been said on the tree of lives, but little need be added respecting his exclusion from present immortality. I would, however, so far anticipate another part of this work as to say here, that the finality of creation, providence, and redemption is, *man upon earth, glorious, honourable, and immortal, in a state of unmingled good*. It was because God loved man, and out of mercy to him, that He drove him out of the garden. Had He been actuated by malignity (a feeling, by-the-bye, that has no place in the heart of God), He would have left him free to involve himself in everlasting misery by eating of the tree of lives. But He did not create the man for such a destiny; nor did He subject his posterity to evil by a stern necessity, that it might in any mode of existence be consigned to interminable torment of mind, of body, or both.

The creed that inculcates this is God-dishonouring, and expresses the foolish thoughts of sinful flesh, unenlightened by His law and testimony. It is the vapouring of the pagan mind, adopted by the Apostasy, and transfused into the symbols of its credulity. As it knows not how to display the divine character in any other light than the propensities, the faintly-illumined intellect, and the perverted sentiments of the flesh exhibit; it presents God to the sons of men as more like the Saturn, or Moloch, of the heathens, who devoured their own offspring, in shrieks and groans, than as one who so loves the world that He beseeches it to be reconciled to Him (2 Corinthians 5:19,20): and to accept, without money or price, the exceeding great and precious things He has in store. Thus the *"religious world"* is ruled by terror. The little faith it professes, works not by love (Galatians 5:6) to the purification of its heart (Acts 15:9); but by the unceasing apprehension of burning in molten lava through endless ages. It works by "fear, which hath torment", and debases the soul; so that were it not for its fears, it would be honest and confess that it cared neither for God nor for His religion. But there is no fear in love; for perfect love casteth out fear. The world of professors, therefore, deceives itself in supposing that it loves God. "He that feareth is not made perfect in love" (1 John 4:17,18). It loves Him not, for its conscience is defiled. "Love is the fulfilling of the law." Its "doubts and fears" demonstrate its consciousness of sin uncovered; and that it either knows not what the truth is, or knowing it, neglects, or refuses, to obey it. It is an egregious contradiction to confess with the same breath that we love God and are yet afraid of Him! Was Adam afraid of God so long as he continued obedient? As soon, however, as he sinned, fear seized upon him, and he fled from the sound of His voice, and hid himself. The righteous man's fear of God is the fear of offending one he loves. God is terrible only to His enemies. His sons and daughters confide in Him with the affection of children; and He protects them with all the love and jealousy of His holy and blessed name.

Being ignorant of "the exceeding great and precious promises" relating to the kingdom of God, the leaders of the people know not in what other way to move them to "get religion", as their phrase is. Hence, they pretend to preach "the terrors of the law". But "religion" got by such a process is worth nothing. Nay; I will retract this. It is worth something. A religion of terror, so long as it is believed, is useful as a system of *ecclesiastical police*; which, associated with the civil

155

and military forces, assists materially in keeping the world in awe. But for the fear of what may be hereafter, professors would be as lawless as the antediluvian giants; and thus, by the ecclesiastical antagonism of society being destroyed, the earth would be filled with violence as before the flood. Superstition is useful in maintaining order until the period shall arrive to supersede it by "wisdom and knowledge", which will be the stability of the times pertaining to the kingdom of God (Isaiah 33:6). But as a means of inheriting this kingdom, and of entitling men to the crown of righteousness, a religion which works by terror is utterly worthless. Remove the terror, and the religion's gone; except in so far, indeed, as the possession of it is necessary to the preservation of its "temporalities", "vested interests", and worldly advantages.

But the "pure and undefiled religion" of God has no present temporalities or worldly interests. It has no "lands, tenements, and hereditaments"; nor "states", colleges, or "sacred edifices". It is like the Son of God in the days of his flesh; homeless, houseless, and poverty-stricken among the sons of men. It has great riches, and good things in store for the poor in this world *who are rich in faith* (James 2:5); it *promises* them the possession of the world (1 Corinthians 3:22) with all the honour, and glory, and riches of it, with endless life for the enjoyment of them; but it requires faith in God with filial obedience to His law, in a time of tribulation (Acts 14:22; 2 Timothy 3:12), as the condition of the inheritance.

It is perfectly absurd to imagine that men who are revelling in all the luxuries, conveniences, and comforts of life; enjoying the honour, glory, and friendship of the world, as do the ecclesiastics of antichristendom in their several ranks, orders, and degrees; to suppose, I say, that such can inherit the Kingdom of God with Jesus, and that "cloud of witnesses", of whom Paul says "the world was not worthy", is preposterous. If men would reign with Christ they must believe his doctrine, and suffer with him (2 Timothy 2:12), in enduring persecution for the word's sake (Mark 10:29-30; Luke 18:29). They must separate themselves from "the churches", both State and Nonconformist, which have a name to live, but are dead in trespasses and sin. The whole system is rotten; and awaits only the manifestation of the Lord's presence to be abolished with signal marks of his displeasure. Therefore, let all honest men, lay and clerical, who shall believe the truth, come out from among them, and be separate. Better stand alone for the Kingdom of God's sake, than be numbered with the multitude in the day of Christ, who will be denied permission to "eat of the tree of life and live for ever".

When man was expelled from Paradise, the Lord God, apprehended some new act of presumption, placed a guard over the tree of lives. This tree, it will be remembered, was planted *in the midst* of the garden. Now, when Adam was driven out, "the Lord placed *at the east* of the garden of Eden, CHERUBIM, and *a flaming sword* which turned every way, to keep the way of the tree of life". This would seem to indicate that Adam was driven out in an easterly direction; had he gone westward, the tree of life would have been between him and the Cherubim; so that it would still have appeared accessible, and have tempted him to try to get at it; which would doubtless have been his destruction. The Cherubim and sword were to guard *the Way of the Tree*, so that it could not be approached. If they were disposed to make a circuit to avoid the Cherubim, the flaming sword, or devouring flame, flashed on every side; "it turned every way to keep it" from being invaded by their presumption.

From this arrangement, they either saw the tree of life no more; or, saw it only in the distance. The latter is the more probable. The sight of it from time to time would remind them of what they had lost; and, from what they had learned of the effect producible upon the eater of its fruit, it suggested the possibility of mortal man *putting on immortality*. This was a thing to be desired. But they could not get at the tree; how could they then attain it? There were but two of them, and neither of them could answer the question. There were no scriptures testifying to them as to us, "This is the way, walk ye in it". They were ignorant of "the way leading unto life" (Matthew 7:14); and, if they had not been *"taught of God"*, they would have remained ignorant of it for ever. The thinking of the flesh could never have discovered it; for the obtaining of immortality involved the belief and practice of things which it was utterly impossible for the heart of man to conceive.

We have an illustration of this in the endeavour of the heathen philosophers to solve the problem. Being ignorant of God's knowledge they ran into the most absurd speculations. They thought that immortality was a sort of ghost inside of a man that went to the fields of Elysium when death dissolved its union with the body. They regarded this innate principle as a particle of the divine essence from which proceeded all virtuous actions; while vice was the natural result of the operation of the matter of the body, which was essentially malignant. The apostle refers to this in part when he says, "Professing themselves to be wise, they became fools" (Romans 1:22). Hence, he styles "the wisdom of the wise" "foolishness"; and, as the Corinthians had received the gospel of the kingdom, which teaches a very different doctrine, he inquires of them, "Hath not God made foolish the wisdom of the world?" (1 Corinthians 1:20). Has He not shown the absurdity of their speculations about "*souls*", "immortality", and "*the nature of the gods*"?

They had no idea of immortality being conferred only upon men who might be accounted worthy of a certain kingdom. This was a doctrine which the flesh, with all its thinking, and with all its logic, had no conception of. It never thought of the kingdom of God and the name of a particular personage, as the channel through which immortality was to flow. It was lost in reveries about Elysium and Tartarus: and the river Styx which flowed between them; and about Charon and his ferry-boat; and ghosts; and three-headed Cerberus; and the snake-haired Furies; and Pluto, "king of hell". But of "glory, honour, incorruptibility, and life", an incorruptible and unde-filed inheritance, the recompense or reward to the subjects of a righteousness by faith — of such a "prize" as this, to be sought after by doing the will of God, they were as utterly ignorant as an unborn babe. Well might the apostle say in the language of the prophet, "Eye hath not seen, ear hath not heard, neither have entered into the heart of men, the things which God hath prepared for them that love him. But God hath revealed them *to us* by his spirit" (1 Corinthians 2:9-16); that is, to those who received the gospel of the kingdom.

Immortality, then, and *the way to it*, are things about which man must have remained for ever ignorant, so long as their discovery depended upon the thinking of the flesh. In other words, they are matters purely of divine testimony; and as faith is the belief of testimony, men can have no *faith* in them beyond what is stated in the written word of God. The carnal mind, by reflecting upon its own consciousness, may be "of *opinion*" that what it terms "I myself" is immaterial *because it thinks*, and "therefore immortal"; but beyond that it can never go. Opinion implies doubt; for if a matter be beyond doubt, it is no longer opinion, but faith or knowledge. Where, then, is the man, be he philosopher or theologist, who can demonstrate the existence of an "immortal soul" in the animal man, by a "thus it is written", or a "thus saith the LORD"? A few phrases in scripture may be twisted, and tor-tured into *an inference* — which, however, becomes lighter than vanity before the direct testimonies of the word to the contrary. With these words, then, by way of preface, I shall proceed to offer a few remarks upon

THE CHERUBIM

BUT little is said about the *Cherubim* in the Mosaic narrative. The word is a plural noun, and represents, therefore, more objects than one. But, in what did this plurality consist? I should say, judging from a text in the next chapter, that it had especial regard to a plurality of *faces*; for when the Lord God sentenced Cain to a fugitive and vagabond life, the fratricide answered, "Behold, then, from THY FACES (*plural in the Hebrew*)* shall I be hid" (Genesis 4:14); that is, "I shall no more be permitted to come before the Cherubic faces, which thou hast placed at the east of the garden, to present an offering for my sin". As he truly observed, "Mine iniquity is greater than that it may be forgiven". He was exiled from the Faces of God still further to the east as a murderer doomed to eternal death (John 3:15) at the end of his career.

That the faces were connected with the Cherubim seems unquestionable from other passages of scripture where cherubim are described. The Lord spoke of them to Moses in the Mount. Having commanded him to make an ark, or open chest, overlaid with gold, with a crown along its upper margin, he said, "Thou shalt make a *mercy-seat* of pure gold. And thou shalt make *two cherubim* of beaten gold in the two ends of the mercy seat". In another place, this is explained thus— "Out of the mercy seat made he the cherubim on the two ends thereof". Then it is continued, "And the cherubim shall stretch forth *wings* on high, covering the mercy-seat with their wings, and their *faces* one to another, toward the mercy-seat shall the faces of the cherubim be. And thou shalt put the mercy-seat *above upon* the ark, and *in the ark thou shalt put the testimony* that I shall give thee" (Exodus 25:10-21).

It is probable that the reason why Moses gave no description of them in Genesis was because he intended to speak more particularly when he came to record their introduction into the most holy place of the tabernacle. In the text above recited they are described as having wings and faces; and being made out of the same piece of gold as the mercy-seat, upon which they looked down, beholding, as it were, the blood sprinkled upon it; it is evident, they were symbols connected with the institution of atonement for sin through the shedding of blood. But they were still more significative. They were God's throne in Israel. Hence, the psalmist saith, "The LORD reigneth; he *sitteth* between the cherubim". This throne was erected upon mercy: and for this reason it was, that the

---

*The word is plural *only* in the Hebrew; even in the case of Jacob and the angel (Genesis 32:30; compare also Ezekiel 10:14).

covering of the ark containing the testimony, the manna (Exodus 16:33; John 6:33), and the resurrected rod (Numbers 17:8; Isaiah 11:1), was styled the Mercy-seat or throne, where the Lord covered the sins of the people. It was also the Oracle, or place from which God communed with Israel through Moses. "There", said the Lord, "will I meet with thee, and I will commune with thee from above the mercy-seat, from between the two cherubim which are upon the Ark of Testimony, of all things which I will give thee in command-ment unto the children of Israel."

But, though Moses informs us of two cherubim with a plu-rality of faces and wings each,* he does not tell us what kind of faces or how many wings they had. This deficiency, howev-er, seems to be supplied by Ezekiel. Those he saw had each of them *four faces* and *four wings*; a human body with feet like a calf's, and the hands of a man under their wings. Of their faces, one was like a man's; a second, like a lion's; a third, like that of an ox; and a fourth, like an eagle's. The things of his first chapter, taken collectively, evidently represent *the Messiah upon his throne, surrounded by his saints, and all energized and made glorious by the Spirit of God*. The rings of Ezekiel's wheels were full of eyes; but in the cherubim which John saw, the wheels were not introduced, but two more wings were added, and the eyes were transferred to the six wings (Revelation 4:8). In this place, the cherubim are styled "beasts", more properly, *living creatures* (τὰ ζῶα); and are associated with "twenty-four elders".

Now, by attending to what is affirmed of them in another place, we shall see who are represented by the four cherubim of Ezekiel with four faces each, and their wheels; and the four of John with one different face each, and twenty-four typical elders. It is written, that "they fell down before the Lamb, having every one of them harps, and golden vials full of odours, which are (or represent) the prayers of the saints. And *they* sung a new song, saying, Thou art worthy to take the book, and to open the seals thereof; for thou wast slain, and hast redeemed *us* to God by thy blood out of every kin-dred, and tongue, and people, and nation; and hast made *us* unto our God kings and priests; and WE *shall reign on earth*" (Revelation 5:8-10). *From this it is evident that the cherubim,*

---

*They would of necessity have two wings each; but the scripture does not here specify a plurality of faces *each* (Exodus 25; 37). We read of "the face of a cherub" (Ezekiel 10). *"The* cherubim" of Eden (Genesis 3:24—RV) appear to be the angels (compare the incident of Balaam, Numbers 22:31); those of Moses and Solomon were manufactured figures of divine specification, that ritually represented men of God made one in Christ and "equal unto the angels". The cherubim and living creatures of Ezekiel and John represent this "one body" in the relations here graphically described by Dr. Thomas.

etc., represent the aggregate of those redeemed from the nations in their resurrection state. The Lamb, the four cherubs, and the twenty-four elders are a symbolical representation of what is expressed by the phrase, "them that are sanctified *in* Christ Jesus, called *saints*"; that is, those who have been constituted the righteousness of God in Christ *in a glorified state.*

The cherubim are the *federal* symbol; and *the eyes*, representative of the *individuals* constituted *in him* who is signified by the Cherubim. The Lamb is introduced to represent the relationship between the holy eyes, or saints, and the Cherubic Faces; that is, between them and the Lord Jesus; while the *"twenty-four elders"* are indicative of their constitution as "the Israel of God". There are *twenty-four*, because the Kingdom of God, being an Israelitish Commonwealth, is arranged with the *twelve sons of Jacob* as its gates (Revelation 21:12); and with *the twelve apostles of the Lamb* as its foundations (Revelation 21:14; Ephesians 2:20); the former being the entrance into present life of the *fleshly* tribes, or *subjects*; and the latter, the foundations of the *adopted* tribes, or HEIRS of the kingdom; so that twenty-four is the representative constitutional number of the spiritual Israel of God; for without the natural the spiritual could not be; any more than there could be adopted Americans, if there were no American nation.

But the Mosaic Cherubim were deficient of several of the characteristics which distinguish those of Ezekiel and John. They had simply the wings and the faces. His cherubim were not only of beaten gold continuous with the substance of the mercy-seat; but they were embroidered into the Veil, made of blue, purple, and scarlet, and fine twined linen, which divided the holy and the holiest places of the tabernacle. Now, when "Jesus cried with a loud voice, he expired (ἐξέπνευσε) and *the Veil of the Temple was rent in twain from top to bottom*" (Mark 15:37,38). Thus, we see the breaking of the body of Jesus identified with the rending of the Cherubic Veil; thereby indicating that the latter was representative of the Lord.

We have arrived then at this, that the Mosaic Cherubim were symbolical of *"God manifest in the flesh".* We wish now to ascertain upon what principles His incarnate manifestation was represented by the Cherubim? First, then, in the solution of this interesting problem, I remark, that the scriptures speak of God after the following manner: "God is *light*, and in him is no darkness at all" (1 John 1:5); again, "God is a *Spirit*; and they that worship him, must worship him in spirit and in truth" (John 4:24); and thirdly, "Our God is a consuming *fire*" (Deuteronomy 4:24). In these three texts, which are only a sample of many others, we perceive that God is represented by *light, spirit,* and *fire*; when, therefore, He is symbolized as manifest in *flesh*, it becomes necessary to select certain *signs* representative of light, spirit, and fire, derived from the *animal* kingdom. Now, the ancients selected the *lion*, the *ox*, and the *eagle* for this purpose, probably from tradition of the signification of these animals, or the faces of them, in the original Cherubim. They are called God's Faces because His omniscience, purity, and jealousy are expressed in them. But the omniscient, jealous, and incorruptible God was to be manifested in a particular kind of flesh. Hence, it was necessary to add *a fourth face* to show in what *nature* He would show Himself. For this reason, the *human* face was associated with the lion, the ox, and the eagle.

These four faces united in one human shape, formed out of beaten gold; and two such, not separate and distinct symbols, but standing one on each end of the mercy-seat, and the same in continuity and substance with it;—taken as a whole, represented Jesus, the true blood-sprinkled mercy-seat, or propitiatory, "in whom dwelleth the fulness of the Godhead bodily" (Romans 3:25; Colossians 2:3,9). All four faces were to look upon the mercy-seat, so as to behold the sprinkled blood of the yearly sacrifice. To accomplish this, two cherubs were necessary; so that the lion and the ox faces of the one; and the man and the eagle faces of the other, should all be "mercy-seat-ward".

It will be seen from this view of things, how important a place the Cherubim occupied in the worship of God connected with "*the representation of the truth*". They were not objects of adoration; but symbols representing to the mind of an intelligent believer the Seed of the woman as God manifested in the likeness of sinful flesh. This I take it was the significance of the Cherubim which the Lord God placed at the east of the garden; and which became the germ, as it were, of the shadowy observances of the patriarchal and Mosaic institutions; whose substance was of Christ.

THE FLAMING SWORD

"A Flaming Sword which turned every way."

THE things represented by the lion, ox, and eagle faces were visibly manifested in the sword of flame. This was light, spirit, and fire flaming around the cherubim as the glory of God. It turned every way to keep the way of the tree of life. This is all Moses says about it; and were it not for other testimonies, we should be at a loss to understand its allegorical signification. The cherubim set up in the tabernacle and first temple were enveloped in a cloud of thick darkness (2 Chronicles 5:14; 6:1). At night, the cloud, which was visible without the former, appeared like a blaze of fire (Exodus 40:35-38); but in the day, it towered aloft as a pillar of cloud. Darkness and fire were frequent accompaniments of the divine presence; indeed, always so upon great occasions. The presence of the Lord upon Mount Sinai was a magnificent and terrible example; and when Jesus expired in blood, Judea was veiled in darkness, and God looked upon it.

With the exception of the thunder, the earthquake, the tempest, and the flashing lightning, God's communings with Moses, and after him with the High Priests, were conducted from between the Cherubim, as upon Sinai—"The LORD descended upon it in fire; and the smoke thereof ascended as the smoke of a furnace; and God answered him by a voice" (Exodus 19:18); so that the thick darkness became luminous and indicated His presence. The illumination of the darkness without the voice would be sufficient to give assurance of acceptance. The Priest having witnessed this on the great day of atonement, when he came out to the people, looking for him with anxiety to know the result, would be enabled to report to them that the Lord had shined forth. This was the sign to them of a typical salvation. Hence, Asaph prays, "Give ear, O Shepherd of Israel; thou that dwellest between the cherubim *shine forth* ... stir up thy strength, and come and save us. Turn us again, O God, *cause thy face to shine*; and we shall be saved" (Psalm 80:1-3).

But the flaming sword in Eden is more strikingly illustrated as to its probable appearance by Ezekiel's description of the cherubic glory. He says he beheld "a great cloud, and a *fire infolding itself*, and a brightness was about it, and out of the brightness thereof as the colour of amber, out of the midst of the fire; whence issued forth the likeness of four living creatures", or cherubim. "The appearance was like burning coals of fire, and like the appearance of lamps: it went up and down among the living creatures: and the fire was bright, and out of *the fire went forth lightning*. And the living creatures ran and returned as the appearance of a *flash of lightning*."

It was customary for the Lord to answer men by fire, when any great principle, or new institution was to be established. Thus, the covenant with Abraham was confirmed by fire (Genesis 15:17); there also came out a fire from before the Lord, and consumed the offering on Aaron's induction as high priest (Leviticus 9:24); when the plague was stayed at the intercession of David, the Lord answered him by fire from heaven upon the altar of burnt offering, and thus indicated the place He had chosen to place His name there (1

Chronicles 21:16,18,26; 22:1); and also at the dedication of the temple, fire consumed the sacrifices in the same way (2 Chronicles 7:1). From these examples, I think it is a fair inference, that the flaming sword in Eden was applied to a similar purpose, namely, to flash forth its fire for the consumption of the sacrifices offered by the family of Adam before the Lord.

The fire described by Ezekiel represented the spirit of God in its cherubic relations; for as the fire flashed its lightning so they moved to and fro. It also represented the glory, or brightness, of the Messiah as he will appear upon his throne. "I saw", saith he, "as the appearance of a man above upon the throne: as the colour of amber, as the appearance of fire round about within it, from the appearance of his loins even upward, and from thence downwards, as it were the appearance of fire, and it had brightness round about. As the appearance of the bow that is in the cloud in the day of rain, so was the appearance of the brightness round about. This was the appearance *of the likeness of the glory of the LORD*" (Ezekiel 1:4,13,14,26-28).

The apocalyptic representation of the Lord's glory when seated on the throne of David is a repetition of Ezekiel's, though under some modification, so as to adapt it to circumstances which had arisen out of the things concerning Jesus. "I beheld", says John, "a throne was set in the heaven, and one sat on the throne. And he that sat was to look upon like a jasper and sardine stone: and there was a rainbow round about the throne, in sight like unto an emerald. And out of the throne proceeded lightnings and thunderings, and voices: and there were *seven lamps of fire* burning before the throne, which are *the seven spirits of God*" (Revelation 4:2-5).

From these passages, it is evident, that *fire* which is also *light*, is in symbolic representation significative of the *spirit* of God. If more proof were necessary, the outpouring of the spirit on Pentecost and at the house of Cornelius, would be sufficient to settle the matter (Acts 2:2-4; 11:15). Now, when this appearance envelops men and things, it is called *glory*, or majesty. Hence, referring to the transfiguration of Jesus on the Mount, the apostle says, "We were eye-witnesses of his *majesty*; for he received from God the Father *honour* and *glory*" (2 Peter 1:16). Such glory, or brightness, so beautifully represented by Ezekiel and John, will clothe the saints, as well as the Lord Jesus, when they shall appear in the kingdom of God: as it is written, "They that be wise shall shine as the brightness of the firmament; and they that turn many to righteousness as the stars for ever and ever" (Daniel 12:3). The apostle also speaks of the brightness of the sun, moon, and stars, as an illustration of the glory of the risen saints (1

Corinthians 15:41,42); and what is symbolically represented in Ezekiel and John of the glory of the Lord, is plainly affirmed by the prophet in these words: "The moon shall be confounded, and the sun ashamed, when the LORD of Hosts shall reign on Mount Sion, and in Jerusalem, and before his ancients *gloriously*" (Isaiah 24:23).

From the whole, then, I conclude that the cherubim and flaming sword at the east of Eden's garden were representative, *first*, of God manifest in the woman's nature as "the word made flesh"; and by being bruised in the heel, set forth as the blood-sprinkled mercy-seat, or propitiation for sin; and *secondly*, of God manifested in the spiritual nature, clothed with dazzling brightness, surpassing the sun and moon in splendour. The cherubim were the throne of the Lord in relation to the antediluvian world. There He communed with men. His presence was there, and the altar He had set up. When men went to sacrifice before Him, there they presented their offerings. If these were according to His appointment, He accepted the worshipper; and, probably, answered him by fire flashing forth from the cherubic glory, and consuming the sacrifice upon the altar. If the worshipper were faithless and disobedient, *the faces were hid* by thick darkness, and the offering remained unconsumed. This was the case with Cain, His countenance fell, and he expressed himself with anger. Then the Lord God "answered him with a voice", and the conversation ensued which is recorded in the Mosaic narrative. Having, then, ascertained the signification of the cherubim and flaming sword, I shall proceed now to speak of *the principles of religion*.

THE WAY OF THE TREE OF LIFE

"Strait is the gate and narrow is the way which leadeth unto life, and few there be that find it."

RELIGION is not coeval with the formation of man; neither had it any existence during his novitiate. Though it was instituted in the paradise, it was not for his observance there; for while he continued the *sinless* tenant of the garden, he stood in no need of the *healing* consolations it affords. Until he ate of the forbidden fruit, there was no *breach* of friendship, no misunderstanding, no alienation, between him and the Lord God; there needed not, therefore, any means or system of means, for the *reconciliation* of estranged parties. But, as soon as the good understanding was interrupted by disobedience to the Eden law, sentence of condemnation to the dust was pronounced upon the offenders; and *means were institut-*

ed to put them *at one again* with the Lord, that He might bring them back from the ground, no longer naked and ashamed of their condition; but clothed with glory and honour, incorruptibility and life, as a crown of righteousness that should never fade away. These *instituted means* made up the way of life, which Moses terms *"God's way"* (Genesis 6:12). David styles it *"the path of life"* (Psalm 16:11); which the apostle, in quoting, renders *"the ways of life"* (Acts 2:28); ὁδοὶ ζωῆς; that is, the way leading to life in which man must walk now; and the way into the kingdom from the house of death.

In the beginning, God's way was styled *"the Way of the Tree of Life"*; which in the passage where it occurs, must be taken literally, and then allegorically. In its literal sense, it was the *path* leading to the Tree in the midst of the garden; but allegorically it signified *the things to be believed and practised by those who desired to live for ever*. To believe and do, is to walk "in the Way which leadeth unto life"; because *immortality* will be a part of the recompense of reward for so doing. Until the crucifixion, the Way was marked out, first by the patriarchal arrangement of things; and secondly, by the Mosaic law; all of which pointed to the Shiloh. But, when Jesus appeared, he announced, saying, *"I am the Way*, the Truth, and the Life; no man cometh to the Father, but by me" (John 14:6). Whosoever would attain to life must believe the truth concerning Jesus, and the kingdom, which is the most holy place. Hence, it is written, "We have boldness to enter into the Holiest by the blood of Jesus, by *a New and Living Way*, which he hath consecrated for us, through *the Veil*, that is to say, *his flesh"* (Hebrews 10:19,20). The old Way was but typical of the new; but both are purely matters of revelation. Nothing is left to conjecture. Man may corrupt the Way of the Lord; but he cannot improve it: and as surely as he attempts to adapt it to circumstances, he converts it into "the Way which leadeth to destruction", which is both broad and easy to walk in, being in perfect harmony with the lusts and thinking of the flesh.

The things of the Way of Life constitute RELIGION. As a word, it is derived from the Latin *religio* from *religare*, which signifies *to bind again*; hence, *religion* is the act of *binding again*, or that which *heals a breach* previously existing between two parties. This traditional idea the Romans expressed by *religio*. They believed as the foundation of their mythology that mankind and the gods were at enmity; but how it originated they had lost the knowledge of. Their impression was that they were angry, but not implacable; nevertheless, so estranged from men that there could be no direct communication with them. Mediatorial converse with the gods was an idea universally prevalent in the world. The pagans had derived it by tradition from the family of Noah;

with whom were deposited the revealed principles of the Way of God instituted in the beginning. The idea of *mediate communication for the appeasement of divine wrath* was incorporated in all the domestic and temple worship which constituted their religion. They poured out abundantly the blood of victims; and, from the tradition of Abraham's sacrifice of Isaac in obedience to the divine mandate, the Carthaginians, who migrated from Palestine, probably concluded that the most acceptable offering for sin was that of human life. Be this as it may, the principle that "without the shedding of blood there is no remission", which is an axiom of God's truth, took deep root among all the descendants of the sons of Noah. Their system was a corruption of God's Way. They were without faith, and erred, not knowing "His thoughts".

The word used by the Greeks for *religion* was θρησκεία, from θρησκεύω, *to worship*. This may be derived from σκεῦος, taken metonymically for a *minister*; and θρέω, to *shout* or *make a clamour*; because, in that worship which results from the thinking of sinful flesh, the performers rend the air with their *shouts*; and if idolaters, they "call upon the name of their gods" with frantic cries, "cutting themselves with knives and lancets till the blood gushes out upon them" (1 Kings 18:28). The worship of God recognizes no such practices as these. When persons make their meeting houses to echo with clamorous prayers, such as may often be heard among some who profess the religion of Christ—shouting, I say, like the priests of Baal, as though God were "talking, or pursuing, or on a journey, or peradventure sleeping, and needed to be awaked"—such persons evince that they are σκεύη ὀργῆς, *vessels of wrath*, who comprehend not the genius of the truth; and not σκεύη ἐλέους, *vessels of mercy*, whose thoughts are in harmony with the divine law.

How different was the prayer of Elijah! From him ascended the "still small voice" of fervent, but tranquil supplication. He knew that God was neither deaf nor asleep; but a God everywhere present by the universality of His spirit. His words were few (Ecclesiastes 5:1,2). He did not expect to be heard for his much speaking; knowing that God is not to be moved by "vain repetitions", or volubility of speech; but by the love He has for His children, and for the glory of His name.

While men consider that there is a want of harmony between them and divine wisdom and power, and admit that they are deserving of divine wrath; they do not understand, that *as offenders they have no right to institute the means of reconciliation.* They act upon the principle, that God has left it to them to worship Him according to the dictates of their own reason. Hence the world is full of modes of worship as diversified as the thoughts of sinful flesh. The notions that men may invent religious services; and that the divine displeasure can be appeased by human contrivances are fallacies which are characteristic of false religion wherever they are found. Men have no right to invent religions, or modes of worship. Even reason dictates this when the question is viewed as a breach between friends. When a misunderstanding occurs between such, the initiatory of a reconciliation of right appertains to the party offended; and he only has the privilege of dictating the terms of agreement. Hence, in the breach between God and man, it is God's prerogative alone to prescribe; and all that men have liberty to do is to accept, or reject, the conditions of amity and peace.

This view of the case precludes entirely the idea of appeasing the wrath of God by human ingenuity. God needs not to be appeased by man; and every system, therefore, which is predicated upon the notion that it is necessary, is not only unscriptural, but *essentially* false. He is already reconciled to the world, which He has always loved; although it acts the part of, and therefore is, the enemy of God. "He so loved the world that he gave his only begotten Son that whosoever believeth in him should not perish, but have everlasting life" (John 3:16). The fact of a divine religion being instituted is proof of the love He bears the human race. He seeks to appease men by His goodness, which invites them to repentance (Romans 2:4). His love is manifested in all that He has done for the world. He has sought to enlighten it, and to exalt it to a participation in the divine nature by the ameliorating influences of the truth. He has sent messengers to it with their lives in their hands, ready to lay them down in the divine work of beseeching mankind to be reconciled to God. Is it not strange that men should besiege heaven with vain and clamorous repetitions, "praying and beseeching" God to "come down and convert these soul-stricken penitents", whom they are "bearing up in their arms before a throne of grace"; representing them as quite ready and willing to be reconciled if He would only grant His spirit, and so assure them that all was peace between them:—is it not extraordinary, I say, that this should be the order of things in the face of the revelation that "God was in Christ, *reconciling the world unto himself*, not imputing their trespasses unto them"; and so "winking at the times of their past ignorance"? (Acts 17:30).

The case is exactly the reverse of the pulpit theory. This represents the world as reconciled, while God is unreconciled and hard to be persuaded. Hence, the world is full of religions, all of which have been invented, and continue to be observed for the purpose of appeasing His wrath, and disposing Him to peace. He is represented by pulpit orators as in a rage; as ready to launch mankind into the flames of hell, and only prevented from hurling His thunderbolts at them by Christ seizing Him by His arm, as it were, and pointing to his wounds! But this is purely mythological. God stands in no such attitude to the world, nor Christ to Him. The Lord Jesus is not contending with the Father upon any such principle. There is no antagonism between them. They agree in one; and what God conceived is committed to the Son to execute. The world is not reconciled to God; nor has it the least disposition for reconciliation upon any other principles than it has itself decreed. These principles are subversive of His supremacy in the universe; they are annihilative of His truth; they demoralize His character—therefore He will accept no homage predicated upon them.

He has long since proclaimed the conditions of peace, which He is waiting to ratify in every case where they are accepted. This proclamation is styled *"the Word of Reconciliation"*, which, saith the apostle, "God hath committed unto us". Not, be it most distinctly understood, to me; nor to the ecclesiastics of any sect, party, or denomination, extant. The Word of Reconciliation hath been committed to no man, or set of men now living. It was committed to the apostles and their divinely inspired co-labourers, and to them only. So that they could say in the words of one of them, "We are of God: he that knoweth God heareth us: he that is not of God heareth not us. Hereby know we the spirit of truth, and the spirit of error" (1 John 4:6). And they were perfectly justified in saying so. For Jesus said to them. "It is not ye that speak, but the Spirit of your Father which speaketh in you" (Matthew 10:20); therefore he said in another place, "He that heareth you, heareth me; and he that heareth me heareth him that sent me".

The word of reconciliation, then, was committed to the apostles, whom God appointed as His ambassadors to the world. And, be it observed, that their ambassadorial character did not rest upon assumption, like that of their pretended successors. God attested them, as He had done His Son before them. Their credentials were in the miracles which accompanied their word. They produced the signs of their apostleship; and multitudes acknowledged them, as Nicodemus did their Lord, saying, "We know thou art a teacher come from God: for no man can do these miracles that thou doest, except God be with him" (John 3:2). They would not have been received as ambassadors of heaven if God had not attested them by His power; but being so attested, they were prepared, and did present themselves at Satan's court—that is, before Caesar—to invite the world to be at peace with Him.

The pulpit orators of this age are either greatly deceived, or, if their eyes be open, most egregiously impose upon the credulity of the public, in pretending to be Christ's ambassadors to the world. Why, they are the world's allies; the friends and supporters of the institutions of Satan's kingdom; whose subjects pay them their wages on condition of *preaching such doctrine as suits them!* Talk of being ministers and ambassadors of Jesus Christ, how perverted must their own minds be to imagine it; and how spoiled by "philosophy and vain deceit" the people, who can acquiesce in so unfounded a pretension. "Have they seen Jesus?" or what special message have they to the world from God, that men cannot read for themselves in the scriptures of truth? If they have any *new* light from Him, He will attest it as He has always done by a display of power. Men will then be justified in receiving them as plenipotentiaries of the Divine Majesty, provided always that what they speak be in strict accordance with what Paul preached; otherwise not (Galatians 1:8). "God hath given to *us*", say the apostles, *"the ministry* of reconciliation. Now then *we* are ambassadors for Christ, as though God did beseech by us; we pray in Christ's stead, be reconciled to God" (2 Corinthians 5:18-20). These are the men whom He appointed, who sought not to please the public, but to enlighten them; "for", saith one of them, "if I yet pleased men, I should not be the servant of Christ".

The church was associated with the apostles in the ministry of reconciliation. By "the church", I mean, not that multiform thing called "the church" by the world in these times; but that one, undivided body of disciples, collected together by the personal labours of the apostles and evangelists; and all through subsequent generations, who should believe and practise *the same truth.* To this *"one body"*, energized by the *"one spirit"* (Ephesians 4:4), and "perfectly joined together in the same mind and in the same judgment" (1 Corinthians 1:10; Acts 4:32), and styled "THE BRIDE"—is committed the work of making known "the manifold wisdom of God" (Ephesians 3:10), as contained in the word; and of inviting the world to be reconciled to God (Revelation 22:17). No member of this body is exempt from the obligation of co-operating in this work. It is the duty and privilege of every one in his own sphere to endeavour to turn men to righteousness; for there is no distinction of *"clergy"* and *"laity"* in the family of God.

In the days of the apostles, things were very different to what they are now. There were many congregations, or churches, but they were all *one flock*, or "denomination", and men endowed with spiritual gifts were their rulers. But even these were not distinguished from their brethren as "clergy", or priests; but as *ministers*, or servants. Well knowing the presumption, pride, and arrogance of the flesh, the Spirit commanded them especially to feed the flock, and not to fleece it; to oversee it willingly and of a ready mind, but not for the sake of compensation; and to be examples to the flock, and not to lord it over *the heritages* (1 Peter 5:2,3).

The word *"clergy,"* as the title of an order, is assumed by men who have no right to it. It is a word which comes from the Greek κλῆρος, *a lot or portion*; and is applied by the apostle in the text quoted to a single congregation of disciples: so that when he speaks of all the *congregations* of the flock, he styles them *"the heritages"*, τῶν κλήρων. But, in after years, the ministers of the heritages, or clergies, disregarded the commandment, and set themselves up as lords of the heritages, which they fleeced, and oppressed for lucre's sake. They even made the clergies of God believe that they were nothing more than mere commoners; while they themselves, the usurpers of the believers' rights, were God's peculiar lot, or portion, as the tribe of Levi were among the Israelites; and the distinction was then set up of *"clergy"* and *"laity"*, from οἱ λαοί, *the multitude!* But the distinction belongs to the apostasy, and not to God's oppressed and scattered sheep. When "clergy" get in among them, it is "as grievous wolves, not sparing the flock, but speaking perverse things to draw away disciples after them" for their own worldly gain (Acts 20:29,30). They have nothing to do with the word of reconciliation except to pervert it, and to bring it into disrepute.

The principles of the apostasy, and indeed of all false religion, are such as result from the thinking of the flesh when left to its own communings. This is illustrated in the case of Adam and Eve. They sought to cover their sin by a device of their own. "They sewed fig-leaves together, and made themselves aprons." Their shame was covered, indeed; but their consciences were not healed. But it was the best they could do in their ignorance. They were as yet unacquainted with the great principle that without the shedding of blood there could be no remission of sin (Hebrews 9:22). They were not aware of this necessity; for it had not been revealed: neither did they understand that as offenders they would not be permitted to devise a covering for themselves. They had everything to learn as to the ground of reconciliation with God. They had no idea of *religion*; for hitherto they had needed none. It yet remained to be revealed as *the divinely appointed means of healing the breach which sin had made between God and men.*

Man having been made subject to evil, and consigned to the bondage of a perishing state, the Lord God repudiated their fig-leaf invention, and "appointed coats of skins" for their covering. In this testimony there is much expressed in few words. To appoint coats of skins implies a command for the sacrifice of animals whose skins were converted to this purpose. It also implies that Adam was the priest on the occasion who presented himself before the Lord with the mediatorial blood. When the sacrifice was accepted, the offence was *provisionally* remitted; for the scripture saith, that it is not possible for the blood of animals to take away sins (Hebrews 10:4). It was impossible, because sin was to be condemned in sinful flesh. This required the death of a man; for the animals had not sinned: so that, if the whole animal world, save man, had been made an offering for sin, sin would still have been uncondemned in his nature. Besides the necessity of a human sacrifice, God deemed it equally necessary that the victim should be free from personal transgressions; and that when he had suffered, he should rise from the dead so as to be "a living sacrifice".

If the death of a transgressor would have sufficed, then, Adam and Eve might have been put to death at once, and raised to life again. But this was not according to the divine wisdom. The great principle to be compassed was *the condemnation of sin in sinful flesh, innocent of actual transgression*. This principle necessitated the manifestation of one, who should be born of a woman, but not of the will of man. Such a one would be the Seed of the Woman, made of her substance, with Him for his Father who by His over-shadowing spirit should cause her to conceive. He would be Son of God by origination; and Son of Mary by descent, or birth of sinful flesh. Now, it is not to be supposed that Adam and Eve did not understand this: God doubtless explained it to them; for they had none to teach them but Him; and without His instruction, they would not have known what they should believe. It was from them that Abel derived the knowledge which was the foundation of his faith, to which God testified in the acceptance of the firstling of his flock and the fat thereof.

Adam and his wife had faith, or God would not have accepted the sacrifices with whose skins they were clothed; for it was as true then as it is now, that "without faith it is impossible to please God". Faith, then, in the Seed of the Woman, first as a sacrifice for sin, wounded to death by his enemies; and afterwards the destroyer of the sin-power; in connexion with the sacrifice of animals as representative of the bruising of his heel—was the ground of their acceptance with the Lord God. It was the Way of Life. If they walked with God in this way, they would be as pleasing to Him as Enoch afterwards was, who was translated about 57 years after Adam's death. It was the way which was corrupted by the antediluvians; and although the sacrifices have been interrupted, the faith and hope which gained celebrity and commendation to Abel, Enoch, Noah, Abraham, Moses, and a cloud of other witnesses, comprehended substantially the same things, but less in detail than in that faith which was preached by the apostles as the gospel of the kingdom and name of Christ, for the justification of all who should believe. The things believed by Abel as compared with the faith preached on Pentecost, were as the acorn to the oak. The gospel of the kingdom in the name of Jesus was the revelation in full of the things communicated in the beginning; and afterwards more considerably amplified in the promises made to the fathers of the people of Israel. When the saints are all gathered into the kingdom, they will not find themselves in an unexpected situation. They will all be there by virtue of believing the same things; though some, contemporary with the later history of the world, will have had the advantage of more abounding testimony. Their sins will have been covered upon the same principle—*by the raiment of righteousness derived from the sacrifice, by faith in whose blood they had been cleansed.*

There is no true religion without faith; nor any true faith without the belief of *the* truth. Now, although a scriptural faith is the scarcest thing among men, it is exceedingly simple, and by no means difficult to acquire, when it is sought for aright. Paul gives the best definition of faith extant. He says, *"Faith is a confident anticipation (ὑπόστασις) of things hoped for, a full persuasion (ἔλεγχος) of things not seen"* (Hebrews 11:1). This is the faith without which, he tells us afterwards, God is not, and cannot by any possibility be, pleased. It is a faith which lays hold of the past and the future. The person who possesses it knows what is testified concerning Jesus by the apostles, and is fully persuaded of its truth; he also knows the exceeding great and precious promises which God has made concerning things to come, and he confidently anticipates the literal fulfilment of them. Laying hold of these things with a firm faith, he acquires a mode of thinking and a disposition which are estimable in the sight of God; and being like Abraham in these particulars, he is prepared, by induction into Christ, to become a son of the father of the faithful, and of the friend of God.

This faith comes by studying the scriptures; as it is written, "Faith comes by hearing, and hearing by the word of God" (Romans 10:17). This word contains the "testimony of God". When this testimony is understood, and allowed to make its own impression in "a good and honest heart", faith establishes itself there. There is no more mystery in this, than how one man comes to believe another guilty of a crime when he is made acquainted with all the testimony in the case. The ability to believe lies in a sound understanding, a candid disposition, and knowledge of the testimony of God. Where there is ignorance of this there can be no faith. It is as impossible for a man ignorant of God's word to have faith, as it is for a man to believe another guilty of an alleged crime who knows nothing at all about the matter.

But, one may say, there are multitudes who believe in Christ who are very ignorant of the scriptures. Yes, they believe in Christ as Turks believe in Mohammed. But this is not the faith defined by Paul. The mere belief that Jesus is the Son of God is not believing in him. To believe in him is to believe what God testifies concerning him. The faith of the "religious world" is like a stool with only one leg. It *professes* to believe in Jesus; but it is ignorant, and therefore faithless, of *the message* he was sent to deliver to Israel. His message had relation to "the things hoped for"—to the things of the kingdom which the God of heaven will set up upon the ruin of the kingdoms which now exist. Men are invited to believe in the Messenger of the Covenant, and in the message which unfolds the things of the covenant. To believe the one and reject the other is stultification. The "religious world" has placed itself in this predicament; and unless it believes the whole truth, which is not likely, it will be cut off as was Israel in the days of old.

"Love is the fulfilling of the law" (Romans 13:10). "He that hath my commandments, and keepeth them, he it is that loveth me"; "If any man love me, he will keep my words"; and "He that loveth me not, keepeth not my words" (John 14:21,23,24). In the face of these sayings of Jesus, what is the love of "professors" for God and His Son worth? It is like their faith, of no account whatever. God asks men for their hearts; but they give Him only their lips. They profess to love Him, but give their affections to the world. From the ecclesiastical throne, or pulpit, to the humblest "layman", can they give a scriptural demonstration of obedience to the faith? They offer verbal sacrifices without end; at least *they* do, who are compensated for their words; the "laity" are possessed of a legion of dumb spirits, and sit only as the listless hearers of the "eloquence" presented according to their taste:—but where is obedience to the gospel of the kingdom in the name of Jesus? Who ever thinks of obeying this? And yet he comes to take vengeance on all who obey it not (2 Thessalonians 1:8).

I cannot too earnestly commend the words of Samuel to the attention of the reader in this place. "Hath the LORD", saith he, "as great delight in burnt-offerings and sacrifices as in obeying the voice of the LORD? Behold, to obey is better than a sacrifice, and to hearken than the fat of rams. For rebellion is as the sin of witchcraft, and stubbornness is as iniquity and idolatry" (1 Samuel 15:22,23). A great principle is set forth in these words. It is that which can alone place men in harmony with the religion of God. Without it a man may indeed know the truth; but he must believe *and do* if he would inherit the kingdom which has been preparing from the foundation of the world.

Religion is of two kinds—that, namely, which is invented by the thinking of sinful flesh; and that which is revealed of God. The former is superstition, and leads men to do a vast deal more than God requires of them, or less than He has appointed. In what is called "Christendom" most improperly (for instead of being Christ's dominion, as the word implies, it is the arena of his sufferings in the persons of his disciples and in the suppression of his truth), these extremes of superstition in its plus and minus exhibitions, are illustrated in all their diversity from popery, which is superstition in excess, down to Quakerism, which is superstition in its homoeopathic proportion.

The religion of God, on the contrary, is the *juste milieu*, occupying a commanding and dignified position between the two extremes. It does not require men to abase themselves in the dust, and to afflict their bodies for their sins; nor to plant themselves as so many statues of clay, with downcast or upturned visage in the silence of the sepulchre, under pretence of waiting for Him to move them to preach or pray. There is no fanaticism nor pietism in His religion. When in the exercise of it men are moved to action, they are acted upon by an intelligent and earnest conviction of the truth. This is the instrumentality by which He rouses men to religious exercise—*by the spirit which is the truth* (1 John 5:6)..

When, therefore, they are really "moved by the spirit" they are moved by the truth, and do not talk nonsense. They speak according to "the law and the testimony"; and thus evince to all who understand the scriptures, that they have *"light within"*. Everything spoken not according to the word is nonsense; and the spirit never moves men to speak nonsense: nor doth the light of truth within ever teach men to undervalue the institutions of religion; or to live in neglect of them under pretence of a refined spirituality, or superior sanctity. "By their fruits ye may know them." This is an excellent rule by which to discern the spirits. Men pray for the Holy Spirit; profess to preach under its guidance; and often in a very bad spirit, protest that they received it when converted. But the spirit dwells only with those who understand, believe, and obey the gospel of the kingdom; and who walk according to its precepts. No man, be he preacher or "layman", has the spirit, or anything else to do with it than as resisting it, who does not preach and believe the gospel Paul preached. The "religious world" is utterly destitute of the spirit which belongs to God's religion; because it is ignorant of the gospel, and understands not "the voices of the prophets".

If, therefore, it be sincerely desirous of the spirit of God, let it renounce the traditions of *"the fathers"* and *"mothers"* of the apostasy, from Origen to Joanna Southcott, Jemima Wilkinson, and Ann Lee; let it shake off the thrall of Rome, Oxford, Wittenburg, Geneva, and Nauvoo; all of which make of none effect the word of the living God: and let it *"search the scriptures"* according to the divine command, "proving all things and holding fast that which is good", that it may believe the truth and obey it in the love of it. Christ will then dwell in its heart by faith (Ephesians 3:17); it will be rooted and grounded in love, having attained to the obedience of faith, which is the sole criterion of love to God; and the well-intentioned and conscientious, though unenlightened members of its community, will have no longer ground of lamentation on account of "the decay of spirituality, and the prevalence of formality and worldliness in the churches". All the Most High requires of men is just to believe what He has done, what He teaches, and what He promises: to obey the law of faith; to take care of the poor of His flock, and keep themselves unspotted from the world. This is pure and undefiled religion (Titus 2:11-14; James 1:27). But, alas! where is it to be found?

Religion being the divine remedy for sin, it is evident that when the sin of the world is taken away, religion will be abolished. So long as sin exists in the earth, so long will there be separation between God and men; for it is sin, and that only, which interrupts man's fellowship with God and His angels, as it obtained before the fall. When sin is eradicated from the world there will be no more death; for death and sin are boon companions; as it is written, "The wages of sin is death". The abolition of death presupposes the extinction of sin in the flesh; and consequently that the *animal nature* of man has been transformed (not evaporated, but changed) into the *spiritual nature* of the Elohim. Man will then be no longer subject to evil. His race will have passed through its 7,000 years of probation; and all of its individuals, who have been the faithful subjects of God's religion, will become the incorruptible and perpetual inhabitants of the earth, emancipated from every curse; God will then dwell in men by His Spirit as He now fills the Lord Jesus Christ. All distinction of church and world, saints and sinners, righteous and wicked, shall cease for ever; for there will be none of the Serpent's seed alive. They will have been utterly destroyed; for only "the meek shall inherit the earth, and delight themselves with abundance of peace" (Psalm 37:11).

Religion begins in the third chapter of Genesis, and finds the record of its end in the last two chapters of the Revelation. Its abolition is expressed in these words: "Behold, the tabernacle of God is with men, and he will dwell with them, and they shall be his people, and God himself shall be with them as their God. And he shall wipe away all tears from their eyes: and *there shall be* NO MORE DEATH, neither sorrow, nor crying, neither shall there be any more pain: for the former things are passed away. And he that sat upon the throne said, Behold, *I make all things new. And there shall be* NO MORE CURSE" (Revelation 21:3-5; 22:3). Then will the victory be complete. *The Sin-power and all its works will be finally abolished; and an eternal jubilee gladden the hearts of men, in whom God will be all and in all* (1 Corinthians 15:28).

As it is highly important that the reader should have a distinct understanding of the religion of God, if he would profit by it, it may not be amiss, in order to facilitate its comprehension, to present the following

SUMMARY OF PRINCIPLES

1.   Religion is that *system of means* by which the *breach* made by sin between God and man is repaired; and the wound inflicted upon the latter is healed.

2.   Man's defilement was first a matter of conscience; and then corporeal. For this cause, his purification is first a cleansing of his understanding, sentiments, and affections; and afterwards, the perfecting of his body by spiritualizing it at the resurrection.

3.   An *evil* conscience is made manifest by the truth, and is evinced by shame and by "doubts and fears".

4.   A *good* conscience is characterized by a full assurance of faith and hope, founded upon an understanding of the gospel of the kingdom in the name of Jesus, and an obedience to it. The obedience of faith gives the subject "the answer of a good conscience".

5.   A *seared* conscience has no compunctions. It is that condition of thinking flesh which results from the absence of all divine knowledge, and habitual sin. It is incurable.

6.   Religion is a system of *faith* and *practice*.

7.   The *faith* of religion embraces what God has done, what He promises to do, and what He teaches in His word; all of which is presented for the elaboration of a godlike disposition, termed "the Divine Nature" in the believer.

8.   To be of any value, religion must be entirely of divine appointment.

9.   The *obedience* of religion is a conformity to "*the law of faith*" resulting from the belief of "the things concerning the Kingdom of God and the name of Jesus Christ". It is termed "*the obedience of faith*"; for believers only can yield it.

10.   The *repentance* of religion is the *thinking contrary* to the flesh, and *in harmony with* the testimony of God: accompanied with an Abrahamic disposition as the consequence of believing it.

11.   The *morality* of religion is the taking care of the widows and orphans of Christ's flock, and "keeping one's self unspotted from the world". Collectively, it is the "fruits meet for repentance".

12.   Religion hath its *"elements"*, which are styled *"weak and beggarly"*. These are "days, and years, and months, and times"; "meat and drink"; sacrifices, ablutions, ordinances of divine service, holy places, veils, altars, censers, cherubim, mercy-seats, holy days, sabbaths, etc., "which were a shadow of things to come; but the substance is of Christ" (Colossians 2:17).

13.   The elementary doctrinal principles of religion are few and simple: and no other reason can be given for them than that *God wills them.** They may be thus stated: —

a.   No sinner can by any means redeem his brother, nor give to God a ransom for him, that he should still live for ever, and not see corruption (Psalm 49:7,9).

b.   Sin cannot be covered, or remitted, without the shedding of blood.

---

*With reference to paragraph 13 above, the fact that *God wills* the elementary doctrinal principles of religion is all sufficient, but here and there allusions in the scriptures suggest *reasons why* He so wills them. For example when Nadab and Abihu set aside His will and offered strange fire He struck them dead, and Moses recognized the reason: "This is it that the LORD spake, saying, I will be sanctified in them that come nigh me, and before all the people I will be glorified" (Leviticus 10:3). Moses himself afterwards died on Mount Nebo (as Aaron had previously died on Mount Hor) without entering the promised land, and God said it was "because ye sanctified me not in the midst of the children of Israel" (Deuteronomy 32:51). The Lord's prayer, in its opening words, places the same principle in the forefront: "Our Father which art in heaven, Hallowed be thy name". "If I be a father, where is mine honour?" said God to apostate Israel (Malachi 1:6). "I am a great King, saith the LORD of Hosts, and my Name is dreadful among the heathen" (verse 14). God set forth Jesus as a Mercy seat, not only for man's sake, but that "He might be just", and that "boasting" on man's part might be "excluded" (Romans 3:4,25-27). He committed the treasure of the truth to "earthen vessels", that "the excellency of the power might be of God" and not of man (2 Corinthians 4:7). Thus He "chose the base things of the world ... that no flesh should glory in his presence" (1 Corinthians 1:28-29). These and similar scriptures convey the idea that the reasons of God's appointments in His principles of religion are that, in the first place, He may be "justified", "honoured", "sanctified", and "hallowed"; and next, that man, taking this truly reasonable, humble, and obedient attitude, may be saved from death and live for ever. No one more strenuously upholds this doctrine than Dr. Thomas.

c.   The blood of animals cannot take away sin.

d.   Sin must be condemned in sinful flesh innocent of transgression.

e.   Sins must be covered by a garment derived from the purification-sacrifice made living by a resurrection.

14.   To be naked is to be in an unpardoned state.

15.   The proximate principles of religion are "repentance from dead works, faith towards God, doctrine of baptisms, and of the laying on of hands, and of resurrection of the dead, and of eternal judgment" (Hebrews 6:1,2).

RUDIMENTS OF THE WORLD

CHAPTER VI

THE PRESENT WORLD IN RELATION TO
THE WORLD TO COME

God the builder of all things—Nothing elaborated by chance, but all things the result of divine premeditation—Whatever exists He created for His own pleasure and glory—The purpose of God in the work of creation and providence, revealed in the scriptures—The present order of things merely provisional—The economy of the fulness of appointed times the true "Intermediate State" of a thousand years duration—The tower of Babel builders, peacemen, and socialists—The principle upon which men attain to the angelic nature, and dignity, defined—God's two-fold purpose in the foundation of the world stated—The means by which it is accomplishing—Dissertation on the Elohim.

AMONG the many and various titles of the Supreme Being in the scriptures of truth, is that of a Builder, or Architect; as it is written, "the BUILDER of all things is God". Pursuing this suggestion, I remark, that "a wise master builder" never begins to build without a *design*. He draughts this after a scale of so much to the foot. This is the extension, or *time*, so to speak, of the building, or edifice, to be erected. Having well considered the whole, he concludes that it is the best possible plan that can be devised in harmony with the rules and principles of architecture. The plan then becomes his "purpose", his "fore-ordination", "predestination", or design. All subsequent arrangements are made to conform to this recorded purpose, because it is the very best his most deliberate wisdom and ingenuity could devise; and no extraneous suggestions, or considerations, will cause him to diverge in the smallest iota from his predestination.

The next thing the Builder does is to collect together all the necessary materials, whether of brick, stone, lime, sand, wood, or aught else that may be needed. If a spectator desired to know what all these crude matters were heaped up together in one place for, the architect would reveal to him *"the mystery of his will which he had purposed in himself"* (Ephesians 1:9), by submitting the draught of his plan, in all its lines, circles, angles, etc.; and he would describe to him such an arrangement of the materials as would impress the spectator's mind with an image of the edifice, though it would fall infinitely short of the reality when perfected.

If we suppose the edifice, call it temple, or palace, to be now finished, the architect would next order the rubbish, or materials which were left as unfit to work into the building, and therefore worthless, such as broken brick, splinters, shavings, sand, and so forth, to be cast out to be trodden under foot, to burn (Malachi 4:3; Matthew 5:13), etc. Thus the edifice is built out of the accumulated materials, according to the outline of the draught, or purpose of the Builder; and the work is done.

Now, as the scripture saith, the Great Builder of the heavens and earth is God. "His hand hath laid the foundations of the earth, and his right hand hath spanned the heavens." The Builder of all things either left the elements of the world to a random and accidental aggroupment, or, He "ordered them in all things". Where is the man among "philosophers" who will stultify, or idiotize himself by saying that the Creator permitted chance to elaborate the terrestrial system? The thing is absurd. Chance is defined to be the *cause* of fortuitous, or accidental events. What is that cause? The fool says in his heart it is not God. Why does he say so? Because he would make the cause of all things, a mere physical disposition in matter, destitute of all intellectual and moral attributes, *in order that he may get rid of all responsibility to such a Being*. He hates truth, righteousness, and holiness, and therefore he vainly strives to persuade himself that there is no God of a truthful, righteous, and holy character.

But no man of any pretensions to sound mind would affirm this. Nothing has been elaborated by chance. The scriptures declare that everything was measured, meted out, and weighed; and that the Spirit of the Lord executed His work without any to counsel or instruct Him. As it is written, "He has *measured* the waters in the hollow of his hand, and *meted out* heaven with a span, and comprehended the dust of the earth *in a measure*, and *weighed* the mountains in scales, and the hills in a balance. Who hath directed the Spirit of the LORD, or being his counsellor, hath taught him? With whom took he counsel, and who instructed him, and taught him in the path of judgment, and taught him knowledge, and showed to him the way of understanding?" (Isaiah 40:12-14).

God, then, had in His own mind a pattern, or design, of all the work that was before him, before He uttered a word, or His spirit began to move. This design, or archetype, which placed the beginning and the end of all things before Him in one panoramic view, was constructed in harmony with the principles—the eternal principles of His vast, unbounded realm; which coincide with the immutable attributes of His character. The work He was about to execute was for His own pleasure; as, saith the scripture, "Thou hast created all things; and for thy pleasure they are, and were created". But, when the work is finished, which, for His own pleasure, God labours to elaborate, *what will it consist in?*

This inquiry we make as the spectators of the wonders of creation, providence, and redemption. We behold the materials of these departments of Eternal Wisdom, and we ask to what are all things tending? What temple, or edifice, is the Divine Architect raising for His own pleasure and glory? If we turn our thoughts within us, there is no voice there which unfolds the philosophy of His doing; if we soar into the heavens, or descend into the sea; if we search through the high places of the earth—we find no answer; for "Who hath known the mind of the LORD, who hath been his counsellor, or who hath instructed him?" If we would ascertain what God designs to elaborate out of the past, the present, and the future, we must be content to assume the attitude of listeners, that He may reveal to us from His own lips what He intends to evolve in the consummation of His plans.

God, then, has caused a book to be written for our information as to His design—His ultimate purpose in the works of creation, providence, and redemption, which are the three grand divisions of His labour; and which are all tending to the development of one great and glorious consummation. This Book, so graciously bestowed, and so inimitably written, is vernacularly styled THE BIBLE (ὁ βίβλος); or, scripturally, THE WRITINGS (αἱ γραφαί) and sometimes THE HOLY WRITINGS. These are divided into two parts, popularly styled the Old and New Testaments. The appeals made by Jesus and his apostles to the writings were to what is now termed the Old Testament; for there were no other writings acknowledged then. The New Testament was not written in the beginning of the apostolic era. Indeed it was not so much needed then; for the apostles taught orally the things, which afterwards they in part committed to writing. The breathings of the spirit, enunciated through the spiritual men of the churches, supplied the place which the New Testament now occupies. The writings of the prophets, which are the root and foundation of the New Testament, and without the understanding of which the latter is unintelligible aright, are divided into "the law and the testimony"; or "the law, the prophets, and the psalms"; altogether they are styled THE WORD. This, with "the testimony for Jesus" left on record by the apostles, makes the *"word of the Lord"* to us, which lives and abides for ever.

All writers and speakers must be unceremoniously tried by this; for, God hath said, that "if they speak not according to this word, it is because there is no light in them". It matters not who the sinner may be; pope, cardinal, archbishop, bishop, minister, or their admirers; or, even one of the saints of God, or an angel himself; nothing he may say, or write, must be received unless in strict conformity to this word; and of this the people must judge for themselves upon their own responsibility; and in the face of their eternal weal, or rejection from the Kingdom of God. To this Book, then, we appeal for light—for information concerning the things which shall be hereafter.

If we take up an ordinary book, how could we proceed to ascertain the end the author had in writing his book? We should read it through carefully, and thus having made ourselves acquainted with its contents, we should be prepared to answer the question intelligently and accurately. *Why do men not do so with the Bible?* God is admitted by all sensible persons to be the author; Moses, the apostles, and the prophets, are but His amanuenses to whom He dictated what to write. If then the questions be put, what end had God in view in the six day's work of the creation? in His subsequent providential arrangements in relation to men and nations? and in the propitiatory sacrifice of the Lamb of God?—we proceed in the same way with the Bible in which He tells His own story; and answer according to the light we may have acquired.

Now the Book of God is peculiar in this; it narrates the past, the present, and the *future* all in one volume. We learn from the accuracy of its details in relation to the past and the present, to put unbounded confidence in its declaration concerning the future. In ascertaining, therefore, the ultimate design of eternal wisdom in the creation of all things, we turn to the end of the Bible to see what God hath said *shall be* as the consummation of what has gone before; for what He has said *shall be the permanent constitution of things, must be the end which He originally designed before ever the foundation of the earth was laid.*

Turn we then, to the last two chapters of the Book of God. What do we learn from these? We learn from them, that there is to be a great physical and moral renovation of the earth. That every curse is to cease from off the globe; and that it is to be peopled with men who will be deathless, and free from all evil. That they will all then be the sons of God, a community of glorious, honourable, incorruptible, and living beings; who will constitute the abode of the Lord God Almighty and the Lamb, the glory of whose presence will evolve a brilliancy surpassing the splendour of the sun. *The globe a glorious dwelling place, and its inhabitants an immortal and glorious people, with the indwelling presence of the Eternal Himself*—is the consummation which God reveals as the answer to the question concerning His ultimate design. The following testimonies will prove it:

184

"The inheritance of the saints in light" (Colossians 1:12). "An inheritance incorruptible, and undefiled, and that fadeth not away, reserved in heaven" (1 Peter 1:4)—"I, John, saw a new heaven and a new earth, and *there was no more sea*. And I saw the holy city, new Jerusalem, coming down from God out of heaven, prepared as a bride adorned for her husband. And I heard a great voice out of heaven, saying, The tabernacle of God is with men, and He will dwell with them, and they shall be His people, and God Himself will be with them, their God. And God shall wipe away all tears from their eyes: and there shall be no more death, neither sorrow, nor crying, neither shall there be any more pain; for the former things (or the "heaven and earth" in which they existed) are passed away. And he that sat upon the throne said, Behold I make all things new, And he said unto me, Write; for these words are true and faithful. And he said unto me, It is done; I am Alpha and Omega, the beginning and the end. I will give unto him that is athirst of the fountain of the water of life freely. He that overcometh shall inherit all things; and I will be his God, and he shall be my son" (Revelation 21:1-7); "and there shall be no more curse" (22:3).

Now, *the creating of all things new* implies that the constitution of things which precedes the new creation was *an old system*, that had answered the end for which it was arranged in the first instance. This old system, styled by John "the former heaven and earth", is manifestly the system of the world based upon the six days' creation; for "the former things" which had passed away in the vision were the sea, death, sorrow, sin, the curse, and all their correlates. This old creation, with its temporary mediatorial constitution, then, is but a grand system of means, elementary of a still grander and inconceivably more magnificent creation, which will be of an unchangeable and eternal constitution. The old Mosaic physical heavens and earth are to the new creation as the accumulated materials of a building are to the edifice about to be built: and hold the same relation to the new heavens, as the natural system does to the spiritual. We repeat, then, that the creation of the six days, which we have termed Mosaic, because Moses records their generations, was not a finality; but simply the beginning, or ground-work of things, when God commenced the execution of His purpose which He had arranged; the *ultimatum* of which was, to elaborate BY TRUTH AND JUDGMENT, as His instrumentality, a world of intelligent beings, who should become the glorious and immortal population of the globe, under an immutable and eternal constitution of things.

Such is the superlative of the matter. The physical creation of the six days is positive; there was *an ulterior*, however, as well as

185

an ultimate purpose in the work. The ulterior is the comparative; the ultimate, the transcendent excellency of the design. The Almighty Builder of all things intended not to translate the whole human race from a state of sin and death at once into a state of good and glory. He foresaw that the living race would never be fit for this; but that they must be previously disciplined and prepared for the transition. Hence, he proposed to develop an INTERMEDIATE STATE *upon the earth*, and among the nations of mortal men contemporary with it; in which, good and evil would still be commingled, but differing from the preceding state (the present) in this, that, though evil would continue to be, sin should not have dominion over the world, but be dethroned by righteousness. We have styled this state *intermediate*, because it is designed to occupy *a middle place between* the present times of the Gentiles, and the unchangeable constitution of the globe, when there will be "no more sea", and all men will be immortal.

This ulterior, but not ultimate, constitution of things is alluded to in these words: "God *hath made known* unto us the Mystery of his will, which he hath purposed in himself according to his good pleasure: that in the dispensation of the fulness of the times appointed (*εἰς οἰκονομίαν τοῦ πληρώματος τῶν καιρῶν*) he might gather together in one, all things in Christ, both which are in the heavens, and the things upon the earth, in him" (Ephesians 1:9,10). This elliptical allusion to the revelation of God's will, or purpose, is strikingly interpreted by the following passages from the word. "The Iron Kingdom (the Roman) shall be divided into ten kingdoms. And in their days shall the God of heaven set up A KINGDOM, which shall never be destroyed: and the kingdom shall not be left to other people; but it shall break in pieces and consume all these kingdoms, and it shall stand for ever." They shall become "like the chaff of the summer threshing-floors; and the tempest shall carry them away, that no place shall be found for them: and the stone (or power) that shall smite them shall become a great mountain, and fill the whole earth" (Daniel 2:41,44,35).

"There shall be given to the Son of Man dominion, and glory, and a kingdom, that all people, nations, and languages, may serve him; his dominion is an EVERLASTING DOMINION which shall not pass away, and his kingdom shall not be destroyed, and all dominions, or rulers, shall serve and obey him" (7:14,27).

"The LORD," Jesus, "shall be king over all the earth; in that day shall there be one LORD, and his Name one" (Zechariah 14:9).

"The LORD of Hosts," Jesus, "shall reign on Mount Zion, and in Jerusalem, and before his ancients gloriously" (Isaiah 24:23). "I, Jesus, was born that I might be a King."

"The righteous dead shall live again
A thousand years with Christ to reign." (Revelation 20:6)

"The nations shall beat their swords into ploughshares, and their spears into scythes: nation shall not lift up sword against nation, neither shall they learn war any more" (Isaiah 2:4).

From these testimonies, it is manifest to all minds, unspoiled by a "vain and deceitful philosophy", that, in the Economy of the Future Age, all kingdoms, states, and empires; and all people, nations, and languages, are to be gathered together into one dominion under Jesus Christ. These are the "things in the heavens", and the "things on the earth", which, grouped together into one imperial dominion, will constitute an economy of things that will be wonderful and glorious. We see, then, what God hath declared *shall be* — an IMPERIO-REGAL HIERARCHY OF IMMORTALS, *which*, UNDER ONE CHIEF, *shall possess all power and authority over subject nations in the flesh.* By such a constitution of things as this upon the globe for 1,000 years, the human race will have furnished from the foundation of the world a sufficient multitude of righteous men to people the earth when there shall be "no more sea". Till this economy begins, the previous 6,000 years will have furnished scope sufficient to obtain an adequate number of kings and priests from Israel and the nations for the kingdom of the Future Age.

After this exhibition who will lack the ability to answer the question — Why hath God made of one blood all nations of men to dwell on all the face of the earth; and determined the previously-appointed times; and the bounds of their habitation? The answer is, He created a human pair and subjected them to the law of procreation, that they might so multiply as to refill the earth; He divided their posterity into nations by the confusion of tongues; determined the times of their self-dominion; and set limits to their territorial extension — that, in the fulness of time, the materials of A KINGDOM AND EMPIRE OF NATIONS might exist, which He would confer upon a king, and such other regal associates as in His own good and sovereign pleasure He should think proper to appoint.

The segregation of mankind into nations, then, is not accidental, or the result of mere human policy. It is a divine appointment. Human wisdom was opposed to it in the beginning; and if Socialists, Peace Societies, and such like, could carry out their schemes, they would commingle the nations into one indiscriminate "universal brotherhood", and abolish all times and bounds of habitation.

The projectors of the city and tower of Babel announced in their programme that the enterprise was intended to secure to the patrons of the scheme "*a Name*"; and to prevent them from being "scattered abroad upon the face of the whole earth". They were opposed to nationalization; they preferred a *fraternal communism*, and proceeded to build a temple of social fraternity for all mankind. But God and His purposes were in none of their thoughts. They were concocting schemes utterly subversive of them; therefore He interfered, saying, "Behold, the *people is one*, and they have all one language; and this they *begin* to do; and now nothing will be restrained from them which they have imagined to do. Let us go down, and there confound their language, that they may not understand one another's speech. So the LORD scattered them abroad from thence upon all the face of the earth: and they left off to build the city" (Genesis 11:4).

The development of this imperio-regal constitution of nations is the one grand idea of the divine writings. It is the subject matter of the gospel of the kingdom and peace of God. All other divine arrangements concentre in this as the great focal truth of human redemption and terrestrial regeneration. The needle is not more true to the pole, nor planetary attraction to the sun's centre, than are the things of the prophets and apostles to this idea of an Israelitish kingdom and empire of nations. To lose sight of this is to remain in hopeless ignorance of the faith and hope, which God has graciously set before us in His word; and to lay ourselves open to every species of delusion that the carnal mind, so fertile of evil fruits, may enunciate in opposition to the "mystery of the divine will".

Enlightened by the scriptures of truth, we are enabled to discern that the present system of the world is but the aggregate of the means through which God purposes to accomplish *two grand developments*—the one *near*; and the other a *thousand years more remote*. The creation of the six days, and the peopling of the earth with nations of mortal men, is the mere preparation and collection together of the raw materials for a great, glorious, and magnificent display of wonders upon the earth. Hitherto, these materials have been shaped, or reduced, from chaos into form, by the *modifying influence of truth and divine judgment*. But for these agencies "a universal brotherhood" of savages, such as we behold in the vast howling wilderness of Africa and America, would have shared the globe with the nobler beasts of the forest; unmitigated socialism after this type would have effectually superseded all ecclesiastical and civil association; or, if this extreme had given place to another, the world would have groaned under the ferocious despotism of a "brother of the sun and moon", a Nero, or of a Pope Alexander VI.

But truth and the sword of God have been thrown into the scale of human events. Multitudes have embraced that truth in whole or part; vastly more, however, in part than as a saving whole. According to their apprehensions of it, they have resolved themselves into party groups. A minority—a great minority, so great as to be styled "*a few*", have seized upon it in letter and spirit. These contend against everything opposed to it without regard to fame, property, or life; they contend, however, not with the sword of the flesh, but with "the sword of the spirit, which is the word of God". Not so, however, they who embrace it in part, corrupt it by admixture with human tradition, or reject it altogether. They fight for their opinions, as their means enable them. They who corrupt or reject it endeavour to suppress it *vi et armis*, by force, not of argument, but by clamour, misrepresentation, and proscriptive laws; and where they can find no scope, by imprisonment, war, and murder.

But there are others who understand the theory of the truth to a considerable extent, but have only that spirit of liberty and sense of justice in them which the truth inspires; without that disposition to suffer patiently and unresistingly for it, which it inculcates. Men of this class take the sword for liberty and the rights of men; and contend against all who would destroy them with a courage which strikes terror into their enemies. By such agency as this, by action and re-action, by agitating the truth revealed, and the warlike conflict it produces among the nations, things have been shaped into the civil, ecclesiastical, and social constitution of things, which prevails upon the earth in the present age; and which, having waxed old, is ready to vanish away.

In view of these things we come upon a very interesting, and indeed, immensely important enquiry, namely: "Upon what principle, or principles, did the God of heaven propose to carry out His purposes in relation to the developing of rulers for the kingdom and empire of nations; and for the peopling of the globe under its eternal and incorruptible constitution?" Was it upon a purely intellectual, or a purely moral, or a purely physical and mechanical, principle; or was it upon all these conjoined? For example, He peopled the present world by first creating a human pair, and then placing them under the natural, or physical, laws. Will he provide kings and priests for his kingdom, and afterwards people the globe in its perfect constitution, by natural generation, and physical regeneration; or, upon some other principle revealed in His word? Will He bestow the honour, glory, and dignity of His kingdom and empire upon men, because they are men; or because they are descended by natural birth from righteous ancestors? Or, will men inhabit the globe for ever, because they are flesh, and the offspring of His creative power?

It will doubtless be admitted, that upon whatever principle God might determine to operate, it would certainly be such a one as would redound most to the glory of His wisdom, justice, and sovereign power. This being conceded, we would enquire, would it have been to the glory of God, if He had made man a mere machine?—had He made *inexorable necessity* the law of his nature, which he must yield to as the tides to the moon, or the earth to the sun? No reasonable man would affirm this. The principle laid down in the scripture is that MAN HONOURS GOD IN BELIEVING HIS WORD AND OBEYING HIS LAWS. There is no other way in which men can honour their Creator. This honour, however, consists not in a mechanical obedience; in mere action without intelligence and volition, such as matter yields to the natural laws; but in an enlightened, hearty, and voluntary obedience, while the individual possess the power not to obey if he think best. There is no honour, or glory, to God as a moral being, in the falling of a stone towards the earth's centre. The stone obeys the law of gravitation *involuntarily*. The obedience of man would have been similar had God created and placed him under a physical law, which should have necessitated his movements, as gravitation doth the stone.

Does a man feel honoured, or glorified, by the compulsory obedience of a slave? Certainly not; and for the simple reason, that it is involuntary, or forced. But, let a man by his excellencies command the willing services of free men—of men who can do their own will and pleasure; yet voluntarily obey him, and, if he required it, are to sacrifice their lives, fortunes, and estates, and all for the love they bear him; would not such a man esteem himself honoured, and glorified, in the highest degree by such signal conformity to his will? Unquestionably; and such is the honour and glory which God requires of men. Had He required a necessitated obedience, He would have secured His purpose effectually by at once filling the earth with a population of adults, so intellectually organized as to be incapable of a will adverse to His own—who should have obeyed Him as wheels do the piston rod and steam by which they are moved—the mere automata of a miraculous creation.

But, saith an objector, this principle of the *enlightened voluntary obedience of a free agent* is incompatible with benevolence; it would have prevented all the misery and suffering which have afflicted the world, if the globe had been at once with a sufficient number of inhabitants, who should all of them have been created perfect.

If the character of the All-wise were constituted of one attribute only, this might have been the case. But God is the sovereign of the universe, as well as kind and merciful; and all His intelligent creatures are bound to be in harmony with His name. He might have operated on the objector's principle had it pleased

Him; but it did not; for He has pursued the directly opposite course. Instead of creating a human pair, He could, indeed, have filled the earth with immortals, and left them blessed for ever. But then they would have been without character, neither virtuous nor vicious; and, like themselves, their world would have been without a history. God is not merely an intellectual, He is also a moral, being. "The LORD, whose name is Jealous, is a jealous God"; yet "merciful and gracious, longsuffering, and abundant in goodness and truth; visiting the iniquity of the fathers upon the children unto the third and fourth generations of *them that hate me*; and showing mercy unto thousands of *them that love me, and my commandments*".

Such is the name, or character, of God; hence, as all His works must glorify Him, they must redound to His praise as a merciful and gracious, a just, holy, and truthful, being. The sun at noonday, the moon walking in brightness, and the stars in their courses, illustrate His eternal-power and superhumanity; but it is only His relations with intellectual and morally constituted creatures—the image and likeness of Himself—that can illustrate His moral glory, and redound to the honour of His name.

Seeing that God had rejected the principle of *stern necessity and immediate physical perfection*, there remained but one other, according to which He could officer His kingdom and empire; and at length fill the globe with an order of beings "equal to the angels". Upon this principle He has worked from the foundation of the world to this day. He made man a reasonable creature, and capable of being acted on by motive, either for weal or woe. He placed him under a law, which required *belief of God's word and obedience*. He could obey, or disobey, as he pleased ; he was "free to stand and free to fall". He disbelieved God's word; he believed a lie, and sinned. Here was voluntary disobedience; hence, the opposite to this is made the principle of life namely, belief of *whatsoever* God saith, and voluntary obedience to His law. This is the principle to which the world is reprobate; and to a conformity with which all men are invited, and urged by the motives presented in the scriptures; even all who would inherit the kingdom of God, and afterwards inhabit the earth for ever, on an equal footing with the angels of the universe.

The following testimonies will elucidate the principle of the divine economy. "I will give *unto him that is athirst* of the fountain of the water of life freely; and *he that overcometh* shall inherit all things";—"Blessed are they that *do his commandments* that they *may have right* to the Tree of Life, and that they may enter through the gates into the city";—"To him that overcometh will I give to eat of the Tree of Life which is in the midst of the Paradise of God";—"He shall not be hurt by the second death";— 'To him that overcometh and *keepeth my works to the end*, I will give POWER OVER ALL NATIONS: and he shall RULE THEM with a rod of iron";—"If thou doest well thou shalt be accepted"; —"These things are written that ye may believe, and that *believing* ye may have LIFE *through his name*";—"As many as received Jesus, to them gave he power to become the sons of God, *to them that believe on his name*, which are born, not of blood, nor of the will of the flesh, nor of the will of man, but which are born of God";—"Except a man be born of water and the spirit he cannot enter into the kingdom of God";—"He that believes the gospel and is baptized shall be saved";—"God will render to every man *according to his deeds*; to them, who *by patient continuance in well doing* SEEK FOR glory, honour, and immortality—ETERNAL LIFE".

But of testimonies there is no end. The law of the Lord is perfect, and *without a single exception*. There are no "perhapses" or "maybes"; it is not "yea and nay, but Amen in Christ Jesus". The only way to the kingdom of God, and to a participation in the eternal constitution of the world, is in the path of a faithful obedience to the law of God.

Now from these testimonies it is plain, that to attain the rank of the sons of God in the eternal world—where, indeed, all are sons without exception—human beings, without respect to age, sex, or condition, must *believe and obey the truth*; for "without faith it is impossible to please God". This rule provides for no exceptions; but declares the principle without qualification. If faith then be required, it is manifest that God designed to move men *by motive*, not by necessity—but *by intellectual and moral considerations*.

Now the carrying out of this principle necessarily involves great loss of human, or animal life; for if virtue be the subject of reward, vice must also be of punishment. Because, if vice were unrestrained, it would gain the ascendancy; eradicate virtue from among men as before the flood; and defeat the principle upon which it is proposed to effectuate the work, and thus destroy the original design.

The mere fact of dust, by the power of God expressed in creation and the physical laws, assuming the form of men, does not, therefore, entitle them to the glory of the Future Ages; or expose them to the alternative of damnation in eternal death. These are doctrines predicated upon a *moral*, not a physical constitution of things. The destiny of the animal world, and that of men, is physically the same; they are all under God's physical laws, and consequently have "no pre-eminence" the one over the other. Man differs from other animals, as these differ from one another;

and if his *race* attain to the angelic nature, which God designs it shall, it will not be because it is human, but because it is *voluntarily obedient to His laws*.

The peopling of the Future World upon this principle we have proved from the Word. It is a principle which annihilates all human sophisms and traditions about "the salvation of all mankind"; the "predestination of some to salvation, and of others to damnation by a stern, inexorable necessity"; "physical regeneration before death"; "the disembodied existence of immortal souls in heaven or hell for ages before the resurrection"; the "damnation and salvation of infants, idiots, and pagans"; "purification by death and resurrection without previous remission"— and much more unscriptural, irrational, and absurd jargon of the schools and systems of the age.

Universalism, a wide-spreading pernicious influence in the world, which teaches that all human beings, of whatever age or character, shall dwell with God eternally, is based upon a mistaken notion of God's purpose in the formation of the animal world. It is assumed by that shallow system of speculative theology that His intention was "the greatest possible good to the whole creation". This certainly was not His design; for the principle I have demonstrated is utterly subversive of it. The *voluntary obedience of free men* implies the possibility, as well as the probability, of their *voluntary disobedience* predicted upon the known capriciousness of human nature. Now, as the very existence of God upon His throne depends upon the suppression, and therefore punishment, of sin (which is sorrow and pain so long as life lasts), the greatest possible good to *all* men, in the universal sense of the word, was no part of His design, being incompatible with the principle and end in view. "The greatest possible good of the whole creation", then, being no part of His purpose, it is a mere conceit, the idea that God wills the immortalization and glorification of every member of the human family. He has purposed no such thing. His design requires only *the separation from the nations of a sufficient number of men and women to occupy the globe when constituted on an eternal basis, without sea, be that many or few*.

"What a paltry, contemptible few", exclaims one, "compared with the immense mass of human flesh and blood which will have existed on the earth for 7,000 years!" Granted; but what is needed more than a sufficient population for the renovated earth? If this immense mass of corruption and sin, living and dead, had listened to the voice of reason, if it would have believed God and obeyed Him, an adequate provision would have been made for them; but they would not, and the consequences inevitably follow. The principle is an eternal one. It is persistent as God Himself; a principle without an exception, and as uncompromising as the truth.

The case of the thief on the cross only establishes the rule. He believed in the kingdom of God, and acknowledged Jesus while in his lowest estate as "King of the Jews", and therefore future monarch of the nation. He was *by constitution* one of "the children of the kingdom" (Matthew 8:12), though he had proved himself a very disreputable citizen. It was only necessary in his case that his faith and change of mind and disposition should be counted to him for repentance and remission of sins; for without this he could not enter the kingdom of God. The Lord Jesus, who then alone upon the earth had power to forgive sins, granted his petition, and so constituted him an heir of the righteousness which is by faith in the gospel of the kingdom. The case of the thief was unique, and one to which there has been none like, before or since.

It is proved, that the revealed mystery of God's will, which He has purposed in His own mind, is first *to found a kingdom and empire of nations, which He will bestow on the crucified and resurrected King of the Jews, and upon all those who believe the doctrine, or word, concerning it, and become obedient to the faith*; and secondly, at the end of 7,000 years from the foundation of the world, *to renovate the globe, and to people it with immortal men "equal to the angels", who shall all have attained to the eternal state and to the possession of all its transcendent glories, on the principle of believing His "exceeding great and precious promises", and of lovingly and voluntarily obeying His laws.*

Behold, then, the conclusion of the matter. There are two systems, or worlds—the one the animal and natural; the other the spiritual and incorruptible; and between these a mixed state, being partly animal and partly spiritual, which may be termed *the transition state.* Out of the natural system, as the materials and scaffolding the building, God purposes to elaborate "the ages of the ages" with all that shall pertain to them. Thus constituted, the globe will become a glorious province of the universe, and a new imperial abode of the Divine Majesty. It will then be a sealess (Revelation 21:1) and luminous sphere, and peopled with myriads of inhabitants of equal rank and station with the angels of God.

The means by which, from the beginning, He determined to accomplish this magnificent work, were, first, by His creative energy to lay the foundation; secondly, by constitutional arrangement and angelic oversight, which men term "providence", to shape and overrule all things, so as to work out the end proposed; thirdly, by the moral force of truth, argued and attested;

fourthly, by judicial interference in human affairs; and lastly, by re-creative energy in the renovation of the earth. When the gigantic work is perfected, the edifice will be complete; and the top stone imposed with joyous acclamations, saying, "Grace! grace unto it!"

DISSERTATION ON THE ELOHIM

THE principles of universal grammar require in general that a "*verb agree with its nominative in number and person*"; as, the spirit moves, the waters roar. Here *the spirit* is of the singular number, and third person; and so is the verb *moves*; hence they agree in number and person: "the waters" is of the third person plural, and so is *roar*; hence they also agree. But in the first chapter of Genesis, this rule appears to be disregarded by the spirit, under whose guidance Moses wrote. In the first verse it reads, *Berayshith bara Elohim*, *i.e.*, in the beginning Elohim created. In this sentence *bara* is the verb in the third person singular, and *Elohim* a noun in the third person plural; so that they do not agree according to the rule. For an agreement to ensure, either the noun should be *Eloah*, or *El*, in the singular, or it should remain as it is in the plural, and the verb should be changed to *barau*; as *barau* ELOHIM (*they*) created. But it does not stand thus; it reads literally (the) Elohim (he) created.

Speaking of Elohim, Dr. Wilson says "That this noun, which is not unintentionally here joined with the singular verb *bara*, is nevertheless really plural, appears not merely from its termination *im*, but by its being frequently joined with adjectives, pronouns, and verbs in the plural. *Vayyomer Elohim nashah adam betzalmainu*, *i.e.*, Elohim said, 'Let *us* make man in *our* image'." Mr. Parkhurst, in his lexicon under the word *alah*, cites many passages where Elohim is associated with other plurals. Upon close examination there will be found no good reason to question the conclusion, that Elohim is a noun plural, and signifies "*gods*".*

But why the plural Elohim, gods, should have been associated with a singular verb in this chapter, Hebraists have been much perplexed to answer satisfactorily to themselves or others. Grammar failing, they have had recourse to dogmatism to explain the difficulty. Dr. Wilson truly remarks, that "Elohim is not unintentionally here joined with the singular verb"; though

---

*But *Elohim* has also a singular usage: "Thy throne, O God" (*Elohim*)— Psalm 45:6, spoken of Jesus. See also Jacob and the angel (Genesis 32), and other instances.

in my opinion Messrs. Wilson and Parkhurst have widely mistaken the intention. They imagine that it was intended to reveal a trinity of *persons* in one *essence*, or, as some express it, "society in God". Dr. Wilson observes that *"Let us make man* is an expression of consultation, and marks a difference in man's creation from that of other creatures in point of importance. 'Let us make *man*' regards the animal nature; 'in our *image*' denotes his spiritual nature, which alone could resemble the Deity. 'Let us make', *etc.*, 'in our image, after our likeness.' Here is the plurality three times expressed, and that in the first person: a manifest agreement with, and proof of, the scriptural doctrine of a *plurality of the Deity*, to which, as God is one in essence, we give the name of *persons"*.

Elohim, "a name", says Parkhurst, "usually given in the Hebrew scriptures to the ever-blessed Trinity". He wrote a pamphlet against Dr. Priestley and Mr. Wakefield to prove a plurality of Elohim in Jehovah! If the reader understand who the Elohim are, this will appear an extraordinary instance of learned ignorance and folly. It is equal to undertaking to prove, that there are three princes in one king; or three angels in an archangel. In one thing, however, I agree with him entirely, namely, that a *plurality of agents* is denoted in the Mosaic history of the terrestrial creation. By faith we understand that the spirit, or word, operated in, by, and through them, in the formation of all things terrestrial; but that all these agents were in the divine essence, constituting "society in God", is too great a camel for my power of deglutition.

A first principle with me in all reasonings upon this subject is, that "There is one God and Father of all, who is above all, and through all, and in all" His spiritual family. Another axiom is, that "He is the blessed and only Potentate, the King of kings, and Lord of Lords; who ONLY hath immortality, dwelling in *the light which no man can approach unto*; WHOM NO MAN HATH SEEN, *nor can see"* (1 Timothy 6:15; 1:17). And again, "God is spirit" (John 4:24); and He is "incorruptible" (Romans 1:23). THE INCORRUPTIBLE SPIRIT DWELLING IN LIGHT is the scripture revelation of the undefinable essence of the self-existent Eternal One, who is from everlasting to everlasting, God. What His essence consists in, He has not revealed; He has made known to us His name, or character, which is enough for men to know; but to say that, because He is a spirit, He is therefore "immaterial", is to speak arrant nonsense; for immateriality is nothingness; a quality, if we may so speak, alien to the universe of God.

"No man", says Jesus, "hath seen God *at any time"*; but Adam, Abraham, Jacob, and Moses, saw the Elohim and their Lord;

therefore Elohim does not necessarily mean the Everlasting Father Himself.

Elohim is a name bestowed on *angels* and *orders of men*. It is written, "Worship him, all Elohim" (Psalm 97:7). This is quoted by Paul* in the first chapter of Hebrews, as a command of the Everlasting Father to the angels, that they should do homage to the Lord Jesus as His Son, when He shall introduce him into the world again at the opening of the Future Age. It is also written concerning him, "Thou hast made him a little lower than the Elohim". Paul applies this to Jesus, saying, "We see Jesus, who was made a little lower than the angels". He continued inferior to them a little upwards of thirty years, from the birth of the flesh to his resurrection; when he was exalted far above them in rank and dignity, even to the "right hand of power", which is enthroned in light, where dwells the Majesty in the heavens.

Those to whom the word of God came through Moses are styled Elohim, as it is written, "I have said, Ye are Elohim; and all of you children. of the Most High; but ye shall die like men, and fall like one of the princes" (Psalm 82:6; John 10:34). "Thou shalt not revile the Elohim, nor curse the Ruler of thy people" (Exodus 22:28); that is, thou shalt not revile the magistrates, nor curse the high priest, or king (Acts 23:5).

Furthermore, it is a well established principle of the sacred writings, that *what the Everlasting Father* does by His agents, He is considered as doing Himself. There is a maxim in law similar to this, which runs somehow thus, *qui facit per alios, facit per se*, what one doth by, or through, others, he does of himself. If this be borne in mind, many seeming incongruities will be harmonized. Thus, *the Lord* is said to have appeared to Abraham, as he sat in his tent-door (Genesis 18:1); but when he first caught sight of the visitant, he did not see the Lord but "three men", or Elohim, of whom one was the chief. Read the whole chapter and to verse twenty-nine of the next, and it will be seen that the Everlasting God talks and acts by, or through, these Elohim, but chiefly through one of them, styled the Lord God.

In another place, God is said to appear to Jacob (Genesis 35:9), and, in the eleventh verse, to say to him, "I am God Almighty"; and in the thirteenth, "God went up from him in the place where he talked with him". He was then at Bethel, where formerly "the Elohim were revealed unto him". On that occasion he dreamed that he saw a ladder reaching from earth to heaven, "the LORD standing above it, and the angels of God ascending and descending on it". These angels were the Elohim, or "minis-

*See note, page 41.

197

tering Spirits sent fort to minister for them who shall be heirs of salvation" (Hebrews 1:14). On one occasion, they declared to Jacob the promises made to his father and grandfather in the name of the "Invisible God"; he wrestled with God in wrestling with one of them, etc. Hence, they speak in the first person as personators of the Invisible and Incorruptible Substance, or Spirit, who is the real author of all they say and do.

On a certain occasion, the Invisible God spake to Job out of the whirlwind, and said, "Where wast thou when I laid the foundation of the earth? Declare, if thou hast understanding. Who hath laid the measures thereof? Declare, if thou knowest. Or, who hath stretched the line upon it? Or, who laid the corner stone thereof: when *the Morning Stars sang together, and all the sons of God shouted for joy?*" Job could not answer these questions. He knew, doubtless, what the Elohim had done; but "touching the Almighty", by whose spirit they operated, "we cannot", said Elihu, "find him out". The Elohim were these Morning Stars and Sons of God. Jesus is styled "the Bright and the Morning Star", "the Day Star", and the Son of God. To say, therefore, that the Elohim are Morning Stars and Sons of God, is to speak in the language of scripture.

The relation of the Elohim to Him that dwelleth in the light in the work of creation and providence may better appear by the following illustration. Experimental philosophers can form water, air, and earths; they can bring down lightning from the expanse; they can weigh, or rather calculate the weight of, the sun, moon, and stars; they can speak by electricity; paint by sunlight; and outstrip the wind by fire. These are wonderful combinations of their genius. But what have these they did not receive? And from whom did they receive it? They subject certain substances to certain conditions. They do not originate a single principle. The elements and the laws to which all simple and compound bodies are subject, are independent of the experimenters. They may say, "Let water be formed"; and by passing the electric spark through the gaseous mixture, water will be formed; but it is the power of God that doth it, and not theirs.

After a like manner, the Elohim gave the word; they brought the latent elements of the globe into play; they gave direction and application to power; and the Spirit of the Invisible God accomplished all they were commanded to arrange. The *Spirit* of the Incorruptible God through the Elohim *created* the heavens and the earth. *They* said, "Let there be light"; *they* saw that it was good; *He* made the expanse: *they* called it heaven:—He did it all through them; and they executed by His power what He enjoined. This power, or Spirit, being committed to them, it became *"the Spirit of the Elohim"*. Hence, in the beginning, *the*

Spirit of the Elohim created; which being plainly indicated in the second verse of the first chapter of Genesis, needed not afterwards to be repeated; so that throughout the chapter, "Elohim" is written instead of *"the Spirit of the Elohim"* and is found in connection with a singular verb, not as its nominative, but as the governed word of the nominative singular, *ruach*, Spirit, understood. This is the solution I offer of this grammatical enigma.

It is a part of the "strong delusion" which has supplanted the truth, to suppose that the Invisible God left the throne of the universe on a visit to this region of immensity, where, like a mechanic building a house, He worked in creating the earth and all things therein. After this fashion He is supposed to have made man; and when His mechanism was complete, to have applied His mouth to his nostrils, and "breathed into him a particle of His own divine essence, by which he became a living and immortal soul".

Such a procedure on the part of the "Only Potentate", whose abode is in the light, and whose servants, the Elohim, are innumerable, would have been unfitting His dignity and underived exaltation. He has revealed Himself to us as a Potentate, a King, a Lord, etc.; now, they who fill these stations commit to others the service of executing their will and pleasure. And thus it is with the Invisible and Eternal Potentate. His kingdom ruleth over all. His angels, or Elohim, mighty in strength, do His commandments, hearkening unto the voice of His words. They are His hosts; His ministers, that do His pleasure (Psalm 103:19-21).

In the light of this revelation I understand the Mosaic record of the creation. It pleased the King Eternal nearly six thousand years ago to add a new habitable province to His dominion; not by an original creation of a globe, but by the re-constitution of one already existing as one of the solar planets. He commanded His angels to go and execute the work according to the order detailed by Moses. They hearkened unto the voice of His word; and in six days finished all they were commanded to do. But without His power they could have effected nothing: therefore, in the history all things are referred to Him. He willed; the Elohim executed by His Spirit.

All the lower animals are more or less observant; but the Serpent was the most so of all the Lord of the Elohim had made. It noted the objects around it, and among these observed the *"gods"*, or "Morning Stars and Sons of God", to whom it told Eve she should be like if she ate of the Tree of the Knowledge of good and evil. In the Hebrew the word rendered "gods" is Elohim, the same as occurs throughout the first chapter. From what other source but the sight of its eyes, unless by divine inspiration, could the serpent have derived information about the "gods"? It spoke of what it had seen and heard. But the animals were still without a king; therefore, said the Chief of the Elohim, "Let *us* make man in *our* image". There was none like the Elohim of all the creatures they had made; therefore, they determined to make an animal after their *form*. They shaped him with head, limbs and body like their own; so that he stood before them the earthly image of the celestial Elohim. As much their image as Seth was the image of his father Adam (Genesis 5:3).

We have not said that man's *likeness* to the Elohim consisted in his being "very good"; but that the Spirit of God formed him "very good" in the same sense that it formed all other animals so. They were without character; so was he: his goodness was physical, not moral; that of the Elohim was both.

Yet, in a certain sense, man was formed in the likeness of the Elohim. This likeness, we have already shown, but may repeat here, consisted in the man's *ability to manifest mental phenomena like theirs; and in his susceptibility of an exaltation to their nature and rank, upon the same principles as they had attained thereto.* By this similitude he was distinguished from all the other animals they had formed. He was constituted like to the Elohim, though of inferior nature. He could manifest intellect and disposition even as they, and he could know evil as they had done.

Dr. Wilson observes that the phrase " 'Let us make man' is an expression of consultation, and marks a difference in man's creation from that of other creatures *in point of importance.*" To this I have no objection, and I believe that the "subtle serpent" overheard the consultation, and was, therefore, able to tell Eve that there was a particular in which she should be like the Elohim, *ka-elohim*, by eating the fruit, in which she could not resemble them unless she did eat—viz., in "knowing good *and* EVIL". In this point, man was unlike the Elohim when pronounced "very good". Nor was this item of the temptation a falsehood, for the Lord of the Elohim said to His celestial companions, "Behold, the man *hath become* AS *one of us*, to know good and evil" (Genesis 3:22). In this, then, the man became still more like the Elohim, and in this likeness he hath continued ever since. But thanks to the Invisible God and Father of the saints, man is placed under a law of progression. His prototype has gone before. He was himself made "a little lower than the Elohim", for he took not upon him *their nature*, but assumed that of the seed of Abraham. His nature, however, is now like theirs, being *spiritual*, that is INCORRUPTIBLE AND IMMORTAL. "We shall be like him", says John; hence, also, "equal to the angels", as Jesus hath himself affirmed (Luke 20:36).

The Arch-Elohim said that the man had become LIKE *one* of themselves in the matter of knowing good and evil. This also is an argument for his likeness to a plurality of persons; and it further shows that the Elohim were once in a condition similar to man after he had transgressed. The Lord of the Elohim himself declares that they also had been *experimentally sensible* of evil, for this is the idea expressed by the Hebrew word YADA, *to know*. In short, it is credible that none of the Elohim of the only Potentate's dominion were created immortal; but earthly, or animal, like Adam. The eternal King is the only being who is originally immortal in any sense, hence it is written that "He *only* hath immortality". The immortality of all other intelligences is derived from Him as a reward for the "obedience of faith". Just men at the resurrection of the First Fruits will be equal to Elohim.

Shall we say that these "Morning Stars and Sons of God" did not attain to the spiritual nature by a progression similar to man; seeing that he "who was made so much better than they", even Jesus, the "Bright and the Morning Star", was "made perfect through sufferings"? Have they had no trials to endure; no probation to pass through for the refining of their faith as gold is tried? It is credible, rather, that they were once animal men of other spheres; that in a former state, they were "made subject to vanity not willingly"; that while in the flesh they believed and obeyed God with the self sacrificing disposition afterwards evinced by Abraham; that their faith was counted to them for righteousness; that they succumbed to death as mortal men; that they rose from the dead, and so attained to incorruptibility and immortality as the Elohim of the Invisible God.

Our mundane system is but the pattern of things in other worlds, which may ere this have attained to that perfection which awaits the earth; and probably an illustration of what may even now obtain in other planets where the inhabitants have not yet progressed beyond the animal and probationary era of their history. *Our* angels, or Elohim, those I mean of the heavenly hosts, to whose superintendence terrestrial affairs are consigned, until the Lord Jesus shall assume the reins of government; not all the Elohim, but those of them related to us "always behold the face of God", and minister His will towards the sons of men. This is their glory—a part of their reward. He sent them to form and fill the earth with living souls. They executed their commission according to His purpose.

BEHOLD THEN THE CONSUMMATION! Mortal and corruptible beings like ourselves become Elohim, mighty in strength, and framers of new worlds, of which the planet we inhabit, even in its present state, is a grand and glorious specimen. "Behold", says

Jesus, once an infant at the breast, powerless in death, but now endued with all power, *"I make all things new."* He will educe from the things which exist, a new and magnificent world, as a fit and appropriate habitation for his companions, redeemed by his blood from the sons of men. This is the destiny set before those who shall become "equal to the angels" by a resurrection to eternal life.

PART SECOND

THE THINGS OF THE KINGDOM OF GOD, AND THE NAME OF JESUS CHRIST

CHAPTER I

THE GOSPEL OF THE KINGDOM IN RELATION TO ISRAEL AND THE GENTILES

THE truth indicated—None but the believers of the truth can inherit the Kingdom of God—Abraham "the Heir of the World"—To inherit with him, men must believe what he believed; and become his children by adoption through Jesus Christ—The Gospel and the things of the Kingdom one and the same—It was preached to Abraham, Israel, and the Gentiles by the Lord God, by Moses, by Jesus, and by the apostles—Gospel things susceptible of a threefold classification—The Keys of the Kingdom—Entrusted only to Peter—The Mystery of the Kingdom—The Fellowship of the Mystery—"Apostolic Succession"—Qualifications of an apostle of Christ—Import of the phrase "the end of the world"—"The sign" of its approach—The Gospel preached to every creature by the Apostles—Modern missionaryism inadequate to the end proposed.

IN the former part of this work, I have shown that it has been the purpose of God from the foundation of the world to set up a kingdom and empire of nations which shall supersede all others previously existing upon the globe. We have now arrived at that part of our subject which relates to the development of this *imperial constitution of the world*, which, when brought to the birth, will have occupied six days of a thousand years each in its formation. No topic can surpass this in interest and importance to every man that breathes the breath of life. God has made the belief of the things concerning it a condition of partaking in the glory, honour, and incorruptibility which belong to it. Whatever ignorance may be overlooked, ignorance of the things pertaining to this kingdom alienates men from the life of God. This is equivalent to saying that no man can attain to eternal life who does not believe that gospel; for the subject matter of the gospel is this very Kingdom which it is the purpose of God to establish for the Son of Man and the saints.

It is of primary importance that we believe the truth, and not a substitute for it; for it is by the truth only we can be saved; "the truth as it is in Jesus", neither more nor less, is that to which our attention is invited in the word. "The truth" is set forth in the law and the prophets; but we must add to these the apostolic testimony contained in the New Testament if we would comprehend it *"as it is in Jesus"*. The kingdom is the subject matter of "the truth"; but, "as it is in Jesus", is the truth concerning him as the king and supreme pontiff of the dominion; and *the things concerning his name*, as taught in the doctrine of the apostles. As a whole, "the truth" is defined as *"the things concerning the Kingdom of God and the Name of Jesus Christ"* (Acts 8:12). This phrase covers the entire ground upon which the *"one faith"*, and the *"one hope"*, of the gospel are based; so that if a man believe only the *"things of the kingdom"*, his faith is defective in the *"things of the name"*; or, if his belief be confined to the "things of the name", it is deficient in the "things of the kingdom". There can be no separation of them recognized in a "like precious faith" (2 Peter 1:1) to that of the apostles. They believed and taught all these things; God hath joined them together, and no man need expect His favour who separates them, or abolishes the necessity of believing the things He has revealed for faith.

There can be no doubt of the truth of these statements in view of Paul's emphatic declaration that, "though we (apostles), or an angel from heaven, preach any other gospel to you than that which we have preached unto you, *let him be accursed*. As we said before, so say I now again, if any man preach any other gospel unto you than that ye have received, let him be accursed" (Galatians 1:8). Here, then, he pronounces a curse upon even an angel, if he should come and offer to us any other gospel than that which was preached by himself and the other apostles. It is our wisdom, therefore, to receive nothing which has not the sanction of their authority. Paul styles everything else but what he preached "another gospel", that is, "a perversion of the gospel of Christ"; and, as we can only be saved by belief of the truth, such a gospel is both useless and injurious.

"Gospel" is a word which signifies *good news*, or glad tidings; and *the* gospel some particular good news. "Blessed", say the scriptures, "are they who know the *joyful sound*", or the gospel; and the reason is, because it makes known the "blessedness" which is to come upon the nations, and will give every one an interest in it who believes and accepts it. The gospel of God is the good news of blessedness promised in the scriptures of the prophets, and *summarily* expressed in the saying, "In thee, Abraham, shall all the nations of the earth be blessed". The making of this promise to Abraham is termed by Paul the preaching of the gospel to Abraham; for, says he, "The scripture, foreseeing that God would justify the heathen through faith, preached before the gospel to Abraham, saying, In thee shall all nations be blessed" (Galatians 3:8-9). This he styles "the blessing of

Abraham", which is to come upon the nations through Jesus Christ.

Abraham holds a conspicuous place in relation to the blessedness of the gospel. He is named by Paul six times in the third chapter of Galatians, which he concludes by saying, "If ye be Christ's then are ye *Abraham's seed* and *heirs* according to the promise". Hence, men are required to be Christ's that they may be Abraham's seed. But why is it so important to be of the seed of Abraham? For the very obvious reason that, as the promise was made to Abraham, it is only by being *constitutionally* "in him" that any son of Adam can obtain a participation in what belongs to Abraham.

This idea may be illustrated by reference to the law of inheritance among all civilized people. If a man be possessed of an estate, the members of his family alone have any right to it at his decease. Though all the world may be his friends, unless they are named in his will, they can have no part in the inheritance he may leave behind. And again, if he have no heir, his estate and property would escheat to the lord of whom he happened to hold his title; but, to avoid this, it would be quite competent for him to *adopt an heir* according to the law. The person so adopted would become his seed in every respect save that of natural birth. In the case before us, God hath promised an estate to Abraham; therefore he is styled "THE HEIR OF THE WORLD" (κόσμος)—that is, of the glory, honour, and power, of the nations throughout the globe in their millennial blessedness—a gift worthy of Him that hath *promised* it.

Now the promise of this to Abraham and his seed is a promise to no one else. No stranger can lay claim to it. He must be Abraham's seed, or he has no right to Abraham's property. On this principle, no one who is not a lineal, or fleshly, descendant of Abraham can inherit the world with him when God fulfils the promise. This is the view taken of the matter by the Jews, who found their hope of participation in the world when it becomes Abraham's and his seed's, upon the acknowledged fact that they are Abraham's flesh and blood. This would be very well, if no other condition of inheritance were specified. But the word saith, that "the children of the flesh are not the children of God; but the children of the promise (*those who believe it*) are counted for the seed" (Romans 9:8). If the children of the flesh had a right to share with Abraham when he obtains possession of the world which God has promised him, then all descended from Ishmael and Esau, his son and grandson, as well as from Isaac, would have equal rights. But God, who not only promises the estate, but specifies the conditions of heirship, has restricted the inheritance to those termed the "children of the promise as Isaac was"

(Galatians 4:28). He has proclaimed the great truth that "the son of the bond-woman shall not be heir with the son of the free-woman" (Galatians 4:30).

To be a son of the free-woman, a man, although a Jew, must *believe in the promise made to Abraham*; he must be of a like disposition with Abraham; he must be obedient like Abraham; he must have faith in Jesus as the seed of Abraham associated with him in the promise; he must believe in his name; he must be constitutionally inducted into Christ by immersion into the Father, Son, and Holy Spirit:—being the subject of these conditions he is included in the Family of God, to whose members it is said, "Ye are all the children of God in Christ Jesus through the faith. For as many of you as have been baptized into Christ have put on Christ. There is no distinction of Jew or Gentile, bond or free, male or female among you; for ye are all *one* in Christ Jesus. And *if* ye be Christ's *then* are ye Abraham's seed, and heirs according to the promise" (Galatians 3:26-29). These are the children of the promise, the children of God, the brethren and joint-heirs of Jesus Christ, the sons of the free-woman, and Abraham, Isaac, and Jacob's seed, who are alone entitled to possess the world with him.

Jesus came to preach the gospel. "The Spirit of the Lord" saith he, "is upon me, because he hath anointed me to preach the gospel to the poor; and to preach the acceptable year of the Lord" (Luke 4:19). It is admitted, then, that Jesus fulfilled his mission; consequently, in his proclamation he preached the *good news of the acceptable season,* or BLESSED ERA of the Lord. But, what was the great focal truth of this acceptable year? Let Jesus answer the question in his own words: "*I must preach the kingdom of God; for therefore am I sent*" (Luke 4:43): and so much did he preach about this kingdom that the people become impatient and sought to take him by force and make him King. But he would not permit it; "and because they thought that the kingdom of God was immediately to appear, he spake a parable to them", in which he gave them to understand that he must first take a journey into a far country to be presented before the Ancient of Days to receive from Him the kingdom, and then to return; when he would bestow upon his servants power and authority over the cities of the world (Daniel 7:13,14; Luke 19:11,17; Daniel 7;18,27). According to this arrangement, Jesus rose from the dead and took his departure; when he ascended to the right hand of the Majesty in the heavens, where he is now. He has not yet received the kingdom, glory, and dominion, or he would have already returned. He is waiting for this, "sitting at the right hand of God *until* his foes are made his footstool" (Psalm 110:1).

He will then appear in his kingdom and rule as King over all the earth.

The gospel, then, was preached to Abraham by the angel of the Lord; and it was preached by Jesus to his own nation, and to them only; for "he was not sent, save to the lost sheep of the house of Israel" (Matthew 15:24). Paul also declares that it was preached to that generation of Israelites whose carcases fell in the wilderness; but it did not profit them *because they did not believe it* (Hebrews 4:2). Therefore, God sware in His wrath that they should not enter into the rest it proclaimed (3:18,19). Before he suffered on the accursed tree, Jesus sent his apostles, and seventy others, throughout the land to "preach *the kingdom* of God". In recording their obedience to his command, Luke says, "They went through the towns preaching *the gospel*" (Luke 9:2,6); so that it is clear that to preach the kingdom is to preach the gospel; and to preach the gospel is to preach the kingdom of God.

This is a most important demonstration; for *it enables us to determine when we hear the gospel*. The gospel is not preached when the things of the kingdom are omitted. And this is one grand defect in modern preaching. Either there is nothing said about the kingdom; or a kingdom is preached which is a mere matter of speculation; a kingdom of heaven in principle, in the hearts of men, or somewhere beyond the skies! But the gospel does not treat of such a kingdom as this; a mere fiction indoctrinated into men's minds by "the cunning craftiness of those who lie in wait to deceive". So inseparable is the idea of gospel from that of kingdom that we find them, not only substituted for each other, but associated together as terms of explanation.

Thus, "Jesus went throughout every city and every village, preaching and showing *the glad tidings of the kingdom of God*" (Luke 8:1; Mark 1:14); and in the prophecy of Mount Olivet it is written: "THIS *gospel of the kingdom* shall be preached in all the habitable (ἐν ὅλῃ τῇ οἰκουμένῃ, *Roman Empire*) for a testimony to all nations; and then shall come the end" (Matthew 24:14). After he rose from the dead, he commanded the apostles, saying, "Go, preach *the gospel* to every creature: he that believes and is immersed shall be saved; and he that believes not shall be condemned"; and "Lo, I am with you always, until the end of the world". In view of these texts, can anyone be so mystified as not to see that salvation is predicted on believing the gospel of the kingdom, and being baptized into Jesus Christ?

They were to preach "*this* gospel of the kingdom" in the name of Jesus. How did they execute the work? "They went forth and preached everywhere, *the Lord working with them*, and confirming THE WORD with signs following" (Mark 16:20). They began at

Jerusalem, passed throughout Judea, then went to Samaria, and lastly to the end of the earth. They began on the day of Pentecost, and preached only to Jews for several years; at the end of which, Peter and Paul began to proclaim the kingdom to Gentiles also. The labours of the apostles were indefatigable. They filled the Roman empire with their doctrine, and made such an impression upon it that tumults were excited; and they were charged with treason against the state, because they proclaimed another king than Caesar (Acts 17:7), who should rule the world in righteousness (verse 31), as the sovereign Lord of all the earth. "They spake the word of God with boldness ... The multitude of them that believed were of one heart and of one soul"; and great kindness was among them all. In about thirty years, the gospel of the kingdom was proclaimed in all the world, to every creature under the heaven (Colossians 1:6,23). They finished their work, and fell asleep, the Lord having abundantly fulfilled his promise of co-operating with them to the end of the world.

Thus, the same gospel that was preached to Abraham was preached also to Jews and Gentiles by the apostles after the ascension of Jesus to the right hand of power. There was, however, this difference: when it was preached to Abraham and to the generation which perished in the Wilderness, *it was altogether a matter of promise*; but when preached by the apostles to the Roman nations, *some things connected with the promise were fulfilled*: so that the gospel of the kingdom, as they preached it, was partly a matter of promise, partly a matter of history, and partly doctrinal. It was thus presented to mankind in a threefold point of view, which may be stated in this form:—

I.   Promises to be fulfilled; or, things concerning the kingdom of God.

II.   Promises fulfilled already; or, things concerning Jesus.

III.   The doctrinal import of the fulfilled promises; or, things concerning his Name.

A man might believe all the promises and the doctrinal import, but if he did not believe that Jesus of Nazareth was the subject of them, he would make a very good believing Jew under the law, but he would not be a Christian under grace. This is the great turning point in the faith of an enlightened Jew, and Christian. Is Jesus of Nazareth the personage described in the law and the prophets; has he right and title to the throne of David, and to the dominion of the world?

The Jew says, "No, we look for another": but the Christian replies, "He unquestionably is the person: we look for no other; but assuredly expect the re-appearance of 'this same Jesus' on earth, to restore the throne and kingdom of David; to occupy them as the King of the Jews; and to be the Melchizedec High Priest and the Ruler of the nations". Hence, it is the foundation truth of the gospel of the kingdom, that Jesus of Nazareth is the Anointed King, the Son of the living God. He is the Rock, or Strength, of Israel; whose power will never be restored till he sits upon the throne of their Kingdom, and is acknowledged as King by the nation.

On the other hand, a man may believe that Jesus is the Son of God; that he was sent of God as a messenger to Israel; that there is remission of sins through the shedding of his blood; that he is the saviour; and that he rose from the dead:—if he believe these things, but be ignorant, and consequently faithless, of "the things of the kingdom", he cannot obtain glory, honour, incorruptibility and life in that kingdom. The condition of salvation is the *belief of the whole gospel and obedience to it*. It is not, "He that believes in Jesus Christ, and is immersed, shall be saved"; but "He who shall believe THE GOSPEL, and is immersed" (Mark 16:15,16). Simply to believe in Jesus is to believe no more than in "THE MESSENGER"; but, he was sent to preach the gospel to the poor; to show the glad tidings of the kingdom of God: this was his MESSAGE, the message of God to the Jew first, and afterwards to the Greek. Let it be remembered, then, that salvation is predicated upon *belief in the* MESSENGER *and in the* MESSAGE *he brings from God*.

The unhappy condition of the professing world at the present time is, that they have no faith in the message of God, but rather ridicule it, and heap insult upon those who contend for it. "I came to preach the kingdom of God", says Jesus.

"Oh! we believe that thou camest from God, because no man could do the miracles thou doest unless God were with him; but we do not believe a word in a kingdom in Judea under thy rule. We have no idea of thy coming to this cursed earth again to reign in Jerusalem, and to sit as a priest upon a throne there. This is nothing but the day dream of those who take thy words, and the saying of the prophets, as if they were to be understood in the carnal, or literal sense. It would be derogatory to the interests of God to suppose or desire such a consummation. No, no; we believe thou art at the right hand of the Majesty in the heavens, now reigning over mankind; that we are thy ministers and ambassadors on earth; and that in enriching us, the world is giving its substance and doing homage to thee; and that when we die, we shall come to thee, and kingdoms rule beyond the skies! Our churches are thy kingdom here, and it is our deep and pious conviction, that the more they confide in us, and the less they trouble themselves about the millennium, the better it will be for them, and for the peace of the denominations to which they belong."

This is in effect the language of the religious leaders of the world, and of those who surrender their understandings to the traditions with which they make of none effect the "word of the kingdom of God". But these traditions are sheer nonsense, and without the least foundation in the scriptures. They belong to a dark and foolish generation, and find their origin in the speculations of men of corrupt minds and reprobate concerning the faith.

When the apostles preached on the day of Pentecost, they announced that God had raised up Jesus to sit upon the throne of David (Acts 2:30). In the porch of the temple, they told the Jews that God would send Jesus Christ to them at the time of the restitution (Acts 3:21). When Philip preached the word concerning Christ to the Samaritans, he announced "the things concerning the kingdom of God and the name of Jesus Christ" (Acts 8:12). In the convention of the apostles and elders, James invited their attention to Peter's narrative and the prediction of Amos. He stated that the work to be done was to *take out of the nations a people for the name of God*, as it is written, "AFTER THIS I *will return*, and raise up the dwelling place of David that is fallen, and close up the breaches thereof; and I will raise up his ruins, and I will build it *as in the days of old*; that they may possess the remnant of Edom, and all the heathen which are called by my name. And I will bring again the captivity of my people Israel, and they shall build the waste cities, and inhabit them; and they shall plant vineyards and drink the wine thereof; they shall also make gardens, and eat the fruit of them. And I will plant them upon their land, and they shall no more be pulled up out of their land which I have given them, saith the LORD" (Acts 15:14-18; Amos 9:11).

In Athens, Paul announced that God intended to rule the world in righteousness by Jesus Christ; and that He had raised him from the dead as an assurance of its verity (Acts 17:31). In the Ephesian synagogue he disputed for three months, persuading the things concerning the kingdom of God (Acts 19:8; 20:20,21-25,27). Paul stood at the bar of Agrippa, and was judged "for the hope of the promise made of God unto the fathers; unto which promise the twelve tribes of Israel, instantly serving God, day and night, hope to come" (Acts 26:6,7). Hence, he preached the hope of Israel's twelve tribes, as set forth in Amos, and all the prophets; and directed their attention to Jesus as the personage whom God had raised up to accomplish their desire. Indeed, he told the Jews at Rome plainly, that he was a prisoner in chains on account of the hope of Israel; and in illustration of it, "he expounded and testified the kingdom of God, both out of the law of Moses and the prophets, and teaching those things which concern the Lord Jesus Christ". According to the law and the testimony he spoke, diffusing the light of the glorious gospel of the blessed God, for two whole years in Rome, "the great city which reigns over the kings of the earth" (Acts 28:20,23,31).

To understand the relations of things, it must be known that the gospel stands related to Abraham's descendants before the preaching of John the Baptist; to Israel from John to the day of Pentecost; from this epoch until the calling of the Gentiles; and then to the Gentiles at large. "The law and the prophets were until John, then the kingdom of God was proclaimed" to Israel by John, Jesus, the seventy, and the twelve.

There was "*a mystery*", however, connected with the gospel which was not manifested in the proclamation of it before the day of Pentecost. The people were taught in parables, but the apostles were favoured with an interpretation of them in private; for, said Jesus to them, "To you it is given to know the *mystery of the kingdom of God*, but to them it is not given" (Mark 4:2; Matthew 13:11). Referring to this, Paul says, "My gospel and the preaching of Jesus Christ according to the revelation of *the mystery*, which was kept secret since the world began, but *now* is made manifest, and by the scriptures of the prophets ... made known to all nations for the obedience of faith" (Romans 16:25,26). "Pray for me", says he, "that I may open my mouth boldly, to make known *the mystery of the gospel*, for which I am an ambassador in bonds" (Ephesians 6:19). Again, "By revelation God hath made known unto me, Paul, *the mystery*, which in other ages was not made known to the sons of men, *as it is now revealed* unto the holy apostles and prophets by the spirit; that the Gentiles should be fellow-heirs, and of the same body, and partakers of his promise in Christ by the gospel ... To me was given to make all men see what is the FELLOWSHIP *of the mystery*, which, from the beginning of the world (ἀπὸ τῶν αἰώνων) hath been hid in God, who created all things: to the intent that now unto the principalities and powers in the high places might be made known through the church the multifarious wisdom of God" (Ephesians 3:3-10).

From these writings we learn that the gospel of the kingdom of God is a phrase which embraces the whole subject; and that the mystery of the kingdom, and the fellowship of the mystery, are things pertaining to the gospel of the kingdom in a special sense, but unknown until revealed to the apostles. The mysteries of the kingdom were placed on record in the sacred writings but their signification was hidden from the prophets themselves, until "THE KEYS" thereof were vouchsafed to the apostles. Hence, says Peter, "Of the salvation of souls (ψυχῶν) the prophets have inquired and searched diligently, who prophesied of the *grace* that should come *unto you*: searching what, or what manner of time the spirit of Christ which was in them did signify, when it testified beforehand *the sufferings of Christ*, and the glory that should follow. Unto them it was revealed that *not unto themselves*, but unto us did they minister the things which are now reported unto you by them that have preached the gospel unto you with the Holy Spirit sent down from heaven; which things the angels desire to took into" (1 Peter 1:10-12).

The mystery of the kingdom, then, has been made known, and we find that it had relation to *the sufferings of the Christ; and repentance, remission of sins, and eternal life in his name, to the Jews first and afterwards to the Gentiles*. The prophets, who foretold these things, were not able to penetrate the mystery of them; and the angels themselves, who brought the word to them, desired to understand them. But this was not permitted; and it was preserved as a *secret* until after the sufferings of Christ, which were to be the foundation of the manifestation.

When the "point of time" drew nigh for "the finishing of the transgression, the making an end of sin-offerings, the making reconciliation for iniquity, and the bringing in of everlasting righteousness" (Daniel 9:24), Jesus who had been anointed the Most Holy, the sealed prophet of the Father, and fully confirmed as Messiah the Prince, selected one man of the twelve (who had the least reason to exalt himself above his brethren as "the prince of the apostles"), as the depository of the keys of the Mysteries of the Kingdom of God.

This highly-honoured individual was Simon Peter, son of Jonas, who denied his master with oaths and curses. But, being converted, and restored to favour by his gracious Lord, he was prepared to be the unaspiring "servant of the least"; and to strengthen his brethren in all the trials and afflictions they were called upon to endure for the truth's sake. "I will give unto thee, Simon Bar-jona", said the king, "the keys of the kingdom of God; and whatsoever thou shalt loose on earth shall be loosed in heaven" (Matthew 16:19). Here was an appointment of Peter in a special sense to the particular function of binding and loosing men on earth.

But we would ask any reasonable man, unspoiled by human folly and absurdity, If a power be conferred on A, nineteen hundred years ago, is it therefore bestowed on B, living nineteen centuries after? The keys were promised to Peter, and not to successors of Peter, if it were possible for him to have them in such an office; which none but the most stupidly ignorant of the scriptures would venture to affirm. The custody of the keys by a successor of Peter is the most farcical assumption that ever poor crazy mortals were guilty of. When we come to see what the keys of the Mysteries of the Kingdom of Heaven are, we shall see at once that the very use of them for the first time operates upon Peter's own possession of them, as the telling of a secret to all the world does upon his power over it afterwards by whom it was told.

Had Peter, instead of using the keys, hid them till his death-hour, and then imparted them to a single person, this individual might truly be said to have "succeeded to the keys". But this he did not, dared not, do. He communicated them to such multitudes of Jews and Gentiles that they became the common property of the world; and none but men "earthly, sensual, and devilish" as the priests, "seducing spirits, speaking lies in hypocrisy", whose trade it is to "make gain of godliness";—none but such as these would have conceived of the possibility of a transfer of the keys of the Mysteries of the Kingdom of Heaven to a successor; especially to such a succession of impious impostors as the prophets of the Roman See.

A key is used in scripture as a symbol of the power of revealing, or interpreting, secret things; also for power in general. As a key is to a lock, so is power to things intellectual, moral, and political. The scriptures say of Messiah, "The keys shall be upon his shoulder"—*i.e.*, "The government shall be possessed by him". And again, "I have", says Jesus, "the key ($\kappa\lambda\varepsilon\tilde{\iota}\varsigma$) of Hades ($\ddot{a}\delta ov$) and of death"; which is to say, that Jesus hath the power to open the abode, or chamber, of the dead, and to restore them to life. In these instances, a key is the symbol of political, and physical power; but it also represents scientific or knowledge-imparting power. Thus, under the law of Moses, it was divinely appointed that "the priest's lips should keep knowledge, and Israel should seek the law at his mouth; for he was the messenger of the LORD of Hosts". The priests, however, became so corrupt and ignorant that Israel sought in vain for knowledge at their lips, and therefore perished for lack of it. The Lord charged this home upon them by the hand of Malachi. "Ye are", says he, "departed out of the way, O ye priests; ye have caused many to stumble at the law; ye have corrupted the covenant of Levi, saith the LORD of Hosts. Therefore have I also made you contemptible and base before all the people, according as ye have not kept my ways, but have been partial in the law" (Malachi 2:8-9).

This was precisely the state of things when "THE MESSENGER OF THE COVENANT" made his appearance in Judea. He denounced them for their corruptions. "Ye have made", said he, "the commandment of God of none effect by your tradition. Hypocrites that ye are, ye draw nigh to God with your mouth, and honour him with your lips, but your heart is far from him. But in vain do ye worship him, teaching for doctrines the commandments of men." Among these hypocrites were the lawyers, who, feeling the keenness of his reproaches, remonstrated against it. But he turned upon them, and said, "Woe unto you, lawyers! for ye have taken away the KEY OF KNOWLEDGE: ye enter not in yourselves, and them that were entering in ye hindered" (Luke 11:52).

This was the unhappy condition of the Jewish nation at the appearing of Jesus; as it is of all the nations at the present time against whom the kingdom is shut by clerical traditions. The Lord Jesus came to restore to Israel the key of knowledge. "They erred, not knowing the scriptures": but he was about to open them, so that in spite of the hypocrites, they might enter into the kingdom of God. O that men could be induced now to devote themselves to the study of the scriptures without regard to articles, creeds, confessions, and traditions! These things are mere rubbish; monuments of the presumption and folly of former generations indoctrinated with the wisdom from beneath. If a Berean spirit could be infused into them; if they could be persuaded to "search the scriptures daily" (Acts 17:11,12) for the truth as for hid treasure; they would soon leave their spiritual guides alone in all their glory of mysticism and patristic lore, and rejoice in the liberty of that truth which can alone make them "free indeed".

The gospel invites men to enter into the Kingdom of God. The way of entering is made exceedingly plain in the Bible. There is now *no hidden* mystery concerning it as there was before the sufferings of Christ were manifested. The mystery of the kingdom has been unlocked. The key of knowledge has been given; but unfortunately it has been stolen again by Peter's pretended successors; and, upon a smaller scale, by every other ecclesiastic who would discourage or throw hindrances in the way of a free, unbiassed, and independent examination and avowal of Bible truth in their churches; or, an unrestricted advocacy of it, though at variance with the institutes of dogmatic theology, in all the pulpits of the land.

The leaders of the people dare not permit such a course to be pursued; for the Bible is hostile to their systems, and sets forth things which, if believed, would empty their rostrums, disperse their flocks, and close their doors; and elaborate such a social revolution, that truth and righteousness would triumph in the midst of the earth; and the people be enlightened in the knowledge which comes from God. Such a consummation, however, need never be hoped for, so long as the instruction and government of the nations are in the hands of the existing orders or rulers, lay and ecclesiastical; for "like priests, like people", and *vice versa*; they are corrupt and altogether gone out of the way; and, therefore, are devoid of all power to resuscitate the things which remain, and which are ready to vanish away.

Before a man can enter into the Kingdom of God, he must be unloosed from his sins in the present state; and liberated hereafter from the prison-house where the dead lie bound in chains of intense darkness. The unloosing from sins, Jesus committed to Peter; but the enlargement from the chamber of death he reserved to himself (Revelation 1:18; 20:1).

Knowledge is the *key* to remission, or release from sins, and to an entrance into the Kingdom of God. No one can enter this kingdom in his sins, and destitute of a character approved of God; and none could answer the question, "How can a man obtain the remission of sins; and what kind of a character would God henceforth account worthy?"—until the apostle Peter revealed the secret, communicated to him by the spirit, on the day of Pentecost. If the reader peruse the second chapter of the Acts, he will there learn how Peter used one of the keys of the kingdom given to him by its King. On that occasion, I say, he used but one of the keys. He revealed the mystery of the gospel of God's kingdom to Jews only.

They believed in the kingdom, glory, and dominion, promised to the Son of Man in Daniel and the prophets; they were well aware that the kingdom was to belong to their nation; that the King was to be David's son, and to live for ever; and that the righteous were to take the kingdom with him: these things were the substance of the national hope; but they did not then know upon what conditions the obtaining of them was predicated. Hence, it was Peter's duty to instruct them. He first recalled to their recollection certain notable things concerning Jesus. That the wonders he performed by the power of God evidently showed that God approved him; that *they* had been guilty of his death in clamouring for his crucifixion; but that all this was predetermined of God; that God had "loosed him from the pains of death" by raising him from the dead. He then proceeded to show by their prophets that the things which had thus happened to Jesus were verifications of certain predictions. He adduced the testimony of David, that the Christ was to be *"raised up to sit upon David's throne"*, and consequently, must previously suffer death; and that after he was resurrected, he was to ascend to the right hand of God. He then concluded by saying, "Let all the house of Israel know assuredly that God hath made that same Jesus whom ye have crucified, both Lord and King Anointed (Χριστύς, *Messiah*)". For the truth of this statement he appealed to what they saw and heard; to the cloven tongues like fire sitting upon their heads, the "sound of a rushing mighty wind", and the many languages spoken by Galilean fishermen without previous study.

The result of the Apostle's reasoning was their conviction that Jesus was indeed the King of Israel, even the Shiloh that had been promised them for so many ages. They acknowledged him to be the "Son whose NAME should be called Wonderful, Counsellor, the Mighty God, the Father of the Future Age (*Avi Ad*), the Prince of Peace" (Isaiah 9:6). This belief, however, also convinced them that, being this great personage, they had committed an enormous crime; and had "killed the Prince of life". Their consciences smote them; "they had denied the Holy and Just One, and desired a murderer before him"; and had imprecated his blood upon themselves and their posterity. Of what use was their faith to them in this extremity? They believed *in the kingdom*, they believed *in Jesus*, they were penetrated with remorse, but still they were conscious only of guilt, and of judgment well deserved. It was yet a *hidden mystery* to them what should be done for pardon of this great transgression. What was "*the righteousness of God*" which He required of them? Should they go to the high priest, and offer a whole burnt offering, and confess their sin? This would have been impracticable. Caiaphas would have offered sacrifice for them upon the altar upon no such confession as this; for in confessing themselves sinners for killing Jesus, they would have charged the high priest as a principal in the crime. To what, or to whom, were they to look for a solution of "the mystery"? Who could *unlock* it, and *open* to them the *door* of liberty, and *loose* them from their sins?

Is not the reader prepared to answer, "The Holy Spirit alone could reveal to them of righteousness, because Jesus had gone to the Father"? (John 16:7,10). This is true; and the time had arrived to do it. But how, or through what channel, was the Spirit to do this? Was it to be by words thundered from heaven; by a still, small voice whispering in their ears; by a feeling that they were forgiven; by words of inspiration spoken by the tongues of angels; or by the mouth of man? After what has been said, the reader will be prepared to say, "The keys of knowledge, or the power to reveal the secrets of the kingdom of heaven, were committed to Peter; therefore, the new doctrine concerning righteousness, or justification to life, was to be revealed through him". This is also true, but the "devout Jews" were ignorant of this arrangement; therefore, instead of addressing Peter alone, they inquired of all the apostles, saying, "*Men and brethren what shall we do?*" (Acts 2:37). Mark, reader, though the question was put to all, only one of them, and that one, Peter, replied to the inquiry. He was the spokesman of the twelve, by whose mouth God had chosen that Israel should hear the word of the gospel, and believe; or, as Paul writes, "The gospel of the circumcision was committed to Peter, in whom God wrought effectually for the purpose" (Galatians 2:8).

The answer given by Peter announced for the first time, what believers of the gospel of the kingdom and in the things concerning Jesus, *must do*, in order to become joint-heirs with him of the promise made to the fathers. To these *devout* Jews, who now believed what both the prophets and apostles had spoken, who were now humbled in disposition as little children, swift to hear, and anxious to do, whatever the spirit should dictate; the holder of the keys to unlock the mystery of the gospel, said, "REPENT *and* BE BAPTIZED *every one of you* IN THE NAME *of Jesus Christ* FOR THE REMISSION OF SINS" (Acts 2:38; see also page 142).

Such an annunciation as this had never been made before. In this way "repentance and the remission of sins" were "preached *in the name of Jesus*". This is God's way of righteousness, and besides this, there is no other way of salvation; "for there is *none other name* under heaven given among men, whereby we must be saved" (Acts 4:12). God's salvation is placed in the name of Jesus; and this name is accessible to mankind only upon the condition of believing "*the things concerning the kingdom of God and the name of Jesus*", and being baptized in his name—"He that believes the gospel and is baptized shall be saved" is the unrevoked fiat of the Son of God.

The words of the Spirit by the mouth of Peter went home to the hearts of these devout Jews. "They that *gladly* received his word were baptized: and the same day there were added to the congregation about three thousand souls. And they continued steadfastly in the apostle's doctrine and fellowship, and in breaking of bread, and in prayers" (Acts 2:41,42). These disciples were "a kind of first-fruits of God's creatures begotten of his own will *by the word of truth*" (James 1:18), which "lives and *abides for ever*".

But, though the mystery of the gospel was thus made known in the name of Jesus, even Peter, to whom the keys of the mystery were given, did not yet understand "the FELLOWSHIP *of the mystery*". The keys were not given to him when Jesus spoke the words; nor were both of them given to him on the day of Pentecost. The mystery was revealed to the Jew first: and several years elapsed before it was known, or supposed, that the Gentiles would be admitted to a joint-heirship with Jesus on an equality with the Jews. During this period of about seven years, the body of Christ consisted solely of believing Israelites, sons of Abraham by flesh and faith.

At the end of this time, however, God determined to "visit the Gentiles, *to take out of them a people for his name*". He graciously resolved to invite men of all the nations of the Roman territory to accept honour, glory, and immortality, in the kingdom and empire about to be established on the ruins of all others. Hitherto He had only invited His own people Israel to this high destiny; but now He was about to extend the gospel call to the nations also.

Before this, however, could be accomplished according to the principles laid down in God's plan, it was necessary to prepare Peter for the work. Although an apostle, he was still a Jew, and had all the prejudices of the Jew against the Gentile. He considered it "unlawful for him to keep company, or come unto one of another nation". The Jews had no more social dealings with the Gentiles than the Samaritans. And if any had suggested the propriety of his going and preaching the Kingdom of God and the Name of Jesus to the Gentiles, he would have positively refused. If, however, he had been ever so willing, he could not have done it for various other reasons.

In those days, no one could preach effectually unless he were sent; and, as he had not been sent of God, his mission would have been a failure. Then, he did not know whether God would accept the Gentiles on the same conditions as the Jews, if indeed, He would admit them to a joint-heirship at all. But, the law was a sufficient wall of separation to keep Jewish preachers and Gentiles apart until God's time should arrive to do it away, and to bring them together into "one body".

Peter, then, had to be prepared for the work. The narrative of his preparation is contained in the tenth chapter of Acts. A direct attack was made upon his prejudices. He became very hungry about 12 o'clock in the day. While waiting for something to eat on the housetop, an amazement came over him. In this state, he saw a great sheet full of all sorts of unclean creatures, fit and appropriate emblems of the moral condition of the Gentiles. At this crisis, the spirit said, "Rise, Peter, kill and eat". But Peter preferred hunger to defilement; and would not consent, until it was repeated for the third time, that the legal distinction between clean and unclean was done away:— "What God hath cleansed, call not thou common", or unclean.

The impression made upon Peter by this vision is best expressed in his own words. "God hath showed me", said he, "that I should not call *any man* common, or unclean. Therefore came I to you, Gentiles, as soon as I was sent for." In this way the second key of the kingdom was imparted to him. Its use was to make known the Fellowship of the Mystery.

As soon as Peter's preparation was complete, even while he was debating within himself the meaning of the vision, three Gentile messengers from Cornelius, a centurion of the Italian regiment, arrived from Caesarea, to request him to visit him. The Spirit told Peter to go with them, nothing doubting, for He had sent them.

Now, while God was preparing Peter's mind for a ready obedience, He had sent a messenger to tell Cornelius to send for Peter. It would be well for the reader to reflect on the character of Cornelius before the angel visited him. He was not a pagan Gentile, or a wicked sinner in danger of hell fire; but a proselyte of righteousness, or an outer-court worshipper. "He was *a just and devout* man, and *one that feared God* with all his house; gave much alms to the Jews, among whom he was of good report; and he prayed to God always." No better man, lay or clerical, can be produced from any modern sect than Cornelius. He was a God-fearing, "pious", and generous-hearted man. He was not a perverse, hot-headed, ignorant disciple of some sect; but a man approved of heaven, whose prayers and alms ascended before God as a memorial of him.

But why dwell so on the character of this excellent man? Because a special messenger was sent from heaven to tell even this good man, this just and devout Gentile, to send for the apostle Peter, that *he* might come from Joppa, and tell him *what he ought to do*. But, as though this were not explicit enough, the angel stated that "Peter should come and tell him *words, whereby he and his house might be saved*". Now it is worthy of especial note by the religionists of this self-complacent generation, that this just person was not in a saved state under the new order of things: that he had both to *hear words* and to *do* something for his salvation which he had then as yet neither heard nor done. And let it be observed, furthermore, that *the angel* of God was not permitted to preach the gospel to Cornelius; or, in other words, to tell him what he ought to do; or "the words by which he and his house might be saved". He was only allowed to tell him to *send for Peter*.

According to modern notions, this was quite unnecessary; for, cries popular ignorance, it would have saved both time and trouble if the angel had told Cornelius at once what it was necessary for so excellent a man to believe and do, instead of sending three men through the broiling sunshine to fetch Peter to Caesarea. O what a lesson is contained in this interesting narrative for the "clergy", "ministers", and people of these times! How it convicts them of infidelity to the gospel, and sinfulness before God; or, if sincerity be granted to them, and, doubtless, there are among them many honest and well-intentioned persons, who "err, not knowing the scriptures"; grant, then, that they sincerely love truth in the abstract, yet comparing their creeds and preaching, and practices, with the testimonies contained in the second, tenth and eleventh of the Acts, to say nothing of others—how condemned are they as vain talkers, and deceived leaders of the blind. It is really painful to listen to the superficial dissertations of the textuaries, retailed to the people from the pulpits of the day. Theological speculations on isolated scraps of scripture are substituted for the words of Peter and the other apostles, by which alone even the "pious" can be saved. They talk of true religion, of primitive Christianity, of the gospel, of churches of Christ, and of an evangelical ministry; but where among Papist or Protestant, Church or Dissent, are these things to be found, reflecting the precepts, precedents, and morality of the "pure and undefiled religion" of the New Testament?

This New Testament Christianity is the grand desideratum of the Protestant world; which, however, we despair of beholding even in theory until Messiah shall appear in his kingdom, and abolish all existing names and denominations, which serve, indeed, as a kind of ecclesiastical police, but are perfectly useless as institutions capable of indoctrinating mankind with the things which they ought to believe and do, if they would become joint-heirs with Jesus of the kingdom, glory, and empire of the Ancient of Days.

From the testimonies before us, then, we learn,

1.   That "piety" and morality alone, will not save men;

2.   That good and pious men must believe certain things, and do certain others, for salvation;

3.   That these things, indispensably necessary to salvation, are set forth in Peter's words spoken to his contemporaries;

4.   That Peter's words are the keys to the mystery, and fellowship, of the gospel of the kingdom;

5.   That there is no difference between Jews and Gentiles in relation to this mystery;

6.   That God hath appointed men, and not angels, to preach the gospel;

7.   That Peter was to be sent for, because to him alone the keys were given;

8.   That, though piety and morality alone cannot save; neither can faith, unaccompanied by fruits meet for repentance, give a man inheritance in the kingdom of God.

Peter having arrived at the house of Cornelius, announced to all present, "the things which God had commanded him to speak". Having stated the great discovery made to him by the spirit, how that "God was no respecter of persons; but that in every nation he that fears him (not however with that fear "which is taught by the precepts of men"), and works righteousness (such as God requires) is accepted of him":—he directed their attention to "that WORD which God sent unto the children of Israel by Jesus Christ", preaching peace. He told them that they were acquainted with that word; for it was published throughout all Judea, beginning from Galilee after John's proclamation. As they knew it, he did not occupy time in repeating it in detail. The reader knows what the word was that God sent to Israel by Jesus Christ, for we have already spoken of it; but, lest it should have escaped him, we will reiterate it.

"I was sent", says Jesus, "to preach the kingdom of God." This was his message to Israel. Hence, he styles it in the parable of the sower, "the word of the kingdom". This word was so notorious to all that sojourned in the land of Israel, that it was as familiar as any question could possibly be. It was known also to every one, how that Jesus was anointed, or christened, with the Holy Spirit at his immersion in the Jordan by John; and how he went about doing good and healing the infirmities of the people; and none knew better than Roman centurions, that he was slain and hanged on a tree. These were matters of household notoriety and belief. A far more comprehensive faith than that of the moderns; but yet impotent to the justification of Cornelius and his house. More words were yet to be reported to them.

Peter therefore affirmed that God had raised him from the dead; and shown him openly, not to the public in general, but to certain witnesses previously chosen for the purpose, even to the apostles, who could not possibly have been deceived, because they ate fish and bread with him, and drank with him, after he rose from the dead. These things they heard and believed. The next thing he declared to them was, that God has commanded them to preach to the people Israel, and to testify, that Jesus was he that is appointed of God to be the Judge of the living and the dead (2 Timothy 4:1). Now, said Peter, and this was the fellowship of the mystery, "To him give all the prophets witness, that WHOSOEVER *believeth in him* SHALL RECEIVE REMISSION OF SINS THROUGH HIS NAME".

This was new doctrine to Gentiles. They had heard of it before as preached to Jews; but they heard it now for the first time, that "*whosoever* believed", whether Jew or Gentile, should receive remission of sins through his Name. Peter had made a very straightforward and simple statement of truth to them. This he called preaching "repentance and remission of sins in the name of Jesus". There was no sermonizing, or text-weaving; no scratching of itching ears; every thing was delivered in a concise and dignified manner, which carried the impress of truth upon its very front. But, he not only opened the mystery of the Gospel of the Kingdom to these Gentiles, but he "preached the gospel to them with the Holy Spirit sent down from heaven"; for, "while he yet spake these words, the Holy Spirit fell on all them who heard the Word". When the six Jewish Christians, who accompanied Peter, *saw* this, they were astonished, because that on the Gentiles was poured out the gift of the Holy Spirit as on the apostles themselves on the day of Pentecost. They could make no mistake about this, for "they heard them speak with tongues and magnify God".

Here, then, was the Word preached, and the Word *confirmed* by the Lord working with Peter. No one that heard the account of these things could doubt for a moment, whether "God had purified their hearts by faith", and accepted them. But still there was something wanting. Peter had told them of remission of sins through the name of Jesus to every one that believes in him; but he had not informed these believers, *how they could avail themselves of this omnipotent Name.* How were they to be washed, sanctified, and justified by this Name? How were they to take it upon them? In what manner was it to be named upon them? The apostle says, that when the Spirit fell upon them, he had only "begun to speak". If he had not been interrupted by this extraordinary effusion, he would doubtless have fully explained himself upon this point; for, he was not only commanded to preach the name of Jesus, but to command *believers* to be immersed "INTO THE NAME ($\varepsilon i \varsigma$ τo $\check{o}\nu o\mu a$) of the Father, and of the Son, and of the Holy Spirit" (Matthew 28:19).

Here, then, is a great matter. *The* NAME OF JESUS *is placed in the institution of immersion, based on an intelligent, child-like belief of "the things of the kingdom of God, and the name of Jesus Christ".* God has always placed His name in His institutions. Under the law He placed it in the Tabernacle, and afterwards in the Temple at Jerusalem; but, under grace, He has placed it in such a baptism as we have just defined, in conformity to which we can "worship him in spirit and in truth", without going to Jerusalem or Samaria. Cornelius and his household were in Caesarea, and in a private house. Peter did not require them to go to Jerusalem, or to a synagogue, in order to worship, or do homage to God, in spirit and in truth. They had believed the truth spoken by the Spirit through Peter; and they awaited the command of the Spirit as to the manner in which they might work the righteousness of God. Peter, feeling his way with caution, because of his six brethren of the circumcision who accompanied him, inquired, "Can any man forbid water, that these should not be immersed, who have received the Holy Spirit as well as we?"

From this question we learn that there were cases in those days in which the use of water was forbidden, or considered as improper. The apostles did not preach water to the people as the moderns do. They permitted no one to have access to the water unless they believed he was a proper subject. They were sometimes deceived, but that was not their fault; they did their best to discharge their duty faithfully. If a man did not believe the gospel of the kingdom of God and the name of Jesus Christ, they would not immerse him; for it was commanded them that "he that believeth not should be condemned", *i.e.*, should not be unloosed from his sins in the name of Jesus.

The paidorhantists do well to refuse to be immersed; and the Baptists do wrong to urge it upon them. For the sprinklers do not believe the gospel of the kingdom, and neither have they the spirit of the gospel; and therefore, they are not fit to be immersed. The institution of God's name ought not to be desecrated by the immersion of such misbelievers into its formula. Water should be forbidden them. It is not water, but faith, they need at present — that one, heart-purifying faith, such as Cornelius and his household possessed, and "without which it is impossible to please God".

It cannot be said that the paidorhantists (from παιδές, *infants*, and ῥαντισταί, *sprinklers*, that is, *infant sprinklers*) make too little of water; one great offence against high heaven which they commit, is making infinitely too much of it. The efficacy the apostles put in the heart-purifying faith and conscience-cleansing name of Jesus, they place in a few drops of "*holy*" or common, water, and a physical regeneration of a hypothetic principle in the flesh! They require no faith, no repentance, no confession to qualify their subjects for the water and formula of the Name. They ask only a suckling of eight days, with godfathers and godmothers, whose characters are not even inquired into, to answer questions, which oftentimes they do not understand, and oftener have no intention to conform to the requirements of; or, dispensing with these godless gods, give them the infant with a proxy parental faith in the dogmas of a sect, and it will suffice.

Paidorhantist "ministers", with solemn mockery of the holy and august name of the Father, Son, and Holy Spirit, will sprinkle the face of the mindless weakling, and impiously proclaim to the people that such is the "one baptism" of the religion of Christ! Is it not wonderful, that God has witnessed this blasphemy for ages, and not rent the heavens with indignation upon them? Great indeed, is the forbearance of the Most High; but the time shall at length come when His patience will have an end. How astounding is the presumption of such! "The people of the Lord", say they, "are we! Wisdom will die with us !" Yet they are *faithless* of the words of Peter, for they do them not; and have changed the ordinance of God, and made it contemptible. A rhantized, but unbaptized, community is the vast majority of the professing world; and therefore "without Christ, being aliens from the commonwealth of Israel, and strangers from the covenants of promise, having no hope (no true one) and without God in the world". Them that honour God, He will honour; but they who seek honour one of another, and desecrate His name, are fattening their hearts for the day of slaughter; and are fit only for capture and destruction.

Cornelius and his household differ from these *in toto*. They all believed the words of Peter, awaiting his commands. He had inquired if there were any present who could, in the face of what they saw and heard, "forbid water that they should not be baptized". He doubtless paused a reasonable time that objections might be urged if any could possibly exist. But all Jewish prejudices were abolished by "the demonstration of the spirit", and they held their peace. Things being brought to this crisis, it only remained for the Spirit of God to pronounce the word. Therefore, Peter opened his mouth, and "COMMANDED *them to be* BAPTIZED IN THE NAME OF THE LORD".

After this manner Peter used the keys of the kingdom of heaven given to him by the Lord Jesus Christ. When he had accomplished this work, *he no longer retained the power of the keys.* They were transferred to the multitude of the believing Jews and Gentiles. The spirit had revealed the mystery of the kingdom, and the fellowship of the mystery, by the mouth of Peter on Pentecost, and at Caesarea; so that the keys became the common property of all believers. The Lord "who hath the key of David, hath opened, and no man can shut" (Revelation 3:7-8); He hath set before the Gentiles "an open door, and no man can close it", so long as the scriptures are in the hands of the people. The false prophet may dangle keys at his girdle, and affect the power of the Son of God; but so long as "THE LAW AND THE TESTIMONY" are accessible "whosoever is athirst may come; and whosoever will may take the water of life freely". The scriptures contain the keys. Popes, priests, clergy, and ministers may suppress, torture, and garble the truth, and throw hindrances in the way; but the man who discards their authority, and thinks for himself, may, by the enlightening efficacy of the living word, become "wise unto salvation by the faith which is in Jesus Christ". Let the people then help themselves, if they would that God should aid them.

From what has been advanced it is manifest that "the word of the kingdom" presents itself to us in the scriptures in a three-fold relation:

1.   As the gospel preached to Abraham, etc.

2.   As the same gospel preached in the name of Jesus on Pentecost, or the mystery of the gospel of the kingdom; and

3.   As the fellowship of the mystery of the gospel preached first by Peter to circumcised Gentiles; and afterwards by Paul to the worshippers of idols.

There are not three gospels; but one and the same gospel, as before stated; originally all promise; then promise, history, and doctrine preached to Jews only; and afterwards offered to the Gentiles upon the same terms as to the Jews. But though I have set forth these things with some minuteness, the reader will still feel that the treatise is incomplete so long as I have not set forth "the things concerning the kingdom of God", to which such frequent reference has been made, as the grand theme of "the glorious gospel of the blessed God"; and without the knowledge of which a man's faith is destitute of the "one hope of the calling" which is the anchor of the soul both sure and steadfast within the veil in Christ Jesus; who is there "waiting to receive the kingdom and return". This, then, will be the subject of future illustration, in the hope that we shall make it so plain that "he may run who reads". I shall now proceed to say a few words upon

APOSTOLIC SUCCESSION

"DIVINES" contend that the mantle of the apostles fell upon the elders, or bishops, of the churches who survived them; that these survivors were *"the successors of the apostles"*, and that when these died away, the apostolic mantle fell upon those who succeeded to their offices in the churches, being invested by the imposition of hands; and that thus from generation to generation until the present day, the succession has been perpetuated by the institution of ordination, or "holy orders"; so that the living orders of ecclesiastics, composed of pope, cardinals, bishops, priests, and ministers, are "successors of the apostles", endued with like authority and power in the churches, and entitled to the same obedience and consideration.

They found their claim to these high pretensions upon certain passages of scripture, written concerning the apostles and their co-labourers, which they apply to themselves, and argue that the grace of office has been transmitted from one to another by the imposition of "holy hands"! Thus, when an aspirant to apostolic succession presents himself before a bishop for ordination, the latter says to this effect: "Receive thou the Holy Ghost by the imposition of my hands for the office, or work, of a priest, in the house of God; whosesoever sins you remit are remitted, and whosesoever sins you retain are retained". This, says the thirty-sixth article of the national religion, "hath nothing that of itself is superstitious or ungodly". By virtue of this consecration and ordering, absolution, or remission of sins, is pronounced by the priest standing up alone in the midst of the people, who kneel to receive it; and in the form it is declared that "Almighty God hath given power and commandment to His ministers to declare and pronounce to His people, being penitent, the absolution and remission of their sins". Thus, the national parsonocracy claim the apostolic attribute of remitting and retaining sins, of binding and loosing, even as the Papists; with this modification, however that they remit sins in the gross, while the latter do it both wholesale and retail. Thus do the national and Popish clergy speak blasphemy (cf. Matthew 9:2,3,6) continually.

But the state-clergies are not alone in their assumption of apostolicity; the Dissenters are condemnable on the same account. They claim to be ambassadors of Jesus Christ; and they permit none to "administer ordinances" who are not ordained by the imposition of hands. The ordained do not undertake to forgive sins after the manner of the apostles; but they apply to themselves scriptures which relate only to the apostles, by which they constitute themselves their "successors".

But, the truth is, that neither State nor Nonconformist clergies are entitled to be regarded as "successors of the apostles". The nature of the office may be comprehended by the qualifications of the office-holder, which were indispensable. They may be thus stated:—

1.   An apostle of Christ to the circumcision must be one who has companied with the Lord Jesus from his baptism until his ascension; so as to be a witness to his resurrection (Acts 1:21,22,8);

2.   An apostle of Christ to the Gentiles must have seen Jesus, and have conversed with him, as well as the former (1 Corinthians 9:1);

3.   An apostle must be chosen, ordained, and sent of the Lord (John 15:16); and authorized by him to forgive and retain sins (John 20:22,23);

4.   An apostle must be able to work signs, and wonders, and mighty deeds, as signs of his apostleship (2 Corinthians 12:12; Galatians 2:8);

5.   To be an apostle a man must have believed the pure gospel of the Kingdom of God (Galatians 1:8), have been immersed (Luke 7:29; Acts 22:16), and walk according to the truth of it (Galatians 2:14).

With these qualifications, the thirteen apostles (ἀπόστολοι, *men sent with commands*) directed the affairs of the churches, which they had formed and established in the world. Their administration was in fact the administration of the Spirit through them; so that in their word was power (1 Corinthians 4:20,21) to the healing of disease, the infliction of it (1 Corinthians 5:4-5; Acts 13:11), and the destruction of life (Acts 5:9,10). They conferred spiritual gifts upon believers by the imposition of their hands (Acts 8:14-18); and gave commandments to the faithful as the vicegerents of the Lord (Matthew 28:20). Now, reason and common sense teach, that if men are real successors to apostolicity, they will be like Peter and Paul in all their qualifications and attributes; but reason also teaches, that after the ascension of Jesus, no man can be qualified for the apostleship unless the Lord appear to him, as in the case of Paul. But the truth is, that this claim of apostolic succession is as groundless as the claim of the clergy of the apostasy to tithes on the ground of their succession to the rights of the Levitical priesthood. If their apostolicity be granted, it can only be as "false apostles, deceitful workers, transforming themselves into apostles of Christ. And no marvel", continues Paul, "for Satan himself is transformed into an angel of light. Therefore, it is no great thing if his ministers also be transformed as the ministers of righteousness; whose end shall be according to their works" (2 Corinthians 11:13).

It is a stronghold of these pretended apostles, that the Lord promised to be with them always, to the end of the world. They contend (though, as learned men they must know better) that the phrase "the end of the world" indicates a period of time yet future; and, therefore, that Jesus had reference, not to the apostles only, but to their "successors" likewise. Hence, they argue that the command yet remains with them to be executed, which says, "Go ye therefore, into all the world, and preach the gospel to every creature".

But to this I object, *first*, that the end of the world to which Jesus referred, arrived more than eighteen hundred years ago; *secondly*, that the work enjoined upon the persons in the text was fully accomplished by the apostles; *thirdly*, that the Lord is not with them who pretend to be their successors; *fourthly*, that the moderns cannot execute the command, because they are utterly ignorant of the gospel; and, therefore, cannot be the individuals referred to.

THE THINGS OF THE KINGDOM OF GOD

In the first place, the Lord Jesus did not use the phrase, "The end of the world", in the vulgar English sense of it. He said to the eleven, "Behold, I am *with you, πάσας τὰς ἡμέρας, all the days, ἕως τῆς συντελείας τοῦ αἰῶνος, until the end of the age*". Here are *certain days* indicated, which were comprehended in the period to elapse from the time when Jesus made the promise, until the end of the age. These days are termed by Paul, *"these last days"* (Hebrews 1:2); which he characterizes as those in which God spoke to the Israelites by a Son, as well as those in which he was writing to the Hebrews some thirty years after: *"These* last days", says he. Now, the days taken collectively, he styles according to the English version, "the end of the world"; as it is written, "Now once *in the end of the world* hath Jesus appeared to put away sin by the sacrifice of himself" (Hebrews 9:26). The reader will easily perceive by the remark in the text, that the world spoken of was that to which Jesus stood related by death. That it was near its end when he was crucified by it; but if *"the world"* is to be taken in the vulgar English sense, Paul was wrong in saying, that Jesus sacrificed himself *in the end of it*; for surely that period was not the end of the world, which passed away more than eighteen hundred years ago! But the truth is, Paul was perfectly accurate in what he wrote. He knew nothing about the English sense of his words: for there were neither Englishmen, nor English words in his day. He penned Hebraisms in Greek words; that is, he put the things God had taught Israel into a Greek dress. He wrote "the things of the spirit" in the words of the spirit selected from the Greek language. What he said in the text before us was, "But now once for all, *ἐπὶ συντελεία τῶν αἰώνων, at the end of the ages*, hath he appeared to put away sin by the sacrifice of himself". The constitution of Mount Sinai was the founding of the Hebrew world, or *κόσμος;* because it ordered, or arranged, the things pertaining to Israel, as a system *sui generis.* This system had *times peculiar to itself* which were appointed at the promulgation of the law. These are termed in scripture *αἰωνές*, that is, *aions*, from *ἀεί*, *alway* and *ὦν, passing*. The etymology of *αἰών* does not express the duration of the time; its continuance is defined by the Mosaic law. The Hebrew Commonwealth *under the Sinaitic constitution* was not intended to continue always. The time of its existence was predetermined of God, but not revealed in the law, or the prophets, but "reserved in his own power" (Acts 1:7; Mark 13:32). It is termed *αἰών*; and its approaching termination, *συντελεία τοῦ αἰῶνος, the end of the time*, that is, of the Hebrew Commonwealth, under the Mosaic law. But, though the precise duration of this *great time* (1,697 years) was kept secret; the *lesser times*, or *αἰώνες, aions*, of which it was composed, were very minutely specified as in the case of the Jubilees, so that the whole time of the commonwealth was the αἰών τῶν αἰώνων, *the aion of the aions*, the time of the times, or age of the ages. Hence, while the Lord Jesus designated the consummation as *the end of the time*, Paul indicated it *as the end of the times*, or ages.

That the delivering of the law was the beginning of the αἰών, or Hebrew world, is obvious from the words of Peter. Addressing the men of Israel, he said, "God will send Jesus Christ to you; whom the heaven must retain *until* times (χρόνων) of reconstitution of all things, which God hath spoken by the mouth of all his holy prophets ἀπ' αἰῶνος, *from the age*; for Moses truly said to the fathers", etc. (Acts 3:20-22). In the authorized version ἀπ' αἰῶνος is rendered *"since the world began"*. If this be preferred, it is evident that the world referred to was coeval in its beginning with Moses; for he is cited as the first of the holy prophets by whose mouth God spoke of the reconstitution of the Hebrew commonwealth at the appearing of Christ from heaven. Paul refers to the same epoch, saying, "The fellowship of the mystery hath been hid in God ἀπὸ τῶν αἰώνων, *from the ages*"; in the common version, *"from the beginning* of the world" (Ephesians 3:9). From the beginning of the age, or of the ages, is the correct rendering of the Greek in these texts. They both refer to the beginning of the commonwealth of Israel in the giving of the law from Sinai.

To speak in the vernacular, *God promised eternal life to man before the world began*. Such a statement as this would be incomprehensible to a mere English reader; yet such is the import of the saying, "God, who cannot lie promised eternal life before the world began (πρὸ χρόνων αἰωνίων); but *in due times (καιροῖς ἰδίοις*); hath manifested his word in the preaching" (Titus 1:2,3). To whom did He promise it? Certainly not to any one before the formation of man. The world referred to cannot therefore be that founded in the six days; but a constitution of things long subsequent to it. A literal translation removes all difficulty. The phrase πρὸ χρόνων αἰωνίων is, *before the aionian times*; that is, before the times of the Hebrew commonwealth were arranged, God promised eternal life; and in καιροῖς ἰδίοις, *his own times*, such times, namely, as are particularized in Daniel (9:24,26), He made His word, which had before been a hidden mystery, manifest (Romans 16:26) through the apostolic preaching.

In the parable of the sower (Matthew 13:37-40), the phrase *"the world"* is used in different senses, which are not distinguished in the English version. Jesus says there, *"the field* is the *world"*. Did he mean it was "the whole habitable", "the age", or the Israelites; for *world* is applied to them all? If it had been the first he would have said, "The field is the ὅλη οἰκουμένη"; if the second, "The field is the *αἰών*"; and if the third, "The field is the *κόσμος*". The last is the record in the case. He represents himself as the sower; and says that the seed which he sowed was "the word of the kingdom"; that it was "good seed"; and that he sowed it into the hearts of the Israelites, or "children of the kingdom", of whom there were two classes, good and bad" (Matthew 8:12).

These, then, were the field, and therefore, the *κόσμος* or nation-world. But the enemy sowed tares into this field, which were to be gathered out and burnt. This conflagration was to be at harvest-time, concerning which Jesus said, "The harvest is *the end of the world*". Did he mean the end of the nation-world? No; therefore he used another word, namely *αἰών* instead of *κόσμος*. The harvest was to be at the end of the *aion, συντέλεια τοῦ αἰῶνος;* and not at the end of the *kosmos*, or extermination of the nation Israel from among nations. The extinction of Israel from the earth will never take place; though a full end will be made of all other nations.

But at the end of what *aion* was the harvest to be? Jesus replies, "As the tares are gathered and burned in the fire at harvest time; so shall it be *ἐν τῇ συντελείᾳ τοῦ αἰῶνος τούτου*, in the end of this age".* That is, in the end of the *aion* in which he flourished. Then he would send his reapers, namely, the Romans, his angels, or messengers (*ἄγγελοι*) of destruction, to "gather out of his kingdom" of Judea, all the tare-like children of Israel, and cast them into the place of the Lord, "whose fire is in Zion, and his furnace in Jerusalem" (Isaiah 31:9), where there should be wailing, and gnashing of teeth. When this should be accomplished the *aion* would be finished, and the commonwealth of Israel should "be no more until He should come whose right it is to reign" (Ezekiel 21:25-27). "Then shall the righteous shine forth as the sun in the kingdom of their Father."

As Jesus sat on the Mount of Olives, his disciples asked him saying, *"What shall be the sign of the end of the age—τί τὸ σημεῖον τῆς συντελείας τοῦ αἰῶνος?"* or, in the common version, "of the end of the world?" He replied, "This gospel of the kingdom shall be preached *in the whole habitable* (*ἐν ὅλῃ τῇ οἰκουμένῃ*) for a testimony to all the nations: and then shall come the end" (Matthew 24:3,14). Having said this, he gave them *"the sign"*, namely, the standing of the abomination of desolation in the holy place, or city, as foretold by Daniel (Daniel 9:26-27). First, then, the gospel was to be fully preached to every creature by the apostles; and afterwards, the sign was to appear. Did the apostles

---

*But the parable also certainly points to the end of "the times of the Gentiles".

perform their work, or does it yet remain to be accomplished? Their pretended successors answer, *"No*, they did not". They contend that there are vast regions which were unknown to the ancients, where the gospel has never been preached; and, therefore, that, as it is to be preached to every creature, it is incumbent on them to do it; and that the end of the world will not come until they have converted all the nations to Christianity! Hence, they have established societies *de propaganda fide*, both Romish and Protestant. Every principal sect has its missionary society, whose utopian speculation is the conversion of the world under the warrant of the apostolic commission! As if a command given to the apostles to preach *the gospel of the kingdom* were a command given to modern missionaries to go and preach Churchism and Dissenterism, Calvinism, Arminianism, and Popery to all the world! But the apostles were not sent to "all the world" in the Gentile acceptation of the phrase. They were sent to all the nations of the then habitable, or civilized world; principally, and almost exclusively, comprehended in the limits of the Roman dominion. Nor were they sent under the idea of converting them nationally to the gospel; but to preach it *εἰς μαρτύριον, for a testimony*; that is, for their information, that disciples might be made among them all; so that a people might be taken out of them (*ἐξ ἐθνῶν*) for the administration of the affairs of God's kingdom and empire upon earth (Acts 15:14). The apostles left nothing for "successors" to do under the commission given to them. They preached the gospel of the kingdom to "every creature" of the Roman nations; if not in the Gentile sense of "every creature", at least in the sense of the phrase as used by the Lord Jesus.

I feel strong upon this point, sustained as I am by the direct testimony of scripture; which is worth all the theories, and all the logic of the schools *en masse*. The apostle, in speaking of the *"one hope of the calling"* (Ephesians 4:4), contained "in the word of the truth of the gospel", tells the Colossian believers (Colossians 1:5-6), that "it had come to *all the world"* (*παρόντος ἐν παντὶ τῷ κόσμῳ*) in the sense of "every creature", as appears in another verse (verse 23) of the same chapter. In this place he says, *"The hope of the gospel was preached to every creature which is under the heaven"*. This was the result of some thirty years' apostolic labour; for the epistle in which he makes the statement is assigned to AD 62; which was about eight years before the desolating abomination appeared before the walls of Jerusalem, as *"the sign"* of the end of the age.

The gospel of the kingdom, so efficiently preached by the apostles, was soon after perverted by "men of corrupt minds" (2 Timothy 3:1-8; 4:3-4; Titus 1:10-14); whom Paul, who was very severe, but not too much so, upon this class of professors, styles, "seducing spirits, speaking lies in hypocrisy, and having their conscience seared as with a hot iron" (1 Timothy 4:1-3). (Let the reader consult these references.) These characters were the "successors" from whom modern apostles and ambassadors of Christ have originated. When the Hebrew commonwealth was broken up by the Romans, they claimed to be successors to the priests and Levites of the law, as well as to the apostles. Thus they united a worldly priesthood (for all Christ's disciples are kings and priests elected for the purpose of the approaching kingdom) with eldership; and became a *distinct order* unrecognized by the scriptures, by which they are repudiated as "reprobate concerning the faith". This order of men, as I have already stated elsewhere, had the presumption to style themselves *God's heritage*, or "clergy"; as though He had a delight in them above all other professors! But with all their praying and preaching, and profession, neither they nor their successors love the Lord; for they *do not obey* Him: and He has made obedience the test of love, as it is written, "Love is the fulfilling of the law". They corrupted, and perpetuate the perversions of the faith from age to age; therefore, says the scripture, "Let them be accursed when the Lord comes" (1 Corinthians 16:22; Galatians 1:8,9; Matthew 7:21-23).

By the ministerial influence of this order of men multitudes departed from the faith; and by their accession to municipal and state authority, they were enabled to give political existence to the apostasy they had consummated. It is unnecesary to narrate the history of their evil deeds from the beginning to the present time. It would require volumes to do justice to their ignorance, hypocrisy, and crime. As ecclesiastical policemen they have kept the world in order for the advantage and behoof of the oppressors and destroyers of the earth; and have used the people for their own profit under pretence of "curing their souls".

But while this is undeniably true of the order, I am free to admit that there have been, and no doubt are, many sincere, honest, and moral men, who bear the names of "clergyman" and "minister":—many, who conscientiously believe their theories to be the true sense of scripture; and who would suffer the loss of all things, and life itself, rather than surrender what they believe to be the truth. There have been many such; and may still be, should occasion arise to necessitate their manifestation. These are men who are in advance of the systems by which they have been created "clergymen", and "ministers". Their position is an unhappy one. System has made them; and they conscientiously support and perpetuate the system, having been indoctrinated by their predecessors into the belief that the system is the religion of God! But I have hope that if this book fall into the hands of this respectable class of professors, it may be instrumental in opening their eyes to see the deception practised upon them by the traditions of their fathers.

Sincerity, honesty, piety, and morality, are good qualities without which no man can be saved. I admit they have all these. But they should remember that Cornelius was as estimable a man as they; and had the advantage of them in this, that his character was attested of God by the mouth of a special messenger from heaven; whereas they have no attestation beyond what is purely human. Now piety and God fearing did not save Cornelius: they only commended him to God's remembrance. It was necessary for him to believe words, and to be baptized in the name of the Lord, as I have already shown. These words were the gospel of the kingdom of God and His Christ. This necessity has never been abrogated. It is in full force to this day. Clergy and ministers do not believe it. Much of it they sneer at as "the millennial *hypothesis*". If they would attain to the kingdom of God, they must believe the doctrine concerning it. Martyrdom for opinion's sake is no substitute for "the obedience of faith". It is self-deception to say that God is with us to the end of the world, when we neither understand, nor believe and obey, the truth.

Lastly, the clergy and ministers of the age, being utterly ignorant of the gospel of the kingdom, are plainly not the persons referred to in the commission. The Lord is not "*with them*"; and without his co-operation, were they as enlightened and faithful as the apostles themselves, they could do nothing (John 15:5). They point to what *is done* among the heathen in proof of his being "with them". But, there is nothing done there as it ought to be done; or, as things were done when the Lord worked with the apostles. Their missionary societies are but so many institutions for the intellectual, moral, and social training of the heathen in the civilization of European and American religionists. They make Protestants and Catholics of the natives; but beyond this they cannot go. They may extend the civilization of Japheth into the tents of Shem, and compel Ham to be their servant; but to beget them in Christ Jesus *through the gospel*, and so to induct them into the heirship of the kingdom of God, is a thing they could as soon accomplish as to still the raging of the sea. If by their labours they were to make all the earth like England and America, it would still need to be converted to the religion of Christ.

Ecclesiastics have done all they are able to do in "civilized" communities. They are powerless for progress among these; and men of naturally strong minds are either indifferent to their ministrations, or have repudiated them altogether. They lack one thing, namely, the knowledge of "the truth as it is in Jesus". In default of this they occupy the minds of the people with foreign enterprises, benevolent institutions, public meetings, platform and pulpit oratory, fancy fairs, and all sorts of devices to raise the wind to keep the machine in motion. But all will not do. The people begin to flag. The masses take no interest in their preaching. Their churches are cold, formal, and deathlike. Their "spirituality" is gone; and, unless the Lord come to raise the dead, both priests and people will be beyond the reach of cure.

Apostolic succession, then, especially through such a channel, is a mere figment of the carnal mind. The only succession of which any scriptural idea can be formed is, the following in the steps of the apostles' faith; which no one who understands the word of the kingdom would affirm of the ecclesiastical guides of the people. The power and authority of the apostles died with them. Those *who succeed to their faith* are their successors only in this sense. Their word, which is also the Lord's word, dwells in such richly in all wisdom; and where the word of the Lord is found, there, by the belief of it, he dwells in the hearts of men. When they work according to this word, they and the Lord work together. But this is not peculiar to a ministerial class, but is common to all the Lord's people, for he is no respecter of persons. A successor to the faith of the apostles delights to feel that he is a layman; that he is one of the flock; and of the best of the sheep it contains, because his sole anxiety is to know and obey the great shepherd's voice (Hebrews 13:20; John 10:27). He is not a wolf, nor a dog, rending and devouring the flock, and investing himself with its wool; but one who would be the servant of the least, that he may be exalted to an unfading crown of glory, when the good shepherd shall appear to give life to all his sheep for evermore.

CHAPTER II

THE GOSPEL PREACHED TO ABRAHAM: HIS FAITH AND WORKS

Five points of prophetic testimony—The general elements of a kingdom constituents of the kingdom of Christ—The promise made of God to the fathers,
the hope of Israel, and the gospel, the same—Who the fathers are—Abram
originally from Babel, and an idolater—The Lord preaches the gospel to him
in Mesopotamia—He believes it, and emigrates westward in consequence—
Becomes a wanderer in the land of Canaan, which is promised to him and
Christ for ever—His faith counted to him for righteousness—The promise of
a resurrection to eternal life—Confirmation of the covenant of promise—The
extent of the land defined in the Covenant—The personal re-appearance of
Christ necessitated by the nature of things—The phrases "in thee", "in him",
and "in thy seed", explained—The nations God's people in no sense—
Abraham, Christ, and the saints, "heirs of the world"—The token of the
covenant—The signification of circumcision—Modern Israel under the curse
of the law—Circumcision of the heart—The Allegory—The two seeds—
Parable of the Seed—Summary of Abraham's faith

IT is written in the prophet Micah, that "the LORD shall judge
among many people, and rebuke strong nations afar off (from
Jerusalem)"; and as the result thereof, "they shall beat their
swords into ploughshares, and their spears into scythes; nation
shall not lift up sword against nation, neither shall they learn
war any more. But they shall sit every man under his vine and
under his fig tree; and none shall make them afraid". And "in
that day, saith the Lord, I will assemble" Israel, "and make them
A STRONG NATION: *and the LORD shall reign over them in Mount
Zion*, FROM HENCEFORTH, even for ever". And "Unto thee, O Zion,
shall it come, even the FIRST DOMINION; the *kingdom* shall come to
the daughter of Jerusalem" (Micah 4:3-8). And the Judge, who
shall be Ruler in Israel, whose goings forth have been from everlasting, "shall stand and feed in the strength of Jehovah, *in the
Majesty of the Name* of the LORD his God; and Israel shall abide;
for now shall He be great to the ends of the earth. And this man
(Christ the Lord) shall be the peace when the Assyrian (the
Russo-Assyrian) shall come into our (Israel's) land". And
"Assyria shall be wasted with the sword, and the land of Nimrod
in the entrances thereof; thus shall He (the Judge of Israel)
deliver us from the Assyrian (Gog) when he cometh into our
land". "And the remnant of Jacob shall be in the midst of many

people as a dew from the Lord, as the showers upon the grass, that tarrieth not for man, nor waiteth for the sons of men. And the remnant of Jacob shall be among the Gentiles in the midst of many people as a lion among the beasts of the forest, *as a young lion among the flocks of sheep*, who, if he go through, both treadeth down, and teareth in pieces, and none can deliver. Thine hand shall be lifted up upon thine adversaries, and all thine enemies shall be cut off." "And I will execute vengeance in anger and fury upon the heathen, *such as they have not heard*" (Micah 5:1,2,4-9,15).

From this passage, which is only a specimen of the general tenor of the law and the testimony, we are informed,

1.　That the nations are to be *subdued*, and that universal peace shall prevail in consequence;

2.　That when this shall occur, the Israelites shall become a strong nation;

3.　That they shall then constitute A KINGDOM;

4.　That the Judge of Israel, formerly treated with indignity, shall be their King;

5.　That Jerusalem shall be the metropolis, and Mount Zion the throne, of the kingdom.

Such is the revealed purpose of the Most High. But a consummation like this requires preparation; and that, too, a very long one; especially as it is to be developed upon certain moral, as well as political, principles. When the time shall come for the kingdom to be possessed, it will be said to the heirs of it, "Come, ye blessed of my Father, inherit the kingdom *prepared for* you from the foundation of the world". From this, it appears that the work of *preparing* the kingdom takes from the foundation of the world to the resurrection of the dead. All this time the kingdom is preparing; but when the King descends, and rebukes the nations, and wastes the land of Nimrod with the sword, and makes Israel a strong nation, it will then be said that the kingdom is *prepared*.

The reader will probably inquire, what does this work of preparation consist in that it should take so long a time? This is an important question, and, in reply, I remark that if physical force only were employed in preparing the kingdom, it need not take so long. A kingdom may be set up in a few days, and abolished as speedily, as we have witnessed in our own time. But it is not so with the Kingdom of God. The physical is subordinated to the intellectual and moral; and as men, among whom it is being prepared, are so earthly and sensual, the mental progresses much more slowly than the physical; and therefore, a kingdom founded upon moral principles requires longer to prepare, but is more enduring when completed. In the following pages my endeavour will be to set forth an answer to the question in detail.

A *kingdom* is the dominion of a king. An *empire* is also the dominion of a king, but with this difference: the kingdom proper, or "*the first dominion*", is restricted to a regally constituted territory; while the empire, or secondary dominion, though belonging to the same king, extends over other peoples, multitudes, nations, and tongues, than those of the royal domain. This is illustrated in the case of the British kingdoms and empire. The kingdoms are restricted to England and Scotland, which are by constitution regal territories; but the empire is a secondary dominion of the same united crowns, extending over Canada, Hindostan, and other parts of the globe, with all the nations, languages, and people, they contain.

There are various elements necessary to the constitution of a well-organized kingdom. In the first place, *a kingdom must have a territory*. This is only saying, in other terms, that something must be somewhere. To maintain the opposite would be to contend that something is nowhere. A kingdom is not located in feeling, or in heart; though a belief of its future existence, a comprehension of its nature, or an attachment to it, may exist there. It must have a place, a locality, as well as a name.

It would be highly absurd to say that the kingdom of England and the throne of her sovereign were in Spain; yet this would be as reasonable as to say that the kingdom and throne of David are beyond the skies!—an orthodox dogma contained in the fiction that Jesus is now sitting upon the throne of his father David! What conceit after this is too ridiculous for creed-makers and systematizers to promulge?

In addition to a territory, a kingdom requires *subjects*, which compose the nation over whom there is the king. But, simply to set up a man and call him "king" would be unwise. It would be consonant only with the barbarism of savage tribes. A well-regulated monarchy requires graduation of ranks, and orders of the best men, with whom the king may divide his power, and glory, and administer the laws of the kingdom. These laws should be in conformity with the provisions and spirit of the constitution; which defines the principles, and creates and combines the elements, of the State.

Now it is worthy of remark, that *the subjects* of a kingdom do not possess the kingdom. They are simply the inhabitants of the territory, who are defended against external aggression, and protected as civilians by the power, and laws, of the State. The possessors of the kingdom are the king, and those with whom he is pleased to share his authority. This is an important distinction, and must not be forgotten in studying "the things of the kingdom of God". The *subjects* of the kingdom and empire are a totally different class from the *heirs*, or possessors, of the dominion.

From this brief view, then, of the nature and constitution of a kingdom, its elements may be stated as consisting of:

1. A territory;
2. Subjects;
3. A king;
4. A constitution
5. Laws, civil and ecclesiastical;
6. Aristocracy;
7. Attributes, or prerogatives, rights, privileges, etc.

Now, *"the kingdom of God and of his Christ"* will consist of all these things; and will be as material an institution—as real and terrestrial a monarchy as that of Great Britain. It is not now an existent reality; for, though it once existed under a constitution, which hath waxed old and vanished away, its elements are dissolved from their previous combination, and remain dispersed. Their restitution is, however, a matter of promise, attested by two immutable things—the promise and the oath of the living God. His kingdom and empire on earth are a great truth, but not an existing fact; they are visible only to the eye of faith, and are required by their founder to be received in the *"full assurance of hope"*, with rejoicing and confidence to the end (Hebrews 3:6,14; 4:11; 10:38,39).

In studying the things of the kingdom of God, the foundation laid in the beginning must not be forgotten; for at that epoch its preparation was commenced. The system of the world is an adaptation to man in his fallen state; and out of the things thus arranged it is that Christ's imperial dominion is being evolved. By the law of procreation has been provided a population which, by the confusion of tongues, has been distributed into nations, whose habitations have been fixed by the controlling power of the Elohim. Thus nations have been formed which are destined to flourish in the blessedness of the Future Age. Their history records the fiery ordeal through which their generations have passed. For the most part, men see nothing in it but a strife for territory, and glory, for the advantage of their rulers; but the scriptures reveal the workings of an invisible machinery, whose activity is perceived by the believer, in the incidents which occasion the conflicts among them. He discerns the leaven, hid in the three measures of meal, at work leavening the minds of men, and developing the *"enmity"* *between the seeds*. And though the strife is terrible, he feels no dismay, but rejoices with firm and unwavering confidence in the certainty of the triumph of the truth and its adherents; because God has assured him in His word that the King He has provided shall crush the sin-power, and make the nations lick the dust like a serpent (Micah 7:17). Now this implies their subjugation; and it is to this crisis that all things are at present tending. And what then? Obviously, the transfer of the conquered to the sceptre of Jehovah's King, who overcomes them (Revelation 17:14); as it is written, "The Gentiles shall wait for his law" (Isaiah 42:4); and "He shall reign over them" (Romans 15:12). *The nations, then, are the subjects of the theocratic empire.* By the truth and judgments of God brought to bear upon them, exciting and controlling their activity, they are being moulded like clay in the hands of the potter, for the dominion of the saints in the Future Age.

The hope of these things, whose seeds were sown in the constitution of the world at the beginning, was the hope of the gospel then in its most general enunciation. The subjects and territory of the empire, and the rulers thereof, were plainly marked out. The earth, and the conquered seed of the serpent, obedient to the victorious seed of the woman, was the gospel of the kingdom in its most simple form. No particular portion of the globe, however, was indicated as the territory of a kingdom. The Spirit began with universals; but as the world became older, the particulars of the promise were unfolded to the eye of faith. But never, from the foundation of the world to the sealing up of the testimony of God, was such a kingdom, or dominion, promised as that which is believed in, and glorified in the "sacred" psalmody of the Gentiles. Earth, and not the skies, is the region where alone it will appear. I shall show this abundantly; and thereby prove that they who sing such ditties as those of which the following is a specimen, sing what ne'er was, nor is, nor e'er shall be:

"With thee we'll reign, with thee we'll rise,
And kingdoms gain beyond the skies!"

"According to your faith be it unto you." This is the first principle of religion delivered by the Great Teacher himself. It is just and right it should be so. No one can blame God for not bestowing upon them what they do not believe in; and, consequently, do not want, or seek after. This is precisely the position of the present generation of religionists in relation to the kingdom of God. They have faith in a sort of kingdom which He hath not promised; and in the one He has promised they do not believe. Hence, they believe in a non-entity; and, believing in what is nothing, they will get nothing but confusion of face. But we propose to show them a more excellent way; and in so doing invite their attention to

"THE PROMISE MADE OF GOD UNTO THE FATHERS"

"The Hope of Israel"

THERE is no one, I suppose, who reads the scriptures but admits that Paul was persecuted; being imprisoned, scourged, arraigned, and manacled, because he preached the gospel of the kingdom in the name of Jesus. This is admitted by all. It matters not, then, in what terms he states the *cause* of his trials, it will all amount to this declaration, namely, "For the gospel I am called in question, and am judged, and bound with this chain".

But we will let the apostle state his case in his own words. When he stood before Ananias, the high priest, and the council of the Jews, he cried out, "On account of *the hope* and resurrection of dead persons (νεκρῶν) I am called in question" (Acts 23:6). But it may be asked here, "Concerning what hope was the question between the apostle and his persecutors?" He tells us in his defence before Agrippa: "I stand and am judged", says he, "for *the hope of the promise* made of God unto our fathers; unto which promise our twelve tribes, instantly serving God day and night, hope to come. For *which hope's sake*, king Agrippa, I am accused of the Jews" (Acts 26:6-7). Now, from this statement, it appears:

1.   That God had made a certain promise to the fathers of Israel;

2.   That this promise became *the hope of the nation*, and was therefore a national question;

3.   That this promise had been the hope of the twelve tribes in all their generations; was the ground of their worship; and that they hoped to attain it by rising from the dead.

But we have a still plainer avowal, if possible, of the identity of this national hope with the hope for which the apostle suffered so much. The Lord Jesus had appeared to him after his arraignment before Ananias, and said to him, "Be of good cheer, Paul; for as thou hast testified of me in Jerusalem, so must thou bear witness also at Rome". When he arrived at this city, he called the chief of the Jews together, and told them that he had nothing to accuse his nation of; but he had sent for them to inform them how matters really stood. He then told them how it was they found him in the custody of a Roman soldier, with fetters upon his person: "*On account of* THE HOPE OF ISRAEL" said he, "am I bound with this chain" (Acts 28:20). This is conclusive. *The hope of the promise made to the fathers* was, and, indeed, is to this day, *the Hope of Israel*; and for preaching this hope, and inviting the Gentiles to a participation in it without other circumcision than that of the heart, he was denounced as a pestilent fellow, and unfit to live (Acts 24:5-6; 22:21-22).

But what was the hope of Israel about? The answer to this question is easy. Having made the chief of the Jews at Rome acquainted with the cause of his appeal to Caesar, they remarked to him, that they should like to hear of him what he thought upon the question of the national hope, as so strenuously contended for by the sect of the Nazarenes. As it was not, however, convenient then, they appointed a future day when they would meet him, and hear what he had to say upon the subject. Accordingly, at the time appointed, they came together at Paul's lodging, and he proceeded to lay before them his thoughts upon the subject of Israel's hope. But I cannot do better than to state what he did in the words of Luke; who says that "He expounded and testified to them *the kingdom of God,* persuading them concerning Jesus *both out of the law of Moses and out of the prophets,* from morning till evening" (Acts 28:23).

Now who can be so dim of vision as not to perceive that the subject-matter of the hope of Israel is the Kingdom of God? And observe, that in giving his thoughts of the national hope, the apostle's persuasions turned upon things concerning Jesus. The Kingdom of God and Jesus were the subjects of Paul's testimony, when he preached "the hope of Israel", or "the hope of the promise made of God unto the fathers". Having begun his testimony with the chiefs of the Jews, some of whom received it, he continued to publish it for two years in his own hired house to all that visited him "preaching the Kingdom of God, and teaching those things which concern the Lord Jesus Christ, with all confidence" (Acts 28:30-31). In this way he bore witness for Jesus in Rome, as he had done before in Jerusalem.

But, one might say, if the hope the apostle preached, and the hope of the twelve tribes, were the same hope, why was he persecuted by the Jews? The answer is, because Paul and the rest of the apostles testified that Jesus whom they had crucified was the king whom God had anointed to be the Judge of Israel in His Kingdom, of which they were the natural born citizens. They had been constituted "a kingdom of priests, and a holy nation", by the covenant of Sinai; and had on that occasion accepted Jehovah as their king. They were therefore the kingdom of God. In after ages, they had demanded a king who might go in and out before them. He gave them David; and promised to *raise up* from among his descendants, sleeping in the tomb, a king, who should be immortal, and reign over them for ever, according to the provisions of a new constitution. Now the apostles testified that God had raised up Jesus from among the dead for this very purpose; and had sent them to the Jews first, to inform them that if they desired to reign as princes over Israel and the nations with his king, it was not enough for them to be natural born descendants of Abraham; but that they must acknowledge Jesus as King of Israel, and walk in the steps of Abraham's faith. They testified furthermore, that if they would not acknowledge him as their king, seeing that the kingdom and empire of God would require kings and priests to administer its affairs, they would turn to the Gentiles, and invite them to accept the honour and glory of the kingdom, upon terms of perfect equality with Israel; for so the Lord had commanded them to do.

This mortified the Jews exceedingly. They despised Jesus because of his poverty and ignominious death. A suffering and crucified king was a reproach to the nation in their esteem; and to be put on a level with Gentiles, whom they regarded as *"dogs"*, filled them with indignation and madness against the preachers of such pestilent heresies. But it was the apostolic mission to withstand their fury with *"the testimony of God"*; and to establish their preaching by what is written in the law of Moses and the prophets, and by what they had seen and heard, and which was attested by the power of God exhibited in the miracles they performed.

We have, then, arrived at a great truth, namely, that the *"one hope of the gospel"* preached by the apostles to the Jew first, and afterwards to the Greek, was *"the hope of Israel"*; that the subject of it was *the kingdom of God and Shiloh*; and that these were the matters of promise made to the fathers. It remains for us now to look into this promise so that we may come to understand it well; for its provisions are the things of the kingdom; and to be ignorant of these is to be without understanding, and therefore faithless, of the gospel of Christ.

The apostle Paul, who will be our interpreter, tells us that the promise, which is the subject of the *"one hope"*, was made to *"the fathers"*. This is a phrase which signifies sometimes the predecessors of the generation of the apostle's time, who were contemporary with the prophets (Hebrews 1:1); and at others the fathers Abraham, Isaac, and Jacob (Exodus 4:5). It is in the latter sense the apostle uses the phrase in connection with "the promises"; for speaking of Abraham, Isaac, and Jacob he says: "These all died in faith *not having received the promises*"; that is, the things contained in the promise: and after adding "a cloud of witnesses", who lived in after ages, and who illustrated their faith in the promise made to the fathers, he concludes by saying, "These all, having received a good report through faith, *received not the promise*: God having provided some better thing for us, that they without us should not be made perfect" (Hebrews 11:13,39,40), by a resurrection from the dead to inherit the kingdom. They must rise from the dust before they can receive the promise. They are imperfect now, being in ruins. But when they are re-fashioned by the Spirit of God, and spring forth glorious, incorruptible, and powerful men, "equal to the Elohim", they will have been *"made perfect"* and fit for the kingdom of God. But they are not to be thus perfect until all the believers of the promise are brought in; for all the faithful of all previous ages are to be perfected together.

The study of the promises unconnected with the study of the fathers is impossible. Those who are ignorant of the biographies of Abraham, Isaac, and Jacob must be ignorant of the gospel; for these patriarchs were the depositories of the promises (Hebrews 11:17) which constitute the gospel-hope; and of them, Abraham is especially designated as *him that hath the promises* (7:6)—τòν ἔχοντα τὰς ἐπαγγελίας. It is for this reason that a man must become of Abraham's seed by adoption through Jesus Christ. Unless a son of Abraham by a like faith and disposition with him, neither Jew nor Gentile can share in Abraham's estate. It is only Abraham's spiritual family that can divide with him the promises he holds. God has made him the spiritual father of mankind; and the Lord Jesus, the elder brother of the family. If, therefore, a man become a brother of Jesus, he at the same time becomes a son of Abraham; for Jesus is Abraham's seed, and was in the loins of Isaac, when Abraham offered his only son, and received him from the dead again, in a figure. If the reader understand this matter, he will fully comprehend the meaning of the apostle's saying, that believers "are all the children of God (being Abraham's) by faith in Christ Jesus. For as many as have been baptized into Christ have put on Christ. And *if Christ's,* THEN *Abraham's seed, and* HEIRS *according to the promise"* (Galatians 3:26-29).

After what has been advanced, no more, I think, need be said upon the importance of the subject before us. I shall, therefore, proceed now to a more particular illustration of the glad tidings of the kingdom by an exposition of

THE PROMISE MADE TO ABRAHAM

THE descendants of Noah were beginning to tread in the footsteps of the antediluvians. They became ambitious of making *"a name"* for themselves, irrespective of the name of the Lord. This their way was their folly; yet their posterity approved their endeavour. Idolatry was beginning to prevail; and they proceeded to build a city, and a tower, whose top should reach to heaven, in honour of their god. But the Lord came down and put a stop to their enterprise by confounding their language, and scattering them abroad over the earth.

Noah had lived 292 years after the flood, when three sons were born to Terah a descendant of Shem, Terah being 70 years old. Shem was a worshipper of the true God, whom Noah styled "the LORD God of Shem" (Genesis 9:26). Terah, however, seems to have departed from the simplicity of the truth; and was, probably, engaged in the mad scheme of making "a name" for the sons of men in the land of Shinar. But that undertaking being interrupted, it is probable he migrated from Babel, the name of the city they were building, in a southerly direction. Be this as it may, we find him in Chaldea at a place called Ur (Genesis 11:28). At this place, eastward of "*the great river Euphrates*", Abram, Nahor, and Haran were born to Terah. They lived there many years, serving the gods of Shinar. The idolatry of Terah's family appears from the testimony of God Himself, who said to Israel, "Your fathers dwelt on the other side of the flood (Euphrates) in old time, even Terah, the father of Abraham, and the father of Nachor: and *they served other gods*". When Joshua reported this to the people, he admonished them, saying, "Put away *the gods which your fathers served on the other side of the flood, and in Egypt*, and serve ye the LORD. And if it seem evil to you to serve the LORD, choose you this day whom ye will serve; whether the gods which your fathers served that were on the other side of the flood, or the gods of the Amorites, in whose land ye dwell; but as for me and my house, we will serve the LORD". And the people said unto Joshua, "The LORD our God will we serve, and his voice will we obey" (Joshua 24:2,14,15,24).

While Terah's family dwelt in Ur of the Chaldees, the Lord appeared to them, and said to Abram, "Get thee out of thy country, and from thy kindred, and come into the land *which I shall show thee*" (Genesis 15:7; Acts 7:2,3). This command caused them to remove from Ur, and to journey towards the land of Canaan; on their way to which, they arrived at Haran, and dwelt there (Genesis 11:31). Thus Terah, Abram, Sarai, and Lot, obeyed the voice of the Lord, and separated themselves from the idolaters of the Chaldean district of Mesopotamia. They remained in Haran till the Lord appeared again to Abram. On this occasion, the Lord came to show him the land he was to go to; but did not immediately name it, He appears only to have told him to travel westward until He met him again; for it is written that he went in that direction, "not knowing whither he went".

At this interview in Haran, the Lord said to Abram, "*I will make of thee* A GREAT NATION, and I will bless thee and make thy name great; and thou shalt be a blessing: and I will bless them that bless thee, and curse him that curseth thee: and *in thee shall all the families of the earth be blessed*" (Genesis 12:2,3). Alluding to this promise, the apostle says, that in making it, "*the gospel* was preached to Abraham"—the glad tidings of blessedness to the nations, when Abraham and his descendants should be great, and renowned throughout the earth. Abraham believed this gospel promissorily announced to him by the Lord God. Nor was his faith inoperative. It was a living, moving faith—a faith through which he obtained a good report. By the influence of that faith, which embraces the things hoped for, it is testified that Abraham "when he was *called* to go out into a country which he should after receive for an inheritance, *obeyed*; and he went out, not knowing whither he went. For he looked for *the city* having foundations, whose architect and builder is God" (Hebrews 11:8,10). He turned his back on Babel, and with Sarai and his nephew, Lot, and all his substance, he left his father's house, crossed the Euphrates and the Jordan, and entered *the land of Canaan*, still travelling onward until he arrived at Sichem, in the plain of Moreh. Having come thus far into the country, the Lord appeared again to Abram to let him know that he was in the land He intended to show him; and added this remarkable promise, saying, "*Unto thy* SEED *will I give this land*" (Genesis 12:7).

Let us pause here in the biography of Abram, and consider this promise. Here was a country, lying between the Euphrates and the Mediterranean, in which were Abram and all his house, with his flocks and herds, and which was in the actual possession of warlike tribes, living in cities walled up to heaven. Concerning this country, the Lord, to whom heaven and earth belong, said to Abram, *I will give it to thy Seed*, when as yet he had no child. But it is particularly interesting to know who is intended by Abram's Seed in this promise. Is it the "*great nation*" spoken of in the former promise? or is it some particular personage to whom the Land of Canaan is here promised *as an inheritance*? I shall offer no opinion upon the subject, but let the apostle to the Gentiles answer the question. In writing to the disciples in Galatia about the inheritance, he says, "The promises were made to Abraham and to his Seed. God saith not, And *to seeds*, as of many persons; but as of one person, as it is written, And unto thy Seed, *which is Christ*" (Galatians 3:16). The apostle here tells us that *the Land of Canaan was promised to the Christ*, when God said to Abram, "Unto thy Seed will I give this land". Let the reader, then, bear this in mind as one of the first principles of the gospel of the kingdom. Deny this, and there is an end to all understanding of the truth.

Having built an altar at Sichem to commemorate the Lord's promise concerning his Seed's inheritance, and sojourned there a while, he removed to a mountain between Bethel and Hai, where be built another altar, and called upon the Name of the Lord. After this he journeyed, going on still toward the South.

Having been driven into Egypt by famine in the Land of Canaan, he sojourned there for a time, and acquired much wealth. After it had subsided, he left Egypt and returned to the station between Bethel and Hai, where he called on the Name of the Lord. Soon after this, Lot separated from Abram, and went and dwelt among the cities of the plain, now submerged under the Dead Sea. After this separation, the Lord appeared to him again, and said, "Lift up now thine eyes, and look from the place where thou art, northward, and southward, and eastward, and westward: for all the land which thou seest, *to* THEE *will I give, it, and to thy Seed* FOR EVER. And I will make thy seed (*plural here*) as the dust of the earth; so that if a man can number the dust of the earth, then shall thy seed also be numbered. Arise, walk through the land in the length of it, and in the breadth of it: *for I will give it unto thee*" (Genesis 13:14-17).

This was an amplification of the promise given at Haran and Sichem. At the former place, the promise of blessing which was to come upon him and the nations, and in which his seed in the sense of a multitude was to become great—was given in general terms; at the latter place, the Christ was promised as descending from him to inherit the Land of Canaan; but in these promises, nothing was said about what Abram was to have, nor as to *how long* the Christ was to possess the country. In the promise, however, amplified near Bethel, these desiderata were supplied. Abram was informed that he should inherit the country as well as Christ; and that they should possess it *"for ever"*. Having received this assurance, he removed his tent from Bethel, and went and pitched it near Hebron in the plain of Mamre, and builded there an altar to the Lord.

When Abram had resided nearly ten years in the Land of Canaan, the whole country was in arms east of the Jordan, and to the north and south of Abram's encampment. A rebellion had broken out against Chedorlaomer, king of Elam, who appears to have been the principal potentate of the time. During the war, Sodom was attacked and taken, and Lot, and all his goods, carried away with the spoil of the city, for he dwelt there. Abram having heard of this, hastily collected a company of three hundred and eighteen retainers, and started in pursuit of the spoilers, whom he overtook and put to the rout as far as Hobah, on the west of Damascus. He recovered all the spoil, and returned south, considerably disturbed in mind, doubtless, on account of the danger of the times.

At this crisis, *the word* of the Lord came to Abram in a vision, and comforted him with the assurance, saying, "Fear not, Abram, I am thy shield, and thine *exceeding great reward*". Abram was now eighty-five years old, and he had no child. How, then, could the promise made of God at Haran, and repeated at Sichem and Bethel, be fulfilled, seeing that he was childless? He was even now an old man, and had concluded to make Eliezer of Damascus his heir; how then could the great, the exceeding great, reward be realized by him? Prompted by these considerations, but in no wise distrusting God, Abram said, "Lord GOD, what wilt thou give me, seeing I go childless, and the steward of my house is this Eliezer of Damascus? Behold, to me thou hast given no seed; and, lo, one born in my house is my heir". But, "the word of the LORD came to him, saying, This (Eliezer) shall not be thine heir; but he that shall come forth out of thine own bowels shall be thine heir." The Lord's messenger, who brought this word to Abram, then led him forth from his tent, and directed his attention to the heavens, saying, "Count the stars if thou art able to number them: and he said unto him, *So shall thy seed be*". This was a great draft upon the faith of an old man of upwards of fourscore with a wife of seventy-five years of age. But, it is testified of him, that "against hope he believed in hope, that he might become the father of many nations, according to that which was spoken, saying, So shall thy seed be. And being not weak in faith, he considered not his own body now as good as dead (he being about a hundred years old), neither yet the deadness of Sarah's womb; he staggered not at the promise of God through unbelief; but was strong in faith, giving glory to God; and being fully persuaded that what he had promised he was also able to perform" (Romans 4:18-21). Such was the manner of Abram's faith; his *mode of thinking* upon the things reported to him in the word of the Lord: and his *disposition* in relation to them. So pleased was God with him that "*he counted it to him for righteousness*".

Abram, having first sought the kingdom of God in leaving his father's house to "seek the city, whose architect and builder is God", had now become the subject of the righteousness of God by faith so that the Lord was now prepared to add all other things to him (Matthew 6:33). He reminded him of the purpose for which He had brought him into the Land of Canaan, saying, "I, the LORD, brought thee out of Ur of the Chaldees *to give thee this land to inherit it*". Abram had been in the country ten years. He had become well acquainted with the land, and he perceived that it was a noble and desirable inheritance. When, therefore, the angel referred to the Lord's promise, Abraham requested a sign, saying, "Lord GOD, whereby shall I know that I shall possess it?"

In reply to this, he was commanded to take "a heifer of *three years old*, and a ram of *three years old*, and a turtle dove, and a young pigeon". Having killed them, "he divided them in the midst, and laid each piece one against another, but the birds divided he not". This sacrifice was representative of the qualities of the Christ, concerning whom confirmation was about to be made, attestative of Abram's and his Seed's possession of the land in the fullness of the times afterwards to be arranged. From the time of the sacrifice until the going down of the sun, Abram was engaged in watching the carcases, so as to keep off the birds of prey. It is probable that the sacrifice was exposed about three hours; at all events, "when even was come" (Matthew 27:46; Mark 15:42), and the sun was going down, Abram fell into a state of figurative death, by a deep sleep and horror of great darkness coming over him.

This is a very remarkable feature in the case before us. Abram had built altars, and had called upon the name of the Lord before; but there were no such attendant circumstances as these. Here, however, he stands watching the exposed sacrificial victims until even; and then is laid powerless in the similitude of death, and of the intense darkness of the grave. While he was in this state, the Lord revealed to Abram the fortunes of his descendants in the ensuing four hundred years ; the judgment of the nation that should oppress them; their subsequent exodus from bondage with great wealth; his own peaceful death in a good old age; and the return of his descendants into the Land of Canaan again. The following are the words of the testimony: "Know of a surety that thy seed shall be a stranger in a land that is not theirs, and shall serve them; and they shall afflict them four hundred years; and also that nation whom they shall serve, will I judge: and afterwards shall they come out with great substance. And thou shalt go to thy fathers in peace; *thou shalt be buried in a good old age*. But in the fourth generation they shall come hither again: for the iniquity of the Amorites is not yet full".

I suppose the reader need hardly be informed that all this was literally accomplished. Jacob and his family, consisting of seventy persons, migrated into Egypt *two hundred and five years after the revelation was made to Abram*. When a king arose in Egypt who knew not Joseph, the saviour of the country under God, the Israelites were sorely oppressed *till the end of four hundred years from Abram's deep sleep*. After this four hundred years had expired, even thirty years after, God having judged the Egyptians, they left the country with great substance; and in the fourth generation re-entered the land of Canaan, as God had said. The iniquity of the Amorites was then full; and Israel, under Joshua, became the executioners of divine vengeance upon them.

But God had said to Abram at Bethel, *I will give* THEE *the land of Canaan* FOR EVER: and in the answer to this question, "Whereby shall I know that I shall inherit it?" here tells him that he should die, and be buried in a good old age! Now the promise to Abram rests upon the veracity of God. If we attempt to interpret it by the history of the past, we are brought to the conclusion that the promise to Abram has failed. Stephen alludes to this *apparent* failure of the promise to Abram in his speech before the Sanhedrin in these words: "God said to him, Come into the land which I shall show thee. Then came he into this land in which ye dwell. And *he gave him none inheritance in it*, no, not so much as to set his foot on: YET *he promised that he would give it to him for a possession*, and to his seed (τῷ σπέρματι, *in the singular*, to one person called *the seed*) after him, when as yet he had no child" (Acts 7:5).

What shall we say then? Shall we dare to say that God hath lied to Abram, or that He meant something else than what He promised? Far be it from the writer or the reader to insult God by any such insinuation, but rather let us say with the apostle in reference to this particular incident, that "God cannot lie"; that in promising to Abram *an everlasting possession of the Land of Canaan*; and, nevertheless, afterwards declaring that he should die and be buried, and his posterity be oppressed for four hundred years—"He promised" to him *a resurrection to "eternal life"* before the arrangement of the times (πρὸ χρόνων αἰωνίων) (Titus 1:2). If Abram were sentenced to die, how could the promise of God concerning the land be fulfilled, unless he were raised from the dead? And as he is to possess it *for ever*, when he is raised, he must be also made incorruptible and immortal to enable him to possess it everlastingly. *The promise of eternal life*, then, consists *in promising a mortal man and his son possession of a terrestrial country for ever*; and this promise to the two becomes a promise to all who believe it, and are constituted one in them.

Abram understood this, and so do all who become Abraham's seed through Jesus as the Christ, concerning whom the promise was made. The apostle says he saw the promises in their fulfilment afar off, but was persuaded of them, and embraced them, and confessed that he was a stranger and pilgrim in the Land. And, in saying such things, he plainly declared that he was seeking a country. And truly, if he had been mindful of the Mesopotamian Chaldea from whence he migrated, he might have

249

returned if he had pleased. But no; he desired a better country than that beyond the Euphrates—that is, the Land of Canaan *under a heavenly constitution*: wherefore God is not ashamed to be called the God of Abraham, Isaac, and Jacob, and the God of all whose faith is like theirs in word and spirit: for He hath prepared for them a city (Hebrews 11:8-16).

This manner of teaching the doctrine of a resurrection—namely, *by promising, or declaring something that necessitates it*—is not peculiar to the case before us. There are other instances; one, however, will be sufficient at present. I refer to the dispute between Jesus and the Sadducees. The latter, who admitted as authority only the writings of Moses, denied the resurrection of the dead. In proving it, therefore, to their conviction, it was necessary to demonstrate it from his testimony. This Jesus undertook to do. He first stated the proposition, saying, *Moses has shown that the dead are raised*. He then directed their attention to the place where Moses teaches this resurrection (Exodus 3:6). It is there written, "I, the LORD, am the God of Abraham, the God of Isaac, and the God of Jacob"; in recording this, Moses teaches the resurrection of Abraham, Isaac, and Jacob. "But", says one, "I see nothing said about resurrection there." Nor did the Sadducees. "No", continues the objector, "nor about the dead either; for Abraham, Isaac, and Jacob are not dead, but alive in heaven, where Christ, and Lazarus, and the thief are. They are all living; and therefore God is their God." This is very good Platonism, but very bad logic, and egregious nonsense. When Jesus quoted the passage, it was to prove that "the dead are raised". The question therefore is, How does this testimony of Moses prove it? In this way—Abraham, Isaac, and Jacob are dead; but "God is not the God of the dead", yet He is called "their God": therefore in order to be their God, they must be made alive, "for God is the God of the living": hence, to style Him "God of Abraham" teaches the resurrection by implication; "for all live to him" in the age to come (Luke 20:27-38). But why call Him the God of these fathers now? By anticipation; for, says the apostle, "God, who makes alive the dead, styles *the not being* (τὰ μὴ ὄντα) *as being*" (ὡς ὄντα) (Romans 4:17)—that is, God's promise is so certain to be fulfilled, that *He speaks of what is to be as though it were past*. He has promised to raise Abraham, Isaac, and Jacob, who, while dead, have no being; and as He cannot lie their restoration to being is inevitable. God therefore speaks of them as though they had already been raised from the dead, and "is not ashamed to be called their God". God is not the God of dead men who are not to rise again. He is the God only of those who become His children by being the children of the resurrection, and who can die no more, because they are equal to the angels

(Luke 20:36). Such, then, is the way in which the doctrine of the resurrection is taught by the Lord God in Moses and the prophets: plainly, indeed, but in such a manner as to require the exercise of the reasoning faculties of men.

But to return to Hebron. Eternal life having been promised to Abram and Christ by constituting them heirs of the land of Canaan for ever; the Lord proceeded to grant Abram a sign whereby he might know assuredly that he and his seed should inherit it. The sun having gone down entirely, which was figurative of the setting of "the sun of Righteousness" below the horizon of life, Abram beheld "a smoking furnace, and a flame of fire pass between the pieces". This was a sign which could not be mistaken. The animals he had slain, and watched, and defended so long from the birds of prey, were consumed by fire from heaven. By this he knew, and was assured, that he and his seed, the Christ, should inherit the land for ever. But this was not all. On the same day, the Lord converted his promise made at Sichem, and repeated near Bethel, into a covenant with Abram, as Moses testifies, saying, "In the same day the LORD made a covenant* with Abram, saying, *Unto thy seed have I given this land*, from the river of Egypt unto the great river, the river Euphrates": inhabited by "the Kenites, and the Kenizzites, and the Kadmonites, and the Hittites and the Perizzites, and the Rephaim, and the Amorites, and the Canaanites, and the Girgashites, and the Jebusites" (Genesis 15:18-21).

In commenting upon these things, the apostle saith, "The covenant previously confirmed by God, the law which came into existence (γεγονὼς) four hundred and thirty years after, cannot

---

*Through the next four or five pages to the end of this section, this term *covenant* is retained, to the exclusion of "will" and "testament," which appeared in the old editions. The exposition is thereby rendered more consistent in its parts. There is a lack of true analogy between "the last will and testament" of a mortal man, and the "everlasting covenant" of the ever-living God. How the Authorized Version came to use both the terms "testament" and "covenant" in Hebrews 7,8,9, the following note from the Oxford *Helps to the Study of the Bible* incidentally explains. — "Paul in a notable passage calls the books of Moses, if not the whole of the Hebrew Canon, 'the old covenant' ('at the reading of the old covenant'—2 Corinthians 3:14, RV). In the same context he describes himself and his fellow-labourers as 'Ministers of a New Covenant' (2 Corinthians 3:6). These terms, ἡ παλαιὰ διαθήκη, the Old Covenant, and ἡ καινὴ διαθήκη, the New Covenant, were employed at the close of the second century by ecclesiastical writers to denote the Jewish and Christian scriptures respectively. The Latin rendering of διαθήκη fluctuated at first between *instrumentum* and *testamentum*, but *testamentum* prevailed. Hence in the languages of the West, the two collections of writings which make up the Bible came to be called 'the Old Testament' and 'the New Testament'. *But the original idea of a Covenant must not be lost sight of.*"

disannul, that it should make the promise of none effect. For if the inheritance (the land of Canaan and its attributes) be of the law, it is no more of promise: but God gave it to Abraham by promise" (Galatians 3:17,18). To understand this we must know that a question agitated the congregations of Galatia, namely, *that it was necessary for the disciples from among the Gentiles to be circumcised, and to keep the law of Moses, as well as to believe the gospel and be baptized, or they could have no part in the inheritance covenanted to Abraham and Christ.*

The apostle styles this Judaizing and preaching "another gospel". It was the beginning of that awful apostasy, the fruit of which we behold in the ecclesiastical system of our day. He contended strenuously against this perversion of the truth in all places. The Judaizers argued that a right to Canaan when made a heavenly country under Christ, was derived from the law of Moses; the apostle denied this, and maintained that the law could give no title to it. That it could only be obtained *"through the righteousness of the faith"*; "for the promise that he should be *the heir of the world* was not to Abraham, or to his seed, through the law, but through the righteousness of faith. For if they who are of the law be heirs, faith is made void, and the promise is made of none effect: because the law worketh wrath. Therefore it is of faith, that it might be by grace; to the end that the promise might be sure to all the seed; not to that (portion of the seed) only which is of the law, but to that also which is of the faith of Abraham; who is the father of us all", both Jews and Gentiles, "before God, whose promises he believed"; as it is written, "a father of many nations have I constituted thee" (Romans 4:13,14,16,17). The Judaizers claimed a right to the inheritance because they bore the seal of the covenant, marked in their flesh by circumcision; the apostle, because he believed the same things that Abraham did, and was the subject of God's righteousness through the faith of Jesus Christ, without any title derived from the law of Moses.

Seeing that he threw the law out of the question altogether, he anticipates the objection, viz., if this be so, wherefore, then, serveth the law? Of what use is it? To this he replies, "It was added because of transgressions, *till the Seed should come to whom the promise was made*". It was "a schoolmaster" until Christ; but when "the things of the name of Jesus Christ" were manifested for faith, or, as he expresses it, "after that faith is come", Israel is "no longer under a schoolmaster. For ye are all", both Jews and Gentiles, "the children of God in Christ Jesus through the faith" (Galatians 3:19-29).

The apostle lays great stress upon the covenant of promise being prior both to circumcision and the law of Moses; consequently Abram could not derive his title to Canaan and the world from either of them; for the promise was given before he became the subject of the righteousness which is by faith of it; and he was constituted righteous before the promise was made a covenant and confirmed; and this confirmation was fourteen years before the institution of circumcision, and 430 years before the promulgation of the Law of Moses. "Faith", says the apostle, "was reckoned to Abraham for righteousness when he was in uncircumcision"; and then it was, he was constituted the father of many nations and Heir of the World.

The promise, before it became a confirmed covenant with Abram, indicated the country he is to inherit; but it did not point out its territorial frontiers. This deficiency was supplied at the confirmation. It was to extend from the Euphrates to the Nile, comprehending a tract of country of considerable extent, and inhabited by the nations enumerated in *"The Covenant"*. Abram, therefore, could be at no loss to know in what direction, or to what limits, his future country was to extend; for he had travelled it all over in its entire length and breadth. Now, if a map of the territorial area indicated in the covenant be examined, it will be seen that the broadest extent is *"from sea to sea"*, as it is expressed in scripture (Psalm 72:8; Zechariah 9:10); that is, from the Mediterranean to the Persian Gulf and its greatest length, *"from the river to the end of the land"* or, from the Euphrates at its junction with the gulf, northward; and from the Pelusiac branch of the Nile to the entrance into Hamath.

But the frontiers of the territory were afterwards more particularly marked out at the time of the captivity in Babylon. The twelve tribes were then all in exile from the land, and it was once more wholly possessed by the Gentiles, as it is now. They were powerless and prostrate under the heel of the oppressor; and without hope of recovering the country by their own efforts. At this crisis, the Lord revealed to them the extent to which in after times they should re-possess their country. "This", said he, "shall be the border, whereby ye shall inherit the land according to the twelve tribes of Israel. And this shall be the border of the land toward the north side, from the great sea (Mediterranean), the way of Hethlon, as men go to Zedad; Hamath, Berothah, Sibraim, which is between the border of Damascus and the border of Hamath; Hazar-hatticon, which is by the coast of Hauran. And the border from the sea shall be Hazar-enan, the border of Damascus, and the north northward, and the border of Hamath. This is *the north side*, of the land. And the east side ye shall measure from Hauran, and from Damascus, and from Gilead, and from the land of Israel by Jordan, from the border unto the East Sea. And this is *the east side* (running along the Euphrates). And the south side southward, from Tamar to the waters of strife in Kadesh, to the river toward the Great Sea (Ezekiel 47:19; 48:28). This is *the south side* toward Teman. The west side also shall be the Great Sea from the (west end of the south) border, till a man come over against Hamath. This is *the west side.* So shall ye divide this land unto you according to the tribes of Israel" (47:13-21).

Now, let it never be forgotten in the investigation of "the things of the kingdom of God", that the Israelites have never possessed the country as defined in this survey since it was revealed to them through the prophet. The twelve tribes have not even occupied the land together; and those of them that have dwelt there after the return from Babylon to the overthrow by the Romans, held but a very small portion of it, while the Gentile Kingdoms lorded it over all the rest. Now either God is a liar, as some people make Him out to be who deny the restoration of the twelve tribes; or, the time He refers to in the promise of the land according to these boundaries, is not arrived. This is the only conclusion a believer in the gospel of the kingdom can come to. All theories opposed to this are mere sublimated infidelity. If Israel be not restored, then the promise to Abraham will have failed. But Abraham's seed are under no apprehension of this kind. They believe in God, who has sworn by Himself, that what He has promised He is able, willing, and determined to perform.

Here, then, is a noble domain, lying between Assyria, Persia, Arabia, the Red Sea, Egypt, and the Mediterranean; capable, when peopled by an industrious, enlightened, and well and strongly governed, nation, of commanding the commerce and sovereignty of Asia, and the wealth of Europe and America. Such is the land, containing, according to the survey of the British Government, 300,000 square miles, concerning which God said to Abram, "To thee will I give it and unto thy seed *for ever.*"

But, the apostle says, that the covenant, confirmed 430 years before the law was promulgated, was "concerning Christ" especially. It was the Father's Covenant of which Christ was the Mediator. This being the case, his death was necessitated; for so long as he was alive, the covenant had no force. Neither Abraham, Isaac, Jacob, nor himself, could inherit the land for ever, until the covenant was ratified by his death. Hence, his was "the blood of the New Covenant, which was shed for many"; that they which are called might receive the remission of sins, and obtain the promise of the inheritance for ever (Matthew 26:28; Hebrews 9:15-17). The covenant of promise, then, was typically confirmed 430 years before the law; and finally dedicated by the death of the mediator; this being accomplished, the covenant could not be disannulled, or added (Galatian 3:15). But when we look at Jesus in the light of this Divine Covenant, we perceive some grand and important deficiencies in its effects, if the history of the past is to be taken as the criterion of its accomplishment. In the historical view of the covenant, we are led to the conclusion that it has not been carried out at all; and that its beneficiaries have received none of their Father's estate. Look at Abraham. He has received nothing. The same is true of all who believed the things hoped for from his day to this. Even the Lord Jesus, who has been perfected, has received nothing of what is assigned to him in the covenant. "I will give", said God, "this land to thy Seed for ever." Now look at the facts in the case. "Jesus came to *his own*, and *his own* received him not (John 1:11). What is to be understood by this? What is signified by "his own" twice repeated in this text? The facts in the case supply the answer. Jesus came "unto his own things" (kingdom, or realm); but his own people, the Jews, who are "the children of the kingdom", did not receive him, but rejected and crucified him. "But to as many as received him, to them gave he power to become the sons of God, *to them who believe in his name*."

But what constituted the land of Canaan *his* realm, more than John the Baptist's, or any other Jew's? Because it was promised to him in the covenant; and because he was the sole surviving heir of David's throne. We see, however, that like his father Abraham, he never possessed even so much as to set his foot upon; and so poor was he, that though "the foxes had holes, and the birds of the air had nests, yet he had not where to lay his head". Under God, he was indebted to some of those who received him, for his daily bread. What significance this fact attaches to that petition of the prayer he taught his disciples, saying, "Our Father, who art in heaven, give us this day our daily bread". There were thirteen of them, himself and the twelve, who had all to be provided for from day to day; and though he could multiply a few loaves and fishes to feed thousands, his own wants were supplied by contribution.

When Jesus was crucified, and buried, his enemies conceived that his claims to the realm and throne of David were extinct. The common people would have taken him and made him king, if he would have permitted them; but the rulers, already possessed of the vineyard, hated him; for they knew that if he should obtain the kingdom they would be cast out. They rejoiced, therefore, at his death. But their joy was soon turned into dismay; for God raised him from the dead. And for what purpose? In the words of the apostle, *God raised up Christ to sit upon David's throne* (Acts 2:30; Luke 1:31-33); for, in the words of David, "The righteous shall inherit the Land, and dwell therein for ever"; and again, "Wait on the LORD, and keep his way, and he shall exalt thee to inherit the Land (Psalm 37:29,34).

But, even after his resurrection, when he was made both Lord and Christ, though "heir of all things", yet were not all things subjected to him. He received neither the land nor the sceptre; but ascended to heaven, having received nothing promised in the covenant. He left the land, the kingdom, Abraham, and all the prophets, behind him. In after years, the land was reduced to a wilderness, its cities laid waste, and the Hebrew commonwealth dissolved. It became the battle ground of Crusaders, Saracens, and Turks; and until this day has been subjected to the worst of the heathen. Forty centuries have passed away since God confirmed His promise of the land to Christ, who has been waiting nineteen hundred years at His right hand for its fulfilment. Is Jesus never to possess the land from sea to sea, and from the rivers to its extremities? Are Turks and Arabs, and a motley crew of Papists, Greeks, and Fellahs to perpetuate its reproach for ever? Or is a Gentile dominion to be established there to lord it over Asia?

Where is there a believer of the gospel of the kingdom to be found who will affirm it? Millions of *"professing* Christians" imagine something of the kind; but they are infidels, and insulters of God—not believers in "the covenants of promise". To affirm any other destiny for Palestine and Syria than that stated in the promise, is, in effect, to tell God that He has spoken falsely. But on the ground that "He cannot lie", what does the nature of the case necessitate in order to fulfil the promise to Abraham and Christ? This is the answer, and let the reader mark it well:—to meet the demands of the covenant, *it is indispensable that Jesus return to Canaan, and that he raise Abraham from the dead.* Reason and scripture agree in this.

Hence, the second advent is as necessary as the first. The appearing in sinful flesh was necessary for the dedication of the covenant by the death of the "Mediator"; and the second appearing in the spiritual nature in power and great glory, for his effectual carrying out of all its provisions. For it is manifest that this cannot be done except by One who is all-powerful. Abraham, Isaac and Jacob, and all constitutionally in them, are the beneficiaries. The things promised to them are eternal life, the land of Canaan, and "a city", or state, "whose architect and builder is God". Hence the Mediator must be able to form them out of the dust, and to give them life for ever. He must be mighty in battle; for he will have to expel the Mohammedans, Catholics, and other barbarians from the land, and to restore the kingdom of David "as in the days of old".

The accomplishment of these, and many other things to be hereafter developed, makes the future pre-millennial advent of Christ a necessity. There is no room for opinion upon the subject, for opinion implies doubt. It is a matter of absolute certainty; and the belief of it is as essential to a participation in the kingdom of God as faith in the death and resurrection of the Lord. For a man to deny the advent of Jesus to Palestine in power and glory before the millennium is to proclaim to men and angels his utter ignorance of the glorious gospel of the blessed God. To talk about his coming at the end of the millennium to make a bonfire of the world is ridiculous. Restitution and renovation, and not destruction of the earth, is the Almighty fiat, as I have already shown at sufficient length. "Come, Lord Jesus, come quickly", is the heart-breathing of the true believer, who, with the hearing ear rejoices in the Bridegroom's voice, which says, "Behold, I come as a thief, and quickly; *and my reward is with me*, to give every man according as his work shall be. Blessed is he that watcheth, and keepeth his garments, lest he walk naked, and they see his shame" (Revelation 22:12; 16:15). The prolonged absence of Christ for ten more centuries would break the hearts of the saints of God, who have long since cried with a loud voice, saying, "How long, O Lord, holy and true, dost thou not judge and avenge our blood on them who dwell on the earth?" No, no; the day is come at length when he is about to gather the vine of the earth, to reward his saints, and to destroy the oppressors of the world (Revelation 11:18; 14:19,20). Then will "the kingdoms of the world become those of Jehovah and of his King; and he shall reign for ever and ever"; and the covenant with Abraham concerning Christ will be fulfilled in every jot and tittle of its details.

ABRAHAM THE HEIR OF THE WORLD

ABRAHAM and Christ are inseparably associated as co-heirs of the covenant of promise. Hence, they are joint-heirs of the country mentioned in the covenant. But out of this arises a question of considerable interest, namely, when they jointly possess the land of Canaan, what will be their relation to the world at large? The answer to this is, that at that time their name will be great in the earth; Abram's descendants will be a great nation; and he and Christ will be a blessing, by all the families of the earth being in them. This was stated in general terms when the gospel was preached to Abraham at Haran. In searching out these matters, the phrases *"in thee"*, and *"in him"*, and *"in thy seed"*, should

257

be particularly attended to. They are little words, but full of meaning.

The reader knows what it is to be *in a house*, and he is aware that he must pass *into it* before he can be *in it*. This is the literal. Now, suppose we call the house *a man*; and in answer to the question, "Where is he?" we say he is *in the man*, this would be to speak figuratively, but still scripturally and intelligibly. Before, however, a person or a nation, or a multitude of nations could be said to be *in the man Abraham*, and *in the man Christ Jesus*, it is equally clear that they must *pass into* Abraham, and *into Christ*. Now although many nations may literally come out of one man, a multitude of nations cannot literally be packed into one man. When, therefore, nations and individuals are said to be in Abraham and in Christ, it is manifest it must be in a figurative sense. Hence, *"in thee"*, *"in him"*, and *"in Christ"* are figurative expressions, or *terms of constitution*. They are things of stubborn import. They do not express a feeling, but a *relationship* which is predicated on belief and obedience. These are literal and actual things; for there is no scriptural faith without belief of the letter, or written, or spoken, word; nor any obedience without conformity to prescribed action. To pass, or to be introduced, into a man is to sustain a relationship towards him of faith, affection, and allegiance, as prescribed.

No person, or nation, can introduce themselves into a man; their induction, in other words, must be according to prescription, and not according to their own appointment. God, or he to whom, as His "Apostle", or Ambassador, He has committed all authority, is the only person that can prescribe *the formula of induction*. Mankind are diseased, and cannot cure themselves. "The blessing of Abraham" is for their restoration to health and happiness. They are, therefore, the recipients of favour, and not the prescribers, or legislators, in the case. The nature of the inducting formula is determined by the kind of subject to be induced. If the subject to be passed into Abraham and Christ be an individual, the formula is spiritual; that is, it places him in a moral and domestic or family relationship to them; but if the subject be a nation or a multitude of nations, then the formula is civil and ecclesiastical, or political. A person in Abraham and Christ (and a man cannot be in one without being in the other) is the subject of *adoption* by a spiritual formula, which will be perfected in "the redemption of his body" at the resurrection; while nations in Abraham and Christ are adopted by a political formula, which is perfected in the blessings of good government, peace, equitable laws righteously administered, the enlightenment of all classes in the knowledge of God, universal prosperity, and so forth.

The formula of spiritual adoption is exhibited in the gospel. It requires a man to believe "the promise made of God to the fathers" concerning the land of Canaan, the Christ, the blessedness of the nations in Abraham and his seed, eternal life by a resurrection, etc.; and to be baptized into the Father, Son, and Holy Spirit. When an individual has done this, he is in Abraham and Christ, and an heir with him of the promises he believes. So that *"the seed"*, though spoken of one person—that is, of Christ—comprehends all the believers of the promises, who, by adoption are *"in him"*. The phrase "the seed" is therefore used in an individual and federal acceptation. Hence, whatever is promised to Abraham and Christ is also promised to their federal constituents—to the sons of Abraham, and brethren of Christ, by adoption into the family of God.

But the formula of national, or political, adoption has not yet been promulgated to the world. No people has ever been politically in God but Israel. The natural descendants of Abraham in the line of Isaac and Jacob became the people of God in a national sense by the adoption provided in the Mosaic law. But no other nation before or since has ever stood in the same relationship to Him. Neither Egypt of old, nor Britain and America of modern times, can say, "We are the people of the Lord." God has never called these nations *"My people"*, for they have never been the subjects of political adoption as Israel were. State religions are established upon the hypothesis that the people are God's people; and, therefore, as acceptable worshippers as the Jews under the law; and that they are constitutionally "in God the Father and in the Lord Jesus Christ". Hence, they call the nations of Europe "Christian nations".

But a greater fallacy was never entertained. There are no Christian nations; neither indeed can there be until the formula of political adoption shall be made known. The nations are now *in Satan their father, and in his vicegerent the Lord Pope.* Hence, it may be said to them as Jesus said to the rulers and clergy of Israel, "Ye are of your father the Devil, and the works of your father ye do". The Devil is their father by birth and constitution. The nations of Europe became the people of Satan by constitution, when they put on the Pope as their high priest and mediator according to the Justinian code. Having received this, they became Satan's seed, and the Pope's brethren; and being thus in Satan and in the Pope, are joint-heirs with them of a "just punishment, even an everlasting destruction," to issue forth "from the presence of the Lord and the glory of his power" (2 Thessalonians 1:9); and which hangs over them, like the hair-suspended sword of Dionysius, ready to fail with death-dealing vengeance on every side.

But a time is coming when the Antichristian, Mohammedan, and pagan nations of the world will all become the people of God, and, therefore, Christian. This is evident from the testimony of scripture, which saith, "In that day shall there be a highway out of Egypt to Assyria, and the Assyrian shall come into Egypt, and the Egyptian into Assyria, and *the Egyptians* SHALL SERVE *with the Assyrians*. In that day shall Israel be the third with Egypt and Assyria, even *a blessing in the midst of the Land*: whom the LORD of Hosts shall bless, saying, Blessed be *Egypt* MY PEOPLE, and Assyria the work of my hands, and Israel *mine inheritance*" (Isaiah 19:23-25). And again it is written of Christ, "He shall come down like rain upon the mown grass; as showers that water the earth. *In his days* shall the righteous flourish; and abundance of peace so long as the moon endureth. He shall have dominion also from sea to sea, and from the river unto the ends of the earth. They (the Arabs) that dwell in the wilderness shall bow before him; and his enemies shall lick the dust. The kings of Tarshish, and of the isles, shall bring presents; the kings of Sheba and Seba shall offer gifts. Yea, all kings shall fall down before him: ALL NATIONS SHALL SERVE HIM. His name shall endure for ever, his name shall be continued as long as the sun; and men shall be *blessed* IN HIM; all nations shall call him blessed" (Psalm 72:6-11,17).

According to this testimony, it is proved that the nations, or families, of the earth will become the people of God as well as Israel, who will have the pre-eminence among them as the inheritance of the Lord; and so Israel and the nations will constitute a kingdom and empire, which will then compose "*the World*", and be blessed in him and Abraham; whose subjects will reciprocate the benefits bestowed upon them, and serve their god-like rulers with heart-felt loyalty, and blessings upon his name for ever.

But when we contemplate the nations now in Satan, and Israel scattered to the four winds, and compare their present condition with what is to be when they all serve Christ and are blessed in him and Abraham, we perceive the womb of futurity to be pregnant of a mighty change; and one, too, which cannot be effected by mild and persuasive measures. The time for persuasives has passed away. The nations turn a deaf ear to everything which is not in harmony with their lusts. Hence, coercion can alone bring them to wait for the divine law. For this reason, it is testified of Christ—"He shall break in pieces the oppressor"; and "will execute vengeance in anger and fury upon the heathen, such as they have not heard. And the nations shall see and be confounded at all their (Israel's) might: they shall lay their hand upon their mouth, their ears shall be deaf. They shall lick the dust like a serpent, they shall move out of their holes like worms of the earth; they shall be afraid of the LORD, Israel's God, and shall fear because of thee" (Micah 5:15; 7:16,17).

This testimony shows that the nations will be reduced to abject submission, even the most powerful among them. Their courage and means of resistance will have departed; for by the sword of the Lord and of Israel they will have been subdued. At this crisis, however, they will find a deliverer in him who hath overcome them (Revelation 17:14; 19:11-21). "Look unto me", saith he, "and be ye saved, all the ends of the earth; for I am God, and there is none else. I have sworn by myself," to Abraham, "the word has gone out of my mouth in righteousness, and shall not return, that unto me every knee shall bow, every tongue shall swear, saying, Surely *in* the LORD have I righteousness and strength: even to him shall men come" (Isaiah 45:22,23). If we turn to this oath of subjection and future blessing we shall see what is meant by every knee bowing to the Lord. "By myself have I sworn, saith the LORD, for because thou, Abraham, hast done this thing, and hast not withheld thy son, thine only son, that in blessing I will bless thee, and in multiplying I will multiply thy seed as the stars of heaven, and as the sand which is upon the sea-shore; *and thy seed* (Christ) *shall possess the gate of his enemies*; and *in* thy seed shall all the nations of the earth be blessed; because thou hast obeyed my voice" (Genesis 22:16-18).

The nations being prepared by coercion, the formula of political adoption is promulgated to them. This is contained in *the law which goes forth from Zion*. The details of this law are not all specified. In general, it establishes the power of the Lord, then become "a great mountain filling the whole earth" (Daniel 2:35), above all other powers; and constitutes the newly erected Temple in Jerusalem "the house of prayer for all nations" (Isaiah 56:7). This law gives the kingdom to the daughter of Jerusalem, which is Zion; where the Lord reigns over them henceforth for ever. (Micah 4:7,8; Isaiah 24:23). The nations accept the law, which saves them from extermination. This is evinced by the effects which follow its promulgation. They all flow to Jerusalem as the centre of the world, and fountain of all blessings; for "my springs", saith the Lord, are "in thee". They go thither for instruction in the ways of the Lord, and return to walk in his paths, to live at peace among themselves, to abandon the study of war, and to devote themselves to agriculture, commerce, and the arts (Isaiah 2:2-4). This is the millennial future state. Abraham and Jesus are, then, the greatest personages upon the earth; the former being the spiritual father of Jesus and the saints, and the political father of a multitude of nations, over whom Christ and his brethren rule until *"the end"* (1 Corinthians 15:24).

Such is *"the world"* of which Abraham and his Seed are the heirs. Speaking of the latter in this relation, the apostle says, "Whom God hath appointed heir of all things, and on account of whom he constituted the Ages" (Hebrews 1:2)—the Age of Jubilees, and the Jubilee Age. And to the joint-heirs of Abraham and Christ he says, "Let no man glory in men: for all things are yours; *the world*, life, death, *things present and things to come*; all are yours; and ye are Christ's; and Christ is God's" (1 Corinthians 3:21-23). And again, "Do ye not know that the saints shall judge the world?" (1 Corinthians 6:2). The verb here rendered *"judge"* is the same as is translated *"go to law"* in the preceding verse. The apostle, therefore, asks if they do not know that they will sit judicially, and dispense justice to the world, according to the divine law; and because this is their destiny he positively forbids believers in the covenants of promise to submit themselves to the judgment of the unjust. It is better, says he, for one to be defrauded than to submit to such a humiliation. Let the heirs of the world arbitrate their own affairs in the present state; for it is a strange thing if men, whose destiny is to judge the world and angels, cannot settle things pertaining to this life.

Thus, then, there are three parties, yet constitutionally *one family*, who are heirs of the world as it will be politically organized in the Future Age—namely, Abraham, Christ, and the believers in the promises made to them, called saints, who are in Abraham as their father, and in his Seed as their elder brother. These are *the inheritors* of the kingdom and empire attached to the land of Canaan—"the children of the promise who are counted for the Seed"; and "not of the world", or *subjects*. These are men in the flesh, Jews and Gentiles, whose lives and fortunes will be at the disposal of the Royal Family of God. The members of this social circle are not known now by the world, which has set its affections upon those who mislead it, teaching it to look for a visionary elysium beyond the skies! But such leaders as these have no light in them, for they do not speak according to the law and the testimony. The word of God converts their wisdom into folly, declaring in the teeth of their traditions that "he that putteth his trust in God shall possess *the land*, and shall inherit his holy mountain" (Isaiah 57:13); while Israel in the flesh "shall be all righteous; they shall inherit the land for ever as the branch of the LORD's planting, the work of his hands, that He may be glorified. A little one shall become a thousand, and a small one a strong nation. "I, saith the LORD, will hasten it in its time" (Isaiah 60:14,18,21,22).

THE TOKEN OF THE COVENANT

IT was fourteen years after the confirmation of the covenant, and when Abram had attained the age of ninety-nine, that the Lord appeared to him to repeat His promises, and to appoint the *token* of the covenant. On this occasion, God talked with him, and changed his name from Abram to Abraham, as an everlasting memorial that He had made him heir of the world, by constituting him a father of a great multitude. "Behold", said God, "my covenant is with thee, and thou shalt be a father of many nations. Neither shall thy name any more be called Abram, but thy name shall be Abraham; for a father of many nations have I constituted thee." And besides this constitutional fatherhood, the Lord assured him that though so old, he should be prolific of multitudes which should descend from his own loins. "I will make thee", said he, "exceeding fruitful, and I will make nations of thee; and kings shall come out of thee." The Lord then announced, that the covenant He had confirmed should be *established* between Him and Abraham, and his fleshly descendants in their generations for an *everlasting* covenant; and that He would be a God to him and to them. He also again declared His oft-repeated promise, saying, "I will give unto thee, and to thy seed after thee, the land wherein thou art a stranger, *all the land of Canaan*, for an *everlasting* possession: and I will be their God" (Genesis 17:1-8).

In the passage from which this is taken, God says, "I *will make* my covenant between me and thee"; and afterwards, "Behold, my covenant *is* with thee." The *"will make"* refers to a covenant subsequent to that confirmed fourteen years before. That to be made was *the token* of that which was already made; and *"the seal* of the righteousness of the faith which Abraham had when it was counted to him for righteousness" (Romans 4:11). "This", said God, "is my covenant which ye shall keep, between me and you and thy seed after thee: every man-child among you shall be circumcised; and it shall be *a token of the covenant betwixt me and you*, Abraham." The appointing of this token in their flesh was the establishment of the covenant with Abraham's seed in the time of Isaac and Jacob in their generations. When, therefore, Israelites behold the mark in their flesh it reminds them that they are "the children of the covenant which God made with their fathers, saying unto Abraham, And in thy Seed shall all the kindreds of the earth be blessed" (Acts 3:25); that the land of Canaan, *all of it*, is promised to them for an everlasting possession; but that an everlasting possession in it can only be attained by belief of the thing promised in the covenant being counted to them for righteousness in the way of

God's appointment. They know, or rather ought to know, that the sign of circumcision and the Mosaic law can give them no title to the *everlasting* occupancy of Canaan, either as individuals, or as a nation. It is circumcision of the heart, of which circumcision of the flesh is but the sign of the circumcised heart of Abraham, that confers a title to the land *and all its attributes,* Before Israel can inherit the land for ever, and so be no more expelled by "the Horns of the Gentiles", they must "circumcise the foreskin of their hearts, and be no more stiff-necked"; and "love the LORD their God with all their heart, and with all their soul, that they may live" (Deuteronomy 10:16; 30:6). This may seem to some to put their restoration a long way off. And so it does, if the circumcision of their hearts is to be effected by the instrumentality of the Society for the Conversion of the Jews. By the well-meant endeavours of this body, it never can be accomplished; for the Society and its agents are themselves deficient in this particular.

But "God is able to graft them in again" (Romans 11:23); and testifies by His prophets, saying, "A new heart also will *I* give you, and a new spirit will *I* put within you, O Israel; and *I* will take away the stony heart out of your flesh and *I* will give you a heart of flesh. And *I* will put my spirit within you, and cause you to walk in my statutes, and ye shall keep my judgments, and do them. And ye shall dwell in the land that I gave to your fathers; and ye shall be my people; and I will be your God. I will also save you from all your uncleannesses; and I will call for the corn, and will increase it, and lay no famine upon you. And I will multiply the fruit of the tree, and the increase of the field, that ye shall receive no more reproach of famine among the heathen" (Ezekiel 36:26-30; 39:25-29). In this testimony, while Moses exhorted them to circumcise the *foreskin* of their hearts, the Lord says that He will change their hearts Himself; not, however, by "the foolishness of preaching", for that has failed even by the mouth of apostles energized by the spirit, but by means in reserve which will astonish Israel and the world and of which He has spoken at large in the holy scriptures. I will anticipate this part of the subject so far as to say, that the Lord has left on record an illustration of the manner in which He changes the heart of a nation, and plants them in a land flowing with milk and honey, in the history of Israel's exode from Egypt, and their settlement in the land of Canaan. This is a representation on a small scale of how He intends to graft them in again, as He has declared by the prophets.

In after times circumcision came to be performed as a mere custom, or ceremony. An institution of God, that was appointed as a memorial of His promise concerning the *everlasting* possession of Canaan and the world; and of that righteousness by faith of the promise which could alone entitle to it: and which was to express the faith of those who practised it—degenerated into a mere form which was observed, like infant sprinkling, by "the pious" and most ungodly characters alike. But it is evident that circumcision, being instituted *after* the covenant of promise was confirmed, and *after Abraham had obtained a title to it* by a righteousness of faith, could confer upon the person circumcised no right to possess the things promised for ever: and certainly none to reprobates who practised it, as Turks and wild Arabs do now, because their fathers have done before them, time immemorial to them.

What obligation, then, did this sign of the covenant, and seal of Abraham's justification by faith without circumcision, impose upon the circumcised? Let the apostle answer the question. "I testify", says he, "to every man that is circumcised, that *he is a debtor to do the whole law*" (Galatians 5:3). This was a fearful obligation for a man to be brought under, who sought to be justified, to the end that he might obtain an *everlasting* inheritance in the land of Canaan, which implies the acquisition of eternal life and glory. The law was weak through the flesh; and gave only the knowledge of sin. It was an unbearable yoke of bondage; and a law which no man born of the will of the flesh had been able to keep without sin. If, then, a man sought to obtain a right to an everlasting possession of the land by obedience to it, he had undertaken an impossibility; for the law, on account of human weakness, could give no one a right to live for ever; and without life eternal a man could not everlastingly possess the land; and this life no one can attain to who is not justified from all his past sins; for if in his sins he is under the sentence of death, as it is written, "the wages of sin is death". The apostle speaks directly to the point; for he says, "If there had been a law given, which could have given (*a title to*) life (*eternal*), verily righteousness (or justification from past sins to life) should have been by the law" (Galatians 3:21); "for if righteousness had come by the law, then Christ is dead in vain" (2:21). He says explicitly, "By the law shall no flesh be justified". A circumcised person is therefore bound to keep that which he cannot possibly keep; and which if he did keep could not benefit him, because justification to life is by faith in the promise, and not by conformity to the Mosaic law.

The relation of the Jews to eternal life as individuals, and to the everlasting possession of Canaan in blessedness and peace as a nation, is manifest. They are circumcised, and therefore bound to keep the whole law; by which law they seek to be justified. But how vain and impossible is their enterprise. The law says, "Cursed is every one that continueth not *in all things* written in the book of the law to do them" (Deuteronomy 27:26); and so unexceptional is this sentence, that it even cursed the Lord Jesus, saying, "Cursed is every one that hangeth upon a tree" (21:23); and in this way he was made a curse for men (Galatians 3:13). Now, the law teaches that without the shedding of blood there is no remission of sins, and prescribed certain sacrifices which must be offered upon an altar in Jerusalem, and there only. To say nothing of other impossible things, these offerings, which are indispensable, the Jews neither do, nor can present. These are things, then, they do not continue in, and therefore they are cursed by the law, and condemned by Moses in whom they trust. They are under sentence of death, and of eternal exclusion from all inheritance in Canaan and the world. They may possibly believe in the promise made to Abraham, that God will give the land to him and the Christ; but they deny that Jesus is the person named in the covenant, which is tantamount to rejecting the covenant itself.

While circumcision obliged Israel to keep the whole law, in which there was an annual remembrance of national offences, it gave them through that law only *a tenant at will occupancy* of the land of Canaan; and that *not to the extent* which pertains to its everlasting possession. This appears from the words of Moses, as it is written, "If thou wilt not observe to do all the words of this law, ye shall be plucked from off the land whither thou goest to possess it" (Deuteronomy 28:58,63). The condition of their tenancy was their good behaviour. If they served God according to the law of the land He had given, He would bless them in their basket and store; but if they served other gods, He would let in the worshippers of those gods upon them, and expel them from the country. Israel has rebelled; and therefore they are in dispersion, until the time appointed shall come to remember the covenant made with the fathers; and therefore to remember the land (Leviticus 26:40-42).

The national tenancy of Canaan under the law being leasehold, no purchases of freehold estates could be made in the land. If Israel had been a freeholder, the case would have been different. But the land belonged to the Lord; and they had no more right to grant it away in parcels for ever, than the tenant under a twenty-one years' lease has to cut up his holding into lots, and sell them to purchasers for ever. Israel were the Lord's tenants; and the law said to them on the part of their Landlord, "The land shall not be sold for ever; for the land is mine, and ye are *strangers and sojourners* with me"; so that "in all the land of your possession ye shall grant a redemption for the land". Hence, if poverty compelled a man to sell his farm, it was always redeemable by himself, or kin, according to certain conditions; but if neither could raise the money to redeem, the estate was not lost to the original owner; for though it remained in the hands of the purchaser, he was obliged to return it for nothing at the year of jubilee (Leviticus 25:23-28). Even under the New Constitution, when the nation obtains everlasting possession, the servants of the Prince will have to surrender his territorial gifts at the year of liberty; while his sons will possess them for ever (Ezekiel 46:16-18).

The covenant of promise confers a more extensive holding of the country than the law of Moses. At no time of their occupation did Israel possess all the land from the Euphrates to the Nile, as promised in the covenant; and even if they had, such holding would not have been in the sense of the covenant, for they have not held possession according to the limits defined *"for ever"*. *"All* the land of Canaan for an *everlasting* possession" is the promise; but the indisputable fact is that Israel have only possessed a *part of it for a limited* and turbulent period. In Solomon's days, when the nation was at its zenith under the law, the land was jointly possessed by Israel, the Tyrians, and the remains of the Hittites, Amorites, Perizzites, Hivites, Jebusites, etc.; but when the age of the covenant arrives, Israel under Shiloh will possess it all; "and there shall be no more the Canaanite in the house of the LORD of Hosts" (2 Chronicles 8:7; Zechariah 14:21).

No uncircumcised person was permitted to be a member of Abraham's family. Home-born, or purchased, slaves, as well as sons, were to be alike circumcised, or else to be cut off; for he that was uncircumcised on the eighth day after the first circumcisions were instituted, or not at all, had broken the Lord's covenant. This was a great calamity; for *none but circumcised persons can inherit the promises*. This may startle; but it is strictly true. It will, however, be remembered that true circumcision is of the heart. Circumcision of the flesh is but an outward sign of Abraham's circumcision of heart; and every one who would inherit with faithful Abraham must be circumcised of heart likewise. When he was circumcised of heart his faith in God was imputed to him for remission of sins that were past. His former idolatry, etc., was forgiven, and the body of the sins of his flesh put off. Now, a man believing what Abraham believed, with the same effect on his disposition and life, is also circumcised of heart, when, *in putting on Christ*, he is "circumcised with the circumcision made without hands by the circumcision of Christ", performed on the eighth day according to the law. In putting on Christ, his faith is counted to him for righteousness as Abraham's was. "The body of the sins of his flesh," is cut off. The foreskin of his heart is circumcised, and he is the subject of "circumcision in the spirit"; and his praise, though not of men, is pronounced of God (Romans 2:29).

Now, I respectfully inquire, will a man who understands the signification of circumcision of the flesh, and the nature of circumcision of the heart jeopardize his reputation for soundness of mind by saying that infant-sprinkling, even if a spiritual practice, was divinely appointed in the room of circumcision in flesh or spirit? That the immersion of a man of the same faith and disposition as Abraham's is connected with circumcision, I have shown; to such a man, immersion into the glorious name is *the token* of his justification by faith, as circumcision of the flesh was to Abraham. It is, indeed, a substitute for circumcision of the flesh; but the accompaniment also for circumcision of the heart: and as all of Abraham's faith were to be cut off from his people who were not circumcised in flesh, so all of his faith now will be cut off who are not immersed; for immersion is the appointed, and only appointed, means of putting on the circumcision of Jesus Christ by which the body of the sins of the flesh are put off (Colossians 2:11,12). But this is a very different affair to infant-rhantism coming in the room of circumcision of the flesh. Suppose it did, then the law of circumcision must have become the law of the substitute—that is, of infant-sprinkling. The rhantized subject, then, is bound to keep the whole law, and in default thereof comes under its curse. The immersion of an unbeliever amounts to nothing. To such a person it is no token. What shall we say, then, of the rhantism of an infant? Is the sprinkling, and marking it with the sign of a cross a token to it, or to others, that it is "justified by faith, and has peace with God through the Lord Jesus Christ"? Or is it a sign of the faith of its godfathers and godmothers, or of its parents, of their being justified by faith, and circumcised of heart? Or is it a token that the clerical administrator has faith in the covenant of promise? Nay, rather, it is a token of the astounding ignorance of the letter and spirit of the gospel, and of the Judaism of all concerned; and a striking illustration of that "*strong delusion*" spread over the face of all people as a covering veil (2 Thessalonians 2:11; Isaiah 25:7).

THE ALLEGORY

ABRAHAM had two sons—Ishmael, the son of Hagar, an Egyptian handmaid; and Isaac, the son of Sarah. Ishmael was fourteen years old when Isaac was born. He was born in the ordinary course of things, and therefore said to be "born after the flesh"; while Isaac was born out of the usual course, Sarah being ninety and Abraham a hundred, she being also strengthened of God, according to the promise, and consequently said to be "born after the Spirit". Hagar was a bondwoman; but Sarah was free: yet, had it been left to Abraham, he would have made Ishmael his heir as well as Isaac, for he loved them both. But Ishmael manifested an evil spirit towards Sarah and Isaac, which he had imbibed from his mother. Moses says he mocked Isaac, or spoke contemptuously of him; which the apostle terms persecuting him, and characteristic of those of Ishmael's class. Sarah's indignation was fired at this; "Wherefore, she said unto Abraham, Cast out this bondwoman and her son: for the son of this bondwoman shall not be heir with my son, even with Isaac". Although Abraham was exceedingly grieved at this, God approved of Sarah's decision; and informed him that Christ should descend from Isaac, and not from Ishmael, saying, "*In Isaac shall thy Seed be called*"; nevertheless, because Ishmael was his son, he would make a nation of him also with twelve princes for its fathers.

This fragment of Abraham's history has a signification beyond what appears on the face of it. The apostle informs us that *the two women* and their characteristics, represent *two covenants*; and *the two sons* of Abraham by them *two seeds*, or classes of persons. The covenants are "the one from Mount Sinai in Arabia", and the other the covenant confirmed of God 430 years before that of Sinai was promulgated; and which, being a matter of promise, the subject of which is Christ as the inheritor of Canaan, and its future king in Jerusalem, now at the right hand of God, is said to be "Jerusalem which is above". The apostle says that Jerusalem is the subject of both these covenants; but in different periods of her history. During her existence as the metropolis of the Hebrew commonwealth under its Sinaitic constitution, she was represented by Hagar the bondwoman; because the covenant from Sinai "gendered to bondage"; and in consequence the citizens of the commonwealth were in bondage with the mother city. They were "entangled with the yoke of bondage", "under the rudiments of the world". They were bound to keep the whole law, by which they sought to be justified, and as they could not do it owing to the weakness of the flesh, they came under the curse.

But this state of things was only provisional. God did not intend the Hebrew commonwealth to exist perpetually under the Sinaitic constitution. Israel was not always to be in bondage to the law of Moses. A great revolution was predetermined of God, which should result in the abolition of the Arabian covenant, and the dispersion of Israel among the nations. This is allegorically styled "*casting out the bondwoman and her son*"; which was necessary for the good and all-sufficient reason that the Sinaitic constitution of the commonwealth of Israel was not adapted for the people and state when Christ should sit upon the throne of his father David, and the saints should possess the kingdom. The law of Moses enjoined ordinances concerning the flesh, such as "the water of separation" (Numbers 19; Hebrews 9:13), which would be quite incompatible with the realities of the Age to Come. Under the law there was "a remembrance again of sins every year" (Hebrews 10:3) but under the New Constitution from heaven, "the sins and iniquities of the people will be remembered no more" (Jeremiah 31:31-34). The Sinaitic constitution was faulty; it was therefore necessary that it should give place to a better, which shall be established on better promises (Hebrews 8:6,7). Hence, the bondwoman was to be cast out to make room for a more perfect arrangement of the commonwealth.

Since the expulsion of Israel by the Romans, Jerusalem and her children are in the situation of Hagar and her son, while wandering in the wilderness of Beer-sheba. She is divorced from the Lord as Hagar was from Abraham, and "being desolate she sits upon the ground" (Genesis 21:16; Isaiah 3:26), and bewails her widowhood. But there is to be *"a restitution of all things"*. Jerusalem is to become a free woman as Sarah was; and to take her stand in the midst of the earth as *"the city whose architect and builder is God"*. She will then "remember the reproach of widowhood no more. For her Maker will be her husband; the LORD of Hosts is his name; and her Redeemer the Holy One of Israel (even Jesus), *the God of the whole earth shall he be called"* (Isaiah 54:4-5). She will then be the metropolis of the world: and her citizens, or children, will be more numerous than those she rejoiced in under the law, as a married wife. The period of her glory will have arrived, the twelve tribes be again the united, peaceful, and joyous inhabitants of the land; the "greater than Solomon", their king; and his city, "the heavenly Jerusalem", which "is free, and the mother of us all".

But, while Hagar represents Jerusalem under the law; and Sarah Jerusalem under the new constitution of the Hebrew commonwealth; Ishmael represents Israel, glorying in their fleshly descent from Abraham, and boasting in the law; and Isaac, those of Israel and the Gentiles, who regard the flesh as profiting nothing, and who are the sons of Abraham by believing the promises made to him and to his seed. Hence, Ishmael and Isaac represent two seeds or classes of mankind, who shall not be heirs together of the promise. Indeed, their natures are so opposite that it would be impossible for them to fulfil in concert the destiny marked out for those who are to inherit the promises. The Ishmaelite-seed are wild men; whose hands are against all who believe the truth. They are mockers; for as Ishmael mocked Isaac, so Israel mocked Jesus, and spoke reproachfully of him

and his brethren, who are one. The kingdom to be established is a righteous dominion, and requires righteous men for its administration; as it is written, *"He that ruleth over men must be just, ruling in the fear of the Lord"* (2 Samuel 23:3). It is impossible, therefore, that the Ishmaelite-seed can be heirs of the promise. All the honour, glory, and power of the state were in their hands under the Arabian covenant; and cruel and unjust was the use they made of their position. They put Jesus to death; and persecuted those to whom "he gave power to become the sons of God", believing on his name; and were "contrary to all men; forbidding the apostles to speak to the Gentiles, that they might be saved" (1 Thessalonians 2:15,16). They were then *"first"*; but power was destined to change hands, when they who were *"the first shall be the last"*. They had killed the heir that the inheritance might be theirs; but they have been destroyed, and the vineyard now remains to be bestowed upon others, who shall render its Lord the fruits in their seasons (Matthew 21:38,41). Thus, as in the case of Ishmael and Isaac, "he that was born after the flesh persecuted him that was born after the spirit, even so", says the apostle, "it is now"; and, we may add, ever will be, until the times of the restitution of the State when "the last shall be first", and beyond the reach of evil.

No one but God had the right, or the power, to appoint *"the heir of all things"*. Abraham could not appoint him, neither could he be self-appointed. Abraham wished that Ishmael might be the heir; or, as he expressed it, "O that Ishmael might live before thee". But God would not consent to this. He therefore promised to give him one for the heir, whom he should call Isaac; and of whom He said, "I will establish my covenant with him for an everlasting covenant, and with his seed after him" (Genesis 17:19). But Isaac was not only born of promise; he believed the promises likewise, for the scripture saith, "By faith Isaac blessed Jacob and Esau *concerning things to come*". Now it is written, *"In Isaac shall thy seed be called"*—that is, Christ shall descend from him, and all *who believe the promises*, and put on Christ, shall be considered as *"in Isaac"*; and being thus "the children of the promise", shall be "counted for *the seed*" (Romans 9:6-8; Galatians 4:28), who shall inherit the land and the world for ever. *"The seed"*, then, is a phrase that must be understood in a two-fold sense—first, as referring to Christ; and secondly, to all who are constitutionally *in him*. Isaac is representative of both: for Christ was in his loins, and all *"in him"* must be constitutionally in Isaac also.

For want of understanding the scripture doctrine of the two seeds, some very fatal mistakes have been made by many well-meaning persons. They have gone so far as to deny that the seed of Abraham after the flesh will ever be restored to the land of Canaan, which is *in effect* to deny the fulfilment of a vast proportion of "the testimony of God". The seed of the serpent, and the seed of the woman, indicated before the Flood, were afterwards distinguished in the seed of Ishmael, and the seed of Isaac. "The children of the flesh are not the children of God; neither are they all Israel, who are of Israel" (Romans 9:8). This is true; but it does not therefore follow that there is nothing more to be done with "the children of the flesh" than to burn them up. *To carry out the allegory, God has yet to make of the Ishmael-seed a great nation*; for though Ishmael was an outcast and a wanderer in the wilderness, God promised that he should be great, and dwell in the presence of his brethren (Genesis 17:20; 16:12). The children of Abraham according to the flesh are "the children of the kingdom" (Matthew 8:12; 13:38) as well as the children of the promise; only, these two classes of children stand in a different relation to the government and glory of the commonwealth, and to the dominion of the nations in the age to come. The Ishmael-children were cast out of the government by the Romans; but the children in Isaac will "shine forth as the sun in the kingdom of their Father", when the kingdom is restored again to Israel (Acts 1:6).

"In the regeneration when the Son of Man shall sit on the throne of his glory", the children in Isaac will reign as *"sons"*; while the children of the flesh will be the king's subjects, or *"servants"*. This distinction is apparent from the following testimony: "Instead of thy fathers shall be thy children, whom thou mayest make princes throughout all the earth" (Psalms 45:16); of whom it is said, "If the Prince give a gift unto *any of his sons*, the inheritance thereof shall be his sons; it shall be their possession by *inheritance*. But if he give a gift of his inheritance to *one of his servants* then it shall be his to the year of liberty; and after it shall return to the prince: but *his* inheritance shall be his sons' *for them*" (Ezekiel 46:16,17). The sons of the prince are joint-heirs with him; but the servants of the prince are only leasehold-ers for a certain number of years. If the natural Israel are not restored to Canaan, the spiritual Israel, that is to say, the prince and his sons, would inherit a kingdom without subjects to serve them. This would be like the Royal family reigning in Windsor Castle over the realm of Britain after all its inhabitants had expatriated themselves to the United States. It requires more than *a staff* to make a regiment; so also it requires a multitude of people as well as princes, priests, and kings, to constitute a Kingdom in Canaan, or in any country.

Now, the children in Isaac become the children of the heavenly Jerusalem by believing "the exceeding great and precious promises" set forth in "the manifold wisdom of God". They hope to see Canaan and Jerusalem under the new covenant, which will constitute them both heavenly. They are even now said to have "come to Mount Zion, and unto the city of the living God, and to the heavenly Jerusalem" (Hebrews 12:22); but it is as yet only in spirit, that is, by faith and hope: and as the city and land will be made heavenly by the Lord from heaven, their glorious attributes are in truth *"above"*; to believe, then, in what will be brought down to the city from above, is for the children of the promise in Isaac to stand related to "Jerusalem which is above, the mother of them all" (Galatians 4:26). Hence, the apostle exhorts them, saying, "If then ye be risen with Christ, seek those things which are above, where Christ sitteth at the right hand of God. Set your affection on things above, not on things on the earth. For ye are dead (to earthly things) and *your life is hid* with Christ in God. *When* Christ, who is our life, shall appear, *then* shall ye also appear with him in glory" (Colossians 3:1-4).

PARABLE OF THE SEED

ABRAHAM was ninety-nine years old, and Ishmael thirteen when they were circumcised (Genesis 17:24,25). Isaac was born when Abraham was one hundred. Between the circumcision of his household and the birth of Isaac, while he was yet living "in the plain of Mamre which is Hebron" the Lord appeared to him, and again promised Sarah a son. At this crisis Sodom and Gomorrha were destroyed, and the Dead Sea formed. After this catastrophe, Abraham journeyed from Hebron towards the south country, and dwelled between Kadesh and Shur, and sojourned in Gerar of the Philistines (Genesis 20:1). On his arrival there, he entered into an agreement with the king of the country, which they confirmed by an oath, by which he was permitted to dwell in any part of Philistia he pleased, and a certain well of water was restored to him, called Beer-sheba, which had been violently taken away by the king's servants (Genesis 20:15; 21:25,31).

After this arrangement, Isaac was born according to promise. On the day he was weaned, Abraham made a great feast. It was then Ishmael was detected mocking at Isaac, which caused his and Hagar's expulsion from the family. These being cast out, Abraham planted a grove in Beer-sheba, and there "called on the name of the LORD, the everlasting God". Having thus settled himself, "he sojourned in the Philistines' land many days" (Genesis 21:33,34). How long he continued there may be learned from the following considerations. In his speech before the Sanhedrin, Stephen says: "When Abraham's father was dead, he removed him into this land wherein ye dwell" (Acts 7:4); that is, he returned from Philistia to "Hebron in the land of Canaan" (Genesis 23:1,2). Now Terah, Abraham's father, was seventy years old when Abraham was born; so that when Isaac was born at Beer-sheba, Terah was a hundred and seventy. But Terah lived two hundred and five years, and then died at Haran; and it was after his death that Abraham removed to Hebron, where Sarah died, aged one hundred and twenty-seven. Now she died two years after Terah; so that it was in this two years that Abraham left Philistia. But Stephen says it was *when* Terah died he moved to Canaan, which makes the *"many days"* he sojourned in the Philistine's land *thirty-five years from the birth of Isaac.* This simple statement of facts removes a difficulty which has puzzled chronologists exceedingly. Moses says Terah died in Haran aged two hundred and five (Genesis 11:32); and Stephen is made to say that Abraham removed from Haran to Canaan when Terah died, *thereby making Sarah a resident of the country only two years!* This is the fault of the English version, which renders κἀκεῖθεν, *"from thence"* instead of *afterwards*, as it ought to be.* "Abraham", said Stephen, "dwelt in Haran; and afterwards"—How long after?—"When his father was dead, he removed him"—Where from? From Beer-sheba of the Philistines. Where to? To Hebron "in this land wherein ye dwell". Thus Moses and Stephen agree.

Now, at some time while Abraham was sojourning in the land of the Philistines, God appeared to him for the purpose of putting his faith to the proof; and of giving him in the person of Isaac, a lively representation of what was to befall his seed, the Christ, then in the loins of Isaac, before he should be exalted to inherit Canaan and the world. The trial was a very severe one. He was commanded to take Isaac, "his only son whom he loved", into the land of Moriah; and "offer him there for a burnt-offering upon one of the mountains", which God should point out. Moriah was itself a mountain upon which Solomon afterwards built the temple (2 Chronicles 3:1); and the land, or region, around, is celebrated by the mounts, afterwards called Zion, Olivet, and Calvary. The mountain chosen of God is not named; I can only therefore express my opinion that it was Calvary. It took him till *"the third day"* to arrive at the place, a distance of forty miles in a straight line from Beersheba. This will not be surprising when it is remembered, that he rode upon an ass, accompanied by two young men, beside Isaac, who conveyed the wood, and other necessaries for the journey. Their progress was therefore slow. "On

---

* And as it is translated in Acts 13:21.

the third day Abraham lifted up his eyes, and saw the place afar off." He then caused the party to halt. He told the young men to stay there with the ass: "and I and the lad", said he, "will go yonder and worship, *and come again to you*". But if he were going to slay Isaac, how could *Isaac* and he come again to them? The apostle explains this, saying, "By faith Abraham when he was tried offered up Isaac; and he that had received the promises offered up his only begotten" of Sarah. "Of whom it was said, That in Isaac shall thy Seed be called: accounting that God was able to raise him up, even from the dead; from whence also he received him in a parable"—ἐν παραβολῇ (Hebrews 11:17-19). Abraham fully intended to slay Isaac; but he firmly believed that God would raise him from the dead again; because all the promises God had made him were to be accomplished in Isaac's Seed; as it is written, "My covenant will I establish with Isaac and his seed after him": therefore, said Abraham to the young men, "we will come again to you".

The parable, or representation, of what was afterwards to happen to Isaac's Seed, the Christ, now began. "Abraham took the wood of the burnt-offering, and *laid it upon Isaac, his son*"; while he carried the fire and the knife. Isaac went on with great readiness, not in the least suspecting that he was the proposed victim. "My father", said he, as they jogged along; and he said, "Here am I, my son." "Behold", said Isaac, "the fire and the wood; but where is the lamb for a burnt-offering?" And Abraham said, "My son, God will provide himself a lamb for a burnt-offering".

Having arrived at the place, built an altar, and laid the wood in order, he bound Isaac his son, and laid him on the altar upon the wood. He then stretched forth his hand, and took the knife, to slay his son. At this crisis, when Isaac was expecting instant death at the hand of his father, who loved him as his only son, the angel of the Lord called to him out of heaven, and commanded him to do the lad no harm. A ram caught in a thicket by the horns was appointed as a substitute for Isaac, who was therefore substitutionally slain; but by his personal deliverance from death, restored to Abraham as by a resurrection. Abraham called the place of this memorable and instructive transaction, Jehovah-jireh; and upwards of 400 years afterwards, it was known by the name of "the Mount of the Lord" (Genesis 22:14).

But before we dismiss the parable of the Seed, it is to be remarked, that it was not completed in the figurative resurrection of Isaac. The sacrificial death and resurrection of Christ had been represented; but then, after these events, what was to be his destiny? The answer to this question is found in the closing incident of the parable. Moses testifies that "the angel of the Lord called unto Abraham out of heaven *the second time*". The first time he announced from heaven the acceptance of the son's sacrifice; but the second time the Lord spoke from heaven, had reference to Christ's triumph over his enemies, and his possession of the world, as preached to Abraham in the gospel at the beginning. "By myself have I sworn saith the LORD, for because thou hast done this thing, and hast not withheld thy son, thine only son: that in blessing I will bless thee, and in multiplying I will multiply thy seed as the stars of the heaven, and as the sand which is upon the sea shore; and thy Seed shall possess the gate of *his enemies*; and in thy Seed shall all the nations of the earth be blessed; because thou hast obeyed my voice." Thus, the parabolic representation was finished, "and Abraham returned to his young men; and they rose up, and went together to Beer-sheba; and Abraham dwelt there".

SUMMARY OF ABRAHAM'S FAITH

ABRAHAM is the father of all them who believe, and who walk in the steps of *that faith* which he had while yet uncircumcised. This is the apostle's testimony. I think I need scarcely say, yet it may be useful to do so, that *no one can walk in the steps of Abraham's faith who does not believe the same things*. This is self-evident. It is to be to Abraham according to his faith; and this is the rule for everyone else. We shall inherit what we have faith in. If we have an understanding faith in the truth, we shall inherit the truth; but if we believe in what is not true, and therefore visionary, we shall inherit nothing but the whirlwind. Now, if it be asked, *What is the truth?*—the answer is, *the things which Abraham believed*, with the acknowledgment that Jesus is the Seed spoken of in the promises made to him. It is, therefore, essential to our salvation that we be familiar with the matters of his faith. To make this as easy as possible then, I shall here subjoin in a summary of the faith which was counted to him for righteousness. I would just remind the reader here that Abraham was justified because *he believed in God*. This does not mean because he believed in the existence of God. This is implied. To believe on God in the scripture sense is the "being fully persuaded that what he has *promised*, he is also able to perform and because this was the case with Abraham, "therefore it was imputed to him for righteousness". Furthermore, this persuasion does not consist in saying, "Whatever it is God has promised I know not, but of this I am persuaded, He will perform it". This is not the sort of persuasion God accepts. *He requires men to acquaint themselves first with what He has promised, and then to consult the testimony He has given until they are fully per-*

suaded, as Abraham was. "Now", says the apostle, "it was not written for Abraham's sake alone, that his full persuasion of the divine promise was counted to him for righteousness; but for us also to whom it shall be imputed if we believe on God" (Romans 4:1,23).

In studying the life of Abraham, his biography presents him—

1. As an idolater under condemnation with the world;

2. As a believer of the gospel preached by the angel of the Lord;

3. As justified from all past sins by faith in its promises; and

4. As justified by works unto eternal life.

These four particulars are affirmable of all Abraham's spiritual children. Born of the flesh, they are denizens of the world, and heirs of condemnation; then they believe the gospel; afterwards they are justified by faith from past sins; and subjected to a subsequent probation by which their faith is tried and made perfect. It is worthy of remark here, that *Abraham believed the gospel ten years before his faith was counted to him for righteousness*. This appears from the fact that the gospel was preached to him at Haran; and it was not until the occasion of the confirmation of the covenant at Hebron, that the Lord vouchsafed him an acquittal from all his past sins; which is implied in the testimony that "he believed in the LORD; and he counted it to him for righteousness". This fact ought to teach the reader, that *it is not at the instant a man believes that he is justified*. A man may believe the truth for many years, and yet not be the subject of the righteousness of God. If so, it may then be asked, "When, or at what point of time, and how, is a man's faith in the truth counted to him for remission of sins?" As to the manner of its imputation, this must necessarily differ from the case of Abraham. The angel of the Lord announced to Abraham his justification *by word of mouth*; but under the present arrangement of things, this is not to be expected. The angel sent to Cornelius did not pronounce his justification but simply put him in the way of attaining it. I trust the reader has not forgotten the use of the key in his case.

The scriptures say that through Jesus is now preached the remission of sins to those who believe the gospel of the kingdom; and that justification by faith is through his Name. That is, God has appointed an institution through which remission of sins is communicated to believers of the things of the kingdom of God and the name of Jesus: so that instead of sending an angel to announce to each individual that his faith is counted to him for righteousness, as in the case of Abraham, He has caused a general proclamation to be made, that *"through Christ's name"* believers may obtain the remission of sins. Now, there is but one way for a believer of the gospel to get at this name, to wit, by being "baptized into the name of the Father, and of the Son, and of the Holy Spirit". The answer to the question, then, is this, that *a man's faith in the gospel is counted to him for righteousness in the act of being baptized into the name*. There is no other way than this, and even a believer of the truth will die in his sins unless he submit to it.

The "articles," then, of Abraham's faith were these—

1.   That God would multiply his descendants as the stars of heaven for multitude, and make them a great and mighty nation;

2.   That at that time his own name would be great;

3.   That out of his posterity should arise ONE, in whom and in himself all the nations of the earth should be blessed;

4.   That he together with this personage should have actual possession of the land of Canaan for ever;

5.   That they two, with all his adopted seed, should possess the world;

6.   That the seed, or Christ, would be an only begotten and beloved son, even the seed of the woman only, and therefore of God; that he would fall a victim to his enemies; and in his death be accepted as an offering by being raised from the dead, after the example in the case of Isaac;

7.   That after resurrection, or at "a second time", Christ would possess the gate of his enemies in triumph, and obtain the land of Canaan, and the dominion of the world according to the promise; and,

8.   That, at that time, he and his adopted seed, would be made perfect, receive the promises, and "enter into the joy of their Lord".

Such was the faith of Abraham in outline and such must be the faith of all who would inherit with him. In conclusion, I would direct the reader's attention to the fact, that Abraham was the subject of a twofold justification, as it were; first, of a *justification by faith*; and secondly, of *a justification by works*. Paul says he was justified by faith; and James, that he was justified by works. They are both right. As a sinner he was justified from his *past sins* when his faith was counted to him for righteousness; and as a saint, he was justified by works when he offered up Isaac. Of his justification as a saint James writes, "Abraham our father was justified by works, when he offered Isaac his son upon the altar. Faith wrought with his works, and *by works was faith made perfect*. And the scripture was fulfilled which saith, Abraham believed God, and it was imputed unto him for righteousness: and he was called the friend of God. Ye see then how that by works a man is justified, and NOT *by faith alone*" (James 2:21-24).

I have termed it a twofold justification by way of illustration but it is, in fact, only one. The two stand related as cause and effect; faith being the motive principle it is a justification which *begins* with the remission of sins that are past, and is *perfected* in obedience unto death. The idea may be simplified thus. No exaltation without probation. If a man believe and obey the gospel *his past sins* are forgiven him in Christ; but, if after this he walk in the course of the world his faith is proved to be dead, and he forfeits his title to eternal life. But if, on the other hand, a man become an adopted son of Abraham, and "by a patient continuance in well-doing seek for glory, honour, and incorruptibility" (Romans 2:7), he will find everlasting life in the Paradise of God.

THE THINGS OF THE KINGDOM OF GOD

CHAPTER III

THE GOSPEL PREACHED TO ISAAC AND JACOB:
THE SCRIPTURE DOCTRINE OF ELECTION

The gospel preached to Isaac—The election of Jacob—The scripture doctrine of election—Not according to popular tradition—How men are elected, and how they may know it—Esau hated—Vision of Jacob's Ladder—Jacob's care for his body after death—Joseph's anxiety about his bones—Jacob's prophecy of the Last Days—Summary of "the faith" at Joseph's death—Things established—Chronology of the Age before the Law

ABRAHAM'S faith having been perfected by the severe trial to which it was subjected on the Mount of the Lord, the remainder of his sojourn among the living appears to have been no further illustrated by angelic visitations. Sarah had died "at Kirjath-arba, the same is Hebron in the land of Canaan", two years after his removal from Beer-sheba, where he continued to reside for the rest of his days, being a period of thirty-eight years. During this time, "the LORD blessed him in all things", and he became great in the midst of Canaan, though he possessed of it only the field and cave of Machpelah, which he had purchased for a burial place of the sons of Heth. The Lord had given him flocks, and herds, and silver, and gold, and men-servants, and maid-servants, and camels, and asses (Genesis 24:35); and so gave him an influence and consideration among the surrounding tribes which riches are sure to create.

But in all his prosperity. he did not forget the promises. He had trained up Isaac in his own faith; and in order to preserve him from the evil and corrupting influence of faithless women, and to contribute to the future welfare of his descendants, he took an oath of his steward that he should not take a wife for his son of the daughters of the Canaanites among whom he dwelt; but from among his kindred in Mesopotamia, who appear to have also believed in God (Genesis 24:50). The steward, however, thought it possible he might not succeed; but Abraham had no such misgiving. "The LORD God of heaven", said he, "who took me from my father's house, and from the land of my kindred, and who spake unto me, and sware unto me, saying, *Unto thy Seed will I give this land*; he shall send his angel before", and prosper thy way.

Isaac was forty years old when he married Rebekah, whom he brought into Sarah's tent. Sarah had now been dead three years. At the end of thirty-five years from this time, Abraham died, being a hundred and seventy-five, having "dwelt in tents with Isaac *and Jacob*, the heirs with him of the same promise" (Hebrews 11:9), for fifteen years. "He was gathered to his people. And his sons Isaac and Ishmael buried him in the cave of Machpelah" in a good old age, as the Lord had told him. "He died having obtained a good report through faith, not having received the promises; that he without the rest of the seed might not be made perfect" (Hebrews 11:13,39,40). Such is the scriptural obituary of all who die in hope of the kingdom of God.

After Abraham's decease, Isaac broke up his encampment at Hebron, purposing to go down into Egypt in consequence of a famine in the land of Canaan. He had travelled south as far as Gerar of the Philistines on his way thither. But the Lord appeared unto him there, and said: "Go not down into Egypt: dwell in the land which I shall tell thee of. Sojourn in this land, and I will be with thee, and will bless thee: for *unto thee* and unto thy Seed will I give *all these countries*, and I will perform the oath which I sware unto Abraham thy father; and I will make thy seed to multiply as the stars of heaven, and will give unto thy seed all these countries: and in thy seed shall all the nations of the earth be blessed: because that Abraham obeyed my voice, and kept my charge and commandments, my statutes, and my laws" (Genesis 26:2-5).

In these words, the gospel was preached unto Isaac as it had been to Abraham before him. He also believed the Lord; for on the faith of these promises he proceeded no farther on his way to Egypt, but "dwelt in Gerar". There was no uncertainty in Isaac's mind. He did not look beyond the grave as to "an undiscovered country whence no traveller returns". The future was no mystery to him. "Heaven" was to him *a state of blessedness upon earth*—a well-defined, and definable constitution of things. "I will bless thee", said God: and mark the grounds upon which this blessing was predicated: *"for"*, continued the Lord,

1.   I will give all these countries *to thee*;

2.   I will give all these countries to thy seed "who is Christ", says the apostle;

3.   I will make thy seed a great multitude;

4.   I will give this multitude of people all these countries; and,

5.   I will bless all nations in thy seed; the Christ.

As Abraham had died without receiving these promises made to him also; and as Isaac knew they were to inherit together; the promise of "all these countries" to him was equivalent to an assurance that he should rise from the dead; when he would see his father and the Christ in possession of the land; and his descendants increased to a great multitude, and then become a mighty nation exclusively occupying it; and all the nations happy and contented under the dominion of Christ. This was the gospel he believed; and the heaven, and blessedness for which he hoped.

After this Isaac sowed in the land, and received that year a hundred-fold; and "he waxed great, and went forward, and grew until he became very great; and the Philistines envied him". And their king said, "Go from us: for thou art much mightier than we". So he left Gerar, and went to Beer-sheba. After this, he received a visit from the king of Gerar accompanied by one of his friends, and the general of his army. But Isaac did not seem pleased at their coming; for he asked them, "Wherefore come ye to me, seeing ye hate me, and have sent me away from you?" Their answer shows that they were aware of the relation Isaac sustained to God and to His promises for they replied, "We saw certainly that the LORD was with thee; we wish therefore to make a covenant with thee that thou wilt do us no hurt"; and they ended by stating their conviction, saying, *"Thou art now blessed of the LORD"*; that is, Abraham being dead with whom we made a covenant before, the blessing of God promised to him now rests upon thee, from whom we seek amity and peace (Genesis 26:29; 21:23).

When Isaac was sixty, and Abraham a hundred and sixty, Esau and Jacob were born. Before their birth, the Lord said to Rebekah, "Two nations are in thy womb, and two manner of people shall be separated from thy bowels; and the one people shall be stronger than the other people; and the elder shall serve the younger". Upon this election, the apostle makes the following remarks, saying, "When Rebekah had conceived by our father Isaac—for the children being not yet born, neither having done any good or evil, that *the purpose of God* according to election might stand, not of works, but of him that calleth, it was said unto her, The elder shall serve the younger. As it is written, Jacob have I loved, but Esau have I hated" (Romans 9:10-13; Malachi 1:2,3). This election had relation to the purpose of God revealed in the promises to Abraham and Isaac. He purposed to make "a mighty nation" of their posterity, out of whom "He shall come that shall have dominion" (Numbers 24:19). This purpose could not be accomplished if left to the undirected will of man. Abraham would have made Ishmael his heir, and Isaac would have elected Esau, both of which, as events have shown, would have defeated, rather than have promoted, "the purpose of God". The wild Arabs of the desert, who have descended from Ishmael; or the Edomites, the posterity of Esau—both of which races illustrate the moral obliquity of their fathers—would have been a sorry election in which the purpose of God might be established. The rejection of Ishmael, and the election of Jacob, prove the wisdom and foresight of Him with whom the fathers had to do. He sees the end of all things from the beginning; and perceiving the future characters of the two races, He said to Malachi, "I loved Jacob, and I hated Esau, and laid his mountains and his heritage waste for the dragons of the wilderness".

It may be remarked here that the election of scripture has reference to "the purpose of God" in relation to the constitution of the kingdom. He has elected *its territory*; He has elected *the nation* to inhabit it for ever; He has elected *the king* to rule over it; and He has elected *its saints* to assist him in the administration of its affairs. The election in all these cases has been "*of him that calleth*". This election, however, is not such as "divines" contend for; *nor does it relate to the subjects of which they treat*. He does not say to this man, "I elect you from all eternity to be saved from the flames of hell, do what you may"; nor does He say to that, "I predetermine you to reprobation and eternal torture, do what you can". To affirm this of God is to blaspheme His name. The scriptures declare that "He is no respecter of persons"; that "He has no pleasure in the death of the wicked; but that the wicked turn from his way, and live"; and that "He is long-suffering, not willing that any should perish, but that all should come to repentance" (Acts 10:34; Ezekiel 33:11; 2 Peter 3:9). Such a statement as this is entirely at variance with "*theology*", whose traditions are the exhalations of the carnal mind of a fierce and gloomy age.

God elects saints for His kingdom, not by foregone conclusions which are irreversible; but men are "elect through sanctification of spirit, unto obedience and sprinkling of the blood of Jesus Christ" (1 Peter 1:2). This reveals to us the means and design of the election in relation to the present time. "Sanctification of spirit" is the means; "obedience and sprinkling of Christ's blood", the end. How this is brought about is explained in these words— "Ye have purified your souls in obeying the truth through the spirit" (1 Peter 1:22). The manner in which men are brought to obedience and purification by the sprinkled blood, through the spirit, is practically explained in the use of the keys by Peter on the day of Pentecost, and at the house of Cornelius. The spirit, through the apostle, convinced men of sin, and righteousness, and judgment to come and confirmed his words by the signs which accompanied them. They believed and obeyed the truth;

and in obeying it were purified from all past sins by faith in the blood of sprinkling. Thus they were "washed, sanctified, and justified by the name of the Lord, and by the spirit of God"; and after this manner elected according to His foreknowledge and predetermination.

No man need flatter himself that he is one of God's elect, unless be believes the gospel of the kingdom and obeys it, and walks in the steps of the faith of Abraham. A man then knows, and feels, that he is elected; because God hath said, "He that believes the gospel, and is baptized, shall be saved". In the prophecy of Mount Olivet the elect are named in connection with the suppression of the Hebrew commonwealth. It is there written, "Except those days be shortened, there should no flesh be saved"—that is, no Jew should survive—"but for the elect's sake those days shall be shortened" (Matthew 24:22). These elect were the servants of the Lord in Israel to whom Jesus had granted power to become the sons of God; as well as the fathers, for whose sake Israel is beloved (Romans 11:28), and for whose future blessedness and glory the nation is preserved.

This preservation of Israel for the elect's sake is beautifully expressed by the prophet, saying, "Thus saith the LORD, As the new wine is found in the cluster, and one saith, Destroy it not: for a blessing is in it: so will I do for my servants' sake, *that I may not destroy them all*. And I will bring forth *a Seed* out of Jacob, and out of Judah *an inheritor* of my mountains; and *mine elect shall inherit it* (the land of Canaan), and my servants shall dwell there. And Sharon shall be a fold of flocks, and the valley of Achor a place for the herds to lie down in, for my people that have sought me" (Isaiah 65:8-10). "God", then, *"has not cast away his people Israel, whom he foreknew"*, and spoke of to Abraham and Isaac, before they had any sons. He has chastised them for their sins; but "there is a remnant according to the election of grace". "The election hath obtained the grace, by accepting Jesus as the Seed, and inheritor of the land; and the rest are blinded until this day". But this blindness is not permanent. They will yet become a great and mighty nation, rejoicing in the service of the Lord Jesus and the elect; for "blindness in part has happened to Israel until the fulness of the Gentiles be come in. And so all Israel shall be saved" (Romans 11:2,5,7,8,25,26); that is, all the twelve tribes shall be reunited into one nation and kingdom upon their own land, and be received into the favour of God (Ezekiel 37:25-28; 36:33-38; 39:25-29); they will then have been grafted in again according to the word of the Lord.

In conclusion, every thing in relation to the kingdom is ordained upon sovereign principles. Nothing is left to the will of man. Hence, the apostle saith, "It is not of him that willeth, nor of him that runneth, but of God that showeth mercy". The call of the Gentiles to take part in the future kingdom is a striking illustration of the truth of this. Had things been left to the apostles they would not have extended the invitation to men of other nations to become with them heirs of the kingdom of Canaan, and of the dominion of the world. They were running to and fro among their own nation, calling upon them to become the children of the promise who are counted for the seed; but it was not of their will, but contrary to it, that "the word" was preached to the Gentiles, opening the kingdom to them. The invitation to our race, as the apostle truly saith, was "of God that showeth mercy".

Pharaoh of Egypt is another illustration of this principle. God purposed to show forth His power that His name might be declared throughout all the earth. This manifestation was not left to the wisdom or pleasure of Moses. The display was to be according to the divine will. The world was overspread with ignorance and superstition; and Pharaoh was the autocrat of the age. He was totally ignorant of who the Lord was, and therefore refused to obey Him. He was *"a vessel unto dishonour"* — an idolater under the dominion of the propensities. Had he been left to himself, he would have continued like all other chiefs of the sin-power, "a vessel of wrath fitted for destruction". His tyranny had come to this crisis, namely, either the Israelites must be exterminated, or the oppressor and his power must be destroyed. The judgment in the case belonged to the God of Abraham, of Isaac, and of Jacob; the result could not, therefore, be for a moment doubtful. He that has power over the clay, had appointed Israel to be *"a vessel unto honour"*, upon whom it was His sovereign pleasure to have mercy. They were, therefore, "vessels fitted for mercy", whom He had before prepared, that on them He might make known the riches of His glory, both then and in a time to come. To effect their deliverance then; to punish Pharaoh and his abettors for their tyranny; and to make Himself known to the surrounding nations — He stirred up the Egyptian king to show all that was in his obdurate and relentless nature. Upon this view of the case, He elected Pharaoh and his host to a terrible overthrow; while He elected Israel to become His people in the land of Canaan. Thus "He had mercy on whom he would have mercy, and whom he would he hardened" (Romans 9:14-33).

Such is the doctrine of election as taught in the scriptures of truth. Let us return now to the further consideration of the case of Esau and Jacob.

The boys grew to be men. "Esau was an expert hunter, and a man of the field." The result of these pursuits was to surround himself with warriors, whose power grew into the future kingdom of Edom. When he was ninety-one years old, he was able to march with four hundred men against Jacob, then on his return from Mesopotamia. But Jacob was of a more peaceful disposition. "He was a plain man, dwelling in tents." While they sojourned with their father, Esau was Isaac's favourite; and Jacob his mother's. One day, while Jacob was preparing a pottage of red len-tiles, Esau come in from hunting very much overcome with fatigue. He requested Jacob to let him partake of the red lentiles. But Jacob was not disposed to part with it without a considera-tion. Esau was the elder, and according to the custom of primo-geniture, was entitled to certain privileges, termed *birthright*. Now Jacob, whose name signifies "*supplanter*", wished to sup-plant him in this right, that he might afterwards be entitled to the precedence over Esau, which God had indicated in saying, "The elder shall serve the younger". Therefore, before he consent-ed to Esau's request, he said, "Sell me this day thy birthright". Esau reflected on the demand a little; at length he said, "Behold, I am at the point to die; what profit shall this birthright do to me?" "Swear then", said Jacob, "to me this day"; and he sware unto him, and sold his birthright to Jacob. Jacob then gave him the red pottage. From this time Esau acquired the surname of Edom, which signifies *red*, and commemorates the fact that "Esau despised his birthright" (Genesis 25:27-34).

When Esau was forty years old, he married two Hittite women, who were a grief of mind to both his parents. About thir-ty years after this, when Isaac was one hundred and thirty-one, he determined to bestow his blessing upon Esau, although he had sold his birthright. But the faithful vigilance of Rebekah circumvented it. The elder was to serve the younger, and she intended that Isaac's blessing should take that direction. Accordingly, in blessing the supposed Esau (for his eyes were too dim to see accurately), he said, "God give thee of the dew of heaven, and the fatness of the earth, and plenty of corn and wine: *let people serve thee, and nations bow down to thee: be lord over thy brethren, and let thy mother's sons bow down to thee*: cursed be every one that curseth thee, and blessed be he that blesseth thee". Here was a blessing, contrary to the will of Isaac, pronounced upon Jacob, whom God had predetermined to bless to the same purpose. Truly, "it is not of him that willeth, but of God that showeth mercy".

Esau had fully calculated on the blessing, although he had bartered away his birthright, seeing that Isaac had promised to bestow it upon him on his return from the field. When, therefore, he entered to receive the blessing, and announced himself as the real Esau, "Isaac trembled very exceedingly" when he found that he had been imposed upon; nevertheless, he confirmed what he had done, saying, "Yea, and he shall be blessed". When Esau discovered what had happened, "he cried with a great and exceeding bitter cry, saying, Bless me, even me also, O my father!" And he lifted up his voice and wept. But the thing that was done could not be revoked, for the hand of God was in it.

The apostle cites the case of Esau as a warning to believers lest any of them should *"fail of the grace of God."* All who are Abraham's seed by being in Christ have obtained the birthright; and are thereby entitled to the blessing of Abraham, Isaac, and Jacob, that hereafter "people should serve them, and nations bow down to them; and that they should be lords over their brethren". But, if for some temporal advantage they should "sin wilfully", and thus barter it away, "there remaineth no more sacrifice for sins, but a certain fearful looking for of judgment, and fiery indignation, which shall devour the adversaries" (Hebrews 10:26-37). There is no scope afforded to such for repentance, for they have placed themselves precisely in Esau's position. Hence, the apostle exhorted his brethren to look diligently to it, that none of them proved to be "a profane person", as Esau, who for one morsel of meat sold his birthright: "for," said he, "ye know how that afterward, when he would have inherited the blessing, he was rejected: for he found no possibility of a change of (Isaac's mind) (μετανοίας τόπον οὐχ εὗρεν) though he sought it carefully with tears" (Hebrews 12:15-17). God is merciful; but He is also jealous; and "will by no means clear the wilful". If His children sell their birthright to the world for anything it can tempt them with, His mind, like Isaac's, is immovable; and transgressors cannot change it, though they may seek carefully to do so with tears, and prayers, and with great and exceeding bitter cries.

Jacob having been involuntarily appointed heir of the blessing by Isaac, Esau conceived a hatred of him, and was overheard to threaten him with death when their father was dead. This determination was reported to Rebekah, who, having sent for Jacob, informed him of Esau's malice, and advised him to escape into Mesopotamia, and remain awhile with her brother Laban at Haran, until his brother's fury should subside. It was necessary, however, to get Isaac's consent, that no breach might be made between him and Jacob, for Esau was his favourite son. Rebekah knew well how to manage this. Isaac as well as herself was sorely annoyed by Esau's wives, whose demeanour appears to have been very disgusting to them. She complained to Isaac of the grief they were to her, and declared to him that if Jacob were to take a wife from among the daughters of the land, her life would be of no value to her. This being also Isaac's feeling in the case, he fell into her views immediately; and having called Jacob, he blessed him, and charged him, saying, "Thou shalt not take a wife of the daughters of Canaan". He then directed him to go and take a wife of Laban's family; and said, "God Almighty bless thee, and make thee fruitful, and multiply thee, that thou mayest be a multitude of people; and give thee *the blessing of Abraham*, to thee, and to thy Seed *with thee*: that thou mayest inherit the land wherein thou art a stranger, *which God gave unto Abraham*" (Genesis 28:14). Such was Isaac's understanding of the blessing in regard to the time of its accomplishment. He did not expect it until the Seed, or Christ, was manifested; but when he appeared in possession, they, even Abraham, Isaac, and Jacob, would be blessed *with him*. Let us proceed now to the consideration of

THE VISION OF JACOB'S LADDER

ON the night after his departure, while asleep under the canopy of heaven, the Lord appeared to him in a dream. In the vision he saw, as it were, "a ladder set up on the land, and the top of it reached to heaven: and behold, the angels of God ascending and descending on it. And the LORD stood above it, and said, I am the LORD God of Abraham thy father, and the God of Isaac; *the land whereon thou liest, to thee will I give it, and to thy seed*: in whom all the families of the earth shall be blessed. And behold, I am with thee, and will protect thee in all places whither thou goest, and I will bring thee again into this land: for I will not leave thee, until I have done that which I have spoken to thee of" (Genesis 28:10-15). Thus, in the blessing that now rested upon Jacob, as well as upon Abraham and Isaac, God promised

1.   That at some future time not specified, He would give Jacob actual and personal possession of the land he was then lying upon, and upon which the town of Bethel stood for ages;

2.   That he should have a seed, or descendant, in whom all nations should be blessed; and,

3.   That Jacob and his seed should have possession of Palestine and Syria *together*—that is, at one and the same time.

The exact time, I say, was not specified in the promise. Jacob, however, was given to understand by the representation in the vision that it would be *a long time* after the epoch of his dream. As the apostle says, "*he saw the promises afar off*, and was persuaded of them, and embraced them, and confessed that he was a stranger and pilgrim in the land". He saw the fulfilment of the things promised afar off *in point of time*; but not afar off as to place: for *the place where* they were to be fulfilled was Bethel, about fifteen miles from Jerusalem. He was at the place; and so well did he understand this that he termed Bethel "*the gate of heaven*."

Now the interval of time between the giving of the promise and the fulfilment of it was represented to Jacob by a ladder of extraordinary length, one end of which stood at Bethel, and the other end against the vault of heaven. Here were two points of contact, the land of Judah and heaven; and the connecting medium, the ladder between them. This was a most expressive symbol, as will be perceived by considering the uses to which a ladder is applied. It is a contrivance to connect *distant points*, by which one at the lower end may reach a desired altitude. It is, then, a connecting medium between points of distance. Now if, instead of distant *localities*, distant *epochs* be substituted, *the ages and generations* which connect them will sustain a similar relation to the epochs as a ladder to the ground on which it rests, and the point of elevation against which it leans. The ladder, then, in Jacob's vision was representative of his seed in their generations and appointed times. One end of it was in his loins; the other, in the Lord Jesus when he should sit upon his throne, reigning over the land upon which Jacob was asleep.

But upon this ladder of ages and generations, with Jacob at the bottom and his seed, the Shiloh, at the top, "the angels of God were seen ascending and descending". This represented to him that the affairs of his posterity, natural and spiritual, in all their relations with the world, would be superintended by the Elohim, who would pass to and fro between earth and heaven, in the performance of their work. Hence, the apostle styles them, "All ministering spirits, *sent forth* to minister for them who shall inherit salvation" (Hebrews 1:14). Israel and the nations are under their vicegerency till the Lord Jesus comes to assume the sovereignty of the world. When he appears in his kingdom, the land of Israel especially will be no longer subjected to their superintendence. The apostle includes Palestine and Syria, when the Hebrew commonwealth is reconstituted upon them, in "*the future habitable*" (Hebrews 2:5) (τὴν οἰκουμένην τὴν μέλλουσαν). When he wrote this, these countries were inhabited by Israel under the Mosaic constitution, mixed up with, and in subjection to, the Gentiles.

Under this arrangement their affairs were superintended by the angels of God. But with the future habitable it will be different; for the apostle says, "God hath not put *it* in subjection to the angels": but "when he brings the first-born back again into the habitable (εἰς τὴν οἰκουμένην) he says, Let all the angels of God do homage to him". This return of the Lord to the habitable cannot be referred to the epoch of his resurrection; because he had not then left it. Indeed, he never left it but once before his resurrection, and that was involuntarily when Joseph and Mary carried him into Egypt. He said himself that he had not been to the

Father before rising from the dead (John 20:17). He was in the habitable, only asleep in death. But when he ascended then he departed into a far country to receive the kingdom; and when he had received it, to return. But he has not yet received it, or he would be at this time reigning in the future habitable land. Till the Lord Jesus, however, sits on his throne as "King of the Jews" (John 18:33-39; 19:12-19), the providential direction of human affairs is committed to the Elohim; who are termed the angels of the little ones *who believe in Jesus* (Matthew 18:3-6,10); because they minister to their profit, in causing all things among the nations to work together for their ultimate good.

When that remarkable change in the constitution of things is brought to pass, when Jesus having received the sovereignty, the angels shall do homage to him, there will be a great national jubilee throughout the earth. The nations which are now groaning under the blood-stained tyrannies of the world, and imprecating curses loud and deep upon the heads of their destroyers, will send up to heaven a shout "like mighty thunderings, saying, Alleluia: for the Lord God, the Omnipotent, reigneth" (Revelation 19:6). Paul evidently had a view to this period of blessedness, when he quoted the saying, "Worship him, all gods." He quoted this from the ninety-seventh psalm,* which celebrates the epoch of the reign in these words: "The LORD reigneth; let the earth rejoice; let the multitude of the isles be glad. Clouds and darkness are round about him; righteousness and judgment are the habitation of his throne. A fire goeth before him, and burneth up his enemies round about. His lightnings enlightened the world; the earth saw and trembled. The hills melted like wax at the presence of the LORD, *at the presence of the Lord of the whole earth.* The heavens declare his righteousness, and all *the people see his glory.* Confounded be all they that serve graven images, that boast themselves in idols: *worship him, all ye Elohim.* Zion heard, and was glad; and the daughters of Judah rejoiced because of thy judgments, O LORD. For thou, LORD, art high above all the earth; *thou art exalted far above all the Elohim.*" Such will be the manifestation when the Father shall bring the Lord Jesus back again to the habitable. At present the Elohim are ascending and descending the ladder, so to speak, *between* the Lord Jesus, who is at the right hand of the Majesty in the heavens, and the earth: but, when "he reigns on Mount Zion, and in Jerusalem, before his ancients gloriously" (Isaiah 24:23), heaven and the habitable will be one; and the Elohim will ascend and descend upon him. Heaven will then be open to the eyes of his saints, and they will behold the wonders of the invisible. For

---

* See note, page 41.

such is the doctrine taught by the Lord himself; who, when Nathanael realized him as the Son of God, and King of Israel, because he revealed his secret actions, said to him, "Thou shalt see greater things than these. Hereafter *ye* shall see *heaven open*, and the angels of God ascending and descending *upon* the Son of Man" (John 1:51). Then will the future habitable have been subjected to the Son.

The ladder of ages and generations, as I have said, connects the commencing and terminating epochs of a long period of time. Of this interval, nearly four thousand years have elapsed. A few more years only remain, and the top of the ladder will be attained by Abraham, Isaac, and Jacob, and by all others with them who shall be accounted worthy of the kingdom of God. They will have reached to heaven; not by flying thither as ghosts upon the wings of angels, but by heaven being brought down to earth, when the Lord Jesus shall descend in glory.

Jacob sojourned with his uncle Laban *twenty years* (Genesis 31:38). While residing in Mesopotamia, eleven sons were born to him. The twelfth, named Benjamin, was born of Rachel, the mother of Joseph, at Bethlehem Ephratah, where she died and was buried. Now, as Joseph was thirty-nine when Jacob went down into Egypt, being at that time a hundred and thirty years old (Genesis 41:46,47; 45:6; 47:9), it follows that Jacob was ninety-one when Joseph was born, and seventy-seven when he fled to Haran. After the birth of Joseph, the angel of God appeared to him, and said, "I am the God of Bethel, where thou anointedst the pillar, and vowedst a vow unto me: now arise, get thee out of this land, and return unto the land of thy kindred". He obeyed. Having secretly collected together all his substance, he fled from Laban, taking up his route "to go to Isaac, his father, in the land of Canaan". Having crossed the Euphrates, he arrived at the river Jabbok, which flows into the Jordan about midway between the Sea of Galilee and the Dead Sea. Not very far from the confluence of these rivers "the angels of God met him", and on this account he named the place Mahanaim—that is, *God's host*. Having sent messengers to Esau in the land of Seir to propitiate him, and got over all that he had, he remained on the north side alone. It was here that he wrestled with one of the angels, who blessed him; and changed his name from Jacob to the more honourable one of Israel, which signifies *a prince of God*. As a memorial of this honour, the angel touched the tendon in the hollow of his thigh, and caused it to shrink. So that Jacob became lame, "and halted upon his thigh".

Having crossed the Jabbok to Penuel, and joined his company, he had an interview with Esau, who received him with apparent kindness, though with evident mistrust on the part of Jacob. A reconciliation ensued. Esau accepted a liberal present, and pressed upon Jacob the unwelcome protection of his warriors. Jacob, however, persuaded him to depart without him; and he would follow "softly, until", said he, "I come unto my lord unto Seir". But as soon as Esau was well on his way Jacob pushed on to Succoth. Having halted there for a time, he crossed the Jordan and pitched at Shalem, in the land of Canaan. After his sons had taken vengeance upon the city on account of Dinah, their sister, God appeared to him again, and told him to go and dwell at Bethel, and erect an altar there to God, who appeared to him when he fled from the face of Esau. The gods of Laban were still in the possession of his family. In obeying the voice of God, therefore, he ordered his household to put them away. This they did, and surrendered their ear-rings with them, and Jacob buried gods and jewels under an oak near Shechem.

When he arrived at Bethel, he built the altar as God had told him. And God said to him there, "I am God Almighty: be fruitful and multiply: *a nation and a company of nations* shall be of thee, and kings shall come out of thy loins: and the land which I gave Abraham and Isaac, *to thee* will I give it, and *to thy Seed after thee will I give the land*" (Genesis 35:12). In this renewal of the promise the additional idea was revealed to Jacob, that the nation constituted of his descendants, would contain a plurality of nations—that is, be *a national association of tribes*. He was to inherit the land with them, and with the Seed, or Christ; and as he knew they were to be oppressed by another nation till four hundred years, after which that nation would be judged, and his children would come out with great wealth, this blessing at Bethel reminded him that he would rise from the dead with Abraham, and inherit the land for ever with his Seed. Having left Bethel, he journeyed towards Bethlehem, on the way to which Rachel died. After her death he spread his tent beyond the tower of Edar, on Mount Zion. From thence he came to Hebron, where his father Isaac dwelt. Twenty-nine years having elapsed after this re-union from Jacob's departure from Laban, Isaac died, having attained the age of one hundred and eighty years; and his sons, Esau and Jacob, buried him (Genesis 35:29).

THE PARABLE OF JOSEPH

A PARABLE is the setting forth of a certain thing as a representative of something else. Hence, it is a comparison, or similitude. It may be spoken, or acted. In the former case, fiction is used to illustrate that which is real; while in the latter, real actions on a smaller scale are representative of remoter and grander events. Whether spoken or acted, parables are dark and unintelligible to those who are not skilled in the things of the kingdom; but when once they come to comprehend these, the things they resemble immediately appear. To allegorize is to represent truth by comparison. For certain features of the kingdom of God to be illustrated parabolically is to speak, or act, allegorically; and is a mode of instruction more calculated to keep up the attention, and to impress the mind permanently, than a set discourse, or formal disquisition. The scriptures are constructed after this ingenious plan, by which they are made so much more interesting, and capable of containing so much more matter, than any other book, on the same subject, and of the same size. They are a study of themselves; and no "rules of interpretation", or of "logic", are of any value to the understanding of the things which they reveal.

A parable was enacted by Abraham in offering up Isaac. The things transacted were real, but they were also parabolic, or figurative, of something else, even of the sacrifice and resurrection of the Seed, or Christ. After the death of Isaac, and when Jacob was waxing old, Joseph was selected from among his sons by the arrangements of God to be the typical representative of the future Seed, through whom the promises were to take effect. Hence, the life of Joseph became a living parable by which was represented to Jacob and his sons, and to believers afterwards, what was to be transacted in the life of Christ. In itself the story of Joseph is an interesting and moving history; but when we read it as though we were reading of Christ instead of him, the narration assumes an importance which highly commends itself to the student of the Word.

Jacob had resided seventeen years in the land of Canaan after leaving Laban: Joseph was then seventeen, and Isaac one hundred and sixty-eight. It was, therefore, when Jacob was one hundred and twenty, and twelve years before the death of Isaac, that Joseph had his remarkable dreams. These are the first examples on record of symbolic prophecy. They represented to Joseph that he should be lord over his brethren; and when repeated to them, they as clearly understood them to indicate his supremacy and their subjection, as though it had been ever so literally predicted. I mention this to show that prophecy by symbols and symbolic action is as intelligible as prophecy in the plainest words.

Joseph was the beloved of his father, and the envied and hated of his brethren, whose conduct caused him to give his father an "evil report" of them. He dreamed that he and they were binding sheaves in the field, and that his sheaf stood upright, and theirs also round about, and that they made obeisance to his sheaf. When he told them his dream, they caught at the meaning at once. "Shalt thou", said they, "indeed reign over us? or, shalt thou indeed have dominion over us? And they hated him yet the more for his dreams and for his words." In his second dream, "the sun and the moon, and the eleven stars, made obeisance to him"; which Jacob interpreted, saying, "Shall I and thy mother and thy brethren indeed come to bow down ourselves to thee to the earth? And his brethren envied him: but his father observed the saying."

Now in these little incidents we read, not only Joseph's exaltation, but the treatment Christ would afterwards receive from the sons of Joseph's brethren and his subsequent exaltation to reign over them, when Abraham, Isaac, and Jacob, and his family shall bow down before him to the earth. Jesus gave an evil report of his brethren, who saw that he was beloved of God; he troubled them with his parables and reproofs; and they envied him and hated him for his words. The fate of Joseph awaited him; for as the eleven conspired against Joseph to kill him, and actually sold him to the Ishmaelites of Midian for twenty pieces of silver, so was the Lord Jesus sold for thirty, and subjected to a violent death by the rulers, thinking thereby to falsify his words, and extinguish his pretensions to lordship over them.

Joseph, having become the property of the Midianitish merchants, was "separated from his brethren", and as good as dead to them. They lost sight of him entirely, and at length forgot him altogether. Their conspiracy to all appearance had perfectly succeeded; they had got rid of "the master of dreams"; and had imposed upon Jacob the falsehood that he had met with a violent death from a savage beast. But "God was with him"; and though they had made everything sure, their sin was certain to overtake them.

Joseph was carried into Egypt when he was seventeen years old; and he was thirty-nine when he was made known to his brethren at their *second interview*; hence, he was separate from his father's house for twenty-two years. During this time his fortunes were varied, but always tending to the promotion of God's purpose through him. The word to be accomplished was to plant the Israelites in Egypt, that they might be strangers in a land not theirs, and serve them, and be afflicted, until the time should arrive for their oppressors to be judged, and their deliverance effected to the glory of Jehovah's name. God works by human instrumentality in the affairs of men. Hence, He selected Joseph, as He has since done the Lord Jesus, whom He has also "separated from his brethren", to be the honoured agent in the developing of His purpose in regard to Israel in relation to their own destiny, and the judgment, and subsequent blessedness, of the nations.

The second chapter of the Josephine parable begins with Joseph in the house of Potiphar. Being there the victim of a false accusation, he was immured in the State-prison. But even here he found favour, as he had in Potiphar's house before; for Joseph was a righteous man, and God was with him. He had been in prison *two full years*, when the King of Egypt had his dreams of *the kine*, and *the ears*. The report of his correct interpretation of the chief butler's, and the chief baker's, dreams, while in durance, caused him to be brought before Pharaoh to interpret his. It was then believed that "interpretations belong to God" (Genesis 40:8); that is, when He causes men to dream prophetically, He reserves the interpretation of them to Himself. This is illustrated in the case before us, and afterwards in that of Nebuchadnezzar. Pharoah consulted all the magicians and wise men of Egypt, but there was none that could interpret his dreams. But God revealed their interpretation to Joseph, who exhibited to the king a luminous exposition of them as indications of what God was about to do; and offered him such advice in the emergency as convinced Pharoah that Joseph was "a man in whom the Spirit of God was", and that "none was so discreet and wise as he." "Therefore", said the king, "thou shalt be over mine house, and according unto thy word shall all my people be ruled; only in the throne will I be greater than you."

When Joseph was thirty-seven years old, the famine began in Egypt. It extended to all the surrounding countries, and was sore in the land of Canaan. Hearing that there was corn in Egypt, Jacob sent "Joseph's ten brothers" to purchase some. Now Joseph, being governor, was the man who sold the grain. This caused the sons of Israel to appear before him; and, as he had predicted, "they bowed themselves before him with their faces to the earth". Joseph knew them; but they did not recognize him. He affected to believe they were spies, and put them in ward for three days; but afterwards released them, retaining one as a hostage, for their re-appearance with their youngest brother; and then sent them back loaded with grain for their father's house. The harsh treatment they experienced from Joseph brought to their recollection the manner they had treated him two-and-twenty years before. Their consciences accused them; and not knowing that Joseph understood Hebrew, for he spoke with them through an interpreter, they confessed their guilt to one another in his presence, saying, "We are verily guilty concerning our brother, in that we saw the anguish of his soul, when he besought us, and we would not hear; therefore is this distress come upon us".

Having visited Egypt *a second time*, they were introduced into Joseph's house, when Simeon was restored to them. On Joseph's entrance, "they bowed down their heads, and made obeisance." They were placed at table in regular order, from the eldest to the youngest; and they ate, drank and were merry with Joseph, still supposing him to be an Egyptian. Having departed on their return to Canaan, Joseph caused them to be pursued, and brought back, under pretence of having stolen his drinking cup. At this *second* interview, *Judah* made supplication for his brethren; and confessed that God had found out the iniquity of himself and brethren; and that they were now fairly the servants of the Lord of Pharaoh's kingdom. Judah having finished, Joseph could refrain no longer, but wept aloud, and announced himself as their brother, whom they had sold into Egypt. They were greatly troubled at his presence; but he tranquillized their fears, and assured them that it was all of God, who had sent him before them into Egypt to "preserve them a posterity in the earth, and to save their lives by a great deliverance".

Jacob having received information of all that had been transacted, proceeded to break up his encampment, and to go down into Egypt as Joseph and Pharaoh had invited him to do. Isaac had been dead ten years, and Jacob had attained the age of one hundred and thirty. Having arrived at Beer-sheba on his way thither, he offered sacrifices to the God of Isaac. On this occasion, God spake unto him, and said, "I am God, the God of thy father; fear not to go down into Egypt: for *I will there make of thee a great nation*: I will go down with thee into Egypt; and *I will also surely bring thee up again*: and Joseph shall put his hand upon thine eyes." In this promise Jacob was re-assured of a resurrection to life. The action of putting the hand upon the eyes represents death; for this was one of the last offices of the nearest relations. Hence, to tell Jacob he should die, and yet that he should *be brought up again*, was telling him in effect that he should rise from the dead again to possess the land.

Seventeen years having passed away after his arrival in Egypt, the time drew nigh that Jacob must die. This residence in the land of Ham had not at all diminished his attachment to the land of Canaan. When, therefore, he found his end approaching, he took an oath of Joseph, saying, "Bury me not, I pray thee, in Egypt: but I will lie with my fathers, and thou shalt carry me out of Egypt, and bury me in their burying-place". And Joseph promised to do as he had said. But why was Jacob thus anxious? Surely it could make no difference to him where he should crumble into dust! Nor would it, if Jacob had been a faithless Gentile; or a religionist whose mind was perverted by Platonism. He would have cared nothing about his body; all his solicitude would have been about his "immortal soul". But in Jacob's death-bed scene, he expressed no anxiety about "his soul"; all his care was for his body after death, that it might be duly deposited in the cave of Machpelah, where Abraham, Isaac, Sarah, Rebekah, and Leah were sleeping (Genesis 47:29-31; 49:29-33). This was equally the case with Joseph; for although Egypt had been the theatre of his glory, and he was venerated there as the saviour of the country, in which he had also lived ninety-three years, yet his last thoughts were upon the land of Canaan and the disposal of his bones. "I die", said he: "and God will surely visit you, and bring you out of Egypt unto the land which he sware to Abraham, to Isaac, and to Jacob"; and he took an oath of them, saying, "Ye shall carry up my bones from hence".

Why, I ask, is all mankind's anxiety now about their "souls", and a heaven beyond the skies, when the friends of God, who had all their pilgrimage been the honoured subjects of His fatherly care, manifested no such carefulness; but on the contrary exacted oaths of their survivors expressive of their love for Canaan, and of their concern that their bodies should moulder there? The reason is that the moderns have no faith in the promises of God. Neither Protestants nor Papists "believe on God". They have a system of faith which bears no affinity to the religion of God; and hence they hope for things which He has not promised; and consequently the most pious of them die with a lie in the right hand. The faith and hope of Protestantism are not the faith and hope of "the fathers", whom God has constituted the "heirs of the world".

The last thoughts of these holy men were on "the exceeding great and precious promises" which are to be manifested in the land of Canaan; where their posterity will yet become "a great and mighty nation" under Shiloh and his saints as the Lords of Israel and the Gentiles. Seeing this, then, though afar off, they gave expression to their faith by giving commandment concerning their bodies; as it is written, *"By faith Joseph, when he died, made mention of the departing of the children of Israel: and gave commandment concerning his bones"* (Hebrews 11:22). He was, therefore, embalmed, and put into a coffin; and at the end of one hundred and fifty-four years his bones were carried out of Egypt by Moses; they accompanied Israel in all their journeyings through the wilderness; and were finally deposited by Joshua at Shechem in the parcel of land purchased by Jacob (Genesis 50:24-26; Exodus 13:19; Joshua 24:32). When professors believe the truth, they will have as much interest in Canaan, and the disposition of their bodies, expressive of their faith, as we find testified of Israel and Joseph by those who are high in the favour of their God. We must believe the promises concerning Canaan, if we would be immortal of body in the kingdom of God.

JACOB'S PROPHECY OF THE LAST DAYS

JACOB being a hundred and forty-seven years old, and about to die, called his sons together to tell them "what should befall them in *the last days*." From what has been already advanced on "the end of the world," the reader will understand to what period the prophecy of Jacob principally refers. But, lest any should have forgotten, I will repeat that it relates to events which were to happen in the last days of the Hebrew commonwealth, under the constitution from Mount Sinai. It sketches the political fortunes of the twelve tribes which, with the blessing on Joseph's sons, it now constituted; touches upon the peculiar features of the several portions of Canaan which should be allotted to them: and reveals certain principal events in connection with the tribes of Levi, Judah and Joseph.

It will not be necessary for me to do more than to point out these special incidents as bearing upon the kingdom of God. After Reuben, Simeon and Levi are conjoined in the prophecy. They had slain Hamor and Shechem, and all the males of their city. This circumstance is taken as a characteristic of their tribes in the last days. "Instruments of cruelty", said Jacob, "are in their habitations." Foreseeing the part they would play in relation to the Seed, he exclaimed, "O my soul, come not thou into their secret; unto their assembly (Psalm 22:16; Matthew 26:14), mine honour be not thou united". But why not, Jacob? For in their anger *they slew a man* (Matthew 26:57,59), and in their self-will they digged down a wall, that is, overthrew a city (Genesis 34:25-29). "Cursed be their anger, for it was fierce: and their wrath, for it was cruel." The verification of these things will easily be recognized in the history of the tribe of Levi at the era of the crucifixion. It was the priests who sought and at last accomplished the death of Jesus, to whom Jacob refers; and to mark his sense of their conduct, he said, "I will divide them in Jacob, and scatter them in Israel." This was fulfilled in giving Levi no cantonal inheritance in the land, and in including Simeon's portion within the limits of the canton of Judah (Joshua 19:1,9). From this arrangement Levi, Simeon, and Judah became the tribes principally concerned in the transactions of the last days.

Having spoken of the death of Christ by Levi and Simeon, he then proceeded to speak of things connected with Judah alone. Of this tribe he affirmed:

1. That Judah should be the praise of all the tribes;
2. That it should subdue its enemies;
3. That it should rule over all Israel;

4. That its sovereignty should be monarchical;
5. That Shiloh should arise out of it as a lawgiver;
6. That the gathering of the people should be to him;
7. That he should ride an ass accompanied by its foal;
8. That his garments should be dyed with the blood of his enemies; and,
9. That the fountains and rocks of the country should exuberate with grapes and pasture.

Such are the points into which the members of Jacob's beautiful prophecy concerning the things of the Kingdom, in connection with Judah as the royal tribe, are resolvable when converted into literal, or unfigurative speech. But it is very clear from the past history of the tribe that the prophecy is only partially accomplished. Judah is now "stooping down, and couching as an old lion"; and in view of his present prostration, Jacob inquired, "Who shall rouse him up?" Yes: who shall do it? Who shall start him to his feet again, that he may rend and tread down, and devour the enemies of Jerusalem? Who but the Shiloh, whose goodly horse in the battle Judah is appointed to be? (Zechariah 10:3-5; 12:6; 14:14).

Two appearances of the Shiloh are indicated by Jacob; first after the departure of the sceptre from Judah; and secondly, at the attainment of the tribe to the dignity of giving laws to the gathered people. The sceptre had departed from Judah before the appearing of Jesus; but neither Jesus, nor the tribe, have promulgated *a code of laws* to Israel or the Gentiles. Moses was a lawgiver, not of Judah, but of Levi; but when Shiloh comes as the lawgiver of Judah, then "the law shall go forth from Zion, and the word of the LORD from Jerusalem" (Isaiah 2:3).

The blessing on Judah contains in it the hope of Israel. It shows what views Jacob had of the promises made to him and his fathers. His faith was of things substantial and definable. He looked for a kingdom and an empire, whose royal domain should be the land of Canaan, and especially that part of it allotted to Judah (Ezekiel 48:8-22); and whose imperial ruler should be the Giver of Peace, descended from his loin; in the line of Judah. The Spirit of God in Jacob marked him out to wield the sceptre and to give laws to the world, possessing the gate of his enemies, and blessing all the nations of the earth. It is generally supposed that Jacob saw the sceptre depart from Judah. This is implied by the English version, "Not depart *until* Shiloh come," which is as much as to say, when Christ appears it shall depart: which is not in accordance with the facts of the case.

Having blessed Judah in the terms recorded in scripture (Genesis 49:8-12), he passed over Zebulun, Issachar, Dan, Gad, Asher, and Naphtali, with a brief notice, and then dwelt with emphasis upon Joseph. He described in general terms the fertility of the cantons of Ephraim and Manasseh, and invocated blessings of every kind upon his posterity. Recalling Joseph's history in the past as indicative of his descendants' in the future, he predicted that they would be sorely grieved by their enemies, and separated from the other tribes. Nevertheless, their bow, though unstrung, should abide in strength, and they should be made strong again "by the hands of the Mighty God of Jacob, who should help them", and bless them above what their progenitors enjoyed before they were carried away into captivity. He saw that they would be a royal tribe, and that at some period of their nationality, "the everlasting hills" unto their utmost bound, should bow to his sceptre who is destined to rule them (Habakkuk 3:3-16).

But in the blessing of Joseph, Jacob gave a very remarkable intimation concerning the Shiloh. He styles him *"the shepherd and stone of Israel"* (Isaiah 28:16). In his blessing on Judah, he foretold his descent from him; but in the blessing of Joseph, he declares he is from the God of Jacob, and (being thus spoken of in connection with Joseph) after the parable of his history. In other words, that the Seed should be both son of Judah and Son of God; and that his relation to the tribe of Israel should be after the representation of Joseph's to his brethren. "The archers should sorely grieve him, and shoot at him, and hate him; but his bow should abide in strength, and his arms be made stronger by the God of his fathers, who should help him; and cause all blessings to rest upon his crown, who should be long separated from his brethren."

SUMMARY OF THE FAITH AT JOSEPH'S DEATH

AFTER the death of Joseph, which occurred two hundred and seventy-six years after the confirmation of the covenant concerning Christ, Levi and his sons Kohath, Amram, and Moses, may be regarded as the more especial conservators of the faith with which God is pleased. Many of Jacob's family in the period which elapsed between the death of Joseph and their glorious exodus under Moses, had given themselves up to the service of Egypt's gods (Joshua 24:14). This, however, was not the case with all. Some still kept the promises of God before them; and we find it testified of Moses when only forty years old, and before he fled from Egypt, that "he supposed that his brethren would have understood how that God by his hand would deliver them; *but they understand not"* (Acts 7:25). This was forty years before their deliverance, and one hundred and fourteen years after Joseph's death. Seventy-four years after this event Moses was born to Amram the grandson of Levi. The supposition he entertained concerning his brethren's spiritual intelligence is an indication of his own; for he evidently judged them by his own understanding of the divine promise.

Although "he was learned in all the wisdom of the Egyptians", this did not divert him from the faith. He had been indoctrinated into this in his tender years by his parents. For it is testified that "by faith they hid him three months, not being afraid of the king's commandment" (Hebrews 11:23); thus becoming heirs of the righteousness which is by faith of the promises. This testimony to their faith shows that, however delinquent others might be, "the faith," the one faith of the gospel, dwelt in them. They instilled this faith into Moses, on the fleshy table of whose heart it was so indelibly inscribed, that not all the blandishments of the court of Egypt could efface it. The result of the parental instruction he had received was that "by faith when he came to years he refused to be called the son of Pharaoh's daughter; choosing rather to suffer affliction with the people of God, than to enjoy the pleasures of sin for a season; esteeming *the reproach of Christ* greater riches than the treasures of Egypt; for he had respect to *the recompense of the reward.* By faith he forsook Egypt, not fearing the wrath of the king; for *he endured,* as seeing him who is invisible" (Hebrews 11:24-27).

From this testimony, then, we learn that the faith in Amram's family was concerning Christ, and the recompense of the reward; that this was so little sympathized with, that those who embraced it were subjected to reproach, and called upon to endure on account of it; and that the things connected with Christ were esteemed by those who understood them, as of greater value than the most enlightened, wealthy, and powerful of kingdoms, possessed in all its glory. Now, as the faith of Amram's family is the "faith without which it is impossible to please God" in any age, it will be of advantage to us to have as distinct a view of it as possible. Omitting, then, the general principles of religion, stated on pages 177 to 179 of this work, in which all the faithful were instructed, I shall present in this place a summary of the things which were "all the salvation and all the desire" of Abraham's family, though for a long time "God made it not to grow". I shall begin the enumeration with the most elementary principle, and ascend to the more complex in the order of their development in the promises of God. They believed, then,

1.   That a son of Eve would take away the sin and evil of the world;

2.   That until the sin-power should be subdued, there would be perpetual strife between his adherents and the partisans of sin;

3.   That in this war the Son of the woman and his allies would suffer much adversity, and be temporarily overcome; but afterwards, conquer all their foes;

4.   That Eve's son would descend from Abraham in the line of Isaac, Jacob and Judah;

5.   That Abraham's descendants in the line of Jacob would become "a great and mighty nation"; and that when this came to pass, Abraham's name would be great in all the earth;

6.   That all nations should be blessed, in a social, ecclesiastical, and civil sense, in Abraham and his Seed, whom I shall hereafter term Christ;

7.   That this personage, the hope of Abraham's family, should possess the gate of his enemies—that is, gain the victory over them;

8.   That Christ should possess the land of Canaan from the Euphrates to the Nile; that he should possess it "for ever", and therefore be immortal;

9.   That Abraham, Isaac, and Jacob should possess Canaan with Christ for ever;

10.   That Abraham was the constitutional father of nations, and, with his sons—namely, with Christ and his brethren—the "heir of the world", which was memorialized by the change of his name from Abram to Abraham;

11.   That kings would descend from Abraham in the line of Judah, etc.; and that, therefore, the twelve tribes would constitute *a kingdom in the land of Canaan*, of which Judah would be the royal tribe;

12.   That through Judah, as the lion of Israel, their enemies should be subdued;

13.   That "the Shepherd and Stone of Israel" would be a Son of Judah and Son of God; and that he would be the Lawgiver and King of all nations to the utmost bound of the everlasting hills;

14.   That Christ would be slain by the tribe of Levi after the parable of Isaac;

15.   That as Christ and Abraham are to inherit the land of Canaan for ever, they would rise from the dead to possess it; and that the same thing must occur in the case of all others who should inherit with them;

16.   That after this resurrection and exaltation to power and dominion, ten tribes of Christ's brethren after the flesh would go down into Egypt a second time; and meeting them there, he would make himself known to them; receive their humble and sincere submission; and, we may add, like another Moses and Joshua in one person, lead them out of Egypt and plant them in the land of Canaan;

17.   That to share in this consummation would be the reward of a righteousness counted to those who believed the things promised;

18.   That every one of whom this righteousness was reckoned must be a circumcised person; or otherwise be cut off from his people; and that circumcision was the token of the covenant of promise, and the seal of the righteousness by faith.

In the exposition of the things of the kingdom, as unfolded in "the promises made of God to the fathers", the following points have been fairly established:

1.   That the *territory* of the kingdom of Shiloh is not beyond the skies, but all the land of Canaan from the Euphrates to the Nile; and from the Gulf of Persia and Red Sea to the Mediterranean;

2.   That the twelve tribes of Israel are the natural born *subjects* of the kingdom;

3.   That Christ in the line of Judah is its *King*;

4.   That those of like faith and disposition with Abraham, and who walk in the steps of his faith, are the joint inheritors with its king; in other words, its *aristocracy*; who will share in the glory, honour, power, and blessedness of the kingdom for ever: and,

5.   That all nations will be subject to this kingdom, and constitute its *empire*.

These five points, however, do not comprehend all the things concerning the kingdom of God. Shiloh, or the Anointed One of God, was promised in the line of Judah; but the question remained open from Jacob's decease for many centuries after, as to the particular family of the tribes of Judah he was to descend from. Besides this, there is nothing said respecting the constitution, laws, and ecclesiastical institutions of the kingdom. It will, therefore, be necessary for us to look into these things, that we may fully comprehend the system of the world to be established by the God of heaven, when all other dominions shall have passed away.

It may facilitate a clear and distinct conception of the contents of this chapter to bring the dates quoted into a tabular form;

I shall, therefore, conclude this part of my subject by presenting the reader with the following chronology.

CHRONOLOGY OF THE AGE BEFORE THE LAW

Years
after
Flood

2	Shem beget Arphaxad, and lived afterwards 500 years.
292	Terah aged 70; and Abram born.
350	Noah died; Abram 58 years.
367	Abram leaves Haran, aged 75.
377	The promise concerning Christ confirmed on the 14th day of Abib at even; Abram 85.
378	Ishmael born.
391	Circumcision instituted; Abraham circumcises all his males.
392	Isaac born; Abraham 100 years. Sojourns in the Philistines' land.
427	Terah dies, aged 205; Abraham 135; leaves Philistia after residence there of 35 years.
429	Sarah dies at Hebron, aged 127.
432	Isaac marries Rebecca; Abram 140.
452	Esau and Jacob born; Isaac 60.
467	Abram dies, aged 175; Jacob 15 years.
492	Esau marries, aged 40.
502	SHEM, or Melchizedec, disappears. Jacob 50; Isaac 110.
529	Jacob leaves Isaac; sees the Vision of the Ladder: arrives at Laban's, aged 77.
543	Joseph born.
549	Jacob leaves Laban having served him 20 years, aged 97. Isaac 157.
560	Joseph sold into Egypt aged 17. Jacob 108 years.
572	Isaac dies aged 180. Jacob 120.
582	Second year of the great famine. Jacob 130; removes into Egypt: Joseph 39 years.
599	Jacob dies, aged 147. Joseph aged 56.
653	Joseph dies, aged 110 years. From confirmation of covenant 276 years.
727	Moses born. Aaron 3 years old.
767	Moses flies from Egypt.
807	The Israelites return from Egypt 430 years from the confirmation of the covenant. Moses 80 years.

THE THINGS OF THE KINGDOM OF GOD

CHAPTER IV

THE GOSPEL IN RELATION TO THE
MOSAIC ECONOMY

State of Egypt and Israel before the Exodus—The time of the promise arrives—Call of Moses—God's everlasting memorial—Moses is sent to Israel—He is accepted as a ruler and deliverer—He declares glad tidings to them, but they refuse to listen—The Exodus—Israel baptized into Moses—The song of victory—They are fed with angels' food—The Lord's passover—How to be fulfilled in the kingdom of God—The Lord's supper—The Twelve Tribes constituted the kingdom of God—The gospel preached to Israel—They reject it—Of the Rest—The Royal House of the Kingdom—The sure mercies of David—The kingdom and throne of David—David's kingdom also God's kingdom under its first constitution

D
URING the one hundred and fifty-four years that elapsed between the death of Joseph and *the returning* of the Israelites from Egypt, they multiplied so much as to excite the apprehensions of the Egyptians. "Behold", said Pharaoh, "the people of the children of Israel are more and mightier than we; come on, let us deal wisely with them, lest they multiply, and it come to pass, that when there falleth out any war they join also unto our enemies, and fight against us, *and so get them up out of the land.*"

From this it would seem that the idea prevailed in Pharaoh's court that the Israelites contemplated a wholesale emigration to some other country. His policy, however, was to prevent it, and to maintain the numerical superiority of the Egyptians, by exhausting the Israelites by oppressive toil, and destroying their children at birth. But what can the policy of kings effect when they undertake to combat the purposes of God? The cup of Egypt's iniquity was well-nigh running over. They had not retained God in their thoughts, being wholly given up to the basest superstition and idolatry. They had forgotten their obligations to God, who had saved their nation by the hand of Joseph, whose posterity they had enslaved, and cruelly destroyed. What, then, remained, but that God should judge them? That He, the Lord of all the earth, should step in between the profane tyrant and those whom He purposed to be His people, and give to Egypt according to its works? Israel's four hundred years of affliction were accomplished. They had served the oppressor long enough; and the time had at length arrived when the nation which had reduced them to servitude should be judged, and themselves remunerated for their past sufferings and services, by the spoil of their adversaries.

This was a just and equitable decree; the illustration of which is yet to be exhibited on a grander scale, "when God shall set his hand again A SECOND TIME to recover the remnant of his people which shall be left, from Assyria, *and from Egypt*, and from Pathros, and from Khush, and from Elam, and from Shinar, and from Hamath, and from the islands of the sea. And when he shall utterly destroy *the tongue of the Egyptian sea* (the Red Sea); and with his mighty wind shall shake his hand over *the river* (Nile), and shall smite it in the seven streams, and make men (Israel) go over dry-shod. And there shall be a highway, for the remnant of his people, which shall be left, from Assyria; *like as it was to Israel in the day that he came up out of the land of Egypt*" (Isaiah 11:11,12,15,16). I quote this passage here by way of a hint to the reader that if he would understand how Jehovah will arbitrate between Israel and the existing nations when He grafts them in again, he must give himself to know the particulars of their deliverance under Moses: for the exodus under him is the type, or representation, of their future exodus under the Lord of Hosts.

But, spiritually dark as were the Egyptians with all their wisdom, the Israelites could boast of little more light than they. The relative condition of these two people was very similar to what it is now in regard to the Jews and papal nations among whom they are scattered. The Jews have a vague idea of the promise made to Abraham, and, therefore, cherish the hope of restoration to Canaan; but of the name of God they are as ignorant as the generation to whom Moses was sent. "Who is Yahweh" said Pharoah, "that I should let Israel go? I know not who the LORD God of Israel is." This is the predicament of existing nations. They are called by the name of Christ, but as to God's character, they are as ignorant of it as of His person. As to Israel of "the fourth generation", we have seen that "they understood not" when Moses supposed they would have recognized in him their deliverer; and, when God was about to send him for that very purpose forty years after, Moses inquired what he should say unto them when the elders of Israel should say to him, *"What is his name?"*—the name of Him Whom he styled "the God of their fathers" (Exodus 3:13,16). Thus, without understanding of the promises, ignorant of the God of Abraham, Isaac, and Jacob, and serving the gods of Egypt, they differed only from the Egyptians in being the oppressed instead of the oppressor, and "beloved for the fathers' sake"—a type of their present condition, preparatory to their everlasting emancipation from the tyranny of nations as ignorant as, but more brutal than, themselves.

Such was the benighted condition into which God's people Israel had fallen "when *the time* of the promises (the end of the four hundred years) drew nigh, which God had sworn to Abraham". But though Israel had forgotten them, God had not. They were overwhelmed and absorbed in their personal sufferings which elicited a cry of great distress. This was the crisis of their fate. "Their cry came up to God by reason of the bondage. And God heard their groaning, and *God remembered his covenant with Abraham, with Isaac, and with Jacob. And God looked upon the children of Israel, and had respect unto them.*"

He sent an angel to deliver them. Moses was tending the flock of Jethro, his father-in-law, in the vicinity of Horeb. Seeing a bush on fire yet not consumed, he drew near to take a closer view of it. As he approached, the angel addressed him in behalf of the Lord, saying, "I am the God of thy fathers, the God of Abraham, the God of Isaac, and the God of Jacob. I have surely seen the affliction of my people who are in Egypt, and have heard their cry by reason of their taskmasters; for I know their sorrow and I am come down to deliver them out of the hand of the Egyptians, and to bring them up out of that land unto a good land and a large, unto a land flowing with milk and honey; unto the place of the Canaanites, etc. Come, now, therefore, and I will send thee unto Pharaoh, that thou mayest bring forth my people, the children of Israel, out of Egypt" (Exodus 3:2,6-10). Thus Moses, whom forty years before "they refused, saying, Who made thee a ruler and a judge? the same did God send to be a ruler and a deliverer by the hand of the angel who appeared to him in the bush" (Acts 7:35).

Moses being thus called of God, was first sent to the elders of Israel to make proclamation to them of the good news of deliverance from Egypt, and of national independence in the land promised to their fathers. Moses was not only called and sent, but he was also equipped for the work; and prepared to prove that he was Jehovah's ambassador to them and Pharaoh. The Lord knew how incredulous they would reasonably be of the validity of Moses' pretensions to the high office of His plenipotentiary. They had refused Moses forty years before when he was in favour at the court of Egypt; it was not likely, therefore, that they would accept him as a returned exile. Hence, something more was wanting than Moses' bare assertion that he was the ambassador of God. He was, therefore, endued with divine power by the exercise of which his claim to their acceptance might be attested. His staff could be turned into a serpent; his hand could become leprous as snow by putting it into his bosom; and water of the Nile spilled upon the ground converted into blood. By these three signs given him to perform as his credentials, he was assured by the Lord they would recognize him. He was to execute them in their presence "that they might believe that the LORD God of their fathers, the God of Abraham, the God of Isaac, and the God of Jacob, *had appeared unto him*. And I will be with thy mouth", said God, "and teach thee what thou shalt say." "I have made thee a god to Pharaoh, and Aaron thy brother shall be thy prophet" (Exodus 7:1).

Having received his appointment after this manner, he was commanded to go and introduce himself to the elders of Israel in his new capacity. He was ordered to say to them, "The LORD God of your fathers, the God of Abraham, the God of Isaac, and the God of Jacob, *hath sent me unto you*: this is my name *for ever*, and this is my *memorial* unto all generations. This, the LORD God, hath appeared unto me, saying, I have surely visited you, and seen that which is done to you in Egypt; and I have said, I will bring you up out of the affliction in Egypt (Genesis 15:13,14,16) into the land of the Canaanites, etc.; into a land flowing with milk and honey" (Exodus 3:15-17).

In obedience to the voice of God, Moses presented himself before the elders of Israel, accompanied by his prophet. He announced himself as the messenger of God, and laid before them his *"memorial unto all generations"*. As I have shown on page 246, this memorial, which is *God's name for ever*, reveals the resurrection of Abraham, Isaac, and Jacob, the last of whom had then been dead two hundred and eight years. This was an important announcement, and amounted to this, *"I, Moses, am sent to you by the God of your fathers, who are to rise again"*. This was a startling declaration for a fugitive from Egyptian vengeance, and a Midianitish shepherd, to make to a whole people. "I am *'called and sent'* of Him, who is the God of the living, and hath appeared unto me, to inform you that He hath come down to deliver you by my hand from your grievous bondage in this country of the Nile."

This was as astounding a pretension as that of the "ministers" and "clergy" of this time, who also claim to be "called of God as Aaron was", and to be sent with the word of the Lord to the people as His ambassadors! The important difference, however, in the case is, that God attested the truth of Moses' pretensions, but does not confirm theirs. Clerical and ministerial ambassadorship rests upon their own word, and is predicated upon a feeling which no one can perceive but themselves. It is assertion without proof; and until they can adduce credentials divinely attested as in all other cases of real appointments in scripture, if they are not set down at once as impostors (which would be quite justifiable after waiting for credentials many centuries), mankind are at all events under no obligation to attend to the word they profess to have received.

When Moses received his commission, he objected to go to Israel, for, said he, "They will not believe me, nor hearken unto my voice: for they will say, The LORD hath not appeared unto thee". It was then the Lord empowered him to work the first sign; and if that did not convince them, then the second; but if still incredulous, afterwards the third; which would be irresistible. Now, when through Aaron he had spoken all the words commanded, "he did the signs in the sight of the people". If they had believed his simple word, the signs would not have been given; but as they were all given, it is evident that they did not believe his bare assertion. When they saw the wonders, however, they came to the conclusion of Nicodemus in relation to "the prophet like unto Moses", that he was a person "sent from God, for no man could do the miracles he did except God were with him" (John 3:2); as it is written, "And he did the signs in the sight of the people, and they believed that the LORD had visited the children of Israel, and that he had looked upon their affliction" (Exodus 4:31).

Being accepted as a ruler and a deliverer, he and his prophet, accompanied by the elders of Israel, presented themselves before Pharaoh. Moses announced himself as the bearer of a message to him from the Lord God of Israel, saying, "Let my people go, that they may hold a feast unto me in the wilderness". This demand astonished Pharaoh exceedingly. "Who", said he, "is the LORD, that I should obey his voice to let Israel go? I know not the LORD, neither will I let Israel go. Wherefore do ye, Moses and Aaron, hinder the people from their works? Get you to your burdens." The only effect of this application was to double their toil, and to cause the officers of Israel to be beaten, because they were not successful in extorting from their brethren what was impossible. They remonstrated with the tyrant, but to no other purpose than to be spurned from his presence as idle fellows. They perceived that they were in an evil and desperate case; and as their condition was worse since Moses came among them, they looked on him as the cause of all the aggravated evil that had befallen them. Moses, indeed, could not deny it. He had nothing to say in extenuation; but in his extremity returned to expostulate with the Lord. "Wherefore, Lord", said he, "hast thou so evil-entreated this people? Why is it that thou hast sent me? For since I came to Pharaoh to speak in thy name, he hath done evil to this people; neither hast thou delivered thy people at all" (Exodus 5:22).

After this manner, being made to feel the need of deliverance, Moses was sent again to them with glad tidings of a sure and speedy redemption. In communicating it to Moses, the Lord prefaced the message with a reiteration of the memorial. "I am the LORD", said He: "and I appeared unto Abraham, unto Isaac, and unto Jacob, by the name of God Almighty, but by my name JEHOVAH (*He who shall be*) (Isaiah 42:8,9) was I not known unto them. And I have also established my covenant with them, *to give them the land of Canaan*, the land of their pilgrimage, wherein they were strangers. And I have also heard the groaning of the children of Israel, whom the Egyptians keep in bondage: *and I have remembered my covenant.*"

Such was the preamble. The God of Abraham was about to *begin* the fulfilment of the covenant in that part of it which related to "the fourth generation" of the natural seed. He was therefore in relation to Israel about to become known as the performer of His word. Abraham, Isaac, and Jacob knew Him as Almighty; but as they had died without receiving the promises covenanted, they knew Him not as Jehovah; yet as Jehovah is now the name of Abraham's God unto all generations, Abraham, Isaac, and Jacob will know Him as set forth in His memorial, when they rise from the dead. He will then be Jehovah to them.

Because, then, after nearly 430 years from its confirmation, God had remembered His covenant, He said to Moses, "Say unto the children of Israel, I am Jehovah, and I will bring you out from under the burdens of the Egyptians, and I will rid you out of their bondage, and I will redeem you with a stretched out arm, and with great judgments; and *I will take you to me for a people*, and I will be to you a God: and ye shall know that I am the LORD your God, who bringeth you out from under the burdens of the Egyptians. And I will bring you unto the land, concerning the which I did swear to give it to Abraham, to Isaac, and to Jacob; and I will give it you for a heritage: I am Jehovah." According to all these words Moses spoke to them, "but they hearkened not to him, for anguish of spirit, and for cruel bondage".

After this the judgments of God fell fast and heavy upon Pharaoh and the Egyptians, until at length they rose and thrust the Israelites out of Egypt. The record of this event is thus given by Moses. "Now the *returning* (*vemuseb*) of the children of Israel who dwelt in Egypt was four hundred and thirty years, even the self-same day it came to pass, that all the hosts of the LORD went out from the land of Egypt. It is a night to be much observed unto the LORD, for bringing them out from the land of Egypt; this is that night of the LORD to be observed of all the children of Israel in their generations" (Exodus 12:40-42). The period here indicated was 430 years from the confirmation of the covenant now remembered of God, which occurred on the 14th of Abib, or Nisan, at even; the month when the Jewish year and calendar begin (Exodus 12:2), answering to the latter half of March and the former part of April.

The terrible display of power by the hand of Moses, while it filled the minds of the Egyptians with dismay, convinced Israel at length that God was able and willing to perform what He had covenanted to do. He had said to Pharaoh, "Israel is my son, even my first-born; therefore, let my son go, that he may serve me; and if thou refuse to let him go, behold, I will slay thy son, even thy first-born" (Exodus 4:22,23). This threat had at length been carried into execution; and: "there was not an house in Egypt where there was not one dead". First-born for first-born. If Pharaoh destroyed God's first-born, God would retaliate upon him, and not spare his. Let the reader mark the style here. "Israel is my son, my first-born." What does this import? Did not God tell Abraham, that He had constituted him a father of many nations? Then these nations are in effect his sons; for a father implies sons. But of this family of nation-sons, which of them is the first-born son? The testimony before us declares that Israel is. The nation of Israel then is the heir, and nearest to the throne in the empire of the world. But it is now, and will be for a few more years, as it was in the days of Pharaoh. Israel, God's first-born, is scattered, oppressed, and destroyed, by the tyrants of the nations, and a subject of reproach among the people. But the sentence of God is still unrepealed; and at a coming crisis, he says to the Autocrat, "Let my son, Israel, go, that he may serve me; and if thou refuse, I will slay thy son, even thy firstborn." When the events in Egypt shall be re-enacted in the latter day, "a nation," even Israel, "shall be born in a day"; and other nations will soon after follow him in a birth into Christ and the political family of Abraham. When this comes to pass, all the nations of the earth will be Abraham's sons, and rejoice in Israel their elder brother.

But, when Israel was brought to the birth, and stood trembling on the shore of the Red Sea, they were about to be introduced into Moses. They had been begotten of God as His national first-born "but were they to be born of water into the everlasting possession of Canaan?; or into a possession in which they were only "strangers and sojourners" in the land? That would depend upon the question of their national baptism into Moses, or into Christ: if into Moses, they could only inherit according to his law; but if into Christ, then they would obtain an everlasting national possession of the land, of which no other nation, or confederacy of nations, could deprive them. But they could not be nationally baptized into Christ, for Christ had not come; and until he came, and as the mediator of the New Covenant, suffered death, neither individual nor nation could have everlasting inheritance in the land; for the covenant was of no force while the mediator was alive.

But there is an end of all question in the case. The apostle, in reference to the passage of the Red Sea, writes, "I would not that ye should be ignorant, how that all our fathers were under the cloud, and all passed through the sea; and were all *baptized* INTO *Moses* (εἰς τὸν Μωσῆν) *in* the cloud and *in* the sea (1 Corinthians 10:1,2) (ἐν τῇ νεφέλῃ and ἐν τῇ θαλάσσῃ)." This was the national baptism: an entire obscuration of a whole nation from the view of all beholders on either shore. It was buried, not in the sea only, but in the cloud *and* in the sea—a cloud, which was black with darkness to the Egyptians, but light to Israel between the icy walls of the sea. But though buried, the nation rose again to a new life upon the opposite shore, leaving all their tyrant taskmasters, and all their bondage behind them, washed away by the returning waters of the deep. First, then, believing in Moses and in the Lord, they were baptized into Moses, and so "saved that day out of the hands of the Egyptians", who were washed up "dead upon the seashore" (Exodus 14:26-31).

In celebration of this great deliverance, they sang the song of Moses. What a thrilling incident was this! Six hundred thousand men, besides women, children, and a mixed multitude, encamped upon the shore, and singing the song of the Lord's victory over their enemies! After magnifying the gloriousness of His power, and the great salvation with which He had delivered them, they rejoiced in the future that awaited their return, when it should realize the possession of the land of Canaan under the sceptre of Shiloh "for ever and ever". "Thou shalt bring them in, and plant them in the mountain of thine inheritance; in the place, O LORD, which thou hast made for thee to dwell in; in the sanctuary, O Lord, which thy hands have established. The LORD shall reign for ever and ever" (Exodus 15:17,18).

Let the reader peruse the song of Moses, and bear in mind that it is not only a magnification of the past, but also prophetic of as great, or greater, a deliverance of the nation under Shiloh. Under Moses, they were saved by the angel of God (Exodus 14:19); but when the time of the second exodus from Egypt arrives, they will be saved by the Lamb of God, whose prowess will be applauded by God's harpists of the crystal sea, who will sing the *new* song of Moses, the servant of God, *and the song of the Lamb*, saying, "Great and marvellous are thy works, Lord God Almighty; just and true are thy ways, thou King of saints. Who shall not fear thee, O Lord, and glorify thy name? for thou only art holy; for *all nations shall come and worship before thee*; for thy judgments are made manifest" (Revelation 14:1-5; 15:2-4). The song of Moses, we have seen, celebrated the overthrow of the

Egyptians; the song of the Lamb, "the prophet like unto Moses", "will celebrate his future triumph over all the nations in his deliverance of the twelve tribes from their tyranny; a redemption which will result in the submission of all nations to his sovereignty, as predicted in the song. And it is to be observed that the Lamb's victory being the accomplishment of the prophecy in Moses' song, and a victory gained on a similar occasion, and in connection with the same nation, the Lamb's song is styled, in the Apocalypse, "the song of Moses *and* the song of the Lamb."

The generations of Israel's nation are reckoned from Abraham. Between seven of them there is a remarkable relationship in the way of type and antitype. These are the fourth, the fifth, and fourteenth, the fifteenth, the thirty-second, the forty-second, and, possibly, the rising generation of the present time. The events of the fourth occurred under Moses; of the fifth, under Joshua; of the fourteenth, under David; of the fifteenth, under Solomon; of the thirty-second, under Zorobabel; of the forty-second, under Christ; and of the last, the substance of all that have preceded it, and as yet in the undeveloped, but not unrevealed, future. The six generations present so many pictures, as it were, of what will be transacted in the seventh. But want of space forbids more than allusion to the fact. Referring to the remarkable incidents of Jewish history, the apostle says, "All these things happened unto them for types (τύποι, *representative things*): and they are written for our instruction upon whom the ends of the ages (τὰ τέλη τῶν αἰώνων) are come."

Having been baptized into Moses, they looked to him for meat and drink. The angel had brought them out by his hand into a waste and howling wilderness, under a promise to give them a land flowing with milk and honey. But after three days the nation found itself without water; and though soon after they found some, it was so bitter they could not drink it. And they murmured against Moses. The Lord heard them, and healed the waters. A month after their departure from Egypt their provision failed them. Again they murmured against Moses and his prophet; and turned back in their hearts to the land of their affliction. But God heard them, and gave them bread and meat to the full, and continued to them this sustenance for forty years, until they came to the borders of the land of Canaan.

One would have supposed that having been given bread from heaven all their murmurings would have ceased. But when they came to Rephidim and found no water, they murmured again, and were ready to stone Moses, and tempted God, saying, "Is the LORD among us, or not?" Though the manna still fell, the rebellious-hearted Israelites questioned the presence of the Lord among them! Though tempted, He still bore with them. He commanded Moses to go to the rock in Horeb, on the top of which He would take his stand. He was then to *smite* it before their eyes that it might give forth water. And Moses did so; and the place was called Massah, and Meribah (Temptation, and Strife)— Exodus 17. On a later occasion, at Kadesh (Numbers 20), God commanded Moses to speak to the rock. But, having convened the assembly, he addressed them, saying, "Hear now, ye rebels; must *we* fetch you water out of this rock? And he *smote* the rock *twice*; and the water came out abundantly, and they drank" (Exodus 17:6; Numbers 20:10,12,24). In this Moses exceeded his commission; therefore the Lord said, "Because ye believed me not, to sanctify me in the eyes of the children of Israel, therefore ye shall not bring this congregation into the land which I have given them".

These incidents had a secondary import which is found in the antitypes of the forty-second generation. Thousands of Israelites and Gentiles believed the gospel of the Kingdom, and were baptized into Christ. As a whole they constituted "a holy nation"—a nation within the nation—which fed upon the true bread of heaven, and drank of the water of life by faith in the things of Christ. But they were, and are, still strangers and sojourners in the world, which to them is like the wilderness of Arabia to Israel of the fourth generation. But there have been multitudes in Christ, as there were in Moses, who did run well but were afterwards hindered. They turned back in their hearts to Egypt, loving the present world, and not having faith enough to get the mastery over it. Now, the apostle likens such to those of the fourth generation who were murmurers, and faithless, and whose carcases fell in the wilderness, from which they will never arise to enter the land of Israel under Shiloh. "They did all eat the same spiritual meat", says he; "and did all drink the same spiritual drink; for they drank of that spiritual rock that followed them: and that rock was (or represented) Christ. But with many of them God was not well-pleased; for they were overthrown in the wilderness. Now these things were our examples, to the intent we should not lust after evil things, as they also lusted" (1 Corinthians 10:3-6). Their faith was addressed through sensible objects; ours through written testimony. But for the most part professors look not beyond "the things which are seen and temporal". Whether in Moses, or *professedly* in Christ, they are mere creatures of sensation, who walk by sight and not by faith. Let us, reader, not be of this number; but let us rejoice in hope of the promise made to the fathers, though at present it seemeth not to the eye of sense to grow. "If a man eat of this bread (the spiritual) he shall live for ever" and, drinking of the blood of Christ, which is the spiritual drink represented by Horeb's stream, the rock of Israel will raise him up at the last day to life in the age to come. But if, after their example, we love the present world, though we may have believed and obeyed the truth in the beginning, we shall come under the sentence of exclusion from "the rest which remains for the people of God".

THE LORD'S PASSOVER

ON the tenth day of Abib, the first month of the year, being 430 from the confirmation of the covenant, the Israelites were commanded to put up a lamb for each house, and to kill it upon the fourteenth day in the evening. They were to take its blood and to sprinkle it upon the door-posts of their houses, and to eat its flesh that same night, roast with fire, with unleavened bread, and bitter herbs. Nothing of it was to be left till morning. They were also to eat it in haste, as if about to hurry off upon a journey. The meaning of this was, that God was about to destroy the first-born of every family in Egypt, which would cause them to be thrust out of Egypt with great haste; and that when the destroying angel should see the blood on the door-posts, he would pass over that house, and not destroy the first-born there. For this cause the lamb was termed the Lord's Passover (Exodus 12). Not a bone of it was to be broken. No stranger, foreigner, hired person, or uncircumcised individual, was to eat of it; a servant, however, bought with the money of an Israelite, provided he were circumcised, was permitted to partake of it.

But this institution represented more than the facts upon which it was founded. It pointed to events which would be connected with later generations of Israel. The apostle styles Christ the believers' passover, who was sacrificed for them (1 Corinthians 5:7); and exhorts them to "keep the feast with the unleavened bread of sincerity and truth". Jesus was the Lamb of the feast whom God had provided. Not a bone of him was broken. His blood was sprinkled, not upon the door-posts of houses, but upon the doors of believers' hearts by faith in the blood of sprinkling. None can eat his flesh, if they would, but those who are circumcised in heart; for *to eat his flesh is to digest, and be a part of our mental selves, the truth concerning the kingdom of God and Jesus Christ*. This is the spiritual food upon which the believer's spiritual existence is sustained. As Jehovah's first-born son was saved by the blood of the Passover lamb in Egypt; so also is the believer in the kingdom saved by the blood of Christ so that when the day of retribution comes, and the first-born of all the nations, "who know not God, and obey not the gospel", are destroyed, the angel of death will *pass over* him, and he shall not be harmed.

But while the passover has this spiritual signification, it also represents facts, or events, which will be made manifest in connection with Israel at the appearing of their king in glory. This is evident, from the saying of Christ while partaking of the Passover with his apostles, the future sovereigns of the tribes. "With desire", said he, "I have desired to eat this Passover with you before I suffer: for I say unto you, I will not any more eat thereof, *until it be fulfilled in the kingdom of God*"; and "I will not drink of the fruit of the vine, *until the kingdom of God shall come*". And, of this kingdom, he said, "I appoint unto you a kingdom, as my Father hath appointed unto me; *that ye may eat and drink at my table in my kingdom, and sit on thrones judging the twelve tribes of Israel*" (Luke 22:15,16,18,29,30; Matthew 19:28). From this, then, it is clear that the passover was prophetic of what is to be fulfilled in the kingdom of God. Has that kingdom come? If it has, as some very erroneously affirm, then Christ has eaten another passover, and has again drunk of wine with his apostles; for he said he would do so when the kingdom had come. But no man in his senses will affirm this. Another passover could not be celebrated till a year after; so that Jesus could not eat it with his disciples before that. Where is the testimony to his eating it with them then? There is none; but much of a contrary nature every way. The gracious declaration of Jesus is, *I will eat of this passover, and drink of the fruit of the vine, with you in the Kingdom of God when it shall be come.* He did not say, *when you shall go to the kingdom beyond the skies*, but when the kingdom shall come, which he had taught them to pray for.

It is perfectly ridiculous to talk about the kingdom having come, and of the apostles being on their thrones. To affirm this proves that the professor is totally ignorant of the gospel. A pretty sitting upon thrones it was, when they were all arraigned at the bar, condemned, imprisoned, and scourged, for preaching the gospel of the kingdom in the name of Jesus! What havoc the apostasy has made with the truth! The gospel preached no such stuff as this. It treats of a kingdom which the God of heaven shall set up in Judea: which shall never be removed from thence; in which the whole twelve tribes shall rejoice; which the saints of all ages shall possess; and which shall rule over all. Its elements at present are all scattered. It is not a matter of fact; but a thing of hope; in which only they rejoice who believe the promises made of God to the fathers.

The passover must be restored before it can be eaten of by Christ and his apostles in the kingdom of God. This is one of the things to be re-established at "the restitution of all things"; and the law of its restoration is in the following words: "In the first month, in the fourteenth day of the month, ye shall have the passover, a feast of seven days; unleavened bread shall be eaten. And upon that day shall (Messiah) the Prince prepare for himself and for all the people of the land a bullock for a sin-offering" (Ezekiel 45:21,22). This was spoken by the prophet to Israel of the fourteenth generation, concerning the observance of the passover by Israel of the generation contemporary with the "restoration of the kingdom again to Israel", when it should be constituted under the Prince. Moses' law said all about the observance of the passover before the Prince appeared; but as Moses ceased to be the law-giver when he came, a New Code is revealed through Ezekiel which will become the law of the kingdom under Shiloh. When Ezekiel's passover is observed at Jerusalem, Christ will be there, the apostles also, Abraham, Isaac, and Jacob, and all the prophets, and many from the four winds of heaven,—all of them the first-born redeemed from the earth, saved by the sprinkled blood of the true paschal Lamb of God, and who shall find themselves in Canaan as inheritors of its attributes; celebrating their own redemption, and the overthrow of all their enemies by the Lord Jesus at his revelation in flaming fire, attended by the angels of his power.

The bread and wine of *"the Lord's supper"* are the remains of the passover, which are to be shared by the circumcised of heart and ears, until Christ comes in power and great glory. I am informed by a Jew that when they eat the passover they eat no Lamb, but have a dry bone of one on a dish; and that all who celebrate take hold of the lip of the dish, and unitedly offer a petition. This is remarkable. They have slain the true Lamb, which believers of the gospel feed upon: while only a dry bone remains to them, strikingly illustrative of themselves. Faith in the Lamb of God supplies the absence of the lamb in the Lord's Supper. The broken bread and poured-out wine memorialize his sacrifice for believers; and the testimony, "This do in remembrance of me *until I come*", keeps alive the hope of his appearing in the kingdom of God. When hope becomes a reality, the supper will give place to the passover; for when Christ *is come*, the memorial of his coming ceases to be prophetic of the event.

THE TWELVE TRIBES CONSTITUTED THE KINGDOM OF GOD

THE Israelites being born into national existence under Moses as a ruler and a deliverer, he led them from the Red Sea to the foot of Mount Sinai to meet with God. On their arrival there, the

Lord commanded Moses to say to them, "Ye have seen what I did to the Egyptians; now, therefore, *if ye will obey my voice* indeed, *and keep my covenant,* then ye shall be a peculiar treasure unto me above all people: for all the earth is mine: and ye shall be UNTO ME *a kingdom of priests and a holy nation"* (Exodus 19:3-6). This was an offer on the part of God to become their King, predicated upon what He had done for them. If they closed with the proposal, they would henceforth be a kingdom. Hitherto they had been a crowd of slaves subject to the will of the kings of Egypt. But He proposed to organize them; to give them a constitution, religion, and laws; to appoint them a government; to exalt them by His instructions, to the freedom, independence, and moral excellence, which are attainable only by the influence of divine truth; to make them the envy and admiration of surrounding nations; to make them, in short, His kingdom, and His beloved nation. This was a proposal rich with blessings. All God would require of them was *obedience,* and *adhesion to the covenant* He had made with their fathers. The terms of the compact were highly eligible. No nation had received such a liberal and honourable proposal before, or since. Would they accept it, and abide by it? Moses was sent to see.

Having arrived at the encampment, he convened the elders of the people, and laid the proposition before them. Having consulted the nation, they returned answer to Moses, saying, "All that the LORD hath spoken we will do". Upon this, Moses returned the words of the people to the Lord. In this transaction a formal agreement was entered into between Israel and the Lord. In the word they sent back by Moses, they accepted the Lord as their King, and became His subjects, or "the children of His kingdom". The relation of God to the tribes as their king is undoubted; for when they demanded a visible king like other nations, the Lord told Samuel that they had not rejected him, but the Lord Himself, whose representative among them he was.

By this political compact, Abraham's natural seed became "THE KINGDOM OF GOD". It was the first, and the only kingdom, He has ever had among the sons of men. He will yet have other kingdoms. All the kingdoms of the world will become His; and will yet acknowledge the King He has provided to rule over them (Revelation 11:15). But even then, the kingdom founded at the beginning of the ages, the Kingdom of Israel, will be His "peculiar treasure above them all". If, then, we would understand "the things of the kingdom of God," we must never lose sight of Israel in connection with the kingdom. Indeed, without them there is no kingdom of God; and to affirm the contrary is to believe in a kingdom of which there is no nation to rule! No misconduct of Israel can dissolve the covenant entered into between them and

God. The rebellion of a nation does not do away with the rights of the king. If they set His laws and government at defiance it becomes a question of might. If the rebellion triumph the king is dethroned; but if the rights of the throne prevail, the rebel nation has no alternative but to submit to whatever terms the conqueror may prescribe.

This is precisely the state of things between God and Israel. The tribes have rebelled against Him. He has anointed Jesus of Nazareth to be King of the Jews. But they say, no good thing ever came out of Nazareth, and they will not have him for their king. They have no other king, they say, but Caesar; hence they crucified Jesus, and have served Caesar ever since. But has God surrendered His rights? Will He allow Himself to be dethroned by rebels, and His Viceroy to be treated as a malefactor? All who deny the restoration of Israel in effect say, "They have rebelled successfully against God and His Christ". But this cannot be. God will restore them "for His name's sake". He will plant them in Canaan; settle them in the land according to their old estates; and place Jesus upon David's throne in triumph: for He has sworn that "at the name of Jesus every knee shall bow, and every tongue confess that he is Lord, to the glory of God the Father" (Philippians 2:9-11). The great rebellion will then be suppressed; God will have recovered His rights; His kingdom will be re-established; and Israel will thenceforth "obey His voice, and keep His covenant", as they originally agreed to do.

The nation being adopted as the kingdom of God, and having received its constitution three days afterwards, which was fifty days from its redemption as Jehovah's first-born of nations; and also having received its religion and civil laws, as related in Exodus and Leviticus—all things were prepared for transferring the tribes from the wilderness to the land of Canaan. Moses had announced this consummation to them while groaning in Egypt. But they hearkened not for anguish of spirit. When, however, they were "baptized into Moses in the cloud and in the sea", they came to believe on the Lord, and in him as His servant. But their probation in the wilderness was too much for their faith. They were continually turning back in their hearts to Egypt. The time, however, had now arrived to put this fourth generation to a final test.

Twelve principal men, one for each tribe, were sent from the wilderness in Paran to view the land of Canaan, and to bring back a report to the people. After an absence of forty days they returned. They said the land was all that could be desired, and flowing, indeed, with milk and honey; but as to being able to take possession of the country, that was impossible; for the inhabitants were gigantic and strong, living in well-fortified cities, and could not be overcome by Israel, who were but as grasshoppers when compared to them. But Caleb and Joshua, who believed on God, testified to the contrary; and encouraged the people to go up at once, and possess it; for they were well able to overcome it. "The land", said they, "which we passed through to search it, is an exceeding good land. If the LORD delight in us, then he will bring us into this land, and give it us; a land which floweth with milk and honey. Only rebel not ye against the LORD, neither fear ye the people of the land; for they are bread for us; their defence is departed from them, and the LORD is with us: fear them not" (Numbers 14:7-10).

Now, when all the people heard the evil report, they cried and wept all night. They murmured against Moses, and wished they had died in Egypt, or in the wilderness, before they had been brought into this extremity. They proposed, at length, to make a captain, and march back into Egypt. As for Caleb and Joshua, they bade stone them to death.

The reader's attention is particularly requested to this passage of Jewish history. The apostle in commenting upon these incidents, says that *the gospel was preached to them on this occasion*; and that the land spied out was connected with God's rest. His words are these — "They could not enter into his rest because of unbelief": then addressing his brethren, he says, "Let us therefore fear, lest a promise being left of entering into his rest, any of you should seem to come short of it. For unto us was the gospel preached *as well as unto them*; but the word preached did not profit them, not being mixed with faith in them that heard it" (Hebrews 3:18,19; 4:1,2). In the context of this passage the apostle had been speaking of Moses and Christ, the former, as a faithful servant in another's house; and the latter as a son over his house: whose house the believers in the things spoken of the land are, *"if* they hold fast the confidence and rejoicing of *the hope* firm unto the end". He then introduces the case of the fourth generation as a warning of the fatal consequences of letting go *the hope of the promise*. He quotes from a scripture written in the fourteenth generation, in which the Holy Spirit repeats the sentence upon them, and upon all like them, who harden their hearts, saying, *"they shall not enter into my rest"* (Psalm 95:7-11). What rest is here spoken of? The peaceable possession and enjoyment of the land so highly commended by Caleb. They did not enter in, but were turned back towards the Red Sea, and wandered in the wilderness for forty years, until the carcases of all the rebels above twenty years old fell to their lowest estate. But did not the fifth generation obtain the rest under Joshua when they possessed the land? No, says the apostle, they did not; "for if Joshua had given them rest, then would

God not have spoken afterward by David of another day". The rest which Joshua gave the nation was only transitory. When he and his associates of the fifth generation died, the nations which God had not driven out were as thorns in their sides, which gave them but little rest in after years. "There *remaineth* then", saith he, "a rest for the people of God"; even Canaan in the age to come, under Shiloh, the Prince of Peace, whose "rest shall be glorious" (Psalm 132:11-18), and undisturbed by war's alarms.

Now this rest under Shiloh was preached unto them. The possession under Joshua was the first step to full accomplishment of the covenant. Had the nation continued to obey the Lord's voice and to keep the covenant, and, when Christ came, received him as king on the proclamation of the gospel, they would doubtless have been in Canaan until now; and he might have come ere this, and be now reigning in Jerusalem, King of the Jews and Lord of the nations. But had this been the case we Gentiles would have had no part in the kingdom. We might attain to eternal life at the end of the reign; but in the glory of the kingdom, and in the administration of its affairs, as heirs of the world with Abraham and his seed, we should have had no part; for it was the unbelief of the forty-second generation of Israel that became the riches of the Gentiles.

The fourth generation "could not enter in because of unbelief". Neither can we unless we also believe *what they rejected*; for the same gospel that was preached to them, was preached by the apostles to the forty-second generation, but cannot be said to be preached to us of this century. I am endeavouring, however, to set it before the people in this book; although I feel it a difficult work, seeing that men's minds are so mystified, and preoccupied with the jargon of the schools. God's rest in Canaan—by which is not meant that all his saints will be living there, though all that abide there will be a righteous people: the things which belong to Canaan will overspread the world; and where there are nations to be governed, there will there be saints to rule—but this rest, I say, is the great theme of the gospel, whether preached by Moses, by Jesus, or by the apostles. The rest and the kingdom are but different terms, though substantially the same. They will both be of Canaan, and are both the subject of the promise made of God to Abraham and his seed for ever.

THE ROYAL HOUSE OF THE KINGDOM

THE covenant made with Abraham promised an immortal inheritor of Canaan; and in Jacob's last prophecy it was plainly revealed that he should be its King, and should descend from

Judah. By this it was understood that Judah would be the royal tribe: but it was not known what family of Judah he would be born of. This was a matter which remained in abeyance until the fourteenth generation. The nation had been long settled in Canaan. For four hundred and fifty years the laws of the kingdom had been administered by judges, until at length the people demanded a king who should go in and out before them, as among the neighbour nations. This happened in the days of Samuel the prophet, who laid their request before the Lord. Though He was displeased at the demand, as it was in effect a rejection of Him, He nevertheless granted their request, and gave them Saul, of the tribe of Benjamin, until another man upon whom He had set His heart should have been sufficiently trained in the school of adversity to take his place. This was David, the son of Jesse, and of the tribe of Judah. God ordered Samuel to anoint him king over Israel. By this act, David became the Lord's anointed, or Christ; and when he ascended the throne, ruled the nation as Jehovah's king.

In the former part of his reign he was much engaged in war, which was at length terminated by the Lord giving him rest from all his enemies. At this crisis of his history, it came into his heart to build a magnificent temple for the ark and cherubim of glory. Though the Lord highly approved of the feeling which prompted the resolution, He forbade his carrying it into effect. The work was too momentous to be undertaken by one in David's case. Jehovah being the real king of Israel, did not permit a national temple to be erected in His kingdom by a subordinate ruler without His primary direction. David had shed much blood, which was urged as an objection to his doing more than collecting the materials which his son should put together after his decease.

At this time the word of the Lord came to Nathan, saying, "Go and tell David my servant, Thus saith the LORD, Thou shalt not build me a house to dwell in. But the LORD telleth thee that *he will make thee a house*". What follows is an explanation of what is meant by this. "And when thy days be fulfilled, and thou shalt sleep with thy fathers, I will set up thy seed after thee, which shall proceed out of thy bowels, and *I will establish his kingdom*. He shall build a house for my name, and I will establish the throne of his kingdom *for ever*. I WILL BE HIS FATHER, AND HE SHALL BE MY SON. Even in suffering for iniquity I will chasten him with the rod of men, and with the stripes due to the children of Adam. But my mercy shall not depart away from him as I took it from Saul, whom I put away before thee. *And thy house and thy kingdom shall be established for ever* BEFORE THEE: thy throne shall be established for ever" (2 Samuel 7:11-16).

These promises are styled *"an everlasting covenant, even the sure mercies of David"* (Isaiah 55:3; Acts 13:34). There can be no doubt to whom they refer, for the apostle has applied them to Christ (Hebrews 1:5). In his last words, David thus expresses himself concerning them: "The God of Israel spake to me, saying, He that ruleth over men must be just, ruling in the fear of God. And he (the just One) shall be as the light of the morning when the sun riseth, even a morning without clouds; as the tender grass springing out of the earth by clear shining after rain. Although my house be not so with God: yet he hath made with me an everlasting covenant, ordered in all things and sure: for this is all my salvation and all my desire, although he make it not to grow" (2 Samuel 23:3-5).

This covenant of the throne and kingdom was David's desire and salvation, because it promised him a resurrection to eternal life, in the assurance that his house, kingdom, and throne, with God's son and his son, one person, sitting upon it, should be established in his presence for ever. "I have made a covenant with my chosen, I have sworn unto David my servant, saying, Thy seed will I establish for ever, and build up thy throne to all generations. He shall cry unto me, Thou art my Father, my God, and the Rock of my salvation. Also I will make him my first-born, higher than the kings of the earth. My covenant will I not break, nor alter the thing which has gone out of my lips. Once have I sworn by my holiness that I will not lie unto David. His seed shall endure for ever, and his throne as the sun before me. It shall be established for ever as the moon, and as a faithful witness in heaven" (Psalm 89:3,4,19-28,34-37).

After these testimonies there requires no further proof that David's family was constituted by a solemn covenant the Royal House of God's kingdom; and that that one of David's posterity whom God should acknowledge to be His son, should be its everlasting king. The claims of Jesus to be David's seed and God's Son have been fully established by his resurrection from the dead; which is an assurance to all men, both Jews and Gentiles, that God hath appointed him as the Holy One of Israel their king; to rule the world in righteousness, and to establish truth and equity among the nations; as God sware to Moses, saying, *"Truly as I live, all the earth shall be filled with the glory of the LORD"*. Let us then proceed now to some further inquiries about

THE KINGDOM AND THRONE OF DAVID

THERE are, as we have seen, *two everlasting covenants of promise* upon which the kingdom of God is based—the one made with Abraham, and the other with David. The former gives the land of Canaan to their Seed for ever; the latter, the kingdom and throne established upon it, as long as the moon endures. They are called David's because his family alone can possess the kingdom. David's kingdom, however, is also *"the kingdom of God and of his Anointed"*, or Christ; for, whether David, or David's Son of the twenty-eighth generation after him, sit upon the throne, they are both the Lord's Anointed, and ruling as His representatives in His kingdom. The great difference between the two in regard to the anointing is, that David the First was anointed with holy material oil by the hand of Samuel; whereas Jesus was anointed with the Holy Spirit, at his emergence from the Jordan, direct from the excellent glory. Hence, Jesus, who is David the Second as well as the second Adam, is Jehovah's Christ, or Anointed King, in a higher sense than "his father David." The Lord Christ and king David are associated in several prophecies, because the everlasting covenant of promise made with the latter declares its mercies to them both, at one and the same time. David is to witness the fulfilment of its promises; for the record is, "Thy house and thy kingdom shall be established *for ever*". But when? "BEFORE THEE." From this it is evident, the everlasting establishment of his kingdom cannot take place under the circumstances which have obtained since the death of David until this present time; because, if it is to exist perpetually *"before"*, or in the presence of, David, David must be raised to life for immortality; for, if mortal, he could not behold his throne occupied by Christ for ever. But "David is both dead and buried, and his sepulchre", said Peter, "is with us until this day"—"He is not ascended into the heavens" (Acts 2:29,34). If, then, he *"is dead"*, and not "gone to heaven", as the phrase is, he is alive in no sense; and consequently the covenant promises are not fulfilled. David must be alive when they are accomplished. Christ, his divine son, has been manifested and glorified, and God has recognized him as His Son; but in no other particular has the covenant been fulfilled: for he has inherited neither the land of Canaan, nor the kingdom and throne of David once upon it.

But where are the kingdom and throne of David? "In heaven, beyond the skies, where Christ is at the right hand of God, and where precious souls go when they die." Such is the answer given by Gentile theology! Need we wonder at Jews having such a contempt for what is called "Christianity", when they hear its professors gravely affirm such absurd nonsense as this? Have Canaan, Jerusalem, and the twelve tribes been translated beyond the skies? Oh no, say they, these things remain, but then they are types of things which exist where Jesus is! Alas, what sorry stuff, what shilly-shally twaddle is this, to come out of the mouths of "great and good and pious men". It is admitted that David's and Solomon's reigns were typical, or representative, of Christ's reign; not beyond the skies, however; but upon their throne and in their kingdom upon the veritable land promised to Abraham. But, inquires one, if not beyond the skies, where are the kingdom and throne of David? In answer to this question, reader, mark it well—*at present they exist nowhere*. They once existed, and while they had a being they were the kingdom and throne of God among men. He has kingdoms and thrones in other orbs; but we have nothing to do with them, and have no more right, had we the power, to go and take possession of them either as "souls", or bodies, than the angels have to come and seize upon all the thrones and kingdoms of earth, which belong to Christ and his brethren by inheritance. But let us leave to the owls and bats the idols of the schools, the worshipful phantasmata of the apostasy, and let us turn to the enlightening testimony of God.

The scripture, foreseeing that God would temporarily abolish the kingdom of David, saith in view of the covenant, "But thou hast cast off and abhorred, thou hast been wroth with thine anointed. Thou hast *made void the covenant* of thy servant: thou hast *profaned his crown* by casting it to the ground. Thou hast broken down all his hedges; thou hast brought his strongholds to ruin. All that pass by the way spoil him; he is a reproach to his neighbours. Thou hast made his glory to cease, and *cast his throne down to the ground*. The days of his youth hast thou shortened: thou hast covered him with shame" (Psalm 89:38-45). This is descriptive of the state of the kingdom of God and of David for twenty-five centuries past. The crown and throne are in the dust, and the territory and people a by-word among the nations. Instead of the covenant being fulfilled, if the present state of things were final, it would be "*void*", and the promise of God have failed. In view, then, of the promises and things as they are, the scripture inquires, "*How long*, Lord? Wilt thou hide thyself for ever? Lord, where are thy former loving-kindnesses, which thou swearest unto David in thy truth?" (verses 46-49). Yes: where are they? *In promise still.*

In the face of facts, what are we to say to the testimony, that "*David shall never want a man to sit on the throne of the House of Israel*"? Thus saith the Lord, "If ye can break my covenant of the day, that there should not be day in its season; then may also my covenant be broken with David, my servant, that he should not have a son to reign upon his throne" (Jeremiah 33:17,20,21). What shall we say to this? There has been no son of David reigning upon his throne since the dethronement of Zedekiah by Nebuchadnezzar five hundred and ninety-five years before the birth of Christ. But it is not a question of *uninterrupted succession*; but of the everlasting occupation of the throne according to the covenant. When the time comes for this to be fulfilled, noted by David's resurrection, from thenceforth shall his son fill the throne of Israel's kingdom for ever. But what saith the scripture?

Just before the fall of Jerusalem by the Chaldeans, the sins of Judah and its king had attained the full. Zedekiah was then on the throne wearing the crown of David. Ezekiel was commanded to say to him, "Thou profane wicked prince of Israel, whose day is come, when iniquity shall have an end, thus saith the Lord GOD, Remove the diadem, and take off the crown: this (Zedekiah) shall not be the same (son of David spoken of in the covenant): exalt him that is low (even Jesus), and abase him that is high"— that is, dethrone Zedekiah. But then, what is to become of the kingdom of David? Hear the Lord by His prophet—"I will overturn, overturn, overturn, it: and *it shall be no more* UNTIL *he* (Shiloh) *shall come whose right it is*: and I will give it him" (Ezekiel 21:25-27). According to this word so has it been to the letter. The king's eyes were put out; Zion was ploughed as a field; and not a tribe remained in the land. After seventy years' captivity, there was a restoration under Ezra, Zerubbabel, Joshua, and Nehemiah. But until BC 165, the Israelites in Canaan were not even a kingdom, but a subject province of the Persian monarchy, and afterwards of the Macedonian. About the year named they became a kingdom again, but not David's. The throne was that of the Asmoneans, who were of the tribe of Levi. Their dynasty was superseded by the Roman senate, which set up Herod's family instead. He was an Idumean, and reigned till after the birth of Jesus, whom he sought to put to death. He was succeeded by Archelaus, who was deposed by the Romans, and Judea reduced into the form of a province under a procurator; thus verifying, as is supposed, that the sceptre should depart from Judah when Shiloh came: and so it came to be when God called His Son Jesus out of Egypt. From that time to this, there has been no kingdom, or throne of Israel, in Canaan. The Hebrew commonwealth was broken up by the Romans about thirty years or so after the crucifixion; and it has been, and will be, no more, until the Lord Jesus come, who is the King of the Jews, and whose sole right it is to reign.

In reference to this good time which is near at hand, it is written, "Behold the days come, saith the LORD, that I will perform that good thing which I have promised to the house of Israel, and to the house of Judah. In those days, and at that time, will I cause the Branch of Righteousness to grow up unto David; *and he shall execute judgment and righteousness in the land.* In those days shall Judah be saved, and *Jerusalem shall dwell safety*; and this is the name whereby he shall be called, The LORD our Righteousness" (Jeremiah 23:5,6; 33:14-16; Ezekiel 48:35; Isaiah 24:23).

The Kingdom of God, then, has existed once, but, for the present, exists "*no more*". It existed from the fourth to the twenty-eighth generation, a period of rather more than a thousand years; but it has been extinct upwards of two thousand five hundred years—a time so long that the promise of its restoration has become a mere fable, or speculation, in the estimation of the world! But the believer in the gospel of this kingdom rejoices in the sure and certain hope of its restitution, and glorious and triumphant existence for a thousand years, at the expiration of which kingdoms on earth will be no more, but God will be all and in all.

The reader, then, will perceive from this exposition that the kingdom of God must be studied in the two periods of its existence—in the thousand years of the past, and in the thousand years of the Age to come. As God's kingdom of the past, it is the grandest theme of ancient or modern history; but as His kingdom of the future, it is the sublime topic of "*the truth as it is in Jesus*". In the past, it existed under the law of Moses, which made nothing perfect. Its kings and priests were frail and mortal men, who held the kingdom for a brief space, and then "*left it to other people*". Its subjects were rebellious, and its realms invaded and wasted by the hands of ruthless and barbarous foes. But how changed will be its fortunes in Messiah's age! The same land and nation will then be under the law of the New Covenant which goes forth from Zion. All things will be perfected. Its king and pontiff will be the King immortal from the right hand of God. The rulers of the tribes will be the fishermen of Galilee, "shining as the stars for ever and ever". The chiefs of its cities, and the possessors of its glory, its honours, and its dominion will be the holy ones of God, "equal to the angels", and subject unto death no more. In short, "the saints of the Most High will take the kingdom, and possess the kingdom for ever, even for ever and ever" (Daniel 7:18; 2:44), never receding from their position, nor leaving it to be possessed by others.

THE THINGS OF THE KINGDOM OF GOD

CHAPTER V

THINGS CONCERNING THE NAME OF
JESUS CHRIST

Israel unable to redeem themselves; and the nations equally powerless to their own regeneration—The reconstruction of the social fabric the work of Omnipotence by the hand of the Lord Jesus at his approaching manifestation—He will re-establish the kingdom and throne of David—The priesthood of Shiloh—The Ezekiel temple to be built by Christ—Of the Name of Jesus—Of repentance, remission of sins, and eternal life—Death-bed and gaol repentance

BY this time, I presume, the reader well understands what the Lord has promised, or covenanted, to do. Let him, then, in view of these "exceeding great and precious promises", take a mental survey of Canaan, of Israel, and of the nations—of Canaan in its desolation, of Israel in their dispersion, and of the nations in the abyss of mortal ignorance, and of dark and cruel superstitions; and prostrate under the iron heel of blood-stained and murderous tyrannies. This is truly a bottomless abyss from which neither Israel nor the Gentiles are able to extricate themselves. The Strength of Israel has hid His face from them; they are therefore powerless among the nations, and can neither "restore all things", nor return to their country. As for the pagan, Papal, Protestant, and Mohammedan peoples, their case is equally desperate with that of the Jews. They groan under the armed oppressor; they sigh after "liberty, fraternity, and equality"; they long for the regeneration of society; but instead of looking to heaven for deliverance, they curse God and despise His laws; and grasping the sword, undertake the amelioration of society by deeds of blood! Mankind have not yet learned that the world's redemption from all its evils is from God; nor are they aware, such is the impenetrability of human ignorance, that they have neither virtue, knowledge, power, nor wisdom, enough to deliver themselves from their miseries, and to reconstitute society to the promotion of their own happiness, and to the glory and honour of the Most High. There is no man, nor any combination of men, under the heavens, that is competent to the work of social regeneration. If individuals be unable to regenerate themselves, which is unquestionable, no association of persons, however multitudinous, can renew the world, and make it what it ought to be. That it needs regeneration is self-evident to all the "sons of light"; and that it cannot of itself compass that necessity is equally apparent to all, save those who are of the night. What, then, is the hope of the believer in the world's extremity? Let the "testimony of God" be our oracle; and let Him reveal to us the help He has provided, the deliverance in reserve.

In the testimony a voice is heard addressing the nations in these words, saying, "Listen, O isles, unto me; and hearken, ye people, from afar: the LORD hath called me from the womb; *from the bowels of my mother hath he made mention of my name.* He hath made my mouth like a sharp sword; in the shadow of his hand hath he hid me, and made me a polished shaft: and said unto me, Thou art my servant, O Israel, *in whom I will be glorified*". Need the reader be told who this great and mighty one is? Whose name was mentioned by the Lord before his birth? Hear the scriptures—"And Gabriel said to Mary, Behold thou shalt conceive in thy womb, and bring forth a son, and shalt call his name JESUS (*Heb.* Jehoshua, or Jehovah-tzidkenu, the LORD our righteousness), for he shall save his people from their sins. He shall be great, and shall be called the Son of the Highest; and the Lord God shall give unto him *the throne of his father David*: and he shall reign *over the house of Jacob for ever*; and of his kingdom there shall be no end" (Matthew 1:21; Luke 1:31-33).

But he was born, and has departed, and is hid in the shadow of the Lord's hand; and has neither received David's throne, nor does he reign over Israel, who, though yet to be ruled by him, "curse their king and their God, and look upwards" (Isaiah 8:21). We shall see how this is. In the oracle quoted, the Lord Jesus, who makes proclamation to the isles of the Gentiles, announces himself as *the Servant of Jehovah in whom He will be glorified.* Now *a servant* implies *work to be performed* for, and in behalf of, another. What work, or service, then, has the Lord Jesus to execute for the Father? "Behold, the LORD will come with strong hand, and his arm shall rule for him: behold *his reward* is with him, *his work* before him" (Isaiah 40:10). We want to know what this work is. Hear then what the word saith. "The LORD formed me from the womb to be his servant *to bring Jacob again to him.*" But is the restoration of the tribes of Israel all he will have to do? We shall find not; for Jehovah says to him, "It is a light thing that thou shouldest be my servant to raise up the tribes of Jacob, and to restore the desolation of Israel: *I will also give thee for a light to the Gentiles, that thou mayest be my salvation to the ends of the earth*" (Isaiah 49:1-3,5,6,8).

The Lord Jesus, the servant of Jehovah, then, is in reserve at the right hand of the Majesty in the heavens, for the purpose of a future manifestation, not to destroy the earth, and to burn up the wicked, but to fulfill the covenants of promise; in putting an end to the desolation of Canaan, restoring the tribes to their native land, re-establishing the commonwealth of Israel, enlightening the nations, regenerating society, filling the earth with the glory of the Lord, establishing his sovereignty in the world, and in rewarding the saints. All this is to be accomplished when the Lord comes. The God of the fathers will then remember the covenants which He *began* to fulfil when He called Israel out of Egypt under Moses; and when He called Jesus out of Egypt in the days of Archelaus. These were but earnests of the good things to come, in the manifestation of which the promises will be perfected in every jot and tittle of the word.

This is the sense in which James understood the testimony of God. "Simeon", said he, "hath declared how God at the first did visit the Gentiles, *to take out of them a people for his name.*" Then, in quoting the words of Amos, he continues, "*After this I will return*, and will build again the tabernacle of David which is fallen down; and I will build again the ruins thereof, and I will set it up: that the residue of men (Edom) might seek after the Lord, and all *the Gentiles upon whom my name is called*, saith the Lord" (Acts 15:14-17). This was adduced as a quietus upon the Judaizers to prove the acceptance by the Lord of Gentiles as well as of Jews, and upon the same terms. But I have introduced it here to show the arrangement of things in relation to the work to be performed. We see that there is a certain labour to be finished—to wit, the taking out a people from among the nations for the Lord's name. By the time this is accomplished, *the Lord will return*. But what does the text before us say he returns for? *To set up David's kingdom which is in ruins*. But again, what ulterior purpose is to be effected through this restitution? The turning the Gentiles from their delusions, to serve God according to the institutions of the Age to come. *The people for the Lord's name* are the saints or "heirs of the kingdom". Such an institution requires administrators; and as from its nature only righteous and immortal men can inherit it, it became necessary to *call them out*, first from Israel, and then from the nations, upon the principle of *the obedience of faith*. This is one reason why so many ages have elapsed from the *promise of it* to Abraham until now. If it had been possible to set it up in Abraham's time, where would have been the kings and priests to answer its requirements, seeing it is to rule over all nations? It would have been a kingdom without rulers. Hence, the gospel, or glad tidings, concerning it have been preached for the purpose of obtaining kings, priests, and princes of all ranks and degrees, for the kingdom, when the time comes for the God of heaven to establish it by the hand of His servant, the Lord Christ.

333

If Jew or Gentile aspire to this glorious station in the Age to come, *"the prize"* is attainable on the simple condition of believing the things concerning the Kingdom and the name of Jesus Christ, and of being baptized; and thenceforth walking as becomes men who are to be, not only the rulers, but the companions of Christ, and examples of the nations in righteousness, equity, and faith. The time, however, for collecting together *the nobility of the kingdom* is almost elapsed. It has been continuous with the desolation of Jerusalem. She was to be "trodden down of the Gentiles until the times of the Gentiles should be fulfilled" (Luke 21:24). These times are almost accomplished. Only a few more years remain, and then "the accepted time and day of salvation" will have passed. The door into the kingdom will be shut, and no more can obtain a right to enter it. Men who may survive the worse than Egyptian plagues coming upon them, may live in the future age in hope of immortality when the age has passed away; but in the glory and honour of Shiloh's "everlasting dominion", they will have neither part nor lot.

THE PRIESTHOOD OF SHILOH

IN the everlasting covenant made with David, the son promised him, who is to sit upon his throne and to wear his crown for ever, is also set forth as a sacrificial victim; as it is written, "In suffering for iniquity I will chasten him with the rod of men, and with the stripes due to the children of Adam". So the passage is rendered by Adam Clarke. It is in strict accordance with the truth in the case; and in agreement with the testimony, which says, "He hath borne our griefs, and carried our sorrows; yet we did esteem him stricken, smitten of God, and afflicted. But he was wounded for our transgressions, he was bruised for our iniquities; the chastisement of our peace was upon him; and with his stripes we are healed" (Isaiah 53:4,5).

But, being a sacrifice for sin, who should be the priest in the case, and enter into the Most Holy with his blood to make atonement, or reconciliation, for his people? Where there is a sacrifice there is also of necessity a priest. There were priests under the law of Moses, who went into the Most Holy with the blood of the slain beasts, and sprinkled it upon the lid of the ark called the propitiatory, or mercy-seat, upon which the cherubic faces looked. But the blood of David's Son was not to be sprinkled there. It was not to be carried into the Most Holy made with hands, either by himself, or by the high priest of the law: and wherever its memorial was presented, it could only be exhibited by a high priest. The Son of David could not officiate as a priest on earth so long as the covenant from Sinai continued the law of the land; because it permitted only the tribe of Levi to minister in holy things. He belonged to the tribe of Judah, "of which Moses said nothing concerning priesthood". He could not enter into the temple after his resurrection and present himself before the Lord in its most holy place; neither could the Levitical high priest enter heaven with the memorial of Shiloh's death. What, then, was to be done? David's son must appear in heaven in his own person, and as the high priest of a new law offer himself before God.

But the covenant made with David, while it speaks of his son as a sacrifice, and, by implication, of his resurrection, and future occupation of his throne for ever; says nothing about him as high priest of his kingdom. Hence, in order that he might enter his divine Father's presence as a high priest, and hereafter sit as a priest upon the throne of David's kingdom, *"the word of the oath"* (Hebrews 7:28) was given for the purpose. This was necessary; for "no man taketh this honour upon himself, but he that is called of God, as Aaron was". David's son was called to the high priesthood of the kingdom, as distinctly as Aaron was to the same honour under the Mosaic law. "He glorified not himself to be made a high priest; but he that said unto him, Thou art my Son, today have I begotten thee; saith also in another place, Thou art a Priest for ever after the order of Melchizedec" (Hebrews 5:4-6; Psalm 110:4).

Here, then, are *two orders of priesthood*—the Order of Melchizedec, and the Order of Aaron. Melchizedec's was contemporary with Abraham; Aaron's was not instituted until 430 years after the confirmation of the covenant. Of Melchizedec, the apostle could have said much more than he did say; but he has said enough to give us an idea of his order of priesthood. In this he was without predecessor, or successor, without sacerdotal genealogy, and without beginning of official days, or end of life; but, assimilated to the Son of God, abideth a priest continually; of whom also it is testified that he liveth (Hebrews 7:3,8). The Aaronic priesthood was the reverse of all this. Its priests were descended from Aaron, their mothers were of the tribe of Levi, their fathers in office before them, upon which they entered at thirty years, and vacated it at fifty. But the priesthood of Shiloh is not like this. His pedigree is royal, and not sacerdotal. He had no predecessor, nor will he ever vacate the office that another may take his place.

It is probable that Shem was the personage to whom Abraham paid tithes on his return from the slaughter of the kings. Abraham died thirty-five years before Shem reached his five hundred and second year, after the flood. At this date, Isaac was one hundred and ten, and Jacob fifty; so that they were contemporary with Shem for these periods of their lives. There is no account of Shem's death in the scripture; on the contrary, it is testified, as we have seen, that the person called Melchizedec still lives. Now, Melchizedec is a word expressive of the character of the person who bore it. It signifies king of righteousness, or righteous king. He was the greatest king in Canaan, and reigned in Salem, which signifies *peace*, and is afterwards called Jerusalem; so that this righteous king was King of Peace. Shem, king of righteousness, and king of peace, and priest of the Most High God, is the type, contemporary with the holder of the promises, of the Seed, or Christ, on the throne of the Kingdom of God.

The word of the oath, saying, "I have sworn, and will not repent, Thou art a priest for ever after the order of Melchizedec" having changed the priesthood of the kingdom, "there is made of necessity also a change of the law" (Hebrews 7:12) of the State. No revolution was more complete and radical than that necessitated by the substitution of the Melchizedec for the Aaronic priesthood of the commonwealth of Israel. Under the Mosaic code the regal and pontifical offices were divided, and held by two distinct orders of men. The regal was hereditary in the family of David, and the pontifical was hereditary in the family of Aaron; but when the new code shall be promulgated, that, namely, which is to "go forth from Zion" when Christ shall give peace to the world, and judge among the nations, the kingly and priestly offices will be united, and their functions exercised by one person, even Jesus, "who is King of Righteousness and King of Peace, the Priest of the Most High God", as Melchizedec was. Jesus the High Priest will inherit the throne of David by virtue of the covenant made with him. If there had been no other oaths than that with Abraham, and this with David, David's son could not have been a priest upon his throne; but *the word of the oath* coming in, the throne and pontificate of the kingdom become the right of Christ, the Lord.

SHILOH TO BUILD A TEMPLE

IN the everlasting covenant made with David it is declared of his immortal son by the Lord, saying, *"He shall build a house for my name"*. David wished to execute this great national work, but was forbidden. It was afterwards accomplished by Solomon, and in this he eminently typified the "greater than Solomon", who is to construct a similar edifice, only on a vastly more magnificent scale. This will appear from the following testimony. After

Solomon's temple was laid in ruins, and while the Jews, after their return from Babylon, were erecting a new one upon the site of the old, the word of the Lord came to the prophet, saying, "Behold the man whose name is THE BRANCH: and he shall grow up out of his place, and he shall build the temple of the LORD; even *he shall build the temple of the LORD*; and he shall bear the glory, *and shall sit and rule upon his throne; and shall be a priest upon his throne.* And they that are far off shall come and build in the temple of the LORD" (Zechariah 6:12,13,15).

Let the reader turn to the following texts, and he will have no doubt as to the person styled the Branch (Zechariah 3:8; Isaiah 11:1; Jeremiah 23:5; 33:15; Revelation 22:16). The Melchizedec Son of David, then, is to build the Millennial Temple in Jerusalem to the name of Jehovah; and as the Tyrian Gentiles aided Solomon to rear his edifice, so those who are far off from Jerusalem, where the prophecy was delivered, are to co-operate in the erection of Shiloh's, which is to be *"a house of prayer for all people"* (Isaiah 56:7), when the Lord shall "plant the heavens, and lay the foundations of the earth, and say unto Zion, Thou art my people" (Isaiah 51:16). If the reader wish to know more about the temple to be built by Shiloh in Jerusalem, he can consult Ezekiel (40; 41; 42). The description comes in between the battle of Armageddon, in which Nebuchadnezzar's image is broken to pieces on the mountains of Israel, and the earth shining with the glory of the Lord. The first nine verses of the forty-third chapter show that the era of the temple described is when Shiloh "dwells in the midst of the children of Israel for ever, and his holy name they shall defile *no more*". This is conclusive; for ever since their exode from Egypt until the present time, they have incessantly defiled the Lord's name; but the prophecy contemplates a period when they shall do it *"no more"*.

When the Lord Jesus shall sit upon the throne of his father David, as high priest of the nation, and has dedicated the temple to the Most High, what then? "Many people shall go and say, Come ye, and let us go up to the mountain of the LORD, to the house (or temple) of the God of Jacob; and he will teach us of his ways, and *we will walk in his paths"* (Isaiah 2:3). "The sons of the stranger, that join themselves to the LORD, to serve him, and to love the name of the LORD, to be his servants, every one that keepeth the sabbath from polluting it, and taketh hold of my covenant; even them will I bring to my holy mountain, and make them joyful in my house of prayer; their burnt offerings and their sacrifices shall be accepted upon mine altar." And "there shall be no more the Canaanite in the house of the LORD of hosts" (Isaiah 56:3-6; Zechariah 14:16-21).

THE THINGS OF THE KINGDOM OF GOD

THE NAME OF JESUS CHRIST

IF I have been successful in making a distinct impression upon the reader's mind as to the nature of "the kingdom of God and of his Christ"; and that impression has originated within him a desire to know *what he must do to inherit it*, it remains now to direct his attention to the things of the name of Christ. This is a subject which would occupy very much space if all were to be said about it that would be profitable. I find myself, however, compelled to confine myself to a mere sketch, which the reader must more highly finish as the result of his own investigations.

The *name* of Jesus Christ comprehends all that is affirmable of him; and is, therefore, the summary of his character as a prophet, sacrifice, priest, and king. Hence, to understand his name we must know what is testified of him in the law, the prophets, the psalms, and the apostles. From the Old Testament we may become acquainted with the Shiloh's name. This is absolutely necessary: for unless we understand what sort of a person Christ was to be, how can we, when we learn the name of Jesus as described by the apostles, be able to say that the name of Christ as set forth in the prophets, and the name of Jesus, are the name of one and the same person? But by comparing the apostolic *history* with the testimony of *prophecy*, we can intelligently confess that "Jesus of Nazareth is the Christ the Son of the living God". This, then, is a first principle of the name of Jesus. Admit that he is the Shiloh, and all things predicted of the Shiloh are solely applicable to him.

Now there are certain things affirmed of Jesus Christ, the belief of which is highly essential to the constituting of a believer an heir of the kingdom. These things have regard to Jesus *as an offering for sin*. He died, was buried, and rose again. These are facts. But what is the truth, meaning, or doctrine of the facts? "He was delivered for *our* offences, and raised again for *our* justification" (Romans 4:25; Isaiah 53:5,10); that is, for the justification of those who believe the gospel of the kingdom. It is a great mistake to suppose that the belief in the sacrificial part of the name of Jesus Christ, is sufficient for salvation. Salvation in the kingdom is not promised to those who only believe that Jesus is the Son of God, and died and rose again for sin. It is *equally* necessary to believe in the promises of the covenants; not more so, but equally so; for if one believed the things of the kingdom, but rejected the sacrifice of Jesus, and his resurrection, he could not be saved. The gospel must be taken as a whole, and not cut up into pieces, and one or two selected which suit the taste, and the rest set aside as unimportant and non-essential. Without the sacrificial ingredient of the name, there would be no means of justification by the name; but then *Jesus as a sin-offering* is not the end of faith; but a means to the end, which is the inheritance of the kingdom with him in all his glory.

A very circumscribed and superficial view of the gospel is that which finds it stated in the words, "Christ died for our sins according to the scriptures, was buried, and rose again the third day according to the scriptures" (1 Corinthians 15:3,4). The *"our"* for whom Christ died are those who believe in the gospel of the kingdom, not those who are ignorant of it; or, as the apostle expresses it, those *"who keep in memory* A CERTAIN WORD *I preached unto them"*. What word? That which he taught among them a year and six months; and which he preached wherever he went. The word concerning *"the hope of Israel"*, on account of which he was taken prisoner to Rome; and which the Jews listened to patiently (Acts 18:4), so long as he did not mention the name of Jesus; but when that was introduced, they opposed themselves and blasphemed (Acts 18:5,6,11). Because the apostle is made to say in the common version that he "delivered *first of all"* the death and resurrection of Christ, persons, who know no other than their mother tongue, conclude that the sacrifice of Jesus for sin was the first thing spoken, and the very gospel itself! But the apostle did not write *"first of all"*; his words are ἐν πρώτοις, that is, *among the first things*. And why does he call up the things mentioned in the third and fourth verses in preference to the other things he delivered? Because he was about to refute the Platonic notion taught by some in Corinth, to wit, "that there is no resurrection of the dead"; and to do so it was necessary to remind them of his having preached to them the sacrificial death and resurrection of Jesus; which was all a fable, if there were no future resurrection as they said, because it had "passed already" (2 Timothy 2:18): "Ye are then", said he, "yet in your sins, and they who are fallen asleep in Christ are perished."

Three things were to be preached in the name of Jesus Christ to them who believed in the promises made of God to the fathers. These were, first, *repentance*; secondly, *remission of sins*; and third, *eternal life* (Luke 24:44-47; John 20:31). To preach the kingdom in the name of Jesus Christ was to expound the things concerning it; and to offer them to all who would become the subjects of repentance and remission of sins in his name. Neither *"flesh and blood"*, nor *"sinners"*, can inherit the kingdom of God (1 Corinthians 15:50). These are fixed principles. But why not? Because *"the kingdom shall not be left to other people"*, and because those who inherit it are to possess it for ever. Now "flesh and blood" is *mortal*; how then can mortality inherit immortality? It is a physical impossibility. In other words, a man who only lives seventy years, cannot hold office for a thousand years; he must be made deathless before he can retain it for ever. Again, it is a moral impossibility for sinners to possess the kingdom, because the law of the kingdom is that "he that ruleth over men must be just, ruling in the fear of God". It is the inheritance of saints, to whom the Lord will not impute sin. Two things are therefore indispensable before Jew or Gentile can inherit the kingdom—first, a moral purification; and secondly, a physical, or corporeal, purification. The first is compassed in obeying the truth; the last, by a resurrection unto life.

Now, the repentance which results from believing the gospel of the kingdom is not "sorrow for sin"; nor does it contain the least bitterness or remorse of feeling in it. The scripture word translated *repentance is μετάνοια*, and signifies *a change of mind and purpose*. When such a change takes place from believing the truth, it is a disposition and mode of thinking such as characterized Abraham, who is the model of the faith and temper which precedes justification in the name of the Lord. But a change of mind and purpose, however "evangelical", is only granted for repentance in the name of Jesus Christ. That is to say, though a believer of the gospel of the kingdom might possess this state of mind and child-like disposition, he would not be regarded as in repentance any more than in Jesus until the name of Christ was named upon him according to *"the law of faith"*. It imports not how much a woman loves a man, she is not his wife, and therefore entitled to none of the benefits he is able to confer, until she puts on his name according to law. The name of Christ consummates everything. "Complete in him"; but out of him everything is imperfect. Faith is unfinished, and the change of mind and disposition is incomplete, until the believer of the gospel of the kingdom puts on the name of Christ. In the act of doing this, his faith is counted to him for righteousness, or remission of sins that are past; and his change of mind and disposition is granted to him for repentance (Acts 5:31; 11:18).

But *a right* to eat of the tree of life in the paradise of God is also imparted to the believer through the name of Christ. The life-giving efficacy of his name is derived from his resurrection as the first-fruits of them that sleep. Had Jesus not risen from the dead, men could not have obtained a right to eternal life through his name. This is the doctrine of the apostles and the prophets. An unrisen sacrifice is only a temporary propitiation for sin. This was the nature of the sacrifices under the Mosaic law. Hence the law had no vitality in it; "for if there had been a law given that could have given life, verily righteousness should have been by the law" (Galatians 3:21). But this was impossible. Moses was the mediator of the covenant from Sinai. He died, and the Lord buried him; but there was no testimony added of his resurrection: and though he lives (for he appeared to Jesus on the Mount), it was after the law came into force. The Mosaic law is, therefore, a minister only of death and cursing. But Jesus died and rose again, and lives for evermore. Hence, the gospel in his name, and the new code hereafter to be promulgated from Zion, are efficacious to the bestowal of a right to eternal life upon all who believe through his name.

While a believer is out of Christ, he is in his sins, and while he is in his sins he is under the sentence of death; for "the wages of sin is death". As soon, however, as his sins are forgiven through Christ's name, in the act of forgiveness he passes from under the sentence of death; and as there is no middle, or neutral position, he comes under the sentence of life, and rejoices in hope of the kingdom of God. Thus Jesus Christ hath abolished death, and brought life and incorruptibility *to light in the gospel of the kingdom* (2 Timothy 1:10). There is no other way of obtaining them than through his name, and by a resurrection from the dead; or, if living at the setting up of the kingdom, by a change in the twinkling of an eye. Such is the doctrine of Christ as opposed to the vain philosophy of Plato. The Papist and Protestant admirers of this heathen speculator, contend for the hereditary immortality of an immaterial essence, innate in sinful flesh; while the Lord Jesus has made known that life and incorruptibility are attributes of the kingdom of God, which they only can obtain who are accounted worthy on gospel principles of inheriting it. In fine, incorruptible life is part of the reward of the righteous; and nowhere in the Bible is immortality predicated of, or promised to, men who die in their sins. Out of Christ, immortality there is none.

DEATH-BED AND GAOL REPENTANCE

BY *"the great salvation"* is meant deliverance from the grave by a resurrection to life, and a share in the kingdom of God. This, as we have seen, is predicated on faith in the promises made to the Fathers, an Abrahamic disposition, baptism into the name of the Holy Ones, and faith made perfect by works. In other words, salvation is promised to those only who walk in the steps of Abraham's faith. To deny this is to deny the testimony of God. His own Son was not exalted until he was made perfect by suffering. "He that believes the gospel, and is baptized, shall be saved; and he that believes not shall be condemned." This fiat has never been revoked; it is, therefore, as valid and exceptionless as when it fell from the lips of the Son of God.

THE THINGS OF THE KINGDOM OF GOD

Now, in view of this irrefutable truth, what shall we say of that system which holds out assurances of "heaven" to men of earthly, sensual, and devilish lives, when they find themselves prisoners of disease, and convicts in the clutches of the law? When death stares them in the face, they are exhorted by their "spiritual guides" to "make their peace with God"; and even when preparing for the scaffold are taught by "gaol chaplains" to expect to meet in heaven the companions of their crimes; and that by partaking of the "sacrament" they are making their souls ready "to meet their God"! And upon what is all this "consolation of religion" founded? Upon a terrible apprehension of the molten and flaming sulphur in hell's cauldron, into which the "penitents" are taught their "immortal souls" will be plunged by God, and where they will be tormented by the Devil for all eternity. A gaol-chaplain at Coventry actually burned a female convict's hand with the flame of a candle as a foretaste of her tortures after death if she did not repent! This was his plan of proceeding in the "cure of her soul"! But if disease, or crime, had not captured the "penitents", their career would have been still onward in iniquity. Finding there is no escape from death, either by the rope, or in the ordinary way, their audacity and impiety are suspended. They are imposed upon by the clerical assurance that the Lord is "waiting to be gracious"; they are directed to the thief upon the cross; and they are deceived by the falsehood that "while the lamp holds out to burn, the vilest sinner may return". All is ready, the gospel feast is prepared, and nothing is wanting but for them to believe that Christ died for them, to be sorry for the past, profess themselves at peace with God and all mankind, and to pray for forgiveness through Jesus Christ.

Thus the "spiritual guides" of the people shrive them to perdition. An act of the mind, prompted by terror and their persuasions, is proposed by them as a set off for a whole life of impiety and crime! What base views must such men have of the God whose ministers they pretend to be! Their "consolations" are unmitigated blasphemy, and false from first to last. Need they be surprised at the little impression they make upon the public mind by their preaching; and that mankind are daily increasing in infidelity? The million, though ignorant, are not fools. "What necessity for us", say they, "to trouble ourselves about religion? We can be shrived in half-an-hour for all the offences of a long life of sin." It is the preachers that make men infidels by the preposterous absurdities they preach in the much-abused name of Christianity.

But the worst, and most repulsive, form of ministerial blasphemy is exhibited in gaol-chaplain consolations. These are a striking manifestation of clerical ignorance of the letter and spirit of the truth. The scripture saith, that *"no murderer hath eternal life abiding in him"*; and that even "he that hateth his brother is a murderer", and, consequently, beyond the pale of mercy. Murder can only be pardoned through a faith in the truth that works by love and purifies the heart, and made perfect by obedience. If after this such a believer fail of the grace of God, and hate and murder his brother, there is no forgiveness with God, "he shall not see life: but the wrath of God abideth upon him". What with sprinkling infants in the name of the Lord, and calling it Christian baptism; shriving reprobates at the gates of death, and calling it repentance; and committing their loathsome carcases to the earth under a repetition of *"common* prayer" read over myriads of times, and styling it Christian burial; surely there is superabundant reason to conclude, were we even ignorant of the truth itself, that both priests and people are deceiving and being deceived.

To call the popular system of religion by which we are surrounded the religion of Christ, is not only a misnomer, but an imputation on the wisdom of God. Infant-sprinkling, death-bed repentances, and "Christian burials", as they are termed, are mere human inventions. They belong to the apostasy, and are no part of the "things of the kingdom of God and the name of Jesus Christ". If a man serve the lust of his flesh all his life, no remorse, or resolves on a bed of death will serve in the least. "He that sows to his flesh shall of the flesh reap corruption for whatsoever a man soweth that shall he also reap" (Galatians 6:7,8); and again, "to be carnally minded is death"; and "they that are in the flesh cannot please God"; and "if ye live after the flesh ye shall die" (Romans 8:6,8,13). These are testimonies which, in few words, show that there is no salvation for a man who serves himself all the days of his life, and when he is no longer able to grasp the world, offers the extreme fag-end of his existence to God. It is like eating all the meat of a joint, and throwing the bone to your friend. If he would feel himself insulted, in what estimation would God hold a similar treatment of His majesty; would He not spurn the hypocrite from His presence, and justly too?

It is because of these abominations that the judgments of God are falling upon the nations. Ministerial and popular iniquities have brought the pestilence upon this people; and war and famine upon others. They are but the beginning of sorrows. The present storm may lull; but it is only that it may gather force to sweep before it all refuges of lies. "Woe to the world because of offences!"

In former pages I have endeavoured to show the reader what the truth is. I have advanced nothing, that I can recollect, but what I have adduced "the law and the testimony" to prove. Let him view the landscapes of the moral world by the light of the truth, and he will behold the darkness visible. He will see its drapery in tatters, and its rags falling to pieces from very rotten-ness. Its fabric is rent from the dome to its foundations; and its structure is like a bowing wall and a tottering fence. There is no safety under its roof. Even the owls and the bats of its crannies are panic-stricken. Come out, then, dear reader, and leave the den, if unhappily you sojourn there. Believe the truth for its own sake, and obey it; and if you stand alone, be of good courage. There is more real satisfaction in knowing, and being able to prove, the truth, and in contending single-handed for it, than in all the honour and enjoyment derivable from the applause of men, or the abundance of the world's goods a man may possess.

If the righteous "scarcely be saved" what scope is there for the ungodly and the sinner; and if judgment began at the house of God in the persecutions it endured, "what shall the end be of them that obey not the gospel of God?" (1 Peter 4:17,18). Be not deceived by the traditions of the Gentile scribes and orators. Their ministrations have no vitality in them, and leave their flocks in their own predicament, "dead in trespasses and in sins." Therefore "come out from among them, and be ye separate, and touch not the unclean; and I will receive you, and will be a Father to you, and ye shall be my sons and daughters, saith the Lord Almighty (2 Corinthians 6:17,18).

PART THIRD

THE KINGDOMS OF THE WORLD IN RELATION TO THE KINGDOM OF GOD

CHAPTER I

NEBUCHADNEZZAR'S IMAGE—THE HAND OF GOD IN HUMAN HISTORY

The pandemonianism of the world—The Press its organ to a great extent—Its conductors greatly deficient in political prevision—A divine agency the real source of the world's revolutions—God hath revealed what shall come to pass—Nebuchadnezzar's Image explained—It represents an Autocracy to be manifested in these Latter Days—The Toe-kingdoms enumerated—The Vision of the Four Beasts—Of the Saints and the two Witnesses

HAVING laid before the reader in the former parts of this work "the things concerning the kingdom of God and the name of Jesus Christ", and, I trust, enabled him to be "ready always to give an answer to every man that asketh him a reason of the hope that is in him", and also to know, without doubt, what he must do to be saved, I propose now to give an outline of the things set forth in "the sure word of prophecy" in relation to that crisis in human affairs which has come upon the world, and which is destined to be the occasion of the introduction of the kingdom of God.

The Lord hath truly said by the prophet, "I have a long time holden my peace; I have been still, and refrained myself" (Isaiah 42:14). It is now nearly nineteen hundred years since He spoke by His servant John to the seven congregations in Asia Minor; and so entirely hath He refrained Himself from further revelation of His will, that men have at length almost generally concluded that He hath ceased to take any interest in human affairs. They speculate upon passing events as though they thought that mankind were formed for no nobler destiny than to fret out a brief and crushing existence in a precarious competition for food and raiment; and to labour with asinine endurance for the behoof of those who, by violence, avarice, and fraud, have gained the ascendancy over them. God is not in their thoughts when they treat of the affairs of men. They deal only with secondary causes, while the agency of the great First Cause is supposed to be confined to the saving of "immortal souls" from purgatory, or from burning in liquid brimstone underneath. "Order" at any price is, with them, the chief good. They ascribe glory and honour to Satan, though he has established a despotism over the nations which rivals the mythic dominion of Pluto. Everything dear to truth, righteousness, and liberty must be suppressed by armed mercenaries, provided only that bank, stock-exchange, and commercial speculations, and the "vested interests" of public plunderers in church and state be protected and preserved intact.

Such is the pandemonianism of the world. Sin in its most heartless and hateful deformity reigns the universal despot of the nations. It is enthroned, and decorated with crowns, tiaras, coronets, and mitres; and is gathering strength by fraud, hypocrisy, and murder, for a last and final effort to crush all future endeavours to cast it out unto the earth, and its angels with it. A corrupt and vicious press is the ignoble and servile apologist of its treachery and blood. It flatters the grim assassins of the people, the soul of whose institutions is the ignorant stolidity and cruel superstition of a dark and iron age. Its sympathies are with profligate kings, blasphemous priests, and savage generals; while no epithet is too vile or opprobrious for those who, having endured to the uttermost the debasing and ruinous oppression of their destroyers, seek to break their bonds, expel them from their thrones, and to diffuse truth and science among the people.

While a Christian would take no part in the armed *mêlée*, he is convinced that nothing but violence in the beginning, in order to punish and crush the tyrants, can prepare the way for the amelioration of society. This is the order, as I shall show, which God has ordained as preliminary to the setting up of His kingdom. But the conductors of the press do not understand this. It is not more corrupt and vicious than it is blind to the scriptural philosophy of the things of which it treats. It cannot see afar off, and the objects which are near, it cannot comprehend. How applicable to its scribes is the exclamation of the Lord, "O ye hypocrites, ye can discern the face of the sky; but how is it ye cannot discern the signs of the times!"—signs, which are announcing to the nations with a voice of thunder that Jehovah hath aroused Himself in His holy habitation; that the time hath at length come when He will be still and refrain Himself no longer; but that He will make bare His holy arm, and "destroy them that destroy the earth" (Revelation 11:18), or oppress mankind.

But, though the Lord hath a long time held His peace, He hath not been unmindful of His people, nor heedless of human affairs. The great incidents of history which have given rise to successive kingdoms and dominions, from the overturning of the kingdom and throne of God, and of David, His anointed, in

Judea, by the Chaldeans, to the present time, are but events pre-determined and arranged in the purpose of God, and revealed in the "sure word of prophecy". Not a kingdom has been established, nor a king dethroned, but it has formed a move, which has contributed to the maturity of the present crisis, which will ultimate in the introduction of the kingdom of God. This truth is beautifully expressed in the words of the prophet, saying, "Blessed be the name of God for ever and ever; for wisdom and might are his: and *he changeth the times and the seasons*; HE REMOVETH KINGS AND SETTETH UP KINGS: he giveth wisdom unto the wise, and knowledge to them that know understanding: *he revealeth the deep and secret things*: he knoweth what is in the darkness, and the light dwelleth with him" (Daniel 2:20-22). It is He to whom all things are subjected; "for he ruleth in the kingdom of men, and giveth it to whomsoever he will, and *setteth up over it the basest of men*" (Daniel 4:17). This is the reason why men and women with so little wisdom, or rather possessed of so much positive folly and imbecility, are able to rule the nations without "setting on fire the course of nature". When their wickedness and stupidity become obstacles to His purpose, He removes them out of the way, and introduces other actors upon the stage. In this way, He controls and regulates the world's affairs; but in every interference He shapes the course of events towards the consummation predetermined from the foundation of the world.

In ages past, God has had among the nations a people of His own. These are wise in the wisdom of God, and venerate His word above all things. Though not His counsellors, He has graciously condescended to inform them what He intends to do before it comes to pass. Hence, it is testified by the prophet that "the Lord GOD will surely do nothing, but he revealeth his secret unto his servants the prophets" (Amos 3:7). This revelation is made that His people's faith may be confirmed and enlarged, and that in every generation they may know the times and seasons to which they stand related. Knowing the signs, they are enabled to discern the times; and while consternation and dismay cause men's hearts to fail they are courageous, and rejoice in perceiving the approach of the Kingdom of God.

This is the proper use of the prophetic word. It was thus that the ancients used it, and were enabled to live in advance of their contemporaries. This appears from the exhortation of the apostle, who says, "We have a sure word of prophecy whereunto you do well to take heed, as unto a light that shineth in a dark place until the day dawn, and the day-star arise in your hearts: knowing this first, that no prophecy of scripture is of one's own disclosure. For prophecy came not at any time by the will of man; but the holy men of God spake being moved by the holy Spirit"

(2 Peter 1:19-21). Some were not unmindful of this exhortation, which is as applicable to us as to them; for the day has not yet dawned, nor has the day-star arisen. Were it not for the prophetic word, the "heirs of the kingdom" would be in as utter darkness as gaol-chaplains, who burn the flesh to cure the soul, or administer the "Sacrament" to gallows-thieves about to die! The sure prophetic word is itself a shining light, but, having been "put under a bushel", mankind are left enshrouded in Egyptian night. "Be mindful", saith the scripture, "of the words spoken before by the holy prophets"; and on the ground that this was the case, the apostle adds, "Therefore, beloved, *seeing ye know these things before*, beware lest ye, being led away with the error of the wicked, fall from your own steadfastness" (2 Peter 3:17). The words of the prophets to which he referred, related to the destruction of the Hebrew commonwealth. His brethren were acquainted with these prophecies and, therefore, knew what was about to happen, though not the day or the hour. Hence, this knowledge was to be their caution and security against being led away by the spiritualizers of the time, who wrested the scriptures to their own destruction (2 Peter 3:2,16).

From these premises we may conclude that, as the Lord has also revealed what is to come to pass in these latter days, it is both our duty and privilege to make ourselves acquainted with it, that our faith may grow and be strengthened; that our affections be detached from the fleeting present, and set more firmly on things to come; that our minds may be fortified against error; and that we may be prepared to meet the Lord as those who have kept their garments, and shall not be put to shame (Revelation 16:15). It is our own fault if we are not "light in the Lord". He has plainly set before us what is happening in our day, and what is yet to occur. Hence, while the Priests of the State Church are drowsily exclaiming, while war and political murders abound, "Give peace in our time, O Lord!"—and while peace-societies are with infidel voices crying "Peace and safety", they who take heed to the prophetic word "know before" that the hour of God's judgment is come, and that destruction is at the door.

In pursuance, then, of the work before us, namely, that of unfolding the train of events which are to ultimate in the setting up of the kingdom of God, I shall proceed to show the things represented in:—

NEBUCHADNEZZAR'S IMAGE

THIS was a colossus in human form, which appeared to the king of Babylon in a dream. The head was of gold; the breast and the arms of silver; the belly and the thighs of brass; the legs of iron; and the feet part of iron and part of clay. While the king continued to behold it, a stone poised in the air, unsustained by hands, fell with great force upon the feet, and broke them to pieces. After they were smitten, the iron, the clay, the brass, the silver, and the gold, were all broken to pieces together, and became like chaff, which the wind so completely swept away that no vestige of the image remained. The image being thus destroyed and abolished, the stone that smote it became a great mountain, and filled the whole earth.

The interpretation given to the king informed him that the head of gold represented the dominion of which he was the head; that the silver part symbolized the monarchy which would succeed his; the brazen part, a third power which should bear rule over all the earth; and the iron part, a fourth dominion strong as iron, that should subdue everything before it. This fourth kingdom, he was told, should be divided, inasmuch as there were two iron legs, and ten toes. But as *the toes* of the feet were part of them of iron and another part of clay, the dominion represented by the ten toes would be partly strong and partly broken. But as there was a mingling of iron and clay in the structure of the feet, while the toes constituted unitedly the iron dominion, they should not cleave to one another, but should be independent and antagonistic kingdoms.

Lastly, the king was given to understand that the smiting of the image by the stone on the feet represented the breaking in pieces and consumption of all the toe-kingdoms by the God of heaven, who should set up in their place a kingdom which shall never be destroyed, nor left to other people.

Such was the prophetic interpretation which was given with the dream about twenty-five centuries ago. I shall now briefly outline the *historical* interpretation, and then consider what yet remains to be accomplished.

The interpreter has determined the commencement of the image. It goes no further back than the time of Nebuchadnezzar, whose dynasty was superseded by a two-armed monarchy, in the reign of his son's son, Belshazzar, BC 542. This was the silver dominion of the Medes and Persians. After 208 years, this was overturned by Alexander of Macedon, BC 334. His dominion exceeded that of Babylon and Persia, extending from the remote confines of Macedonia to the Indus, or as it is expressed, "bearing rule over all the earth". This was the dominion of "the brazen-coated Greeks", answering to the brazen parts of the image. After a few years the empire of brass was divided into four kingdoms, *two* of which had especial relations with the land of Canaan upon which the kingdom of the Stone is to be established. These two, therefore, are alone represented in the image. They answer to the two brazen thighs; and are known in history as the Syro-Macedonian kingdom of the north, that is, from Jerusalem; and the Greco-Egyptian kingdom of the south. The northern kingdom continued till BC 67, when it became attached to the iron leg; the southern kingdom, however, "continued more years than the king of the north", even thirty-seven, when it also merged into the iron dominion.

From this epoch, the iron monarchy prevailed over all antagonists. It is known in history as the Roman. In the fourth century after Christ it was finally divided into the Eastern Roman, and the Western Roman, empires, answering to the two legs of iron. Though divided thus, the Roman majesty was considered as one. The date of the decision was AD 396.

In about ninety-seven years from this epoch ten kingdoms appeared upon the Western Roman territory answering to the ten toes. They were not all strong kingdoms. Part of them were absorbed into a new dominion, which arose after them beyond the limits of the Roman territory. These strong and broken toe-kingdoms have existed upwards of thirteen centuries. They are still in being; but not as originally established. This the prophecy does not require. All that is necessary, is that there should be ten kingdoms at the time the image is smitten by the stone. And these kingdoms, I am satisfied, should be on "*the earth*", and not upon "*the sea*"; that is to say, they should be found upon the Roman continent, and not upon the islands; and that the enumeration of them belongs to the time of the end, rather than to the period of their foundation. With this view, then, I enumerate the toe-kingdoms as follows:*

1, Belgium; 2, France; 3, Spain; 4, Portugal; 5, Naples; 6, Sardinia; 7, Greece; 8, Hungary; 9, Lombardy; 10, Bavaria.

I have not named Britain, although the island was a part of the Roman dominion. It is, however, no more imperative that she should be included in the ten than Egypt, which is also on the Roman territory. Existing theories require Britain to be counted in; but I have nothing to do with them; I propose to show a more consistent interpretation that shall harmonize with other important and interesting parts of the prophetic word.

---

* See footnote on page 352.

The ten kingdoms enumerated above are all within the Roman limits. There are many other kingdoms beyond its frontiers, resting upon territory that never belonged to Rome, or the iron dominion; therefore they must not be named in the same category. Nebuchadnezzar's image has to do only with powers occupying the area of the golden, silver, brazen, and iron dominions; other prophecies survey the rest.

Thus far, then, history runs parallel with the prophetic interpretation. We are not informed in this vision how many of the toes were weak. It simply affirms the fact and defers further details for illustration by other symbols. What, then, remains to be accomplished? The testimony informs us that the ten kingdoms are all to be broken to pieces; and *after* they are smitten that the whole image in all its different metals is to be "broken to pieces *together*". But how can this be? Where are the dominions represented by the gold, the silver. the brass, and the iron? How can they be broken to pieces together, seeing that they have been broken to pieces *one after the other* many centuries ago? The answer to this question is important, and must be given; for without it no interpretation can be received as satisfactory. And here I would remark, that the image was presented to the mind of the King of Babylon, not so much to represent *a succession of empires*, as to exhibit the catastrophe which should usher in the Kingdom of God. The idea I would convey is well expressed by the prophet, saying, "The God in heaven, who revealeth secrets, maketh known to the king *what shall be in the latter days*" (Daniel 2:28,29). That is, there will be in the latter days a dominion, ruling over all the countries mainly comprehended in the limits of the successive empires of Babylon, Persia, Greece, and Rome: and represented by the image as a whole; and which will be broken by a power from heaven, which will utterly destroy it, and set up an empire which will cover all the territory it possessed.

Now, there has never yet existed a single dominion, contemporary with the toe-kingdoms, and of course comprehending them in its jurisdiction, which could claim to be represented by Nebuchadnezzar's image. In order, then, to prepare for the catastrophe, the image which is now in antagonistic parts, *must be confederated*:* in other words, a dominion must arise before the setting up of the kingdom of God, which shall rule over the toe-kingdoms, and the Turkish and Persian territories, till it meets the British Power in the East. The description of the dream says that the feet were smitten; and *"then* was the iron, the clay, the brass, the silver, and the gold, broken to pieces *together"*; thereby intimating that the breaking of the power of the ten kingdoms would precede that of the conjoint destruction of all the other

351

parts. That when they are conquered, the dominion of the conqueror will be overturned by the revelation of power from above.

I shall be able to show, from other parts of the prophetic word, that the power destined to play the conspicuous part indicated above is RUSSIA. That it will dominate all the ten kingdoms, subdue Turkey, and incorporate Persia into its empire; but that when it has reached its zenith, it will in turn be precipitated into the abyss, and its dominion suppressed for a thousand years. When I come to unfold these things, the reader will see why Britain is not included in the ten toes. She is reserved of God to antagonize Russia, as she did France, when all Europe was prostrate at the feet of "Napoleon le Grand". The ten toes belong to the image as a united dominion; hence Britain cannot be included among them unless it is first conquered by the overshadowing power, which it will not be, as is clearly demonstrable from many parts of the divine testimony. Russia will command the land, and Britain rule the sea. *They will contend for the dominion of the East; but neither will obtain it.* It is not for mortal man to rule the world, and grasp the sole dominion of the globe. This is an inheritance, the divine legacy of Omnipotence, to Abraham, Shiloh, and the saints.

It is evident that the dominion of the Image is not broken by a human power. The stone which destroys it is represented as not in hands; that is, it symbolizes a supernatural power. If the stone had been poised in a man's hands ready to smite the image, we might look for an earthly conqueror to overthrow the dominion of the Autocrat, as he will overthrow the rest. But the power that wields the stone is plainly declared in the interpretation. It is the God of heaven who pulverizes the image, and sweeps its chaffy dust away by the whirling tempest which wrecks the kingdoms of the world and transfers them to His saints. The kingdom of the stone grinds to powder whatsoever it falls upon, and then becomes a great mountain, or empire of nations, and fills the whole earth.

---

* Many things have happened since this was written in 1848, and considerable progress has been made in the confederation of the parts of the image. For instance, with reference to some of the kingdom named:—Naples, Sardinia, and Lombardy have been incorporated with Italy. Bavaria became confederate with Germany in 1870. Through the last fourteen centuries there have been many changes, but always resulting in about ten kingdoms. The time of the end will reveal the final enumeration, as Dr. Thomas says, page 350.

THE VISION OF THE FOUR BEASTS

THERE were certain important particulars to be revealed in connection with the empires and kingdoms of the Metallic Image, which could not be suitably expressed through a symbol of the human form. It became necessary, therefore, to introduce other representations, that would admit of appendages more in harmony with them. Wild beasts were selected to represent dominions instead of parts of a metallic figure; and as there were four different metals, four different animals were selected, according to the following order:

1. The *head of gold*, was illustrated by a LION;

2. The *breast and arms of silver*, by a BEAR;

3. The *belly and thighs of brass*, by a LEOPARD; and,

4. The *legs, feet, and toes of iron*, by a FOURTH BEAST WITH TEN HORNS.

OF THE LION,

THE beasts being substituted for the metals represent of course the same dominions. The lion was a very appropriate symbol for the Assyrian dynasty; as was well understood in the days of the prophets. Hence, speaking of the overthrow coming upon Judah by Nebuchadnezzar, Jeremiah says, "I will bring evil *from the north*, and a great destruction. The *Lion* is come up from his thicket, and the destroyer of the Gentiles is on his way. He is gone forth to make thy land desolate; and thy cities shall be laid waste without an inhabitant" (4:7).

But in Daniel (chapter 7), the Assyrian lion appears under different aspect. He is represented first, as a lion with eagle's wings, crouching; and, secondly, as a lion without wings, standing erect.

The lion in these two aspects represents the Assyrian monarchy in two phases; first, while Nineveh was its capital; and secondly, when by conquest the seat of government was transferred to Babylon. Esarhaddon was king of Assyria while Merodach-Baladan was king of Babylon, and both were contemporary with Hezekiah, king of Judah; Baladan, the father of Merodach-

Baladan, was probably the founder of Nebuchadnezzar's dynasty. Merodach was doubtless an important member of the family; for Nebuchadnezzar named his son Evil-Merodach, after him. About 106 years elapsed from the embassy of Merodach-Baladan to inquire after the health of Hezekiah, and concerning the bringing back of the shadow ten degrees by which it had gone down on the dial, to the first year of Nebuchadnezzar's reign; which was equivalent to the third of Jehoiakim, king of Judah. It was by the Merodach-Baladan dynasty, that "the wings of the Assyrian lion were plucked"; that is, the Esarhaddon dynasty of Assyria was superseded by the king of Babylon, as the destroyer of the Gentiles.

Before this revolution was effected, the Assyrian dominion was represented by a winged lion, having the form of a man down to the waist, and furnished with arms. This is satisfactorily demonstrated by Mr. Layard in his "Nineveh and its Remains". In his excavations at Nineveh he laid bare sculptured lions, twelve feet high and twelve feet long. In one hand, a goat was held; and in the other, hanging down by the side, a branch with three flowers. From the shoulder sprang forth expanded wings which spread over the back. The body was that of a lion with five legs,* two on the fore-end, and three on the side. The head, breast, and arms were human, and as low down as the waist. A knotted girdle ending in tassels, encircled the loins.

But when Nineveh's dominion was transferred to Babylon by a conqueror, a change came over the Assyrian lion. Daniel says, "I beheld till its wings were plucked, and it was lifted up from the earth." In consequence of its eagle's wings being plucked— that is, of Armenia and Persia being subdued—the Assyrian dominion was prostrated to the earth; completely overthrown, but not destroyed; for Daniel says furthermore, that "the lion was made to stand upon the feet as a man". Nebuchadnezzar was at once the conqueror and rebuilder of the Assyrian Monarchy. He made it stand erect, and gave it a more civilized constitution. Shalmaneser had destroyed the kingdom of the ten tribes of Israel, and Sennacherib had blasphemed Jehovah, and the posterity of his son Esarhaddon had become effete: this was a dynasty which had become a pest, a plague spot upon the nations; but Nebuchadnezzar, though an idolater, was a man better suited to the purposes of God. There was more of the man, and less of the wild beast, in him than in the kings of the dynasty he had overthrown. Therefore, when the Assyrian lion was made to stand erect upon its hind feet like a man, Daniel says, that "a man's heart was given to it". Its golden, or imperial

---

* The fifth leg was added to give an appearance of symmetry to the side view.

lion-head, was responsive to divine impressions, and gave utterance to sentiments which were entirely alien from the heart of the kings of Nineveh. "I blessed the Most High", said Nebuchadnezzar, "and I praised and honoured him that liveth for ever, whose dominion is an everlasting dominion, and his kingdom is from generation to generation; and all the inhabitants of the earth are reputed as nothing; and he doeth according to his will in the army of heaven; and among the inhabitants of the earth: and none can stay his hand, or say unto him, What doest thou? I praise, and extol, and honour the King of Heaven, all whose works are truth and his ways judgment; and those that walk in pride he is able to abase" (compare Daniel 4:34,35,37, with Isaiah 36).

But this *"man's heart"* was not the disposition of Belshazzar, his son's son. Instead of praising, and extolling, and honouring the God of Israel, he defied Him; and "lifted himself up against the Lord of heaven; and out of the holy vessels of His temple he, and his lords, his wives, and his concubines, drank wine; and he praised the gods of silver and gold, and of brass, iron, wood, and stone, which see not, nor hear, nor know: and the God in whose hand his breath was, and whose were all his ways, *he had not glorified*". This was his offence, on account of which the Lord of heaven passed this sentence upon him: "God hath numbered thy kingdom, and finished it; thou art weighed in the balances, and art found wanting. And thy kingdom is divided and given to the Medes and Persians." Nor was the execution of the decree long delayed, for "on that night was Belshazzar the king of the Chaldeans slain. And Darius the Median took the kingdom" (Daniel 5:31).

OF THE BEAR

THE Lion dominion being overthrown, the dynasty of the Bear took its place when " Darius the son of Ahasuerus, of the seed of the Medes, was made king over the realm of the Chaldeans", in 542 before Christ. It was a dominion to be extended by the sword, a particular expressed in the words addressed to the Bear, "Arise, devour much flesh."

In the symbolography, or description of the symbol, the prophet saith, that "it raised up itself on one side". Hence, one side was "higher than the other"; but before it raised itself up the higher side was the lower; therefore, the higher side acquired its more elevated position last. Compare this characteristic of the Bear with what is said of the horns of the Ram (Daniel 8:3). The inequality of the sides of the Bear represents the historical fact that the dynasty of the Bear-dominion was mixed; that is, it was first Median and then Persian. Darius was a Mede, and his successor Cyrus, a Persian. They were allies in the overthrow of the Chaldean kingdom. When the crown was to be assumed, the Mede preceded the Persian; but when Darius died, instead of the crown descending to a Mede, it passed to a Persian, whose race continued to wear it until the dominion of the Bear was superseded by the Leopard. Thus the Persian side of the Bear was raised up last.

But the Bear had also "three ribs in the mouth of it, between the teeth of it". This indicates that in devouring much flesh, the result was that its prey was reduced to "three ribs", which had become firmly fixed to its head. In other words, that the Medes and Persians had made extensive conquests, which were reduced to three divisions for the better administration of public affairs. A rib of the dominion, then, represents an imperial presidency, or as we should say, vice-royalty; each satrapy comprehending a number of principalities. This organization of the Bear is thus expressed by the prophet: "It pleased Darius to set over the kingdom a hundred and twenty princes, which should be over the whole kingdom and *over these* THREE PRESIDENTS; of whom Daniel was first; that the princes might give accounts unto them, and the king (or Bear's head) should have no damage." By the reign of Ahasuerus, or Artaxerxes the second, the dominion of the Bear extended "from India to Ethiopia over one hundred and twenty-seven provinces". Though the principalities may have been increased in number, or extent, the presidencies remained the same. A dominion represented by the Bear, its dynastic branch by the higher side, and its three presidencies by the three ribs, were the principal points which distinguished the realm of the Chaldeans, under the Medo-Persian sovereignty, from that of the Lion, or the Head of Gold. And it is worthy of remark here, with reference to the image at the crisis of its fate, that the Power which shall possess Persia *in the latter days* will be the Bear, and consequently answer to the breast of silver. We have already in the heraldry of nations an intimation of the Power destined to act the part of the Bear, when the Four Beasts have "their dominion taken away". This Power is the Russian, whose symbol is a Bear. This is so well-known that the phrase "the Russian Bear" is as familiar as household words. Russia, which already comprehends some of the Persian territory in its bounds, is destined to conquer Persia, and to possess it from India to Ethiopia. This is not conjecture but an absolute certainty; for God has declared by Ezekiel that Persia in the latter days shall be a constituent of the dominion of Gog; and that Gog is the autocratic dynasty of Russia will be seen when we come to treat of that prophecy in its proper place. We proceed now to the consideration of the Third Beast, or

FOUR-HEADED AND FOUR-WINGED LEOPARD

THIS beast represents the Macedonian dominion which superseded that of the Bear, as the belly and thighs of brass did the breast and arms of silver. The Leopard-dominion was more extended than its predecessors; for it embraced all that belonged to the Lion and the Bear, with the addition of that which had been established by Philip of Macedon, the predecessor of Alexander "the Great". It bore rule "over all the earth", or Image-territory, thus far subjugated to "civilization", such as it was at that era of the world.

In the year 301 before Christ, the Macedonian dominion in its divisions, and their relative position, is illustrated by the Four Wings of a fowl, and the four Leopard-heads. Alexander ruled his conquests for the short space of six years, when he died in Babylon of intoxication. After a long period of war, his unwieldy empire was resolved into several kingdoms of which the four principal ones are represented by the Four Heads of the Leopard. These were its mighty Powers to which the others looked up as the lesser States do now to the great military potentates of the age.

The four great Powers, or heads, of the Grecian Leopard were:

1.   The kingdom of the South, which comprehended Egypt, Libya, Arabia, Coele-Syria, and Palestine, under the Greco-Egyptian dynasty;

2.   The kingdom of the North-west, including Thrace, Bithynia, etc.; or the Thraco-Macedonian;

3.   The kingdom of the North-east, comprehending the rest of Asia, and beyond the Euphrates to the Indus; India beyond the river, though allotted to this dominion, revolted; so that the Indus became its boundary: this was the Assyro-Macedonian; and,

4.   The kingdom of the West, which embraced Macedonia and Greece.

Such were the heads. But how was it to be determined that they should stand related to these four points of the compass? This was indicated by the wings of the Leopard—interpretation made evident from the words of the prophet, saying, "The Lord shall gather Judah from the four corners (in Heb., *the four wings*) of the earth" (Isaiah 11:12; Daniel 11:4). The addition of the wings, then, to this beast, signifies that the kingdoms represented by the heads would be towards the east, west, north and south, of Judea.

A Leopard is sometimes used to indicate the British power. During the war in the Peninsula, Napoleon and his generals often threatened to "drive the leopard into the sea"; by which they meant, that they would drive the British out of Spain and Portugal. Now, in Daniel (8:5) the dominion of Alexander, which extended into British India, is represented by a Unicorn—that is, a goat with one horn. Hence, the Leopard, without additional heads, and without wings, represents the same dominion as the Unicorn. Now it occurs to me, that the British Unicorn is a symbol representing a similar thing to the Ægean Unicorn of Alexander; and, therefore, identifies the British power with the Grecian Leopard. I do not say that the mind which designed the heraldry of the British power had the part predestined for Britain to enact in the latter days before it when it inserted the leopard Unicorn. But divine wisdom sometimes impels men to do things the import of which they very imperfectly understand; and the insertion of the Unicorn may have been an act of this nature. Be this as it may, there are indications which make the idea more than probable. In the first place, the British power is the constitutional protector of the Ionian Islands contiguous to the Morea and ancient Macedonia; and secondly, it possesses a part of Alexander the Great's dominion in India, and is absorbing more and more of it every war it wages in the Far East. When the Bear pushes for Constantinople, it is not unlikely that the British Unicorn will make extensive seizures of the islands in the Mediterranean* as an antagonistic compensation for the continental territory acquired by the Autocrat in European Turkey. Britain is bound to maintain a maritime ascendancy in the Mediterranean; not because she has any continental territory washed by its waters, but because of her vast interests in India, which would be greatly endangered by an uncontrolled military power in Anatolia and Egypt. When the power of the British Unicorn shall be fully developed in maritime Greece, Egypt,* Palestine, the Red Sea, and India, a leopard dominion will again appear upon the stage of action, and be prepared for the catastrophe of the latter days.

---

* Since this was written in 1848, the Ionian Islands were ceded to Greece in 1864, but on the other hand Cyprus has been ceded to Britain by the Anglo-Turkish Convention of 1878; and Egypt was occupied by Britain from 1882, though since 1922 she has been nominally independent.

OF THE FOURTH BEAST, OR TEN-HORNED DRAGON

THIS beast was to arise out of the Mediterranean territory as well as the others. The belligerent tempests on every side were to give rise to it; for, says Daniel, "the four winds of the heaven strove upon the Great Sea. And Four Great Beasts came *up from the sea*, diverse one from another"; and, when he has finished the description of them, he states that "they are four kings (kings being used in scripture oftentimes for their kingdoms and *vice versa*) which shall arise *out of the earth*"; which explains, that when he says "up from the sea", he means the countries of the Mediterranean, which in scripture geography is styled the Great Sea.

That this beast is identical in signification with the iron part of the image, and incorporates within its dominion the territory of the kingdoms of the brazen thighs, is indicated by "its teeth of iron and claws of *brass*". A beast of prey destroys with its teeth and claws. Like the iron kingdom of the image, this iron-toothed dominion was to devour and break in pieces all that came in its way, and to stamp the undevoured residue with its brazen-clawed feet. It was "exceeding dreadful and terrible, and strong exceedingly"; and, though not named by the prophet, may, by the aid of history and the Apocalypse, be correctly termed the GRECO-ROMAN DRAGON.

This Fourth Beast was shown to Daniel for the purpose of representing certain things predestined to come to pass in connection with the ten toes of the image, which could not be suitably displayed in symbolic feet. The things to be illustrated were:

1.   The eradication of the power of *three toe*-dynasties: or royalties; and the subjection of their territories to an imperial dominion;

2.   The peculiar character and constitution of this imperiality;

3.   The part this militant power was to play in relation to the saints;

4.   the time the image's feet were to continue before they should be smitten by the stone;

5.   The *consumption* of the militant power which was to precede the destruction of the image;

6.   The personage through whom the destructive power of the stone should be manifested;

7.   The giving of the kingdom to Him, and the saints; and,

8.   The nature of the mountain which should fill the whole earth.

These eight points constitute a summary of the things designed to be represented by the Eleven Horns which made their appearance on the head of the Forth Beast. The first point is symbolised by the coming up of a Little Horn among the Ten Horns, which "*subdues* Three Horns", so as to "pluck up by the roots" the regal dynasties they represent; and in this way leaving only seven independent royalties, besides its imperial self.

The second and third points are presented by this Little Horn having inserted into it Human Eyes and Mouth; and described as having a more audacious look than his fellow horns, or contemporary dynasties; and "speaking very great things", or blasphemies, "against God, to blaspheme his name, and his tabernacle (or saints, styled the temple of God in the scripture), and them that dwell in heaven". its character is also further illustrated by its "making war upon the saints and prevailing against them", and changing God's times and laws.

The fourth and fifth points are set forth by the slaying and burning of the Fourth Beast with his appendages at the end of "a time, times, and the dividing of time".

And the sixth, *seventh and eighth*, points, are revealed by the verbal declaration, that "the Son of Man came with the clouds of heaven, and came to the Ancient of Days, and there was given him dominion, glory, and a kingdom, that all people, nations, and languages, should serve him; his dominion is an everlasting dominion which shall not pass away, and his kingdom one which shall not be destroyed". Again, "the saints of the Most High shall take the kingdom, and possess the kingdom for ever, even for ever and ever"; and again, "*the time came* that the saints possessed the kingdom"; "and the kingdom, and dominion, and the greatness of the kingdom under the whole heaven shall be given to the people of the saints of the Most High, whose kingdom is an everlasting kingdom, and ALL DOMINIONS SHALL SERVE AND OBEY HIM" (Daniel 7:13,14,18,22,27). This is the dominion of "the great Mountain that fills the whole earth".

There is nothing said about *the heads of this* Fourth Beast, whether there was one or more. Hence, the chronology of the symbol must be restricted to the Horns. The dynasties of the leopard-heads were all superseded by the Forth Beast before the birth of Christ; but the ten horns, answering to the ten toes of the image, did not make their appearance till the fifth century after Christ. The life of the Beast is measured by the continuance of the horns; and the duration of these by the time allocated for the Little Horn to prevail against the saints. It is to prevail "until a time, times, and the dividing of time" shall have elapsed from some determinate epoch. Nothing is more obvious to one of these saints than that these "times" have not yet run out; because the power still exists and prevails against them. Upwards of 1,260 years have elapsed since the Horns established themselves on the western Roman territory; so that the chronology of the symbol is not to be calculated from the rise or growth of the horns out of the Dragon's head. Indeed, if we had no other data than what are furnished us in the vision of the Fourth Beast, we could not tell when "the time, times, and dividing of time" should commence. The vision only informs us when it shall end, namely, with the casting down of the thrones, or Horn-dynasties; and the destruction of the Beast's dominion in all its parts by the "burning flame"; a process which has been steadily approaching since February, 1848, and thereby indicating that the consummation is at hand.

The fall of three horns before the Little Horn which overthrows them, by which it becomes an eighth power on the Dragon's territory, suggests its identity with "the eighth which goeth into perdition" treated of in the Apocalypse (17:11). Speaking of the signification of the Seven Heads of the Roman Beast, it is stated that they have a double interpretation; that is, they represent the seven mountains on which Rome is situated; and seven heads of government which have prevailed there. The seventh dynasty had not appeared when John saw the vision. When it was manifested, it was to continue in the seven-hilled city only "a short space". After this had passed away, and, as history shows, 246 years after its entire destruction, an eighth head appeared in Rome. This was an outlying dynasty, thrusting itself in among the horns from a country lying beyond the geographical limits of the old Roman territory. It was a dynasty growing out of a foreign country, and, therefore, styled "another Beast". Hence, the reason why it is written in the text referred to, "the Beast that was and is not, even he is the eighth, and is of the seven, and goeth into perdition". This is also affirmed of the Ten-horned Beast, as well as of the Two-horned Beast, or Eighth Head; because there is the same intimate connection between these two Beasts, or dominions, as that which exists between the Little Horn and Seven Horns of the Greco-Roman Dragon.

John was favoured with a vision of "the wilderness", or territory of "the Holy Roman Empire" as it is styled. He saw it as it was in the first century after Christ. Then, the dominion which now exists there had no being. In spirit he viewed it as it would appear several centuries after when the dominion had arisen. It was then "the Beast that IS"; again, he saw the wilderness after the power had passed away; he then speaks of the dominion as "the Beast that WAS", and "the Beast that IS NOT", because it will then have gone into perdition. We can now say of the holy Roman

Beast *"it is"*; and from present appearances, shall be able to say in a few years, *"it was and is not"*, because it is destroyed by "the burning flame."

The Little Horn's character has been more obvious to interpreters than its constitution. In certain respects it is like the other Ten Horns. These were all SECULAR *dynasties*. If they had individually possessed "eyes and a mouth", they would all have been episcopal and speaking Horns, like the Little Horn. But they possessed neither. They were simple horns, evincing power, secular and not spiritual, in their operations. When eyes look more stout than existences around them, and their mouth speaks blasphemies against God, angels, and the saints, they become symbolical of ecclesiastical power; and inserted into a horn, they present a symbol which represents a CONJUNCT DYNASTY; that is, a dominion whose executive is imperial, and which is constituted, either of an imperial pontiff and a secular emperor, or of one Head in whom is vested the imperial administration both of secular and ecclesiastical affairs, as was the case with the pagan Roman emperors.

The Little Horn of the Greco-Roman Dragon, or fourth beast, is a two-fold dynasty or dominion. Its eyes and mouth represent one horn; and *the rest of the horn*, another. The former is the over-seeing and blaspheming horn; the latter, the secular, or military horn, which co-operates with it, and does all the fighting. Hence, when we find the little horn fully developed, we may expect to discover TWO PERSONAGES, who, through subsequent ages, are conspicuous as imperial chiefs of the western world. These, it is almost needless to add, are the Pope and the Emperor.

OF THE SAINTS AND TWO WITNESSES

WHEN the little horn appeared among the ten horns, Daniel was particularly struck by his blasphemous talking, and enmity against the saints of the Most High. The mouth of this horn is evidently the same as the mouth of the ten-horned, and two-horned, beasts of the Apocalypse (chapter 13). It was the mouth of a lion, because of its roaring for prey, seeking whom it might devour; as well as for its Babylonish affinities. "It spake as a dragon", with the ferocity of the old pagan emperors against the saints. Describing this mouth, John says, "It spake great things and blasphemies against God, to blaspheme his name, and his tabernacle, and them that dwell in heaven." These blasphemies Daniel styles "great words against the Most High", which, of course, were very offensive to the servants of God, and aroused their indignation. They "contend earnestly for the faith once delivered to the saints" against its blasphemies; and advocated the liberty of the truth, the equality of the faithful, and the fraternity of the children of God. This brought down upon them the hatred and revenge of the Popes, who stirred up all the horns of the beast against them, as it is written, "He made war upon them, and overcame them, and killed them."

Daniel speaks of "*the saints*" and of "*the* PEOPLE *of the saints*". I apprehend that there is the same distinction to be drawn here as between "*a Jew inwardly*" and "*a Jew outwardly*". "The saints" is a term which includes them both; even as "Israel" includes both the natural and the believing seed of Abraham.

Because a person is one of the saints it does not therefore follow that he is a righteous man. This is clear from the fact that the twelve tribes as a company of nations are termed "the Lord's witnesses"; concerning whom He says, "This people have I formed for myself; they shall show forth my praise". They are styled "a holy nation", or a nation separated from all other nations by a divine constitution, by which they are made the people of God. Now this "holy nation" has proved itself to be "a stiff-necked and perverse race"; nevertheless, it is "holy", or separate, on the same principle that the temple, Jerusalem, the land, etc., are holy.

But pagan nations are sometimes termed holy, or sanctified. Hence, the Lord says, "I have commanded my sanctified ones, I have also called my mighty ones for mine anger, etc. They come from a far country, from the end of heaven, even the LORD and the weapons of his indignation to destroy the whole land." This is from a prophecy against Chaldea. These saints are declared to be the Medes and Persians, who were pagan nations associated together in the overthrow of the Babylonian dynasty. "I will stir up the Medes against them, who shall not regard silver; and as for gold, they shall not delight in it. Their bows also shall dash the young men to pieces; and they shall have no pity on the fruit of the womb; their eye shall not spare children" (Isaiah 13:3,17,18).

A class of persons separated in the providence of God to execute any work for Him are His sanctified ones, irrespective of their moral relations to the gospel. They are designated in scripture by various names. They are styled witnesses, prophets, olive trees, candlesticks, as well as saints; because they are exercised in these several capacities. They may have to bear witness for civil and religious liberty; to preach against the lion-mouth and his clergy; to stand forth as a lamp before God to enlighten the nations of the earth, etc.; they may discharge all these functions, and yet be neither believers of the gospel of the kingdom, nor even "pious" as the term is. This class of people may be found figuring largely in the history of all European nations. They are the hostile party to the beast in all "religious wars", and wars for liberty against the despotism of popes, emperors, kings, and priests. In these sanguinary wars their uniform has been sackcloth; yet they have devoured their enemies with fire and sword, and smitten the earth with all the plagues of war as often as they pleased. With various fortune they have combated with the tyrants of the world. Cromwell "tormented them (the Royalists) who dwelt in" England, and who drew the sword for the "right divine of kings to govern wrong"; he struck terror into those in Ireland who worshipped the beast, and devoured them with fire and brimstone from the cannon's mouth. In France, the Huguenots did good service against the beast. They shut up the political heaven, and suffered not the rain of peace to descend upon Piedmont, and the south, where the blood of Albigenses, and Waldenses, was crying out from the ground, like Abel's, for vengeance upon those who dwelt upon the earth. But, however successful for a season, they were destined to succumb for a while; as it is written, in Daniel, "The little horn made war with the saints, and prevailed against them: UNTIL the Ancient of Days came, and judgment was given to the saints of the Most High: and the time came that the saints possessed the kingdom."

Now, it must not be forgotten that, by reason of the Little Horn's empire comprehending the three subjugated horns, it is a part of the ten-horned apocalyptic beast as well as the independent horns; therefore what is affirmed of it, is also affirmed of the beast as a whole, including its mouth and horns. Hence, John writes the same thing of the ten-horned beast, and of the two-horned beast, and the image of the former beast's imperial head, that Daniel does of the Little Horn, saying, "The beast that ascendeth out of the bottomless pit", or sea, "shall make war upon them, and shall overcome them, and kill them" (Revelation 11:7); and in another place, the ten-horned beast "shall make war with the saints, and overcome them" (Revelation 13:7); and again, the two-horned beast "causeth them that dwell in the earth to do homage to the (imperial head of the) first beast, whose deadly wound was healed. And he causeth those that dwell upon the earth to err through the deeds it was given him to do against the beast; saying to them that dwelt on the earth that they should make an Image of the Beast, which had the wound by a sword and did live. And it was given to him to give breath (πνεῦμα) to the image of the beast, that the image of the beast should both *speak*, and cause as many as would not worship the image of the beast *that they should be killed*. And he caused all, the small and the great, the rich and the poor, the free and the bond, that a sign (χάραγμα, mark or sign) should be made upon them on their right hand, or upon their forehead: and that no man might be qualified (δύνηται, *be able*, in a moral sense) to buy or sell, except he have the sign, or the name of the beast, or the number of his name" (verses 12-17).

Now it is the saints who refuse to adore the imperial Roman image, or Eyes and Mouth of the Little Horn; and who have not the sign ✠ upon their foreheads, or in their right hands. These are the parties whom the image has caused war to be made upon, and who have been prevailed against, and killed with all the attendant enormities of promiscuous massacre. The slaughter of the Albigenses in Languedoc; of the Vaudois in the valley of the Piedmontese mountains, in the thirteenth and fifteenth centuries; and of the Huguenots on St. Bartholomew's, and at the Revocation of the Edict of Nantes; the dragonnades, drownings, etc., are instances of the cruelties inflicted upon the saints by the roaring lion of the "eternal city". In the face of these teeming testimonies of history, the special pleaders of the Papacy have the hardihood and effrontery to declare that the Head of their church has put none to death; that their church is the pure, sinless spouse of Christ! But the spirit denounces it as "drunk with the blood of the saints", because, in stirring up the secular powers to murder and massacre the opponents of Romanism and the advocates of human rights, it has "*caused* the saints *to be killed*"; and become so dyed in wickedness, and steeped in crime, that its iniquity hath at last reached unto heaven, and the burning flame of war is consuming and destroying it unto the end.

But, says the apostle, "the weapons of our warfare are not carnal, but spiritual". In his letter to the Ephesians (6:14-17), he enumerates them as the girdle of truth, the breast-plate of righteousness, the preparation of the gospel of peace for sandals, the shield of faith, the helmet of salvation, and the sword of the spirit which is the word of God. This is the "whole armour of God" which "the *people* of the holies" are permitted to use. The two-edged sword of the spirit is the only offensive weapon they are allowed to wield in combat with the Beast. The impulses of the flesh would lead them to crush the tyrants who have drenched the earth with their blood, and to bruise their heads like serpents, but their Captain has said, " Vengeance is mine, I will repay". It is the impulse of the flesh, hostile to the truth of God, which urges the Beast to war against those who adhere to that truth. The people of the holies are forbidden to act under such an impulse, but to imitate Jesus, who resisted not, but committed his cause to God. Unresisting suffering is the law of their spiritual warfare. If persecuted they must fly; if smitten, they must not smite again; if reviled, they must bless; but withal "fight the good fight of faith" with the word of God, without favour, affection, or compromise, with any thing that exalts itself against the knowledge of God.

But this may be thought to be a contradiction of what has been said of the witnesses inflicting the plagues of war as often as they pleased. How can they do this unless they contend in battle against the Beast? The answer is, that the Anti-Papal instrumentality of God in the earth consists of *three classes of persons*; two of these classes are political, but the third is that class spoken of by the apostle as his brethren. The prophecy of the two witnesses is concerning *two great parties* in the ten-horned beast's dominion, which antagonize it in its civil and ecclesiastical policy. One party is purely secular, and styled *"the earth"*, or democracy; the other party is *"religious"*, and termed *"the woman"*. The mission of these is to make war upon tyranny, and to take vengeance upon it, and finally to be the means, or occasion, of breaking it up in its ten-horned and Papal constitution. "The earth", or secular witness, is the helper of "the woman", or religious witness. They have co-operated since the reign of Constantine more or less intimately until the present time; their co-operation consisting in a determined hostility to State-Churchism, and to its monarchical allies. They are both more or less Republican in their principles. "The earth" especially is animated by a hatred of oppressors. Its spirit in all ages has shown itself in a terrible form. It is ferocious as the tiger, but it is a ferocity which is required by the nature of the work assigned it. The civil and ecclesiastical tyranny it has to combat, which is itself horribly terrific and blasphemous against God and His truth, must be encountered by a spirit as fierce. In history, we see it exhibited in the Circumcellions of the first century of its operations, in the men of Münster of the sixteenth, the Camisards of the seventeenth, the Terrorists of the eighteenth, and the Red Republicans, Socialists, etc., of the nineteenth. Like God's "sanctified ones, the Medes", the heart of *"the earth"* is steel, and its eye unpitying. It is ready to dash out the brains of sucklings, to spoil the property of the rich, and to reduce the social fabric of the Beast to its elemental chaos. Its political representative in Europe was "THE MOUNTAIN" in the French legislature—a body of men who were the abomination and terror of the Jesuit-priest-party throughout the world.

"The woman" is constituted of heterogeneous sects. *"Dissent"* and *"Non-conformity"* are terms which define the religious witness in this country. In France she is styled *"Calvinist"*. Her tendencies are Republican, as illustrated in the Cromwellian commonwealth, and in the constitution of the United States of

America, which was the conjoint work of *"the earth"* and *"the woman"*. This great religious witness is made up of an infinite variety of factions, whose contempt of popes, emperors, kings, priests, and aristocrats is profound; yet, with all their hatred, they conscientiously repudiate the excesses of *"the earth"*, or secular witness. These two witnessing parties, however, are of one theory, which is *death to tyranny*, if not to tyrants; and, in some sense or other, rally around the standard of "liberty, equality, and fraternity" —three principles which are utterly destructive of the dominion of the Little Horn, and its audacious fellows of the Roman Beast.

But there is *a third party* which, although it has the deep-rooted enmity of truth against every form of Satanism in Church and State, Papal and Protestant; and wishes success to the Two Witnesses in their war with civil and ecclesiastical tyranny, yet it is distinct from them both. It is that party described by the apostle in the passage above quoted. It is composed of the saints of God in the highest sense of the word. It is the One Body of Christ, having the one faith, the one hope, one Lord, one spirit, one baptism, and one God and Father (Ephesians 4:4-6). It is styled *"the holy city"* in the Apocalypse (11:2); and is trodden under foot of the Gentiles for forty-two months of years, till the Ancient of Days appears. It is by this class that "the faith once for all delivered to the saints" is preserved from being entirely lost. In the twelfth of Revelation they are termed "the *remnant* of the Woman's seed, who keep the commandments of God, and have the testimony of Jesus Christ". They are a people who believe the gospel of the kingdom of God and the things of Christ's name as set forth in "the law and the testimony"; for "the testimony of Jesus is the spirit of the prophecy". They are also an immersed people; for they keep the commandments of God as well as believe His word. It is their mission to "contend earnestly for the faith". Hence they come into collision with all parties; being antagonistic to "every high thought that exalts itself against the knowledge of God", whether entertained by the enemy, or by witnesses, who torment him with their insurrections, or with prophesyings in behalf of civil and religious liberty.

Such, then, is the antagonism ordained of God to keep the Beast, or European governments, in check, and to preserve the light of truth and liberty from extinction among the nations. It is to this agency the world is indebted for the little liberty it rejoices in. This has been conquered from the Beast at a great cost of human life. The United States of America is a specimen of its handiwork; and but for the incurable condition of society in the old world by human efforts, as happy a state of things would ere this have been established on the European continent, as in

367

some degree hath been in this island. The Roundheads, Puritans, and Lollards, or Bible-men, laid the foundation of American institutions on the soil of Britain. They successfully resisted the encroachments of an Act-of-Parliament-religion on the rights of men; and by contending for the Bible (without very well understanding it themselves) in opposition to human authority in religion, gave an impulse to the minds of men which all the powers emanating from the "bottomless pit" can no longer prevail against or control.

But while the liberty provided by the constitution of the United States, and practically enjoyed in England, is much to be appreciated by the people of these respective countries, there are but few of them who have tasted the sweets of that liberty which dwells in "the Holy City". "If the truth shall make you free", says Christ, "ye shall be free indeed." So long as a people practically venerate a professional ministry, whether in the pay of the State, or of the people, to preach what pleases them more than "the law and the testimony"; so long as they are ignorant and faithless of "the things concerning the kingdom of God, and the name of Jesus Christ", and glorify themselves in religious systems, which nowhere on the sacred page meet the eye of the unbiased student of God's word; so long as their pulpits are closed against men who would reason with the people out of the scriptures "concerning righteousness, and temperance, and judgment to come", *irrespective of party shibboleths and decrees,*—so long are they strangers to the liberty, equality, and fraternity which belong to the truth of God alone.

The eye of faith sees the fairest spots of earth veiled in thick darkness. Its hope is not in "the earth"; for man can neither regenerate himself, nor society. Any organization of the world fabricated by human wisdom, must perish; for men have neither knowledge, wisdom, nor virtue enough to build a social fabric conducive to the honour and glory of God, or to the general happiness of mankind in their several relations of life. Our hope is in the Ancient of Days. "The earth" may "help the Woman", and consume the dominions of the Horns; but the Son of Man can alone deliver the holy city, crush the Dragon's head, and reconstitute society to the glory of God, and the happiness of all the families of mankind.

When the remnant ceased to "contend earnestly for the faith once delivered to the saints", "the earth" began to fail in its efforts to establish civil and religious liberty in the countries where "the remnant of the woman's seed" had witnessed for the truth so long. The reactionists on the side of arbitrary power began to prevail against both classes of witnesses, and the holy city; and to succeed in re-establishing what they call "ORDER";

that is, such a state of society as existed in France from AD 1685 to 1789, or in England under Charles II; or of which we have more recent illustrations in the case of France under Louis XVIII and Charles X; and of Italy under Austria and the Pope, etc., in 1815! It is the "order" established by Satan, when he triumphs over the rights of men, and the truth and righteousness of the untraditionized gospel of the kingdom of God. Satan's adherents sigh for that "order" in Church and State which will enable them to increase their power, augment their earthly treasures for the gratification of their lusts, and perpetuate their grinding and debasing tyranny over the nations. For a time they appear to triumph. Indeed, their ascendancy is permitted in the wisdom of God; but its *limited* continuance is expressly revealed. The champions of "order" are destined to preserve their ascendancy until, not "the earth", but the Lord Jesus Christ shall appear in power, and gloriously accomplish what "the saints" have hitherto been unable to effect.

It is because of this permitted ascendancy of the dynasties of the world for 1,260 years, that the popular insurrections in the territories of the Beasts and their image, have been invariably superseded by reactions which have re-established the reign of tyranny, hypocrisy, and superstition. Even the torment with fire and brimstone in war inflicted by Napoleon on the guilty dynasties which had murdered the saints in past ages, at length receded before the resuscitation of the old order of things, which this MAN OF THE EARTH had so signally demolished. But what Napoleon failed *permanently* to accomplish will as assuredly come to pass as there is a God in heaven who punishes the guilty.

Of the witnesses and holy city, without discriminating them, REINERIUS, the Inquisitor-General, who shed their blood, writes thus concerning them as a whole: "Among all the sects which are or have been, there is not any more pernicious to the Church (*i.e.*, of Rome) than that of the Leonists. And this for three reasons. The first is, because it is *older*; for some say that it hath endured from the time of Pope Sylvester (fourth century), others from the time of the apostles. The second, because it is more general, for there is scarce any country wherein the sect is not. The third, because when all other sects beget horror in the hearers by the outrageousness of their blasphemies against God, this of the Leonists have a great show of piety; because they live justly before men, and believe all things rightly concerning God and all the articles which are contained in the Creed; only *they blaspheme the Church of Rome and the clergy*, whom the multitude of the laity is easy to believe."

"The causes of their estrangement", says Acland, "from the Roman Church are thus stated: 'It is because the men and women, the young and old, the labourer and the learned man, do not cease to *instruct themselves*; because they have translated the Old and New Testaments into the vulgar tongue, and *learn these books by heart, and teach them*; because, if scandal be committed by anyone, it inspires them with horror, so that when they see anyone leading an irregular life, they say unto him, The apostles did not live so, nor shall we who would imitate the apostles: in short, they looked upon all that a teacher advances, *unsupported by the New Testament*, as fabulous.'"

It is with such people as these my sympathies are found: and it is to multiply such in the world that I write this book. If the reader would be numbered with this class of witnesses, he must "instruct himself" by the study of the word; he must cease to surrender himself to the clergy of Church or Dissent; but treat all their hypotheses "as fabulous", unsupported by the law and the testimony: for "the scriptures are able to make us wise unto salvation through the faith which is in Christ Jesus" (2 Timothy 3:15). What more do we want than to be saved in the kingdom of God? Ask the clergy, "What must you do to be saved?" They will repeat like parrots, "Believe on the Lord Jesus Christ and thou shalt be saved"; but ask them, "What does believing on the Lord Jesus for salvation consist in?" and I hesitate not to say—indeed, with the preceding pages as my premises, which I firmly believe to be the only scriptural exegesis of the gospel, I am necessitated to say—*they cannot tell*.

Then, like the Leonists of old, away with the clergy, the "blind leaders of the blind", "dumb dogs that cannot bark", "who neither enter into the kingdom themselves, and them who would they hinder". "All scripture is given by inspiration of God, and is profitable for teaching, for reproof, for correction, for instruction in righteousness: *that the man of God may be perfect*, thoroughly furnished unto all good works" (2 Timothy 3:16,17). Here Paul teaches that the scriptures can make a man perfect in all these things; how perverse, then, of mankind to neglect this instrument of perfection, and lean upon such broken reeds. The Leonists, Paulicians, Albigenses, Waldenses, etc., had more wisdom than this. They drank from the fountain head of truth; and it was only in later times, when their minds were diverted from this by the dazzling demonstrations of the protesting Romanists, who, under their early leaders, were rebelling against the Pope, and laying the foundation of State religions in Germany, England, etc., that they were ensnared in the toils of mercenaries. They merged into Protestantism, and thus an extinguisher was placed upon their lamp, which for 1,260 years had illuminated the darkness around.

A writer on prophecy has well remarked, that "there is no nation existing which, first and last, has produced such a number of faithful witnesses against Papal corruptions, and tyrannies, as France. No people have so long a list of martyrs and confessors to show as the Huguenots of that country; and there is no royal family in Europe which has shed, in the support of Popery, half the blood which the Capets have shed. Who deluged the earth with the blood of the Waldenses and Albigenses that inhabited the southern parts of France, and bore testimony against the corruptions and usurpations of Rome? The cruel kings of France slew above a million of them. Who set on foot, and headed, the executioners of the massacre of Bartholomew in 1572, which lasted seven days, and in which, some say, near 50,000 Huguenots were murdered in Paris, and 25,000 more in the provinces? The royal monsters of France. A massacre this, in which neither age nor sex, nor even women with child, were spared; for the butchers had received orders to slaughter all, even babes at the breast, if they belonged to the Huguenots. The king himself stood at the windows of the palace, endeavouring to shoot those who fled, and crying to their pursuers, 'Kill them, kill them!' For this massacre public rejoicings were made at Rome, and in other Papal countries. A medal was struck at Rome commemorative of this tragical event. In the words of the Apocalypse, 'They that dwell upon the earth shall rejoice over them, and make merry, and shall send gifts one to another; because these two prophets tormented those who dwelt on the earth' (11:10)".

This dreadful massacre was 1,260 years from the separation established between State-church Christians, and the remnant of the Woman's seed. In 312-3, the man child was born of the Woman as the military chieftain destined to cast the pagan dragon out of the Roman heaven. A great revolution was consummated. The world's religion was changed; and the foundation laid for that awful despotism in Church and State, which has made all the families of the earth to wail. Constantine and his successors "ruled the nations with a rod of iron"; and united in adulterous alliance, an apostasy from apostolic Christianity to the kingdom of the world. Thus, a Satanic system was established, which persecuted all "who kept the commandments of God, and had the testimony of Jesus Christ" (Revelation 12:7-9,17). The troubles of the witnesses commenced with the institution of State Christianity, and they will not cease until every State Religion is abolished from the earth.

This Bartholomew massacre of 1572 marks the epoch of the terminating of the testimony of the two witnesses. From 1572 till 1685 was a period of war, during which unnumbered thousands fell in defence of their civil and religious rights. The war was waged with various fortune on both sides. At first, the Huguenots were so far successful, that their valour and devotedness raised their leader, Henry of Navarre, to the throne of France. Though a Huguenot, he could not withstand the temptation of an earthly crown, for which he changed sides, and professed himself a Papist. He could not, however, forget his companions in arms, but granted them in 1598 the celebrated Edict of Nantes. This charter accorded to them the right to celebrate their worship in every place in which they were resident previous to the year 1597. It permitted them to publish books in certain towns, to convene their synods, to open academies and schools for the education of youth, and to fill public offices. It also gave to them a number of cities as cautionary towns, or pledges of security, with the privilege of keeping them garrisoned, and levying taxes on their own account. Thus there was a little State within the State. The Romanists and Huguenots were like two armies, or two nations, in view of each other. They had concluded a treaty of peace, in which the king himself was the mediator; and it was necessary that each of the contracting parties should obtain their guarantees for the future. This singular state of things resulted from the violation of their engagements by the Papists, and from the priests inculcating the treacherous policy of not keeping faith with heretics.

Henry IV was assassinated in 1610, by Ravaillac, a fanatic of the Jesuit order. Upon this troubles immediately recommenced between the warlike Huguenots and Papists. The former were conquered; they lost all their strongholds; and in 1628, Rochelle, their last bulwark, fell into the hands of Cardinal Richelieu. Thus disappeared in this kingdom of the Beast their power to "devour their enemies by fire proceeding out of their (cannon) mouth" (Revelation 11:5). They had no longer "power to shut heaven that it should not rain"; nor could they any more turn the waters of Piedmont and the departments of France, into blood, and smite the earth with the plague of war "as often as they willed". Their political power was gone, and their affairs grew worse and worse, until their total wreck in the reign of Louis XIV.

"Soon after he came to the crown", says Mr. Claude, "there arose in the kingdom a civil war, which proved so sharp and desperate, as brought the State within a hair's breadth of utter ruin. Those of the reformed religion still kept their loyalty so inviolable, and accompanied it with such a zeal, and with a favour so extraordinary, and so successful, the king found himself obliged to give public marks of it by a declaration made at St. Germains in the year 1652. Then as well at Court as in the armies, each strove to proclaim loudest the merits of the reformed." Now, however commendable Mr. Claude and others may deem them on account of this loyalty, the simple import of the matter is, that their devotion to Louis XIV proved that their *testimony was finished*. Instead of standing aloof, and testifying against the despotism of Church and State, and "contending earnestly for the faith once delivered to the saints", their pastors and congregations had sunk down into the formalism of Calvinism; and actually drew the sword for a horn, or dynasty, of the very Beast which had "made war against the saints", with all the attendant cruelty of massacre, rapine and ravishment; and which was destined finally to "kill them". Calvinists in the imperio-papal, and royal, armies, of the Beasts and their horns, have forfeited all claims to divine favour as His witnesses of either class. Their mission is ended, and the sentence of death rests upon them. In about thirty years after this fatal demonstration of loyalty to the monster of the sea, God permitted their enemies to destroy them.

Moved by the Jesuits, who flattered his pride by persuading him that for him was reserved the glory of re-establishing religious unity in his dominions, Louis XIV determined to accomplish the suppression of Huguenotism in France. The plan was arranged in the spirit of Jesuitism, and pursued with dreadful perseverance. Referring to their newborn zeal for the Bourbon dynasty, their enemies said, "If on this occasion the Huguenots could preserve the State, this shows likewise that they could have overthrown it; this party must therefore by all means be crushed." Hence, Louis, and the abettors of the tyranny, immediately set about it. "A thousand dreadful blows", says M. Saurin, "were struck at our afflicted churches before that which destroyed them: for our enemies, if I may use such an expression, not content with seeing our ruin, endeavoured to taste it." They were persecuted in every imaginable way. They were excluded from the king's household; from all employments of honour and profit; all the courts of justice, erected by virtue of the Edict of Nantes, were abolished, so that in all trials their enemies only were their judges, and in all the courts of justice the cry was, "*I plead against a heretic*"; "I have to do with a man of a religion odious to the State, and which the king is resolved to extirpate."

"Orders were printed at Paris, and sent from thence to all the cities and parishes of the kingdom, which empowered the parochial priests, churchwardens, and others, to make an exact inquiry into whatever any of the reformed might have done, or said for twenty years past, as well on the subject of religion as otherwise; to make information of this before the justices of the peace, and punish them to the utmost extremity. Thus the prisons and dungeons were everywhere filled with these pretended criminals; orders were issued, which deprived them in general of all sorts of offices and employments, from the greatest to the smallest, in the farms and revenues; they were declared incapable of exercising any employ in the custom-houses, guards, treasury, or post-office, or even to be messengers, stage coachmen, or waggoners. Now a college was suppressed, and then a church shut up, and at length they were forbidden to worship in public at all by the Revocation of the Edict of Nantes in 1685. Rude Popish missionaries, without learning, or decency, went from house to house, for the purpose of inducing them to abjure their religion; they interrupted the preachers; and, if the congregation forcibly ejected them, they complained to the magistrate, who seized the opportunity thus presented to suppress the meeting-house.

"Consciences were bought up like articles of merchandise. Pastors were forbidden to preach beyond the place in which they resided, under penalty of several years' imprisonment. Children of tender age were authorized to embrace Popery in spite of the opposition of their parents; who, without regard to rank, condition, or merit, were declared unworthy to serve the State.

"The great majority continued steadfast. Promises of wealth and honours, seductions, artifices, threats, failed to shake their constancy: so that their persecutors resorted to the still more energetic measures, commonly known as THE DRAGONNADES.

"These were a species of punishment unthought of by the Inquisition. Profligate and merciless soldiers were sent into the houses of the Huguenots. They had orders to resort to every method except assassination to convert their victims to Papalism! They laid waste their property, destroyed their household goods, treated mothers, wives, and maidens, in an infamous manner, brutally struck the men; and, by a refinement of cruelty, hindered them from taking an hour's rest until they had signed a derisive abjuration. Some, crushed beneath such accumulated sufferings, lost their reason: others, led away by despair, suffered death by their own hands. The Dragonnades still live in the memory of Frenchmen, as a fearful and horrible memento of bygone days. But even these atrocities were insufficient to consummate the conversion of the Huguenots to Romanism.

"In 1685, as we have said, Louis the Fourteenth signed the revocation of the Edict of Nantes. The preamble of this ordinance made the king say, 'We now see, with the gratitude we owe to God, that our endeavours have had the result which we proposed, since the best and greatest portion of our subjects of the pretended reformed religion have embraced the Catholic faith.' But this did not express the truth. Hundreds of thousands emigrated from France, to seek asylums in foreign lands; into every part of Europe, and from the Cape of Good Hope to the American wilderness, they carried their faith, industry, laborious habits, and their example; and besides these, two millions remained in the land of their birth, who persevered in their opinions beneath the sword of the executioner. and in the sight of the fires of martyrdom.

"Those who had not quitted France were in the most deplorable condition. Deprived of their leaders, and having no regular means of religious instruction, pursued like rebels, they met at distant intervals, in some wild retreat. When they were surprised, the soldiers fired on them, as if they had been ferocious animals. Thousands of poor victims were condemned to the galleys, and were there confounded with the vilest wretches. Others were hung, beheaded, or burned. If a dying man, moved to remorse, disavowed in his last moments the Popish religion, to which he had conformed during his life, his dead body was dragged through the streets by the hangman, and was afterwards cast into a receptacle for filth, like the carcase of an unclean beast."—*Abridg. of G. De Felice.*

Speaking of the Revocation, M. Saurin says, "Now we were banished, then we were forbidden to quit the kingdom, on pain of death. Here we saw the glorious rewards of those who betrayed their religion; and there we beheld those who had the courage to confess it, haled to a dungeon, a scaffold, or a galley. Here, we saw our persecutors drawing on a sledge the dead bodies of those who had expired on the rack; there we beheld a false friar tormenting a dying man, who was terrified on the one hand with the fear of hell if he apostatized; and on the other, with the fear of leaving his children without bread, if he should continue in the faith." "They cast some", says M. Claude, "into large fires, and took them out when they were half roasted; they hanged others with ropes under their armpits, and plunged them several times into wells till they promised to renounce their religion; they tied them like criminals on the rack, and poured wine with a funnel into their mouths till, being intoxicated, they promised to turn Catholics. Some they slashed and cut with pen-knives; some they took by the nose with red-hot tongs, and led them up and down the rooms till they agreed to turn Catholics. These cruel proceedings made 800,000 persons quit the kingdom."

Thus, Oct. 18th, 1685, became the epoch of the death of the witnesses. The war had been long, but the Beast had subdued them at last. The voice of testimony against Papalism in Church and State was silenced. The stillness of death pervaded not France only, but Europe likewise; and if I were called upon to point out the darkest period of BIBLE CHRISTIANITY from the time of Constantine to the present time, I should point to the interval from the revocation of the Edict of Nantes to the breaking out of the French Revolution in 1789. During this time the holy city was laid low, and the symbolic witnesses lay dead, though unburied. Their lamps were extinguished, and "before the God of the earth" there was no light; no Illuminati; none to torment them that dwelt upon the earth with a faithful testimony against tyranny and State religion. Everything was sunk into cold formality, and the Beasts and their Images (Revelation 13:1,11,15) were triumphant everywhere.

CHAPTER II

ROMAN BABYLON AND THE RESURRECTION OF
THE WITNESSES

The Sin-Power in its war against the seed of the woman in the West, symbolized by the Beasts and their Image—God will surely avenge His saints—The crimes for which the nations are being judged stated—The geography of the "Lake of Fire" where the judgment sits—The saints the executioners of the Little Horn—They are raised from political death for this purpose—Events connected with their resurrection—The three days and a half of their unburied state explained—Their ascension—End of 1,260 years—Of the time of the Beast

THE fourth beast of Daniel's vision, the ten-horned and two-horned beasts, and the image of the sixth head of the ten-horned beast, are so many different symbols, which represent the Sin-power in its European constitution. The apocalyptic beasts and their image are introduced into the thirteenth chapter of Revelation to represent certain things in relation to the Little Horn, to its Eyes, and to its Mouth, which could not have been set forth in the symbol of the Roman dominion seen by Daniel. In this prophet the Eyes of the Little Horn are said to be "like the eyes of a man", which gave it "a look more stout than its fellow-horns". Of the mouth it is said that "it spake very great things," which were "words against the Most High"; and that "because of the voice of these great words", consumption and final destruction came upon the whole beast.

This is the nearest approach the Eyes and Mouth make to that order of men called the Popes. They are represented as an audacious and blasphemous power, "wearing out the saints of the Most High, and changing times and laws"; and concerning the saints, it is added, "They were given into his hand until a time, times and the dividing of time".

Under a new symbol, some additional information is given respecting the Eyes and Mouth in the exercise of their power, etc. They are inserted into an image, which is said to resemble that head of the ten-horned beast which had been wounded in its power, throne, and jurisdiction over the third part of the Roman world (Revelation 8:12; 13:3,14). This was the sixth, or imperial, head. Hence, the Eyes and Mouth were part of an imperial Image. Now, when we look into the testimony, we find that it did not set up itself; but is the puppet of another power represented by a beast with two horns, which answers to the Little Horn itself, minus the Eyes. The Mouth of the Little Horn, of the two-horned, and of the ten-horned Beasts, is common to the three symbols—it is mouth to them all. It is said to be like the mouth of a dragon; hence it is Roman and Imperial—the speaking organ of the three. Now, the same things are affirmed of it by John as by Daniel. He says, "It speaks great things and blasphemies against God, to blaspheme his name and his tabernacle, and them that dwell in the heaven". And then it is added that "it was given to him to make war with his saints and to overcome them". It also continues the same length of time which is expressed by "forty-two months" instead of by "time, times, and dividing of time"; for it is clear that as long as the beast lives, so long will its mouth continue to speak.

Now, in the exercise of the power given to it, the imperial or Papal image spoke, and in consequence of its speaking it *caused* all to be killed who would not do homage to it. It also caused all its subjects to be marked with the sign of a cross *"in their right hand"* in ordination, and *"on their foreheads"* in paidorhantism; and unless a man had this mark it would not permit him to *"buy or sell"* as a spiritual soul-merchant in its bazaars.

The symbols of this chapter of Revelation, it may also be remarked, represent the Gentiles in their civil and ecclesiastical constitution, who tread down the holy city (11:2). This is evident from the testimony, that the beast with its ten horns and mouth of a lion, possessed "power over all kindreds, and tongues, and nations". From what has been advanced the reader will then perceive that two parties are represented which are antagonists, namely, the saints and the sin-power. Hence, he has before him a symbolical exhibition of the sentence upon the serpent, saying, "I will put enmity between thee and the woman, and between thy seed and her seed; it shall bruise thy head, and thou shalt bruise his heel". The saints are marshalled on the side of the woman; and their persecutors on the side of the serpent. The war has been long, fierce, and bloody; but the saints' victory is certain and the destruction of the beasts and their image inevitable and sure.

In the previous chapter I have briefly sketched the cruelties practised by the Ten Horns, the Little Horn, and the ecclesiastical image upon the witnesses and the holy city (called the saints in the aggregate) in all the countries in which they have appeared. France and the "bloody house of Austria" have been pre-eminent in the strife. They are dyed in infamy of every kind, which they have enacted on the most virtuous of the human race. In all their deeds of fiendishness they have been applauded by the archdemon of the Papacy, who styles them his "beloved sons", and the mercenary instruments of his cruelty, his "dear children". Does the reader suppose that the just and merciful Father of the Lord Jesus Christ, and of those who keep His commandments and have His testimony, hath looked on the fiendism of the sin-power with indifference; and that He will permit their wrongs to die unavenged? If he do, he has greatly mistaken God's character, and knows nothing at all of the awful judgments He has decreed against those who "bruise the heel" of His beloved. Did He judge Egypt for oppressing Israel, though at the time idolaters; did He sink Sodom into the volcanic abyss for its crimes; and did He punish Judah with pestilence, famine, sword, and scattering for eighteen centuries, because of unbelief of "the truth *as it is in Jesus*", and for killing His servants—and will He not avenge His elect whom He hath chosen, upon the demoniac powers which have continued to crush them? The scripture saith, "Precious in the sight of the Lord is the death of his saints"; and "precious shall their blood be in his sight". If the blood of the murdered Abel, crying from the ground, was heard of God and avenged, what shall be said of that exceeding great and piercing cry, which upon the same principle, ascends to His throne from that ocean of blood which has been poured out like water from the hearts of his slaughtered saints? Doth it not cry aloud to heaven against popes, emperors, kings, hypocritical and blaspheming priests, and their hordes of mercenaries; and against all ecclesiastical abettors of arbitrary power in Church and State? Yes, that voice, though unheard and unheeded by those who worship the beasts and their image, continually ascendeth, and hath "entered into the ears of the Lord of sabaoth", saying, "How long, O Lord, holy and true, dost thou not *judge and avenge* our blood on them that dwell on the earth?" (Revelation 6:10). The hour has come, and the death-knell of the destroyer hath sent forth its clangour throughout the dominion of the Roman beast. As in the case of Sodom, though unseen by the eye of the flesh, God hath "come down to see if they have done altogether according to the cry". He has found it even so. "Their sins have reached unto heaven", therefore He will reward them double for all the evil with which they have afflicted His saints.

Such, then, is the case before us. The great national crime has been committed, and perpetuated, *of converting the truth of God into a lie, of blaspheming His name, and of bruising the heel of His saints*. All nations are guilty of this; and as national offences can only, and must necessarily, be punished by national judgments, retribution is pouring out upon them according to the word of the Lord. The outline I have sketched has brought us down to the epoch of the death of the two witnesses. Daniel beheld this, and at the same time received the information, that the Little Horn was to triumph over "the saints" to the end of the beasts's life, which it arrives at by the end of 1,260 years. This long period having elapsed, he beheld a sight, the knowledge of which must rejoice the heart of every one who sympathizes in the award of justice to them who are oppressed. He saw a revolution in human affairs that completely reversed every thing that had previously existed. Instead of "the saints" being worn out any longer, he saw the power of judgment given to them to take away the dominion of the Little Horn (Daniel 7:22,26,11), to slay the beast, and to destroy his body with the burning flame, so that nothing represented by the symbol should be left.

The territory which is to be the scene of this judgment is all that region comprehended in the Roman Dragon, and in the Austrian and German domain. By the Roman Dragon, I mean the old Roman territory, extending from the Euphrates to the German Ocean, including Turkey, Italy, Switzerland, Roman Africa, and the other countries contained within the limits of the ten toe-kingdoms. Upon this territory, then, our attention must be fixed if we would discern the progress of the events by which the beast's destiny is fulfilled. He is to be destroyed by the burning flame. It is evident, therefore, that the territory of his dominion will be turned into a region of flame, in which the populations being everywhere insurgent, and contending with fire and sword against their oppressors, it will become "a lake of fire burning with brimstone" (Revelation 19:20). Into this are cast alive the two-horned beast of the earth, and the image, which before the end of its existence is stripped of its imperial character, and reduced to the humbler dignity of a "prophet", and that a false one.*

What remains of this chapter will be occupied in explaining these words of the prophet—"The judgment shall sit, and *they* shall take away *his* dominion, to *consume* and *to destroy* it unto the end" (Daniel 7:26). The judgment sits upon the whole beast, and consists of slaying and burning. This distinction is preserved in the Apocalypse; for whilst the beast and false prophet are cast alive into a lake of fire, "*the remnant*", or the horns that remain, are "slain with the sword of him that sits upon the horse, which sword proceedeth out of his mouth". "With the breath of his lips shall he slay the wicked." This implies a prolongation of existence to certain powers beyond that of the beast and false prophet. These will be totally destroyed by "the saints"; but "the remnant" are reserved for a future fate at the hand of the King of

---

* The complete fulfilment of this came to pass in 1870, in the fall of the Temporal Power of the Pope.

kings and Lord of lords. Daniel makes the same distinction in the judgment of the fourth beast. Speaking of it as a whole, he says, "I beheld till *the beast was slain*, and *his body* given to the burning flame". The *consuming* affects the body; and the *destroying*, "the remnant" of his political carcase by the sword. Turkey, and the Austro-Papal dominions, constitute the body and Little Horn of the beast. These go into perdition first. They entirely disappear from among "the powers that be"; as completely as a carcase cast into Nebuchadnezzar's furnace. After their fate is sealed, a power arises to conquer the toe, or horn-kingdoms, which are not suppressed, but made tributary to the conquering power; and are incorporated as vassal kingdoms into his dominion; and under his banner meet the Lord of hosts in battle in the plains of another Waterloo, called Armageddon, where both he and they are overcome, and lose their crowns for ever.

Speaking of the Little Horn, or Austro-Papal power, the prophet says, "*They* shall take away his dominion". Now the context shows that the agents indicated in "*they*" are the "saints" with whom the horn has contended so long. In the twenty-second verse he says, "*Judgment was given to the saints*". Having received power to judge, what use did they make of it? This is answered in the twenty-sixth verse—"to take away his dominion"; and if a further inquiry be made, by what means? The reply is by consuming and destroying it with fire and sword. There is a fitness in this. The Austro-Papacy has been established by fraud and violence; and shored up to the end of its existence by murder. It has fattened on the blood of the two witnesses in all countries of its dominion: and therefore the rule of the judgment is to "give them blood to drink, for they are worthy" (Revelation 16:6). This is the fate impending over Austria and all thrones which have given their power to execute the will of the Roman prophet.

But to this some may object, How can the saints execute the judgment written (Psalm 149:5-9), seeing that the beast overcame them and killed them in the reign of Louis XIV? It is very certain that they cannot, unless they are the subjects of a political resurrection; and this the testimony affirms they should be. But before they rose from political death, they were to remain politically dead, but unburied, for three symbolic days and a half; after which the spirit of political life from God was to enter into them; and in consequence they were to stand upon their feet, ascend to power, and strike terror into all their enemies who beheld them (Revelation 11:8-12). They were to lie dead and unburied "upon the broad way (ἐπὶ τῆς πλατείας) of the great city, which spiritually is called Sodom and Egypt, where also our Lord was crucified". Jesus was put to death in Judea; but then Judea was a Roman province at the time, and therefore a part of *"the great city"*; for all the Roman provinces were regarded merely as an extension of Rome which ruled over them, inasmuch as the Roman city was made co-extensive with the empire by the edict of Caracalla. This empire, then, as a whole, is figuratively designated by the Spirit as Sodom and Egypt—as Sodom, because of its filthiness, and as Egypt, because of its darkness; and as Sodom and Egypt conjointly, because the fate of Sodom awaits Rome, and the judgments of Egypt, the nations that acknowledge its spiritual dominion.

The ten horns of the Roman Dragon are ten parts of this great city; the most ample of which, as will be seen by consulting a map of the Roman empire, is the realm of France. It is, therefore, styled *"the broad way"* by the Spirit. Here the witnesses received their death blow, which was speedily followed by their political death in all other parts of the great city. Though politically dead the witnesses were still visible, or unburied. The democracy and the Calvinists still existed in France; and democracy and dissent in England, where thousands of the Huguenots found refuge; but in all countries of the beast they were at zero in political affairs.

In their exile from Europe, multitudes found an asylum in the American wilderness. There they mingled with their brethren, whose progenitors had expatriated themselves from Britain to escape the galling yoke of Church and State Toryism which was carrying itself with a high hand. Thus, by the tyranny of the beast, liberty and democracy were crushed in Europe, and simultaneously planted in American soil. But even there the witnesses were not permitted to rest, for they lived in the other hemisphere, though dead in this. Home tyranny claiming the right to tax the unrepresented, the descendants of the Puritans and Huguenots resisted, and refused to pay. A profligate and extortionate government goaded them into insurrection, by which they became entitled to the honourable distinction of "rebels", and by their success, to that of "patriots". The struggle was between might and right. An arbitrary government demanded tribute, and an ignorant clergy tithes; and the democracy, religious and secular, gave them lead and steel. This was the old fashion in which they had been accustomed to "devour their enemies" during their 1,260 years' contest with the beast. But the conflict was unequal; and but for the suicidal policy of one of its horns, the witnesses would have again been overcome.

The liberty-hating, and the heretic-slaying, Bourbons sent a fleet and army to enable "liberty, equality and fraternity" to triumph in America! Not that they hated sectarianism and democracy less than formerly, but that they hated England more. La Fayette and his companions, though scions of nobility, became the sons of freedom. Britain was check-mated; and the model republic founded, and acknowledged by all the horns of the beast. There, then, beyond the broad waters of the mighty deep, the tree of liberty, planted by the two prophets of human rights, spreads its ample and expanding branches, affording shade and shelter for the persecuted and oppressed of all nations, who may be fortunate enough to escape the "great iron teeth" and "brazen claws" of the all-devouring monster of the sea.

Peace being proclaimed, the French army returned to Europe in 1783. This proved a refreshing breeze to the democracy of that kingdom. "Philosophers" were hard at work teaching the people to despise the superstition of Rome, and the creatures that fattened upon it. They miscalled it Christianity; as if the religion of Christ had the remotest affinity to that of "Sodom and Egypt"! But Romanism was the only view the people had of Christianity; for there had been no testimony borne against it in France for ninety-eight years. The priests taught them that Romanism was the religion of the Bible, but would not permit them to look into it to see. Need one be surprised, then that when the democracy arose to judgment it should abolish such a Christianity as that which had destroyed them; treat the Bible with contempt; and even deny the existence of a God, who was supposed to sanction the falsehoods of Romanism, or to approve its hypocritical and licentious priests? The liberalism of the American auxiliaries manifested itself soon after their return, in the appearance of an American party in French politics. The influence of this in connection with the scepticism of "the philosophers", became "the breath of (political) life from God". It entered into the unburied witnesses; and "they stood upon their feet", ready for action. Thus they drew their first breath in the very city where they had received their death-blow.

A few words may be offered here respecting the time signified by *"three days and a half"*, during which the two witnesses were deprived of political life. The Apocalypse as a whole is a *miniature* representation of "the things which are, and the things which shall be hereafter" (1:1,19); that is, of things in existence while John was in Patmos, and of the things shortly to happen after he wrote, and until the setting up of the kingdom. Everything is exhibited on a smaller scale than the reality; and the time of the symbols is in keeping with them. Thus, multitudes of witnesses are reduced to two; and the years of their prophesying to days. It would have been a violation of the fitness of things to have made them testify for 1,260 years, because this is far beyond the duration of human life, which is the rule of speaking in the case. So in indicating the time of their unburied state, the real time must be expressed in accordance with the physical laws. A dead body might lie in the open air for "three days and a half" without disappearing; but not three years and a half, or three months and a half. Hence, the symbol required the smallest possible period *capable of expressing the real time* of their political non-existence; and that is "three days and a half".

The time that elapsed between their death in 1685, and their resurrection in 1790, was 105 years. This is a period contained in three lunations and a half, on the day for a year principle. It is harmoniously related to the "forty-two months" of the down-treading of the Holy City mentioned in Revelation 11:2. That is to say, forty-two months equals three-and-a-half years, which, in prophetic language, would be expressed as "three days and a half".

This consideration led Mr. Bicheno, a Baptist Pastor in Newbury, England, in 1793, to conclude that *lunar* days were intended. Taking the Jewish month of 30 days (for the 42 months of Revelation 11:2 are coupled with the 1,260 days in verse 3), Mr. Bicheno found that three-and-a-half times thirty, or 105 days (years), gave just the interval from the death of the witnesses in 1685 to their political resurrection in 1790, in the time of the Great French Revolution. Mr. Bicheno, though cloudy on some points, was nevertheless sufficiently sound to be regarded as one of the witnesses. He did well in stirring up his own generation to the study of the Apocalypse; and in discovering for us the true import of the "three days and a half". His labour was not lost; and we thank our Heavenly Father for raising up such witnesses, whose memory the faithful in Christ Jesus do always delight to honour.*

Now, "*after* three days and a half, the breath of life from God entered into the witnesses"; that is, after the three months and a half of day-years had fully expired, "they stood upon their feet". The death-period elapsed on Feb. 18, 1789, and in two months and fourteen days after, being May 4, they accepted the invitation of "a great voice from the heaven", saying to them, "Come up hither!" This great voice was the royal proclamation by which the States General were convened, and in which the witnesses took their seats as the third estate of the kingdom. They soon proved their existence there by the events which followed. They ascended to power in a portentous cloud, which burst upon the devoted heads of their enemies; and in the earthquake which followed they shook the world.

The resurrection of the Calvinist and Secular democracies in the great city, constitutes a great and remarkable epoch in

---

* The preceding two paragraphs have been re-written on the basis of *Eureka*, a later work by the author of *Elpis Israel*.

prophetic time. It was 1,260 years from A.D. 529. Now when we turn to the history of that period, we find that it also is dignified as a notable epoch of the times of the Gentiles. From 529 to December 16, 533, a period of four years and eight months, there were published the celebrated code, pandects, institutes, and novels of Justinian. "These were declared", says Gibbon, "to be the legitimate system of civil jurisprudence; they alone were admitted in the tribunals; and they alone were taught in the academies of Rome, Constantinople, and Berytus. He addressed them to the senate and provinces as his eternal oracles; and his pride, under the mask of piety, ascribed the consummation of this great design to the support and inspiration of the Deity." These documents became the civil and ecclesiastical constitution of the Roman empire; and as the new kingdoms of the west looked up to the majesty of Constantinople and the episcopate of Rome as the founts of jurisprudence, civilization, and religion, they gradually came to adopt the Justinian as the common law code of their kingdoms. An incident recorded in the memoirs of Lavallette will illustrate the truth of this. "The events that preceded the grand drama of 1789", says he, "took me by surprise in the midst of my books, and my love of study. I was then reading the *Esprit des Lois*, a work that charmed me by its gravity, etc. I wished also to become acquainted with the code of the laws of France; but Dommanget, to whom I mentioned my desire, laughed, and pointed to the Justinian code as the common law code of the kingdom." The institutes were published in 533, and in that year, in the case of an appeal by the Emperor Justinian to the ecclesiastical decision of the Bishop of Rome, he addressed him as *the head of all the holy churches* of the empire.

But the Justinian code was not adopted by Europe simultaneously, nor in 534, when his labours were complete. He had made the Roman bishop spiritual head of the empire, but his supremacy was not acknowledged by the toe-kingdoms until about seventy-five years after. Students flocked from all of them to the schools of Rome, Constantinople and Berytus, where they studied the law of the empire; and from these centres also priests and missionaries were sent to propagate the faith, and to convert the governments of the west to the religion of the Roman bishop. When this was accomplished, Roman law and Roman superstition struck deep root among the institutions of the west. The Roman high priest was regarded as their spiritual father; and the emperor, as the imperial head of the divided, but still Roman, dominion of the east and west. This work required years to complete; but when finished, as it was about 606 or 608, we find the contest between the Bishop of Rome and the Patriarch of Constantinople, for the spiritual supremacy of the world, brought to a conclusion by the former being proclaimed *universal bishop* by the Emperor Phocas. From 529 to 604 is a period of 75 years; and from 533 to 608 is also 75 years; and between 604 and 608, the Bishop of Rome obtained his legal recognition, which was celebrated by the erection of a statue to Phocas, with the date of 608 inscribed upon it.

This period of 75 years with a double beginning and a double ending of four years, is the period of the civil and ecclesiastical constitution of the ten-horned beast, when the Roman Dragon "gave him his power, and his throne, and great authority" (Revelation 13:2). Now this symbol is to *"continue forty and two months"*, which is the representative time of the continuance of the things represented by the symbol expressed in miniature. It is the symbolical duration of the decemregal and imperial constitution of Roman Europe. Daniel expresses the same duration by the phrase, *"time, times, and dividing of time"*; which also represents 1,260 years. The beasts and their image, and the little horn and his eyes and mouth, are to prevail against the saints until the end of that period. The little horn, and the two-horned beast and the image, do not exist all that time; for they did not appear till 270 years *"after"* the Justinian epoch: but although they did not all rise from the earth and sea, and attain to dominion at one and the same time, yet it is plainly revealed, that they are all to lose their independence, and finally their sovereignties, at the end of the 1,260 or forty-two months of years; so that while the ten horns will have practised 1,260 years from the time of Phocas, the little horn and his apocalyptic synonyms will have existed only somewhat more than 1,000. The Bishop of Rome, however, as lion mouth of the ten horns, will have passed through his 1,260 years.

Not to interrupt the train of thought before us, I shall finish what I have to say about the time of the beast before I return to the subject of the witnesses. The prophet saith, "Blessed is he that waiteth, and cometh to the 1,335 days" (Daniel 12:12). The end of this period is a time of blessedness to the saints of the Holy City, because like Daniel they shall "stand in their lot in the end of the days". But so long as the fourth beast "prospers" this cannot be; for the Gentiles tread down the Holy City until the 42 months expire ... There will, however, be no delay of the resurrection on account of the "practising" of the beast, because it will have to be destroyed out of the way by the Holy City. The prophet informs us, that all things shown to him are to be finished after a "time, times, and a half", or 1,260 years; and among these wonders is the resurrection of many of the dead to everlasting life (12:7,2).

"Justinian's legislation (AD 530-3) was all devoted to the building up and strengthening of the Catholic Church; while the legislation of the National Assembly (AD 1790-3) was all directed to its destruction. It is a remarkable fact that these two mutually antagonistic and subversive systems of legislation flourished exactly 1,260 years apart from epoch to epoch, and that the one hour of 30 years added to it, or 1,290, brings us to the beginning of the outpouring of the sixth vial (AD 1820) 'upon the great River Euphrates' ... Is this, indeed, the true ending of Daniel's 1,290? And, if so, is AD 1865-6 the ending of the 1,335, as well as of John's forty and two months? *If it be*, then there is an epoch upon us of four years in any day of which Christ may come as a thief ... This appears to me, at this writing, to be the correct interpretation of the times. *It is, of course, impossible to say that the interpretation is without error. The ensuing years will determine this point beyond dispute*. While I write, it is the most satisfactory to my own mind. I have thought that Daniel's 1,290 terminated in 1864, and his 1,335 in 1909. But in writing the exposition of this chapter, the fact of the great earthquake-resurrection of the witnesses being exactly 1,260 years after the promulgation of the civil law of the city, and the hour of 30 years added, bringing us to the beginning of the pouring out upon the desolator of the Holy Land, that which is determined (Daniel 9:27), or 1,290 years afterwards—I do not feel at liberty to persist in rejecting my original conviction that the 1,290 ends in 1820; and the 1,335 forty-five years after, or in the epoch current with 1865-6 or thereabouts."*

In AD 800 came the restoration of the Roman empire of the west, or establishment of the little Latin Horn of Daniel, and two horned beast, and the image, of the Apocalypse. This was 270 years from the publication of the Justinian code; and 240 from the settlement of Italy, according to the articles of the Pragmatic sanction, by which "Rome was degraded to the second rank" among the cities of the empire. The fourth trumpet, which proclaimed the smiting of the sixth head of the Beast in its jurisdic-

---

* This paragraph is taken from a later work by Dr. Thomas, *Eureka*, an exposition of the Apocalypse, vol. 2, p. 680. "The ensuing years" in the language of Dr. Thomas, *have* "determined the point beyond dispute." The 1,335 years are not yet ended, for the event that marks their termination is *still in the future*. The erroneous interpretation has therefore been omitted from this edition of *Elpis Israel*.

tion over a third part of the Roman territory, still continued its soundings. The events which pertained to it yet showed themselves in the wars between Justinian and the Vandals, Goths, and other people, until Italy was depopulated of many millions of its inhabitants. Under this trumpet, the sovereignty of the eternal city suffered a total eclipse; so that the imperial day shone not upon her "for a third part of it, and the night likewise" (Revelation 8:12). This was a day and night of years, the minimum of time demanded by the nature of the eclipse.

A day of years, and a night of years, are each 360 years long; for as a day in symbolic time represents a year, or 360 days, so if the decorum of the symbol require it, each of these days may represent a year. A scripture, or Jewish, day contains 12 hours; and a night likewise. Hence, the third part of a day is four hours; and the third part of a night, four hours also. An hour being a twelfth part is equal to 30, which multiplied by 4 gives 120 years for the third part of the day; and 120 years for the third part of the night, which added together make 240 years. Now, if my calculation and interpretation be correct, it follows that Rome (in which there had been seven sovereignties from the foundation of the city till the fall of the Gothic kingdom of Italy in AD 553) should be no more the seat of empire, from the degradation by the Pragmatic sanction until the end of 240 years. In other words, that at the end of that period her eclipse should terminate, and she should once more shine forth with imperial splendour.

Now, no interpretation of prophecy is worth anything which is not sustained by *facts*; for prophecy is not a prediction of opinions, principles, or feelings, but of tangible and stubborn facts. What, then, are the facts in the case before us? I give the answer to this question in the words of Gibbon. "On the festival of Christmas", says he, "the last year of the eighth century (*i.e.*, 800) Charlemagne appeared in the church of St. Peter. After the celebration of the holy mysteries, Leo suddenly placed a precious crown upon his head, and the dome resounded with the acclamations of the people, 'Long life and victory to Charles, the most pious Augustus, crowned by God the great and pacific emperor of the Romans!' The head and body of Charlemagne were consecrated by the royal unction; after the example of the Caesars, he was saluted or adored by the pontiff; his coronation oath represents a promise to maintain the faith and privileges of the Church; and the first fruits were paid in his rich offerings to the shrine of the apostle". Gibbon styles him "the Restorer of the western empire", which included France, Spain, Italy, Germany, and Hungary; and from the restoration of which "Europe", says he, "dates a new era". Thus, Rome's eclipse passed away, and her system was again illumined by the shining forth of the imperial sun, moon, and stars over the third part from which they had been so long obscured.

THE KINGDOMS OF THE WORLD

CHAPTER III

THE "VIALS OF THE WRATH OF GOD"
—ARMAGEDDON

Doings of the witnesses when invested with power—They execute justice on their enemies—A great earthquake—The seventh trumpet—Divided into seven vial-periods—The third, fourth, and fifth vials, and Napoleon—England and the second vial—Turkey and the sixth vial—All Europe and the seventh vial—The prophecy of the Frogs explained—The mission of the unclean spirits—Their operation the sign of Christ's stealthy and sudden return—The great desideratum in view of the Advent

"THE time of the end" (Daniel 8:17; 11:40), styled also by Daniel "*the latter days*" (2:28; 10:14), is the period of the Beast's trouble by sword and flame at the hands of the saints. They are to "consume and destroy his dominion to the end". Their success, however, in this work of blood will be the occasion of bringing up a power upon them, which will overcome them in turn; and by his conquests build up the Image of Nebuchadnezzar, and bring out again to view the Lion, the Leopard, and the Beast; by which the Image will be broken to shivers; and the Beasts "have their dominion taken away by the Ancient of Days"; though their existence will be prolonged for "a season and a time", or 1,000 years, during which their destinies will be at the disposal of the inheritors of the Kingdom of God.

There elapsed four years and eight months between the publication of the Justinian code, and that of the pandects and institutes. A second edition of the code, amended and enlarged, was proclaimed in rather less than six years after its first publication. Now it is remarkable, that about the same space of six years was occupied by the antagonists of the Beast, in the national assembly of its principal kingdom, in repealing, by its 8,370 decrees, the Justinian constitution of the empire by which the Bishop of Rome became the lion-mouth of the dominion, and the Roman superstition the State religion of the Horns. In 533, the supremacy of Rome in ecclesiastical affairs was recognized by Justinian: and in 1,260 years after, that is, in 1793, the new constitution was adopted, and the Roman religion abolished. There are other notable considerations of the same kind which the reader may observe for himself in studying the history of these periods. Want of space forbids my going more into detail upon this part of the subject; I shall, therefore, return to a brief outline of what remains concerning the witnesses after their ascension to supremacy in the sight of their enemies.

Having responded to the "great voice from the heaven, saying unto them, Come up hither!" they were not long in making their power felt. They converted the States General into the National Assembly on June 17, 1789; abolished the feudal system, and all privileges; and declared ecclesiastical property to be the property of the nation. In 1790 they continued to shake the monarchy with great violence. They suppressed all religious orders; and destroyed "*seven thousand names of men*" (ὀνόματα ἀνθρώπων); that is, completely abolished all titles of nobility, not even sparing the king's. These things were only preliminary to the fall of the throne. "*The tenth of the city fell*", for, in 1792, they abolished the monarchy, and proclaimed a republic. On Jan. 31, 1793, they executed "*national justice*" upon Louis XVI, the representative of the king who, in 1685, had massacred them by thousands in cold blood. His Queen soon met with the same fate; and to crown all, the worship of Reason was substituted for the vile superstition of Rome. The national justice having been carried to this extent, "*the remnant were affrighted*". The reign of terror was established. They sent a revolutionary army over the departments with artillery and the guillotine to take vengeance on their enemies. Priests, aristocrats, and their adherents, became bread for the avenger. The *dragonnades* were retributed by wholesale drownings, and pitiless slaughters. They slew 2,160 nobles and priests at Nantes; drowned and shot 2,000 infants, 7,641 women, and 5,300 artisans. Thus the broad way of the great city became a field of blood from one end of the domain to the other. In the hour of their vengeance, they did not omit an act of justice to the heirs of their brethren, the murdered Huguenots. They restored to them all their confiscated estates which remained unsold; and declared all Frenchmen who were not Papists admissible to all offices, civil and military.

In 1794 the saints had nearly completed the national justice for the present upon the French horn of the beast for its cruelties upon their brethren, and its impiety and licentiousness down to this time. It was truly "a great earthquake", and had produced terrible devastation. The real character of the events of this epoch has never been appreciated so far as I am informed. They have been viewed too much as the incidents merely of a sanguinary conflict between political factions. Viewed in this light indeed, the actors in the scenes can only be looked upon with horror and detestation. They were exceedingly wicked and depraved men; and so were God's "*sanctified ones*" the unpitying Medes, whom He had prepared to execute vengeance upon

Babylon. "The wicked are the sword of the LORD"; hence, it is in this light His "saints" of the Median character must be regarded. Viewed through a scripture medium, we see in the democracy of the eighteenth century, the sword of God "bathing itself in the heaven, and coming down upon the people of His curse to judgment" (Isaiah 34:5).

If the saints to whom the judgment of the beast is committed were men disposed to mercy, they would be unqualified for their work in the absence of the captain of their salvation. *The saints of the holy city* are not appointed to take vengeance at present. This work is for the wicked, that the wicked may destroy the wicked. But with all their depravity, the saints of the sword were no worse, nor, indeed, so detestable, as Charles IX, Louis XIV, the Popes, the Inquisition, and the savage mercenaries by whom their orders were executed. There has been this redeeming quality in these saints, that they have "helped the woman"; and in their conflicts protected "the remnant of her seed" against the Beast; while kings, priests, and nobles, have soaked the soil of Europe with their blood; and celebrated their sufferings with illuminations, gifts, and merry-makings (Revelation 11:10).

A most unexpected event marked the end of the second woe which has hitherto been under consideration. It was revealed to John that the reign of terror would pass away by their giving "glory to the God of heaven". The democracy, which had been trained to atheism and blasphemy by the Roman superstition and the "philosophers", had decreed that there was no God when they abolished the Papal worship. The nation, however, did not maintain this edict for many months; for on May 7, 1794, Robespierre obtained a decree from the convention, proclaiming the existence of the Supreme Being; and another on June 8, decreeing a national festival to his honour, which was celebrated accordingly in Paris with popular demonstrations of joy. Thus ended the sixth trumpet, which was to be quickly succeeded by the seventh and last.

THE SEVENTH TRUMPET

IN the days of the voice of the seventh angel *when he shall sound* (ὅταν μέλλῃ σαλπίζειν) the secret of God shall be finished, *as he hath declared* to his servants the prophets" (Revelation 10:7). Here is *a continuance of time* specified, namely, *"in the days of the voice* of the angel"; that is, the sounding of the last trumpet would be no exception to those which had gone before; but, that as they had occupied years in sounding, so the seventh would sound through a succession of years, even until the kingdom of

God should be established as revealed in the writings of the prophets (Daniel 2:44). This is the declared mystery, to the manifestation of which all things are tending.

The things which will have been accomplished when the seventh trumpet shall have ceased to sound are stated summarily in the following words; "And the seventh angel sounded; and there were great voices in heaven, saying, The kingdoms of this world are become the kingdoms of our Lord and of his Anointed (Χριστός); and he shall reign for ever and ever". This is the consummation, which is introduced by these foregoing events, to wit: "The nations were angry, and thy wrath is come, and the time of the dead, that they should be judged, and that thou shouldest give the reward to thy servants the prophets, and to the saints, and them that fear thy name, small and great; and shouldest destroy them that destroy the earth." In connection with these wonderful events, "the temple of God was opened in the heaven, and there was seen in his temple the Ark of his testament"; and this exhibition is to be accompanied by "lightnings, and voices, and thunderings, and an earthquake, and great hail" (Revelation 11:15-19); the result of which will be the translation of the kingdom under the whole heaven to the prophets, and saints, and to them who fear the name of the Lord.

The eleventh chapter of the Revelation terminates with the glorious and terrible advent of Christ. The thirteenth verse records the end of the sixth trumpet or second woe; and the nineteenth, the end of the seventh trumpet, or of the third woe, which is consummated in the destruction of the tyrants who have for so many ages been the demoralizers and destroyers of the people; and in the introduction of the era of blessedness to the world. As I have said, the sounding of the last trumpet is not an instantaneous blast, but a series of blasts in regular succession. He is the trumpeter who summons the nations to war throughout the time of the end, after which "the judgment sits to take away the dominion of the fourth beast to consume and to destroy it unto the end".

While this trumpet is sounding, seven angels, or messengers, are engaged in pouring out "the wrath of God upon the earth", or continental Europe and Asia, especially that portion of them comprised in the Greco-Roman Dragon. The portions of wrath committed to these symbolical angels are termed "*vials*", which were to be emptied upon certain territories and powers of the Roman world. The first five were consecutive in their beginnings, but afterwards concurrent for several years. The vengeance they contained fell upon the ten horns of the beast, the two-horned beast, and the image of the beast; while the agent, or executioner, was the French democracy, to which "power was given". They had first plagued God's enemies, and those of His people, in France; and having finished their work there, they were let loose upon the other horns of the beast, and upon his little horn and its appendages to plague them for their crimes against God and man. The democracy were invited to their work abroad by the continental coalition against France, in which Austria was a principal.

The reader can consult the history of the period for details; it will be sufficient for me to say here, that with every disadvantage in the outset, the *sans-culottes*-soldiery became at length everywhere triumphant. They were without funds, imperfectly armed and disciplined, and led on by inexperienced generals; they were opposed by well-appointed armies, with all the military talent of Europe to direct them: but God's power was with them in a way not visible to flesh. They were contending with His foes, and avenging the blood of His saints, therefore no power could withstand them so long as they did not transcend their mission. The history of these events ought to teach politicians that God can punish the destroyers of the earth by an agency which in itself is without strength or wisdom. When He takes the work in hand, the feeble become strong; and the poor despise riches. His saints of Media "did not regard silver; and as for gold they delighted not in it". Politicians speculate as though money were omnipotent; and we hear "financial reformers" predicting the inactivity of Russia and Austria for want of funds! Where did the barbarians procure funds for the overthrow of the western empire in the fifth and sixth centuries? Did they not support themselves by the spoil? Let the Russian treasury be as empty as it is said to be, and its expenditure exceed its revenue by double the alleged deficit, it will only operate as a pressure from within, causing her Autocrat to "enter into the countries and to overflow and pass over", and to enrich himself with the spoil of those he is destined to subdue.

The Third Vial.—From among the lowest of the people there arose a military hierarchy, headed by a chief who became the sword of God and scourge of Europe. It is scarcely necessary to say that this was NAPOLEON and his generals. To him, as the man of the earth and sword of the democracy, it was given to carry on the vengeance upon Daniel's fourth beast. He appears pre-eminent in the pouring out of the third vial upon "the rivers and fountains of waters", which, under his hand, "became blood". His celebrated campaigns in the Alpine regions and plains of Italy, abounding in springs, lakes, and rivers, strikingly illustrate this vial of wrath. The Austro-Papal, or little horn, was the principal in the war with whom he had to contend.

The "Italian fields"* were the arena of the dreadful massacres of the witnesses by the "holy Roman" power, whose mercenaries on the same *Aceldama* received blood to drink at Napoleon's hand. This righteous retribution is the subject of angelic celebration, saying, "Thou art righteous, O Lord, which art, and wast, and shalt be, because thou hast judged thus. For they have shed the blood of saints and prophets, and thou hast given them blood to drink; for they are worthy." To this, a voice is represented as issuing forth from the symbolic altar, responding in these words: "Even, so, Lord God Almighty, true and righteous are thy judgments" (Revelation 16:5-7). This vial began in 1796 with the war against Piedmont, and ended with the destruction of the little horn, or two-horned beast's, dominion over Italy; and with the establishment of the sovereignty of the military democracy of France.

The Fourth Vial.—But the vengeance of the "earth" upon the little horn did not stop here. They next proceeded to pour out God's wrath upon *"the sun"* of Roman Europe. They had eclipsed him in Italy; and their Corsican chieftain received imperial power, and in the exercise of it literally "scorched men with fire". Being now himself the sun of a great part of Europe, he would tolerate no rival. The house of Hapsburg still claimed to be the sun of the Roman world, which the head of the now imperial democracy resolved should not be. He therefore "scorched men with great heat" in his German wars. He executed all the wrath of the fourth vial upon the Austrian empire, till at length the time arrived to "fill the beast's kingdom with darkness". This could only be accomplished by a total eclipse of the Roman sun.

The Fifth Vial was, therefore, poured out upon the beast's throne. The vengeance was terrific. The people of the beast "gnawed their tongues for pain, and blasphemed the God of heaven because of their pains and their sores, but repented not of their deeds". The power of the little horn was *"consumed"*, but not yet *"destroyed to the end."* The battle of Austerlitz in 1805 decided the fate of its dominion for a time. Francis of Austria still retained possession of his hereditary domain, which included Hungary and Bohemia; but "THE HOLY ROMAN EMPIRE", says Sir Walter Scott, "having lasted full 1,000 years, was declared to be no more, and of its ancient influence, the representation was to be sought for not at Vienna, but at Paris."

But the work was yet unfinished while the Papal Jupiter remained temporal sovereign of Rome. Napoleon having to contend with the British Leopard in Spain, the Beast and the Image

---

* See Milton's sonnet, "On the Massacre in Piedmont, 1655."

deemed it a favourable opportunity to break the yoke of their consumer. Napoleon had required the Pope to declare war against England. But England was too good a friend to receive such treatment. He therefore refused; and replied to his demand by hurling the thunders of the Vatican at his head; while Austria, energized by British gold, assembled 500,000 men for the war. This was in 1809. In five days this mighty host was broken and dispersed. The battle of Wagram reduced the little horn once more to inactivity; and the Corsican avenger obtained leisure to extinguish the Image of the Beast. By a decree dated from the palace of the little horn at Schoenbrunn, he annexed the Ecclesiastical State of the kingdom of Italy; and by a second decree, dated at Vienna, May 17, 1809, he *suppressed the temporal sovereignty of the Pope*; incorporated Rome with the French Empire; declared it to be his *second* city; appointed a committee of administration for its civil government; and settled a pension on the Pope in his spiritual capacity; all of which came to pass exactly 1,260 years from the capture of Rome by Totila and his Goths.

Thus, by the power given to "the earth", the dominion of the ten-horned, and two-horned, Beasts and their Image, was completely taken away till the fall of their consumer. The kingdoms, or horns, of the Beast were all reduced to vassalage, while the imperial chief of the democracy created thrones, and made kings and princes of whomsoever he pleased. It was a glorious sight to the eye of faith to behold him and his democratic nobles with the Beast writhing at their feet. He claimed for his immediate liege subjects a population of 42,000,000 of souls; with Italy, Carniola, and the Illyrian provinces, as a portion of his personal empire. His authority was almost absolute in Switzerland. He was Lord of the confederation of the Rhine. The King of Naples was one of his generals; and the Peninsula seemed on the verge of final subjugation. Thus, an empire of 800,000 square miles, and containing a population of 85,000,000, in territory one fifth part, and in number of inhabitants one half, of united Europe, was either in quiet subjection to Napoleon's sceptre, or on the point, as was supposed, of becoming so.

But the time had not then arrived either for the *final destruction* of the Beast's dominion; or, for *the saints* to possess the kingdom for ever; nor, indeed, are the saints of the Median class the persons for whom everlasting dominion is intended. These are merely the consumers and tormentors of the fourth beast; and not "the possessors of the kingdom under the whole heaven for ever, even for ever and ever". This is reserved for the saints of the holy city, styled by Daniel, "the people of the saints". It was necessary, therefore, to energize the prostrate Beasts, and to enable them, once more to prevail against the saints, but not to kill them, as in 1685; for their agency was still needed for the perfecting of the plagues that yet remain to be executed for the tormenting of the Little Horn to the end.

To compass this necessity, God had reserved powers on the east and west of Europe which had not been subdued. These were the great rival dominions of England and Russia. To the former had been assigned the pouring out the wrath of *the second vial upon the sea*. England began her work in 1793, and, with little interruption, made the sea "as the blood of a dead man" for two-and-twenty years. The maritime parts of the Beast's dominion suffered the vengeance of her power; and so completely did she clear the sea of his ships of war and commerce, that it might be truly said of them, "every living soul in the sea died"; and the waves were ruled by Britain's fleets alone.

In attacking Russia, the democracy exceeded the limits of its commission; for the Russian dominion is not yet of the ten-horned Beast of the sea, or two-horned Beast of the earth. While Russia, indeed, was combating for the Beasts in Italy and Germany, her hosts were at length everywhere defeated; but when they stood upon their own soil, God shielded them from the Avenger, whose strength was wasted by His frost and snow. Repelled within the limits of Roman Europe, the power of Napoleon dried up more rapidly than it prevailed. By the armies of Russia on the east, and by those of England on the south, the beasts were again enabled to stand. The Eagle fled before the Leopard and the Bear, who at length wrested from him the prey, and restored it to liberty and dominion, just 1,260 years from the defeat and death of Teias, the last of the Gothic kings of Italy; and the defeat of the Franks and Allemanni there.

Thus far the seventh trumpet had sounded with terrible effect against the Greco-Roman dragon; which was plagued not only in Europe, but in Egypt and Syria. In 1815, peace was finally proclaimed; "the holy alliance" formed; the *"holy Roman empire"* resuscitated; and the Papal Jupiter reinstated on his throne; and the rest of Europe portioned out according to the interests of the old dynasties of the Beast, and the good pleasure of the Congress of Vienna. But the Beast and his allies can settle nothing upon a permanent basis any more. "For ever" in its decrees, extends only to the end of the blasts of the seventh trumpet. The "holy alliance" was pledged to keep down the democracy, and to maintain the *"order"* in which the blasphemers of God's name, and the destroyers of the earth, delight. But after a few years, God dissolved it like a thing of air.

The Sixth Vial.—The time at length arrived to make *preparation* for the restoration of Israel. The *"abomination that maketh desolate"* had prevailed under divers forms from the celebrated epoch 529-33, beginning the third year of Justinian's reign upon the throne of Constantinople. The dragon, of whose dominion this city became the seat after Constantine transferred the government from Rome, was the desolator of the Hebrew commonwealth. He destroyed the city and temple, scattered Judah, and consumed the land with fire and sword. These have been its works for nearly 1,900 years. But of this long period, a portion has been separated which should reach to the time when "that determined should be poured upon the desolator" (Daniel 9:27). Now, that "which is determined" is the wrath of God contained in *the sixth vial*, and which is appointed to be poured out upon the eastern division of the Greco-Roman Dragon.

When we look into the history of our own time, it is easy to perceive that the sixth vial began in 1820-3. The other vials had been exhausted principally upon the western division of the empire, with the exception of the *second*, which affected the east and west alike. The *sixth*, however, is poured out primarily upon the east, and drying up the desolator's dominion there, pours on until its stream is commingled with that of the seventh, by which both the east and west are wrapped in a universal conflagration, which terminates in the final destruction of the little horn, or two-horned beast and his prophet; the subjection of the ten kingdoms to the dragon of Constantinople; and lastly, their combined overthrow at the battle of Armageddon by the Lord of hosts. The details of the sixth and seventh vials are amplified in that portion of the Apocalypse beginning at the fourteenth verse of the seventeenth chapter, and ending at the sixth of the twentieth. But to return to the sixth.

The sixth *trumpet* brought up the four dynastic powers from the Euphrates, which was the western boundary of their domain. They crossed this river under Alp Arslan, who, at the head of an immense cavalry, invaded the Roman dragon. After "an hour and a day, and a month, and a year" from the invasion; that is, 360 years added to 30, added to 1 year and 30 days, which is equal to 391 years 30 days—the period of Turkish preparation to seize the dragon's throne was complete. On May 29th, 1453, Constantinople fell into the hands of the Turks, who have retained it to this day. The predecessor of Alp Arslan was Togrul Beg, who was constituted lieutenant of the prophet by the last of the Califs. Togrul's successors down to the last Sultan inherited this lieutenancy, by which they were regarded as the political and spiritual head of the Mohammedan world.

The judgment of the sixth *vial* is to take away his supremacy, and to wrest from him the dragon's sceptre. This is termed "drying up the waters of the Euphrates"; which occurs for the purpose of bringing about the restoration of Israel, who by the constitution of Sinai, are "a kingdom of priests, and a holy nation", and to whom belongs the adoption, through which "the kings of the east" are provided. Now, when the Turks obtained possession of Constantinople, the Catholics were doomed to one of three things—to turn Mussulman, to pay tribute, or to suffer death; and for apostates there was no mercy.

In June, 1844, which was 391 years and 30 days from the capture of the city, and the imposition of these conditions upon the conquered, religious liberty and the right of apostasy were conceded at the instance of the western powers. This was 782 years and 2 months from Alp Arslan's invasion. These facts suggested to me a principle of calculation in relation to the passing away of the Sultan's supremacy. It was 396 years 131 days from Togrul Beg's investiture by the commander of the faithful, to the taking of Constantinople. I argued, therefore, from the analogy before us, that it would be 396 years 131 days after the capture, to the time when the Sultan would be about to lose his supremacy at the hand of Russia, who was then fully occupied in the Hungarian war. This time would terminate Sept. 29, 1849. I made this statement in my lectures in various parts of England and Scotland, when all the country was expressing its sympathy for the Hungarians, and the news of their victories abundant. My calculation was too late by ten days. All relations were broken off between Russia and Turkey on Sept. 19th instead of the 29th. This event was a recommencement of sorrows for the Sublime Porte.

The following events will give the reader some idea of the manner in which the sixth vial has been pouring out "on the great river Euphrates". In 1820, the Greeks rebelled against the Sultan and after several years of war succeeded, by the aid of the western powers, in establishing the kingdom of Greece. In 1826, the Janissaries revolted, and thousands of them were massacred by order of the Sultan. In 1827, Turkey lost 100 ships in the battle of Navarino. In 1828, war with Russia, and a general revolt throughout Albania. From 1821 to 1831, ravages of cholera and plague, and depopulation of the eastern provinces. From 1829 to 1848, the Algerine war by which Algeria was annexed to France. In 1839, Egypt and Syria wrested from the Porte by Mehemet Ali. War between Egypt and Turkey, in which the Turkish fleet revolts to Egypt. In 1844, massacres by the Turks in Syria; and exterminating war between the Maronites and Druses there. And in 1848, Russia moved her forces south, and took up her position in the Turkish Principalities of the Danube, to be in readiness to avail herself of subsequent events. All these disasters so weakened the Porte that the dominion of the Sultan could not be preserved for a month, but for the jealousies of England and France against Russia, which only awaits the opportunity of re-planting the Greek cross on the dome of St. Sophia.*

Ten years after the commencement of the sixth vial, its second series of plagues began to affect the political constitution of the Beast. By the judgment of the sixth, a ninth horn was brought out upon the Greco-Roman dragon, which at present wears a crown. This is the Greek kingdom. But there was still another wanting to make up the ten. This tenth horn was brought to light by the second series, whose beginning was marked by the revolution in Paris in 1830. The congress of Vienna had constituted the kingdom of the Netherlands, part of which lay in Roman Europe, and part of it, namely, Holland, beyond it. The sixth vial, however, paid no respect to the political geography of the "holy alliance". The beast required ten crowned horns to answer the prophetic symbol at the epoch of its destruction; for they are then to be unjewelled that they may become the vassal-horns of the Greco-Roman Dragon. Hence, when the air of the Roman world was touched, an electric shock passed through all its kingdoms, producing "voices, and thunders, and lightnings" on every side. A thunderbolt fell upon the Netherlands, striking the throne, and dividing it into two. The result was the establishment of the kingdom of Belgium as the tenth horn of the beast.

It is unnecessary for me to enumerate the ten horns, for they are the same as the ten toe-kingdoms of Nebuchadnezzar's image which are already named. The constitution of France was changed; Louis Philippe, the citizen king, being substituted, by a ruse upon the democracy, for the elder branch of the Bourbons imposed upon them by the "holy alliance". The kingdom of Poland was suppressed, and incorporated as a conquered province with the Russian empire. In Spain and Portugal their several thrones were disputed by pretenders; and even England, though not included in either of the beasts, or in the dragon of "the time of the end", did not escape the vibrations of the air. Events on the Continent gave a salutary impulse to the reform movement, and passed "the bill" (1832).

In 1848 eighteen years had passed away since the blending of these first and second periods. Two years before, a new Pope was elected to the Papal throne. He intended to rule, he said, according to the New Testament! His professions deceived the simple

---

* See Foreword.

hearted, and alarmed the despots of the kingdoms. When Satan undertakes to cast out Satan his kingdom is sure to be convulsed. The reforms of Pius IX satisfied nobody, and tended only to create a longing after liberty, and a determination to free the country from the rule of priests. The hopes of the democracy throughout Europe were inflamed; and "the earth" began to tremble until in 1848 every throne was shaken to its foundation. The events of this wonderful year are too recent to require to be chronicled in this place. It will be enough to say that the democracy broke loose, and commenced a movement, which, though it has been restrained to prevent it progressing too rapidly, cannot be suppressed until the little horn, or two-horned beast and his prophet, be destroyed to the end, and the dominion of the ten-horned beast be taken away.

The events of February, 1848, have developed the "unclean spirits" of the sixth vial. These are precursory to the earthquake of the Apocalypse (11:19). Its first shocks will be terrific; but they are only the premonitions of worse to come. The earthquake, or political convulsion, which followed the resurrection and ascension of the Witnesses in 1789, was awful, as all know who are versed in the history of the time. But that fell far short of what God is preparing for Europe. The tumult of the peoples, and the tempest whose howlings are heard even now, are thus intimated by the prophet, saying, "There shall be a time of trouble such as never was since there was a nation to that same time: and at that time Israel shall be delivered, every one that shall be found written in the book" (Isaiah 4:3). "And many of them that sleep in the dust of the earth shall awake, some to everlasting life, and some to everlasting shame and contempt" (Daniel 12:1,2).

This "time of trouble" is contemporary with the resurrection of a portion of the dead. It is the epoch of Israel's deliverance, both of the Ishmael, and Isaac, seeds; and of the casting down of the thrones of the beast (Daniel 7:9). The convulsion which affects their overthrow is described by the apostle as "a great earthquake, such as was not since men were upon the earth, so mighty an earthquake, and so great" (Revelation 16:18). Ascertain the calamities of former ages, and however terrible they may appear, this will exceed them all. The Flood, Sodom, Egypt, Jerusalem, the fall of the Roman empire, were all judgments which chill the heart, and make the blood run cold to contemplate; but times have now come over the world which will have been hitherto unsurpassed. The wrath of the sixth and seventh vials which remains, is about to overwhelm the nations with "torment and sorrow", for the cup of their iniquity is full.

The more remote effect of past events will be the subdivision of Roman Europe, styled "the great city", into "three parts". This division will be the result of war, for which governments are now preparing themselves, perhaps unwittingly. The tripartite division is attended by the fall of the cities of the nations, as it is written, "The great city was divided into three parts, and the cities of the nations fell." That is, as I take it, that in consequence of the approaching contest, growing out of the Frog-power manifestation of 1848, the ten kingdoms will lose their independence; by which a new partition of the Roman world will ensue; and that when this is brought to pass, events will flow more directly eastward. But before "the cities fall", or as Daniel expresses it, "the thrones are cast down", Rome comes in for her final overthrow. I say, "before", because these kings are to be parties to her tormenting, and are to "bewail and lament for her", to them, unexpected doom. "Judgment" hath then to be given to Zion; for as yet she hath in no part performed her mission. Then are prostrated the horns, the little horn, and the image of the beast, and consumed their dominion; but in connection with this earthquake of the last vial, she has "to destroy it to the end".

They are repressed for the moment: but things are progressing in such a direction as to bring the power of the democracy to bear against Austria and Rome, perhaps through France and Prussia.* When they have done their work, the earth must be again repressed and suppressed, as they were in 1814 and 1815, by a power, however, that will subdue all for itself. There will be no more resuscitation of the old governments, but all things will be absorbed into one continental dominion upon the old Roman domain. In the midst of this great commotion, Britain promotes the colonization of Judea, which is an event pertaining to the sixth vial. By this time, Turkey is no more; and Constantinople acknowledges the sceptre of the Autocrat. England and the Russian lead on the world to the day of doom. They advance their hosts to "the wine-press without the city" (Revelation 14:20), which is called Armageddon (Revelation 16:16) in the Hebrew tongue, and geographically situated in the land of Israel (Ezekiel 39:4; Daniel 11:41,45). There "as a cloud to cover the land" the armed multitudes are assembled, and preparing to decide the fate of Asia by the sword.

But there falls upon them "a great hail out of heaven". Their power is broken; Judah is saved; Messiah appears "as a thief"; the Roman Dragon is bound; and the restoration of the kingdom and throne of David is commenced. Such is an outline of the results to be brought about by the "mighty earthquake" whose premonitions have already revealed what is hereafter to come to pass. In the coming tumult, "great Babylon comes into remem-

---

* And so it has come to pass (1866-1870).

brance before God, to give unto her the cup of wine of the fierceness of his wrath. And every island disappears, and the mountains are not found. And there falls upon men a great hail out of heaven, every stone about the weight of a talent; and men blaspheme God because of the plague of the hail; for the plague thereof will be exceeding great" (Revelation 16:19-21).

"THREE UNCLEAN SPIRITS LIKE FROGS"

BUT the "mighty earthquake" having commenced in 1848, and the democracy which caused it having been repressed to a considerable extent, what agency remains, as revealed in the scriptures of truth, by which is to be brought about the wonderful consummation we have been considering? The answer to this question is contained in the following words. "I saw", says the apostle, "three unclean spirits like frogs out of the mouth of the dragon, and out of the mouth of the beast, and out of the mouth of the false prophet. For they are the spirits of demons (δαιμόνων) working wonders (ποιοῦντα σημεῖα), and they go forth to the kings of the earth, and of the whole habitable (οἰκουμένης ὅλης) to assemble them to the war (εἰς πόλεμον) of that great day of God the Almighty. And he gathered them together into a place called in the Hebrew tongue, Armageddon" (Revelation 16:13-16).

In this passage we have to consider the "THREE UNCLEAN SPIRITS like frogs", THE THREE MOUTHS out of which they proceed, the parties to whom they go forth, and THE FRUIT OF THEIR MISSION. There are three spirits, and three mouths, that is, one spirit proceeding out of each mouth; but as they are all three like frogs and unclean, though proceeding from three different mouths, they are in nature, origin, and tendency, the same. They are called "the spirits of demons", not because of their uncleanness, or wickedness; but because the mouths from which they issue are the demons, or chiefs, of the dominions represented by the dragon, the beast, and the false prophet.

Now the throne of the dragon is *Constantinople*; that of the two-horned beast *Vienna*; and that of the image of the beast, *Rome*. The thrones being in these cities, it follows that the demon of the dragon is the Sultan; the demon of the two-horned beast, the Emperor of Austria; and the demon of the image, the False Prophet himself. It is worthy of observation here, that the text says, "out of the mouth of the false prophet", and not "out of the mouth of the image of the beast". In the beginning of the chapter, while the first vial is supposed to be pouring out, the Papal Jupiter is styled the beast's image; but in the thirteenth verse of the same chapter (Revelation 16), while the spirits are at work, he is termed the false prophet; and in verse twenty of chapter nineteen also, where it speaks of his perdition. This change of style is by no means accidental.

If the reader take a view of the Papal dominion at the close of the eighteenth century, then view it as it is now, and compare the views together; he will doubtless come to the conclusion, that the Pope is no longer the image of the imperial head of the beast. He has no dominion really, for it is so far consumed, that what remains is of little, or no account. He has good will enough to make terrible examples of the democrats who caused his flight from Rome; but he cannot carry it into effect, because the French will not permit him. He is a fugitive in exile, and though pressed to return to Rome, he is afraid to go.* He is, then, no longer imperial, and consequently, has fallen from his Iconism, and become a simple *prophet*.

Protestant and Papal scribes are in the habit of applying the epithet *"false prophet"* to Mohammed, and therefore do not perceive its applicability to the Roman bishop. But neither Mohammed, nor his successors, are termed "the false prophet" in the Apocalypse. The Arabian was false enough, doubtless; but he was a far more respectable character than any Pope that has ever reigned; and were I to choose between the two superstitions, I would rather be a Moslem than a Papist. It was the glory of Mohammed to destroy idolatry: it is the infamy of the Popes to be the high priests of the "queen of heaven". The Saracens were God's locusts to torment, and the Ottomans, God's cavalry to slay with political death, the Catholic image-worshippers of the Asiatic third part of the Roman dragon. Mohammed was the star; and his successors, the "commanders of the 'faithful'", the "angel of the bottomless pit; whose name in the Hebrew tongue is Abaddon, but in the Greek tongue hath his name Apollyon" (Revelation 9:1,11). These names in English signify *Destroyer*, which is indicative of the mission of those who marshalled themselves under the standard of the Arabian.

The epithet "false prophet" is singularly applicable to the Roman bishop. It is a part of his function to preach or prophesy; that is, to "speak unto men to edification, and exhortation, and comfort" (1 Corinthians 14:3). From him these blessings are supposed to flow to all "his children", Aaron was given to Moses to be his prophet because he could speak well. As Aaron, then, was speaker, mouth, or prophet, to Moses; so the Pope is now the

---

* Written in 1849. Pius IX fled from the Revolution to Gaeta in November, 1848, and returned to Rome in 1850. It was not until 1870 that the fall of the Temporal Power was perfected.

mouth, or prophet, or speaker, of the Papacy, and no more. He is virtually stripped of his dominion; he can prophesy, but his rule is a thing of name, and not a fact. A false prophet is he; truthless as Satan; sporting himself with his own deceivings, and thereby provoking a speedy fate, which is "capture and destruction".

But, before he and the two-horned beast before whom he is now working, perish in the European fiery lake they are blowing into a flame, they must fulfil the mission to which they are appointed under this series of the sixth vial. The Sultan, the Pope, and the Emperor, are the "demons" of the crisis, and the mouths, or speakers, of the systems to which they belong. Forth from them are to proceed such measures of policy as will produce a general war. These political measures are symbolized as "unclean spirits". They are *"spirits"*, or influences, exerted through the policy of the three governments; and *"unclean"*, because nothing clean can proceed out of such mouths. Rome, Vienna, and Constantinople, are so many centres of intrigue, whence proceeds the evil that is to ruin the beast. From these are to go forth to "the kings of the earth", and to "the kings of the whole habitable", the results of the intrigues, which will stir up all their propensities to war. The "kings of the earth" are here distinguished from the "kings of the habitable". The former are the kings of Germany and Russia, etc.; while the latter are the kings of Roman Europe, such as of Belgium, France, Spain, Portugal, Sardinia, Naples, and Greece. They are all to be involved in war by the "unclean spirits" of the three demons, whose policy will bring about results that will ruin themselves, and astonish the world.

But why are these three political influences likened to frogs? "I saw", says the apostle, "three unclean spirits like frogs come out of these mouths." The interpretation, I conceive, is this. The frogs are *the heraldic symbol of a power*, which at the prophetic crisis is to be the proximate cause of the several policies which characterize the demon-mouths. That is to say, if this frog-power had not struck out a new course of operation which deranged everything, there would have been no ground for the Sultan, the Emperor and the Pope, to change their policy, and all things would have gone on as usual. The frogs, therefore, and "the spirits", stand related to each other as cause and effect, the *"demons"* being only the *media* through which the frog-power brings about the fatalities of the two-horned beast and the false prophet; and at the same time brings upon the arena a power which is to overtop the horns, repress the frog-power itself, and build up the image of Nebuchadnezzar, preparatory to its being shivered to pieces on the mountains of Israel.

In other words, the scenery of the thirteenth and fourteenth verses of this chapter is a symbolical representation of the working of things unto the judgment, when *"they* shall take away his dominion to consume and *to destroy it to the end"* (Daniel 7:26). Who *"they"* are to whom the work of destruction is committed is obvious from the twenty-second verse, where it is written, "judgment was given to *the saints"*, that is, in the higher sense, who do their work coevally with "the people of the saints", or saints of the holy city, assuming the ruling-judgment "under the whole heaven".

Now, from the evidence I am about to adduce, I think I shall be able to convince the reader that *"the Frogs"* are the symbol of the *French democracy*, the old enemy of the Beasts and their Image. The testimony to establish this is as follows, gleaned from Elliott's *Horæ Apocalypticæ*.

1. Montfaucon, in his *Monuments de la Monarchie Française*, page 4, plate vi, gives a Frog as one of the monuments of the French king, Childeric; thus writing respecting it, "3. Another medal representing *a frog*, which was also an Egyptian symbol." This was found AD 1653, at St. Brice, near Tournay, with other things belonging to Childeric. He reigned AD 456. That is, before the Franks acknowledged the Roman Bishop.

Medal of a Frog found in the tomb of Childeric I

2. In the *Monde Primitif, comparé avec le Monde Moderne*, par M. Court de Gebelin, Paris, 1781, the author thus writes, page 181, "Nous venons de voir que les Armoiries de la Guyenne sont un *leopard*, celles des Celtes (surtout les Belgiques) etoient un *lion*, et celles des *Francs* un *crapaud*. Le Crapaud designe les marais dont sortirent les Francs." And again, on page 195, "La Cosmographie de Munster (1. ii.) nous a transmis un fait très remarquable dans ce genre. Marcomir, Roi des Francs, ayant pénetré de la Westphalie dans le Tongre, vit en songe une figure à trois têtes, l'une de *lion*, l'autre d'*aigle*, la troisième de *crapaud*. Il consulta là dessus, ajoute-t-on, un célèbre Druide de la contrée, appelé Al Runus; et celui-ci l'assura que cette figure

designoit les trois puissances qui auroient régné successivement sur les Gaules; les Celtes dont le symbole étoit le lion, les Romains designés par l'*aigle*, et les *Francs* par le *crapaud*, à cause de leurs marais."*

3. In the sixth century, xlvi of the prophecies of *Nostra Damus* (page 251), translated by De Garencières of London, 1672, occur the following lines:

> Un juste sera en exil envoyé
>
> Par pestilence aux confins de mon seigle;
>
> Response au rouge le fera desvoyé,
>
> Roi retirant à la Rane et à l'aigle.

On which, De Garencières observes: "By the eagle he meaneth the Emperor; and by the frog, the King of France; for, before he took the *fleur-de-lis*, the French bore *three frogs*."

4. In Pynson's edition of *Fabyan's Chronicle*, at the beginning of the account of Pharamond (the first king of the Franks, who reigned at Treves about AD 420), there is a shield of arms bearing *three frogs* (page 57, Ellis' edit.), with the words beneath:

"This is the Olde Armys of France"

---

* The following translation will serve for those who do not understand French.—In M. Court de Gebelin's work, styled "The Primitive World compared with the Modern World", he says, "The armorial bearings of Guyenne are *a leopard*; those of the Celts (especially of the Belgians) are *a Lion*; and of the French *a frog*. The frog represents the marshes whence the French sprung." And again, "The Cosmography of Munster has transmitted to us a very remarkable fact of this kind. Marcomir, king of the French, having penetrated from Westphalia into Tongres, saw in a dream a figure with three heads, the one of *a lion*, the other of an *eagle*, and the third of a *frog*. He consulted there, it is added, a celebrated druid of the country, named Al Runus; who assured him that this figure represented the three powers which had reigned successively over the Gauls; the Celts whose symbol was the lion; the Romans designated by the eagle, and the Franks by the *frog*, because of their marshes."

The banner of Clovis (left), having upon it the *three frogs*, is from an ancient tapestry in the cathedral of Rheims representing battle scenes of Clovis, who is said to have been baptized there upon his conversion to Christianity.

The Banner of Clovis

Armorial Shield of Clovis

The next illustration (right) is from the Franciscan church at Innsbruck*; where is a row of tall bronze figures, twenty-three in number, representing principally the most distinguished personages of the House of Austria; the armour and costumes being those chiefly of the 16th century, and the workmanship excellent. Among them is Clovis, king of France, and on his shield *three fleurs-de-lis* and *three frogs*, with the words underneath, "*Clodovæus der i Christenlich König von Frankreich*"; that is, Clovis the first Christian king of France.

5. *Uptonus de Militari Officio*, page 155, states that three frogs were the old arms of France, without specifying what race of kings.

6. *Professor Schott* supposes the three frogs to have been distinctly the original arms of the Bourbons; *bourbe* signifying *mud*. This may have been the case. When their family became the dynasty of France, they probably assumed the frogs as their arms, being kings of the Franks, whose symbol it had been so long. The Bourbons

---

* The illustration is from a photograph taken in Innsbruck in 1999.

arose out of the mud which is natural to frogs, and by the revolution of 1848 are deep in the mud again!

7. *Typotius*, page 75, gives as the device on a coin of Louis VI, the last French king before Hugh Capet, the first of the Bourbons, *a frog* with the inscription, *Mihi terra lacusque*, land and water are mine.

8. In the *Encyclopædia Metropolitana*, on Heraldry, it is stated that "Paulus Emilius blazons the arms of France, argent three diadems gules"; others say they bear *three toads*, sable in a field vert (ap Gwillim. c. 1), which, if ever they did, it must have been before the existence of the present rules.

Such is the testimony I have to offer in the case before us. The conviction produced on my mind is, that *the Frogs in the prophecy are the symbol of the French democratic power*. It will be seen from the armorial shield of Clovis that the frogs and the lilies were both used as symbols. They are both indigenous to wet, or marshy, lands, and therefore very fit emblems of the French, who came originally from the marshes of Westphalia.

But on the shield of Pharamond so far back as AD 420, the *frogs* without the lilies appear in the armorial bearings of the Franks; and in the medal of Childeric I there is no lily, but the frog only. It would therefore seem from this, that the lilies were not in the original arms, but superadded many years after; and at length adopted by the Bourbons, as the symbol of their race in its dominion over the frogs. These, then, represent the nation, and the lilies, or *fleur-de-lis*, the ruling dynasty. Now, if the apostle had said, "I saw three unclean spirits *like lilies* come out of the mouths", he would have intimated by such a similitude that the French Bourbons were the cause of the "unclean spirits" issuing forth from the Sultan, the Emperor, and the Roman prophet. But he does not say this; he says they were *like frogs*.

The truth, then, is obvious. In AD 96, when John was an exile in Patmos, the Franks were savages in an unnamed country, living by hunting and fishing like American Indians. But the Holy Spirit revealed to him that this people would play a conspicuous part in the affairs of nations; and, foreseeing by what symbol they would represent themselves, He symbolized their nation by it, and styled them *"Frogs"*. He informed John that under the sixth vial their influence would be remarkably apparent. That the Frog-nation would have much to do with the dragon, beast and false prophet; in fact, that so intimate and direct would their dealing be with them, that its effect would be perceived in the warlike tendency and influence of the measures proceeding from the Sultan, the Emperor and the Pope; who, being so completely entangled in the complications created by the policy of the Frog-power, would in their endeavours to extricate themselves, involve the whole habitable in war, which would end in the destruction of the two-horned beast and the false prophet, and in the subjugation of the surviving horns to a new Imperial dominion for a time.

The foregoing analysis of the eleventh, and sixteenth, chapters of Revelation will be found in no other book that I am aware of. It is entirely new. But, as I have said before, no interpretation of prophecy in relation to the past, or present, is worth any thing which is not in harmony with facts. My interpretation must be tried by the same rule, and if it will not stand the test, then let it fade away into everlasting forgetfulness; but if it prove to be correct, I have no apprehension that it will be lost. Facts, then, I remark, are in strict accordance with the exposition given, as I shall briefly point out.

In the last week of February, 1848, the Parisian democracy, ever foremost in revolution, plucked the Bourbon Lily from its throne, and thrust it deep into its native mud. This dynasty of a thousand years was abolished, and the nation resumed its original Westphalian right of choosing a ruler better suited to its taste. The *Fleur-de-lis* being thrown aside, the Frogs by a vote of six millions set over themselves the nephew of their democratic emperor, who had done such good service in executing judgment upon their enemies. The President of the French Republic* is therefore the incarnation of the Frog-power, as the Bourbons were of the Beast while ruling the tenth of the kingdoms. From February the outbreaks of the democracy in other countries became frequent and formidable; and the National Assembly and its Provisional Government constituted in fact the Parliament and executive of the democracy throughout Europe. Under the shadow of their favour Germany and Italy became insurgent, and Hungary followed in the wake of insurrection. The earth shook on every side. Urged on by its democracy, Sardinia attacked the Beast; and, provoked by the treachery of the false prophet, the people of Rome rose, and scared him into exile. After this, the plucking up of the Lombard kingdom by the roots, and the defeat of the Sardinian horn at Novara, by which the Little Horn became triumphant in Italy, caused the Frogs to seize on Rome, that their interests in the Peninsula might be preserved from annihilation.

---

* That is, of course, the Second Republic. In 1852 the President, Louis Napoleon, revived the Empire, being Proclaimed Emperor as Napoleon III, and declaring that "The Empire is Peace!"

By this move the Frog-nation placed itself in antagonism to the two-horned Beast and the false prophet. The Frogs invite the prophet to return to Rome; in other words, to put himself in their power, for which, with the experience of French hospitality towards his predecessors before his eyes, and the treatment he has already received in Rome, he has not the smallest inclination, notwithstanding all his professions to the contrary. If he were to return, he could not remain there twenty-four hours in the absence of a strong military force; and the Frogs will consent to no other than their own; for they occupied Rome, not out of love to the Pope, but as a check upon Austria in Italy. The truth is, Austria and the Pope are natural allies; and are as intimately related as the eyes and mouth of a man are to the man himself. Their fortunes are inseparable. The fate of one is the fate of both, even perdition by the burning flame of war.

The army of the Frog-power has seized upon Rome, and the false prophet will not return, because he regards the Frogs as his real foes. If the Austrians had possession of the city he would go back in triumph: but this not being the case, he is obliged to temporize until the times be more propitious. After this manner, then, the Frogs have become an obstacle in the way of Austria and the Pope, who are both desirous of their expulsion from Rome. They have become the occasion of unclean spirits proceeding from the Emperor and the Roman prophet, which will yet embroil them all, and in the end accomplish the destruction of the Austro-Papal dominion.

In regard to the Sultan, the Frogs are seen exerting their influence upon him. They have assured him of their support in case of his being attacked by Russia. *This promise is sure to bring on a war between the Porte and the Autocrat.** If the Sultan had been left to himself, being weak, he would have yielded and so have avoided war; but being energized by France and England, two strong military and naval powers, the Sultan feels himself a match for Russia, and prepared to assume a bold and warlike attitude. But these assurances will only lure him on to ruin. No powers, however strong, can save dominions foredoomed of God. Their friendship for the Sultan will be as fatal to him as the friendship of England for Austria and the Pope was to them in the days of Napoleon. The Autocrat, being God's sword upon Turkey, will be too strong for them both;† for in the tumult and confusion created by the measures of the Sultan, the emperor, and the Roman bishop, their several dominions will be abolished, and the Autocrat remain lord of the ascendant.

---

* It did (1853).

† Ultimately it will be so; although Russia was checked by the Crimean War.

If the reader take a survey of Europe as exhibited in the events of the last two years, he will see the view I have presented still further illustrated.* The Pope and the Emperor have been the principals who have brought about the wars on the Continent. The unclean spirit of the Little Horn went forth to Russia and brought down its hosts upon Hungary; it is also going forth to Prussia in opposition to the democratic constitution it is developing at Erfurt; and, in concert with Russia, it has gone forth to the Sultan, with whom it has interrupted its former amicable relations. Before the Pope consented to be restored by France, an unclean spirit went forth from him likewise, and brought the Austrians, Neapolitans, and Spaniards, into his States, when he found the Frogs could not be excluded.

I pointed these things out to thousands of people in my lectures, and told them that in regard to Hungary, they were deceiving themselves if they imagined the Magyars would succeed in their war of independence; that Hungary was a brittle toe-kingdom, and one of the three horns which were to be "plucked up by the roots" by the Little Horn. Meetings of sympathy for the Hungarians were being held throughout England; and news arriving every week of Austrian defeats, and Magyar victories. Still, I said, if I have fallen upon the true principles of interpretation, it is impossible for the Hungarians to triumph. So certainly incorrect did some regard this view of the matter, that they said, when I returned to London I should have to expunge what I had advanced about Hungary from the manuscript before I published this book. A preacher who had listened to me at one place, was so convinced of my error, that in his next discourse he predicted the certain triumph of the "brave Hungarians" over all their enemies. But, alas for him! Men should never prophesy of the future from present appearances.

Though these were against my exposition, I was persuaded it would turn out in the end as I had said; and I added, furthermore, that "an unclean spirit" was to go forth out of the mouth of the dragon, as well as from the mouths of the beast and of the false prophet; but that while we could discern "the spirits" issuing forth from these, we did not yet perceive one issuing from the Sultan: nevertheless, though then calm and tranquil, we should soon see a warlike disposition manifest itself in his policy growing out of the Hungarian war. The unclean spirit of the Little Horn had brought the Russians into Hungary, which would only whet their appetites for Turkey, whom they would prepare to devour next. In two or three weeks after making these statements, which as I have said before, were not whispered in a

---

* See Foreword.

corner, but spoken before thousands, all Europe was astounded by the news of Görgey's surrender, and the ruin of the Magyar cause. The details are known to every one. And as I had said, so it came to pass, Turkish sympathy with the Hungarians, and hospitality to the refugees, was made a *casus belli* by the Autocrat; and on the refusal of the Sultan to violate it, diplomatic relations were broken off between Russia, Austria, and Turkey; and the *"unclean spirit"* energized by the Frogs, exhibits even the Sultan as a belligerent.

The mission, then, of these three demons for the period which remains of their political existence, is to stir up the nations to war, which will redound to their own confusion. The Press is prophesying smooth things, and persuading the world of the moderation of the Autocrat, and of the good intentions of Austria and the Pope! It has told us several times that the extradition affair was composed and that peace between Russia and Turkey will not be interrupted; and as often it unsays what it had before affirmed. But the reader need place no reliance upon newspaper speculations. Their scribes know not what God has revealed, consequently their reasonings are vain, and sure to take a wrong direction. As records of facts the journals are invaluable; but if a person permit his opinions to be formed by the views presented in leading articles, and the letters of "our own correspondents", he will be continually misled, and compelled to eat his own words for evermore.

The Bible is the enlightener. If men would not be carried about by every wind that blows, let them study this. It will unfold to them the future, and make them wiser than the world. *The coming years will not be years of peace.* The policy of the Autocrat will be to throw his adversaries off their guard, and take the Sultan by surprise. He is to "come against him like a whirlwind, with chariots, and with horsemen, and with many ships; and he will enter the countries, and overflow and pass over. And many countries shad be overthrown" (Daniel 11:40,41). This is the career marked out for him; which neither France, nor England, nor the world combined can obstruct or circumvent.

"BEHOLD, I COME AS A THIEF!"

IN dismissing this part of the subject, it is necessary to call the attention of the reader to a very important intimation in connection with the prophecy of the "unclean spirits like frogs". This part of the prediction is contained in four verses, that is, from the thirteenth to the sixteenth inclusive. Now, if the reader will examine the passage, he will find that there is a break in the prophecy. That is to say, the subject of the spirits of demons gathering the kings of the whole habitable to war, is suddenly and entirely dropped; and an altogether different subject introduced.

This new topic is nothing less than the appearance of him who sent and signified the contents of the Apocalypse to his servant John (1:1). "Behold", says he, "I COME AS A THIEF. *Blessed is he that watcheth*, and keepeth his garments, lest he walk naked, and they see his shame."

Then, in the next verse, the former subject is revived, and it is revealed, that the angel of the sixth vial gathers the kings and their armies into the battlefield of Armageddon; where, as we learn from other testimony, they encounter the Lamb, upon whom they make war, without knowing, probably, that he is the Commander of the forces with which they are contending (Revelation 17:14; 19:19,21).

Now, does it not strike the reader as remarkable that the coming of the Lord should be introduced in a prophecy like that concerning the frogs? But singular as it may seem it is by no means accidental; but the best possible place for it, because it is intimately connected with their operations. It is mercifully introduced as *a warning* of what is about to happen at the crisis, that the believer may not be taken unawares. It speaks to us in effect, saying, "When you perceive the policy of the Frog-power acting upon the demon of Turkey, the demon of Austria, and the demon of Romanism, so as to cause them to assume an attitude tending to embroil the nations, you may then know that I, the Lord, am about to revisit the world stealthily."

Christ says, "Behold, I come *as a thief*". That is, he comes as a thief comes when he is bent on stealing. A thief not only comes unexpectedly, but he gets into the house with secrecy. John, indeed, says, "He cometh with clouds, and every eye shall see him, even those (*καὶ οἵτινες* who pierced him; and all the tribes of the land shall mourn over him (*ἐπ' αὐτόν*)" (Revelation 1:7). This, however, is affirmed of his appearance in Israel, when he shall make himself known to his brethren after the type of Joseph (Zechariah 12:10-14); which will be subsequently to the great battle in the valley of Megiddo.

The 185,000 Assyrians in the reign of Hezekiah felt the vengeance of the destroyer, but they saw him not; so I believe it will be at the battle of Armageddon, the kings and their armies will be overcome with dreadful slaughter, but they will not see the Avenger's person. The work of the succeeding years requires that so signal a revelation be withheld from them. Israel and the saints of the holy city will see the Lord, but not the nations at large. The divine majesty is not prodigal of its manifestations. Men in the flesh, therefore, will, I apprehend, believe in the presence of the Lord on earth as its imperial and pontifical Ruler, as nations now believe in the existence and sovereignty of the Autocrat, the Sultan, the Emperor, or the Pope, of whom they have heard by the report of others, but whom they have not seen, and perhaps may never behold. Men profess now to believe that the Lord Jesus is at the right hand of God; but hereafter they will believe that he is "reigning in Jerusalem before his Ancients gloriously" (Isaiah 24:23); and their faith if made perfect by works, will, doubtless, as now, be counted to them for righteousness.

But, let the reader observe, that in connection with the warning given, a blessing is pronounced on those who are heedful of the signs of the times. "Blessed", says Jesus, "is he that watcheth." Now no one can watch without light. If the heavens be dark, the watchman must be provided with a light, or he cannot watch. By gazing at the natural luminaries as some professors are accustomed to do, no light can be derived, nor signs observed premonitory of the coming of the Lord. This is "the way of the heathen", and "a custom which is vain" (Jeremiah 10:2,3). The natural heavens are impenetrably dark in relation to his appearing. The believer, or spiritual watchman, must rake "the sure word of prophecy", which is the only "light" capable of enlightening him in the surrounding gloom. This world is "a dark place", and its cosmopolites who understand not the prophetic word, mere embodiments of fog. If we understand "the word of the kingdom" we shall "shine as lights in the world", and be enabled to rejoice in the approach of "the day of Christ." By the "shining light of prophecy" we shall be able to interpret the signs which God has revealed as appearing in the political heavens and earth. Events among the nations of the Roman habitable, and not atmospheric phenomena, are the signs of the coming of the Lord as a thief; whose nature, whether signs or not, can only be determined by "the testimony of God".

From the whole, then, there can be no doubt in the mind of a true believer. He discerns the sign given under the sixth vial as manifestly, and believes as assuredly that the Lord is at hand as they who observed the sun setting in Syrian splendour knew that the coming day would be glorious. Be not deceived, then, by the siren-voices of the peace-prophets. Ere long, the last and most terrible of wars will break out. The Beast and the False Prophet will be plagued, and the Lord will come as a thief in the night. Let this conviction work out its intended results. The blessing is not simply to him that watcheth; but to him that "watcheth and *keepeth his garments*". Simply to believe that the Lord is near, and to be able to discern the signs of the times, will not entitle a man to the blessing. He must "buy gold tried in the fire; and white raiment, that he may be clothed, and that the shame of his nakedness do not appear; and anoint his eyes with eye-salve, that he may see" (Revelation 3:18). In other words, he must believe "the things concerning the kingdom of God and the name of Jesus Christ"; follow the example of the Samaritans and the baptized into the name of Jesus Christ; and thenceforth perfect his faith by his works, as Abraham did. He will then be a lamp, well oiled and trimmed, and fit to shine forth as a glorious light at the marriage of the Lamb.

A community of such persons in a city, constitutes the Lamb's wife there, prepared for the coming of the Lord. She is arrayed in fine linen, clean and white; for the fine linen represents the righteousness of the saints (Revelation 19:7,8); who have "washed their robes, and made them white in the blood of the Lamb". Therefore they will be "before the throne of God, and serve him day and night in his temple (or kingdom): and he that sitteth upon the throne shall dwell among them. They shall hunger no more, neither thirst any more; neither shall the sun light on them, nor any heat. For the Lamb which is in the midst of the throne shall feed them, and shall lead them unto living fountains of water; and God shall wipe away all tears from their eyes" (Revelation 7:14-17). The representative number of their aggregate is 144,000 (14:1-3); and their representative measure 144 cubits (21:17). "These are they who (in the days of their flesh) were not defiled with women; for they are virgins. These are they who follow the Lamb whithersoever he goeth. These were redeemed from among men, being the first-fruits unto God, and to the Lamb. And in their mouth was found no guile: for they are without fault before the throne of God." At present they are the "holy city trodden under foot of the Gentiles"; but when changed and raised from the dead, and exalted to meet the Lord in the aerial, and seen descending there as Zion, they are "the great city, the new and holy Jerusalem, having the glory of God" (11:2; 21:2,9,10,11).

This, then, is the great desideratum of the age—namely, *the preparation of a people for the Lord*; a people whose character shall answer to the testimonies adduced. "The churches" do not contain such a people, neither can their pulpit ministrations produce them. In fact, "the churches" are precisely what college divinity is alone competent to create. "The truth as it is in Jesus" is not taught in the schools. They are mere nurseries of pride, professional religion, and conceit; and "the droppings of the sanc-

417

tuary" which their nurslings are appointed to distil, wear away the intelligence of the people, and leave them irresponsive to "the testimony of God". Nothing short of this, unmixed with the traditions of men, can make people what they must be if they would inherit His kingdom. Other gospels will make other kinds of Christians than those who believe the gospel the apostles preached. We must forsake the pulpits, and devote the time usually spent in dozing over their superficial expositions, to the Berean scrutiny of the scriptures for ourselves. These alone are able to make us wise unto salvation through the faith which is in Christ Jesus.

Hearing "sermons" is not "hearing the word". It is this we must hear if we would have faith; for "faith comes by hearing the word of God". If the gospel of the kingdom were preached in "the churches", and believed, there would be no more complaints of want of spirituality and life. There would be so much of these, that they would be too hot to hold the worldlings who overshadow them with the wings of death. They would go out from them, because they were not of them. Let the well-disposed in "the churches" try the experiment, and they will soon discover the truth of what is here stated. The time is come in which there must be no faint-heartedness, and when a courageous testimony must be borne for the word of the kingdom. Ministerial favour and popularity must be utterly disregarded; and the question be, not "What saith the minister?" or "What will people think?" It matters not what they say, or think, in the case; the simple question is, "How is it written?" "What saith the word?" Let this course be pursued in candour, and I doubt not, but in a short time a people will spring up in these islands prepared for the Lord, whom he will acknowledge at his return.

CHAPTER IV

THE EASTERN QUESTION BEFORE CHRIST

The vision and prophecy of the East—Of the Ram and the Unicorn—The Four Horns of the Goat—Of the fifth, or Little Horn—Of the Seventy Weeks—Of the 1,290 years—Summary of the eleventh of Daniel—Paraphrase of the first thirty-five verses of Daniel 11—Of the King and the strange god—*"Mahuzzim Bazaars"*

THE Greco-Roman Dragon, or Fourth Beast, is a symbol which represents the dominion of the whole habitable; of a greater extent or territory than the empire of pagan Rome, by so much as is included in the countries of the Little Horn, which lie beyond the frontiers of the old dominion. But although this symbol covers all this territory, as it were, it was as impossible to signify by it everything necessary to be represented as it was by Nebuchadnezzar's Image. The Four Beasts were illustrations of the Image. This was especially the case with the fourth. But even by these additional symbols many very important details were left unrepresented. Hence, the Fourth Beast has been itself illustrated by the apocalyptic symbols of the dragon, the ten-horned Beast, the two-horned Beast, and the image of the sixth head of the ten-horned Beast, which was also the sixth head of the dragon.

But notwithstanding all these symbols have been given, all of them in some particular illustrative of the Image, there remains a highly interesting portion of *literal* prophecy unsymbolized. The above-named symbols introduce us to the knowledge of things which history has verified, and to events which belong to "the time of the end". They represent the great truth of the destruction of the Sin-power, and the setting up of the kingdom of God; but of the events connected with the *subjects* of that kingdom, there is a representation that needs to be supplied by other symbols with their appropriate description. These are found in Daniel's *vision of the east*.

But why, it may be asked, has all this symbology been introduced into the Bible? The answer is, to illustrate the relations of the Sin-power to "the holy people" (Daniel 8:24; 12:7) in the eastern and western divisions of the Roman empire. By the holy people is meant the twelve tribes of Israel, and the two witnesses, including also the saints of the holy city among the Gentiles. The Roman power, under its several constitutions, has been the destroyer of "Judah and his companions", and the slayer of the Christians grafted into the stock of Israel, and of those associated with them for their defence against the Beast. The ten horns and Little Horn of the Fourth Beast represent the Roman power *of the West* in its contest with the two witnesses; but there still remained to be represented, the Roman dragonic power *of the East*, as the desolator of Canaan and the destroyer of the Jews, who are *the political subjects* of the kingdom which the God of heaven will set up when He demolishes the Image on the mountains of Israel.

To supply this desideratum the symbols of the eighth chapter, and the exposition of them in the ninth and eleventh chapters, were revealed to Daniel. These may be styled *the vision and the prophecy of the East*; while the Fourth Beast is *the vision of the West*; both of which are set forth briefly and unitedly in the image of divers metals. Having said as much as is necessary to the comprehension of our subject respecting the things which relate to the saints and the Western powers, our attention will henceforth be confined to a brief exposition of the vision and prophecy of the East.

The reader is invited to peruse the eighth chapter of Daniel.

About three years after the vision of the Four Beasts, the prophet saw another vision in which there were only two, namely, a Ram and a He-goat. The former had two horns of unequal height, and *"the higher came up last"*. In the twentieth verse we are informed that the horns represent "the kings of Media and Persia". Hence the Ram symbolizes the Medo-Persian power, with its two dynasties which were not contemporary, but came up one after the other, the Median first, and then the Persian. Having established itself, the Medo-Persians pushed their conquests westward towards Greece (Daniel 11:2), northward towards Armenia, and southward towards Egypt and Ethiopia; so that no powers could stand before them, nor was there any dominion strong enough to deliver the conquered nations from their yoke.

Things continued thus about two centuries from the death of Belshazzar, when a power arose in the west which was represented to Daniel by a Unicorn, that is, by a goat with one horn. This was the Macedonian kingdom; and the horn, its first king, or Alexander the Great. He is styled in *the vision* "a notable horn"; and in *the prophecy* "a mighty king, ruling with great dominion, and doing according to his will" (Daniel 11:3). The

Ram's dominion is represented by the silver part of the image, and the Goat's by the brazen, "which bare rule over all the earth". War broke out between these two powers, which ended in the breaking off of the Ram's two horns; so that the hundred and twenty-seven provinces of the Ram, stretching from India to Ethiopia, were transferred to the Macedonian victor. Now "when he stood up," or "was strong", "his kingdom", or "great horn was broken, and instead of it came up four notable horns towards the four winds (wings) of heaven"; that is, "four kingdoms stood up out of the nation". These have been enumerated on page 357 in speaking of the four heads of the Leopard, which represent the same things as the four horns. Of the horns, it is said, "they stood up not in his power", which is interpreted to signify that the power of the kingdoms did not accrue "to the first king's posterity"; for his kingdom was plucked up for others beside them.

Now, in the latter time of these four Macedonian kingdoms, a fifth power made its appearance among them, and subdued them all. This is represented in *the vision* by a Little Horn growing up out of one of the four horns; and in *the prophecy*, as "a king doing according to his will" (Daniel 11:36). Though relatively small in its beginnings, this fifth power "waxed exceedingly great, toward the south, or Egypt; towards the east, or Euphrates; and toward the pleasant land of Canaan". The history of the kingdoms into which Alexander's dominion was broken, enables us to determine what fifth power is represented by the little horn of the goat, and upon which of the four horns it made its appearance in relation to the land of Israel, which is the arena of the latter time of the vision and prophecy.

The Little Horn, then, is representative of the dragon's power in the East—that is, of the Roman; which was planted on the Assyro-Macedonian Horn BC 65, when it became a province of the dragon empire. It continued to wax exceeding great in these countries until it established its dominion over Syria, Palestine, part of Arabia, and Egypt. The tenth, eleventh, and twelfth verses represent the part it was to enact in the overthrow of the Jewish State; and the twenty-fifth, outlines its ecclesiastical policy, and its exaltation against the Prince of princes in "the last end of the indignation", when it *"shall be broken without hand"* — that is, *by the Stone of Israel when he smites the Image on the feet*.

We see, then, that *Daniel treats of* TWO LITTLE HORNS; the one the "Holy Roman" power of the West that came up *"after"* the Ten Horns; and the other, the Pagan Roman power of the East that appeared in Syria and Palestine in the latter end of the Macedonian kingdoms, and *before* the Ten Horns by many centuries. The Little Horns are representative of powers on certain territories, *not of races*. It matters not whether they be Pagan Romans, Catholic Greeks, Moslem Turks, or Greek-Catholic Russians, the power that rules in Constantinople and plants its standard in Assyria, is the Little Horn of the Assyro-Macedonian Horn of the Goat; and begins its careers by crucifying "the Prince of the Host" (Daniel 8:11); destroying Jerusalem and the temple (Daniel 9:26); sets up a god in Rome whom his fathers knew not (Daniel 11:38); and ends by standing up against Michael, the Prince of princes, who brings him to his end, with none to help him (Daniel 8:25; 11:45; 12:1). All the power of the dragon in relation to Israel and the land of promise is embodied in the Little Horn of the East. The smiting of the Image, the breaking of the Goat's little horn, and the binding of the Dragon, are synchronous and synonymous catastrophes; and "the Stone", "the Prince of princes", "Messiah the prince", and "Michael, the great prince who stands up for Israel", are but different titles by which the Lord Jesus is designated, who is to descend from heaven and fight the battle of God Almighty against them.

Such, then, was "the vision", which was understood by none. At the time it was revealed, Jerusalem and the temple were in ruins, and Israel dispersed among the Gentiles. The time, however, had approached to within two years of the period of restoration. Daniel being aware of this from the testimony of Jeremiah, made confession of sins, and supplicated the return of national prosperity. His prayer was heard, and "the man Gabriel", who had given him the interpretation of the symbols of the vision, was sent forth to "give him skill and understanding" of that part of the vision of the Ram and the Goat which had reference to the subject of his prayer; and to communicate some additional particulars. "The matter" revealed is termed *the prophecy of the seventy weeks*. In this he was informed that a decree should be made for the restoration of the Jewish State; but that at a subsequent period the city and temple should be again destroyed; and that this second destruction should be followed by a desolation of the country which should continue till that determined should be poured out upon the desolator, that is, on the Little Horn of the goat in "the time of the end".

But he was informed that, between the restoration from Babylon and the second destruction of the city, the following important events would come to pass—namely, *first*, the transgression of the law of Moses would be put an end to; *secondly*, an end would be made of sin-offerings by causing the sacrifice and oblation to cease; *thirdly*, reconciliation would be made for iniquity by cutting off Messiah the Prince; *fourthly*, everlasting righteousness, as opposed to the temporary righteousness of the law, would be brought in; *fifthly*, the vision and the prophecy would be sealed up in the confirmation of the covenant; and *sixthly*, the Most Holy would be Anointed. These things were to be brought about by the instrumentality of the Little Horn of the goat; who should "magnify himself against the Prince of the host (of Israel), and by him the daily (sacrifice and oblation) should be taken away, and the place of his sanctuary (the temple) be cast down." To effect this, "an army (the people of the Prince that should come) should be given him against the daily"; because the transgressors in Israel "had come to the full". Therefore he should "cast down the truth (the law and covenant of Sinai) to the ground," and "prosper and practise, and destroy the mighty and the holy people".

But when should this second destruction of the city and temple be? This was a question which Gabriel could not answer. When Jesus was discoursing upon the same topic, four of the apostles addressed him privately, saying, "Tell us, when shall these things be?" But, after giving them certain signs by which they might know that the desolation was approaching, he added, "Of that day and hour knoweth no man, no, not the angels which are in heaven, neither the Son, but the Father" (Mark 13:3,4,32). It was a secret reserved in the power of the Father only.

But if the time when "a host should be given to the Little Horn of the Goat against the city and temple" was withheld, precise information was granted concerning the time when the things testified in the twenty-fourth verse of the ninth chapter, and the cutting off of Messiah the Prince, should come to pass. They were to be accomplished in a period of seventy weeks of years from the promulgation of a certain decree that is, after 490 years. Two years after this was revealed to him, Daniel's heart was rejoiced by the proclamation of Cyrus in the first year of his reign, for the rebuilding of the temple in Jerusalem (2 Chronicles 36:22,23). But had he reckoned the 490 years from this date, they would have terminated 13 years before Messiah was born. The seventy weeks, however, were not to commence with a decree for rebuilding the temple; but "from the going forth of the commandment *to restore and build Jerusalem*"; in other words, to restore the wastes of the city by setting up the wall and the gates thereof, that Israel's reproach might cease (Nehemiah 2:1,5,17). This was issued by Artaxerxes on the first day of Nisan in the twentieth year of his reign, from which it was exactly 490 years to the crucifixion. No date of any other decree answers the demand of "the matter"; therefore there is no option but to receive it as a demonstration by fact.

Gabriel divided the *seventy weeks of years* into *three portions*, namely, into one of *seven weeks*; *another of sixty-two weeks*; and into *a third of one week*, which he subdivided into two half parts.

423

The seven weeks, or 49 years, were allotted to the restoration of the state; after the end of which, 434 years, or sixty-two weeks more, were to elapse to the manifesting of Messiah the prince. This was 483 years to "the beginning of the gospel concerning Jesus Christ" announced by John the Baptist (Mark 1:1), who came baptizing in water that he might be made manifest to Israel (John 1:31). From this date there remained seven years to the end of the 490.

The seventieth week was the week in which the covenant was confirmed in the attestations which the Father gave to Jesus as His Son, and as the Seed of Abraham and of David, to whom He had promised the land of Canaan, and the kingdom and throne of David for an everlasting inheritance. The week of confirmation was divided between the ministry of John and that of Jesus. The former was engaged in baptizing the people into the hope of Messiah's immediate manifestation; and when he was about finishing this work, Jesus was baptized, and publicly recognized before the assembled people, as the Son of God by a voice from the excellent glory. He was also anointed at the same time, and sealed, as the Most Holy One of Israel. John having now finished his ministry, was thrown into prison by Herod the tetrarch (Luke 3:15,19,20-23); and Jesus being thirty years old, entered upon the work of the latter half part of the week, or three years and a half remaining to complete the 490. After he had passed some months of his ministry, he was warned by some Pharisees that Herod would kill him; to which he replied, "Go tell that fox, Behold, I cast out devils, and do cures to-day and to-morrow, and the third day I shall be perfected. Nevertheless I must walk to-day and to-morrow, and the day following; for it cannot be that a prophet perish out of Jerusalem" (Luke 13:31-33).

Besides showing that a day is sometimes used prophetically for a year, the Lord's reply shows also the period of his ministry as equivalent to the latter half part, at the end of which he expected to die, and afterwards to be perfected by a resurrection to life. Exactly to the month "he was cut off, but not for himself", 490 years after the decree of Artaxerxes in the twentieth of his reign. *"The matter"* revealed to Daniel, who was at the same time exhorted to *"consider the vision"*, to a part of which it referred, was all accomplished as far as the seventy weeks were concerned. There only remained now the destruction of the city and temple, the taking away of the sacrifice and the oblation, and subsequent desolation of the land, by the Little Horn of the Goat. Was that to succeed the crucifixion instanter? or after how long a time were these calamities to come to pass? As I have already shown, no one but God could tell; for He withheld the knowledge of it from everyone but Himself; and left it to reveal itself when the time of the judgment of Gehenna should arrive.

At the end of the latter half-part of the week the Lord "caused the sacrifice and oblation to cease" as an acceptable offering for sin. The sacrifice of himself put an end to sin-offerings as far as believers in him were concerned. They still continued to be offered by the nation; but when the people of the Little Horn should come to execute the work assigned them, even these should be violently interrupted; for "the daily was to be taken away, and the place of its sanctuary cast down". This was fully accomplished about 37 years after the crucifixion, that is to say, in about seventy years from the birth of Christ. But why was it removed? Why might not the Mosaic religion continue to be prac-tised in Canaan, as well as the false religions of the Gentiles in the several countries of the earth? Because "an abomination that maketh desolate" was to be "set up". Now, so long as the daily and its holy place continued, there would be no place for this abomination. The daily must therefore be removed to make way for it. They could not exist contemporarily: neither does it follow that "the abomination" was to succeed the suppression of the daily, immediately. The facts in the case forbid this conclusion. Palestine and Syria were for ages after, populous and wealthy provinces of the Roman habitable.

The notion that the duration of the abomination was to be dated from AD 70 is derived from the English version of Daniel; twelfth chapter and eleventh verse. It is there written, "And from the time *that* the daily *sacrifice* shall be taken away, and the abomination that maketh desolate be set up, *there shall be* 1,290 days." In the Hebrew the italic words are not in the text. Leaving out these words, or rather, giving a more literal version without supplying any words at all, the passage appears intelligible enough. "And at the time of vengeance the daily shall be taken away, in order to set up an abomination that maketh desolate a thousand two hundred and ninety days." This rendering agrees with the facts in the case. The daily was taken away at the time of vengeance (Luke 21:22), and 461 years after, an abomination was set up which continued 1,290 years, ending AD 1821. Desolation, it is true, still continues, but this is no objection to their termination then. We are not to suppose that the 1,290 years being ended, internal improvement was to begin the year after. All it justifies is the expectation that when they expired "that that is determined" should begin to be "poured out upon the desolator"; an expectation that has been literally verified in the opening of the sixth vial upon the Ottoman empire in the epoch of 1820-3.

But is the little horn of the goat that destroyed the mighty and holy people, to experience simply a drying up of its power over Palestine and Syria, or what shall be its destiny? It is to be broken to pieces without hand. Its present Ottoman dynasty being changed, it is to "destroy wonderfully, and to magnify himself in his heart, and to stand up against the Prince of princes", that he may receive the blow on the head that shall disable him for a thousand years.

"The matter" of the vision concerning the taking away of the daily was made known to Daniel in the first year of Darius, BC 542. Three years after—that is, in the third of the joint reign of Cyrus and Darius (Daniel 1:21; 10:1)—"a thing was revealed" to him, "the appointed time" of which "was long". In connection with this revelation, or prophecy, "a vision" was also presented before him. It was a representation of the Son of Man in his glory. After he had recovered from the overpowering effect caused by what he saw, he was informed by one that he came to make him understand *what should befall Israel in the latter days* (Daniel 10:14). In carrying out this gracious intention, the revelator added furthermore that he would show him "that which *is noted* in the scripture of truth"; by which he meant, he would make known to him what yet remained to be communicated explanatory of the vision of the Ram and He-Goat, which he had seen in the third year of Belshazzar.

The Lord then proceeded to reveal the things contained in the eleventh and twelfth chapters of Daniel, which have respect, *First*, to the pushing of the Ram westward against Greece in the reign of the fourth king *after* Cyrus; *Secondly*, to the power of Alexander of Macedon, and the division of his kingdom into four lesser ones, which should be inherited by others not descended from him. These matters occupy the first four verses, and constitute a kind of preface to what follows; and serve to establish the connection of "the prophecy" with "the vision of the evening and morning" contained in the eighth chapter. *Thirdly*, the revelation relates to the Greco-Egyptian, and to the Assyro-Macedonian, horns of the goat, styled "the king of the south", and "the king of the north". The wars and policy of these two Powers as far as they compromised the land of Israel and the Jews, form the subject of the eleventh chapter from the fifth to the thirty-fifth verses, inclusive. *Fourthly*, from the thirty-sixth to the fortieth verse, the prophecy relates to the Little Horn of the goat and the Accursed One whom he should acknowledge and increase with glory. *Fifthly*, it refers to the time of the end, or "the latter days", when "the king of the south", and "the king of the north", should re-appear on the stage of action, and the power of the Little Horn, and that of the king of the north, should coalesce, and form *one power*, as when the Roman and Assyro-Macedonian were blended together, BC 67. *Sixthly*, it reveals the invasion of the land of Israel by the Little Horn's northern king, who over-runs Egypt, and finally encamps before the holy mountain. And *seventhly*, the revelation closes with the prediction of his final destruction at the hand of Michael, the great prince of Israel, their consequent deliverance, the resurrection of many of the dead, and the exaltation of the wise in the kingdom of God (Daniel 12:1-3).

Such are the general topics of this remarkable prophecy, which in a chapter of forty verses covers a period of 2,408 years from the third of Cyrus to the breaking of the Little Horn. I propose now to give the reader a more particular, yet necessarily brief, interpretation of this "difficult passage" of the sure prophetic word. I shall paraphrase the text. The words in italics will be those of the scripture and the Roman type, the interpretation of the text, after the following manner.

PARAPHRASE OF DANIEL'S ELEVENTH CHAPTER
To the thirty-fifth verse inclusive

THE date of the prophecy is the third year of Cyrus, BC 540, and runs thus: —

Behold, there shall stand up yet three kings in Persia, namely, Ahasuerus, Smerdis, and Darius; *and the fourth*, or Xerxes, *shall be far richer than they all: and by his strength through his riches he shall stir up all against the realm of Grecia*. 3. *And* Alexander the Macedonian, *a mighty king shall stand up, ruling with great dominion and doing according to his will.* 4. *And when he shall stand up*, having suffered no defeat, *his kingdom shall be broken, and shall be divided* into four kingdoms *toward the four winds of heaven: but* their glory and power shall fall *not to his posterity, nor according to* the extent of *his dominion which he ruled: for his kingdom shall be plucked up, even for other* rulers, *beside those of* his family.

5. *And the king of the south*, Ptolemy Soter, *shall be strong, and shall be one of his*, Alexander's, *princes*, or generals; *and he shall be strong above him, and have dominion; his dominion shall be a great dominion*, extending over Egypt, Libya, Cyrenaica, Arabia, Palestine, Cœle-Syria, and most of the maritime provinces of Asia Minor; with the island of Cyprus, and several others in the Ægean Sea, and even some cities of Greece, as Cicyon and Corinth. Such was the dominion of Ptolemy Soter, the first Macedonian king of Egypt.

427

6. *And in the end* of fifty-two *years* from BC 301, *they*, the kings of Egypt and Assyro-Macedonia, *shall associate themselves together; for the king's daughter of the south*, Berenice, the daughter of Ptolemy Philadelphus, *shall come*, or be conducted, to Antiochus Theos, *the king of the north, to make a marriage agreement; but she shall not retain the power of the arm* of her father Ptolemy Philadelphus. *Neither shall he*, her husband Antiochus, *stand*; for Laodice, his repudiated wife, whom he shall receive again when he divorces Berenice after her father's death, shall cause him to be poisoned. *Nor shall his arm*, Berenice, *stand; but she shall be given up* to suffer death; *and they*, the Egyptians also, *that brought her* to Syria; *and he*, her son, *whom she brought forth, and he that strengthened her in these times*, shall die; and thus leave her to the mercy of Laodice, which will be treachery and death.

7. *But out of a branch of her* parent *roots shall* Ptolemy Euergetes,* her brother, *stand up in his estate*, or kingdom, *and come with an army, and shall enter into* Antioch the capital, and *the fortress of the king of the north, and shall deal*, or make war, *against them*, even against Laodice and her son Seleucus, *and shall prevail*; 8. *and* Euergetes *shall also carry captive into Egypt their gods, with their princes, and with their precious vessels of silver and of gold; and he shall continue* to reign nine *more years* than the king *of the north*, who shall die a prisoner in Parthia five years before the king of Egypt. 9. *So the king of the south shall come into his kingdom, and shall return into his own land*, BC 244.

10. *But his*, Seleucus Callinicus' *sons*, Seleucus Ceraunus, and Antiochus, *shall be stirred up* to war; *and shall assemble a multitude of great forces: and one of them*, even Antiochus the Great, *shall certainly come and overflow* through the passes of Libanus, *and pass through* into Galilee, and possess himself of all that part of the country, which was formerly the inheritance of the tribes of Reuben and Gad, and of the half tribe of Manasseh. *Then*, the season being too far advanced to prolong the campaign, *shall he return* to Ptolemais, where he shall put his forces into winter quarters. *But*, early in the spring BC 217, Ptolemy Philopator shall march with a large army to Raphia, by which Antiochus *shall be stirred up* again to war, and defeated with great slaughter, so that he shall retreat *to his fortress*. 11. Thus, *shall the king of the south be moved with choler, and come forth and fight with the king of the north; and* the king of the north *shall set forth a great multitude*, even 72,000 foot and 6,000

---

* This is the Ptolemy of "The Decree of Canopus", found in "the field of Zoan" in 1866, and now in the Gizeh Museum, Cairo (Copy in the British Museum).

horse; *but the multitude shall be given into the hand* of the king of Egypt.

12. *And when he*, the king of the south, *hath taken away the multitude* by a signal defeat of Antiochus, *his heart shall be lifted up*, for he will desire to enter the most holy place of the temple. But while he was preparing to enter, he was stricken, and carried off for dead. In his victory over Antiochus *he shall cast down ten thousands*, even 10,000 foot and 300 horse. *But*, not following up his advantages, Philopator *shall not be strengthened* by his victory.

13. *For* Antiochus the Great, *the king of the north, shall return, and set forth a multitude* of troops, *greater than the former, and shall certainly come after certain,* that is, nineteen *years* after the battle of Raphia, or BC 198, *with a great army and with much riches,* and shall subjugate all Palestine and Cœle-Syria.

14. *And in those times,* when Ptolemy Epiphanes* shall reign over Egypt, *many shall stand up against the* infant *king of the south,* even the kings of Macedonia, and of Syria, and Scopas, the general of his deceased father. *But the deputies of* the Romans, *the breakers of thy people,* Daniel, *shall interfere to establish the vision.* They became the guardians and protectors of Epiphanes during his minority; and appointed *three deputies,* who were ordered to acquaint the kings with their resolution, and to enjoin them not to infest the dominions of their royal pupil; for that otherwise they should be forced to declare war against them. The deputy, Emilius, one of the three, after delivering the message of the Roman senate, proceeded to Alexandria, and settled everything to as much advantage as the state of affairs in Egypt would then admit. In this way the Romans began to mix themselves up with the affairs of Egypt, Palestine, and Syria; and in a few years established themselves as lords paramount of the East, and so constituted a power in Asia, symbolized by the Little Horn of the Goat, and in the thirty-sixth verse, styled "THE KING". *But,* though they should be "the breakers of Israel", the assurance was given to Daniel, saying, *they shall fall.*

15. So *the king of the north,* being checked by the Romans, *shall come* into Palestine, *and cast up a mount* against Sidon, where he shall besiege the forces of the Egyptians; *and he shall take* Jerusalem, *the city of munitions,* from the castle of which he shall expel the Egyptian garrison; *and the arms of the south shall not withstand, neither his chosen people, neither shall there*

---

* This is the Ptolemy of "The Rosetta Stone", found near Rosetta, 1799, now in the British Museum.

be any strength to withstand Antiochus. 16. *But* Antiochus the Great, *who cometh against* Ptolemy Epiphanes, *shall do according to his own will in* Cœle-Syria and Palestine, *and none shall stand before him*: *and he shall* make a permanent *stand in the glorious land* of Israel, *which by his hand shall be consumed.*

17. *He shall also set his face to enter* into Greece, *with the strength of his whole kingdom, and Israelites (Ishrim) with him. Thus shall he do* to incorporate Greece into his dominion, by which the Romans, who had recently proclaimed it free, would be stirred up against him. Therefore, to secure the neutrality of their Egyptian ally, *he shall give* Cleopatra, *the daughter of women*, or princess royal, to Epiphanes, to wife, *corrupting her* to betray him by resigning to him Cœle-Syria and Palestine as her dower, but on condition that he should receive half the revenues. Thus, the land of Israel was given over as a bribe to bind Cleopatra to her father's interests, that she might influence Epiphanes either to remain neutral, or to declare against the Romans, his protectors. But *she shall* cleave to her husband and *not stand, neither be for him*, but shall join with her husband in congratulating the Roman Senate on the victory they had gained over her father at Thermopylæ (BC 191).

18. *After this shall* Antiochus, at the earnest solicitation of the Ætolians, *turn his face unto the isles* of Greece, *and shall take many*; *but a military commander (kotzin)*, L. Scipio, the Roman consul, *shall cause the reproach offered by him to cease; without his own disgrace he*, Scipio, *shall cause it to turn upon* Antiochus, by defeating him at Mount Sipylus, and repulsing him from every part of Asia Minor. As the condition of peace, the Romans required him to pay 15,000 talents; 500 down, 2,500 on the ratification of the treaty, and the rest in twelve years at 1,000 talents per annum. These terms being acceded to, 19. *he shall turn his face toward the fortress*, or capital, *of his own land*, being much at a loss how to raise the tribute. While in the province of Elymais, he heard of a considerable treasure in the temple of Jupiter Belus. He accordingly broke into it in the dead of night, and carried off all its riches. *But he shall stumble and fall, and not be found*; for the provincials, exasperated at the robbery, rebelled against him, and murdered him and all his attendants (BC 187).

20. *Then shall stand up in* Antiochus' *estate*, or kingdom, his son Seleucus Philopator, *one who causeth an exactor to pass over the glory of the kingdom*; the business of his reign being to raise the tribute for the Romans. *But within few days*—that is, twelve years—*he shall be destroyed, neither in anger, nor in battle*, being poisoned by Heliodorus, his prime minister, having reigned long enough to pay the last instalment to the Romans.

21. *And in his*, Seleucus Philopator's, *place shall stand up* Heliodorus, *a vile person*, being both a poisoner and usurper, *to whom they*, the authorities of the nation, *shall not give the honour of the kingdom; but* Antiochus Epiphanes *shall come in peaceably, and obtain the kingdom by flatteries* bestowed on the party of Heliodorus.

22. *And with the arms of a flood* by which they shall be formidably invaded, *shall they*, the Egyptians, *be overflown from before* Antiochus, whom they excite to war by demanding the restitution of Cœle-Syria and Palestine. *And they shall be broken*, or subdued; *yea, also* Onias *the prince*, or high priest, *of the* Mosaic *covenant*, shall be murdered, as in BC 172, it came to pass. 23. *And after the league made with* Ptolemy Philometor, Antiochus *shall work deceitfully* after his second invasion of Egypt, BC 170; *for he shall come up to* Alexandria, *and he shall become strong with a small people*, or army. By his deceit, 24. *he shall enter peaceably even upon the fattest places of the province* to which he reduces Egypt; *and he*, Antiochus, *shall do, that which his fathers*, or predecessors, *have not done, nor his fathers' fathers*; namely, *he shall scatter among* his followers, *the prey, and spoil, and riches*: *yea, he shall forecast his devices against the strong holds* of Egypt, *even for a time*. 25. *And he shall stir up his power and his courage against the king of the south with a great army; and the king of the south shall be stirred up to battle with a very great army*; *but he shall not stand*: *for* the Alexandrians seeing him in the hands of Antiochus, and lost to them, *shall forecast devices against him*, and place the crown of Egypt upon the head of his brother Euergetes II. 26. *Yea, they that feed of the portion of* Philometor's *meat*, even his courtiers, *shall separate*, or renounce, *him; and his*, Antiochus', *army shall overflow* Egypt; *and many* of the Egyptians *shall fall down slain*. 27. *And the hearts of both these kings shall be to do mischief, and they shall speak lies at one table, but shall not prosper; for the end is yet at the time appointed.*

28. *Then shall* Antiochus Epiphanes *return into his land with great riches; and his heart shall be against the Holy Covenant; and he shall do* terrible things against Jerusalem, taking it by storm, butchering 80,000 men, making 40,000 prisoners, and causing a like number to be sold for slaves. *And then shall he return to his own land*, laden with the spoils of the temple, amounting to 1,800 talents, or £270,000 (BC 169).

29. *At the time appointed*, under pretence of restoring Philometor to the throne, *he shall return, and come toward the south* against Alexandria to besiege it. *But it*, this fourth invasion, *shall not be as the former, or as the latter*. He raised the siege, and marched towards Memphis, where he installed

431

Philometor as king. As soon, however, as he had departed, Philometor came to an understanding with Euergetes, and they agreed to a joint reign over Egypt. This coming to the ears of Antiochus, he led a powerful army against Memphis for the purpose of subduing the country. Having nearly accomplished this project, he marched against Alexandria, which was the only obstacle to his becoming absolute master of Egypt. But the Roman Embassy, sent at the request of the Ptolemies, met him about a mile from the city. They had left Rome with the utmost diligence. When they arrived at Delos, they found a fleet of Macedonian, or Greek, ships, on board of which they embarked for Alexandria, where they arrived at the crisis of his approach. Popilius delivered him the decree of the Senate, and demanded an immediate answer. Sorely against his will, he agreed to obey its mandate, and draw off his army from Egypt. Thus his invasion terminated very differently from the former: 30. *for the ships of Chittim shall come against him,* and prevent him from incorporating Egypt into his Assyrian kingdom of the north (Numbers 24:24).

All his wrath was kindled at this interference; *therefore he shall be grieved, and return, and have indignation against the Holy Covenant*; for in his return march through Palestine, he detached 20,000 men under Apollonius with orders to destroy Jerusalem, BC 168. *So shall he do; he shall even return, and have intelligence with them that forsake the Holy Covenant.*

31. *And arms shall stand on his part* under Apollonius; *and they,* the Assyro-Macedonian troops, *shall pollute the* temple, or *sanctuary of strength,* by shedding the blood of the worshippers in its courts; *and they shall take away the daily sacrifice; and they shall place* a strong fort and garrison to command the temple, even *the abomination that maketh desolate,* and overawes the nation.

As soon as Antiochus Epiphanes was returned to Antioch, he published a decree by which all his subjects were required to conform to his religion. This was aimed chiefly at the Jews, whose religion and nation he was resolved to extirpate. Atheneus, a man advanced in years, and extremely well versed in all the ceremonies of the Grecian idolatry, was commissioned to carry the edict into effect in Judea and Samaria. As soon as he arrived at Jerusalem, he began by suppressing *the daily,* or burnt offering of continuance, and all the observances of the Jewish law. He caused the sabbaths and other festivals to be profaned; forbade the circumcision of children; carried off and burnt all copies of the law wherever they could be found; and put to death whoever acted contrary to the decree of the king. To establish it the sooner in every part of the nation, altars and chapels filled with idols were erected in every city, and sacred groves were planted. Officers were appointed over these, who caused the people generally to offer sacrifice in them every month, on the day of the month on which the king was born, who made them eat swine's flesh and other unclean animals sacrificed there. The temple in Jerusalem was dedicated to Jupiter Olympus, whose statue was placed within it. Thus he did in his great indignation against Jehovah and His people Israel.

32. *And such* of the Jews *as do wickedly against the covenant shall* Antiochus *by flatteries cause to dissemble.* These not only "forsook the holy covenant", but "had intelligence" with the king, and aided him all they could in the desolation with which he was overspreading their country. *But the* Maccabees and their adherents, *people who do know their God shall be strong, and do* valiantly in war. 33. *And they*, even Mattathias and his five sons, etc., *that understand among the people shall instruct*, and encourage, *many*; *yet they* of their party *shall fall by the sword, and by flame, by captivity, and by spoil, days.*

34. *Now when they shall fall* by these calamities *they shall be holpen with a little help*; for whilst Antiochus was amusing himself by celebrating games at Daphne, Judas Maccabæus had raised the standard of independence, and was helping his countrymen in Judea. He levied a small army, fortified the cities, rebuilt the fortresses, threw strong garrisons into them, and thereby awed the whole country. He defeated and killed Apollonius, and made great slaughter of the troops. With 3,000 men he defeated Lysias with 47,000; and another army of 20,000 under Timotheus and Bacchides; and in the year BC 170, he gave Lysias a second defeat at Bethsura, by which he dispersed 65,000 of the enemy. Yet, *many shall cleave to them*, the Maccabees, *with flatteries*, for it was a time of trial. 35. *And* therefore *some of them of understanding shall fall to try them, and to purge, and make them white* FOR THE TIME OF THE END; *because it*, the time of the end, *is yet for a time appointed.*

The thirty-fifth verse of this eleventh chapter brings us down to the end of 430 years from the destruction of the city and temple of Jerusalem by the Chaldeans. There is here a break in the prophecy. Nothing more is said about Israel and the king of the north, until the prediction is resumed in the fortieth verse, which may be regarded as continuous with verse thirty-five. The latter speaks of their being tried and made white to, or till, the time of the end, and then the fortieth re-introduces the king of the south and the king of the north, and outlines the events they were to bring to pass in that time, and which will end in the resurrection, when they who have been tried and made white in the long interval, will stand in their lot with Daniel at the end of the 1,335 days. With the exception of the "little help" derived from the victories of the Maccabees, the history of Israel has been a series of calamities to this day; and will so continue to be till the "time appointed" for their deliverance arrives.

But the Maccabean epoch is particularly interesting as the termination of Ezekiel's 430 years. The house of Israel, and the house of Judah, had been great transgressors of the holy covenant from the foundation of the temple in the fourth year of Solomon to the sack of the city in the 19th of Nebuchadnezzar. This was a period of 430 years, which was divided into two periods—namely, one of forty years from the foundation of the temple to the apostasy of Rehoboam and Judah; the other, of three hundred and ninety from this apostasy to the destruction of the temple. God determined that this long national transgression should be punished by as long a retribution. He therefore gave Israel "*a sign*" of what was coming upon them (Ezekiel 4:1-8). This consisted in Ezekiel lying on his left side 390 days, and then upon his right 40 days more. By this sign was represented the prostrate condition of Israel for 430 years. The 430 years of transgression had not quite ended when the sign was appointed in the fifth of Jehoiachin's captivity. The thing signified began to take effect in the sacking of Jerusalem. Israel then began to "eat their defiled bread among the Gentiles"; so that the 430 years would end BC 161, according to my chronology.

These four centuries of punishment were a very calamitous period of Jewish history. They endured a captivity in Babylon for 70 years: for several years more their times were "troublous"; they were vassals to the Persians till their dominion was overthrown by Alexander; afterwards, as we have seen, they were alternately subject to the king of the south and the king of the north, and their land became a field of battle for the hosts of these Powers, who defiled the temple, and at length converted it into a house for the worship of Jupiter. But, a very few years before the 430 years were about to expire, Judas Maccabæus commenced a war against Antiochus Epiphanes, which ended in the recovery of Jerusalem, the purification of the temple from the heathen worship, its re-dedication to God, and the erection of Judea into an independent kingdom under the Asmoneans, which continued until it was placed under Herod the Idumean by the Romans, about 39 years before Christ.

THE KING AND THE "STRANGE GOD"

THE 430 years of national retribution being ended, and with it the prophecy concerning Israel and the king of the northern horn of the Macedonian Goat, a new power is introduced as superseding that of the northern king. This power appeared on the territory of the north, and absorbed its dominion into itself, so that it became all in all. In "the vision of the evening and the morning" (Daniel 8), it is represented by a Little Horn standing upon another horn, and is styled "a king of fierce countenance, and understanding dark sentences". Moses describes the same power in these words, saying to Israel, "The LORD shall bring a nation against thee from far, from the end of the earth, swift as the eagle flieth; a nation whose tongue thou shalt not understand; a nation of fierce countenance; and he shall besiege thee in all thy gates" (Deuteronomy 28:49,50,52). "His power shall be mighty", said Gabriel, but not by his own power: and he shall destroy wonderfully, and he shall prosper and practise, and shall destroy the mighty and the holy people. And *through his policy*, also, he shall *cause craft to prosper* in his hand", or by his power: "and he shall magnify himself in his heart, and in prospering shall destroy many: he shall also stand up against the Prince of princes; but he shall be broken without hand" (Daniel 8:23-25). This is a general description of the power which should rule over the Assyro-Macedonian territory as well as over the Greco-Egyptian, when "their kingdom" should come to an end for a time, that is, until their revival "in the time of the end".

I am particularly desirous that this part of the prophecy should be understood. Perhaps what I mean may be better comprehended by the following homely illustration. Suppose we were to take a goat's horn, and with a fret-saw were to cut out a small piece of its surface. Then fix this piece upon a spring, the lower end of which should be fixed inside the horn itself. Now if pressure be applied to the small piece it would be brought down to a level with the general surface of the horn. In this state, the horn would represent the Assyro-Macedonian kingdom under the Selucidæ; but remove the pressure and the small piece of horn would start up to the height of the spring's length. Let this represent the Little Horn upon the Goat's horn, and we have the symbol of the power which prevails from the conquest of Assyro-Macedonia, BC 65, until "the time of the end". But if pressure be afterwards applied to the small piece, it is brought down to a level with the surface of the horn, and it again appears like one horn, for by the pressure the Little Horn is merged into it. This last action and its result will represent the merging of the Little Horn power of Constantinople into the Assyro-

Macedonian, or Russian, Horn of the Goat in the time of the end; so that the Constantinopolitan, and Russo-Assyrian, powers, become one horn, as before the Little Horn arose. In the time of the end, the Horn of the North in its enmity against Israel, plays a similar part to that it did of old by the hand of Antiochus Epiphanes in the days of Judas Maccabæus. Therefore, he may be fairly taken as the type of Israel's last and greatest enemy, who shall come to his end, with none to help him.

This Little Horn power, or "King of fierce countenance", is, in the thirty-sixth verse of the eleventh chapter, styled "the King who doth according to his will". This federal potentate must be studied in his secular and ecclesiastical characters. His secular, with a hint or two of his spiritual character, is given in the eighth chapter; while his ecclesiastical is exhibited more fully in the eleventh, from the thirty-sixth to the thirty-ninth verses inclusive. His policy was to be of a remarkable description; for "through his policy he shall *cause* craft to prosper by his power". Hence, his doings with regard to another, and that person's words and deeds, are all affirmed of this wilful king; for, it is by his power as well as through his policy, that this person is enabled to do. Thus, putting them both together, for they are one in policy and action, the power is thus outlined by the prophet who says, "And the King shall do according to his will; and he shall exalt himself, and magnify himself above every god", or ruler, "and shall speak marvellous things against the God of gods, and shall prosper *till the indignation be accomplished*; for that that is determined shall be done. He shall disregard all the gods of his fathers *(ἐπὶ πάντας θεοὺς τῶν πατέρων αὐτοῦ οὐ συνήσει—Septuagint)* and the desire of wives, nor shall he regard any god: for he shall magnify himself above all."

This is evidently not descriptive of the Pagan Roman power, but of that power invested with a new ecclesiastical character. In other words, it is descriptive of the imperial Constantinopolitan Catholic power. Of all who swayed this sceptre from Constantine, the founder of the city, to Palæologus, who lost it to the Turks, the Emperor Justinian is the best illustration of the wilful king in his secular aspect. "Never prince", says Dupin, "did meddle so much with what concerns the affairs of the church, nor make so many constitutions and laws upon this subject. He was persuaded that it was the duty of an emperor, and for the good of the State, to have a particular care of the church, to defend its faith, to regulate external discipline, and to employ the civil laws and the temporal power to preserve it in order and peace."

"Justinian", says Gibbon, "sympathized with his subjects in their superstitious reverence for living and departed saints; his code, more especially his novels, confirm and enlarge the privileges of the clergy; and in every dispute between the monk and the layman, the partial judge was inclined to pronounce, that truth and innocence are always on the side of the church. In his public and private devotions, he was assiduous and exemplary; his prayers, vigils, and fasts displayed the austere penance of a monk; his fancy was amused by the hope, or belief, of personal inspiration; he had secured the patronage of the Virgin, and St. Michael the archangel; and his recovery from a dangerous disease was ascribed to the miraculous succour of the holy martyrs, Cosmas and Damian. Among the titles of imperial greatness, the name of *Pious* was most pleasing to his ear; to promote the temporal and spiritual interest of the (Greco-Roman) church was the serious business of his life; and the duty of father of his country was often sacrificed to that of *defender of the faith* ... While the Barbarians invaded the provinces, while the victorious legions marched under the banners of Belisarius and Narses, the successor of Trajan, unknown to the camp, was content to vanquish at the head of a synod."

"The reign of Justinian was a uniform yet various scene of persecution; and he appears to have surpassed his indolent predecessors, both in the contrivance of his laws, and rigour of their execution. The insufficient term of three months was assigned for the conversion or exile of all heretics; and if he still connived at their precarious stay, they were deprived, under his iron yoke, not only of the benefits of society, but of the common birthright of men and Christians."

Antiochus Epiphanes and Justinian represent "the king" as he will be manifested, when, as the king of the north, he appears upon the arena, standing up to contend with the Prince of princes, on the field of Armageddon; for he is to "prosper till the indignation be accomplished" against Israel. Impious and cruel as Antiochus, and superstitious and fanatical as Justinian, with the arrogance, ambitions and profanity of the Roman Bishop in his halcyon days, this incarnation of the sin-power in the crisis of its fate, will fully answer to all that has been predicated of the king who does according to his will, and "for whom Tophet is ordained of old" (Isaiah 30:27-33; 31:8,9). At present he is represented by the Sultan, who "divides the land for gain".* But when the Little Horn's sceptre is wrested from his feeble grasp by the Autocrat, we shall see in him a potentate, unrivalled in presumption and impiety by any of his fathers, not excepting Pharaoh of the olden time.

In times past, the little horn of the goat has admirably illustrated the prophecy concerning him. "Through his policy he shall

---

* See Foreword.

cause craft to prosper by his power." In studying the reign of Justinian this is remarkably apparent. But before the Horn could find scope for the promotion of the species of craft referred to, it was necessary that he should "disregard all the gods of his fathers", that is, embrace some other religion than Paganism; in other words, become a Greco-Roman Catholic, such as Justinian, who occupied the throne, but did not inherit the peculiar superstition of the Caesars. Having discarded the gods of his fathers, it suited the Horn's policy to bestow his patronage upon another, who should be a god upon the earth, and residing in Rome instead of above the heights of Olympus.

The testimony of Daniel is that "In his estate he shall honour the god of forces"; or more intelligibly, "In his kingdom shall he do honour to *a god of guardians*". The word rendered "guardians" is *mahuzzim* and signifies *munitions*. Hence, any real, or supposed, persons adopted as protectors, guardians, or patrons, are *mahuzzim*, or munitions of strength and safety. Now the god whom the Little Horn of the Goat honoured in his kingdom, was a god of guardian saints, who are regarded by his worshippers as protectors and towers of strength and security against all "the ills that flesh is heir to". Such a god is the Bishop of Rome; who to the pagan officials of the Little Horn, was unknown, being in their reign only a simple bishop, undistinguished from the rest of his class, save that he flourished in the capital, and they in the provinces, of the empire. He is therefore styled in the scripture, "*a god whom his* (the Little Horn's) *fathers knew not*"; hence he is also termed "*a strange god*". But though "strange" and unknown to Trajan and the Antonines, he was afterwards brought into notice by Constantine and his successors. In 313, he was made chief magistrate of Rome, or, as we would say, Lord Mayor, for life. His jurisdiction was confined to the city. In 378, however, the Little Horn of the Goat then reigning over the east and west, extended his spiritual authority over all the churches of Italy and Gaul; and by the time of Justinian, he was prepared for presentation to the nations as spiritual head of the whole Roman habitable. He was the god of a new system of idolatry, whose idols were the images of Mahuzzim, or "the ghosts" of pretended saints and martyrs, the demi-gods, or demons, of the New Roman mythology.

In a celebrated letter written by the Emperor Justinian to this god of patron saints, dated March 533, and which thenceforth became part and parcel of the civil law, he is recognized as the legal head of all the churches of the eastern and western provinces of the empire. "We suffer not", says the imperial writer, "any thing that belongs to the state of the churches to be done without submitting it to your holiness, *who art head of all the churches.*" In this way, "the king, who did according to his will," "*acknowledged*" (Daniel 11:39) this "strange god" as of supreme spiritual authority in the most strong holds".

The work of recognition thus far advanced by Justinian was perfected by the edict of the Emperor Phocas, who began to reign in 603. He also wrote to the Roman Bishop in 604, and *acknowledged* his spiritual supremacy. He was very liberal to the churches, and allowed the Pantheon, a temple dedicated to *all the gods* by his fathers, to be turned into a church, or "most strong hold", to *all the saints*. Phocas was a monster in crime, and therefore the better qualified for a patron of the Roman Bishop, who hailed him as the pious avenger of the church. By this kind of flattery a decree was obtained from him by Boniface III, in 606, declaring the Roman god UNIVERSAL BISHOP. Two years after, a pillar with a gilt statue on the top of it, was erected in Rome to the honour of Phocas, with the following inscription—*Pro innumerabilibus Pietatis ejus beneficiis, el pro quiete procuratâ, ac conservatâ libertate.* Thus was memorialized the fulfilment of the sure word of prophecy, that the Little Horn of the Goat should "in his kingdom do honour to a god of guardian saints".

When the Bishop of Rome was honoured as a god by the Little Horn of the Goat, the other Little Horn had not yet made its appearance among the ten-horned kingdoms of the Beast. There elapsed 266 years from the date of Justinian's letter, and 193 from the decree of Phocas, before this came to pass; for Charlemagne was not crowned Emperor of the western third part of the Roman Empire till AD 800. Upon this occasion, he also "acknowledged and increased with glory" the Universal Bishop as a god "*above every god*" of his dominions. Through his policy he also caused craft to prosper by his power. Priestcraft gained an ascendancy in Europe which it had never attained before the rise of the Germano-Roman Little Horn among the kingdoms of the west. By forming an alliance with "the Accursed One", all the powers were cemented together by a bond far stronger than the sword. The Emperors perceived this, and shaped their policy accordingly. The influence of the Popes in strengthening the imperial authority is well shown in the following quotation:

"There was no general connection existing between the States of Europe till the Romans, in endeavouring to make themselves masters of the world, had the greatest part of the European States under their dominion. From that time there necessarily existed a sort of connection between them, and this connection was strengthened by the famous decree of Caracalla, by the adoption of the Roman laws, and by the influence of the Catholic religion, which introduced itself insensibly into almost all the subdued states. After the destruction of the empire of the west in

493, the Hierarchical system naturally led the several Papal states to consider themselves in ecclesiastical matters as *unequal members of one great society*. Besides the immoderate ascendancy the Bishop of Rome had the address to obtain as the spiritual chief of the church, his consequent success in elevating the Germano-Roman emperor to the character of temporal chief, brought such an accession of authority to the latter, that most of the nations of Europe showed for some ages so great a deference to the emperor, that in many respects Europe seemed to form *but one society*, consisting of unequal members subject to one sovereign."

Thus, then, the "Wicked One" was manifested by the working of Satan with all the power of the Little Horn of the Goat, and afterwards, of the Little Horn of the west. Strange and unknown to the Pagan emperors, he became a god to the wilful king, and Eyes and Mouth to the Little Horn of the west; so that until the capture of Constantinople in 1453, he was in some sort a connecting link between the two imperial horns. The prophecy before us, however, not only foretells his recognition by the Roman power, but sets forth other particulars of a striking and interesting character.

"MAHUZZIM BAZAARS"

THE text, when literally rendered, throws much light upon the subject. Thus, it reads, "In his kingdom shall he do honour to *a god of guardians*, even an Accursed One whom his fathers knew not shall he *honour with gold, and with silver, and with precious stones, and with things desired*. Thus shall he do *in Bazaars of Guardians* with an Accursed Dissembler, whom he shall acknowledge and increase with glory; and he shall cause *them* to exercise authority over multitudes, and he (the Little Horn) shall divide the land for gain."

There are peculiarities in this translation which I shall notice presently; of the whole text, it may be remarked here, that it is in strict accordance with history, and therefore worthy to be received. It testifies that the Little Horn of the Goat should do honour to a god of guardians with riches, and things desired. Now, to honour a god of guardians with such things, is to enrich the institutions dedicated to the guardian saints, whose high priest Rome's episcopal god is. In meeting the suggestions of the Accursed One, the Little Horn was honouring him with "things desired". Justinian was a remarkable instance of liberality to the church and its chief. Besides the magnificent temple of St. Sophia, he dedicated twenty-five others in that city and its suburbs to the honour of the Virgin and the saints: most of these edifices were decorated with marble and gold. His munificence was distributed over the Holy Land; throughout which monasteries for both sexes were amply spread. Almost every saint in the calendar acquired the honour of a temple; and the liberality with which he honoured them was boundless. He employed 10,000 workmen in the erection of St. Sophia, which he finished in five years, eleven months, and ten days from the first foundation. No wood except the doors was admitted into its construction. Paul Silentiarius, who beheld its primitive lustre, enumerates the colours, the shades, and the spots of ten or twelve marbles, jaspers, and porphyries, which nature had profusely diversified, and which were blended and contrasted as it were by a skilful painter.

The triumph of Antichrist "was adorned with the last spoils of Paganism, but the greater part of these *costly stones* was extracted from the quarries of Asia Minor, the isles and continent of Greece, Egypt, Africa, and Gaul. A variety of ornaments and figures was curiously expressed in mosaic; and the images of Christ, of the Virgin, of saints, and of angels, were exposed to the superstition of the Greeks. *According to the sanctity of each object, the precious metals were distributed in thin leaves, or in solid masses.* The spectator was dazzled by the glittering aspect of the cupola; the sanctuary contained forty thousand pounds weight of *silver*; and the holy vases and vestments of the altar were of the purest *gold*, enriched with *inestimable gems*."

Such are the words of Gibbon; and no description of things could more palpably demonstrate the applicability of the text to any other person, than this does to Justinian as the individual emperor of the little Greek Horn, who "in his kingdom honoured an accursed god of guardian saints in their bazaars with gold, with silver, and with precious stones, and with things desired". "Thus shall he do," saith the scripture, "in the most strong holds with a strange god", or accursed dissembler. In the margin of the passage instead of "*in the most strong holds*", it reads, "*in fortresses of munitions*", which does not help the matter at all. The Hebrew words are *le-mivtzahrai mahuzzim*. The root of *mivtzahrai* is *bahtzar*, and signifies "to enclose with a wall, or the like, for safety. As a noun, it signifies *store*, or *treasure so secured*. Derivative—*a bazaar*, a kind of covered market-place among the eastern nations, somewhat like our Exeter 'Change, but frequently much more extensive" (*Parkhurst's Lexicon*). "In the strong-holds of Mahuzzim", or "in Mahuzzim-Bazaars", comes nearer to the original. Understanding that Mahuzzim are deified ghosts, worshipped as patrons and protectors, the question need only be asked, what are their strong holds, or bazaars?

and every reflecting mind will answer immediately—"Why, the churches to be sure!"

This is the truth. The churches, chapels, and cathedrals are the strong holds, and houses of merchandise, dedicated by the prospering craft to guardian-saints and angels. There are the images and pictures of the saints. They are saints' houses in which are deposited their shrines; silver, gold, and ivory crucifixes; old bones, and various kinds of trumpery. They are literally "dens of thieves", without ever having been the houses of the Father, where people are robbed of their money under divers false pretences. They are places where pews are sold by auction; where fairs are held for "pious objects"; and where spiritual quacks pretend to cure souls in exchange for so much per annum. In view of these facts, the scriptural epithet bestowed upon the church-houses of the apostasy is most appropriate. They are truly Bazaars of spiritual merchandise; and *the prospering craft*, "the great men of the earth", made rich by trading in their wares, are the bazaar-men, who extort all kinds of goods from their customers by putting them in fear, and comforting them with heavenly pay. They buy and sell under license from the State, having received the mark on their foreheads, and in their hands.

The reader may find the catalogue of sale in the eighteenth of Revelation. Among the articles of merchandise are (σωμάτων, καὶ ψυχὰς ἀνθρώπων) bodies, and souls of men. But the trade of these soul-merchants is fast falling into disrepute. Their customers growl exceedingly at being compelled to deal at Bazaars, where the profit is all on one side. This state of things, however, will not last much longer; for the time cometh, it is written, when "no man buyeth their merchandise any more". There is often more truth than fiction, though not much elegance, in the proverbs of the vulgar; but the reader will now perceive the scripture origin of the term *"gospel shop"*, as applied to places of religious convocation, where men preach gospels at so much per sermon, or per annum. I am aware that Paul says, "the Lord hath ordained that they which preach the gospel should live of the gospel". This is just and proper. But this ordinance does not apply to those who do not preach the gospel, but preach mere human tradition instead. These are preachers of other gospels; and to pay them is "to take the bread out of the children's mouths, and cast it to dogs", even to "dumb dogs that cannot bark".

The places where they deal out their traditions are well and truly designated shops, or bazaars; for the system which sanctifies them is mere trading in religion, and haggling for a crust of bread. But then, bazaars of priestly wares are distinguished from places of honourable trade by being *dedicated to Mahuzzim*. This is a remarkable feature in the prophecy, which finds its counterpart in the dedication of the churches to guardian saints and angels. St. Sophia at Constantinople, St. Peter's at Rome, Our Lady's at Paris, St. Paul's at London, and innumerable other bazaars, dedicated to all conceivable kinds of saints; and, lest any should be forgotten, to "All Saints", and even to "All Souls",—are examples in point. In these bazaars of guardians, then, the two Little Horns, and the other Horns, "through their policy have caused craft to prosper by their power; and have done honour to the god of guardians with gold, and silver, and precious stones and things desired."

THE KINGDOMS OF THE WORLD

CHAPTER V

THE EASTERN QUESTION IN THE TIME OF THE END

It is impossible that the Holy Land can be for ever subject to the Gentiles—It is to be wrested from them in the crisis of "the time of the end"—Of Daniel's 2,400 days—Of the beginning of "the time of the end"—Of the king of the south at that time—The Autocrat of Russia the king of the north at "the time of the end"—England and the Jews—Of Gogue and Magogue—Ezekiel's and John's two different and remote confederacies—Daniel's king of the north of "the time of the end", and Gogue of "the latter days", the same—The Gogue of Ezekiel proved to be the Emperor of Germany and Autocrat of all the Russias—Gomer and the French—Sheba, Dedan, the Merchants of Tarshish and its young lions, identified as the British power

OUR paraphrase was discontinued (page 433), at the end of the thirty-fifth verse of the eleventh chapter of Daniel. It left Antiochus Epiphanes, the king of the north, at war with the Jews under Judas Maccabæus, who were fighting against fearful odds for their existence as a nation.

The prophecy about the Little Horn king led our attention off from events in the land of Israel to others in Italy and Constantinople where we beheld the Little Greek Horn, and after him, the Little Latin Horn, doing honour to the Roman Bishop, and converting him into a god in their respective dominions. But, though the testimony directed our attention to Rome, in order that we might be able by the transactions of which that city was the centre, to identify the power represented by "the king who did according to his will", before it dismisses the Little Horn by pressing it down into the Assyrian Horn of the Goat, our thoughts are again turned upon Israel and their interesting country, by the prophet telling us that the Little Greek Horn *"shall divide the land for gain"*. This treatment of the Holy Land is particularly characteristic of the Ottoman power which possessed the country from 1509, when it was incorporated with the Turkish empire by Selim IX. It has been divided by his successors to their Pashas literally "for gain": by which the ruin of the country was made sure and expeditious.* Having purchased principalities in it at enormous prices, they make a conscience of reimbursing themselves in the shortest possible time by every

---

* And "the Little Latin Horn" has done the like through all its section of Anti-Christendom, as the division of the land into "parishes", and the "tithes", testify to this day. See Foreword also.

kind of extortion; well-knowing, in past times at least, that if a higher price were offered than they had given, their heads would soon appear at Constantinople, in attestation of their dangerous posts being occupied by equally unscrupulous exactors.

But is the Holy Land to continue for ever as it is at this day? Is the Little Horn of the Goat always to divide it for a price among his pashas? These are questions of great interest to all who believe the gospel of the kingdom of God and his Christ. If the reader has accompanied me through this volume, he will, I doubt not, be ready to answer in full assurance of faith and hope, with an emphatic "No, it is impossible". Yea, verily, it is impossible that it can always be desolate and subject to the horns of the Gentiles. If it were, the kingdom of God could never be established; for the Holy Land is the territory of the kingdom. To all, then, who believe "the things of the kingdom of God and the name of Jesus Christ", how intensely interesting must the future destiny of this country be! Well may it be said by the prophet, "Ye that make mention of the LORD, keep not silence, and give him no rest till he establish, and till he make Jerusalem a praise in the earth" (Isaiah 62:6,7).

But *when* and *how* shall the land of Israel be wrested from the Little Horn of the Goat? As to *the when*, the prophecy contained in the last six verses of the eleventh chapter plainly informs us, that it shall be *in the Time of the End*; "for at the time of the end shall be the vision" (Daniel 8:17). This period is also termed, "the last end of the indignation; for *at the time appointed* the end shall be" (verse 19). In others words, *the winding up of the vision shall be at the expiration of a given time*. The next question is, What given time is this, and when does it expire? In reply to this, I remark that the only time given in connection with the vision of the Ram and He-goat, and the prophecy connected with it, is a long interval of 2,300 years from the evening to the morning of the vision-period. The Septuagint reads 2,400;* and the Hebrew may not be better authority than the Greek translation here, and that says 2,300 as in the common version. Assuming, then, 2,400 is correct, the question is still before us, When does this period expire? A similar inquiry is made in the text, namely, "How long the vision?" "At", or till "the time of the end shall be the vision." Then the 2,400 years are to reach no further than the time of the end, the duration of that end not being defined by the time of the vision … To repeat the question, "How long the vision (concerning the taking away of) the daily, and the treading down by that which maketh desolate, to give both the holy (land) and the host

---

* Only the printed version of the Vatican MS. *Documentary* evidence so far does not seem to warrant the "2,400".

(of Israel) to be trodden under foot?" To this question it was replied, "Unto 2,400 days; then shall the holy (land) be cleansed". We are not to understand by this, that the Holy Land would be cleansed in the 2,401st year; but that the 2,400 years being expired, the subsequent event to be brought about would be the cleansing of the land of Israel. This is a work that requires time, and cannot possibly be accomplished till after the battle of Armageddon.

I say that "the cleansing of the sanctuary" is the cleansing of the land of Israel; and I cannot conceive how any other interpretation can be put upon it, in the face of Ezekiel's testimony, short of this. He predicts the fighting of a great battle in the land of Israel "*in the latter days*", which is synonymous with "*the time of the end*". He describes it as taking place between the Lord God and a great northern power, which is signally defeated upon the mountains of Israel. The heaps of slain are enormous; for it takes seven months to bury them, and seven years to use up their weapons as fire-wood for domestic purposes. "Seven months", says Ezekiel, "shall the house of Israel be burying of them, *that they may cleanse the land.*" Then describing the thorough manner in which the buriers shall do their work, so that not a single bone shall be left visible, he finishes this part of his prediction by saying, "THUS *shall they cleanse the land.*"

But, if the 2,400 years terminate at the time of the end, when do they commence, that we may know when the time of the end begins?

The solution of this problem will be found in the pamphlet *Chronikon Hebraikon*. It is there shown that the "*evening-morning*" period of Daniel 8:14, should read 2,400 instead of 2,300; and that the reed or rule by which the beginning of this time of the vision should be ascertained is, *that the time of a vision must be computed from the first event foreshadowed in the vision*; inasmuch as it cannot be perceived that there is any valid reason for the exclusion of any of the events of a vision from its time. My suspicion was not awakened with regard to the correctness of the reading of this text on the publication of the former editions of this work. I am, however, now satisfied that 2,300 is a corruption of some of the Hebrew manuscripts in the hands of Western Jews, from which it found its way into modern versions.

In this vision of Daniel 8, the first event the prophet sees is *the last horn of the Ram Power overtopping the first*—verse 3. This event came to pass BC 540, when the Persian Dynasty of the Ram represented by Cyrus superseded the Median at the death of Darius the Mede. Can any good reason be given why this coming up of the higher horn last, should not be included in the

2,400? I can see none. I accept it, therefore, as the beginning of the vision's evening-morning time. Hence the question, "How long the vision of the Daily and of the transgression making desolate, to give both the Holy and the Host for a trampling?"—must be understood as an inquiry, "How long shall it be from the Persian Horn overtopping the Median Horn to the Time of the End, when the Holy and the Host shall no longer be given over for a treading down?"—for "to the time of the end shall be the vision"—verse 17. The answer to the question reveals the terminal epoch. So long a time was to elapse before "THE DAY OF VENGEANCE" came. The 2,400 would not include the day of vengeance, but would conduct to that terrible epoch, concurrent with the end of the Sixth, and all the quadragintal period of the Seventh, vials; that is, an epoch commencing with the opening of the third section of the Frog Sign in which the advent occurs, and continuing in all the period of the Seventh Vial, in which the Seven Thunders utter their voices, and ending with this last vial, which occupies the forty years of Israel's Exodus testified of in Micah 7:15.

Now, if my computation be correct, namely, that the 2,400 years terminated in 1860, and that this was the beginning of the time of the end, we ought to find on the political map a "king of the south", a "king of the north", and the Little Horn of the Goat, all contemporary. Besides this we ought to find the king of the south making war on the Little Horn, and the land of Israel should be the subject of the strife. I say we ought to find these things in the time of the end, because the time of the vision, or 2,400 years, is to be the time of the end; "for at *the time appointed* the end shall be": and it is also written, "He", the Little Horn of the Goat, "shall divide *the land* for gain. And AT *the time of the end* the king of the south shall push at him; and the king of the north shall come against him" (Daniel 11:39,40). It is evident from this that at the time of the end, there are to be *two horns of the Goat and the little horn* all co-existent, and as hostile in their policy as in the days of Antiochus Epiphanes.

These are the things which ought to be, but what do we find? The answer is just what the prophecy requires. There is the reigning king of Egypt, or of the south;* the Russian Autocrat, king of the north, and the Sultan, the representative of the Little Horn of the Goat. The two former were brought up upon the territories of the ancient kings of the north and south, by the pouring out of that determined upon the Little Horn, subsequently to 1820, when the sixth vial began. There had been no kings of the north and south upon the Eastern Roman territory for many cen-

---

* Egypt has seen many changes since 1848; but see note on page 450.

turies previous to this period. The war between Russia and the Porte, however, in 1828, advanced the frontiers of the Russian empire to Asia Minor, Ararat, and thence to the Caspian; by which a considerable portion of the territory of the old Assyro-Macedonian kingdom is included in the dominions of the Autocrat. He is, therefore, in relation to Judea, the king of the north and representative of Antiochus Epiphanes. He is also *"the Assyrian"* of the latter days, for whom Tophet is ordained of old.

Very soon after the Russian war, which ended in 1829, Mehemet Ali established himself as king of the south. He attacked and conquered Syria, and for a time was lord ascendant of the east. This exaltation opened new prospects to Mehemet, and he aspired to the throne of the Sultan. The time of the end was not far off, there being only a few years of the 2,400 years to expire. In 1838, Mehemet Ali, king of the south, *"pushed at"* the Sultan. Hitherto he had confined his operations to Egypt and Syria, but now at the closing of the war he pushed for Constantinople, and advanced as far as Smyrna; and but for the interference of the great powers, unconsciously "to establish the vision", he would doubtless have dethroned him. Wearied of this state of affairs, which endangered "the balance of power", England, Russia, Prussia, and Austria undertook to establish peace, and to place things on a permanent footing. They ordered the king of the south to surrender Syria, including Palestine, to the sovereignty of the Little Horn; and to restore the Turkish fleet, which had revolted from the Sultan during the war. Mehemet refused to do either; contending that Syria was his as a part of his kingdom for ever by right of conquest; and the fleet, as the spoils of war. These great powers, however, were not to be trifled with. They were willing that the throne of Egypt should be hereditary in his family; but determined that he should only be Pasha of Syria for life. But Mehemet would not yield, and the result was that the allied fleet bombarded the cities of the Syrian sea-board and took possession of St. Jean d'Acre. They again offered him "all that part of Syria, extending from the gulf of Suez to the lake of Tiberias, together with the province of Acre for life", if he would restore the Turkish fleet. But he still refused, and in the autumn of 1840, they compelled the Egyptians to evacuate the country, and determined he should not have it at all; and threatened that if he did not restore the fleet in ten days, they would bombard him in Alexandria. Prudence at length overcame the obstinacy of Mehemet; he therefore yielded, and surrendered the ships within the time. Thus, the land of Israel was returned to the sovereignty of the Little Horn, and Mehemet restricted to the kingdom of Egypt; so that as the result of the sixth vial down to 1840, the political geography of the east had been so changed, that there now existed the king of the south in Egypt, the king of the north towards Ararat, and the dominion of the Little Horn of the Goat between them, extending to the Euphrates.

Such are the important events which mark the end of the 2,400 years, and the approach of the time of the end. They are evidential of the time soon arriving to which the Lord refers, saying, "*I will remember my covenant* with Abraham, Isaac, and Jacob, and *I will remember the land*" (Leviticus 26:42). Mehemet Ali claimed the land as his for ever; but Jehovah hath said, "The land shall not be sold for ever; for the land is mine". If, then, the Lord would not permit the Israelites to alienate it from one to another for ever, He would be far from permitting Mehemet to possess it, or the Allies to grant it to him, for ever. The hand of God may be clearly discerned in the events of this epoch. He hardened the king of Egypt's heart not to accept the land on any other terms than his own, which were certain not to be granted. If they had yielded to his demand, "the Eastern Question" would have been diplomatically settled, and the course of events regarding Israel turned into a different, and perhaps opposite, channel; but as the affair of 1840 has left the country, its destiny remains to be the subject of a future arrangement, when the dominion of the Little Horn subsides into that of the Russo-Assyrian Horn of the Goat.

The eleventh chapter of Daniel is therefore fulfilled as far as the first colon of the fortieth verse.* The things which remain to be accomplished in the time of the end are briefly outlined in the remaining part of the chapter. The king of Egypt having pushed at the Little Horn, as we have seen, the next event of the prophecy is an attack upon him by the king of the north, as it is written, "And the king of the north shall come against him like a whirlwind, with chariots, and with horsemen, and with many ships"; that is, the Russo-Assyrian autocrat shall attack Constantinople by sea and land, and with such whirlwind impetuosity that the Sultan's dominion shall be swept away. The whirlwind nature of the attack implies, I think, not only its overwhelming character, but that when it is made, the allies of the Sultan will be off their guard; that is, by the Autocrat's assurances of peace and moderation for which they will give him credit, Constantinople will be left unprotected, and it will fall into his hands before they can come to the rescue. To "*push at him*", and to "*come against him*" are phrases which imply more than simple invasion; they indi-

---

* Query: May not a British "push" at Russia in Turkey bring on the overwhelming storm? Mehemet Ali's rebellion of 100 years ago does not now (1958) seem more than an incipient fulfilment.

cate likewise the *direction* that invasion is to take. In the case of the king of the south, when he "pushed at him", he directed his course towards Constantinople, but he did not "come against him", because he was stopped by "the powers". The king of the north, however, is to do more than push, he is actually to "come against" the Sultan, which can only be done by sitting down before Constantinople.

It is not to be supposed that the Autocrat would attack the Porte without some provocation, real or pretended. It is therefore the mission of the Frogs, as we have seen in a former chapter, to bring about such a state of things as will involve the Autocrat and Sultan in war.* The reader will perceive, then, that the operation of the Frog-power comes in between the attacks of the king of Egypt and the Russo-Assyrians upon the Porte. The policy they originate is to involve the whole habitable in war, the more immediate effect of which will be, that "the king of the north shall enter the countries, and shall overflow and pass over". To "enter into the countries" implies invasion; but to "overflow and pass over" indicates conquest. The result of the conquest will be that "many countries shall be overthrown".

Of the horn-kingdoms, it is predicted, saying, "These shall make war with the Lamb, and the Lamb shall overcome them" (Revelation 17:14); and again, "The Beast and the kings of the earth, and their armies, gathered together to make war against him that sat upon the horse, and against his army. And (these) the remnant were slain with the sword of him that sat upon the horse, which sword proceeded out of his mouth; and all the fowls were filled with their flesh" (Revelation 19:19,21,17,18; Ezekiel 39:17-21). Now, this field of battle is to be the valley of Megiddo in the land of Israel. In view of this, has the question ever occurred to the reader, what possible inducement could there be for the rulers of Belgium, Spain, Portugal, Italy; etc., to march their armies into Palestine? What inducement was there for the kings of Europe to meet Napoleon at Dresden, and to march their armies into Russia in 1812? It was compulsion, and not inclination. A similar cause will operate on them again. When the king of the north "overflows and passes over" their countries, they will become subject to him as their emperor; and when his autocracy shall attain the extent marked out for it in the Word, his dominion will be fitly represented by Nebuchadnezzar's Image, of which they will be the toes. They must exist as regal parts of a great dominion until Christ comes: because they are to war with him in person; and because God will set up His kingdom in their time; and, having broken to pieces the power of their imperial

---

* See page 412, footnote.

ruler on the mountains of Israel, by that same kingdom He will "break in pieces and consume all theirs".

The overthrow of the Sultan will not be contemplated by the British Government with indifference. They have already beheld continental Europe to the confines of Russia subject to the will of one man, and they are destined to witness it again. They will unquestionably adopt all possible measures to circumvent the Autocrat. England's Indian Empire, and its contiguity to Asiatic Russia, make Britain his natural enemy. It will be Britain's policy to prevent the Autocrat from taking possession of Egypt and the Holy Land; for if he were to do this, he would intercept all communication between England and India by the Red Sea. Hence, while Britain is the natural enemy of the Autocrat, she is also the natural friend of Egypt and the Jews. The triumph of Russia in the west will cause Britain to strengthen herself in the east; and, as I shall show, she will take possession of Sheba, Dedan, Edom, Moab, and part of Ammon; colonize Judea with Israelites, and form an intimate alliance of offence and defence with Egypt. Thus the Red Sea will become a British lake; and by holding Gibraltar, Aden, and some commanding position at the entrance of the Persian Gulf, Britain will be enabled to retain for a short time longer her commercial and maritime ascendancy.

But these measures of the British will be the means of luring on the Autocrat to his destruction. Having fulfilled the mission of his "sacred Russia" to put down rebellion, to plant the Greek cross on the dome of St. Sophia, and to prostrate Europe at his feet, he will next address himself to the work of establishing his dominion over the east. The prosperity of Egypt and Judea will tempt him to seize them for himself; for, as the prophet saith, "He shall enter also into the glorious land, and many shall be overthrown; but these shall escape out of his hand, even Edom, and Moab, and the chief of the children of Ammon." He will have proclaimed war against the east; and at the head of his vassal kings and their armies have invaded Syria. The war will be bloody, and his hosts like a cloud to cover the land. Having overrun Syria and Persia, he will invade Egypt, Libya, and Ethiopia. For it is written, "He shall stretch forth his hand also upon the countries: and the land of Egypt shall not escape. But he shall have power over the treasures of gold, and of silver, and over all the precious things of Egypt; and the Libyans and Ethiopians shall be at his steps." This subjugation of Egypt arouses all the indignation of Britain.

England's interference* troubles him; for "tidings out of the east and out of the north shall trouble him: therefore he shall go forth with great fury to destroy, and utterly to make away many". Judea will now feel the weight of his power. He will lay siege to Jerusalem, and take it; for, "He shall pitch his palatial tents in the glorious holy mountain." "Yet", though thus far triumphant, "he shall come to his end, and none shall help him." As a further elucidation of this portion of the book of Daniel, I shall now proceed to speak of the prophecy in relation to

GOGUE AND MAGOGUE†
Τὸν Γώγ καὶ τὸν Μαγώγ

THESE names occur together in two remarkable prophecies, the one delivered through Ezekiel (Ezekiel 38:2-3; 39:6), and the other through the apostle John (Revelation 20:8). No portion of scripture has been more mangled, perhaps, than these; yet there is none, as it appears to me, more easy to be understood. An illustration of popular opinion on the subject may be seen in Guildhall, or in "the Lord Mayor's Show", where two huge giants appear, whom the wise men of Gotham have rhantized "Gog and Magog"! Interpreters have enlightened the public upon this subject about as much as the wooden giants themselves. They generally confound the Gogue and Magogue of Ezekiel with the Gogue and Magogue of the Apocalypse; but if the reader carefully examine the two testimonies, he will find that they have reference to different times exceedingly remote from each other. The Apocalyptic Gogue and Magogue are the nations and their leader, who rebel against the government of Christ and his saints, 1,000 years after the binding of the Greco-Roman Dragon is finished. They are the then existing nations outlying the land of Israel on the north, south, east, and west; who, being seduced from their allegiance, revolt and invade Canaan, and lay siege to Jerusalem, but are destroyed by fire from heaven. They are styled Gogue and Magogue because the confederacy is similar to that of Ezekiel's prophecy; being a combination of the posterity of the same populations to invade the same land, and take possession of the same city, and for the same purpose—namely, to seize

---

* The "tidings" seem rather to have to do with the *subsequent* interference of "Michael the Great Prince". Sennacherib was troubled by tidings or a "rumour" of Tirhakah's advance, and drawn off *from* Jerusalem to Libnah, where his blasphemies were avenged in the angelic destruction of his army. The King of the North is troubled by tidings out of Jerusalem, and is drawn *against the city* to encounter the Lord (Zechariah 14).

† I spell these names as they should be pronounced.

the sceptre of universal empire, which has been the matter of contest since God first put enmity between the seed of the serpent and the seed of the woman.

If the reader compare the two prophecies, he will discern the following diversities, which prove them to be confederacies belonging to different epochs.

1. The Gogue of Ezekiel invades Judea *"in the latter days"*; but the Apocalyptic Gogue does not invade the land till 1,000 years after the binding of the dragon;

2. Ezekiel's Gogue goes forth from the north; John's from the four corners of the earth;

3. The Ezekiel-Gogue's invasion is the occasion of the Lord's manifestation, and therefore pre-millennial; but that of John's Gogue is after the Lord has reigned with his saints on earth 1,000 years, and therefore post-millennial;

4. The Lord himself brings the Ezekiel-Gogue against his land; but some arch-rebel stirs up hitherto loyal nations against the government, and as the Apocalyptic Gogue and Magogue defy the King already in Jerusalem;

5. The Lord brings the Ezekiel-Gogue up to battle against Jerusalem, that He may be made known to the Nations; but John's Gogue has known Him for 1,000 years.

The prophecy of Ezekiel concerning Gogue evidently relates to a power that is to arise hereafter; for the Lord says in his address to its chief, *"In the later years* thou shalt come into the land that is brought back from the sword, and *is gathered out of many people*, against the mountains of Israel, which have been always waste: but it is brought forth out of the nations, and they shall dwell safely all of them." In another verse of this chapter, the "latter years" are termed "latter days", as it is written: "And thou shalt come up against my people of Israel, as a cloud to cover the land; *it shall be in the latter days*, and I will bring thee against my land." This testimony shows that there will have been a gathering of the Jews to some extent before Gogue invades their land; and that this gathering is subsequent to a long desolation of the country. Hence, those acquainted with Jewish history will perceive directly that the prediction has not yet been fulfilled; but is yet in the future, and belongs to "the time of the end", which is synchronous with "the latter days".

The prophecy of Gogue synchronizes with the events set forth in the forty-first verse of the eleventh chapter of Daniel. In short, Ezekiel's prophecy of Gogue is an amplification of Daniel's concerning the king of the north. That these two powers are the same will be manifest from the following considerations:

1.   Gogue, or the Prince of Ros, is king of Meshech and Tubal, therefore he is the king of the north geographically; those countries being north of the Holy Land, which, according to the covenant, extends to Amanus and the Euphrates;

2.   Gogue is to invade the land of Israel "from the north parts" and "in the latter days"; and the king of the north is to enter into the same country at the same time; therefore, as they come against the same enemy and at the same time, they must be one and the same power;

3.   The Libyans and Ethiopians belong to Gogue's army; and Daniel testifies, that "the Libyans and Ethiopians are at the steps of the king of the north", that is, they march among his troops;

4.   Hostile tidings come to Gogue from Sheba and Dedan eastward;* and from "the Merchants of Tarshish and the young lions thereof" northward:† so, also, "tidings out of the east and out of the north", says Daniel, "shall trouble the king of the north";

5.   Gogue is to "fall upon the mountains of Israel", where he and his multitudes are to be buried; so the king of the north having encamped "between the seas in the glorious holy mountain", the hill country, "comes to his end" there, "with none to help him"; and,

6.   Gogue unexpectedly encounters the Lord God in battle on the mountains of Israel; and the king of the north contends with Michael the great prince, who standeth up for Israel, and delivers them; they are both defeated and deprived of dominion by the same supernatural power.

Here, then, are six particulars, which clearly establish the identity of Gogue with the king of the north. The multitudes they are destined to lead into the Holy Land are the "all nations" which Zechariah has predicted the Lord will gather together against Jerusalem, to destroy them in battle with a small exception (Zechariah 14:2), and whose slain are "the carcases of the men that have transgressed against the LORD, whose worm shall not die, nor their fire be quenched; and who shall be an abhorring to all flesh" (Isaiah 66:24), who pass through "the valley of the passengers on the east of the sea" (Ezekiel 39:11); for the consumption of their bodies by the worm will commence while they are yet standing alive upon their feet (Zechariah 14:12); so

---

* Say rather, southward: "the Queen of the South" (Matthew 12:42; 2 Chronicles 9:1).

† "All the young lions thereof"; i.e., from Asia, Africa, America, and Australia. See footnote page 453.

that the stench of their consuming bodies will "stop the noses of the passers by."

ROSH, MESHECH, AND TUBAL

THE prophet Ezekiel is addressed by Jehovah as the type, or representative, of him who is to vanquish Gogue on the mountains of Israel. Hence He says to him, "*Son of Man, set thy face against Gogue, of the land Magogue, the prince of Rosh, Meshech, and Tubal, and prophesy against him*" (RV). In this title to the prophecy, the antagonists are indicated—namely, the Son of Man on one side, and Gogue on the other. But, while it is quite clear who the Son of Man is, it is but little understood what power is represented by Gogue. It will, therefore, be my endeavour in the following pages to identify this adversary of Israel and their King; so that the reader may know which of "the powers that be" is chosen of God to personate the serpent's head when it is crushed by the woman's seed.

The Jews appointed by Ptolemy Philadelphus, king of Egypt, to translate the Old Testament into Greek, gave a different rendering of the title to that which appears in the Authorized English Version. They rendered the original by Γὼγ, ἄρχοντα Ῥὼς, Μεσὸχ καὶ Θοβὲλ, i.e., Gogue, Prince of Ros, Mesoch, and Thobel; so that the difference of the two translations turns upon the Hebrew word *rosh* being regarded as a proper, or a common, noun. The Seventy were sensible that in this place it was not an appellative noun, but *a proper name*; and they rendered it accordingly by *Ros*. But Jerome not finding any such proper name among the nation-families mentioned in Genesis, rather disputed the Septuagint reading, and preferred to consider the word *Ros* as a common noun; and his interpretation, established in the Latin Vulgate, has universally prevailed throughout the west. Jerome, however, was more scrupulous than the editors of later versions, who have unqualifiedly rejected it as a common name; for although he inclined to the other rendering, he did not feel authorized to reject altogether one so ancient, and he has therefore preserved them both, translating the passage thus— "*Gogue, terram Magogue, principem capitis* (sive Ros) *Mosoch, et Thubal.*"

But the question between the phrases "the chief prince", and "the prince of Ros", has been long set at rest by the concurring judgment of the learned, who have adopted the primitive interpretation of the Alexandrine Jews. And although the common English version has not the benefit of their decision, yet the title of the prophecy has been generally received among the erudite portion of the western nations for nearly 200 years, according to the ancient Greek interpretation; that is to say, as uniting the three proper names of nations, *Ros, Mosc*, and *Tobl*. By the insertion of vowels, or vowel-points, the Hebrew words have been made to assume the different forms of *Meshech, Mesoch, Tubal*, and *Thobel*; but, as the meaning of Hebrew words depends not on the points, but upon the radical consonants, or letters, it may be as well to express these names by the forms and elements of the original words, for by so doing we keep nearer to the original idea, and are less likely to be mystified by hypothesis. "Ros," says David Levi, "is not an appellative as in the common translation of the Bible, but a proper name." The word "*chief*" ought, therefore, to be replaced by the proper name *Ros*, or *Rosh*.

But *what nations are signified by these three proper names?* This question has been long since determined by the learned. The celebrated Bochart, about the year 1640, observed in his elaborate researches into Sacred Geography, that '*ℛ𝛴*, Ros, is the most ancient form under which history makes mention of the name Russia; and he contended that Ros and Mosc properly denote the nations of Russia and Moscovy. "It is credible", says he, "that from Rhos and Mesech (that is the Rhossi and Moschi), of whom Ezekiel speaks, descended the Russians and Moscovites, nations of the greatest celebrity in European Scythia." We have, indeed, ample and positive testimony, that the Russian nation was called *ℛ𝛴*, Ros, by the Greeks in the earliest period in which we find it mentioned, as, Ἔθνος δὲ οἱ Ῥὼς Σκύθικον, περὶ τὸν ἄρκτωον Ταῦρον; that is, "the Ros are a Scythian nation, bordering on the northern Taurus". And their own historians say, "It is related that the Russians (whom the Greeks called Ῥώς, Ros, and sometimes Ῥῶσος, Rosos) derived their name from Ros, a valiant man, who delivered his nation from the yoke of their tyrants."

Thus, then, we discern the modern names of Russia and of Moscow, or Moskwa, in the ancient names of Ros and Mosc, or Musc. It is not difficult to recognize in Tobl, Tubl, or Thobel, a name which naturally connects itself with them; and which, in conjunction with them, tends, in a very remarkable manner, to determine and fix the *proper object* of the prediction. The river Tobol gives name to the City Tobol*ium*, or Tobol*ski*, the metropolis of the extensive region of Siberia, lying immediately eastward of the territories of Moscovy, or Mosc. Tobol and Mosc are mentioned together by Ezekiel who characterizes them as nations trading in copper (Ezekiel 27:13); a metal which, it is notorious, abounds in the soil of Siberia; a region which includes all the northern part of Asia which borders on Russia to the west, on the Arctic Ocean to the north, on the Pacific Ocean on the east, and on Central Asia to the south. And thus the three denominations Ros, Mosc, and Tobl, united in prophecy, point out, with equal capacity and conciseness, those widely extended regions, which, at the present day, we denominate collectively THE RUSSIAN EMPIRE.

Gogue is styled the *"Prince of Ros, Mosc, and Tobl"*, that is, Autocrat of the Russians, Moscovites, and Siberians, or of "All the Russias". But he is also styled "Gogue of the land of Magogue", as well. There is something important in this. It affirms that he is sovereign of Magogue as well as prince of all the Russias; for there, at the time of the prophecy, is his proper dominion. "Whoever reads Ezekiel", says Michaelis, "can hardly entertain a doubt that Gogue is the name of a sovereign, and Magogue that of his people; the prophet speaks of *the former*, not as a people but as AN EMPEROR." Let us, then, now inquire, where is the region styled *Magogue*: that we may be enabled to ascertain of what people besides the Russians Gogue will be the Emperor. And as Gomer, and Togarmah of the north quarters, are represented as being connected with him, we shall also endeavour to find out what modern nations will answer to these names.

MAGOGUE AND GOMER

WE know from the Hebrew scriptures that Magogue and Gomer were the names of the two sons of Japheth: and it is to ancient Hebrew authority alone that we can resort to learn where, according to the common repute of the Israelites, the nations which descended from these two heads of families, and which *long retained the proper names* of those heads, were spread and established. Josephus says, "that Japhet, the son of Noah, had seven sons; who, proceeding from their primitive seats in the mountains of Taurus and Amanus, ascended Asia to the river Tanais (or Don); and there entering Europe, penetrated as far westward as the Straits of Gibraltar, occupying the lands which they successively met with in their progress; all of which were uninhabited; and bequeathed their names to their different families, or nations. That Gomer founded the Gomari, whom the Greeks, at that time, called Galatæ—τοὺς νῦν ὑφ᾽ Ἑλληνων Γαλάτας καλούμενους—and that Magogue founded the Magogæ, whom the Greeks then called Scythæ, Σκύθαι." It only, therefore, remains for us to ascertain which were the nations that the Greeks, in the time of Josephus, called *Scythæ*, and which they then called *Galatæ*; and to observe whether the geographical affinities of these nations are such as answer to those which are plainly required by the prophecy for Magogue and Gomer.

Herodotus, the most ancient Greek writer accessible, acquaints us "that the name Scythæ was a name given by the Greeks to an ancient and widely extended people of Europe, who had spread themselves from the river Tanais, or Don, westward along the banks of the Ister, or Danube". "The Greeks," observes Major Rennel, "appear to have first used the term Scythia, in its application to their neighbours, the Scythians of the Euxine, who were also called *Getæ,* or *Gothi*; and were those who afterwards subdued the Roman empire: and from which original stock the present race of people in Europe seem to be descended." And again, "the Scythians of Herodotus appear to have extended themselves in length from *Hungary, Transylvania,* and *Wallachia,* on the westward, to the river Don on the eastward." Thus the testimony of Herodotus and Josephus is in perfect agreement concerning the progress of Magogue and Gomer. In these same regions the Scythæ continued many ages after Herodotus, and even long after the time of Josephus; for Dion Cassius, who lived 150 years after Josephus; and above 200 after Christ, relates, that Pompey, in his return into Europe from Asia, "determined to pass to the Ister, or Danube, through the Scythæ; and so to enter Italy". These were the original Scythæ. But Herodotus states further, that a portion of the same people, in an after age, turned back upon the European seats of their fathers, and established themselves in Asia; and from these sprung the Asiatic Scythæ, who, in process of time, almost engrossed the name to themselves.

Since the name of Scythæ, *i.e.,* Magogue is to be considered not by itself, but in geographical connection with Galatæ, or Gomer, we have only to inquire, whether any geographical affinity is really ascribed by the Greeks to the Scythæ and Galatæ; and to ascertain to what regions of the earth those names, so associated were applied. If we can discover these two points, we ought thereby to have discovered specifically the Magogue of the prophecy, which is to be associated with the region, or people of Gomer.

Diodorus Siculus, who lived about a century before Josephus, traces them much further into Europe than the Danube; *even to the shores of the Baltic, and to the very confines of the Galatæ of the Greeks.* In speaking of the amber found upon the shores of that sea, he there places the region expressly denominated, "Scythia above, or north of, Galatia". In which description we at length find the Scythæ, or Magogue, in the immediate neighbourhood of the Galatæ of the Greeks, or Gomer.

Galatia, Γαλατία, is the common and familiar name used by all the earlier Greek historians for Gaul, the Gallia of the Latins; and Galatæ, Γαλάται, is the common Greek name for Gauls, or the Galli of the Latins. Thus, "all the Galatæ" (or Gauls), says Strabo, "were called Celtæ by the Greeks"; and the converse is equally true: "the Celtæ were called Galatæ by the Greeks, and Galli by the Latins." To inquire, *Who* were "the Galatæ of the Greeks"? is, therefore, the same as to inquire, Who were the Galli of the Romans? A colony of these Galatæ, or Galli, indeed, in the third century before Christ, emigrated from Gaul and established themselves in Asia Minor; where they were ever after called by their Greek name Galatians. Diodorus' "Scythia above Gaul extending towards the Baltic", accurately describes that large tract of Europe above the Rhine, *or northern boundary of Gaul*, through which flow the rivers Elbe, Ems, and Weser. Here, and in the countries immediately adjoining, were *the* SCYTHÆ *bordering upon the* GALATÆ *on the north*; that is to say, a considerable part of MAGOGUE, *geographically associated with* GOMER.* Diodorus elsewhere describes the northern part of Galatia, or Gaul, as *confining upon Scythia*. "The Greeks", says he, "call those who inhabit Marseilles and the inland territory, and all those who dwell towards the Alps and the Pyrenean Mountains, by the name of Celts; but those who occupy the country lying to the northward, between the Ocean and the Hercynian mountain, and all others as far as Scythia, they denominate Galatae; but the Romans call all those nations by one collective appellation, Galatae; that is, Galli." These geographical affinities unite in the name of Celto-Scythae, mentioned by Strabo. "The ancient Greeks", says he, "at first called the northern nations by the general name of Scythians; but when they became acquainted with the nations *in the West*, they began to call them by different names of Celts, Celto-Scythæ"; and again, "the ancient Greek historians called the northern nations, collectively, Scythians, and Celto-Scythæ"; which latter name plainly denoted the most western portion of the Scythæ, adjoining Gaul; of the number of whom were the Scythæ on the north of the Galatæ, or the Σκύθαι ὑπέρ Γαλατίαν.

In this general description may easily be discerned that extended portion of *the West of Europe*, comprehending ancient Gaul, Belgium, and the countries bordering upon them, which

---

* "Gomer, ex quo Galatae, id est, Galli", that is to say, "Gomer, from whom proceeded the Galatae, that is, the Gauls."—Isidorus Hispalensis, *Originum sive etymologiarum libri ix*. He wrote about AD 600.

constituted in our day the Napoleon empire.* Gomer, then, points immediately to France. It is a curious coincidence that Louis Philippe paid his visit to England in the *Gomer*. When this vessel was thus named, did they adopt it allusively to their country being originally peopled by the descendants of Gomer? "Scythia above Gaul", or Magogue above Gomer, or to the north of it, through which flowed the Elbe, Ems, and Weser, was the country from whence proceeded principally that renowned people, who, in the early ages of Romanism, formed an extensive confederacy with their kindred nations upon the Rhine, which had migrated successively thither from the regions of the Danube; and who, under the common denomination of FRANKS, overran Gaul, and subdued it; and finally establishing their power and population in the conquered country permanently superseded the name of Gaul by that of FRANCE. "As for the seats of the Franks", says the "Universal History" , "it appears from their constant excursions into Gaul, that they dwelt *on the banks of the Rhine*, in the neighbourhood of Mentz. All historians speak of them as placed there till their settling in Gaul. Their country, according to the best modern geographers and historians, was bounded on the north by the Ocean; on the west by the Ocean and the Rhine; on the south by the Maine; and on the east by the Weser."

These, therefore, were the *Κελτό-Σκύθαι*, or *Σκύθαι ὑπέρ τήν Γαλατίαν*, the Celto-Scythians, or Scythians on the northern confine of Gaul; that is, Magogue in contiguity with Gomer. The Chaldean interpreter applies the name of Magogue to *the Germans*; in short, all the ancients looked for the Magogue of scripture in the West. The Scythae of Asia, who, as we have seen, were only a partial emigration, or reflux, from their ancient stock in Europe, cannot, with any soundness of criticism, be taken account of in this argument.

"Togarmah *of the north quarters*, and all his bands", is also to form a part of the Gogue's confederacy against the Holy Land in "the time of the end". There is little said about Togarmah in history beyond conjecture. He was a son of Gomer, therefore his posterity would migrate originally from the same locality as Gomer's other descendants—namely, from the mountains of Taurus and Amanus; but, instead of going westward with their brethren, they diffused themselves over *"the north quarters"*, that is, relatively to Judea. Ezekiel says, "The house of Togarmah traded in the Tyrian fairs with *horses, and horsemen, and mules*" (Ezekiel 27:14). Hence doubtless they were a nomadic people, tending

---

* See Foreword.

flocks and herds in the pasture lands of the north, where nature favoured their production with little care and expense. Russian, and Independent, Tartary are the countries of Togarmah, from which in former times poured forth the Turcoman cavalry, "which", says Gibbon, "they proudly computed by millions". Georgia and Circassia, probably, are "bands of Togarmah's house".

These, then, are the regions which are to supply the numerous and formidable armies with which their arrogant and mighty Emperor, prophetically denominated Gogue, is hereafter "to ascend as a cloud", against the Holy Land, not long after he shall have gone, "like a whirlwind", against the Little Horn. Let us now consider, as briefly as possible, the applicability of this word to the Prince of Ros, Mosc, and Tobl.

"Gogue of the land Ma-gogue", that is, styling the ruler of Magogue by the latter syllable of the name of the country over which he rules. We have seen that Magogue is the region extending from the Ros, or Russia, to the Rhine, comprehending Wallachia, Transylvania, Hungary, and Germany. Of course, the prophecy must be future, because the Prince of the Ros is the Gogue of Magogue; and as yet no Emperor of Russia has been also Emperor of Germany, etc. But why is the future autocrat of Gomer, Magogue, Ros, Mosc, Tobl, and Togarmah, styled Gogue?

There is no name in the Bible which has more puzzled the critics than this of Gogue. The depths of Hebrew etymology have been explored in vain, and the versatile efforts of ingenuity in vain exerted, in the search for a mystical sense which might attach to this name. But Gogue is a Gentile, and not a Hebrew name; and Michaelis has correctly remarked, "that the origin of a barbaric, or foreign name, ought not to be sought for in the Hebrew, nor in any of its kindred tongues, as many have erroneously done". An early nineteenth century writer, who very incorrectly applied the name to Napoleon, refers to Fredegarius' History as the only satisfactory account of any person of the name of Gogue. Without adopting his application of it to the French Emperor, I will give the substance of what he says concerning it.

It is a proper name well known to continental history: and borne in one notable instance by an ancient ruler, which answers immediately to the Magogue of the scriptures. Gogue was the proper name of the Major Domus Regiæ, or chief of the palace, who, after having been exalted by the voice of the nation to the highest authority, fell by a violent and sanguinary death. The name of this personage appears in the history which is written in Latin under the double form of *Gogo* (*-onis*) and *Gogus* (*-i*); these different terminations and inflexions having been suffixed to the original name. But although modern authors have followed those Latin forms, the name has nevertheless been preserved in the vernacular tongue, with its genuine, original, and simple enunciation of Gogue.

About sixty years after the death of Sigebert, King of Austrasia, AD 575, Fredegarius undertook to write the history of his reign, in which he gives the following account of Gogue:—

"When Sigebert (grandson of Clovis) saw that his brothers had contracted marriages with women of inferior condition, he sent Gogue on an embassy to the King of Spain, to demand his daughter, Bruna, in marriage. The King sent her, with great treasures, to Sigebert; and in order to add greater dignity to her name, it was changed to Brunechildis. Sigebert received her for his consort, with great rejoicings.

"Prior to this event, and during the infancy of Sigebert, the Austrasians had made choice of the Duke Chrodinus, to be Major Domus Regiæ, or chief of the palace; because he was a man of vigorous conduct in affairs, fearing God, endued with patience and possessing no quality but what rendered him dear both to God and men. Chrodinus rejected the honour proffered to him, saying, 'I am unable to establish peace in Austrasia, for all the nobles and gentry of Austrasia are allied to me by blood; and I have not the power of enforcing discipline amongst them, or of taking away the life of any man. They will all rise against me, to follow their own superstitions; and God forbid, that their actions should draw me into the condemnation of hell. Choose ye, therefore, from among yourselves whom ye may approve.'

"When they could find no one they chose Gogue, the tutor of the prince, by the advice of Chrodinus, to be Major Domus Regiae. And on the following morning Chrodinus repaired the first to the dwelling of Gogue, and placed his arm upon his neck; which the rest perceiving, they all followed his example. And thus was the government of Gogue prosperous; until he brought Brunechildis out of Spain. But she soon rendered him odious to Sigebert, who, by her instigation, put him to death."

The high authority of Gogue while he held the reins of the Austrasian Government, is strongly marked in the complimentary poems addressed to him by Fortunatus, Bishop of Poitiers, a distinguished poet of that age; from one of which the following passage, translated from the Latin, may be worthy of selection, on account of its geographical references, so remarkably connecting the proper name of Gogue with the Rhenish section of Magogue.

TO GOGUE HIMSELF

Ye clouds whose course the northern winds impel,
Of my lov'd GOGUE some grateful tidings tell!
Say, with what health his valued life is blest;
What peaceful cares engage his tranquil breast.
If on the banks of *Rhine* awhile he stay,
Where the rich salmon yields itself a prey.
Or where *Moselle* through vineyards guides her stream,
While gentle breezes cool the sultry gleam,
Or flowing waters mitigate the heat
And with fresh waves the bowery margins greet.
Or where the *Meuse* in murmurs soft is heard,
Mid threefold wealth, of vessel, fish, and bird.
Or where the *Aisne* through grassy banks is borne,
Whose waters nourish pasturage and corn.
Or if by *Oise*, by *Sare*, by *Cher*, or *Scheld*,
Somme, Sambre, Saur, the loitering Chief beheld,
Or when the *Seille*, with mouth expanded, laves
Metz' stately bulwarks with her copious waves.
Or if in forest shades he seeks his prey,
With toil, or spear, to capture, or to slay.
Or if on *Ardenne's* wild, or *Vosge's* height,
The echoing woods resound his arrow's flight.
Or if, returned beneath his PRINCELY DOME,
Their lord, a zealous people welcome home.

Of the origin, or family, of Gogue, the first *Maire du Palais*, or
Dux Francorum, of the kingdom of Austrasia, no mention is
made in history; but it is plainly to be collected from the words of
Chrodinus, that he had no consanguinity with either the nobles
or the gentry—the "primates", or "liberi", of that kingdom; and it
seems equally implied in the words of Fredegarius, that he was
not a native of the kingdom, since he was elected to his dignity
because the Austrasians could find no one among themselves.

Thus, it is evident that Gogue is an historical character, and
that he was Regent of a part of Magogue. Now, it is probable
that, because of certain peculiarities in his history in relation to

Magogue, God selected his name as the prophetic title of one who should rule over the same country in "the time of the end". The, resemblance between the historical and prophetic Gogues may be stated as follows. I shall distinguish them as Gogue I and Gogue II.

1.   Gogue I was a foreigner; Gogue II will be one likewise, belonging to the Ros, and not to the Germans;

2.   Gogue I became sovereign *in fact*, though not *de jure*; Gogue II will become sovereign in fact by conquest;

3.   Gogue I became ruler in a time of confusion, because the native princes could not maintain order; weakness of the sovereigns, and anarchy of the people, will precede the *de facto* sovereignty of Gogue II also;

4.   Gogue I, though exalted to the highest post of honour and power, short only of the *legitimate* sovereignty, was precipitated from his high estate by a violent death. This is also the destiny of the prophetic Gogue, who is to "come to his end, and no one shall help him".

With these premises before us, I have no doubt that the following paraphrase will present the reader with the true import of the exordium to the prophecy of Ezekiel concerning Gogue.

"Son of Man, set thy face against Gogue, the Emperor of Germany, Hungary, etc., and Autocrat of Russia, Moscovy, and Tobolskoi, and prophesy against him, and say, Thus saith the Lord God: Behold I am against thee, O Gogue, Autocrat of Russia, Moscovy, and Tobolskoi: and I will turn thee about, and put a bit into thy jaws, and I will bring thee forth from the north parts, and all thine army, horses, and horsemen, all of them accoutred with all sorts of armour, even a great company with bucklers and shields, all of them handling swords: among whom shall be Persians, Ethiopians, and Libyans; all of them with shields and helmet: French and Italians, etc.; Circassians, Cossacks, and the Tartar hordes of Usbeck, etc.: and many people not particularly named besides. Be thou prepared; prepare thyself, thou, and all thy company that are assembled unto thee; and be thou Imperial Chief to them."

From these premises, then, I think, there cannot be the shadow of a doubt that the Autocrat of Russia, when he shall have attained to the plenitude of his power and dominion, is the subject of the prophecy contained in the 38th and 39th of Ezekiel. This personage at present is only "Autocrat of All the Russias", that is, of Ros, Mosc, and Tobl; while the Emperor of Austria holds the position of Gogue and Magogue. But as we have seen elsewhere, the Austrian and German empire is doomed to extinction by fire and sword; so that when this is broken up the

Gogueship will be assumed by the Autocrat, or "prince of Ros, Mosc, and Tobl".

Having proved as I think, that the phrase "Gogue of the land of Magogue" signifies *Emperor of Germany*, and that the particular emperor referred to will also be the "prince of Ros, Mosc, and Tobl"—that is, that at some time hereafter, and that not far off, a Czar of Russia will be both Emperor of Germany and Autocrat of All the Russias—I proceed to remark that, although the Son of Man is his conqueror, he is to be antagonized by another power before he comes to fight his last battle, in which he loses both his life and crown. Ezekiel informs us that Gogue's earthly adversary occupies the countries of Sheba, Dedan, and Tarshish; and that when the Autocrat (for Gogue is an autocrat, *ruling by his own will*) invades the Holy Land for the purpose of spoiling the Jews, the Lion-power of these countries assumes a threatening attitude, and dares him to execute his purpose. "Art thou come to take a spoil? Hast thou gathered thy company to take a prey?" Thus it speaks to Gogue: as much as to say, "Thou shalt not spoil Israel and subdue their country, if we can help it."

The prophet Daniel, however, shows that the only effect of these threatening tidings is to make him furious; for he says, "Therefore shall he go forth with great fury to destroy, and utterly to make away many". But furious as Daniel represents him, Ezekiel testifies that he meets with one more potently furious than himself. But this is not the Lion-power of Tarshish, but the Lord God Himself, "whose fury comes up into his face" when He beholds the extortioner and spoiler (Isaiah 16:4) ravening upon His prey. The lion-and-merchant-power of Tarshish will not be permitted to usurp the glory of the Lion of the tribe of Judah. It is to the latter that Jehovah hath assigned the work of delivering His people from the destroyer. The Lion-power of Tarshish, which will possess Edom and Moab, and Ammon, as well as Sheba and Dedan, will be indeed a covert to Jehovah's outcasts (Isaiah 16:4); and therefore will "Edom, and Moab, and the chief of the children of Ammon escape out of his hand"; but it is only Michael the great prince, who commands the artillery of heaven, that can "break in pieces the oppressor". The men upon the face of the land shall *shake at his presence*; and the solid earth itself will be convulsed. He will turn their swords against themselves; and Judah shall fall upon them, and augment the slain (Zechariah 14:14). Mutual slaughter and pestilence will be aggravated by terrors from above; for "the LORD of hosts will visit them with thunder, and with earthquake, and great noise, with storm and tempest" (Isaiah 29:5-8), and "an overflowing rain, and great hailstones, fire, and brimstone" (Ezekiel 38:18-22). "Thus", saith He, "will I magnify myself, and sanctify myself; and

I will be known in the eyes of many nations, and they shall know that I (Jesus) am the LORD."

But what is the lion-power of which Ezekiel speaks? To ascertain this we must direct our attention to the countries named in connection with "the young lions". Of these, Sheba and Dedan are districts of Arabia. The men of Dedan are in the list given by Ezekiel of the traders in the Tyrian fairs. The Dedanim carried thither the ivory and ebony which they procured from "the many isles" to the eastward, and "precious clothes for chariots". Sheba carried the "chief of all spices, precious stones, and gold". Dedan and Sheba were those parts of Arabia which lay convenient to the ivory, gold, precious stones, and spice countries of Africa and India. The Sultan of Muscat now rules the country of Dedan; while the British have planted their standard on the soil of Sheba, at Aden, the Gibraltar of the Red Sea, and key of Egypt ... The British power is the lion-power of Sheba.*

As to Tarshish, there were two countries of that name in the geography of the ancients. Jehoshaphat built ships at Ezion-geber, a port of the Red Sea, that they might sail thence to Tarshish. Now, it will be seen by the map that they could only sail southward towards the straits of Bab-el-Mandeb, from which they might then steer east, or north, for India. As they did not sail by compass in those days, but coastwise, they would creep round the coast of Arabia, and so make for Hindostan. They might have sailed southward again along the coast of Africa instead of to India; but it is not likely they did, as the commerce of the time was with the civilized world, and not the savage. The voyage occupied them three years. In the days of Solomon the trade was shared between Israel and the Tyrians; for "he had at sea a navy of Tarshish with the navy of Hiram; once in three years came the navy of Tarshish bringing gold and silver, ivory, and apes, and *peacocks*." These products point to India as the Eastern Tarshish—a country which has always conferred maritime ascendancy on the power which has possessed its trade and been its carrier to the nations.

But there was also a Tarshish to the north-west of Judea. This appears in the case of Jonah, who embarked at Joppa, now Jaffa,

---

* In the Scripture genealogies (Genesis 10:6,7; 25:1-3), the names Sheba and Dedan occur both in the third generation of the defendants of Ham, and in the tenth generation of those of Shem: the latter being the grandsons of Abraham by Keturah. These gave their names to the Arabian countries spoken of here by Dr. Thomas. The Hamitic Sheba and Dedan seem to indicate a North African country near Cush, or Ethiopia. British power is now established on the Upper Nile and in the Soudan; and thus, here also "is the Lion-Power of Sheba."

on the Mediterranean, "to flee unto Tarshish from the presence of the LORD". It is evident he must have sailed westward. It is not exactly known where the western Tarshish was situated. It was a country, however, not a city, whose "merchants" frequented the Tyrian fairs. Addressing Tyre, the prophet says, "Tarshish was thy merchant by reason of the multitude of all kinds of riches; with silver, iron, tin, and lead they traded in thy fairs". These metals are the products of Britain, celebrated by the Phœnicians, as Baratanac, or "the land of tin", as some construe it. The merchandise of the northern Tarshish, and of the eastern, identifies Britain and India with the two countries of that name; and Sheba and Tarshish in the prophecy of Gogue are manifestly indicative of the Lion-power of the Anglo-Indian empire.

But, in corroboration of this, I remark further, that the lion-power is represented also *as a merchant power*, in the words, "the Merchants of Tarshish shall say unto Gogue". Having ascertained the geography of Tarshish, it is easy to answer the question, Who are its merchants? This inquiry will admit of but one answer, namely, the *British East India Company*, which is both the merchant and the ruler of the elephant-tooth country of the east. But the association of *"the young lions of Tarshish"* with the "merchants of Tarshish", makes this still more obvious; for it represents the peculiar constitution of the Anglo-Indian government.* As everyone knows, this government is neither purely a merchant-sovereignty, nor a purely imperial one like that of Canada, but a combination of the two. The Honourable Company has no power in Canada, but, with its imperial partner, the firm is omnipotent in India. Now the imperial member is represented in the prophet by "young lions"; that is, the lion is chosen to represent the imperial British power, as the Ram and the Goat, the self-chosen emblems of the nations, were adopted to symbolize that of the Persians and Macedonians. Young rams and young goats were civil and military officials under the ram and goat sovereignties; as also "young lions" are the same under the old Lion of England. This, the lion-power, is represented in the government of India by "the Board of Control", and the imperial forces which serve with the Company's troops in the Indian Army. The merchants of Tarshish govern India under the control of the lion-powers—a constitution of things well represented in the Company's arms, which are a shield whose quarterings are filled with young lions rampant, with the motto, *"Auspicio*

---

* The prophet says *"all* the young lions thereof." The whole British Empire is a "merchant" dominion. The British East India Company, The Hudson Bay Company, The British South Africa Company, etc. are illustrations of the dominion of "the Merchants of Tarshish". See Foreword also.

Senatûs Angliæ". From these facts, it may be concluded, that the united imperial power of Britain and merchant-power of India, is the power of the latter days, destined of God to contend with the Autocrat, when, having laid all Europe prostrate, his ambition prompts him to grasp the sceptre of the east.

But the lion-power of Britain has not yet attained the limit marked out for it by the finger of God: The conquest of Persia by the Autocrat will doubtless cause England to conquer Afghanistan, and to seize upon Dedan that she may command the entrance to the Persian gulf, and so prevent him from obtaining access to India either by land or sea. Possessing Persia and Mesopotamia, the apprehension of his pushing still further southward, and perhaps establishing himself on the north-eastern coast of the Red Sea, and so taking them in the rear and gaining access to India by the straits of Bab-el-Mandeb, will also be a powerful motive for the merchants of Tarshish and its young lions to take possession of all the coast from the Gulf of Persia to the Straits, and thence to Suez, by which the lion-power will not only become the Sheba and Dedan, but also the Edom, Moab, and Ammon, of "the latter days"; for in speaking of the events of these days, the prophets refer not to races of men, but to *powers on territories* designated by the names of the people who anciently inhabited them. Hence, for instance, the Lion-power planted hereafter in the ancient territory of Moab, becomes the Moab of the latter days; so that when the countries before-named are possessed and settled by the British, they will be men of Dedan in Muscat, men of Sheba in Aden and Mocha, and Moabites, Edomites, and Ammonites in their several territories. Thus, the prophecies concerning those countries in their latter-day developments have regard to the power to which they then belong, and which, I have no doubt, will be the British; which, together with the Autocrat's, though henceforth always rival dominions, will endure until both powers be broken up by the Ancient of Days.

It may be as well in this place to recall the reader's attention briefly to the vision of the four Beasts (Daniel 7). The Lion, the Bear, and the Leopard, the symbols of the Assyrian, the Persian, and of a greater dominion than that comprehended in the four heads of the Leopard, or horns of the Goat; therefore, I will call it Alexandrine (Daniel 11:3,4): these three Beasts are represented in the vision as out-living the destruction of the Fourth Beast, or Roman Dragon. Speaking of this, the prophet says, " I beheld till the beast was slain, and *his body* destroyed, and given to the burning flame". Having seen his violent death, he goes on to say, "As concerning the rest of the beasts, they had their dominion taken away; yet a prolonging in life was given them for a season and a time". The meaning of this is, that at the consummation of the judgment, the territories comprehended in the dominions of the four beasts to their full extent will be divided between two independent dominions of the Latter Days—namely, that of Gogue and that of the Lion of Tarshish. Gogue's will include so much of the territory as to entitle his dominion to be represented by Nebuchadnezzar's Image. Assyria proper, Persia, Asia Minor, Armenia, and Mesopotamia; Egypt, Italy, Germany, Belgium, France, Spain, Portugal, Sardinia, Naples, Lombardy, Bavaria, Hungary, and Greece—countries all included in the catalogue given by Ezekiel in his prophecy of Gogue—are symbolized by the head, breast, body, thighs, legs, and toes of the Image. These are at the crisis united together in one dominion, which is broken to pieces as the result of the battle of Armageddon. Gogue's yoke being broken off the neck of these nations, Assyria and Persia resume their independence; but they do not retain it long, for it is "taken away", yet they continue separate states for 1,000 years, only ruled by the saints, whom the Lord may appoint over them.

The Lion of Tarshish is Alexandrine in its dominion, and will then possess much of the territory represented by the Unicorn Goat and the Leopard—all, indeed, not included in the Image. Alexander the Great extended his conquests over Afghanistan, the Punjaub, and into India beyond the Indus. The Lion of Tarshish has already annexed much of his territory, indeed quite sufficient to confer upon it Unicorn and Leopard attributes. Its supremacy over the Ionian Republic still further approximates it to the Macedonian character; which will become still more conspicuous, when it beholds *the prince of Ros, Mosc, and Tobl* possessed of Constantinople, and contending for the Gogueship of Magogue; it will, then, doubtless, make extensive seizures of the Isles of Greece, to strengthen itself in the Mediterranean, and to antagonize, as much as possible, the power of the Autocrat in that direction. Thus, then, answering to the Leopard of the latter days, the Lion of Tarshish survives the destruction of the Image. But subsequent events will affect it in common with the Lion and the Bear; for though it may, in alliance with Assyria and Persia, hold out for a time against the Stone of Israel, its "dominion will be taken away"; for the kingdom he is to establish will "break in pieces and consume all these kingdoms"; yet Assyria, Persia, and Britain will continue to exist as people for "a season and a time", being subject and obedient to the King of Israel, in the light of whose government they will walk with joy, and lay their wealth and honour at his glorious feet.

CHAPTER VI

THE RESURRECTION OF ISRAEL—THE SECOND EXODUS—THE MILLENNIUM—"THE END"

The restoration of Israel indispensable to the setting up of the kingdom of God—Israel to be grafted into their own olive on a principle of faith—Not by Gentile agency, but by Jesus Christ, will God graft them in again—Britain, the protector of the Jews, as indicated by Isaiah 18—The British power in the South, the Moab, etc., of "the latter days"—The second exodus of Israel—The nations of the Image to be subdued by Israel to the dominion of their king—The New Covenant delivered to Judah, and the kingdom of God set up in Judea—The returning of the Ten Tribes to Canaan will occupy forty years—Elijah's mission—Israel reassembled in Egypt—They cross the Nile, and pass through the Red Sea, on foot—They march into Canaan, receive the New Covenant, and, re-united to Judah, form one nation and kingdom under Christ for 1,000 years—The blessedness of the nations, and their loyalty to Israel's king—Of the end of the thousand years

IN the previous chapters the reader has been conducted to the crisis that awaits the world at the conclusion of the time of the end. The two great powers of the day—namely, Gogue, the lord of the earth, and the Lion of Tarshish, the king of the sea, have been brought up in battle array in the region of the Dead Sea. This state of things will have been created by the angel of the sixth vial, whose province it is to gather the kings of the earth and of the whole habitable, with their armies, into the land of Israel, which is "the great winepress of the wrath of God" (Revelation 14:19,20) for a space of 200 miles. This will be brought about upon the same principles as the fulfilment of all other prophecies in ages past—namely, *through the policy of "the powers that be", controlled by God*. The insurrection of "the earth" in 1848 created a situation, in which the Roman question, the German question, and the Turco-Hungarian question, have become the elements of an inevitable war throughout Europe, which will terminate in the final destruction of the Austrian Empire and the Papacy, and the subjection of the Porte and the toe-kingdoms to the Autocrat.

But without some other element to complicate affairs, things might settle down into a mere substitution of one gigantic despotism for the many lesser ones that now exist. It is necessary, therefore, that some other ingredient be introduced into the mess, in order that the course of events may be directed into an

471

eastern channel, by which the crisis may be transferred from Europe to the Holy Land. This political element is found in the commercial interests of Britain in India; in the importance of Syria, Palestine, and Egypt being in the possession of a friendly people to the preservation of those interests; and in the policy of colonizing Palestine with Jews, and so attaching them to the interests of the country by which they are protected. Thus the ascendancy of the Autocrat in Constantinople and the West, by the jeopardy in which it puts the commerce and dominion of the Lion-power, excites the British Government to the adoption of a policy which, in its application to emergencies as they arise, elaborates the restoration of the Jews, and the resuscitation of the East.

The restoration of Israel is a most important feature in the divine economy. It is indispensable to the setting up of the Kingdom of God; for they are the kingdom, having been constituted such by the covenant of Sinai, as it is written, "*Ye* shall be unto me a kingdom of priests, and a holy nation" (Exodus 19:6). The apostles understood this well enough, and so do all who understand the Gospel of the Kingdom. After his resurrection, Jesus conversed with them during forty days, "speaking of the things pertaining to the kingdom of God". This was certainly long enough, under the instruction of such a teacher, to enable them to understand the subject well. It took possession of their minds and hearts, and created in them a desire for its immediate establishment. Hence, they put the question to him, saying, "Lord, wilt thou AT THIS TIME *restore* AGAIN the kingdom to Israel?" (Acts 1:3,6).

It is evident from this, that they regarded Israel as having once possessed the kingdom, and expected the same Israel to possess it again. No other meaning can be put upon their words: for to restore a thing "*again*" to a party implies that they had once possessed it before. When Israel had the kingdom, they were ruled by Israelites, and not by Gentiles, for a foreigner could hold no office under their law. This was not the case in the days of the apostles, for they were ruled by the Roman Senate, and kings of its appointment. But it will not be so when the kingdom is restored to them again. The horns of the Gentiles will then be cast out of the land, and they will be ruled by "Israelites indeed" who will have become *Jews by adoption*; for no Jews or Gentiles after the flesh can have any part in the government of Israel and the Israelitish empire, which will embrace all nations, unless their Jewish citizenship is based upon a higher principle than natural birth. The flesh constitutes a Jew a *subject* of the kingdom, but confers on him no right to sit and rule upon the thrones of the house of David. This is reserved for Christ and his apostles, who "shall sit upon twelve thrones of his glory"; and for all other Jews and Gentiles who shall have become "*Jews inwardly*", for whom the dominion under the whole heaven is decreed in the benevolence of God.

There are several strange fancies in the world concerning the restoration of the Jews. Some deny it *in toto*, and yet impose upon themselves the imagination that they believe the gospel of the kingdom! If any such have followed me through this work, they will, I think, long since have concluded that they have been in error. Others advance a little further, and regard it as an "open question"—a position that may be disputed, but for which more may be said than against it, but concerning which they are not able to decide. This is tantamount to saying that the gospel is an open question, and that they really cannot say whether the kingdom of God will have subjects or not. There are others who believe that Israel will certainly be restored, but they clog it with a condition which in effect makes its fulfilment impossible, or eternally remote. They tell us that they will not be restored until they are converted to Christianity!

By Christianity they mean the inanity preached from the "sacred desks" of the apostasy—the pulpit-gospels of the day; "for", say they, "if they abide not in unbelief they shall be grafted into their own once again." This is quite true; but the fallacy consists in construing this to mean that their restoration is predicated on their believing what the Gentiles teach. The Gentiles themselves are in unbelief. How, then, can they convert the Jews? "Because of unbelief they were broken off, and thou, Gentile, standest *by faith*. Be not high-minded, but fear: for if God spared not the natural branches, take heed lest he also spare not thee"; for "thou also shalt be cut off if thou continue not in his goodness" (Romans 11:20-23). Both Jews and Gentiles are faithless in the gospel of the kingdom in the name of Jesus. The Jews believe one part of it, and the Gentiles another part of it, but even these several parts they adulterate with so many traditions, that neither Jews nor Gentiles believe anything as they ought. Therefore, as He broke off Israel by the instrumentality of the Romans, so He is now about to break off the Gentiles by the judgments soon to be poured out upon them.

The work of grafting Israel into their own olive belongs to God, who, as the scripture saith, "is able to graft them in again". No one, I presume, will dispute His ability. As I have shown elsewhere, He has assigned the work of restoration to the Lord Jesus, who will graft them in again upon a principle of faith. He will bring their unbelief to an end in a way peculiar to the emergency of the case. When the fulness of the Gentiles is come in, then Israel's blindness will be done away.

The restoration of the Jews is a work of time, and will require between fifty and sixty years to accomplish. When Gogue comes to be lord of Europe, like Pharaoh of old he will not permit Israel to remove themselves and their wealth beyond his reach. His dominion must, therefore, be broken before the north will obey the command to "give up", and the south to "keep not back"; and even then Israel must fight their way to Palestine as in the days of old.

The truth is, there are two stages in the restoration of the Jews, the first is before the battle of Armageddon; and the second, after it; but both pre-millennial. God has said, *"I will save the tents of Judah first"*. This is the first stage of restoration. Jesus has already been "a stone of stumbling and rock of offence" to Judah and his companions for 40 years, that is from the day of Pentecost to the destruction of the temple, so that they need not be subjected to a like process any more. But the word saith, "He shall be a stone of stumbling and a rock of offence to *both* the houses of Israel" (Isaiah 8:14): now it is well known that this has not been fulfilled in relation to the ten tribes. They did not inhabit Canaan at the time Jesus sojourned and ministered there. The gospel of the kingdom has never been preached to them in his name; hence, they are only acquainted with him as they have heard of him by the report of Jesuits, and the priests of Gentile superstitions — a report which is incapable of making men responsible for not believing.

It remains, then, after Judah's tents are saved, to make use of them as apostles to their brethren of the other tribes, to preach to them a word from Jerusalem (Isaiah 2:2), inviting them to come out from the nations, and to rendezvous in "the wilderness of the people", preparatory to a return to a land flowing with milk and honey, in which Judah is dwelling safely under the sceptre of the Seed promised to their fathers. Judah's submission to the Lord Jesus, as the result of seeing him, will give them no right to eternal life, or to the glory and honour of the kingdom. It just entitles them to the blessedness of living in the land under the government of Messiah and the saints. So with the Ten Tribes; their faith in the word preached will entitle them to no more than a union into one kingdom and nation with Judah; and a participation in the blessings of Shiloh's reign during their natural lives. If any of them attain to eternal life and glory, it will be predicated on some other premises than those which precede their restoration.

There is, then, a partial and primary restoration of Jews before the manifestation, which is to serve as the nucleus, or basis, of future operations in the restoration of the rest of the tribes after he has appeared in the kingdom. The pre-adventual colonization of Palestine will be on purely political principles; and the Jewish colonists will return in unbelief of the Messiahship of Jesus, and of the truth as it is in him. They will emigrate thither as agriculturists and traders, in the hope of ultimately establishing their commonwealth, but more immediately of getting rich in silver and gold by commerce with India, and in cattle and goods by their industry at home under the efficient protection of the British power. And this their expectation will not be deceived; for, before Gogue invades their country, it is described by the prophet, as "a land of unwalled villages, whose inhabitants are at rest, and dwell safely, all of them dwelling without walls, and having neither bars nor gates; and possessed of silver and gold, cattle and goods, dwelling in the midst of the land" (Ezekiel 38:11,12,13). Now any person acquainted with the present insecure condition of Palestine under the Ottoman dominion must be satisfied from the testimony, that some other power friendly to Israel must then have become paramount over the land, which is able to guarantee protection to them, and to put the surrounding tribes in fear.* This is all that is needed, namely, security for life and property, and Palestine would be as eligible for Jewish emigration as the United States have proved for the Gentiles.

But to what part of the world shall we look for a power whose interests will make it willing, as it is able, to plant the ensign of civilization upon the mountains of Israel? The reader will, doubtless, anticipate my reply from what has gone before. I know not whether the men, who at present contrive the foreign policy of Britain, entertain the idea of assuming the sovereignty of the Holy Land, and of promoting its colonization by the Jews; their present intentions, however, are of no importance one way or the other, because they will be compelled, by events soon to happen, to do what, under existing circumstances, heaven and earth combined could not move them to attempt. The present decisions of "statesmen" are destitute of stability. A shooting star in the political firmament is sufficient to disturb all the forces of their system; and to stultify all the theories of their political astronomy. The finger of God has indicated a course to be pursued by Britain which cannot be evaded, and which her counsellors will not only be willing, but eager, to adopt when the crisis comes upon them.

The decree has long since gone forth which calls upon the Lion of Tarshish to protect the Jews. Upwards of a thousand years before the British were a nation, the prophet addresses them as the power which at *"evening-tide"* should interest themselves in

---

* See Foreword.

behalf of Israel. In view of this, "the time of the end", he says, "The nations shall rush like the rushing of many waters: but God shall rebuke them, and they shall flee far off, and shall be chased as the chaff of the mountains before the wind, and like a rolling thing before the whirlwind"; or, as it is expressed by another, "and they became like the chaff of the summer threshing-floors; and the wind carried them away, that no place was found for them" (Daniel 2:35). "Behold", says the former prophet concerning Israel at this time, "at evening-tide trouble; and before the morning *he* is not. This is the portion of them that *spoil us*, and the lot of them that rob us" (Isaiah 17:13,14)—referring, doubtless, to the overthrow and destruction of Gogue. Now, the invasion of their country by a spoiler at "evening-tide", who robs them, implies their previous return. This finished colonization Isaiah styles, "a present unto the LORD of hosts of a people scattered and peeled"; for, speaking of "the time of the end", he says, "In that time shall the present be brought unto the LORD of hosts of a people scattered and peeled...to the place of the name of the LORD of hosts, the Mount Zion" (Isaiah 18:7). But, then, the question returns upon us, by whom is the present to be made? The prophet answers this question in the first verse, saying, "Ho! to the land shadowing with wings, which is beyond the rivers of Khush: that sendeth ambassadors by sea, and on vessels of papyrus upon the waters, Go, ye swift messengers, to a nation scattered and peeled, to a people terrible from this and onward: a nation meted out and trodden down, whose land the rivers (invading armies—Isaiah 8:7) have spoiled." Now, the geography of this passage points to the Lion-power of Tarshish as "the land shadowing with wings". Taking Judea, where the prediction was delivered, as the place of departure, the word "*beyond*" points to the east; that is, running a line from Judea across the Euphrates and Tigris, "the rivers of Khushistan", it passes into Hindostan, where "the Merchants of Tarshish, and its young lions", rule the land.*

But the British power is still further indicated by the insular position of its seat of government; for the "sending of fleet messengers by the sea", implies that the shadowing-power is an island-state. Ambassadors are sent from the residence of the Court, and if they proceed to their destination by sea, the throne of the power must be located in an island. The text, therefore, points to the north and east, to England and Hindostan, as the land shadowing Israel with its wings. To Britain, then, the

---

* And the British Commonwealth extends "beyond the rivers of Khush" or Ethiopia, in Africa, that is, Egypt, the Soudan, and the far South beyond the Atbara and the Blue and White Nile.

prophet calls as the protector of the Jewish nation *in the evening-tide trouble*, and commands it to send its messengers in swift vessels because the crisis is urgent, and to plant Israel as "an ensign upon the mountains" (Isaiah 18:3); as it is written in another place, saying, "The Lord shall set an ensign for the nations, and shall assemble the outcasts of Israel, and gather together the dispersed of Judah from the four corners of the earth" (Isaiah 11:12).

When this is accomplished to the required extent it becomes a notable sign of the times. It will then be seen that the political Euphrates is evaporated to dryness, and that Israel is walking in the way of the kings of the east. In view of this, the prophet addresses mankind, saying, "All the inhabitants of the world and dwellers on the earth, tremble, when he lifteth up an ensign on the mountains; and when he bloweth a trumpet, shall hear." The ensign being planted on the mountains of Israel by Britain, the Lord will cause the Assyrian Autocrat to "blow a trumpet", summoning the hosts of his nations to war; for He has said, "I will bring thee, O Gogue, against my land". They will "ascend and come like a storm from the north parts, and be like a cloud to cover the land" (Ezekiel 38:9,16); but "they shall be left together unto the fowls of the mountains, and to the beasts of the earth; and the fowls shall summer upon them, and all the beasts of the earth shall winter upon them", for their carcases will lie exposed for "seven months" upon the field (Ezekiel 39:12). Then shall "the present" be brought in full of all the tribes of Israel not previously assembled by "the land shadowing with wings".

But from the subjugation of the Jews for a short time after they have been colonized, the protection of the shadowing-power would seem to have been inefficient. So it will, as far as the mountainous parts of the land are concerned; but, then, it is testified by Daniel, that "Edom, and Moab, and the chief of the children of Ammon, shall escape out of the hand" of the king of the north. These countries will be a place of refuge for those who fly from the face of the spoiler, as Turkey has recently been for the Hungarians, who have fled from the same power. The Lion-power of Tarshish being in military occupation of the countries that escape, is enabled to continue their protection efficiently. Hence, the prophet addresses it, saying, "Take counsel, execute judgment; make thy shadows as the night in the midst of the noon-day; hide the outcasts; bewray not him that wandereth. Let mine outcasts dwell with thee, Moab; be thou a covert to them from the face of the Spoiler." The context shows that this has reference to a future time; for, having shadowed them from the spoiler, who, during their coverture in Moab, has met with his overthrow at the hand of Michael, the great Prince of Israel, —

the prophet goes on to announce the good news, saying, "The extortioner is at an end, the spoiler ceaseth, the oppressors are consumed out of the land."

This cannot be said of any period of Jewish history since the prophecy was delivered; nor can it be said of the land in its present state, for the extortioner and oppressor still keeps it in subjection. But what follows shows conclusively that the time referred to is yet future; for, as soon as the deliverance of the land is declared, and the spoiler is no more, the prophet directs the reader's attention to the setting up of the kingdom, as the next event to come to pass, saying in these words, *"In mercy shall the throne be established: and* HE *shall sit upon it in truth in the tabernacle of David*, judging, and seeking judgment, and hasting righteousness" (Isaiah 16:3-5; Jeremiah 23:5; 33:14-15). But Moab's population is vanished, and the country a mere wilderness, whose solitude is only disturbed by the howl of beasts, or the occasional tramp of the Bedouins. For Moab, therefore, to respond to the prophetic exhortation, a power must take possession of the country capable of outstretching its wings for the defence of a people "whose land the rivers have spoiled", and that power, I believe, is Britain's, the Moab of the latter days.

As I have said elsewhere, the Lion-power will not interest itself in behalf of the subjects of God's kingdom, from pure generosity, piety towards God, or love of Israel; but upon the principles which actuate all the governments of the world—upon those, namely, of the lust of dominion, self-preservation, and self-aggrandizement. God, who rules the world, and marks out the bounds of habitation for the nations, will make Britain a gainer by the transaction. He will bring her rulers to see the desirableness of Egypt, Ethiopia, and Seba, which they will be induced, by the force of circumstances, probably, to take possession of.* They will, however, before the battle of Armageddon, be compelled to retreat from Egypt and Ethiopia; for "the king of the north shall stretch forth his hand upon the land of Egypt, which shall not escape; and the Libyans and Ethiopians shall be at his steps". Hence, these will become the battle-ground for a time, until the seat of war is removed to the mountains of Israel, where, by the Autocrat's discomfiture, the war is brought to an end between the image-giant of Assyria and the Lion of the north and east.

---

* And so it came to pass—1882 and after.

478

The possession, or ascendancy of Britain in Egypt, Ethiopia, and Seba, will naturally lead to the colonization of Palestine by the Jews. Thus the proverb will be verified which saith, "The wicked shall be a ransom for the righteous, and the transgressor for the upright". Though generations of the Jews have been "stiff-necked and perverse", yet their nation is a "holy nation", which other nations are not, inasmuch as Israel is the only nation God has separated to Himself for a peculiar people. In view of what I have been presenting, Jehovah saith to them, "Fear not, O Israel; for I have redeemed thee: I have called thee by thy name: thou art mine. When thou passest through the waters, I will be with thee; and through the rivers, they shall not overflow thee; when thou walkest through the fire, thou shalt not be burned; neither shall the flame kindle upon thee. For I am the LORD thy God, the Holy One of Israel, thy Saviour; *I gave Egypt for thy ransom, Ethiopia and Seba for thee*. Since thou wast precious in my sight, thou hast been honourable, and I have loved thee; *therefore will I give men for thee, and people for thy life*. Fear not; for I am, with thee; I will bring thy seed from the east, and gather thee from the west; I will say to the north, Give up; and to the south, Keep not back; bring my sons from far, and my daughters from the ends of the earth; even every one that is called by my name; for *I have created Israel for my glory*, I have formed him; yea, I have made him" (Isaiah 43:1-7).

Thus the Lord disposes of nations and countries as it pleases Him. To "the land shadowing with wings," which shall proclaim their return to the dust of their fathers, He will give Egypt, Ethiopia, and Seba as their ransom; and enable them, through its power, "to lay their hands upon Edom and Moab"; and to obtain the ascendancy over "the children of Ammon." Thus they will settle in these countries of the Red Sea; to which they will be attracted by the riches to be acquired through their connection with the commerce of the east; which will then resume its channel of the olden time, when Israel and the British, like Solomon's servants and the men of Tyre, will drive a thriving trade between the Indian and China seas, and the nations of the west.

Having thus brought my exposition of the sure prophetic word down to the termination of "the time of the end," I shall conclude my interpretations by exhibiting the truth revealed concerning the things of *the transition period* during which the God of heaven is setting up His kingdom, and breaking in pieces and consuming all the kingdoms of the world, and transferring their glory, honour, and dominion under the whole heaven to the saints of the Most High. These matters will be set forth in brief under the caption of 'The Second Exodus'.

THE KINGDOMS OF THE WORLD

THE SECOND EXODUS

WHEN the Lord has *"broken to pieces together"* all the parts of Nebuchadnezzar's Image—that is, destroyed that power which bound them all together as one dominion—the work next to be accomplished in relation to them is to subdue the gold, the silver, the brass, the iron, and the clay—in other words, the powers represented by them—that they may become "like the chaff of the summer threshing-floors"; so that, being carried away by the tempest of war, "no place may be found for them", and the subjugating power become as "a great mountain, and fill the whole earth".

But a question arises here which must be answered, or our exposition is at fault, and deficient of a very important link in the chain of testimony which connects the kingdom of God with the foundation of the world. It is, By what means are "the kingdoms of the world to become the kingdoms of our Lord and of his Christ", after he has dissolved the imperial bond of union among them by the glorious victory of Armageddon? Is it to be accomplished by sending missionaries of the tribe of Judah to the nations, preaching to them salvation from hell by Jesus Christ, as missionaries are now doing among the heathen, and inviting them to submit to the spiritual authority of the Lord, administered through men of like passions with themselves? Or is it to be brought about by burning up the wicked, and leaving none but the righteous to inherit the earth? Or are the existing orders of bishops, priests, ministers, and missionaries to be employed to bring the nations to the obedience of faith, that they may voluntarily surrender all political power into their hands, as the saints of the Most High God?

I answer unhesitatingly, that the conversion of the world to Christ's supremacy will be accomplished by no such fantastical schemes as are implied in these suppositions. The answer to the question is, *that the nations will be subdued to the sceptre of Shiloh by the sword, and that the tribes of Israel will be his soldiers in the war.* Besides punishing them for their idolatry, and subsequent unbelief of the gospel of the kingdom preached to Judah in the name of Jesus, Israel has been also scattered among all nations, that they may be ready for the work assigned them in *"the time of trouble"*, which intervenes between the battle of Armageddon and their final and complete restoration at the end of forty years. Though the dominion of Gogue be broken, the kingdoms and states which acknowledge him as their imperial chief will not voluntarily surrender themselves to another lord, any more than the populations of the old Assyrian empire did when the power of Sennacherib was broken in one night. The effect of his overthrow was only to prepare them for subjection to a more civilized and powerful ruler. In this case, the Lord used the Chaldeans for their subjugation: but in the coming strife He will use the tribes of Israel.

The Lord Jesus Christ at his appearing in his kingdom finds Judah inhabiting the land. Not all the Jews, but a goodly number of them. Having gained the victory of Armageddon, he convenes the elders of the people, which as their deliverer he has a right to do. Thus "they look upon him whom they have pierced" (Zechariah 12:10); "and one shall say unto him, What are these wounds in thy hands? Then he shall answer, Those with which I was wounded in the house of my friends" (Zechariah 13:6). The effect of this information upon the people is to cause a national lamentation. They will then discover that he to whom they owe their deliverance from Gogue, is Jesus of Nazareth, whom their fathers crucified. They will therefore "mourn for him, as one mourneth for his only son, and will be in bitterness for him, as one that is in bitterness for his first-born. In that day, there will be a great mourning in Jerusalem, as the mourning of Hadadrimmon in the valley of Megiddo" (Zechariah 12:10-14; Revelation 1:7). Two-thirds of the people will have been cut off by the war against Gogue, and the third which survives will have passed through a fiery ordeal. It will have been a refining process in which they will have been refined like silver, and tried as gold is tried. Thus prepared "a spirit of grace and supplications" will be poured upon them, and they will call on the name of the Lord, and He will hear them (Zechariah 13:9), and open for them a fountain for sin and for uncleanness (verse 1). He, will say, "It is my people: and they shall say, The LORD (even Jesus) is my God" (verse 9). Thus will Judah be grafted again into their own olive, and brought to acknowledge Jesus as King of the Jews, and to confess that "he is Lord, to the glory of God the Father".

The New Covenant being made with the house of Judah, the kingdom is established. Not, however, to its full extent. It is but the kingdom in its small beginning, as when David reigned in Hebron over Judah only. The Lord Jesus, as King of Judah, will have to bring the ten tribes and the nations generally to acknowledge him as King of Israel and Lord of the whole earth. What would the reader think of the little kingdom of Greece undertaking to subdue the whole world? Yet when the Lord appears in his little kingdom of Judea, he will undertake to deliver every Israelite in bondage, establish David's kingdom to its full extent, overturn all kingdoms and dominions among the Gentiles, abolish all their superstitions, enlighten them in the truth, and bring them to submit to him joyfully as their lawgiver, high priest, and king. He will begin this mighty enterprise with Judah; for "he hath made them as his goodly horse in the battle. And they shall be as mighty men, which tread down their enemies in the mire of the streets in the battle: and they shall fight, *because the LORD is with them*, and the riders on horses shall be confounded" (Zechariah 10:3-5). "And the governors of Judah shall say in their heart, The inhabitants of Jerusalem shall be my strength in the LORD of hosts their God. In that day", saith the Lord, "I will make the governors of Judah like a hearth of fire among the wood, and like a torch of fire in a sheaf; and they shall devour all the people round about, on the right hand and on the left" (Zechariah 12:5,6).

Such is the illustration of their prowess. The nations will be as wood, or as sheaves, subjected to the action of fire. They may resist, but they are certain to be subdued without further power of resistance. "They shall tread down the wicked; for they shall be ashes under the soles of their feet" (Malachi 4:3). Their conquests will begin with the countries contiguous to Judea. For when the Assyrian shall invade their land, the Judge of Israel having caused him to fall, "Judah shall waste the land of Assyria with the sword, and the land of Nimrod in the entrances thereof: thus shall he" that is to be ruler in Israel "deliver them from the Assyrian when he cometh into their land, and when he treadeth within their borders. And *the remnant* of Jacob shall be in the midst of many people as a dew from the LORD" (Micah 5:1-7).

Having thus conquered the land which God promised to Abraham and his seed for an everlasting possession, and made Judah as a bent bow in the hand of the king, the next thing is for the Lord to fill it with Ephraim as His arrow-headed weapon of war (Zechariah 9:12-16). In other words, "the LORD will seek to destroy all the nations that come against Jerusalem" (Zechariah 12:9) under the banner of Gogue; and to accomplish this so as at the same time to bring back the ten tribes to the land of Canaan, He will cause Judah to make war upon Greece, and blow the trumpet to war against the ten kingdoms of the habitable, and the populations of the west among whom "the remnant of Jacob" is dispersed. These scattered tribes will have been "hissed for" or invited to leave the lands of their oppressors, and to make common cause with Judah. They will respond to the invitation; and as "the arrow of the LORD they will go forth as lightning; and they shall devour and subdue" (Zechariah 9:12-16). "And they shall be like a mighty man, and their heart shall rejoice as through wine. And I will bring them, saith the LORD, again also *out of the land of Egypt*, and gather them out of Assyria; and I will bring them into the land of Gilead and Lebanon; and Ephraim shall *pass through the sea with affliction* and shall smite the waves in the sea, and all the deeps of the river shall dry up; and the pride of Assyria shall be brought down; and *the sceptre of Egypt shall depart away*" (Zechariah 10:7-11; Isaiah 11:15,16).

Let us, then, attend more particularly now to the relation subsisting between the king of Israel and his ten tribes, designated as *"Ephraim"* and *"the remnant of Jacob"* in the word. Addressing them, the Lord says by the prophet, "Thou art my battle-axe and weapons of war; for with thee will I break in pieces the nations, and with thee will I destroy kingdoms; with thee will I break in pieces captains and rulers" (Jeremiah 51:20-23). This has never been the case since the prophecy was delivered; it remains, therefore, to be fulfilled. With Judah as his goodly war horse and well-strung bow, filled with the Ephraim arrow, and wielding the Israel battle-axe, "The LORD will go forth with the whirlwinds of the South". "The remnant of Jacob will" then "be among the Gentiles in the midst of many people as a lion among the beasts of the forest as a young lion among the flocks of sheep: who, if he go through, both treadeth down, and teareth in pieces, and none can deliver." By such a weapon as this, the Lord "will execute vengeance in anger and fury upon the heathen, such as they have not heard" (Micah 5:8,15).

This belligerent state of things between the King of Israel and the nations of Gogue's dominion, styled *"the goats"*, will continue for forty years.* The subjugation will be gradual, as Israel is made to "go through" from kingdom to kingdom. "Feed thy people", saith the prophet, "with thy rod, the flock of thy heritage, which dwell solitarily in the wood; let them feed in Bashan and Gilead as in the days of old." In answer to this petition, the Lord replies, *"According to the days of thy coming out of the land of Egypt* will I show unto Him (Israel) marvellous things". This is forty years; for so long were they in passing from Egypt to Canaan, which was the type of their coming out from among the nations to the Holy Land under the generalship of Elijah, the Lord's harbinger to the Ten Tribes. The "marvellous things" to be shown them will not be performed in private, but will be as notorious as the plagues of Egypt; for "the nations shall see and be confounded at all their might: they shall lay their hand upon their mouth, their ears shall be deaf. They shall lick the dust like a serpent, they shall move out of their holes like worms of the

---

* Micah 7:15 is taken to indicate this period. But the prophet does not say, "According to *the number* of the days", but simply "As in the days." The allusion is to the characteristic wonders of those days, rather than to their duration. Compare the parallel expressions in the following scriptures:—Isaiah 9:4; 11:16; 51:9; Hosea 2:15; 9:9; Zechariah 14:3.

earth; they shall be afraid of the LORD the God of Israel, and shall fear because of thee" (Micah 7:14-17).

The more immediate consequence of these exterminating wars will be the cessation of all further resistance in the north, which will have been thus compelled to *"give up"* the Israelites among them, and to let them go and serve in "the wilderness of the people". They will not march directly into the Holy Land, because the generation of Israelites who leave the north will be no more fit for immediate settlement there than their fathers were who left Egypt under Moses. They would be as rebellious under the government of Shiloh as that generation whose carcases fell in the wilderness, and concerning whom "Jehovah sware in his wrath that they should not enter into his rest". They must, therefore, be subjected to discipline, and trained up under the divine admonition. But, notwithstanding all the "marvellous things" they will have witnessed, they will prove themselves true to the character of their fathers, who were stiff-necked and perverse, and resistant always of the Spirit of God; so that they will not be permitted to enter into the land of Israel. Their children, however, will come thither from "the land of the enemy", and attain to their own border (Jeremiah 31:15-17).

The reader will, doubtless, desire to know upon what ground I affirm these things. This is as it ought to be; for he should set his face like a flint, and refuse credence to anything and everything which is not sustained by "the testimony of God." Turn, then to the prophet Ezekiel, where it is thus written, "As I live, saith the Lord GOD, surely with a mighty hand, and with a stretched-out arm, and with fury poured out, will I rule over you: and I will bring you out from the people, and will gather you out of the countries wherein ye are scattered, with a mighty hand, and with a stretched-out arm, and with fury poured out. And I will bring you into the wilderness of the people, and *there will I plead with you face to face, like as I pleaded with your fathers in the wilderness of the land of Egypt, so will I plead with you*, saith the Lord GOD. And I will cause you to pass under the rod; and will bring you into *a delivering of the covenant*; and I will purge out from among you the rebels, and them that transgress against me. I will bring them forth out of the country where they sojourn, and *they shall not enter into the land of Israel*: and ye shall know that I am the LORD" (Ezekiel 20:36-38).

While they are in this wilderness it is, that the Lord Jesus becomes "a stone of stumbling and rock of offence to the house of Israel", as he had before been to Judah; and the consequence is that "the rebels among them" are excluded from the blessings of Shiloh's government and eternal life and glory in the then world to come. Nothing can be plainer than Ezekiel's testimony. If the reader know how the Lord pleaded with Israel face to face in the wilderness by the hand of Moses, he will well understand the ordeal that yet awaits the tribes to qualify them for admission into the Holy Land. The Lord's power and the angel were with them in the wilderness of Arabia, but they saw not his person; so, I judge, will the Lord Jesus and some of the saints be with Israel in their Second Exodus, seen perhaps by their leaders, as the Elohim were by Moses, Aaron, the elders and by Joshua; but not visible to the multitude of the people, who must walk by faith and not by sight; for, though God is able to graft them in again, He can only do it upon a principle of faith; for the condition of their restoration laid down in His word is, *"If they abide not in unbelief*, they shall be grafted in again."

It would seem from the testimony of Malachi, who prophesied concerning the ten tribes, that while they are in the wilderness of the people they will be disciplined by the law of Moses as their national code, while things concerning Jesus will be propounded to them as matter of faith; for it is testified by Hosea that they shall be gathered, and "shall sorrow a little for the burden of the King of princes" (Hosea 8:10). The person with whom they will have more immediately to do in their Second Exodus is Elijah. There would seem to be a fitness in this. In the days of their fathers, when they forsook the Lord and abolished the law of Moses, Elijah was the person whose ministerial life was occupied in endeavouring to "restore all things". Though he did much to vindicate the name and law of Jehovah, he was taken away in the midst of his labours. For what purpose? That he might at a future period resume his work and perfect it by restoring all things among the ten tribes according to the law of Moses, preparatory to their being planted in their land under a new covenant to be made with them there (Malachi 4:4-6; Jeremiah 31:31).

But it may be objected that Elijah has come already, and that John the Baptist was he. True, in a certain sense he was. John was Elijah to the House of Judah in the sense of his having come "in the spirit and power of Elijah" (Luke 1:17). But John was not the Elijah who talked with Moses on the Mount of Transfiguration. The latter is Elijah to the house of Israel. The scribes taught that Elijah must precede Christ; which Jesus approved, saying, "Elijah truly shall first come, *and restore all things*". He said this after John was put to death. John did not restore all things; but Elijah will, and that too before the Lord Jesus makes himself known to the ten tribes, whom he will meet in Egypt.

The period of Israel's probation drawing to a close, they will have advanced as far as Egypt on their return to Canaan, as it is written, "They shall return to Egypt" (Hosea 8:13). This is necessary, for it is written also in more senses than one, "Out of Egypt have I called my son". As they are to be gathered from the west, north, and east they will have gone through the countries by a circuitous route to Egypt. They are to be gathered from Assyria, or the countries of Gogue's dominion; but I have not yet discovered in the word the line of march they are to follow in arriving at Egypt. But that they are to be assembled there is certain; for it is written, "I will bring them *again* also out of the land of Egypt". This was spoken some two hundred years after the overthrow of Samaria; and it is indisputable that neither Israel nor Judah have been again brought out of Egypt to inhabit their land: the exodus from Egypt is therefore still in the future.

But in coming out of Egypt they will have to cross both the Nile and the Red Sea; and although their march hither will have been one of conquest, it will not have been unattended with defeat, because of their own rebelliousness. The hearts of their enemies will be hardened to their own destruction to the last conflict. The south will still be disposed to *"keep back"* Israel from their country. Therefore, leaving Egypt, "Ephraim shall pass through the sea of affliction, and shall smite the waves in the sea, and all the deeps of the river shall dry up: and the pride of Assyria shall be brought down, and the sceptre of Egypt shall depart away" (Zechariah 10:10,11). The combined forces of Egypt and Assyria shall be broken as the hosts of Pharaoh, and the horse and his rider be drowned in the depths of the sea. For "the LORD shall utterly destroy the tongue of the Egyptian sea and with his mighty wind shall he shake his hand over the river, and shall smite it in the seven streams, and make (Israel) go over dry shod ... like as it was to Israel in the day that he came up out of the land of Egypt" (Isaiah 11:15,16).

They will now sing the song of Moses, and the song of the Lamb, who will have given them such a mighty deliverance from all their enemies. Being now "the ransomed of the LORD, they shall return, and come to Zion with songs, and everlasting joy upon their heads". The prophet "like unto Moses", mightier than Joshua, and "greater than Solomon", will conduct them into the Holy Land, and, having delivered to them the New Covenant, will "settle them after their old estates". Having "wrought with them for his own name's sake", and by them as his "battle-axe and weapons of war", subdued the nations, and brought them to his holy mountain, he will "accept them there", and "there shall all the house of Israel, *all of them* in the land," as one nation and one kingdom under Shiloh "serve the Lord GOD" (Ezekiel 37:21,28; 20:40; 34:22-31).

Thus the little kingdom of Judea will become "a great mountain", or empire, "filling the whole earth". The "Economy of the Fulness of Times" will now have fairly commenced, and the Day of Christ in all the glory of the Sun of Righteousness have opened in all its blessedness upon the nations of the earth. The gospel preached to Abraham, saying, "In thee shall all families of the earth be blessed", will be a reality. The Lord with Judah as his bended bow and Israel for his arrow, having subdued the nations, and "bound their kings with chains, and their nobles with fetters of iron" as his conquests progressed, will have transferred their much-abused power to his saints (Revelation 2:26,27), who shall rule them with a rod of iron which cannot be broken.

Having received his law (Isaiah 42:4), and experienced the justice of its administration, "all nations will call him blessed", and "daily will he be praised". A universal jubilee will celebrate the admiration of mankind, and their devotion to the King of all the earth. The world will no more resound with war's alarms for a thousand years; and among the highest there will be glory to God, on the earth there will be peace, and good-will among men (Luke 2:14). The mission of the Lord Christ will have been gloriously fulfilled. He will have raised up the tribes of Jacob, restored the preserved of Israel, and been the salvation of Jehovah to the end of the earth (Isaiah 49:6). In his days there will be abundance of peace; for the nations will beat their swords into ploughshares, and their spears into scythes, and practice war no more. "At that time they shall can Jerusalem the throne of the LORD; and all the nations shall be gathered to it, to the name of the LORD, to Jerusalem" as the metropolis of the world: *"neither shall they walk any more after the imagination of their evil heart"* (Jeremiah 3:17). The things they now delight in will then be an abomination to them; for "the Gentiles shall come unto the LORD from the ends of the earth, and shall say, *Surely our fathers have inherited lies, vanity, and things in which there is no profit"* (Jeremiah 16:19).

When enlightened by the Lord, this will be their judgment of the "sects and denominations", Pagan, Mohammedan, Papal and Protestant, which now as a covering spread over all nations (Isaiah 25:7), darkens their understandings, and alienates them from the life of God. But when the King of Israel and his Saints shall rule the world, all these superstitions will be for ever abolished, and mankind will be of one faith and practice. They will speak one religious language, and serve Jehovah with unanimity; for, says He, "Then will I turn to the people a pure language, that they may all call upon the name of the LORD with one consent" (Zephaniah 3:9). This must, indeed, be the Lord's doing, for who among men has the wisdom, knowledge, and power to bring the nations to speak intelligibly on religious subjects, and to be of one religion? The sword only, can prepare the way for this. Mankind must be made to lick the dust like a serpent, before they will consent to change their creeds for eternal truth. Judgment will bring them to reason, and they will say at length, "Come, let us go up to the mountain of the LORD, to the temple of the God of Jacob; and *He* will teach us of his ways, and we will walk in his paths: for out of Zion shall go forth the law, and the word of the LORD from Jerusalem" (Isaiah 2:3). Under such teachings as this the work will be accomplished.

As to Israel, the Lord will have gotten them praise and fame in every land where they have been put to shame; and have made them a name and a praise among all the people of the earth (Zephaniah 3:19,20). "All nations shall call them blessed, for they shall be a delightsome land, saith the LORD of hosts" (Malachi 3:12). Instead of being a by-word and a reproach, as at this day, the Gentiles will glory in their patronage; for "in those days it shall come to pass that ten men shall take hold out of all the languages of the nations, even shall take hold of the skirt of him that is a Jew, saying, We will go with you; for we have heard that *God is with you*" (Zechariah 8:23). Yes, the kingdom, and throne of David will then be in their midst again, and Christ the Lord God, and Holy One of Israel, sitting upon it in power and great glory. The gospel of the kingdom will be no longer a matter of hope, but a reality; and those who have believed it, and submitted cheerfully and lovingly to the law of faith in the obedience it requires, and have perfected their faith by works meet for repentance, will be shining "as the brightness of the firmament and as the stars for ever and ever" (Daniel 12:3). This is the Hope of Israel which is set before men in the Gospel, and for which Paul was bound with a chain. It is a very different one from that exhibited in pulpit-theology; yet it is that which must be embraced as the soul's anchorage, if a man would be saved, and inherit the Kingdom of God.

Such will be the order of things for a thousand years. But though truth and righteousness will have gained the ascendancy and have prevailed for so long a period, sin will still exist in the flesh, and in some instances reveal itself in overt acts of disobedience. This is implied by the sayings: "The sinner shall die accursed" (Isaiah 65:20); and, "Whoso will not come up of all the families of the earth unto Jerusalem to worship the King, the LORD of Hosts, even upon them shall be no rain" (Zechariah 14:16-19). There will be no occasion to march an army into a country to put down rebellion; it will be quite effectual, to bring it back to its allegiance, to withhold from it the fruits of the earth. This spirit of insubordination will, however, smoulder among the nations until at the end of the thousand years the *"enmity"* against the Woman's Seed bursts forth again into a flame. If the apostle felt the workings of "the law of sin" within him, though obedient to "the law of the spirit of life"; need we wonder that the same "law of nature" should gather force in the hearts of nations subdued by fire and sword to the sovereignty of Israel's King? Man, unrenewed man, is essentially ungrateful and rebellious. The whole history of his race attests it. A thousand years of peace and blessedness will fail to bind him, by the bonds of love and a willing fealty, to the glorious and benevolent, yet just and powerful, emancipator and enlightener of the world.

Some new demon, who would rather reign as Satan than serve in heaven, will arise among the nations, and unfurl the old satanic standard of the Dragon empire, which will be known to the generation of that remote future as the past existence of the Assyrian, Persian, Macedonian, and Roman empires is known to us; that is, historically. A giant will this rebel be in presumption and crime, and surpassing in hardihood the pre-millennial Autocrat, whom Michael bound with a great chain and cast into the abyss. But what will not a man adventure inspired with the pride of life! Enchanted thus, he becomes the *Adversary* (Satan) of the King of Glory; and goes forth to the remotest nations, to Gogue's Magogian people, and falsely *accuses* his administration, by which means he succeeds in detaching them from their allegiance, and in *deceiving* them into a vain attempt to recover their ancient dominion (Revelation 20:7-10).

The King, instead of nipping the insurrection in the bud, permits the Adversary and Seducer (the Satan and the Devil) to mature his plans, marshal his hosts, and lead them on to an invasion of the land of Israel. The King permits him to come up on "the breadth of the land", and to "compass the camp of the saints about, and the beloved city". Having enclosed the Governor of the world and his ancients in the metropolis, and so hemmed them in as to prevent all escape, with no army in the rear to raise the siege, the sceptre of universal dominion would seem once more to be within the grasp of the Head of the Old Serpent empire. Like our contemporaries, professing to believe the past, but denying, that its scenes will ever be repeated, he remembers the overthrow of the former Gogue, as the Autocrat of Russia now remembers that of Sennacherib in the days of Hezekiah, but believes not in the repetition of so terrible a destruction. He will know, doubtless—and who after that the knowledge of the Lord shall have covered the earth for a thousand years will not know? that "he must reign till he have put all his enemies under his feet", but he will no more believe that it

489

will be so than the Old Serpent, the founder of his dominion, believed that God would subject Adam to death in the day of his transgression though He had declared it. He will persuade the nations that the King of Israel shall not reign for ever, and that the overthrow of his government is possible.

Thus deceived, we find them enrolled under Satan, or the Adversary, and "encompassing the camp of the saints, and the beloved city", full of savage exultation at the expected destruction of the best of kings. But fallacious will be the hopes of the rebel multitude, and dreadful the vengeance to burst upon them. The trembling earth and the blackening heavens warn them of a coming tempest. The dark vapours and thick clouds of the sky, curling in dense and lowering masses, suddenly hiss forth the forked lightning, and the heaven is rent by the deafening roar of the voice of God. Hail, and fire mingled with hail, pour down upon them, and they are destroyed from the face of the land. Thus God will deliver His King; for "fire shall come down from God out of heaven, and shall devour them".

Thus, though corruption of the flesh, *nationally expressed*, was restrained by the overthrow of Gogue, the Dragon-chief, at the pre-millennial advent of the King of Israel, it is finally subdued only when the head of the Serpent-power is crushed at the end of the thousand years. After this victory, another enemy remains to be destroyed to perfect the work of the Son of Man. Death is the last enemy. The power of death is the corruption of the flesh, which is the consequence of sin. But, the wicked all being destroyed by fire, there remain upon the earth only the faithful and true, who are rewarded for their fidelity with the inheritance of the ages. The "law of sin", or law of their flesh, is abolished in the change they undergo from corruption to incorruptibility and life. This is the abolishing of death from the earth, so that its inhabitants can die no more. This being brought to pass, the saying will be fulfilled, and the work accomplished, that "the Son of God was manifested that he might destroy the works of the Devil"; and "him that hath the power of death, that is the Devil".

Such is "the end, when the Son shall deliver up the Kingdom to the Father, that God may be all and in all" (1 Corinthians 15:24-28; Revelation 21:3). The separation between God and Man began with the transgression of the first Adam; it continues till the end of the 7,000 years, when sin and death are utterly eradicated, and harmony again established in this orb of His glorious universe. Earth will have been delivered from moral and physical evil by His power administered and displayed through the Lord Jesus Christ, who, though "subjected to the Father", will have the pre-eminence over all "his brethren" through the endless duration of ages. The last resurrection, which is employed in the development of "the end" (Revelation 20:6), will bring up from the dust the sleeping dead of the previous thousand years.

Those who are accounted worthy of eternal life will receive it, and be added to the saints of the "first resurrection".

Thus a population will have been provided for the earth, which, instead of being destroyed, will be renovated, and all things belonging to it made new (Revelation 21:5). The earth and its inhabitants will be incorruptible, undefiled, and unfading. God, according to His word, will have made "a full end of all nations", except that of Israel; which will be the sole occupant of the globe. and every Israelite, "an Israelite indeed", "equal to the Elohim", and crowned with glory and honour throughout all ages. During the thousand years their nation will consist of three classes, Christ and the saints, righteous Israelites in the flesh, and those who die "accursed"; but when perfection comes there will be but one class, and all will be immortal. The purpose of God, in the formation of the earth, will be accomplished; and "the headstone of the creation will be brought forth with shoutings, crying, Grace, grace unto it."

ELPIS ISRAEL

SUBJECT INDEX

ELPIS ISRAEL

SCRIPTURE INDEX

505

NOTES

NOTES

NOTES